HCSB

THE INVITATION

NEW TESTAMENT

ERC Evangelism Response Center

If you would like to talk to someone about Jesus,
call toll free anytime 888-537-8720

ISBN: 978-1-5864-0334-8

Printed in the United States of America
10 11 12 13 14 – 17 16 15 14
DP

Books of the Bible

New Testament

Features

Introduction to the
Holman Christian Standard Bible®

The Bible is God's written revelation to man. It is the only book that gives us entirely accurate and authoritative information about God, man's need, and God's provision for that need. It provides us with guidance for life and tells us how to receive eternal life. The Bible can do these things because it is God's inspired Word, inerrant in the original manuscripts.

The Bible describes God's dealings with the ancient Jewish people and the early Christian church. It tells us about the great gift of God's Son, Jesus Christ, who fulfilled Jewish prophecies of the Messiah. It tells us about the salvation He accomplished through His death on the cross, His triumph over death in the resurrection, and His promised return to earth. It is the only book that gives us authoritative information about the future, about what will happen to us when we die, and about where history is headed.

Bible translation is both a science and an art. It is a bridge that brings God's Word from the ancient world to the world today. In dependence on God to accomplish this sacred task, Holman Bible Publishers presents the Holman Christian Standard Bible.

Textual base of the HCSB

The textual base for the New Testament [NT] is the Nestle-Aland *Novum Testamentum Graece*, 27th edition, and the United Bible Societies' *Greek New Testament*, 4th corrected edition. The text for the Old Testament [OT] is the *Biblia Hebraica Stuttgartensia*, 5th edition.

Where there are significant differences among Hebrew [Hb] and Aramaic [Aram] manuscripts of the OT or among Greek [Gk] manuscripts of the NT, the translators have followed what they believe is the original reading and have indicated the main alternative(s) in footnotes. With few exceptions, the HCSB uses the traditional verse divisions found in most Protestant Bibles.

Goals of this translation

The goals of this translation are:

- to provide English-speaking people across the world with an accurate, readable Bible in contemporary English
- to equip serious Bible students with an accurate translation for personal study, private devotions, and memorization
- to give those who love God's Word a text that has numerous reader helps, is visually attractive on the page, and is appealing when heard
- to affirm the authority of Scripture as God's Word and to champion its absolute truth against social or cultural ideals that would compromise its accuracy
- to continue making improvements to the translation in each printing

The name, Holman Christian Standard Bible, captures these goals: *Holman* Bible Publishers presents a *Bible* translation, for *Christian* and English-speaking communities, which will be a *Standard* Bible translation for years to come.

Why is there a need for another English translation of the Bible?

There are several good reasons why Holman Bible Publishers invested its resources in a modern language translation of the Bible:

Each generation needs a fresh translation of the Bible in its own language. The Bible is the world's most important book, confronting each individual and each culture with issues that affect life, both now and forever. Since each new generation must be introduced to God's Word in its own language, there will always be a need for new translations such as the HCSB. The majority of Bible translations on the market today are revisions of translations from previous generations. The HCSB is a new translation for today's generation.

<u>English, one of the world's greatest languages, is rapidly changing, and Bible translations must keep in step with those changes.</u> English is the first truly global language in history. It is the language of education, business, medicine, travel, research, and the Internet. More than 1.3 billion people around the world speak or read English as a primary or secondary language. The HCSB seeks to serve many of those people with a translation they can easily use and understand. English is also the world's most rapidly changing language. The HCSB seeks to reflect recent changes in English by using modern punctuation, formatting, and vocabulary, while avoiding slang, regionalisms, or changes made specifically for the sake of political or social agendas. Modern linguistic and semantic advances have been incorporated into the HCSB, including modern grammar.

<u>Rapid advances in biblical research provide new data for Bible translators</u>. This has been called the "information age," a term that accurately describes the field of biblical research. Never before in history has there been as much information about the Bible as there is today—from archaeological discoveries to analysis of ancient manuscripts to years of study and statistical research on individual Bible books. Translations made as recently as the late 20th century do not reflect many of these advances in biblical research. The HCSB translators have taken into consideration as much of this new data as possible.

<u>Advances in computer technology have opened a new door for Bible translation</u>. The HCSB has used computer technology and telecommunications in its creation perhaps more than any Bible translation in history. Electronic mail was used daily and sometimes hourly for communication and transmission of manuscripts. An advanced Bible software program, Accordance®, was used to create and revise the translation at each step in its production. A developmental copy of the translation itself was used within Accordance to facilitate crosschecking during the translation process—something never done before with a Bible translation.

History of the HCSB

After several years of preliminary development, Holman Bible Publishers, the oldest Bible publisher in America, assembled an international, interdenominational team of 100 scholars, editors, stylists, and proofreaders, all of whom were committed to biblical inerrancy. Outside consultants and reviewers contributed valuable suggestions from their areas of expertise. An executive team then edited, polished, and reviewed the final manuscripts.

Features found in the HCSB

In keeping with a long line of Bible publications, the HCSB has retained a number of features found in traditional Bibles:

1. Traditional theological vocabulary (such as justification, sanctification, redemption) has been retained since such terms have no translation equivalent that adequately communicates their exact meaning.

2. OT passages quoted in the NT are set in boldface type. OT quotes consisting of two or more lines are block indented.
3. Traditional spellings of names and places found in most Bibles have been used to make the HCSB compatible with most Bible study tools.
4. Nouns and personal pronouns that clearly refer to any person of the Trinity are capitalized.

Commonly used abbreviations in the HCSB

A.D.	in the year of our Lord	NT	New Testament
alt	alternate	ms(s)	manuscript(s)
a.m.	from midnight until noon	OT	Old Testament
Aram	Aramaic	p.m.	from noon until midnight
B.C.	before Christ	pl	plural
ca	circa	Ps(s)	psalm(s)
chap.	chapter	Sam	Samaritan Pentateuch
DSS	Dead Sea Scrolls	sg	singular
Eng	English	Sym	Symmachus
Gk	Greek	syn.	synonym
Hb	Hebrew	Syr	Syriac
Jer	Latin translation of Psalms by Jerome	Tg	Targum
		Theod	Theodotian
Lat	Latin	v., vv.	verse, verses
Lit	Literally	Vg	Vulgate —an ancient translation of the Bible into Latin
LXX	Septuagint—an ancient translation of the Old Testament into Greek		
		vol.	volume(s)
		vol(s).	volume(s)
MT	Masoretic Text		

Is There Any Hope?

The future is uncertain.
Schools are protected by armed guards.
Many people don't feel safe in their own homes.
Diseases are killing our people.

Is There Any Hope?

Can we have peace and joy in our hearts?
Can we find purpose for our life?
Can we find the strength for tough times?
Does anyone really care?

Yes! Here's Hope:
JESUS Cares for You

The Bible says:

"Now may the God of hope fill you with all joy and peace as you believe in Him so that you may overflow with hope by the power of the Holy Spirit" (Romans 15:13).

In His Word, the Bible, we find the road to hope. The road is clearly marked in the pages of this New Testament. Read the phrase at the top of each marked page and then the underlined verse. You will find the instructions to the next stop on the road at the bottom of the page. Please read all the verses. The journey begins with Romans 1:16 on page 137.

Here's Your INVITATION To Find Hope in Today's World . . .

Turn to Romans 1:16 on page 137.

WHERE TO FIND IT

The New Testament

MATTHEW

1 The historical record[A] of Jesus Christ, the Son of David, the Son of Abraham:

2 Abraham fathered[B] Isaac,
Isaac fathered Jacob,
Jacob fathered Judah and his brothers,
3 Judah fathered Perez and Zerah
by Tamar,
Perez fathered Hezron,
Hezron fathered Aram,
4 Aram fathered Amminadab,
Amminadab fathered Nahshon,
Nahshon fathered Salmon,
5 Salmon fathered Boaz by Rahab,
Boaz fathered Obed by Ruth,
Obed fathered Jesse,
6 and Jesse fathered King David.

Then[C] David fathered Solomon
by Uriah's wife,
7 Solomon fathered Rehoboam,
Rehoboam fathered Abijah,
Abijah fathered Asa,[D]
8 Asa[D] fathered Jehoshaphat,
Jehoshaphat fathered Joram,[E]
Joram fathered Uzziah,
9 Uzziah fathered Jotham,
Jotham fathered Ahaz,
Ahaz fathered Hezekiah,
10 Hezekiah fathered Manasseh,
Manasseh fathered Amon,[F]
Amon fathered Josiah,
11 and Josiah fathered Jechoniah
and his brothers
at the time of the exile to Babylon.

12 Then after the exile to Babylon
Jechoniah fathered Shealtiel,
Shealtiel fathered Zerubbabel,
13 Zerubbabel fathered Abiud,
Abiud fathered Eliakim,
Eliakim fathered Azor,
14 Azor fathered Zadok,
Zadok fathered Achim,
Achim fathered Eliud,
15 Eliud fathered Eleazar,
Eleazar fathered Matthan,
Matthan fathered Jacob,
16 and Jacob fathered Joseph the husband
of Mary,
who gave birth to[G] Jesus who is called
the Messiah.

17 So all the generations from Abraham to David were 14 generations; and from David until the exile to Babylon, 14 generations; and from the exile to Babylon until the Messiah, 14 generations.

18 The birth of Jesus Christ came about this way: After His mother Mary had been engaged to Joseph, it was discovered before they came together that she was pregnant by the Holy Spirit. 19 So her husband Joseph, being a righteous man, and not wanting to disgrace her publicly, decided to divorce her secretly. 20 But after he had considered these things, an angel of the Lord suddenly appeared to him in a dream, saying, "Joseph, son of David, don't be afraid to take Mary as your wife, because what has been conceived in her is by the Holy Spirit. 21 She will give birth to a son, and you are to name Him Jesus,[H] because He will save His people from their sins."

22 Now all this took place to fulfill what was spoken by the Lord through the prophet:

23 **See, the virgin will become pregnant**
and give birth to a son,
and they will name Him Immanuel,[I]

which is translated "God is with us." 24 When Joseph got up from sleeping, he did as the Lord's angel had commanded him. He married her 25 but did not know her intimately until she gave birth to a son.[J] And he named Him Jesus.

2 After Jesus was born in Bethlehem of Judea in the days of King Herod, wise men from the east arrived unexpectedly in Jerusalem, 2 saying, "Where is He who has been born King of the Jews? For we saw His star in the east[K] and have come to worship Him."[L]

3 When King Herod heard this, he was deeply disturbed, and all Jerusalem with him. 4 So he assembled all the chief priests and scribes of the people and asked them where the Messiah would be born.

A1:1 Or *The book of the genealogy* B1:2 In vv. 2-16 either a son, as here, or a later descendant, as in v. 8 C1:6 Other mss add *King* D1:7,8 Other mss read *Asaph* E1:8 = Jehoram F1:10 Other mss read *Amos* G1:16 Lit *Mary, from whom was born* H1:21 *Jesus* is the Gk form of the Hb name "Joshua," which = "The LORD saves" or "Yahweh saves." I1:23 Is 7:14 J1:25 Other mss read *to her firstborn son* K2:2 Or *star at its rising* L2:2 Or *to pay Him homage*

⁵ "In Bethlehem of Judea," they told him, "because this is what was written by the prophet:

⁶ **And you, Bethlehem,** in the land
of Judah,
are by no means **least**
among the leaders of Judah:
**because out of you will come a leader
who will shepherd My people Israel.**ᴬ

⁷ Then Herod secretly summoned the wise men and asked them the exact time the star appeared. ⁸ He sent them to Bethlehem and said, "Go and search carefully for the child. When you find Him, report back to me so that I too can go and worship Him."ᴮ

⁹ After hearing the king, they went on their way. And there it was—the star they had seen in the east!ᶜ It led them until it came and stopped above the place where the child was. ¹⁰ When they saw the star, they were overjoyed beyond measure. ¹¹ Entering the house, they saw the child with Mary His mother, and falling to their knees, they worshiped Him.ᴰ Then they opened their treasures and presented Him with gifts: gold, frankincense, and myrrh. ¹² And being warned in a dream not to go back to Herod, they returned to their own country by another route.

¹³ After they were gone, an angel of the Lord suddenly appeared to Joseph in a dream, saying, "Get up! Take the child and His mother, flee to Egypt, and stay there until I tell you. For Herod is about to search for the child to destroy Him." ¹⁴ So he got up, took the child and His mother during the night, and escaped to Egypt. ¹⁵ He stayed there until Herod's death, so that what was spoken by the Lord through the prophet might be fulfilled: **Out of Egypt I called My Son.**ᴱ

¹⁶ Then Herod, when he saw that he had been outwitted by the wise men, flew into a rage. He gave orders to massacre all the male children in and around Bethlehem who were two yearsᶠ old and under, in keeping with the time he had learned from the wise men. ¹⁷ Then what was spoken through Jeremiah the prophet was fulfilled:

¹⁸ **A voice was heard in Ramah,**

weeping,ᴳ **and great mourning,
Rachel weeping for her children;
and she refused to be consoled,
because they were no more.**ᴴ

¹⁹ After Herod died, an angel of the Lord suddenly appeared in a dream to Joseph in Egypt, ²⁰ saying, "Get up! Take the child and His mother and go to the land of Israel, because those who sought the child's life are dead." ²¹ So he got up, took the child and His mother, and entered the land of Israel. ²² But when he heard that Archelausᴵ was ruling over Judea in place of his father Herod, he was afraid to go there. And being warned in a dream, he withdrew to the region of Galilee. ²³ Then he went and settled in a town called Nazareth to fulfill what was spoken through the prophets, that He will be called a Nazarene.

3 In those days John the Baptist came, preaching in the Wilderness of Judea ² and saying, "Repent, because the kingdom of heaven has come near!" ³ For he is the one spoken of through the prophet Isaiah, who said:

**A voice of one crying out
in the wilderness:
Prepare the way for the Lord;
make His paths straight!**ᴶ

⁴ John himself had a camel-hair garment with a leather belt around his waist, and his food was locusts and wild honey. ⁵ Then people from Jerusalem, all Judea, and all the vicinity of the Jordan were flocking to him, ⁶ and they were baptized by him in the Jordan River as they confessed their sins.

⁷ When he saw many of the Pharisees and Sadducees coming to the place of his baptism,ᴷ he said to them, "Brood of vipers! Who warned you to flee from the coming wrath? ⁸ Therefore produce fruit consistent withᴸ repentance. ⁹ And don't presume to say to yourselves, 'We have Abraham as our father.' For I tell you that God is able to raise up children for Abraham from these stones! ¹⁰ Even now the ax is ready to strike the root of the trees! Therefore, every tree that doesn't produce good fruit will be cut down and thrown into the fire.

¹¹ "I baptize you withᴹ water for repentance,ᴺ but the One who is coming after me is more

---

A2:6 Mc 5:2   B2:8 Or and pay Him homage   C2:9 Or star ... at its rising   D2:11 Or they paid Him homage   E2:15 Hs 11:1   F2:16 Lit were from two years   G2:18 Other mss read Ramah, lamentation, and weeping,   H2:18 Jr 31:15   I2:22 A son of Herod the Great who ruled a portion of his father's kingdom 4 B.C.–A.D. 6   J3:3 Is 40:3   K3:7 Lit to his baptism   L3:8 Lit fruit worthy of   M3:11 Or in   N3:11 Baptism was the means by which repentance was expressed publicly.

powerful than I. I am not worthy to remove[A] His sandals. He Himself will baptize you with[B] the Holy Spirit and fire. [12]His winnowing shovel[C] is in His hand, and He will clear His threshing floor and gather His wheat into the barn. But the chaff He will burn up with fire that never goes out."

[13]Then Jesus came from Galilee to John at the Jordan, to be baptized by him. [14]But John tried to stop Him, saying, "I need to be baptized by You, and yet You come to me?"

[15]Jesus answered him, "Allow it for now, because this is the way for us to fulfill all righteousness." Then he allowed Him to be baptized.

[16]After Jesus was baptized, He went up immediately from the water. The heavens suddenly opened for Him,[D] and He saw the Spirit of God descending like a dove and coming down on Him. [17]And there came a voice from heaven:

> This is My beloved Son.
> I take delight in Him!

4 Then Jesus was led up by the Spirit into the wilderness to be tempted by the Devil. [2]After He had fasted 40 days and 40 nights, He was hungry. [3]Then the tempter approached Him and said, "If You are the Son of God, tell these stones to become bread."

[4]But He answered, "It is written:

> Man must not live on bread alone
> but on every word that comes
> from the mouth of God."[E]

[5]Then the Devil took Him to the holy city,[F] had Him stand on the pinnacle of the temple, [6]and said to Him, "If You are the Son of God, throw Yourself down. For it is written:

> He will give His angels orders
>   concerning you,
> and they will support you
>   with their hands
> so that you will not strike
>   your foot against a stone."[G]

[7]Jesus told him, "It is also written: Do not test the Lord your God."[H]

[8]Again, the Devil took Him to a very high mountain and showed Him all the kingdoms of the world and their splendor. [9]And he said to Him, "I will give You all these things if You will fall down and worship me."[I]

[10]Then Jesus told him, "Go away,[J] Satan! For it is written:

> Worship the Lord your God,
>   and serve only Him."[K]

[11]Then the Devil left Him, and immediately angels came and began to serve Him.

[12]When He heard that John had been arrested, He withdrew into Galilee. [13]He left Nazareth behind and went to live in Capernaum by the sea, in the region of Zebulun and Naphtali. [14]This was to fulfill what was spoken through the prophet Isaiah:

> [15] Land of Zebulun and land of Naphtali,
>   along the sea road, beyond the Jordan,
>   Galilee of the Gentiles!
> [16] The people who live in darkness
>   have seen a great light,
>   and for those living in the shadowland
>   of death,
>   light has dawned.[L,M]

[17]From then on Jesus began to preach, "Repent, because the kingdom of heaven has come near!"

[18]As He was walking along the Sea of Galilee, He saw two brothers, Simon, who was called Peter, and his brother Andrew. They were casting a net into the sea, since they were fishermen. [19]"Follow Me," He told them, "and I will make you fish for[N] people!" [20]Immediately they left their nets and followed Him.

[21]Going on from there, He saw two other brothers, James the son of Zebedee, and his brother John. They were in a boat with Zebedee their father, mending their nets, and He called them. [22]Immediately they left the boat and their father and followed Him.

[23]Jesus was going all over Galilee, teaching in their synagogues, preaching the good news of the kingdom, and healing every[O] disease and sickness among the people. [24]Then the news about Him spread throughout Syria. So they brought to Him all those who were afflicted, those suffering from various diseases and intense pains, the demon-possessed, the epileptics, and the paralytics. And He healed them.

²⁵ Large crowds followed Him from Galilee, Decapolis, Jerusalem, Judea, and beyond the Jordan.

5 When He saw the crowds, He went up on the mountain, and after He sat down, His disciples came to Him. ² Then[A] He began to teach them, saying:

³   "The poor in spirit are blessed,
      for the kingdom of heaven is theirs.
⁴   Those who mourn are blessed,
      for they will be comforted.
⁵   The gentle are blessed,
      for they will inherit the earth.
⁶   Those who hunger and thirst
        for righteousness are blessed,
      for they will be filled.
⁷   The merciful are blessed,
      for they will be shown mercy.
⁸   The pure in heart are blessed,
      for they will see God.
⁹   The peacemakers are blessed,
      for they will be called sons of God.
¹⁰ Those who are persecuted
        for righteousness are blessed,
      for the kingdom of heaven is theirs.

¹¹ "You are blessed when they insult and persecute you and falsely say every kind of evil against you because of Me. ¹² Be glad and rejoice, because your reward is great in heaven. For that is how they persecuted the prophets who were before you.

¹³ "You are the salt of the earth. But if the salt should lose its taste, how can it be made salty? It's no longer good for anything but to be thrown out and trampled on by men.

¹⁴ "You are the light of the world. A city situated on a hill cannot be hidden. ¹⁵ No one lights a lamp and puts it under a basket,[B] but rather on a lampstand, and it gives light for all who are in the house. ¹⁶ In the same way, let your light shine[C] before men, so that they may see your good works and give glory to your Father in heaven.

¹⁷ "Don't assume that I came to destroy the Law or the Prophets. I did not come to destroy but to fulfill. ¹⁸ For I assure you: Until heaven and earth pass away, not the smallest letter[D] or one stroke of a letter will pass from the law

until all things are accomplished. ¹⁹ Therefore, whoever breaks one of the least of these commands and teaches people to do so will be called least in the kingdom of heaven. But whoever practices and teaches these commands will be called great in the kingdom of heaven. ²⁰ For I tell you, unless your righteousness surpasses that of the scribes and Pharisees, you will never enter the kingdom of heaven.

²¹ "You have heard that it was said to our ancestors,[E] Do not murder,[F] and whoever murders will be subject to judgment. ²² But I tell you, everyone who is angry with his brother[G] will be subject to judgment. And whoever says to his brother, 'Fool!'[H] will be subject to the Sanhedrin. But whoever says, 'You moron!' will be subject to hellfire.[I] ²³ So if you are offering your gift on the altar, and there you remember that your brother has something against you, ²⁴ leave your gift there in front of the altar. First go and be reconciled with your brother, and then come and offer your gift. ²⁵ Reach a settlement quickly with your adversary while you're on the way with him, or your adversary will hand you over to the judge, the judge to[J] the officer, and you will be thrown into prison. ²⁶ I assure you: You will never get out of there until you have paid the last penny![K]

²⁷ "You have heard that it was said, Do not commit adultery.[L] ²⁸ But I tell you, everyone who looks at a woman to lust for her has already committed adultery with her in his heart. ²⁹ If your right eye causes you to sin, gouge it out and throw it away. For it is better that you lose one of the parts of your body than for your whole body to be thrown into hell. ³⁰ And if your right hand causes you to sin, cut it off and throw it away. For it is better that you lose one of the parts of your body than for your whole body to go into hell!

³¹ "It was also said, Whoever divorces his wife must give her a written notice of divorce.[M] ³² But I tell you, everyone who divorces his wife, except in a case of sexual immorality,[N] causes her to commit adultery. And whoever marries a divorced woman commits adultery.

³³ "Again, you have heard that it was said to our ancestors,[O] You must not break your oath, but you must keep your oaths to the Lord.[P] ³⁴ But I tell you, don't take an oath at all: ei-

A5:2 Lit *Then opening His mouth*   B5:15 A large basket used to measure grain   C5:16 Or *way, your light must shine*   D5:18 Or *not one iota; iota* is the smallest letter of the Gk alphabet.   E5:21 Lit *to the ancients*   F5:21 Ex 20:13; Dt 5:17   G5:22 Other mss add *without a cause*   H5:22 Lit *Raca,* an Aram term of abuse similar to "airhead"   I5:22 Lit *the gehenna of fire*   J5:25 Other mss read *judge will hand you over to*   K5:26 Lit *quadrans,* the smallest and least valuable Roman coin, worth ¹/₆₄ of a daily wage   L5:27 Ex 20:14; Dt 5:18   M5:31 Dt 24:1   N5:32 Gk *porneia* = fornication, or possibly a violation of Jewish marriage laws   O5:33 Lit *to the ancients*   P5:33 Lv 19:12; Nm 30:2; Dt 23:21

ther by heaven, because it is God's throne; [35] or by the earth, because it is His footstool; or by Jerusalem, because it is the city of the great King. [36] Neither should you swear by your head, because you cannot make a single hair white or black. [37] But let your word 'yes' be 'yes,' and your 'no' be 'no.'[A] Anything more than this is from the evil one.

[38] "You have heard that it was said, An eye for an eye and a tooth for a tooth.[B] [39] But I tell you, don't resist[C] an evildoer. On the contrary, if anyone slaps you on your right cheek, turn the other to him also. [40] As for the one who wants to sue you and take away your shirt,[D] let him have your coat[E] as well. [41] And if anyone forces[F] you to go one mile, go with him two. [42] Give to the one who asks you, and don't turn away from the one who wants to borrow from you.

[43] "You have heard that it was said, Love your neighbor[G] and hate your enemy. [44] But I tell you, love your enemies[H] and pray for those who[I] persecute you, [45] so that you may be[J] sons of your Father in heaven. For He causes His sun to rise on the evil and the good, and sends rain on the righteous and the unrighteous. [46] For if you love those who love you, what reward will you have? Don't even the tax collectors do the same? [47] And if you greet only your brothers, what are you doing out of the ordinary?[K] Don't even the Gentiles[L] do the same? [48] Be perfect, therefore, as your heavenly Father is perfect.

6 "Be careful not to practice your righteousness[M] in front of people, to be seen by them. Otherwise, you will have no reward from your Father in heaven. [2] So whenever you give to the poor, don't sound a trumpet before you, as the hypocrites do in the synagogues and on the streets, to be applauded by people. I assure you: They've got their reward! [3] But when you give to the poor, don't let your left hand know what your right hand is doing, [4] so that your giving may be in secret. And your Father who sees in secret will reward you.[N]

[5] "Whenever you pray, you must not be like the hypocrites, because they love to pray standing in the synagogues and on the street corners to be seen by people. I assure you: They've got their reward! [6] But when you pray, go into your private room, shut your door, and pray to your Father who is in secret. And your Father who sees in secret will reward you.[O] [7] When you pray, don't babble like the idolaters,[P] since they imagine they'll be heard for their many words. [8] Don't be like them, because your Father knows the things you need before you ask Him.

[9] "Therefore, you should pray like this:

> Our Father in heaven,
> Your name be honored as holy.
> [10] Your kingdom come.
> Your will be done
> on earth as it is in heaven.
> [11] Give us today our daily bread.[Q]
> [12] And forgive us our debts,
> as we also have forgiven
> our debtors.
> [13] And do not bring us
> into[R] temptation,
> but deliver us from the evil one.[S]
> [For Yours is the kingdom
> and the power
> and the glory forever. Amen.][T]

[14] "For if you forgive people their wrongdoing,[U] your heavenly Father will forgive you as well. [15] But if you don't forgive people,[V] your Father will not forgive your wrongdoing.[U]

[16] "Whenever you fast, don't be sad-faced like the hypocrites. For they make their faces unattractive[W] so their fasting is obvious to people. I assure you: They've got their reward! [17] But when you fast, put oil on your head, and wash your face, [18] so that you don't show your fasting to people but to your Father who is in secret. And your Father who sees in secret will reward you.[O]

[19] "Don't collect for yourselves treasures[X] on earth, where moth and rust destroy and where thieves break in and steal. [20] But collect for yourselves treasures in heaven, where neither moth nor rust destroys, and where thieves don't break in and steal. [21] For where your treasure is, there your heart will be also.

²²"The eye is the lamp of the body. If your eye is good, your whole body will be full of light. ²³But if your eye is bad, your whole body will be full of darkness. So if the light within you is darkness—how deep is that darkness!

²⁴"No one can be a slave of two masters, since either he will hate one and love the other, or be devoted to one and despise the other. You cannot be slaves of God and of money.

²⁵"This is why I tell you: Don't worry about your life, what you will eat or what you will drink; or about your body, what you will wear. Isn't life more than food and the body more than clothing? ²⁶Look at the birds of the sky: They don't sow or reap or gather into barns, yet your heavenly Father feeds them. Aren't you worth more than they? ²⁷Can any of you add a single cubit to his heightᴬ by worrying? ²⁸And why do you worry about clothes? Learn how the wildflowers of the field grow: they don't labor or spin thread. ²⁹Yet I tell you that not even Solomon in all his splendor was adorned like one of these! ³⁰If that's how God clothes the grass of the field, which is here today and thrown into the furnace tomorrow, won't He do much more for you—you of little faith? ³¹So don't worry, saying, 'What will we eat?' or 'What will we drink?' or 'What will we wear?' ³²For the idolatersᴮ eagerly seek all these things, and your heavenly Father knows that you need them. ³³But seek first the kingdom of Godᶜ and His righteousness, and all these things will be provided for you. ³⁴Therefore don't worry about tomorrow, because tomorrow will worry about itself. Each day has enough trouble of its own.

7 "Do not judge, so that you won't be judged. ²For with the judgment you use,ᴰ you will be judged, and with the measure you use,ᴱ it will be measured to you. ³Why do you look at the speck in your brother's eye but don't notice the log in your own eye? ⁴Or how can you say to your brother, 'Let me take the speck out of your eye,' and look, there's a log in your eye? ⁵Hypocrite! First take the log out of your eye, and then you will see clearly to take the speck out of your brother's eye. ⁶Don't give what is holy to dogs or toss your pearls before pigs, or they will trample them with their feet, turn, and tear you to pieces.

⁷"Keep asking,ᶠ and it will be given to you. Keep searching,ᴳ and you will find. Keep knocking,ᴴ and the doorᴵ will be opened to you. ⁸For everyone who asks receives, and the one who searches finds, and to the one who knocks, the doorᴶ will be opened. ⁹What man among you, if his son asks him for bread, will give him a stone? ¹⁰Or if he asks for a fish, will give him a snake? ¹¹If you then, who are evil, know how to give good gifts to your children, how much more will your Father in heaven give good things to those who ask Him! ¹²Therefore, whatever you want others to do for you, do also the same for them—this is the Law and the Prophets.ᴷ

¹³"Enter through the narrow gate. For the gate is wide and the road is broad that leads to destruction, and there are many who go through it. ¹⁴How narrow is the gate and difficult the road that leads to life, and few find it.

¹⁵"Beware of false prophets who come to you in sheep's clothing but inwardly are ravaging wolves. ¹⁶You'll recognize them by their fruit. Are grapes gathered from thornbushes or figs from thistles? ¹⁷In the same way, every good tree produces good fruit, but a bad tree produces bad fruit. ¹⁸A good tree can't produce bad fruit; neither can a bad tree produce good fruit. ¹⁹Every tree that doesn't produce good fruit is cut down and thrown into the fire. ²⁰So you'll recognize them by their fruit.

²¹"Not everyone who says to Me, 'Lord, Lord!' will enter the kingdom of heaven, but only the one who does the will of My Father in heaven. ²²On that day many will say to Me, 'Lord, Lord, didn't we prophesy in Your name, drive out demons in Your name, and do many miracles in Your name?' ²³Then I will announce to them, 'I never knew you! Depart from Me, you lawbreakers!'ᴸ·ᴹ

²⁴"Therefore, everyone who hears these words of Mine and acts on them will be like a sensible man who built his house on the rock. ²⁵The rain fell, the rivers rose, and the winds blew and pounded that house. Yet it didn't collapse, because its foundation was on the rock. ²⁶But everyone who hears these words of Mine and doesn't act on them will be like a foolish man who built his house on the sand. ²⁷The rain fell, the rivers rose, the winds blew and

---

ᴬ6:27 Or add one moment to his life-span   ᴮ6:32 Or Gentiles, or nations, or heathen, or pagans   ᶜ6:33 Other mss omit of God   ᴰ7:2 Lit you judge   ᴱ7:2 Lit you measure   ᶠ7:7 Or Ask   ᴳ7:7 Or Search   ᴴ7:7 Or Knock   ᴵ7:7 Lit and it   ᴶ7:8 Lit knocks, it   ᴷ7:12 When capitalized, the Law and the Prophets = the OT   ᴸ7:23 Lit you who work lawlessness   ᴹ7:23 Ps 6:8

pounded that house, and it collapsed. And its collapse was great!"

²⁸When Jesus had finished this sermon,ᴬ the crowds were astonished at His teaching, ²⁹because He was teaching them like one who had authority, and not like their scribes.

8 When He came down from the mountain, large crowds followed Him. ²Right away a man with a serious skin disease came up and knelt before Him, saying, "Lord, if You are willing, You can make me clean."

³Reaching out His hand He touched him, saying, "I am willing; be made clean." Immediately his disease was healed.ᴮ ⁴Then Jesus told him, "See that you don't tell anyone; but go, show yourself to the priest, and offer the gift that Moses prescribed, as a testimony to them."

⁵When He entered Capernaum, a centurion came to Him, pleading with Him, ⁶"Lord, my servant is lying at home paralyzed, in terrible agony!"

⁷"I will come and heal him," He told him.

⁸"Lord," the centurion replied, "I am not worthy to have You come under my roof. But only say the word, and my servant will be cured. ⁹For I too am a man under authority, having soldiers under my command.ᶜ I say to this one, 'Go!' and he goes; and to another, 'Come!' and he comes; and to my slave, 'Do this!' and he does it."

¹⁰Hearing this, Jesus was amazed and said to those following Him, "I assure you: I have not found anyone in Israel with so great a faith! ¹¹I tell you that many will come from east and west, and recline at the table with Abraham, Isaac, and Jacob in the kingdom of heaven. ¹²But the sons of the kingdom will be thrown into the outer darkness. In that place there will be weeping and gnashing of teeth." ¹³Then Jesus told the centurion, "Go. As you have believed, let it be done for you." And his servant was cured that very moment.ᴰ

¹⁴When Jesus went into Peter's house, He saw his mother-in-law lying in bed with a fever. ¹⁵So He touched her hand, and the fever left her. Then she got up and began to serve Him. ¹⁶When evening came, they brought to Him many who were demon-possessed. He drove out the spirits with a word and healed all who were sick, ¹⁷so that what was spoken through the prophet Isaiah might be fulfilled:

He Himself took our weaknesses and carried our diseases.ᴱ

¹⁸When Jesus saw large crowdsᶠ around Him, He gave the order to go to the other side of the sea.ᴳ ¹⁹A scribe approached Him and said, "Teacher, I will follow You wherever You go!"

²⁰Jesus told him, "Foxes have dens and birds of the sky have nests, but the Son of Man has no place to lay His head."

²¹"Lord," another of His disciples said, "first let me go bury my father."ᴴ

²²But Jesus told him, "Follow Me, and let the dead bury their own dead."

²³As He got into theᴵ boat, His disciples followed Him. ²⁴Suddenly, a violent storm arose on the sea, so that the boat was being swamped by the waves. But He was sleeping. ²⁵So the disciples came and woke Him up, saying, "Lord, save us! We're going to die!"

²⁶But He said to them, "Why are you fearful, you of little faith?" Then He got up and rebuked the winds and the sea. And there was a great calm.

²⁷The men were amazed and asked, "What kind of man is this?—even the winds and the sea obey Him!"

²⁸When He had come to the other side, to the region of the Gadarenes,ᴶ two demon-possessed men met Him as they came out of the tombs. They were so violent that no one could pass that way. ²⁹Suddenly they shouted, "What do You have to do with us,ᴷ·ᴸ Son of God? Have You come here to torment us before the time?"

³⁰Now a long way off from them, a large herd of pigs was feeding. ³¹"If You drive us out," the demons begged Him, "send us into the herd of pigs."

³²"Go!" He told them. So when they had come out, they entered the pigs. And suddenly the whole herd rushed down the steep bank into the sea and perished in the water. ³³Then the men who tended them fled. They went into the city and reported everything—especially what had happened to those who were demon-possessed. ³⁴At that, the whole town went

---

ᴬ7:28 Lit had ended these words   ᴮ8:3 Lit cleansed   ᶜ8:9 Lit under me   ᴰ8:13 Or that hour; lit very hour   ᴱ8:17 Is 53:4   ᶠ8:18 Other mss read saw a crowd   ᴳ8:18 = Sea of Galilee   ᴴ8:21 Not necessarily meaning his father was already dead   ᴵ8:23 Other mss read to a   ᴶ8:28 Other mss read Gergesenes   ᴷ8:29 Other mss add Jesus   ᴸ8:29 Lit What to us and to You out to meet Jesus. When they saw Him, they begged Him to leave their region.

9 So He got into a boat, crossed over, and came to His own town. ²Just then some men^A brought to Him a paralytic lying on a mat. Seeing their faith, Jesus told the paralytic, "Have courage, son, your sins are forgiven."

³At this, some of the scribes said among themselves, "He's blaspheming!"

⁴But perceiving their thoughts, Jesus said, "Why are you thinking evil things in your hearts?^B ⁵For which is easier: to say, 'Your sins are forgiven,' or to say, 'Get up and walk'? ⁶But so you may know that the Son of Man has authority on earth to forgive sins"—then He told the paralytic, "Get up, pick up your mat, and go home." ⁷And he got up and went home. ⁸When the crowds saw this, they were awestruck,^C,^D and gave glory to God who had given such authority to men.

⁹As Jesus went on from there, He saw a man named Matthew sitting at the tax office, and He said to him, "Follow Me!" So he got up and followed him.

¹⁰While He was reclining at the table in the house, many tax collectors and sinners came as guests to eat^E with Jesus and His disciples. ¹¹When the Pharisees saw this, they asked His disciples, "Why does your Teacher eat with tax collectors and sinners?"

¹²But when He heard this, He said, "Those who are well don't need a doctor, but the sick do. ¹³Go and learn what this means: **I desire mercy and not sacrifice.**^F For I didn't come to call the righteous, but sinners."^G

¹⁴Then John's disciples came to Him, saying, "Why do we and the Pharisees fast often, but Your disciples do not fast?"

¹⁵Jesus said to them, "Can the wedding guests^H be sad while the groom is with them? The time^I will come when the groom will be taken away from them, and then they will fast. ¹⁶No one patches an old garment with unshrunk cloth, because the patch pulls away from the garment and makes the tear worse. ¹⁷And no one puts^J new wine into old wineskins. Otherwise, the skins burst, the wine spills out, and the skins are ruined. But they put new wine into fresh wineskins, and both are preserved."

¹⁸As He was telling them these things, suddenly one of the leaders^K came and knelt down before Him, saying, "My daughter is near death,^L but come and lay Your hand on her, and she will live." ¹⁹So Jesus and His disciples got up and followed him.

²⁰Just then, a woman who had suffered from bleeding for 12 years approached from behind and touched the tassel on His robe, ²¹for she said to herself, "If I can just touch His robe, I'll be made well!"^M

²²But Jesus turned and saw her. "Have courage, daughter," He said. "Your faith has made you well."^N And the woman was made well from that moment.^O

²³When Jesus came to the leader's house, He saw the flute players and a crowd lamenting loudly. ²⁴"Leave," He said, "because the girl isn't dead, but sleeping." And they started laughing at Him. ²⁵But when the crowd had been put outside, He went in and took her by the hand, and the girl got up. ²⁶And this news spread throughout that whole area.

²⁷As Jesus went on from there, two blind men followed Him, shouting, "Have mercy on us, Son of David!"

²⁸When He entered the house, the blind men approached Him, and Jesus said to them, "Do you believe that I can do this?"

"Yes, Lord," they answered Him.

²⁹Then He touched their eyes, saying, "Let it be done for you according to your faith!" ³⁰And their eyes were opened. Then Jesus warned them sternly, "Be sure that no one finds out!"^P ³¹But they went out and spread the news about Him throughout that whole area.

³²Just as they were going out, a demon-possessed man who was unable to speak was brought to Him. ³³When the demon had been driven out, the man^Q spoke. And the crowds were amazed, saying, "Nothing like this has ever been seen in Israel!"

³⁴But the Pharisees said, "He drives out demons by the ruler of the demons!"

³⁵Then Jesus went to all the towns and villages, teaching in their synagogues, preaching the good news of the kingdom, and healing every^R disease and every sickness.^S ³⁶When He saw the crowds, He felt compassion for them, because they were weary and worn out, like

^A9:2 Lit then they   ^B9:4 Or minds   ^C9:8 Other mss read amazed   ^D9:8 Lit afraid   ^E9:10 Lit came, they were reclining [at the table]; at important meals the custom was to recline on a mat at a low table and lean on the left elbow.   ^F9:13 Hs 6:6   ^G9:13 Other mss add to repentance   ^H9:15 Lit the sons of the bridal chamber   ^I9:15 Lit days   ^J9:17 Lit And they do not put   ^K9:18 A leader of a synagogue; Mk 5:22   ^L9:18 Lit daughter has now come to the end   ^M9:21 Or be delivered   ^N9:22 Or has saved you   ^O9:22 Lit hour   ^P9:30 Lit no one knows   ^Q9:33 Lit the man who was unable to speak   ^R9:35 Or every kind of   ^S9:35 Other mss add among the people sheep without a shepherd. ³⁷Then He said to His disciples, "The harvest is abundant, but the workers are few. ³⁸Therefore, pray to the Lord of the harvest to send out workers into His harvest."

10 Summoning His 12 disciples, He gave them authority over unclean spirits, to drive them out and to heal every^A disease and sickness: ²These are the names of the 12 apostles:

> First, Simon, who is called Peter,
> and Andrew his brother;
> James the son of Zebedee,
> and John his brother;
> ³ Philip and Bartholomew;^B
> Thomas and Matthew
> the tax collector;
> James the son of Alphaeus,
> and Thaddaeus;^C
> ⁴ Simon the Zealot,^D and Judas Iscariot,^E
> who also betrayed Him.

⁵Jesus sent out these 12 after giving them instructions: "Don't take the road leading to other nations, and don't enter any Samaritan town. ⁶Instead, go to the lost sheep of the house of Israel. ⁷As you go, announce this: 'The kingdom of heaven has come near.' ⁸Heal the sick, raise the dead, cleanse those with skin diseases, drive out demons. You have received free of charge; give free of charge. ⁹Don't take along gold, silver, or copper for your money-belts. ¹⁰Don't take a traveling bag for the road, or an extra shirt, sandals, or a walking stick, for the worker is worthy of his food.

¹¹"When you enter any town or village, find out who is worthy, and stay there until you leave. ¹²Greet a household when you enter it, ¹³and if the household is worthy, let your peace be on it. But if it is unworthy, let your peace return to you. ¹⁴If anyone will not welcome you or listen to your words, shake the dust off your feet when you leave that house or town. ¹⁵I assure you: It will be more tolerable on the day of judgment for the land of Sodom and Gomorrah than for that town.

¹⁶"Look, I'm sending you out like sheep among wolves. Therefore be as shrewd as serpents and as harmless as doves. ¹⁷Because people will hand you over to sanhedrins^F

and flog you in their synagogues, beware of them. ¹⁸You will even be brought before governors and kings because of Me, to bear witness to them and to the nations. ¹⁹But when they hand you over, don't worry about how or what you should speak. For you will be given what to say at that hour, ²⁰because you are not speaking, but the Spirit of your Father is speaking through you.

²¹"Brother will betray brother to death, and a father his child. Children will even rise up against their parents and have them put to death. ²²You will be hated by everyone because of My name. But the one who endures to the end will be delivered.^G ²³When they persecute you in one town, escape to another. For I assure you: You will not have covered the towns of Israel before the Son of Man comes. ²⁴A disciple^H is not above his teacher, or a slave above his master. ²⁵It is enough for a disciple to become like his teacher and a slave like his master. If they called the head of the house 'Beelzebul,' how much more the members of his household!

²⁶"Therefore, don't be afraid of them, since there is nothing covered that won't be uncovered and nothing hidden that won't be made known. ²⁷What I tell you in the dark, speak in the light. What you hear in a whisper,^I proclaim on the housetops. ²⁸Don't fear those who kill the body but are not able to kill the soul; rather, fear Him who is able to destroy both soul and body in hell. ²⁹Aren't two sparrows sold for a penny?^J Yet not one of them falls to the ground without your Father's consent.^K ³⁰But even the hairs of your head have all been counted. ³¹So don't be afraid therefore; you are worth more than many sparrows.

³²"Therefore, everyone who will acknowledge Me before men, I will also acknowledge him before My Father in heaven. ³³But whoever denies Me before men, I will also deny him before My Father in heaven. ³⁴Don't assume that I came to bring peace on the earth. I did not come to bring peace, but a sword. ³⁵For I came to turn

> a man against his father,
> a daughter against her mother,

---

^A10:1 Or every kind of   ^B10:3 Probably the Nathanael of Jn 1:45-51   ^C10:3 Other mss read and Lebbaeus, whose surname was Thaddaeus   ^D10:4 Lit the Cananaean   ^E10:4 Iscariot is probably "a man of Kerioth," a town in Judea.   ^F10:17 Local Jewish courts or local councils   ^G10:22 Or saved   ^H10:24 Or student   ^I10:27 Lit in the ear   ^J10:29 Gk assarion, a small copper coin   ^K10:29 Lit ground apart from your Father

a daughter-in-law against
her mother-in-law;
³⁶ and a man's enemies will be
the members of his household.^A

³⁷ The person who loves father or mother more than Me is not worthy of Me; the person who loves son or daughter more than Me is not worthy of Me. ³⁸ And whoever doesn't take up his cross and follow^B Me is not worthy of Me. ³⁹ Anyone finding^C his life will lose it, and anyone losing^D his life because of Me will find it.

⁴⁰ "The one who welcomes you welcomes Me, and the one who welcomes Me welcomes Him who sent Me. ⁴¹ Anyone who^E welcomes a prophet because he is a prophet^F will receive a prophet's reward. And anyone who^G welcomes a righteous person because he's righteous^H will receive a righteous person's reward. ⁴² And whoever gives just a cup of cold water to one of these little ones because he is a disciple^I—I assure you: He will never lose his reward!"

11 When Jesus had finished giving orders to His 12 disciples, He moved on from there to teach and preach in their towns. ² When John heard in prison what the Messiah was doing, he sent a message by his disciples ³ and asked Him, "Are You the One who is to come, or should we expect someone else?"

⁴ Jesus replied to them, "Go and report to John what you hear and see: ⁵ the blind see, the lame walk, those with skin diseases are healed,^J the deaf hear, the dead are raised, and the poor are told the good news. ⁶ And if anyone is not offended because of Me, he is blessed."

⁷ As these men went away, Jesus began to speak to the crowds about John: "What did you go out into the wilderness to see? A reed swaying in the wind? ⁸ What then did you go out to see? A man dressed in soft clothes? Look, those who wear soft clothes are in kings' palaces. ⁹ But what did you go out to see? A prophet? Yes, I tell you, and far more than a prophet. ¹⁰ This is the one it is written about:

Look, I am sending My messenger
ahead of You;^K
he will prepare Your way before You.^L

¹¹ "I assure you: Among those born of women no one greater than John the Baptist has appeared,^M but the least in the kingdom of heaven is greater than he. ¹² From the days of John the Baptist until now, the kingdom of heaven has been suffering violence,^N and the violent have been seizing it by force. ¹³ For all the prophets and the Law prophesied until John; ¹⁴ if you're willing to accept it, he is the Elijah who is to come. ¹⁵ Anyone who has ears^O should listen!

¹⁶ "To what should I compare this generation? It's like children sitting in the marketplaces who call out to each other:

¹⁷ We played the flute for you,
but you didn't dance;
we sang a lament,
but you didn't mourn!^P

¹⁸ For John did not come eating or drinking, and they say, 'He has a demon!' ¹⁹ The Son of Man came eating and drinking, and they say, 'Look, a glutton and a drunkard, a friend of tax collectors and sinners!' Yet wisdom is vindicated^Q by her deeds.^R

²⁰ Then He proceeded to denounce the towns where most of His miracles were done, because they did not repent: ²¹ "Woe to you, Chorazin! Woe to you, Bethsaida! For if the miracles that were done in you had been done in Tyre and Sidon, they would have repented in sackcloth and ashes long ago! ²² But I tell you, it will be more tolerable for Tyre and Sidon on the day of judgment than for you. ²³ And you, Capernaum, will you be exalted to heaven? You will go down to Hades. For if the miracles that were done in you had been done in Sodom, it would have remained until today. ²⁴ But I tell you, it will be more tolerable for the land of Sodom on the day of judgment than for you.

²⁵ At that time Jesus said, "I praise^S You, Father, Lord of heaven and earth, because You have hidden these things from the wise and learned and revealed them to infants. ²⁶ Yes, Father, because this was Your good pleasure.^T ²⁷ All things have been entrusted to Me by My Father. No one knows^U the Son except the Father, and no one knows the Father except the

A10:35-36 Mc 7:6 B10:38 Lit follow after C10:39 Or The one who finds D10:39 Or and the one who loses E10:41 Or The one who F10:41 Lit prophet in the name of a prophet G10:41 Or And the one who H10:41 Lit person in the name of a righteous person I10:42 Lit little ones in the name of a disciple J11:5 Lit cleansed K11:10 Lit messenger before Your face L11:10 Mal 3:1 M11:11 Lit arisen N11:12 Or has been forcefully advancing O11:15 Other mss add to hear P11:17 Or beat your breasts Q11:19 Or declared right R11:19 Other mss read children S11:25 Or thank T11:26 Lit was well-pleasing in Your sight U11:27 Or knows exactly

Son and anyone to whom the Son desires[A] to reveal Him.

²⁸"Come to Me, all of you who are weary and burdened, and I will give you rest. ²⁹All of you, take up My yoke and learn from Me, because I am gentle and humble in heart, and you will find rest for yourselves. ³⁰For My yoke is easy and My burden is light."

12 At that time Jesus passed through the grainfields on the Sabbath. His disciples were hungry and began to pick and eat some heads of grain. ²But when the Pharisees saw it, they said to Him, "Look, Your disciples are doing what is not lawful to do on the Sabbath!"

³He said to them, "Haven't you read what David did when he and those who were with him were hungry— ⁴how he entered the house of God, and they ate[B] the sacred bread, which is not lawful for him or for those with him to eat, but only for the priests? ⁵Or haven't you read in the Law[C] that on Sabbath days the priests in the temple violate the Sabbath and are innocent? ⁶But I tell you that something greater than the temple is here! ⁷If you had known what this means: I desire mercy and not sacrifice,[D] you would not have condemned the innocent. ⁸For the Son of Man is Lord of the Sabbath."

⁹Moving on from there, He entered their synagogue. ¹⁰There He saw a man who had a paralyzed hand. And in order to accuse Him they asked Him, "Is it lawful to heal on the Sabbath?"

¹¹But He said to them, "What man among you, if he had a sheep[E] that fell into a pit on the Sabbath, wouldn't take hold of it and lift it out? ¹²A man is worth far more than a sheep, so it is lawful to do what is good on the Sabbath."

¹³Then He told the man, "Stretch out your hand." So he stretched it out, and it was restored, as good as the other. ¹⁴But the Pharisees went out and plotted against Him, how they might destroy Him.

¹⁵When Jesus became aware of this, He withdrew from there. Huge crowds[F] followed Him, and He healed them all. ¹⁶He warned them not to make Him known, ¹⁷so that what was spoken through the prophet Isaiah might be fulfilled:

¹⁸   **Here is My Servant**
         whom I have chosen,

My beloved in whom My soul delights;
I will put My Spirit on Him,
and He will proclaim justice
     to the nations.
¹⁹   **He will not argue or shout,**
     and no one will hear His voice
         in the streets.
²⁰   **He will not break a bruised reed,**
     and He will not put out
         a smoldering wick,
     until He has led justice to victory.[G]
²¹   **The nations will put their hope**
         in His name.[H]

²²Then a demon-possessed man who was blind and unable to speak was brought to Him. He healed him, so that the man[I] could both speak and see. ²³And all the crowds were astounded and said, "Perhaps this is the Son of David!"

²⁴When the Pharisees heard this, they said, "The man drives out demons only by Beelzebul, the ruler of the demons."

²⁵Knowing their thoughts, He told them: "Every kingdom divided against itself is headed for destruction, and no city or house divided against itself will stand. ²⁶If Satan drives out Satan, he is divided against himself. How then will his kingdom stand? ²⁷And if I drive out demons by Beelzebul, who is it your sons drive them out by? For this reason they will be your judges. ²⁸If I drive out demons by the Spirit of God, then the kingdom of God has come to you. ²⁹How can someone enter a strong man's house and steal his possessions unless he first ties up the strong man? Then he can rob his house. ³⁰Anyone who is not with Me is against Me, and anyone who does not gather with Me scatters. ³¹Because of this, I tell you, people will be forgiven every sin and blasphemy, but the blasphemy against[J] the Spirit will not be forgiven.[K] ³²Whoever speaks a word against the Son of Man, it will be forgiven him. But whoever speaks against the Holy Spirit, it will not be forgiven him, either in this age or in the one to come.

³³"Either make the tree good and its fruit good, or make the tree bad[L] and its fruit bad; for a tree is known by its fruit. ³⁴Brood of vipers! How can you speak good things when you are evil? For the mouth speaks from the overflow of the heart. ³⁵A good man produces

---

[A]11:27 Or wills, or chooses   [B]12:4 Other mss read he ate   [C]12:5 = The Torah (the Pentateuch)   [D]12:7 Hs 6:6   [E]12:11 Or had one sheep   [F]12:15 Other mss read Many   [G]12:20 Or until He has successfully put forth justice   [H]12:18-21 Is 42:1-4   [I]12:22 Lit mute   [J]12:31 Or of   [K]12:31 Other mss add people   [L]12:33 Or decayed; lit rotten good things from his storeroom of good,[A] and an evil man produces evil things from his storeroom of evil. ³⁶ I tell you that on the day of judgment people will have to account for every careless word they speak.[B] ³⁷ For by your words you will be acquitted, and by your words you will be condemned."

³⁸ Then some of the scribes and Pharisees said to Him, "Teacher, we want to see a sign from You."

³⁹ But He answered them, "An evil and adulterous generation demands a sign, but no sign will be given to it except the sign of the prophet Jonah. ⁴⁰ For as Jonah was in the belly of the huge fish three days and three nights, so the Son of Man will be in the heart of the earth three days and three nights. ⁴¹ The men of Nineveh will stand up at the judgment with this generation and condemn it, because they repented at Jonah's proclamation; and look—something greater than Jonah is here! ⁴² The queen of the south will rise up at the judgment with this generation and condemn it, because she came from the ends of the earth to hear the wisdom of Solomon; and look—something greater than Solomon is here!

⁴³ "When an unclean spirit comes out of a man, it roams through waterless places looking for rest but doesn't find any. ⁴⁴ Then it says, 'I'll go back to my house that I came from.' And returning, it finds the house vacant, swept, and put in order. ⁴⁵ Then off it goes and brings with it seven other spirits more evil than itself, and they enter and settle down there. As a result, that man's last condition is worse than the first. That's how it will also be with this evil generation."

⁴⁶ He was still speaking to the crowds when suddenly His mother and brothers were standing outside wanting to speak to Him. ⁴⁷ Someone told Him, "Look, Your mother and Your brothers are standing outside, wanting to speak to You."[C]

⁴⁸ But He replied to the one who told Him, "Who is My mother and who are My brothers?" ⁴⁹ And stretching out His hand toward His disciples, He said, "Here are My mother and My brothers! ⁵⁰ For whoever does the will of My Father in heaven, that person is My brother and sister and mother."

13 On that day Jesus went out of the house and was sitting by the sea. ² Such large crowds gathered around Him that He got into a boat and sat down, while the whole crowd stood on the shore.

³ Then He told them many things in parables, saying: "Consider the sower who went out to sow. ⁴ As he was sowing, some seed fell along the path, and the birds came and ate them up. ⁵ Others fell on rocky ground, where there wasn't much soil, and they sprang up quickly since the soil wasn't deep. ⁶ But when the sun came up they were scorched, and since they had no root, they withered. ⁷ Others fell among thorns, and the thorns came up and choked them. ⁸ Still others fell on good ground and produced a crop: some 100, some 60, and some 30 times what was sown. ⁹ Anyone who has ears[D] should listen!"

¹⁰ Then the disciples came up and asked Him, "Why do You speak to them in parables?"

¹¹ He answered them, "Because the secrets of the kingdom of heaven have been given for you to know, but it has not been given to them. ¹² For whoever has, more will be given to him, and he will have more than enough. But whoever does not have, even what he has will be taken away from him. ¹³ For this reason I speak to them in parables, because looking they do not see, and hearing they do not listen or understand. ¹⁴ Isaiah's prophecy is fulfilled in them, which says:

> You will listen and listen,
> yet never understand;
> and you will look and look,
> yet never perceive.
> 15 For this people's heart
> has grown callous;
> their ears are hard of hearing,
> and they have shut their eyes;
> otherwise they might see
> with their eyes
> and hear with their ears,
> understand with their hearts
> and turn back—
> and I would cure them.[E]

¹⁶ "But your eyes are blessed because they do see, and your ears because they do hear! ¹⁷ For I assure you: Many prophets and righteous people longed to see the things you see yet

---

didn't see them; to hear the things you hear yet didn't hear them.

¹⁸"You, then, listen to the parable of the sower: ¹⁹When anyone hears the word^A about the kingdom and doesn't understand it, the evil one comes and snatches away what was sown in his heart. This is the one sown along the path. ²⁰And the one sown on rocky ground—this is one who hears the word and immediately receives it with joy. ²¹Yet he has no root in himself, but is short-lived. When pressure or persecution comes because of the word, immediately he stumbles. ²²Now the one sown among the thorns—this is one who hears the word, but the worries of this age and the seduction^B of wealth choke the word, and it becomes unfruitful. ²³But the one sown on the good ground—this is one who hears and understands the word, who does bear fruit and yields: some 100, some 60, some 30 times what was sown."

²⁴He presented another parable to them: "The kingdom of heaven may be compared to a man who sowed good seed in his field. ²⁵But while people were sleeping, his enemy came, sowed weeds^C among the wheat, and left. ²⁶When the plants sprouted and produced grain, then the weeds also appeared. ²⁷The landowner's slaves came to him and said, 'Master, didn't you sow good seed in your field? Then where did the weeds come from?'

²⁸"'An enemy did this!' he told them.

"'So, do you want us to go and gather them up?' the slaves asked him.

²⁹"'No,' he said. 'When you gather up the weeds, you might also uproot the wheat with them. ³⁰Let both grow together until the harvest. At harvest time I'll tell the reapers: Gather the weeds first and tie them in bundles to burn them, but store the wheat in my barn.'"

³¹He presented another parable to them: "The kingdom of heaven is like a mustard seed that a man took and sowed in his field. ³²It's the smallest of all the seeds, but when grown, it's taller than the vegetables and becomes a tree, so that the birds of the sky come and nest in its branches."

³³He told them another parable: "The kingdom of heaven is like yeast that a woman took and mixed into 50 pounds^D of flour until it spread through all of it."^E

³⁴Jesus told the crowds all these things in parables, and He would not speak anything to them without a parable, ³⁵so that what was spoken through the prophet might be fulfilled:

> I will open My mouth in parables;
> I will declare things kept secret
> from the foundation of the world.^F

³⁶Then He dismissed the crowds and went into the house. His disciples approached Him and said, "Explain the parable of the weeds in the field to us."

³⁷He replied: "The One who sows the good seed is the Son of Man; ³⁸the field is the world; and the good seed—these are the sons of the kingdom. The weeds are the sons of the evil one, ³⁹and the enemy who sowed them is the Devil. The harvest is the end of the age, and the harvesters are angels. ⁴⁰Therefore, just as the weeds are gathered and burned in the fire, so it will be at the end of the age. ⁴¹The Son of Man will send out His angels, and they will gather from His kingdom everything that causes sin^G and those guilty of lawlessness.^H ⁴²They will throw them into the blazing furnace where there will be weeping and gnashing of teeth. ⁴³Then the righteous will shine like the sun in their Father's kingdom. Anyone who has ears^I should listen!

⁴⁴"The kingdom of heaven is like treasure, buried in a field, that a man found and reburied. Then in his joy he goes and sells everything he has and buys that field.

⁴⁵"Again, the kingdom of heaven is like a merchant in search of fine pearls. ⁴⁶When he found one priceless^J pearl, he went and sold everything he had, and bought it.

⁴⁷"Again, the kingdom of heaven is like a large net thrown into the sea. It collected every kind of fish, ⁴⁸and when it was full, they dragged it ashore, sat down, and gathered the good fish into containers, but threw out the worthless ones. ⁴⁹So it will be at the end of the age. The angels will go out, separate the evil people from the righteous, ⁵⁰and throw them into the blazing furnace. In that place there will be weeping and gnashing of teeth.

⁵¹"Have you understood all these things?"^K

"Yes," they told Him.

^A13:19 Gk logos = word, or message, or saying, or thing   ^B13:22 Or pleasure, or deceitfulness   ^C13:25 Or darnel, a weed similar in appearance to wheat in the early stages   ^D13:33 Lit 3 sata; about 40 quarts   ^E13:33 Or until all of it was leavened   ^F13:35 Ps 78:2   ^G13:41 Or stumbling   ^H13:41 Or those who do lawlessness   ^I13:43 Other mss add to hear   ^J13:46 Or very precious   ^K13:51 Other mss add Jesus asked them

52"Therefore," He said to them, "every student of Scripture^A instructed in the kingdom of heaven is like a landowner who brings out of his storeroom what is new and what is old." 53When Jesus had finished these parables, He left there.

54He went to His hometown and began to teach them in their synagogue, so that they were astonished and said, "How did this wisdom and these miracles come to Him? 55Isn't this the carpenter's son? Isn't His mother called Mary, and His brothers James, Joseph,^B Simon, and Judas? 56And His sisters, aren't they all with us? So where does He get all these things?" 57And they were offended by Him.

But Jesus said to them, "A prophet is not without honor except in his hometown and in his household." 58And He did not do many miracles there because of their unbelief.

14 At that time Herod the tetrarch heard the report about Jesus. 2"This is John the Baptist!" he told his servants. "He has been raised from the dead, and that's why supernatural powers are at work in him."

3For Herod had arrested John, chained^C him, and put him in prison on account of Herodias, his brother Philip's wife, 4since John had been telling him, "It's not lawful for you to have her!" 5Though he wanted to kill him, he feared the crowd, since they regarded him as a prophet.

6But when Herod's birthday celebration came, Herodias's daughter danced before them^D and pleased Herod. 7So he promised with an oath to give her whatever she might ask. 8And prompted by her mother, she answered, "Give me John the Baptist's head here on a platter!" 9Although the king regretted it, he commanded that it be granted because of his oaths and his guests. 10So he sent orders and had John beheaded in the prison. 11His head was brought on a platter and given to the girl, who carried it to her mother. 12Then his disciples came, removed the corpse,^E buried it, and went and reported to Jesus.

13When Jesus heard about it, He withdrew from there by boat to a remote place to be alone. When the crowds heard this, they followed Him on foot from the towns. 14As He stepped ashore,^F He saw a huge crowd, felt compassion for them, and healed their sick.

15When evening came, the disciples approached Him and said, "This place is a wilderness, and it is already late.^G Send the crowds away so they can go into the villages and buy food for themselves."

16"They don't need to go away," Jesus told them. "You give them something to eat."

17"But we only have five loaves and two fish here," they said to Him.

18"Bring them here to Me," He said. 19Then He commanded the crowds to sit down^H on the grass. He took the five loaves and the two fish, and looking up to heaven, He blessed them. He broke the loaves and gave them to the disciples, and the disciples gave them to the crowds. 20Everyone ate and was filled. Then they picked up 12 baskets full of leftover pieces! 21Now those who ate were about 5,000 men, besides women and children.

22Immediately He^I made the disciples get into the boat and go ahead of Him to the other side, while He dismissed the crowds. 23After dismissing the crowds, He went up on the mountain by Himself to pray. When evening came, He was there alone. 24But the boat was already over a mile^J from land,^K battered by the waves, because the wind was against them. 25Around three in the morning,^L He came toward them walking on the sea. 26When the disciples saw Him walking on the sea, they were terrified. "It's a ghost!" they said, and cried out in fear.

27Immediately Jesus spoke to them. "Have courage! It is I. Don't be afraid."

28"Lord, if it's You," Peter answered Him, "command me to come to You on the water."

29"Come!" He said.

And climbing out of the boat, Peter started walking on the water and came toward Jesus. 30But when he saw the strength of the wind,^M he was afraid. And beginning to sink he cried out, "Lord, save me!"

31Immediately Jesus reached out His hand, caught hold of him, and said to him, "You of little faith, why did you doubt?" 32When they got into the boat, the wind ceased. 33Then those in the boat worshiped Him and said, "Truly You are the Son of God!"

A13:52 Or every scribe   B13:55 Other mss read Joses; Mk 6:3   C14:3 Or bound   D14:6 Lit danced in the middle   E14:12 Other mss read body   F14:14 Lit Coming out (of the boat)   G14:15 Lit and the time [for the evening meal] has already passed   H14:19 Lit to recline   I14:22 Other mss read Jesus   J14:24 Lit already many stadia; 1 stadion = 600 feet   K14:24 Other mss read already in the middle of the sea   L14:25 Lit fourth watch of the night = 3 to 6 a.m.   M14:30 Other mss read saw the wind

³⁴Once they crossed over, they came to land at Gennesaret. ³⁵When the men of that place recognized Him, they alerted^A the whole vicinity and brought to Him all who were sick. ³⁶They were begging Him that they might only touch the tassel on His robe. And as many as touched it were made perfectly well.

15 Then Pharisees and scribes came from Jerusalem to Jesus and asked, ²"Why do Your disciples break the tradition of the elders? For they don't wash their hands when they eat!"^B

³He answered them, "And why do you break God's commandment because of your tradition? ⁴For God said:^C

> Honor your father
>   and your mother;^D and,
> The one who speaks evil of father
>   or mother
>   must be put to death.^E

⁵But you say, 'Whoever tells his father or mother, "Whatever benefit you might have received from me is a gift committed to the temple"— ⁶he does not have to honor his father.'^F In this way, you have revoked God's word^G because of your tradition. ⁷Hypocrites! Isaiah prophesied correctly about you when he said:

> ⁸   These people^H honor Me with their lips,
>   but their heart is far from Me.
> ⁹   They worship Me in vain,
>   teaching as doctrines the commands
>   of men."^I

¹⁰Summoning the crowd, He told them, "Listen and understand: ¹¹It's not what goes into the mouth that defiles a man, but what comes out of the mouth, this defiles a man."

¹²Then the disciples came up and told Him, "Do You know that the Pharisees took offense when they heard this statement?"

¹³He replied, "Every plant that My heavenly Father didn't plant will be uprooted. ¹⁴Leave them alone! They are blind guides.^J And if the blind guide the blind, both will fall into a pit."

¹⁵Then Peter replied to Him, "Explain this parable to us."

¹⁶"Are you even still lacking in understanding?" He^K asked. ¹⁷"Don't you realize^L that

whatever goes into the mouth passes into the stomach and is eliminated?^M ¹⁸But what comes out of the mouth comes from the heart, and this defiles a man. ¹⁹For from the heart come evil thoughts, murders, adulteries, sexual immoralities, thefts, false testimonies, blasphemies. ²⁰These are the things that defile a man, but eating with unwashed hands does not defile a man."

²¹When Jesus left there, He withdrew to the area of Tyre and Sidon. ²²Just then a Canaanite woman from that region came and kept crying out,^N "Have mercy on me, Lord, Son of David! My daughter is cruelly tormented by a demon."

²³Yet He did not say a word to her. So His disciples approached Him and urged Him, "Send her away because she cries out after us."^O

²⁴He replied, "I was sent only to the lost sheep of the house of Israel."

²⁵But she came, knelt before Him, and said, "Lord, help me!"

²⁶He answered, "It isn't right to take the children's bread and throw it to their dogs."

²⁷"Yes, Lord," she said, "yet even the dogs eat the crumbs that fall from their masters' table!"

²⁸Then Jesus replied to her, "Woman, your faith is great. Let it be done for you as you want." And from that moment^P her daughter was cured.

²⁹Moving on from there, Jesus passed along the Sea of Galilee. He went up on a mountain and sat there, ³⁰and large crowds came to Him, having with them the lame, the blind, the deformed, those unable to speak, and many others. They put them at His feet, and He healed them. ³¹So the crowd was amazed when they saw those unable to speak talking, the deformed restored, the lame walking, and the blind seeing. And they gave glory to the God of Israel.

³²Now Jesus summoned His disciples and said, "I have compassion on the crowd, because they've already stayed with Me three days and have nothing to eat. I don't want to send them away hungry; otherwise they might collapse on the way."

³³The disciples said to Him, "Where could we get enough bread in this desolate place to fill such a crowd?"

^A14:35 Lit sent into   ^B15:2 Lit eat bread = eat a meal   ^C15:4 Other mss read commanded, saying   ^D15:4 Ex 20:12; Dt 5:16   ^E15:4 Ex 21:17; Lv 20:9   ^F15:6 Other mss read then he does not have to honor his father or mother   ^G15:6 Other mss read commandment   ^H15:8 Other mss add draw near to Me with their mouths, and   ^I15:8-9 Is 29:13 LXX   ^J15:14 Other mss add for the blind   ^K15:16 Other mss read Jesus   ^L15:17 Other mss add yet   ^M15:17 Lit and goes out into the toilet   ^N15:22 Other mss read and cried out to Him   ^O15:23 Lit she is yelling behind us or after us   ^P15:28 Lit hour

³⁴"How many loaves do you have?" Jesus asked them.

"Seven," they said, "and a few small fish."

³⁵After commanding the crowd to sit down on the ground, ³⁶He took the seven loaves and the fish, and He gave thanks, broke them, and kept on giving them to the disciples, and the disciples gave them to the crowds. ³⁷They all ate and were filled. Then they collected the leftover pieces—seven large baskets full. ³⁸Now those who ate were 4,000 men, besides women and children. ³⁹After dismissing the crowds, He got into the boat and went to the region of Magadan.^A

16 The Pharisees and Sadducees approached, and as a test, asked Him to show them a sign from heaven.

²He answered them: "When evening comes you say, 'It will be good weather because the sky is red.' ³And in the morning, 'Today will be stormy because the sky is red and threatening.' You^B know how to read the appearance of the sky, but you can't read the signs of the times.^C ⁴An evil and adulterous generation demands a sign, but no sign will be given to it except the sign of^D Jonah." Then He left them and went away.

⁵The disciples reached the other shore,^E and they had forgotten to take bread.

⁶Then Jesus told them, "Watch out and beware of the yeast^F of the Pharisees and Sadducees."

⁷And they discussed among themselves, "We didn't bring any bread."

⁸Aware of this, Jesus said, "You of little faith! Why are you discussing among yourselves that you do not have bread? ⁹Don't you understand yet? Don't you remember the five loaves for the 5,000 and how many baskets you collected? ¹⁰Or the seven loaves for the 4,000 and how many large baskets you collected? ¹¹Why is it you don't understand that when I told you, 'Beware of the yeast of the Pharisees and Sadducees,' it wasn't about bread?" ¹²Then they understood that He did not tell them to beware of the yeast in bread, but of the teaching of the Pharisees and Sadducees.

¹³When Jesus came to the region of Caesarea Philippi,^G He asked His disciples, "Who do people say that the Son of Man is?"^H

¹⁴And they said, "Some say John the Baptist; others, Elijah; still others, Jeremiah or one of the prophets."

¹⁵"But you," He asked them, "who do you say that I am?"

¹⁶Simon Peter answered, "You are the Messiah, the Son of the living God!"

¹⁷And Jesus responded, "Simon son of Jonah,^I you are blessed because flesh and blood did not reveal this to you, but My Father in heaven. ¹⁸And I also say to you that you are Peter,^J and on this rock^K I will build My church, and the forces^L of Hades will not overpower it. ¹⁹I will give you the keys of the kingdom of heaven, and whatever you bind on earth is already bound^M in heaven, and whatever you loose on earth is already loosed^N in heaven."

²⁰And He gave the disciples orders to tell no one that He was^O the Messiah.

²¹From then on Jesus began to point out to His disciples that He must go to Jerusalem and suffer many things from the elders, chief priests, and scribes, be killed, and be raised the third day. ²²Then Peter took Him aside and began to rebuke Him, "Oh no,^P Lord! This will never happen to You!"

²³But He turned and told Peter, "Get behind Me, Satan! You are an offense to Me because you're not thinking about God's concerns,^Q but man's."

²⁴Then Jesus said to His disciples, "If anyone wants to come with Me, he must deny himself, take up his cross, and follow Me. ²⁵For whoever wants to save his life will lose it, but whoever loses his life because of Me will find it. ²⁶What will it benefit a man if he gains the whole world yet loses his life? Or what will a man give in exchange for his life? ²⁷For the Son of Man is going to come with His angels in the glory of His Father, and then He will reward each according to what he has done. ²⁸I assure you: There are some standing here who will not taste death until they see the Son of Man coming in His kingdom."

17 After six days Jesus took Peter, James, and his brother John and led them up on a high mountain. ²He was

^A15:39 Other mss read Magdala   ^B16:3 Other mss read Hypocrites! You   ^C16:2-3 Other mss omit When (v. 2) through end of v. 3   ^D16:4 Other mss add the prophet   ^E16:5 Lit disciples went to the other side   ^F16:6 Or leaven   ^G16:13 A town north of Galilee at the base of Mount Hermon   ^H16:13 Other mss read that I, the Son of Man, am   ^I16:17 Or son of John   ^J16:18 Peter (Gk Petros) = a specific stone or rock   ^K16:18 Rock (Gk petra) = a rocky crag or bedrock   ^L16:18 Lit gates   ^M16:19 Or earth will be bound   ^N16:19 Or earth will be loosed   ^O16:20 Other mss add Jesus   ^P16:22 Lit Mercy to You = May God have mercy on You   ^Q16:23 Lit about the things of God transformed[A] in front of them, and His face shone like the sun. Even His clothes became as white as the light. [3] Suddenly, Moses and Elijah appeared to them, talking with Him.

[4] Then Peter said to Jesus, "Lord, it's good for us to be here! If You want, I will make[B] three tabernacles here: one for You, one for Moses, and one for Elijah."

[5] While he was still speaking, suddenly a bright cloud covered[C] them, and a voice from the cloud said:

This is My beloved Son.
I take delight in Him.
Listen to Him!

[6] When the disciples heard it, they fell face-down and were terrified.

[7] Then Jesus came up, touched them, and said, "Get up; don't be afraid." [8] When they looked up they saw no one except Him[D]—Jesus alone. [9] As they were coming down from the mountain, Jesus commanded them, "Don't tell anyone about the vision until the Son of Man is raised[E] from the dead."

[10] So the disciples questioned Him, "Why then do the scribes say that Elijah must come first?"

[11] "Elijah is coming[F] and will restore everything," He replied.[G] [12] "But I tell you: Elijah has already come, and they didn't recognize him. On the contrary, they did whatever they pleased to him. In the same way the Son of Man is going to suffer at their hands."[H] [13] Then the disciples understood that He spoke to them about John the Baptist.

[14] When they reached the crowd, a man approached and knelt down before Him. [15] "Lord," he said, "have mercy on my son, because he has seizures[I] and suffers severely. He often falls into the fire and often into the water. [16] I brought him to Your disciples, but they couldn't heal him."

[17] Jesus replied, "You unbelieving and re-bellious[J] generation! How long will I be with you? How long must I put up with you? Bring him here to Me." [18] Then Jesus rebuked the de-mon,[K] and it[L] came out of him, and from that moment[M] the boy was healed.

[19] Then the disciples approached Jesus pri-vately and said, "Why couldn't we drive it out?"

[20] "Because of your little faith," He[N] told them. "For I assure you: If you have faith the size of[O] a mustard seed, you will tell this mountain, 'Move from here to there,' and it will move. Nothing will be impossible for you. [[21] However, this kind does not come out ex-cept by prayer and fasting.]"[P]

[22] As they were meeting[Q] in Galilee, Jesus told them, "The Son of Man is about to be-trayed into the hands of men. [23] They will kill Him, and on the third day He will be raised up." And they were deeply distressed.

[24] When they came to Capernaum, those who collected the double-drachma tax[R] approached Peter and said, "Doesn't your Teacher pay the double-drachma tax?"

[25] "Yes," he said.

When he went into the house, Jesus spoke to him first,[S] "What do you think, Simon? Who do earthly kings collect tariffs or taxes from? From their sons or from strangers?"[T]

[26] "From strangers," He said.[U]

"Then the sons are free," Jesus told him. [27] "But, so we won't offend them, go to the sea, cast in a fishhook, and take the first fish that you catch. When you open its mouth you'll find a coin.[V] Take it and give it to them for Me and you."

18

At that time[M] the disciples came to Jesus and said, "Who is greatest in the king-dom of heaven?"

[2] Then He called a child to Him and had him stand among them. [3] "I assure you," He said, "unless you are converted[W] and become like children, you will never enter the kingdom of heaven. [4] Therefore, whoever humbles himself like this child—this one is the greatest in the kingdom of heaven. [5] And whoever welcomes[X] one child like this in My name welcomes Me.

[6] "But whoever causes the downfall of these little ones who believe in Me—it would be better for him if a heavy millstone[Y] were hung around his neck and he were drowned in the depths of the sea! [7] Woe to the world because of offenses. For offenses must come, but woe to that man by whom the offense

A17:2 Or transfigured   B17:4 Other mss read wish, let's make   C17:5 Or enveloped; Ex 40:34-35   D17:8 Other mss omit Him   E17:9 Other mss read Man has risen   F17:11 Other mss add first   G17:11 Other mss read Jesus said to them   H17:12 Lit suffer by them   I17:15 Lit he is moonstruck; thought to be a form of epilepsy   J17:17 Or corrupt, or perverted, or twisted; Dt 32:5   K17:18 Lit rebuked him or it   L17:18 Lit the demon   M17:18; 18:1 Lit hour   N17:20 Other mss read your unbelief, "Jesus   O17:20 Lit faith like   P17:21 Other mss omit bracketed text; Mk 9:29   Q17:22 Other mss read were staying   R17:24 Jewish men paid this tax to support the temple; Ex 30:11-16. A double-drachma could purchase 2 sheep.   S17:25 Lit Jesus anticipated him by saying   T17:25 Or foreigners   U17:26 Other mss read Peter said to Him   V17:27 Gk stater, worth 2 double-drachmas   W18:3 Or are turned around   X18:5 Or receives   Y18:6 A millstone turned by a donkey comes. ⁸If your hand or your foot causes your downfall, cut it off and throw it away. It is better for you to enter life maimed or lame, than to have two hands or two feet and be thrown into the eternal fire. ⁹And if your eye causes your downfall, gouge it out and throw it away. It is better for you to enter life with one eye, rather than to have two eyes and be thrown into hellfire!ᴬ

¹⁰"See that you don't look down on one of these little ones, because I tell you that in heaven their angels continually view the face of My Father in heaven. [¹¹For the Son of Man has come to save the lost.]ᴮ ¹²What do you think? If a man has 100 sheep, and one of them goes astray, won't he leave the 99 on the hillside and go and search for the stray? ¹³And if he finds it, I assure you: He rejoices over that sheepᶜ more than over the 99 that did not go astray. ¹⁴In the same way, it is not the will of your Father in heaven that one of these little ones perish.

¹⁵"If your brother sins against you,ᴰ go and rebuke him in private.ᴱ If he listens to you, you have won your brother. ¹⁶But if he won't listen, take one or two more with you, so that by the testimonyᶠ of two or three witnesses every fact may be established.ᴳ ¹⁷If he pays no attention to them, tell the church.ᴴ But if he doesn't pay attention even to the church, let him be like an unbelieverᴵ and a tax collector to you. ¹⁸I assure you: Whatever you bind on earth is already boundᴶ in heaven, and whatever you loose on earth is already loosedᴷ in heaven. ¹⁹Again, I assure you: If two of you on earth agree about any matter that youᴸ pray for it, will be done for youᴹ by My Father in heaven. ²⁰For where two or three are gathered together in My name, I am there among them."

²¹Then Peter came to Him and said, "Lord, how many times could my brother sin against me and I forgive him? As many as seven times?"

²²"I tell you, not as many as seven," Jesus said to him, "but 70 times seven.ᴺ ²³For this reason, the kingdom of heaven can be compared to a king who wanted to settle accounts with his slaves. ²⁴When he began to settle accounts, one who owed 10,000 talentsᴼ was brought before him. ²⁵Since he had no way to

pay it back, his master commanded that he, his wife, his children, and everything he had be sold to pay the debt.

²⁶"At this, the slave fell facedown before him and said, 'Be patient with me, and I will pay you everything!' ²⁷Then the master of that slave had compassion, released him, and forgave him the loan.

²⁸"But that slave went out and found one of his fellow slaves who owed him 100 denarii.ᴾ He grabbed him, started choking him, and said, 'Pay what you owe!'

²⁹"At this, his fellow slave fell downᵠ and began begging him, 'Be patient with me, and I will pay you back.' ³⁰But he wasn't willing. On the contrary, he went and threw him into prison until he could pay what was owed. ³¹When the other slaves saw what had taken place, they were deeply distressed and went and reported to their master everything that had happened.

³²"Then, after he had summoned him, his master said to him, 'You wicked slave! I forgave you all that debt because you begged me. ³³Shouldn't you also have had mercy on your fellow slave, as I had mercy on you?' ³⁴And his master got angry and handed him over to the jailers to be tortured until he could pay everything that was owed. ³⁵So My heavenly Father will also do to you if each of you does not forgive his brotherᴿ from hisˢ heart."

19 When Jesus had finished this instruction, He departed from Galilee and went to the region of Judea across the Jordan. ²Large crowds followed Him, and He healed them there. ³Some Pharisees approached Him to test Him. They asked, "Is it lawful for a man to divorce his wife on any grounds?"

⁴"Haven't you read," He replied, "that He who createdᵀ them in the beginning made them male and female,"ᵁ ⁵and He also said:

> "For this reason a man will leave
> his father and mother
> and be joined to his wife,
> and the two will become one flesh?ᵛ

⁶So they are no longer two, but one flesh. Therefore, what God has joined together, man must not separate."

ᴬ18:9 Lit gehenna of fire   ᴮ18:11 Other mss omit bracketed text   ᶜ18:13 Lit over it   ᴰ18:15 Other mss omit against you   ᴱ18:15 Lit him between you and him alone   ᶠ18:16 Lit mouth   ᴳ18:16 Dt 19:15   ᴴ18:17 Or congregation   ᴵ18:17 Or like a Gentile   ᴶ18:18 Or earth will be bound   ᴷ18:18 Or earth will be loosed   ᴸ18:19 Lit they   ᴹ18:19 Lit for them   ᴺ18:22 Or 77 times   ᴼ18:24 A huge sum of money that could never be repaid by a slave; a talent = 6,000 denarii   ᴾ18:28 A small sum compared to 10,000 talents   ᵠ18:29 Other mss add at his feet   ᴿ18:35 Other mss add his trespasses   ˢ18:35 Lit your   ᵀ19:4 Other mss read made   ᵁ19:4 Gn 1:27; 5:2   ᵛ19:5 Gn 2:24

⁷"Why then," they asked Him, "did Moses command us to give divorce papers and to send her away?"

⁸He told them, "Moses permitted you to divorce your wives because of the hardness of your hearts. But it was not like that from the beginning. ⁹And I tell you, whoever divorces his wife, except for sexual immorality, and marries another, commits adultery."ᴬ

¹⁰His disciples said to Him, "If the relationship of a man with his wife is like this, it's better not to marry!"

¹¹But He told them, "Not everyone can accept this saying, but only those it has been given to. ¹²For there are eunuchs who were born that way from their mother's womb, there are eunuchs who were made by men, and there are eunuchs who have made themselves that way because of the kingdom of heaven. Let anyone accept this who can."

¹³Then children were brought to Him so He might put His hands on them and pray. But the disciples rebuked them. ¹⁴Then Jesus said, "Leave the children alone, and don't try to keep them from coming to Me, because the kingdom of heaven is made up of people like this."ᴮ ¹⁵After putting His hands on them, He went on from there.

¹⁶Just then someone came up and asked Him, "Teacher, what good must I do to have eternal life?"

¹⁷"Why do you ask Me about what is good?"ᶜ He said to him. "There is only One who is good.ᴰ If you want to enter into life, keep the commandments."

¹⁸"Which ones?" he asked Him. Jesus answered:

Do not murder;
do not commit adultery;
do not steal;
do not bear false witness;
¹⁹   honor your father and your mother;
and love your neighbor as yourself.ᴱ

²⁰"I have kept all these,"ᶠ the young man told Him. "What do I still lack?"

²¹"If you want to be perfect,"ᴳ Jesus said to him, "go, sell your belongings and give to the

poor, and you will have treasure in heaven. Then come, follow Me."

²²When the young man heard that command, he went away grieving, because he had many possessions.

²³Then Jesus said to His disciples, "I assure you: It will be hard for a rich person to enter the kingdom of heaven! ²⁴Again I tell you, it is easier for a camel to go through the eye of a needle than for a rich person to enter the kingdom of God."

²⁵When the disciples heard this, they were utterly astonished and asked, "Then who can be saved?"

²⁶But Jesus looked at them and said, "With men this is impossible, but with God all things are possible."

²⁷Then Peter responded to Him, "Look, we have left everything and followed You. So what will there be for us?"

²⁸Jesus said to them, "I assure you: In the Messianic Age,ᴴ when the Son of Man sits on His glorious throne, you who have followed Me will also sit on 12 thrones, judging the 12 tribes of Israel. ²⁹And everyone who has left houses, brothers or sisters, father or mother,ᴵ children, or fields because of My name will receive 100 times more and will inherit eternal life. ³⁰But many who are first will be last, and the last first.

20 "For the kingdom of heaven is like a landowner who went out early in the morning to hire workers for his vineyard. ²After agreeing with the workers on one denarius for the day, he sent them into his vineyard. ³When he went out about nine in the morning,ᴶ he saw others standing in the marketplace doing nothing. ⁴To those men he said, 'You also go to my vineyard, and I'll give you whatever is right.' So off they went. ⁵About noon and at three,ᴷ he went out again and did the same thing. ⁶Then about fiveᴸ he went and found others standing around,ᴹ and said to them, 'Why have you been standing here all day doing nothing?'

⁷"'Because no one hired us,' they said to him.

"'You also go to my vineyard,' he told them.ᴺ ⁸When evening came, the owner of the vineyard told his foreman, 'Call the workers and

---

ᴬ19:9 Other mss add *Also whoever marries a divorced woman commits adultery;* Mt 5:32   ᴮ19:14 Lit *heaven is of such ones*   ᶜ19:17 Other mss read *Why do you call Me good?*   ᴰ19:17 Other mss read *No one is good but One—God*   ᴱ19:18-19 Ex 20:12-16; Lv 19:18; Dt 5:16-20   ᶠ19:20 Other mss add *from my youth*   ᴳ19:21 Or *complete*   ᴴ19:28 Lit *the regeneration*   ᴵ19:29 Other mss add *or wife*   ᴶ20:3 Lit *about the third hour*   ᴷ20:5 Lit *about the sixth hour and the ninth hour*   ᴸ20:6 Lit *about the eleventh hour*   ᴹ20:6 Other mss add *doing nothing*   ᴺ20:7 Other mss add *'and you'll get whatever is right.'*

give them their pay, starting with the last and ending with the first.'^A

^9 "When those who were hired about five^B came, they each received one denarius. ^10 So when the first ones came, they assumed they would get more, but they also received a denarius each. ^11 When they received it, they began to complain to the landowner: ^12 'These last men put in one hour, and you made them equal to us who bore the burden of the day and the burning heat!'

^13 "He replied to one of them, 'Friend, I'm doing you no wrong. Didn't you agree with me on a denarius? ^14 Take what's yours and go. I want to give this last man the same as I gave you. ^15 Don't I have the right to do what I want with my business?^C Are you jealous^D because I'm generous?'^E

^16 "So the last will be first, and the first last."^F

^17 While going up to Jerusalem, Jesus took the 12 disciples aside privately and said to them on the way: ^18 "Listen! We are going up to Jerusalem. The Son of Man will be handed over to the chief priests and scribes, and they will condemn Him to death. ^19 Then they will hand Him over to the Gentiles to be mocked, flogged,^G and crucified, and He will be resurrected^H on the third day."

^20 Then the mother of Zebedee's sons approached Him with her sons. She knelt down to ask Him for something. ^21 "What do you want?" He asked her.

"Promise,"^I she said to Him, "that these two sons of mine may sit, one on Your right and the other on Your left, in Your kingdom."

^22 But Jesus answered, "You don't know what you're asking. Are you able to drink the cup^J that I am about to drink?"^K

"We are able," they said to Him.

^23 He told them, "You will indeed drink My cup.^L But to sit at My right and left is not Mine to give; instead, it belongs to those for whom it has been prepared by My Father." ^24 When the 10 disciples heard this, they became indignant with the two brothers. ^25 But Jesus called them over and said, "You know that the rulers of the Gentiles dominate them, and the men of high position exercise power over them. ^26 It must not be like that among you. On the contrary, whoever wants to become great among you

must be your servant, ^27 and whoever wants to be first among you must be your slave; ^28 just as the Son of Man did not come to be served, but to serve, and to give His life—a ransom for many."

^29 As they were leaving Jericho, a large crowd followed Him. ^30 There were two blind men sitting by the road. When they heard that Jesus was passing by, they cried out, "Lord, have mercy on us, Son of David!" ^31 The crowd told them to keep quiet, but they cried out all the more, "Lord, have mercy on us, Son of David!"

^32 Jesus stopped, called them, and said, "What do you want Me to do for you?"

^33 "Lord," they said to Him, "open our eyes!"

^34 Moved with compassion, Jesus touched their eyes. Immediately they could see, and they followed Him.

21

When they approached Jerusalem and came to Bethphage at the Mount of Olives, Jesus then sent two disciples, ^2 telling them, "Go into the village ahead of you. At once you will find a donkey tied there, and a colt with her. Untie them and bring them to Me. ^3 If anyone says anything to you, you should say that the Lord needs them, and immediately he will send them."

^4 This took place so that what was spoken through the prophet might be fulfilled:

^5   Tell Daughter Zion,
    "Look, your King is coming to you,
    gentle, and mounted on a donkey,
    even on a colt,
        the foal of a beast of burden."^M

^6 The disciples went and did just as Jesus directed them. ^7 They brought the donkey and the colt; then they laid their robes on them, and He sat on them. ^8 A very large crowd spread their robes on the road; others were cutting branches from the trees and spreading them on the road. ^9 Then the crowds who went ahead of Him and those who followed kept shouting:

    Hosanna to the Son of David!
    He who comes in the name
    of the Lord is the blessed One!^N
    Hosanna in the highest heaven!

---

^A 20:8 Lit starting from the last until the first   ^B 20:9 Lit about the eleventh hour   ^C 20:15 Lit with what is mine   ^D 20:15 Lit is your eye evil; an idiom for jealousy or stinginess   ^E 20:15 Lit good   ^F 20:16 Other mss add For many are called, but few are chosen.   ^G 20:19 Or scourged   ^H 20:19 Other mss read will rise again   ^I 20:21 Lit Say   ^J 20:22 Figurative language referring to His coming suffering; Mt 26:39; Jn 18:11   ^K 20:22 Other mss add [and lor] to be baptized with the baptism that I am baptized with?"   ^L 20:23 Other mss add and be baptized with the baptism that I am baptized with.   ^M 21:5 Is 62:11; Zch 9:9   ^N 21:9 Ps 118:25-26

¹⁰When He entered Jerusalem, the whole city was shaken, saying, "Who is this?" ¹¹And the crowds kept saying, "This is the prophet Jesus from Nazareth in Galilee!"

¹²Jesus went into the temple complexᴬ and drove out all those buying and selling in the temple. He overturned the money changers' tables and the chairs of those selling doves. ¹³And He said to them, "It is written, **My house will be called a house of prayer.**ᴮ But you are making it a **den of thieves!**"ᶜ

¹⁴The blind and the lame came to Him in the temple complex, and He healed them. ¹⁵When the chief priests and the scribes saw the wonders that He did and the children shouting in the temple complex, "*Hosanna* to the Son of David!" they were indignant ¹⁶and said to Him, "Do You hear what these children are saying?"

"Yes," Jesus told them. "Have you never read:

> You have preparedᴰ praise
> from the mouths of children
> and nursing infants?"ᴱ

¹⁷Then He left them, went out of the city to Bethany, and spent the night there.

¹⁸Early in the morning, as He was returning to the city, He was hungry. ¹⁹Seeing a lone fig tree by the road, He went up to it and found nothing on it except leaves. And He said to it, "May no fruit ever come from you again!" At once the fig tree withered.

²⁰When the disciples saw it, they were amazed and said, "How did the fig tree wither so quickly?"

²¹Jesus answered them, "I assure you: If you have faith and do not doubt, you will not only do what was done to the fig tree, but even if you tell this mountain, 'Be lifted up and thrown into the sea,' it will be done. ²²And if you believe, you will receive whatever you ask for in prayer."

²³When He entered the temple complex, the chief priests and the elders of the people came up to Him as He was teaching and said, "By what authority are You doing these things? Who gave You this authority?"

²⁴Jesus answered them, "I will also ask you one question, and if you answer it for Me, then I will tell you by what authority I do these things. ²⁵Where did John's baptism come from? From heaven or from men?"

They began to argue among themselves, "If we say, 'From heaven,' He will say to us, 'Then why didn't you believe him?' ²⁶But if we say, 'From men,' we're afraid of the crowd, because everyone thought John was a prophet." ²⁷So they answered Jesus, "We don't know."

And He said to them, "Neither will I tell you by what authority I do these things.

²⁸"But what do you think? A man had two sons. He went to the first and said, 'My son, go, work in the vineyard today.'

²⁹"He answered, 'I don't want to!' Yet later he changed his mind and went. ³⁰Then the man went to the other and said the same thing.

"'I will, sir,' he answered. But he didn't go. ³¹"Which of the two did his father's will?"

"The first," they said.

Jesus said to them, "I assure you: Tax collectors and prostitutes are entering the kingdom of God before you! ³²For John came to you in the way of righteousness, and you didn't believe him. Tax collectors and prostitutes did believe him, but you, when you saw it, didn't even change your minds then and believe him.

³³"Listen to another parable: There was a man, a landowner, who planted a vineyard, put a fence around it, dug a winepress in it, and built a watchtower. He leased it to tenant farmers and went away. ³⁴When the grape harvestᶠ drew near, he sent his slaves to the farmers to collect his fruit. ³⁵But the farmers took his slaves, beat one, killed another, and stoned a third. ³⁶Again, he sent other slaves, more than the first group, and they did the same to them. ³⁷Finally, he sent his son to them. 'They will respect my son,' he said.

³⁸"But when the tenant farmers saw the son, they said among themselves, 'This is the heir. Come, let's kill him and take his inheritance!' ³⁹So they seized him, threw him out of the vineyard, and killed him. ⁴⁰Therefore, when the owner of the vineyard comes, what will he do to those farmers?"

⁴¹"He will completely destroy those terrible men," they told Him, "and lease his vineyard to other farmers who will give him his produce at the harvest."ᴳ

⁴²Jesus said to them, "Have you never read in the Scriptures:

> The stone that the builders rejected
> has become the cornerstone.ᴴ

ᴬ21:12 Other mss add *of God*   ᴮ21:13 Is 56:7   ᶜ21:13 Jr 7:11   ᴰ21:16 Or *restored*   ᴱ21:16 Ps 8:2   ᶠ21:34 Lit *the season of fruits*   ᴳ21:41 Lit *him the fruits in their seasons*   ᴴ21:42 Lit *the head of the corner*

This came from the Lord
and is wonderful in our eyes?[A]

[43] Therefore I tell you, the kingdom of God will be taken away from you and given to a nation producing its[B] fruit. [[44] Whoever falls on this stone will be broken to pieces; but on whoever it falls, it will grind him to powder!]"[C]

[45] When the chief priests and the Pharisees heard His parables, they knew He was speaking about them. [46] Although they were looking for a way to arrest Him, they feared the crowds, because they[D] regarded Him as a prophet.

22 Once more Jesus spoke to them in parables: [2] "The kingdom of heaven may be compared to a king who gave a wedding banquet for his son. [3] He sent out his slaves to summon those invited to the banquet, but they didn't want to come. [4] Again, he sent out other slaves, and said, 'Tell those who are invited: Look, I've prepared my dinner; my oxen and fattened cattle have been slaughtered, and everything is ready. Come to the wedding banquet.'

[5] "But they paid no attention and went away, one to his own farm, another to his business. [6] And the others seized his slaves, treated them outrageously and killed them. [7] The king[E] was enraged, he sent out his troops, destroyed those murderers, and burned down their city.

[8] "Then he told his slaves, 'The banquet is ready, but those who were invited were not worthy. [9] Therefore go to where the roads exit the city and invite everyone you find to the banquet.' [10] So those slaves went out on the roads and gathered everyone they found, both evil and good. The wedding banquet was filled with guests.[F] [11] But when the king came in to view the guests, he saw a man there who was not dressed for a wedding. [12] So he said to him, 'Friend, how did you get in here without wedding clothes?' The man was speechless.

[13] "Then the king told the attendants, 'Tie him up hand and foot,[G] and throw him into the outer darkness, where there will be weeping and gnashing of teeth.'

[14] "For many are invited, but few are chosen."

[15] Then the Pharisees went and plotted how to trap Him by what He said.[H] [16] They sent their disciples to Him, with the Herodians. "Teacher," they said, "we know that You are truthful and teach truthfully the way of God. You defer to no one, for You don't show partiality.[I] [17] Tell us, therefore, what You think. Is it lawful to pay taxes to Caesar or not?"

[18] But perceiving their malice, Jesus said, "Why are you testing Me, hypocrites? [19] Show Me the coin used for the tax." So they brought Him a denarius. [20] "Whose image and inscription is this?" He asked them.

[21] "Caesar's," they said to Him.

Then He said to them, "Therefore give back to Caesar the things that are Caesar's, and to God the things that are God's." [22] When they heard this, they were amazed. So they left Him and went away.

[23] The same day some Sadducees, who say there is no resurrection, came up to Him and questioned Him: [24] "Teacher, Moses said, if a man dies, having no children, his brother is to marry his wife and raise up offspring for his brother.[J] [25] Now there were seven brothers among us. The first got married and died. Having no offspring, he left his wife to his brother. [26] The same happened to the second also, and the third, and so to all seven.[K] [27] Then last of all the woman died. [28] In the resurrection, therefore, whose wife will she be of the seven? For they all had married her."[L]

[29] Jesus answered them, "You are deceived, because you don't know the Scriptures or the power of God. [30] For in the resurrection they neither marry nor are given in marriage but are like[M] angels in heaven. [31] Now concerning the resurrection of the dead, haven't you read what was spoken to you by God: [32] I am the God of Abraham and the God of Isaac and the God of Jacob?[N] He[O] is not the God of the dead, but of the living."

[33] And when the crowds heard this, they were astonished at His teaching.

[34] When the Pharisees heard that He had silenced the Sadducees, they came together. [35] And one of them, an expert in the law, asked a question to test Him: [36] "Teacher, which command in the law is the greatest?"[P]

[37] He said to him, "Love the Lord your God with all your heart, with all your soul, and all your mind.[Q] [38] This is the greatest and most

A21:42 Ps 118:22-23   B21:43 = the kingdom's   C21:44 Other mss omit bracketed text   D21:46 = the crowds   E22:7 Other mss read But when the (that) king heard about it he   F22:10 Lit those reclining (to eat)   G22:13 Other mss add take him away   H22:15 Lit trap Him in a word   I22:16 Lit don't look on the face of men; that is, on the outward appearance   J22:24 Dt 25:5   K22:26 Lit so until the seven   L22:28 Lit all had her   M22:30 Other mss read God's   N22:32 Ex 3:6,15-16   O22:32 Other mss read God   P22:36 Lit is great   Q22:37 Dt 6:5

importantᴬ command. ³⁹The second is like it: Love your neighbor as yourself.ᴮ ⁴⁰All the Law and the Prophets dependᶜ on these two commands."

⁴¹While the Pharisees were together, Jesus questioned them, ⁴²"What do you think about the Messiah? Whose Son is He?"

"David's," they told Him.

⁴³He asked them, "How is it then that David, inspired by the Spirit,ᴰ calls Him 'Lord':

⁴⁴ The Lord declared to my Lord,
'Sit at My right hand
until I put Your enemies
under Your feet'?ᴱ,ᶠ

⁴⁵"If David calls Him 'Lord,' how then can the Messiah be His Son?" ⁴⁶No one was able to answer Him at all,ᴳ and from that day no one dared to question Him anymore.

23 Then Jesus spoke to the crowds and to His disciples: ²"The scribes and the Pharisees are seated in the chair of Moses.ᴴ ³Therefore do whatever they tell you, and observe it. But don't do what they do,ᴵ because they don't practice what they teach. ⁴They tie up heavy loads that are hard to carryᴶ and put them on people's shoulders, but they themselves aren't willing to lift a fingerᴷ to move them. ⁵They do everythingᴸ to be observed by others: They enlarge their phylacteriesᴹ and lengthen their tassels.ᴺ ⁶They love the place of honor at banquets, the front seats in the synagogues, ⁷greetings in the marketplaces, and to be called 'Rabbi' by people.

⁸"But as for you, do not be called 'Rabbi,' because you have one Teacher,ᴼ and you are all brothers. ⁹Do not call anyone on earth your father, because you have one Father, who is in heaven. ¹⁰And do not be called masters either, because you have one Master,ᴾ the Messiah. ¹¹The greatest among you will be your servant. ¹²Whoever exalts himself will be humbled, and whoever humbles himself will be exalted.

¹³"But woe to you, scribes and Pharisees, hypocrites! You lock up the kingdom of heaven from people. For you don't go in, and you don't allow those entering to go in.

[¹⁴"Woe to you, scribes and Pharisees, hypocrites! You devour widows' houses and make long prayers just for show.ᵠ This is why you will receive a harsher punishment.]ᴿ

¹⁵"Woe to you, scribes and Pharisees, hypocrites! You travel over land and sea to make one proselyte, and when he becomes one, you make him twice as fit for hellˢ as you are!

¹⁶"Woe to you, blind guides, who say, 'Whoever takes an oath by the sanctuary, it means nothing. But whoever takes an oath by the gold of the sanctuary is bound by his oath.'ᵀ ¹⁷Blind fools!ᵁ For which is greater, the gold or the sanctuary that sanctified the gold? ¹⁸Also, 'Whoever takes an oath by the altar, it means nothing. But whoever takes an oath by the gift that is on it is bound by his oath.'ᵀ ¹⁹Blind people!ⱽ For which is greater, the gift or the altar that sanctifies the gift? ²⁰Therefore, the one who takes an oath by the altar takes an oath by it and by everything on it. ²¹The one who takes an oath by the sanctuary takes an oath by it and by Him who dwells in it. ²²And the one who takes an oath by heaven takes an oath by God's throne and by Him who sits on it.

²³"Woe to you, scribes and Pharisees, hypocrites! You pay a tenth ofᵂ mint, dill, and cumin,ˣ yet you have neglected the more important matters of the law—justice, mercy, and faith. These things should have been done without neglecting the others. ²⁴Blind guides! You strain out a gnat, yet gulp down a camel!

²⁵"Woe to you, scribes and Pharisees, hypocrites! You clean the outside of the cup and dish, but inside they are full of greedʸ and self-indulgence! ²⁶Blind Pharisee! First clean the inside of the cup,ᶻ so the outside of itᴬᴬ may also become clean.

²⁷"Woe to you, scribes and Pharisees, hypocrites! You are like whitewashed tombs, which appear beautiful on the outside, but inside are full of dead men's bones and every impurity. ²⁸In the same way, on the outside you seem righteous to people, but inside you are full of hypocrisy and lawlessness.

²⁹"Woe to you, scribes and Pharisees, hypocrites! You build the tombs of the prophets

ᴬ22:38 Lit and first   ᴮ22:39 Lv 19:18   ᶜ22:40 Or hang   ᴰ22:43 Lit David in Spirit   ᴱ22:44 Other mss read until I make Your enemies Your footstool   ᶠ22:44 Ps 110:1   ᴳ22:46 Lit answer Him a word   ᴴ23:2 Perhaps a special chair for teaching in synagogues, or a metaphorical phrase for teaching with authority   ᴵ23:3 Lit do according to their works   ᴶ23:4 Other mss omit that are hard to carry   ᴷ23:4 Lit lift with their finger   ᴸ23:5 Lit do all their works   ᴹ23:5 Small leather boxes containing OT texts, worn by Jews on their arms and foreheads   ᴺ23:5 Other mss add on their robes   ᴼ23:8 Other mss add the Messiah   ᴾ23:10 Or Teacher   ᵠ23:14 Or prayers with false motivation   ᴿ23:14 Other mss omit bracketed text   ˢ23:15 Lit twice the son of gehenna   ᵀ23:16,18 Lit is obligated   ᵁ23:17 Lit Fools and blind   ⱽ23:19 Other mss read Fools and blind   ᵂ23:23 Or You tithe   ˣ23:23 A plant whose seeds are used as a seasoning   ʸ23:25 Or full of violence   ᶻ23:26 Other mss add and dish   ᴬᴬ23:26 Other mss read of them and decorate the monuments of the righteous, ³⁰and you say, 'If we had lived in the days of our fathers, we wouldn't have taken part with them in shedding the prophets' blood.'ᴬ ³¹You, therefore, testify against yourselves that you are sons of those who murdered the prophets. ³²Fill up, then, the measure of your fathers' sins!ᴮ

³³"Snakes! Brood of vipers! How can you escape being condemned to hell?ᶜ ³⁴This is why I am sending you prophets, sages, and scribes. Some of them you will kill and crucify, and some of them you will flog in your synagogues and hound from town to town. ³⁵So all the righteous blood shed on the earth will be charged to you,ᴰ from the blood of righteous Abel to the blood of Zechariah, son of Berechiah, whom you murdered between the sanctuary and the altar. ³⁶I assure you: All these things will come on this generation!

³⁷"Jerusalem, Jerusalem! She who kills the prophets and stones those who are sent to her. How often I wanted to gather your children together, as a hen gathers her chicksᴱ under her wings, yet you were not willing! ³⁸See, your house is left to you desolate. ³⁹For I tell you, you will never see Me again until you say, 'He who comes in the name of the Lord is the blessed One'!"ᶠ

24 As Jesus left and was going out of the temple complex, His disciples came up and called His attention to the temple buildings. ²Then He replied to them, "Don't you see all these things? I assure you: Not one stone will be left here on another that will not be thrown down!"

³While He was sitting on the Mount of Olives, the disciples approached Him privately and said, "Tell us, when will these things happen? And what is the sign of Your coming and of the end of the age?"

⁴Then Jesus replied to them: "Watch out that no one deceives you. ⁵For many will come in My name, saying, 'I am the Messiah,' and they will deceive many. ⁶You are going to hear of wars and rumors of wars. See that you are not alarmed, because these things must take place, but the end is not yet. ⁷For nation will rise up against nation, and kingdom against kingdom. There will be faminesᴳ and earth-

quakes in various places. ⁸All these events are the beginning of birth pains.

⁹"Then they will hand you over for persecution,ᴴ and they will kill you. You will be hated by all nations because of My name. ¹⁰Then many will take offense, betray one another and hate one another. ¹¹Many false prophets will rise up and deceive many. ¹²Because lawlessness will multiply, the love of many will grow cold. ¹³But the one who endures to the end will be delivered.ᴵ ¹⁴This good news of the kingdom will be proclaimed in all the worldᴶ as a testimony to all nations. And then the end will come.

¹⁵"So when you see the abomination that causes desolation,ᴷˑᴸ spoken of by the prophet Daniel, standing in the holy place" (let the reader understandᴹ), ¹⁶"then those in Judea must flee to the mountains! ¹⁷A man on the housetopᴺ must not come down to get things out of his house. ¹⁸And a man in the field must not go back to get his clothes. ¹⁹Woe to pregnant women and nursing mothers in those days! ²⁰Pray that your escape may not be in winter or on a Sabbath. ²¹For at that time there will be great tribulation, the kind that hasn't taken place from the beginning of the world until now and never will again! ²²Unless those days were limited, no one wouldᴼ survive.ᴾ But those days will be limited because of the elect.

²³"If anyone tells you then, 'Look, here is the Messiah!' or, 'Over here!' do not believe it! ²⁴False messiahsᵠ and false prophets will arise and perform great signs and wonders to lead astray, if possible, even the elect. ²⁵Take note: I have told you in advance. ²⁶So if they tell you, 'Look, He's in the wilderness!' don't go out; 'Look, He's in the inner rooms!' do not believe it. ²⁷For as the lightning comes from the east and flashes as far as the west, so will be the coming of the Son of Man. ²⁸Wherever the carcass is, there the vulturesᴿ will gather.

²⁹"Immediately after the tribulation of those days:

The sun will be darkened,
and the moon will not shed its light;
the stars will fall from the sky,
and the celestial powers will be shaken.

³⁰"Then the sign of the Son of Man will appear in the sky, and then all the peoples of the earthᴬ will mourn;ᴮ and they will see the Son of Man coming on the clouds of heaven with power and great glory. ³¹He will send out His angels with a loud trumpet, and they will gather His elect from the four winds, from one end of the sky to the other.

³²"Now learn this parable from the fig tree: As soon as its branch becomes tender and sprouts leaves, you know that summer is near. ³³In the same way, when you see all these things, recognizeᶜ that Heᴰ is near—at the door! ³⁴I assure you: This generation will certainly not pass away until all these things take place. ³⁵Heaven and earth will pass away, but My words will never pass away.

³⁶"Now concerning that day and hour no one knows—neither the angels in heaven, nor the Sonᴱ—except the Father only. ³⁷As the days of Noah were, so the coming of the Son of Man will be. ³⁸For in those days before the flood they were eating and drinking, marrying and giving in marriage, until the day Noah boarded the ark. ³⁹They didn't knowᶠ until the flood came and swept them all away. So this is the way the coming of the Son of Man will be: ⁴⁰Then two men will be in the field: one will be taken and one left. ⁴¹Two women will be grinding at the mill: one will be taken and one left. ⁴²Therefore be alert, since you don't know what dayᴳ your Lord is coming. ⁴³But know this: If the homeowner had known what timeᴴ the thief was coming, he would have stayed alert and not let his house be broken into. ⁴⁴This is why you also must be ready, because the Son of Man is coming at an hour you do not expect.

⁴⁵"Who then is a faithful and sensible slave, whom his master has put in charge of his household, to give them food at the proper time? ⁴⁶That slave whose master finds him working when he comes will be rewarded. ⁴⁷I assure you: He will put him in charge of all his possessions. ⁴⁸But if that wicked slave says in his heart, 'My master is delayed,' ⁴⁹and starts to beat his fellow slaves, and eats and drinks with drunkards, ⁵⁰that slave's master will come on a day he does not expect and at an hour he does not know. ⁵¹He will cut him to piecesᴵ and

assign him a place with the hypocrites. In that place there will be weeping and gnashing of teeth.

25 "Then the kingdom of heaven will be like 10 virginsᴶ who took their lamps and went out to meet the groom. ²Five of them were foolish and five were sensible. ³When the foolish took their lamps, they didn't take olive oil with them. ⁴But the sensible ones took oil in their flasks with their lamps. ⁵Since the groom was delayed, they all became drowsy and fell asleep.

⁶"In the middle of the night there was a shout: 'Here's the groom! Come out to meet him.'

⁷"Then all those virgins got up and trimmed their lamps. ⁸But the foolish ones said to the sensible ones, 'Give us some of your oil, because our lamps are going out.'

⁹"The sensible ones answered, 'No, there won't be enough for us and for you. Go instead to those who sell, and buy oil for yourselves.'

¹⁰"When they had gone to buy some, the groom arrived. Then those who were ready went in with him to the wedding banquet, and the door was shut.

¹¹"Later the rest of the virgins also came and said, 'Master, master, open up for us!'

¹²"But he replied, 'I assure you: I do not know you!'

¹³"Therefore be alert, because you don't know either the day or the hour.ᴷ

¹⁴"For it is just like a man going on a journey. He called his own slaves and turned over his possessions to them. ¹⁵To one he gave five talents;ᴸ to another, two; and to another, one—to each according to his own ability. Then he went on a journey. Immediately ¹⁶the man who had received five talents went, put them to work, and earned five more. ¹⁷In the same way the man with two earned two more. ¹⁸But the man who had received one talent went off, dug a hole in the ground, and hid his master's money.

¹⁹"After a long time the master of those slaves came and settled accounts with them. ²⁰The man who had received five talents approached, presented five more talents, and said, 'Master, you gave me five talents. Look, I've earned five more talents.'

ᴬ24:30 Or all the tribes of the land   ᴮ24:30 Lit will beat; that is, beat their breasts   ᶜ24:33 Or things, you know   ᴰ24:33 Or it; that is, summer
ᴱ24:36 Other mss omit nor the Son   ᶠ24:39 They didn't know the day and hour of the coming judgment.   ᴳ24:42 Other mss read hour; = time
ᴴ24:43 Lit watch; a division of the night in ancient times   ᴵ24:51 Lit him in two   ᴶ25:1 Or bridesmaids   ᴷ25:13 Other mss add in which the Son
of Man is coming.   ᴸ25:15 Worth a very large sum of money; a talent = 6,000 denarii

²¹"His master said to him, 'Well done, good and faithful slave! You were faithful over a few things; I will put you in charge of many things. Share your master's joy!'

²²"Then the man with two talents also approached. He said, 'Master, you gave me two talents. Look, I've earned two more talents.'

²³"His master said to him, 'Well done, good and faithful slave! You were faithful over a few things; I will put you in charge of many things. Share your master's joy!'

²⁴"Then the man who had received one talent also approached and said, 'Master, I know you. You're a difficult man, reaping where you haven't sown and gathering where you haven't scattered seed. ²⁵So I was afraid and went off and hid your talent in the ground. Look, you have what is yours.'

²⁶"But his master replied to him, 'You evil, lazy slave! If you knew that I reap where I haven't sown and gather where I haven't scattered, ²⁷thenᴬ you should have deposited my money with the bankers. And when I returned I would have received my moneyᴮ back with interest.

²⁸"'So take the talent from him and give it to the one who has 10 talents. ²⁹For to everyone who has, more will be given, and he will have more than enough. But from the one who does not have, even what he has will be taken away from him. ³⁰And throw this good-for-nothing slave into the outer darkness. In that place there will be weeping and gnashing of teeth.'

³¹"When the Son of Man comes in His glory, and all the angelsᶜ with Him, then He will sit on the throne of His glory. ³²All the nationsᴰ will be gathered before Him, and He will separate them one from another, just as a shepherd separates the sheep from the goats. ³³He will put the sheep on His right and the goats on the left. ³⁴Then the King will say to those on His right, 'Come, you who are blessed by My Father, inherit the kingdom prepared for you from the foundation of the world.

> ³⁵ For I was hungry
> and you gave Me something to eat;
> I was thirsty
> and you gave Me something to drink;
> I was a stranger and you took Me in;
> ³⁶ I was naked and you clothed Me;

> I was sick and you took care of Me;
> I was in prison and you visited Me.'

³⁷"Then the righteous will answer Him, 'Lord, when did we see You hungry and feed You, or thirsty and give You something to drink? ³⁸When did we see You a stranger and take You in, or without clothes and clothe You? ³⁹When did we see You sick, or in prison, and visit You?'

⁴⁰"And the King will answer them, 'I assure you: Whatever you did for one of the least of these brothers of Mine, you did for Me.' ⁴¹Then He will also say to those on the left, 'Depart from Me, you who are cursed, into the eternal fire prepared for the Devil and his angels!

> ⁴² For I was hungry
> and you gave Me nothing to eat;
> I was thirsty
> and you gave Me nothing to drink;
> ⁴³ I was a stranger
> and you didn't take Me in;
> I was naked
> and you didn't clothe Me,
> sick and in prison
> and you didn't take care of Me.'

⁴⁴"Then they too will answer, 'Lord, when did we see You hungry, or thirsty, or a stranger, or without clothes, or sick, or in prison, and not help You?'

⁴⁵"Then He will answer them, 'I assure you: Whatever you did not do for one of the least of these, you did not do for Me either.'

⁴⁶"And they will go away into eternal punishment, but the righteous into eternal life."

26 When Jesus had finished saying all this, He told His disciples, ²"You knowᴱ that the Passover takes place after two days, and the Son of Man will be handed over to be crucified."

³Then the chief priestsᶠ and the elders of the people assembled in the palace of the high priest, who was called Caiaphas, ⁴and they conspired to arrest Jesus in a treacherous way and kill Him. ⁵"Not during the festival," they said, "so there won't be a rioting among the people."

⁶While Jesus was in Bethany at the house of Simon, a man who had a serious skin disease, ⁷a woman approached Him with an alabaster jar of very expensive fragrant oil. She poured it on His head as He was reclining at the table. ⁸When the disciples saw it, they were indig-

---

ᴬ25:26-27 Or So you knew . . . scattered? Then (as a question)   ᴮ25:27 Lit received what is mine   ᶜ25:31 Other mss read holy angels
ᴰ25:32 Or the Gentiles   ᴱ26:2 Or Know (as a command)   ᶠ26:3 Other mss add and the scribes

nant. "Why this waste?" they asked. ⁹"This might have been sold for a great deal and given to the poor."

¹⁰But Jesus, aware of this, said to them, "Why are you bothering this woman? She has done a noble thing for Me. ¹¹You always have the poor with you, but you do not always have Me. ¹²By pouring this fragrant oil on My body, she has prepared Me for burial. ¹³I assure you: Wherever this gospel is proclaimed in the whole world, what this woman has done will also be told in memory of her."

¹⁴Then one of the Twelve—the man called Judas Iscariot—went to the chief priests ¹⁵and said, "What are you willing to give me if I hand Him over to you?" So they weighed out 30 pieces of silver for him. ¹⁶And from that time he started looking for a good opportunity to betray Him.

¹⁷On the first day of Unleavened Bread the disciples came to Jesus and asked, "Where do You want us to prepare the Passover so You may eat it?"

¹⁸"Go into the city to a certain man," He said, "and tell him, 'The Teacher says: My time is near; I am celebrating the Passover at your place^A with My disciples.'" ¹⁹So the disciples did as Jesus had directed them and prepared the Passover. ²⁰When evening came, He was reclining at the table with the Twelve. ²¹While they were eating, He said, "I assure you: One of you will betray Me."

²²Deeply distressed, each one began to say to Him, "Surely not I, Lord?"

²³He replied, "The one who dipped his hand with Me in the bowl—he will betray Me. ²⁴The Son of Man will go just as it is written about Him, but woe to that man by whom the Son of Man is betrayed! It would have been better for that man if he had not been born."

²⁵Then Judas, His betrayer, replied, "Surely not I, Rabbi?"

"You have said it," He told him.

²⁶As they were eating, Jesus took bread, blessed and broke it, gave it to the disciples, and said, "Take and eat it; this is My body."

²⁷Then He took a cup, and after giving thanks, He gave it to them and said, "Drink from it, all of you. ²⁸For this is My blood that establishes the covenant;^B it is shed for many for the

forgiveness of sins. ²⁹But I tell you, from this moment I will not drink of this fruit of the vine until that day when I drink it in a new way^C in My Father's kingdom with you." ³⁰After singing psalms,^D they went out to the Mount of Olives.

³¹Then Jesus said to them, "Tonight all of you will run away^E because of Me, for it is written:

> I will strike the shepherd,
>   and the sheep of the flock
>   will be scattered.^F

³²But after I have been resurrected, I will go ahead of you to Galilee."

³³Peter told Him, "Even if everyone runs away because of You, I will never run away!"

³⁴"I assure you," Jesus said to him, "tonight, before the rooster crows, you will deny Me three times!"

³⁵"Even if I have to die with You," Peter told Him, "I will never deny You!" And all the disciples said the same thing.

³⁶Then Jesus came with them to a place called Gethsemane,^G and He told the disciples, "Sit here while I go over there and pray." ³⁷Taking along Peter and the two sons of Zebedee, He began to be sorrowful and deeply distressed. ³⁸Then He said to them, "My soul is swallowed up in sorrow^H—to the point of death.^I Remain here and stay awake with Me." ³⁹Going a little farther,^J He fell facedown and prayed, "My Father! If it is possible, let this cup pass from Me. Yet not as I will, but as You will."

⁴⁰Then He came to the disciples and found them sleeping. He asked Peter, "So, couldn't you^K stay awake with Me one hour? ⁴¹Stay awake and pray, so that you won't enter into temptation. The spirit is willing, but the flesh is weak."

⁴²Again, a second time, He went away and prayed, "My Father, if this^L cannot pass^M unless I drink it, Your will be done." ⁴³And He came again and found them sleeping, because they could not keep their eyes open.^N

⁴⁴After leaving them, He went away again and prayed a third time, saying the same thing once more. ⁴⁵Then He came to the disciples and said to them, "Are you still sleeping and

^A26:18 Lit Passover with you   ^B26:28 Other mss read new covenant   ^C26:29 Or drink new wine; lit drink it new   ^D26:30 Pss 113–118 were sung during and after the Passover meal.   ^E26:31 Or stumble   ^F26:31 Zch 13:7   ^G26:36 A garden east of Jerusalem at the base of the Mount of Olives; Gethsemane = olive oil press   ^H26:38 Or I am deeply grieved, or I am overwhelmed by sorrow; Ps 42:6,11; 43:5   ^I26:38 Lit unto death   ^J26:39 Other mss read Drawing nearer   ^K26:40 = all 3 disciples because the verb in Gk is pl   ^L26:42 Other mss add cup   ^M26:42 Other mss add from Me   ^N26:43 Lit because their eyes were weighed down resting?^A Look, the time is near. The Son of Man is being betrayed into the hands of sinners. ⁴⁶Get up; let's go! See, My betrayer is near."

⁴⁷While He was still speaking, Judas, one of the Twelve, suddenly arrived. A large mob, with swords and clubs, was with him from the chief priests and elders of the people. ⁴⁸His betrayer had given them a sign: "The One I kiss, He's the One; arrest Him!" ⁴⁹So he went right up to Jesus and said, "Greetings, Rabbi!" and kissed Him.

⁵⁰"Friend," Jesus asked him, "why have you come?"^B

Then they came up, took hold of Jesus, and arrested Him. ⁵¹At that moment one of those with Jesus reached out his hand and drew his sword. He struck the high priest's slave and cut off his ear.

⁵²Then Jesus told him, "Put your sword back in its place because all who take up a sword will perish by a sword. ⁵³Or do you think that I cannot call on My Father, and He will provide Me at once with more than 12 legions^C of angels? ⁵⁴How, then, would the Scriptures be fulfilled that say it must happen this way?"

⁵⁵At that time Jesus said to the crowds, "Have you come out with swords and clubs, as if I were a criminal,^D to capture Me? Every day I used to sit, teaching in the temple complex, and you didn't arrest Me. ⁵⁶But all this has happened so that the prophetic Scriptures^E would be fulfilled." Then all the disciples deserted Him and ran away.

⁵⁷Those who had arrested Jesus led Him away to Caiaphas the high priest, where the scribes and the elders had convened. ⁵⁸Meanwhile, Peter was following Him at a distance right to the high priest's courtyard.^F He went in and was sitting with the temple police^G to see the outcome.^H

⁵⁹The chief priests and the whole Sanhedrin were looking for false testimony against Jesus so they could put Him to death. ⁶⁰But they could not find any, even though many false witnesses came forward.^I Finally, two^J who came forward ⁶¹stated, "This man said, 'I can demolish God's sanctuary and rebuild it in three days.'"

⁶²The high priest then stood up and said to Him, "Don't You have an answer to what these men are testifying against You?" ⁶³But Jesus kept silent. Then the high priest said to Him, "By the living God I place You under oath: tell us if You are the Messiah, the Son of God!"

⁶⁴"You have said it,"^K Jesus told him. "But I tell you, in the future^L you will see the Son of Man seated at the right hand of the Power and coming on the clouds of heaven."^M

⁶⁵Then the high priest tore his robes and said, "He has blasphemed! Why do we still need witnesses? Look, now you've heard the blasphemy! ⁶⁶What is your decision?"^N

They answered, "He deserves death!" ⁶⁷Then they spit in His face and beat Him; others slapped Him ⁶⁸and said, "Prophesy to us, Messiah! Who hit You?"

⁶⁹Now Peter was sitting outside in the courtyard. A servant approached him and she said, "You were with Jesus the Galilean too."

⁷⁰But he denied it in front of everyone: "I don't know what you're talking about!"

⁷¹When he had gone out to the gateway, another woman saw him and told those who were there, "This man was with Jesus the Nazarene!"

⁷²And again he denied it with an oath, "I don't know the man!"

⁷³After a little while those standing there approached and said to Peter, "You certainly are one of them, since even your accent^O gives you away."

⁷⁴Then he started to curse^P and to swear with an oath, "I do not know the man!" Immediately a rooster crowed, ⁷⁵and Peter remembered the words Jesus had spoken, "Before the rooster crows, you will deny Me three times." And he went outside and wept bitterly.

27 When daybreak came, all the chief priests and the elders of the people plotted against Jesus to put Him to death. ²After tying Him up, they led Him away and handed Him over to Pilate,^Q the governor.

³Then Judas, His betrayer, seeing that He had been condemned, was full of remorse and returned the 30 pieces of silver to the chief priests and elders. ⁴"I have sinned by betraying innocent blood," he said.

---

^A26:45 Or Sleep on now and take your rest. ^B26:50 Or Jesus told him, "do what you come for." [as a statement] ^C26:53 A Roman legion contained up to 6,000 soldiers. ^D26:55 Lit as against a criminal ^E26:56 Or the Scriptures of the prophets ^F26:58 Or high priest's palace ^G26:58 Or the officers, or the servants ^H26:58 Lit end ^I26:60 Other mss add they found none ^J26:60 Other mss add false witnesses ^K26:64 Or That is true, an affirmative oath; Mt 27:11; Mk 15:2 ^L26:64 Lit you, from now ^M26:64 Ps 110:1; Dn 7:13 ^N26:66 Lit What does it seem to you? ^O26:73 Or speech ^P26:74 To call down curses on himself if what he said weren't true ^Q27:2 Other mss read Pontius Pilate

"What's that to us?" they said. "See to it yourself!"

⁵So he threw the silver into the sanctuary and departed. Then he went and hanged himself.

⁶The chief priests took the silver and said, "It's not lawful to put it into the temple treasury,ᴬ since it is blood money."ᴮ ⁷So they conferred together and bought the potter's field with it as a burial place for foreigners. ⁸Therefore that field has been called "Blood Field" to this day. ⁹Then what was spoken through the prophet Jeremiah was fulfilled:

They took the 30 pieces of silver, the price of Him whose price was set by the Israelites, ¹⁰and gave them for the potter's field, as the Lord directed me.ᶜ

¹¹Now Jesus stood before the governor. "Are You the King of the Jews?" the governor asked Him.

Jesus answered, "You have said it."ᴰ ¹²And while He was being accused by the chief priests and elders, He didn't answer.

¹³Then Pilate said to Him, "Don't You hear how much they are testifying against You?" ¹⁴But He didn't answer him on even one charge, so that the governor was greatly amazed.

¹⁵At the festival the governor's custom was to release to the crowd a prisoner they wanted. ¹⁶At that time they had a notorious prisoner called Barabbas.ᴱ ¹⁷So when they had gathered together, Pilate said to them, "Who is it you want me to release for you—Barabbas,ᴱ or Jesus who is called Messiah?" ¹⁸For he knew they had handed Him over because of envy.

¹⁹While he was sitting on the judge's bench, his wife sent word to him, "Have nothing to do with that righteous man, for today I've suffered terribly in a dream because of Him!"

²⁰The chief priests and the elders, however, persuaded the crowds to ask for Barabbas and to execute Jesus. ²¹The governor asked them, "Which of the two do you want me to release for you?"

"Barabbas!" they answered.

²²Pilate asked them, "What should I do then with Jesus, who is called Messiah?"

They all answered, "Crucify Him!"ᶠ

²³Then he said, "Why? What has He done wrong?"

But they kept shouting, "Crucify Him!" all the more.

²⁴When Pilate saw that he was getting nowhere,ᴳ but that a riot was starting instead, he took some water, washed his hands in front of the crowd, and said, "I am innocent of this man's blood.ᴴ See to it yourselves!"

²⁵All the people answered, "His blood be on us and on our children!" ²⁶Then he released Barabbas to them. But after having Jesus flogged,ᴵ he handed Him over to be crucified.

²⁷Then the governor's soldiers took Jesus into headquarters and gathered the whole company around Him. ²⁸They stripped Him and dressed Him in a scarlet military robe. ²⁹They twisted together a crown of thorns, put it on His head, and placed a reed in His right hand. And they knelt down before Him and mocked Him: "Hail, King of the Jews!" ³⁰Then they spit on Him, took the reed, and kept hitting Him on the head. ³¹When they had mocked Him, they stripped Him of the robe, put His clothes on Him, and led Him away to crucify Him.

³²As they were going out, they found a Cyrenian man named Simon. They forced this man to carry His cross. ³³When they came to a place called *Golgotha* (which means Skull Place), ³⁴they gave Him wineᴶ mixed with gall to drink. But when He tasted it, He would not drink it. ³⁵After crucifying Him they divided His clothes by casting lots.ᴷ ³⁶Then they sat down and were guarding Him there. ³⁷Above His head they put up the charge against Him in writing:

**THIS IS JESUS
THE KING OF THE JEWS.**

³⁸Then two criminalsᴸ were crucified with Him, one on the right and one on the left. ³⁹Those who passed by were yelling insults atᴹ Him, shaking their heads ⁴⁰and saying, "The One who would demolish the sanctuary and rebuild it in three days, save Yourself! If You are the Son of God, come down from the cross!" ⁴¹In the same way the chief priests,

---

ᴬ**27:6** See Mk 7:11 where the same Gk word (Corban) means a gift pledged to the temple. ᴮ**27:6** Lit *the price of blood* ᶜ**27:9-10** Jr 32:6-9; Zch 11:12-13 ᴰ**27:11** Or *That is true*, an affirmative oath; Mt 26:64; Mk 15:2 ᴱ**27:16,17** Other mss read *Jesus Barabbas* ᶠ**27:22** Lit "*Him—be crucified!*" ᴳ**27:24** Lit *that it availed nothing* ᴴ**27:24** Other mss read *this righteous man's blood* ᴵ**27:26** Roman flogging was done with a whip made of leather strips embedded with pieces of bone or metal that brutally tore the flesh. ᴶ**27:34** Other mss read *sour wine* ᴷ**27:35** Other mss add *that what was spoken by the prophet might be fulfilled: "They divided My clothes among them, and for My clothing they cast lots."* ᴸ**27:38** Or *revolutionaries* ᴹ**27:39** Lit *passed by blasphemed or were blaspheming* with the scribes and elders,[A] mocked Him and said, [42]"He saved others, but He cannot save Himself! He is the King of Israel! Let Him[B] come down now from the cross, and we will believe in Him. [43]He has put His trust in God; let God rescue Him now—if He wants Him![C] For He said, 'I am God's Son.'" [44]In the same way even the criminals who were crucified with Him kept taunting Him.

[45]From noon until three in the afternoon[D] darkness came over the whole land.[E] [46]About three in the afternoon Jesus cried out with a loud voice, "*Elí, Elí, lemá*[F] *sabachtháni?* " that is, "My God, My God, why have You forsaken[G] Me?"[H]

[47]When some of those standing there heard this, they said, "He's calling for Elijah!"

[48]Immediately one of them ran and got a sponge, filled it with sour wine, fixed it on a reed, and offered Him a drink. [49]But the rest said, "Let's see if Elijah comes to save Him!"

[50]Jesus shouted again with a loud voice and gave up His spirit. [51]Suddenly, the curtain of the sanctuary[I] was split in two from top to bottom; the earth quaked and the rocks were split. [52]The tombs were also opened and many bodies of the saints who had fallen asleep were raised. [53]And they came out of the tombs after His resurrection, entered the holy city, and appeared to many.

[54]When the centurion and those with him, who were guarding Jesus, saw the earthquake and the things that had happened, they were terrified and said, "This man really was God's Son!"[J]

[55]Many women who had followed Jesus from Galilee and ministered to Him were there, looking on from a distance. [56]Among them were Mary Magdalene, Mary the mother of James and Joseph, and the mother of Zebedee's sons.

[57]When it was evening, a rich man from Arimathea named Joseph came, who himself had also become a disciple of Jesus. [58]He approached Pilate and asked for Jesus' body. Then Pilate ordered that it[K] be released. [59]So Joseph took the body, wrapped it in clean, fine linen, [60]and placed it in his new tomb, which he had cut into the rock. He left after rolling a

great stone against the entrance of the tomb. [61]Mary Magdalene and the other Mary were seated there, facing the tomb.

[62]The next day, which followed the preparation day, the chief priests and the Pharisees gathered before Pilate [63]and said, "Sir, we remember that while this deceiver was still alive He said, 'After three days I will rise again.' [64]Therefore give orders that the tomb be made secure until the third day. Otherwise, His disciples may come, steal Him, and tell the people, 'He has been raised from the dead.' Then the last deception will be worse than the first."

[65]"You have[L] a guard of soldiers,"[M] Pilate told them. "Go and make it as secure as you know how." [66]Then they went and made the tomb secure by sealing the stone and setting the guard.[N]

28

After the Sabbath, as the first day of the week was dawning, Mary Magdalene and the other Mary went to view the tomb. [2]Suddenly there was a violent earthquake, because an angel of the Lord descended from heaven and approached the tomb. He rolled back the stone and was sitting on it. [3]His appearance was like lightning, and his robe was as white as snow. [4]The guards were so shaken from fear of him that they became like dead men.

[5]But the angel told the women, "Don't be afraid, because I know you are looking for Jesus who was crucified. [6]He is not here! For He has been resurrected, just as He said. Come and see the place where He lay. [7]Then go quickly and tell His disciples, 'He has been raised from the dead. In fact, He is going ahead of you to Galilee; you will see Him there.' Listen, I have told you."

[8]So, departing quickly from the tomb with fear and great joy, they ran to tell His disciples the news. [9]Just then[O] Jesus met them and said, "Good morning!" They came up, took hold of His feet, and worshiped Him. [10]Then Jesus told them, "Do not be afraid. Go and tell My brothers to leave for Galilee, and they will see Me there."

[11]As they were on their way, some of the guards came into the city and reported to the chief priests everything that had happened. [12]After the priests[P] had assembled with the

[A]27:41 Other mss add *and Pharisees*   [B]27:42 Other mss read *If He . . . Israel, let Him*   [C]27:43 Or *if He takes pleasure in Him*   [D]27:45 Lit *From the sixth hour to the ninth hour*   [E]27:45 Or *whole earth*   [F]27:46 Some mss read *lama*; other mss read *lima*   [G]27:46 Or *abandoned*   [H]27:46 Ps 22:1   [I]27:51 A heavy curtain separated the inner room of the temple from the outer.   [J]27:54 Or *the Son of God*   [K]27:58 Other mss read *that the body.*   [L]27:65 Or *"Take*   [M]27:65 It is uncertain whether this guard consisted of temple police or Roman soldiers.   [N]27:66 Lit *stone with the guard*   [O]28:9 Other mss add *as they were on their way to tell the news to His disciples*   [P]28:12 Lit *After they* elders and agreed on a plan, they gave the soldiers a large sum of money [13]and told them, "Say this, 'His disciples came during the night and stole Him while we were sleeping.' [14]If this reaches the governor's ears,[A] we will deal with[B] him and keep you out of trouble." [15]So they took the money and did as they were instructed. And this story has been spread among Jewish people to this day.

[16]The 11 disciples traveled to Galilee, to the mountain where Jesus had directed them.

[17]When they saw Him, they worshiped,[C] but some doubted. [18]Then Jesus came near and said to them, "All authority has been given to Me in heaven and on earth. [19]Go, therefore, and make disciples of[D] all nations, baptizing them in the name of the Father and of the Son and of the Holy Spirit, [20]teaching them to observe everything I have commanded you. And remember,[E] I am with you always,[F] to the end of the age."

MARK

1 The beginning of the gospel of Jesus Christ, the Son of God. [2]As it is written in Isaiah the prophet:[G]

> Look, I am sending My messenger
>   ahead of You,
> who will prepare Your way.[H]
> [3] A voice of one crying out
>   in the wilderness:
> Prepare the way for the Lord;
>   make His paths straight![I]

[4]John came baptizing[J] in the wilderness and preaching a baptism of repentance[K] for the forgiveness of sins. [5]The whole Judean countryside and all the people of Jerusalem were flocking to him, and they were baptized by him in the Jordan River as they confessed their sins. [6]John wore a camel-hair garment with a leather belt around his waist and ate locusts and wild honey. [7]He was preaching: "Someone more powerful than I will come after me. I am not worthy to stoop down and untie the strap of His sandals. [8]I have baptized you with[L] water, but He will baptize you with the Holy Spirit."

[9]In those days Jesus came from Nazareth in Galilee and was baptized in the Jordan by John. [10]As soon as He came up out of the water, He saw the heavens being torn open and the Spirit descending to Him like a dove. [11]And a voice came from heaven:

> You are My beloved Son;
> I take delight in You![M]

[12]Immediately the Spirit drove Him into the wilderness. [13]He was in the wilderness 40 days, being tempted by Satan. He was with the wild animals, and the angels began to serve Him.

[14]After John was arrested, Jesus went to Galilee, preaching the good news[N,O] of God:[P] [15]"The time is fulfilled, and the kingdom of God has come near. Repent and believe in the good news!"

[16]As He was passing along by the Sea of Galilee, He saw Simon and Andrew, Simon's brother. They were casting a net into the sea, since they were fishermen. [17]"Follow Me," Jesus told them, "and I will make you fish for[Q] people!" [18]Immediately they left their nets and followed Him. [19]Going on a little farther, He saw James the son of Zebedee and his brother John. They were in their boat mending their nets. [20]Immediately He called them, and they left their father Zebedee in the boat with the hired men and followed Him.

[21]Then they went into Capernaum, and right away He entered the synagogue on the Sabbath and began to teach. [22]They were astonished at His teaching because, unlike the scribes, He was teaching them as one having authority.

[23]Just then a man with an unclean spirit was in their synagogue. He cried out,[R] [24]"What do You have to do with us,[S] Jesus—Nazarene? Have You come to destroy us? I know who You are—the Holy One of God!"

[25]But Jesus rebuked him and said, "Be quiet,[T] and come out of him!" [26]And the unclean spirit

---

[A]28:14 Lit this is heard by the governor   [B]28:14 Lit will persuade   [C]28:17 Other mss add Him   [D]28:19 Or and disciple; lit and instruct   [E]28:20 Lit look   [F]28:20 Lit all the days   [G]1:2 Other mss read in the prophets   [H]1:2 Other mss add before You   [I]1:2-3 Is 40:3; Mal 3:1   [J]1:4 Or John the Baptist came, or John the Baptizer came   [K]1:4 Or a baptism based on repentance   [L]1:8 Or in   [M]1:11 Or In You I am well pleased   [N]1:14 Other mss add of the kingdom   [O]1:14 Or gospel   [P]1:14 Either from God or about God   [Q]1:17 Lit you to become fishers of   [R]1:23 Other mss add to the beginning of v. 24: "Leave us alone.   [S]1:24 Lit What to us and to You   [T]1:25 Or Be muzzled convulsed him, shouted with a loud voice, and came out of him.

²⁷Then they were all amazed, so they began to argue with one another, saying, "What is this? A new teaching with authority!ᴬ He commands even the unclean spirits, and they obey Him." ²⁸News about Him then spread throughout the entire vicinity of Galilee.

²⁹As soon as they left the synagogue, they went into Simon and Andrew's house with James and John. ³⁰Simon's mother-in-law was lying in bed with a fever, and they told Him about her at once. ³¹So He went to her, took her by the hand, and raised her up. The fever left her,ᴮ and she began to serve them.

³²When evening came, after the sun had set, they began bringing to Him all those who were sick and those who were demon-possessed. ³³The whole town was assembled at the door, ³⁴and He healed many who were sick with various diseases and drove out many demons. But He would not permit the demons to speak, because they knew Him.

³⁵Very early in the morning, while it was still dark, He got up, went out, and made His way to a deserted place. And He was praying there. ³⁶Simon and his companions went searching for Him. ³⁷They found Him and said, "Everyone's looking for You!"

³⁸And He said to them, "Let's go on to the neighboring villages so that I may preach there too. This is why I have come." ³⁹So He went into all of Galilee, preaching in their synagogues and driving out demons.

⁴⁰Then a man with a serious skin disease came to Him and, on his knees,ᶜ begged Him: "If You are willing, You can make me clean."

⁴¹Moved with compassion, Jesus reached out His hand and touched him. "I am willing," He told him. "Be made clean." ⁴²Immediately the disease left him, and he was healed.ᴰ ⁴³Then He sternly warned him and sent him away at once, ⁴⁴telling him, "See that you say nothing to anyone; but go and show yourself to the priest, and offer what Moses prescribed for your cleansing, as a testimony to them." ⁴⁵Yet he went out and began to proclaim it widely and to spread the news, with the result that Jesus could no longer enter a town openly. But

He was out in deserted places, and they would come to Him from everywhere.

2 When He entered Capernaum again after some days, it was reported that He was at home. ²So many people gathered together that there was no more room, not even in the doorway, and He was speaking the message to them. ³Then they came to Him bringing a paralytic, carried by four men. ⁴Since they were not able to bring him toᴱ Jesus because of the crowd, they removed the roof above where He was. And when they had broken through, they lowered the mat on which the paralytic was lying.

⁵Seeing their faith, Jesus told the paralytic, "Son, your sins are forgiven."

⁶But some of the scribes were sitting there, thinking to themselves:ᶠ ⁷"Why does He speak like this? He's blaspheming! Who can forgive sins but God alone?"

⁸Right away Jesus understood in His spirit that they were thinking like this within themselves and said to them, "Why are you thinking these things in your hearts?ᴳ ⁹Which is easier: to say to the paralytic, 'Your sins are forgiven,' or to say, 'Get up, pick up your mat, and walk'? ¹⁰But so you may know that the Son of Man has authority on earth to forgive sins," He told the paralytic, ¹¹"I tell you: get up, pick up your mat, and go home."

¹²Immediately he got up, picked up the mat, and went out in front of everyone. As a result, they were all astounded and gave glory to God, saying, "We have never seen anything like this!"

¹³Then Jesus went out again beside the sea. The whole crowd was coming to Him, and He taught them. ¹⁴Then, moving on, He saw Levi the son of Alphaeus sitting at the tax office, and He said to him, "Follow Me!" So he got up and followed Him.

¹⁵While He was reclining at the table in Levi's house, many tax collectors and sinners were also guestsᴴ with Jesus and His disciples, because there were many who were following Him. ¹⁶When the scribes of the Phariseesᴵ saw that He was eating with sinners and tax collectors, they asked His disciples, "Why does He eatᴶ with tax collectors and sinners?"

ᴬ1:27 Other mss read *What is this? What is this new teaching? For with authority*   ᴮ1:31 Other mss add *at once*   ᶜ1:40 Other mss omit *on his knees*   ᴰ1:42 Lit *made clean*   ᴱ2:4 Other mss read *able to get near*   ᶠ2:6 Or *thinking in their hearts*   ᴳ2:8 Or *minds*   ᴴ2:15 Lit *reclining* [at the table]; at important meals the custom was to recline on a mat at a low table and lean on the left elbow.   ᴵ2:16 Other mss read *scribes and Pharisees*   ᴶ2:16 Other mss add *and drink*

¹⁷When Jesus heard this, He told them, "Those who are well don't need a doctor, but the sick do need one. I didn't come to call the righteous, but sinners."

¹⁸Now John's disciples and the Pharisees^A were fasting. People came and asked Him, "Why do John's disciples and the Pharisees' disciples fast, but Your disciples do not fast?"

¹⁹Jesus said to them, "The wedding guests^B cannot fast while the groom is with them, can they? As long as they have the groom with them, they cannot fast. ²⁰But the time^C will come when the groom is taken away from them, and then they will fast in that day. ²¹No one sews a patch of unshrunk cloth on an old garment. Otherwise, the new patch pulls away from the old cloth, and a worse tear is made. ²²And no one puts new wine into old wineskins. Otherwise, the wine will burst the skins, and the wine is lost as well as the skins.^D But new wine is for fresh wineskins."

²³On the Sabbath He was going through the grainfields, and His disciples began to make their way picking some heads of grain. ²⁴The Pharisees said to Him, "Look, why are they doing what is not lawful on the Sabbath?"

²⁵He said to them, "Have you never read what David and those who were with him did when he was in need and hungry— ²⁶how he entered the house of God in the time of Abiathar the high priest and ate the sacred bread—which is not lawful for anyone to eat except the priests—and also gave some to his companions?" ²⁷Then He told them, "The Sabbath was made for^E man and not man for^E the Sabbath. ²⁸Therefore, the Son of Man is Lord even of the Sabbath."

3 Now He entered the synagogue again, and a man was there who had a paralyzed hand. ²In order to accuse Him, they were watching Him closely to see whether He would heal him on the Sabbath. ³He told the man with the paralyzed hand, "Stand before us."^F ⁴Then He said to them, "Is it lawful on the Sabbath to do what is good or to do what is evil, to save life or to kill?" But they were silent. ⁵After looking around at them with anger and sorrow at the hardness of their hearts, He told the man, "Stretch out your hand." So he stretched it out, and his hand was restored. ⁶Immediately the Pharisees went out

and started plotting with the Herodians against Him, how they might destroy Him.

⁷Jesus departed with His disciples to the sea, and a large crowd followed from Galilee, Judea, ⁸Jerusalem, Idumea, beyond the Jordan, and around Tyre and Sidon. The large crowd came to Him because they heard about everything He was doing. ⁹Then He told His disciples to have a small boat ready for Him, so the crowd would not crush Him. ¹⁰Since He had healed many, all who had diseases were pressing toward Him to touch Him. ¹¹Whenever the unclean spirits saw Him, those possessed fell down before Him and cried out, "You are the Son of God!" ¹²And He would strongly warn them not to make Him known.

¹³Then He went up the mountain and summoned those He wanted, and they came to Him. ¹⁴He also appointed 12—He also named them apostles^G—to be with Him, to send them out to preach, ¹⁵and to have authority to^H drive out demons.

¹⁶He appointed the Twelve:^I

To Simon, He gave the name Peter;
¹⁷   and to James the son of Zebedee,
    and to his brother John,
    He gave the name "Boanerges"
    (that is, "Sons of Thunder");
¹⁸   Andrew;
    Philip and Bartholomew;
    Matthew and Thomas;
    James the son of Alphaeus,
    and Thaddaeus;
    Simon the Zealot,^J
¹⁹   and Judas Iscariot,^K
    who also betrayed Him.

²⁰Then He went home, and the crowd gathered again so that they were not even able to eat.^L ²¹When His family heard this, they set out to restrain Him, because they said, "He's out of His mind."

²²The scribes who had come down from Jerusalem said, "He has Beelzebul in Him!" and, "He drives out demons by the ruler of the demons!"

²³So He summoned them and spoke to them in parables: "How can Satan drive out Satan? ²⁴If a kingdom is divided against itself, that kingdom cannot stand. ²⁵If a house is divided

^A2:18 Other mss read the disciples of John and of the Pharisees   ^B2:19 Lit The sons of the bridal chamber   ^C2:20 Lit the days   ^D2:22 Other mss read the wine spills out and the skins will be ruined   ^E2:27 Or because of   ^F3:3 Lit Rise up in the middle   ^G3:14 Other mss omit He also named them apostles   ^H3:15 Other mss add heal diseases, and to   ^I3:16 Other mss omit He appointed the Twelve   ^J3:18 Lit the Cananaean   ^K3:19 Iscariot is probably "a man of Kerioth," a town in Judea.   ^L3:20 Or eat a meal; lit eat bread against itself, that house cannot stand. ²⁶And if Satan rebels against himself and is divided, he cannot stand but is finished!^A

²⁷"On the other hand, no one can enter a strong man's house and rob his possessions unless he first ties up the strong man. Then he will rob his house. ²⁸I assure you: People will be forgiven for all sins^B and whatever blasphemies they may blaspheme. ²⁹But whoever blasphemes against the Holy Spirit never has forgiveness, but is guilty of an eternal sin"^C— ³⁰because they were saying, "He has an unclean spirit."

³¹Then His mother and His brothers came, and standing outside, they sent word to Him and called Him. ³²A crowd was sitting around Him and told Him, "Look, Your mother, Your brothers, and Your sisters^D are outside asking for You."

³³He replied to them, "Who are My mother and My brothers?" ³⁴And looking about at those who were sitting in a circle around Him, He said, "Here are My mother and My brothers! ³⁵Whoever does the will of God is My brother and sister and mother."

4 Again He began to teach by the sea, and a very large crowd gathered around Him. So He got into a boat on the sea and sat down, while the whole crowd was on the shore facing the sea. ²He taught them many things in parables, and in His teaching He said to them: ³"Listen! Consider the sower who went out to sow. ⁴As he sowed, this occurred: Some seed fell along the path, and the birds came and ate it up. ⁵Other seed fell on rocky ground where it didn't have much soil, and it sprang up right away, since it didn't have deep soil. ⁶When the sun came up, it was scorched, and since it didn't have a root, it withered. ⁷Other seed fell among thorns, and the thorns came up and choked it, and it didn't produce a crop. ⁸Still others fell on good ground and produced a crop that increased 30, 60, and 100 times what was sown." ⁹Then He said, "Anyone who has ears to hear should listen!"

¹⁰When He was alone with the Twelve, those who were around Him asked Him about the parables. ¹¹He answered them, "The secret of the kingdom of God has been given to you, but to those outside, everything comes in parables ¹²so that

> they may look and look,
> yet not perceive;
> they may listen and listen,
> yet not understand;
> otherwise, they might turn back—
> and be forgiven."^{E,F}

¹³Then He said to them: "Don't you understand this parable? How then will you understand any of the parables? ¹⁴The sower sows the word. ¹⁵These^G are the ones along the path where the word is sown: when they hear, immediately Satan comes and takes away the word sown in them.^H ¹⁶And these are^I the ones sown on rocky ground: when they hear the word, immediately they receive it with joy. ¹⁷But they have no root in themselves; they are short-lived. When pressure or persecution comes because of the word, they immediately stumble. ¹⁸Others are sown among thorns; these are the ones who hear the word, ¹⁹but the worries of this age, the seduction^J of wealth, and the desires for other things enter in and choke the word, and it becomes unfruitful. ²⁰But the ones sown on good ground are those who hear the word, welcome it, and produce a crop: 30, 60, and 100 times what is sown."

²¹He also said to them, "Is a lamp brought in to be put under a basket or under a bed? Isn't it to be put on a lampstand? ²²For nothing is concealed except to be revealed, and nothing hidden except to come to light. ²³If anyone has ears to hear, he should listen!" ²⁴Then He said to them, "Pay attention to what you hear. By the measure you use,^K it will be measured and added to you. ²⁵For to the one who has, it will be given, and from the one who does not have, even what he has will be taken away."

²⁶"The kingdom of God is like this," He said. "A man scatters seed on the ground; ²⁷he sleeps and rises—night and day, and the seed sprouts and grows—he doesn't know how. ²⁸The soil produces a crop by itself—first the blade, then the head, and then the ripe grain on the head. ²⁹But as soon as the crop is ready, he sends for the sickle, because the harvest has come."

A3:26 Lit but he has an end   B3:28 Lit All things will be forgiven the sons of men   C3:29 Other mss read is subject to eternal judgment   D3:32 Other mss omit and Your sisters   E4:12 Other mss read and their sins be forgiven them   F4:12 Is 6:9-10   G4:15 Some people   H4:15 Other mss read in their hearts   I4:16 Other mss read are like   J4:19 Or pleasure, or deceitfulness   K4:24 Lit you measure

[30]And He said: "How can we illustrate the kingdom of God, or what parable can we use to describe it? [31]It's like a mustard seed that, when sown in the soil, is smaller than all the seeds on the ground. [32]And when sown, it comes up and grows taller than all the vegetables, and produces large branches, so that the birds of the sky can nest in its shade."

[33]He would speak the word to them with many parables like these, as they were able to understand. [34]And He did not speak to them without a parable. Privately, however, He would explain everything to His own disciples.

[35]On that day, when evening had come, He told them, "Let's cross over to the other side of the sea." [36]So they left the crowd and took Him along since He was already in the boat. And other boats were with Him. [37]A fierce windstorm arose, and the waves were breaking over the boat, so that the boat was already being swamped. [38]But He was in the stern, sleeping on the cushion. So they woke Him up and said to Him, "Teacher! Don't You care that we're going to die?"

[39]He got up, rebuked the wind, and said to the sea, "Silence! Be still!" The wind ceased, and there was a great calm. [40]Then He said to them, "Why are you fearful? Do you still have no faith?"

[41]And they were terrified and asked one another, "Who then is this? Even the wind and the sea obey Him!"

5 Then they came to the other side of the sea, to the region of the Gerasenes.[A] [2]As soon as He got out of the boat, a man with an unclean spirit came out of the tombs and met Him. [3]He lived in the tombs. No one was able to restrain him anymore—even with chains—[4]because he often had been bound with shackles and chains, but had snapped off the chains and smashed the shackles. No one was strong enough to subdue him. [5]And always, night and day, he was crying out among the tombs and in the mountains and cutting himself with stones.

[6]When he saw Jesus from a distance, he ran and knelt down before Him. [7]And he cried out with a loud voice, "What do You have to do with me,[B] Jesus, Son of the Most High God? I beg[C] You before God, don't torment me!" [8]For

He had told him, "Come out of the man, you unclean spirit!"

[9]"What is your name?" He asked him.

"My name is Legion,"[D] he answered Him, "because we are many." [10]And he kept begging Him not to send them out of the region.

[11]Now a large herd of pigs was there, feeding on the hillside. [12]The demons[E] begged Him, "Send us to the pigs, so we may enter them." [13]And He gave them permission. Then the unclean spirits came out and entered the pigs, and the herd of about 2,000 rushed down the steep bank into the sea and drowned there. [14]The men who tended them[F] ran off and reported it in the town and the countryside, and people went to see what had happened. [15]They came to Jesus and saw the man who had been demon-possessed by the legion, sitting there, dressed and in his right mind; and they were afraid. [16]The eyewitnesses described to them what had happened to the demon-possessed man and told about the pigs. [17]Then they began to beg Him to leave their region.

[18]As He was getting into the boat, the man who had been demon-possessed kept begging Him to be with Him. [19]But He would not let him; instead, He told him, "Go back home to your own people, and report to them how much the Lord has done for you and how He has had mercy on you." [20]So he went out and began to proclaim in the Decapolis how much Jesus had done for him, and they were all amazed.

[21]When Jesus had crossed over again by boat to the other side, a large crowd gathered around Him while He was by the sea. [22]One of the synagogue leaders, named Jairus, came, and when he saw Jesus, he fell at His feet [23]and kept begging Him, "My little daughter is at death's door.[G] Come and lay Your hands on her so she can get well and live."

[24]So Jesus went with him, and a large crowd was following and pressing against Him. [25]A woman suffering from bleeding for 12 years [26]had endured much under many doctors. She had spent everything she had and was not helped at all. On the contrary, she became worse. [27]Having heard about Jesus, she came behind Him in the crowd and touched His robe. [28]For she said, "If I can just touch His robes, I'll be made well!" [29]Instantly her flow

A5:1 Some mss read Gadarenes; other mss read Gergesenes   B5:7 Lit What to me and to You   C5:7 Or adjure   D5:9 A Roman legion contained up to 6,000 soldiers; here legion indicates a large number.   E5:12 Other mss read All the demons   F5:14 Other mss read tended the pigs   G5:23 Lit My little daughter has it finally; = to be at the end of life of blood ceased, and she sensed in her body that she was cured of her affliction.

³⁰At once Jesus realized in Himself that power had gone out from Him. He turned around in the crowd and said, "Who touched My robes?"

³¹His disciples said to Him, "You see the crowd pressing against You, and You say, 'Who touched Me?'"

³²So He was looking around to see who had done this. ³³Then the woman, knowing what had happened to her, came with fear and trembling, fell down before Him, and told Him the whole truth. ³⁴"Daughter," He said to her, "your faith has made you well.ᴬ Go in peace and be freeᴮ from your affliction."

³⁵While He was still speaking, people came from the synagogue leader's house and said, "Your daughter is dead. Why bother the Teacher anymore?"

³⁶But when Jesus overheard what was said, He told the synagogue leader, "Don't be afraid. Only believe." ³⁷He did not let anyone accompany Him except Peter, James, and John, James's brother. ³⁸They came to the leader's house, and He saw a commotion—people weeping and wailing loudly. ³⁹He went in and said to them, "Why are you making a commotion and weeping? The child is not dead but asleep."

⁴⁰They started laughing at Him, but He put them all outside. He took the child's father, mother, and those who were with Him, and entered the place where the child was. ⁴¹Then He took the child by the hand and said to her, "Talitha koum!"ᶜ (which is translated, "Little girl, I say to you, get up!"). ⁴²Immediately the girl got up and began to walk. (She was 12 years old.) At this they were utterly astounded. ⁴³Then He gave them strict orders that no one should know about this and said that she should be given something to eat.

6 He went away from there and came to His hometown, and His disciples followed Him. ²When the Sabbath came, He began to teach in the synagogue, and many who heard Him were astonished. "Where did this man get these things?" they said. "What is this wisdom given to Him, and how are these miracles performed by His hands? ³Isn't this the carpenter, the son of Mary, and the brother of James, Jo-

ses, Judas, and Simon? And aren't His sisters here with us?" So they were offended by Him.

⁴Then Jesus said to them, "A prophet is not without honor except in his hometown, among his relatives, and in his household." ⁵So He was not able to do any miraclesᴰ there, except that He laid His hands on a few sick people and healed them. ⁶And He was amazed at their unbelief.

Now He was going around the villages in a circuit, teaching. ⁷He summoned the Twelve and began to send them out in pairs and gave them authority over unclean spirits. ⁸He instructed them to take nothing for the road except a walking stick: no bread, no traveling bag, no money in their belts. ⁹They were to wear sandals, but not put on an extra shirt. ¹⁰Then He said to them, "Whenever you enter a house, stay there until you leave that place. ¹¹If any place does not welcome you and people refuse to listen to you, when you leave there, shake the dust off your feet as a testimony against them."ᴱ

¹²So they went out and preached that people should repent. ¹³And they were driving out many demons, anointing many sick people with olive oil, and healing them.

¹⁴King Herod heard of this, because Jesus' name had become well known. Someᶠ said, "John the Baptist has been raised from the dead, and that's why supernatural powers are at work in him." ¹⁵But others said, "He's Elijah." Still others said, "He's a prophetᴳ—like one of the prophets."

¹⁶When Herod heard of it, he said, "John, the one I beheaded, has been raised!" ¹⁷For Herod himself had given orders to arrest John and to chain him in prison on account of Herodias, his brother Philip's wife, whom he had married. ¹⁸John had been telling Herod, "It is not lawful for you to have your brother's wife!" ¹⁹So Herodias held a grudge against him and wanted to kill him. But she could not, ²⁰because Herod was in awe ofᴴ John and was protecting him, knowing he was a righteous and holy man. When Herod heard him he would be very disturbed,ᴵ yet would hear him gladly.

²¹Now an opportune time came on his birthday, when Herod gave a banquet for his nobles, military commanders, and the leading men of Galilee. ²²When Herodias's own daughterᴶ

ᴬ5:34 Or has saved you ᴮ5:34 Lit healthy ᶜ5:41 An Aram expression ᴰ6:5 Lit miracle ᴱ6:11 Other mss add I assure you, it will be more tolerable for Sodom or Gomorrah on judgment day than for that town. ᶠ6:14 Other mss read He ᴳ6:15 Lit Others said, "A prophet ᴴ6:20 Or Herod feared ᴵ6:20 Other mss read When he heard him, he did many things ᴶ6:22 Other mss read When his daughter Herodias came in and danced, she pleased Herod and his guests. The king said to the girl, "Ask me whatever you want, and I'll give it to you." ²³So he swore oaths to her: "Whatever you ask me I will give you, up to half my kingdom."

²⁴Then she went out and said to her mother, "What should I ask for?"

"John the Baptist's head!" she said.

²⁵Immediately she hurried to the king and said, "I want you to give me John the Baptist's head on a platter—right now!"

²⁶Though the king was deeply distressed, because of his oaths and the guestsᴬ he did not want to refuse her. ²⁷The king immediately sent for an executioner and commanded him to bring John's head. So he went and beheaded him in prison, ²⁸brought his head on a platter, and gave it to the girl. Then the girl gave it to her mother. ²⁹When his disciplesᴮ heard about it, they came and removed his corpse and placed it in a tomb.

³⁰The apostles gathered around Jesus and reported to Him all that they had done and taught. ³¹He said to them, "Come away by yourselves to a remote place and rest for a while." For many people were coming and going, and they did not even have time to eat. ³²So they went away in the boat by themselves to a remote place, ³³but many saw them leaving and recognized them. People ran there by land from all the towns and arrived ahead of them.ᶜ ³⁴So as He stepped ashore, He saw a huge crowd and had compassion on them, because they were like sheep without a shepherd. Then He began to teach them many things.

³⁵When it was already late, His disciples approached Him and said, "This place is a wilderness, and it is already late! ³⁶Send them away, so they can go into the surrounding countryside and villages to buy themselves something to eat."

³⁷"You give them something to eat," He responded.

They said to Him, "Should we go and buy 200 denarii worth of bread and give them something to eat?"

³⁸And He asked them, "How many loaves do you have? Go look."

When they found out they said, "Five, and two fish."

³⁹Then He instructed them to have all the people sit downᴰ in groups on the green grass. ⁴⁰So they sat down in ranks of hundreds and fifties. ⁴¹Then He took the five loaves and the two fish, and looking up to heaven, He blessed and broke the loaves. He kept giving them to His disciples to set before the people. He also divided the two fish among them all. ⁴²Everyone ate and was filled. ⁴³Then they picked up 12 baskets full of pieces of bread and fish. ⁴⁴Now those who ate the loaves were 5,000 men.

⁴⁵Immediately He made His disciples get into the boat and go ahead of Him to the other side, to Bethsaida, while He dismissed the crowd. ⁴⁶After He said good-bye to them, He went away to the mountain to pray. ⁴⁷When evening came, the boat was in the middle of the sea, and He was alone on the land. ⁴⁸He saw them being battered as they rowed,ᴱ because the wind was against them. Around three in the morningᶠ He came toward them walking on the sea and wanted to pass by them. ⁴⁹When they saw Him walking on the sea, they thought it was a ghost and cried out; ⁵⁰for they all saw Him and were terrified. Immediately He spoke with them and said, "Have courage! It is I. Don't be afraid." ⁵¹Then He got into the boat with them, and the wind ceased. They were completely astounded,ᴳ ⁵²because they had not understood about the loaves. Instead, their hearts were hardened.

⁵³When they had crossed over, they came to land at Gennesaret and beached the boat. ⁵⁴As they got out of the boat, people immediately recognized Him. ⁵⁵They hurried throughout that vicinity and began to carry the sick on mats to wherever they heard He was. ⁵⁶Wherever He would go, into villages, towns, or the country, they laid the sick in the marketplaces and begged Him that they might touch just the tassel of His robe. And everyone who touched it was made well.

7 The Pharisees and some of the scribes who had come from Jerusalem gathered around Him. ²They observed that some of His disciples were eating their bread with unclean—that is, unwashed—hands. ³(For the Pharisees, in fact all the Jews, will not eat unless they wash their hands ritually, keeping the tradition of the elders. ⁴When they come from the marketplace,

---

ᴬ6:26 Lit and those reclining at the table   ᴮ6:29 = John's disciples   ᶜ6:33 Other mss add and gathered around Him   ᴰ6:39 Lit people recline   ᴱ6:48 Or them struggling as they rowed   ᶠ6:48 Lit Around the fourth watch of the night = 3 to 6 a.m.   ᴳ6:51 Lit were astounded in themselves they do not eat unless they have washed. And there are many other customs they have received and keep, like the washing of cups, jugs, copper utensils, and dining couches.[A] [5]Then the Pharisees and the scribes asked Him, "Why don't Your disciples live according to the tradition of the elders, instead of eating bread with ritually unclean[B] hands?"

[6]He answered them, "Isaiah prophesied correctly about you hypocrites, as it is written:

These people honor Me with their lips,
but their heart is far from Me.
[7] They worship Me in vain,
teaching as doctrines the commands
of men.[C]

[8]Disregarding the command of God, you keep the tradition of men."[D] [9]He also said to them, "You completely invalidate God's command in order to maintain[E] your tradition! [10]For Moses said:

Honor your father
and your mother;[F] and
Whoever speaks evil of father
or mother
must be put to death.[G]

[11]But you say, 'If a man tells his father or mother: Whatever benefit you might have received from me is Corban'" (that is, a gift committed to the temple), [12]"you no longer let him do anything for his father or mother. [13]You revoke God's word by your tradition that you have handed down. And you do many other similar things." [14]Summoning the crowd again, He told them, "Listen to Me, all of you, and understand: [15]Nothing that goes into a person from outside can defile him, but the things that come out of a person are what defile him. [[16]If anyone has ears to hear, he should listen!]"[H]

[17]When He went into the house away from the crowd, the disciples asked Him about the parable. [18]And He said to them, "Are you also as lacking in understanding? Don't you realize that nothing going into a man from the outside can defile him? [19]For it doesn't go into his heart but into the stomach and is eliminated."[I] (As a result, He made all foods clean.[J]) [20]Then He said, "What comes out of a person—that defiles him. [21]For from within, out of people's hearts, come evil thoughts, sexual immoralities, thefts, murders, [22]adulteries, greed, evil actions, deceit, promiscuity, stinginess,[K] blasphemy, pride, and foolishness. [23]All these evil things come from within and defile a person."

[24]He got up and departed from there to the region of Tyre and Sidon.[L] He entered a house and did not want anyone to know it, but He could not escape notice. [25]Instead, immediately after hearing about Him, a woman whose little daughter had an unclean spirit came and fell at His feet. [26]Now the woman was Greek, a Syrophoenician by birth, and she kept asking Him to drive the demon out of her daughter. [27]He said to her, "Allow the children to be satisfied first, because it isn't right to take the children's bread and throw it to the dogs."

[28]But she replied to Him, "Lord, even the dogs under the table eat the children's crumbs."

[29]Then He told her, "Because of this reply, you may go. The demon has gone out of your daughter." [30]When she went back to her home, she found her child lying on the bed, and the demon was gone.

[31]Again, leaving the region of Tyre, He went by way of Sidon to the Sea of Galilee, through[M] the region of the Decapolis. [32]They brought to Him a deaf man who also had a speech difficulty, and begged Jesus to lay His hand on him. [33]So He took him away from the crowd privately. After putting His fingers in the man's ears and spitting, He touched his tongue. [34]Then, looking up to heaven, He sighed deeply and said to him, *"Ephphatha!"*[N] (that is, "Be opened!"). [35]Immediately his ears were opened, his speech difficulty was removed,[O] and he began to speak clearly. [36]Then He ordered them to tell no one, but the more He would order them, the more they would proclaim it.

[37]They were extremely astonished and said, "He has done everything well! He even makes deaf people hear, and people unable to speak, talk!"

8 In those days there was again a large crowd, and they had nothing to eat. He summoned the disciples and said to them, [2]"I have compassion on the crowd, because they've already stayed with Me three days and have nothing to eat. [3]If I send them home

---

[A]7:4 Other mss omit and dining couches   [B]7:5 Other mss read with unwashed   [C]7:6-7 Is 29:13   [D]7:8 Other mss add The washing of jugs, and cups, and many other similar things you practice.   [E]7:9 Other mss read to establish   [F]7:10 Ex 20:12; Dt 5:16   [G]7:10 Ex 21:17; Lv 20:9   [H]7:16 Other mss omit bracketed text   [I]7:19 Lit goes out into the toilet   [J]7:19 Other mss read is eliminated, making all foods clean.   [K]7:22 Lit evil eye   [L]7:24 Other mss omit and Sidon   [M]7:31 Or into   [N]7:34 An Aram expression   [O]7:35 Lit opened, the bond of his tongue was untied hungry,[A] they will collapse on the way, and some of them have come a long distance."

[4] His disciples answered Him, "Where can anyone get enough bread here in this desolate place to fill these people?"

[5] "How many loaves do you have?" He asked them.

"Seven," they said. [6] Then He commanded the crowd to sit down on the ground. Taking the seven loaves, He gave thanks, broke the loaves, and kept on giving them to His disciples to set before the people. So they served the loaves to the crowd. [7] They also had a few small fish, and when He had blessed them, He said these were to be served as well. [8] They ate and were filled. Then they collected seven large baskets of leftover pieces. [9] About 4,000 men were there. He dismissed them [10] and immediately got into the boat with His disciples and went to the district of Dalmanutha.[B]

[11] The Pharisees came out and began to argue with Him, demanding of Him a sign from heaven to test Him. [12] But sighing deeply in His spirit, He said, "Why does this generation demand a sign? I assure you: No sign will be given to this generation!" [13] Then He left them, got on board the boat again, and went to the other side.

[14] They had forgotten to take bread and had only one loaf with them in the boat. [15] Then He commanded them: "Watch out! Beware of the yeast of the Pharisees and the yeast of Herod."

[16] They were discussing among themselves that they did not have any bread. [17] Aware of this, He said to them, "Why are you discussing that you do not have any bread? Don't you understand or comprehend? Is your heart hardened? [18] Do you have eyes, and not see, and do you have ears, and not hear?[C] And do you not remember? [19] When I broke the five loaves for the 5,000, how many baskets full of pieces of bread did you collect?"

"Twelve," they told Him.

[20] "When I broke the seven loaves for the 4,000, how many large baskets full of pieces of bread did you collect?"

"Seven," they said.

[21] And He said to them, "Don't you understand yet?"

[22] Then they came to Bethsaida. They brought a blind man to Him and begged Him to touch him. [23] He took the blind man by the hand and brought him out of the village. Spitting on his eyes and laying His hands on him, He asked him, "Do you see anything?"

[24] He looked up and said, "I see people—they look to me like trees walking."

[25] Again Jesus placed His hands on the man's eyes, and he saw distinctly. He was cured and could see everything clearly. [26] Then He sent him home, saying, "Don't even go into the village."[D]

[27] Jesus went out with His disciples to the villages of Caesarea Philippi. And on the road He asked His disciples, "Who do people say that I am?"

[28] They answered Him, "John the Baptist; others, Elijah; still others, one of the prophets."

[29] "But you," He asked them again, "who do you say that I am?"

Peter answered Him, "You are the Messiah!"

[30] And He strictly warned them to tell no one about Him.

[31] Then He began to teach them that the Son of Man must suffer many things and be rejected by the elders, the chief priests, and the scribes, be killed, and rise after three days. [32] He was openly talking about this. So Peter took Him aside and began to rebuke Him.

[33] But turning around and looking at His disciples, He rebuked Peter and said, "Get behind Me, Satan, because you're not thinking about God's concerns,[E] but man's!"

[34] Summoning the crowd along with His disciples, He said to them, "If anyone wants to be My follower, he must deny himself, take up his cross, and follow Me. [35] For whoever wants to save his life will lose it, but whoever loses his life because of Me and the gospel will save it. [36] For what does it benefit a man to gain the whole world yet lose his life? [37] What can a man give in exchange for his life? [38] For whoever is ashamed of Me and of My words in this adulterous and sinful generation, the Son of Man will also be ashamed of him when He comes in the glory of His Father with the holy angels."

9 Then He said to them, "I assure you: There are some standing here who will not taste death until they see the kingdom of God come in power."

[2] After six days Jesus took Peter, James, and John and led them up on a high mountain by themselves to be alone. He was transformed[F]

[A] 8:3 Or fasting [B] 8:10 Probably on the western shore of the Sea of Galilee [C] 8:18 Jr 5:21; Ezk 12:2 [D] 8:26 Other mss add or tell anyone in the village [E] 8:33 Lit about the things of God [F] 9:2 Or transfigured in front of them, ³and His clothes became dazzling—extremely white as no launderer on earth could whiten them. ⁴Elijah appeared to them with Moses, and they were talking with Jesus.

⁵Then Peter said to Jesus, "Rabbi, it's good for us to be here! Let us make three tabernacles: one for You, one for Moses, and one for Elijah"— ⁶because he did not know what he should say, since they were terrified.

⁷A cloud appeared, overshadowing them, and a voice came from the cloud:

This is My beloved Son;
listen to Him!

⁸Then suddenly, looking around, they no longer saw anyone with them except Jesus alone.

⁹As they were coming down from the mountain, He ordered them to tell no one what they had seen until the Son of Man had risen from the dead. ¹⁰They kept this word to themselves, discussing what "rising from the dead" meant.

¹¹Then they began to question Him, "Why do the scribes say that Elijah must come first?"

¹²"Elijah does come first and restores everything," He replied. "How then is it written about the Son of Man that He must suffer many things and be treated with contempt? ¹³But I tell you that Elijah really has come, and they did whatever they pleased to him, just as it is written about him."

¹⁴When they came to the disciples, they saw a large crowd around them and scribes disputing with them. ¹⁵All of a sudden, when the whole crowd saw Him, they were amazedᴬ and ran to greet Him. ¹⁶Then He asked them, "What are you arguing with them about?"

¹⁷Out of the crowd, one man answered Him, "Teacher, I brought my son to You. He has a spirit that makes him unable to speak. ¹⁸Wherever it seizes him, it throws him down, and he foams at the mouth, grinds his teeth, and becomes rigid. So I asked Your disciples to drive it out, but they couldn't."

¹⁹He replied to them, "You unbelieving generation! How long will I be with you? How long must I put up with you? Bring him to Me." ²⁰So they brought him to Him. When the spirit saw Him, it immediately convulsed the boy. He fell to the ground and rolled around, foaming at the mouth. ²¹"How long has this been happening to him?" Jesus asked his father.

"From childhood," he said. ²²"And many times it has thrown him into fire or water to destroy him. But if You can do anything, have compassion on us and help us."

²³Then Jesus said to him, "'If You can'?ᴮ,ᶜ Everything is possible to the one who believes."

²⁴Immediately the father of the boy cried out, "I do believe! Help my unbelief."

²⁵When Jesus saw that a crowd was rapidly coming together, He rebuked the unclean spirit, saying to it, "You mute and deaf spirit,ᴰ I command you: come out of him and never enter him again!"

²⁶Then it came out, shrieking and convulsing himᴱ violently. The boy became like a corpse, so that many said, "He's dead." ²⁷But Jesus, taking him by the hand, raised him, and he stood up.

²⁸After He went into a house, His disciples asked Him privately, "Why couldn't we drive it out?"

²⁹And He told them, "This kind can come out by nothing but prayer [and fasting]."ᶠ

³⁰Then they left that place and made their way through Galilee, but He did not want anyone to know it. ³¹For He was teaching His disciples and telling them, "The Son of Man is being betrayedᴳ into the hands of men. They will kill Him, and after He is killed, He will rise three days later." ³²But they did not understand this statement, and they were afraid to ask Him.

³³Then they came to Capernaum. When He was in the house, He asked them, "What were you arguing about on the way?" ³⁴But they were silent, because on the way they had been arguing with one another about who was the greatest. ³⁵Sitting down, He called the Twelve and said to them, "If anyone wants to be first, he must be last of all and servant of all." ³⁶Then He took a child, had him stand among them, and taking him in His arms, He said to them, ³⁷"Whoever welcomesᴴ one little child such as this in My name welcomes Me. And whoever welcomes Me does not welcome Me, but Him who sent Me."

³⁸John said to Him, "Teacher, we saw someoneᴵ driving out demons in Your name, and we

---

A 9:15 Or *surprised*   **B** 9:23 Other mss add *believe*   **C** 9:23 Jesus appears to quote the father's words in v. 22 and then comment on them.   **D** 9:25 A spirit that caused the boy to be deaf and unable to speak   **E** 9:26 Other mss omit *him*   **F** 9:29 Other mss omit bracketed text   **G** 9:31 Or *handed over*   **H** 9:37 Or *Whoever receives*   **I** 9:38 Other mss add *who didn't go along with us* tried to stop him because he wasn't following us."

³⁹"Don't stop him," said Jesus, "because there is no one who will perform a miracle in My name who can soon afterward speak evil of Me. ⁴⁰For whoever is not against us is for us. ⁴¹And whoever gives you a cup of water to drink because of My name,ᴬ since you belong to the Messiah—I assure you: He will never lose his reward.

⁴²"But whoever causes the downfall of one of these little ones who believe in Me—it would be better for him if a heavy millstoneᴮ were hung around his neck and he were thrown into the sea. ⁴³And if your hand causes your downfall, cut it off. It is better for you to enter life maimed than to have two hands and go to hell—the unquenchable fire, [⁴⁴where

> Their worm does not die,
> and the fire is not quenched.]ᶜ,ᴰ

⁴⁵And if your foot causes your downfall, cut it off. It is better for you to enter life lame than to have two feet and be thrown into hell— [the unquenchable fire, ⁴⁶where

> Their worm does not die,
> and the fire is not quenched.]ᶜ,ᴰ

⁴⁷And if your eye causes your downfall, gouge it out. It is better for you to enter the kingdom of God with one eye than to have two eyes and be thrown into hell, ⁴⁸where

> Their worm does not die,
> and the fire is not quenched.ᴰ

⁴⁹For everyone will be salted with fire.ᴱ,ᶠ ⁵⁰Salt is good, but if the salt should lose its flavor, how can you make it salty? Have salt among yourselves and be at peace with one another."

10 He set out from there and went to the region of Judea and across the Jordan. Then crowds converged on Him again and, as He usually did, He began teaching them once more. ²Some Pharisees approached Him to test Him. They asked, "Is it lawful for a man to divorce his wife?"

³He replied to them, "What did Moses command you?"

⁴They said, "Moses permitted us to write divorce papers and send her away."

⁵But Jesus told them, "He wrote this command for you because of the hardness of your hearts. ⁶But from the beginning of creation Godᴳ made them male and female.ᴴ

> ⁷ For this reason a man will leave
>   his father and mother
>   [and be joined to his wife],ᶜ
> ⁸ and the two will become one flesh.ᴵ

So they are no longer two, but one flesh. ⁹Therefore what God has joined together, man must not separate."

¹⁰Now in the house the disciples questioned Him again about this matter. ¹¹And He said to them, "Whoever divorces his wife and marries another commits adultery against her. ¹²Also, if she divorces her husband and marries another, she commits adultery."

¹³Some people were bringing little children to Him so He might touch them, but His disciples rebuked them. ¹⁴When Jesus saw it, He was indignant and said to them, "Let the little children come to Me. Don't stop them, for the kingdom of God belongs to such as these. ¹⁵I assure you: Whoever does not welcomeᴶ the kingdom of God like a little child will never enter it." ¹⁶After taking them in His arms, He laid His hands on them and blessed them.

¹⁷As He was setting out on a journey, a man ran up, knelt down before Him, and asked Him, "Good Teacher, what must I do to inherit eternal life?"

¹⁸"Why do you call Me good?" Jesus asked him. "No one is good but One—God. ¹⁹You know the commandments:

> Do not murder;
> do not commit adultery;
> do not steal;
> do not bear false witness;
> do not defraud;
> honor your father and mother."ᴷ

²⁰He said to Him, "Teacher, I have kept all these from my youth."

²¹Then, looking at him, Jesus loved him and said to him, "You lack one thing: Go, sell all you have and give to the poor, and you will have treasure in heaven. Then come,ᴸ follow Me." ²²But he was stunnedᴹ at this demand,

ᴬ9:41 Lit drink in the name   ᴮ9:42 A millstone turned by a donkey   ᶜ9:44,46; 10:7 Other mss omit bracketed text   ᴰ9:44,46,48 Is 66:24   ᴱ9:49 Other mss add and every sacrifice will be salted with salt   ᶠ9:49 Lv 2:13; Ezk 43:24   ᴳ10:6 Other mss omit God   ᴴ10:6 Gn 1:27; 5:2   ᴵ10:7-8 Gn 2:24   ᴶ10:15 Or not receive   ᴷ10:19 Ex 20:12-16; Dt 5:16-20   ᴸ10:21 Other mss add taking up the cross, and   ᴹ10:22 Or he became gloomy and he went away grieving, because he had many possessions.

²³ Jesus looked around and said to His disciples, "How hard it is for those who have wealth to enter the kingdom of God!" ²⁴ But the disciples were astonished at His words. Again Jesus said to them, "Children, how hard it is^A to enter the kingdom of God! ²⁵ It is easier for a camel to go through the eye of a needle than for a rich person to enter the kingdom of God."

²⁶ So they were even more astonished, saying to one another, "Then who can be saved?"

²⁷ Looking at them, Jesus said, "With men it is impossible, but not with God, because all things are possible with God."

²⁸ Peter began to tell Him, "Look, we have left everything and followed You."

²⁹ "I assure you," Jesus said, "there is no one who has left house, brothers or sisters, mother or father,^B children, or fields because of Me and the gospel, ³⁰ who will not receive 100 times more, now at this time—houses, brothers and sisters, mothers and children, and fields, with persecutions—and eternal life in the age to come. ³¹ But many who are first will be last, and the last first."

³² They were on the road, going up to Jerusalem, and Jesus was walking ahead of them. They were astonished, but those who followed Him were afraid. Taking the Twelve aside again, He began to tell them the things that would happen to Him.

³³ "Listen! We are going up to Jerusalem. The Son of Man will be handed over to the chief priests and the scribes, and they will condemn Him to death. Then they will hand Him over to the Gentiles, ³⁴ and they will mock Him, spit on Him, flog^C Him, and kill Him, and He will rise after three days."

³⁵ Then James and John, the sons of Zebedee, approached Him and said, "Teacher, we want You to do something for us if we ask You."

³⁶ "What do you want Me to do for you?" He asked them.

³⁷ They answered Him, "Allow us to sit at Your right and at Your left in Your glory."

³⁸ But Jesus said to them, "You don't know what you're asking. Are you able to drink the cup I drink or to be baptized with the baptism I am baptized with?"

³⁹ "We are able," they told Him.

Jesus said to them, "You will drink the cup I drink, and you will be baptized with the baptism I am baptized with. ⁴⁰ But to sit at My right or left is not Mine to give; instead, it is for those it has been prepared for." ⁴¹ When the other 10 disciples heard this, they began to be indignant with James and John.

⁴² Jesus called them over and said to them, "You know that those who are regarded as rulers of the Gentiles dominate them, and their men of high positions exercise power over them. ⁴³ But it must not be like that among you. On the contrary, whoever wants to become great among you must be your servant, ⁴⁴ and whoever wants to be first among you must be a slave to all. ⁴⁵ For even the Son of Man did not come to be served, but to serve, and to give His life—a ransom for many."^D

⁴⁶ They came to Jericho. And as He was leaving Jericho with His disciples and a large crowd, Bartimaeus (the son of Timaeus), a blind beggar, was sitting by the road. ⁴⁷ When he heard that it was Jesus the Nazarene, he began to cry out, "Son of David, Jesus, have mercy on me!" ⁴⁸ Many people told him to keep quiet, but he was crying out all the more, "Have mercy on me, Son of David!"

⁴⁹ Jesus stopped and said, "Call him."

So they called the blind man and said to him, "Have courage! Get up; He's calling for you." ⁵⁰ He threw off his coat, jumped up, and came to Jesus.

⁵¹ Then Jesus answered him, "What do you want Me to do for you?"

"*Rabbouni,*"^E the blind man told Him, "I want to see!"

⁵² "Go your way," Jesus told him. "Your faith has healed you." Immediately he could see and began to follow Him on the road.

11 When they approached Jerusalem, at Bethphage and Bethany near the Mount of Olives, He sent two of His disciples ² and told them, "Go into the village ahead of you. As soon as you enter it, you will find a young donkey tied there, on which no one has ever sat. Untie it and bring it here. ³ If anyone says to you, 'Why are you doing this?' say, 'The Lord needs it and will send it back here right away.'"

⁴ So they went and found a young donkey outside in the street, tied by a door. They untied it, ⁵ and some of those standing there said to them, "What are you doing, untying the

---

^A10:24 Other mss add *for those trusting in wealth* ^B10:29 Other mss add *or wife* ^C10:34 Or *scourge* ^D10:45 Or *in the place of many*; Is 53:10-12 ^E10:51 Hb word for *my teacher* donkey?" ⁶They answered them just as Jesus had said, so they let them go. ⁷Then they brought the donkey to Jesus and threw their robes on it, and He sat on it.

⁸Many people spread their robes on the road, and others spread leafy branches cut from the fields.ᴬ ⁹Then those who went ahead and those who followed kept shouting:

Hosanna!
He who comes in the name
of the Lord is the blessed One!ᴮ
10   The coming kingdom
    of our father David is blessed!
Hosanna in the highest heaven!

¹¹And He went into Jerusalem and into the temple complex. After looking around at everything, since it was already late, He went out to Bethany with the Twelve.

¹²The next day when they came out from Bethany, He was hungry. ¹³After seeing in the distance a fig tree with leaves, He went to find out if there was anything on it. When He came to it, He found nothing but leaves, because it was not the season for figs. ¹⁴He said to it, "May no one ever eat fruit from you again!" And His disciples heard it.

¹⁵They came to Jerusalem, and He went into the temple complex and began to throw out those buying and selling in the temple. He overturned the money changers' tables and the chairs of those selling doves, ¹⁶and would not permit anyone to carry goods through the temple complex.

¹⁷Then He began to teach them: "Is it not written, **My house will be called a house of prayer for all nations?**ᶜ But you have made it **a den of thieves!**ᴰ ¹⁸Then the chief priests and the scribes heard it and started looking for a way to destroy Him. For they were afraid of Him, because the whole crowd was astonished by His teaching.

¹⁹And whenever evening came, they would go out of the city.

²⁰Early in the morning, as they were passing by, they saw the fig tree withered from the roots up. ²¹Then Peter remembered and said to Him, "Rabbi, look! The fig tree that You cursed is withered."

²²Jesus replied to them, "Have faith in God. ²³I assure you: If anyone says to this mountain, 'Be lifted up and thrown into the sea,' and does not doubt in his heart, but believes that what he says will happen, it will be done for him. ²⁴Therefore I tell you, all the things you pray and ask for—believe that you have receivedᴱ them, and you will have them. ²⁵And whenever you stand praying, if you have anything against anyone, forgive him, so that your Father in heaven will also forgive you your wrongdoing. [²⁶But if you don't forgive, neither will your Father in heaven forgive your wrongdoing.]"ᶠ·ᴳ

²⁷They came again to Jerusalem. As He was walking in the temple complex, the chief priests, the scribes, and the elders came ²⁸and asked Him, "By what authority are You doing these things? Who gave You this authority to do these things?"

²⁹Jesus said to them, "I will ask you one question; then answer Me, and I will tell you by what authority I am doing these things. ³⁰Was John's baptism from heaven or from men? Answer Me."

³¹They began to argue among themselves: "If we say, 'From heaven,' He will say, 'Then why didn't you believe him?' ³²But if we say, 'From men'"—they were afraid of the crowd, because everyone thought that John was a genuine prophet. ³³So they answered Jesus, "We don't know."

And Jesus said to them, "Neither will I tell you by what authority I do these things."

12 Then He began to speak to them in parables: "A man planted a vineyard, put a fence around it, dug out a pit for a winepress, and built a watchtower. Then he leased it to tenant farmers and went away. ²At harvest time he sent a slave to the farmers to collect some of the fruit of the vineyard from the farmers. ³But they took him, beat him, and sent him away empty-handed. ⁴Again he sent another slave to them, and theyᴴ hit him on the head and treated him shamefully.ᴵ ⁵Then he sent another, and they killed that one. He also sent many others; they beat some and they killed some.

⁶"He still had one to send, a beloved son. Finally he sent him to them, saying, 'They will respect my son.'

ᴬ11:8 Other mss read *others were cutting leafy branches from the trees and spreading them on the road*   ᴮ11:9 Ps 118:26   ᶜ11:17 Is 56:7   ᴰ11:17 Jr 7:11   ᴱ11:24 Some mss read *you receive*; other mss read *you will receive*   ᶠ11:26 Other mss omit bracketed text   ᴳ11:25-26 These are the only uses of this word in Mk. It means "the violation of the Law" or "stepping over a boundary" or "departing from the path" or "trespass."   ᴴ12:4 Other mss add *threw stones and*   ᴵ12:4 Other mss add *and sent him off*

⁷"But those tenant farmers said among themselves, 'This is the heir. Come, let's kill him, and the inheritance will be ours!' ⁸So they seized him, killed him, and threw him out of the vineyard.

⁹"Therefore, what will the owner[A] of the vineyard do? He will come and destroy the farmers and give the vineyard to others. ¹⁰Haven't you read this Scripture:

> The stone that the builders rejected
> has become the cornerstone.[B]
> ¹¹ This came from the Lord
> and is wonderful in our eyes?"[C]

¹²Because they knew He had said this parable against them, they were looking for a way to arrest Him, but they were afraid of the crowd. So they left Him and went away.

¹³Then they sent some of the Pharisees and the Herodians to Him to trap Him by what He said.[D] ¹⁴When they came, they said to Him, "Teacher, we know You are truthful and defer to no one, for You don't show partiality[E] but teach truthfully the way of God. Is it lawful to pay taxes to Caesar or not? ¹⁵Should we pay, or should we not pay?"

But knowing their hypocrisy, He said to them, "Why are you testing Me? Bring Me a denarius to look at." ¹⁶So they brought one. "Whose image and inscription is this?" He asked them.

"Caesar's," they said.

¹⁷Then Jesus told them, "Give back to Caesar the things that are Caesar's, and to God the things that are God's." And they were amazed at Him.

¹⁸Some Sadducees, who say there is no resurrection, came to Him and questioned Him: ¹⁹"Teacher, Moses wrote for us that **if a man's brother dies,** leaves his wife behind, and **leaves no child, his brother should take the wife and produce offspring for his brother.**[F] ²⁰There were seven brothers. The first took a wife, and dying, left no offspring. ²¹The second also took her, and he died, leaving no offspring. And the third likewise. ²²So the seven[G] left no offspring. Last of all, the woman died too. ²³In the resurrection, when they rise,[H] whose wife will she be, since the seven had married her?"[I]

²⁴Jesus told them, "Are you not deceived because you don't know the Scriptures or the power of God? ²⁵For when they rise from the dead, they neither marry nor are given in marriage but are like angels in heaven. ²⁶Now concerning the dead being raised—haven't you read in the book of Moses, in the passage about the burning bush, how God spoke to him: I am **the God of Abraham and the God of Isaac and the God of Jacob?**[J] ²⁷He is not God of the dead but of the living. You are badly deceived."

²⁸One of the scribes approached. When he heard them debating and saw that Jesus answered them well, he asked Him, "Which command is the most important of all?"[K]

²⁹"This is the most important,"[L] Jesus answered:

> Listen, Israel! The Lord our God, the Lord is One. ³⁰Love the Lord your God with all your heart, with all your soul, with all your mind, and with all your strength.[N][O]

³¹"The second is: Love your neighbor as yourself.[P] There is no other command greater than these."

³²Then the scribe said to Him, "You are right, Teacher! You have correctly said that He is One, and there is no one else except Him. ³³And to love Him with all your heart, with all your understanding,[Q] and with all your strength, and to love your neighbor as yourself, is far more important than all the burnt offerings and sacrifices."

³⁴When Jesus saw that he answered intelligently, He said to him, "You are not far from the kingdom of God." And no one dared to question Him any longer.

³⁵So Jesus asked this question as He taught in the temple complex, "How can the scribes say that the Messiah is the Son of David? ³⁶David himself says by the Holy Spirit:

> The Lord declared to my Lord,
> 'Sit at My right hand
> until I put Your enemies
> under Your feet.'[R]

A12:9 Or lord **B**12:10 Lit the head of the corner **C**12:10-11 Ps 118:22-23 **D**12:13 Lit trap Him in [a] word **E**12:14 Lit don't look on the face of men; that is, on the outward appearance **F**12:19 Gn 38:8; Dt 25:5 **G**12:22 Other mss add had taken her and **H**12:23 Other mss omit when they rise **I**12:23 Lit the seven had her as a wife **J**12:26 Ex 3:6,15-16 **K**12:28 Lit Which command is first of all? **L**12:29 Other mss add of all the commands **M**12:29 Or The Lord our God is one Lord. **N**12:30 Other mss add This is the first commandment. **O**12:30 Dt 6:4-5; Jos 22:5 **P**12:31 Lv 19:18 **Q**12:33 Other mss add with all your soul **R**12:36 Ps 110:1

³⁷ David himself calls Him 'Lord'; how then can the Messiah be his Son?" And the large crowd was listening to Him with delight.

³⁸ He also said in His teaching, "Beware of the scribes, who want to go around in long robes, and who want greetings in the marketplaces, ³⁹ the front seats in the synagogues, and the places of honor at banquets. ⁴⁰ They devour widows' houses and say long prayers just for show. These will receive harsher punishment."

⁴¹ Sitting across from the temple treasury, He watched how the crowd dropped money into the treasury. Many rich people were putting in large sums. ⁴² And a poor widow came and dropped in two tiny coins worth very little.ᴬ ⁴³ Summoning His disciples, He said to them, "I assure you: This poor widow has put in more than all those giving to the temple treasury. ⁴⁴ For they all gave out of their surplus, but she out of her poverty has put in everything she possessed—all she had to live on."

13 As He was going out of the temple complex, one of His disciples said to Him, "Teacher, look! What massive stones! What impressive buildings!"

² Jesus said to him, "Do you see these great buildings? Not one stone will be left here on another that will not be thrown down!"

³ While He was sitting on the Mount of Olives across from the temple complex, Peter, James, John, and Andrew asked Him privately, ⁴ "Tell us, when will these things happen? And what will be the sign when all these things are about to take place?"

⁵ Then Jesus began by telling them: "Watch out that no one deceives you. ⁶ Many will come in My name, saying, 'I am He,' and they will deceive many. ⁷ When you hear of wars and rumors of wars, don't be alarmed; these things must take place, but the end is not yet. ⁸ For nation will rise up against nation, and kingdom against kingdom. There will be earthquakes in various places, and famines.ᴮ These are the beginning of birth pains.

⁹ "But you, be on your guard! They will hand you over to sanhedrins,ᶜ and you will be flogged in the synagogues. You will stand before governors and kings because of Me, as a witness to them. ¹⁰ And the good newsᴰ must first be proclaimed to all nations. ¹¹ So when

they arrest you and hand you over, don't worry beforehand what you will say. On the contrary, whatever is given to you in that hour—say it. For it isn't you speaking, but the Holy Spirit. ¹² Then brother will betray brother to death, and a father his child. Children will rise up against parents and put them to death. ¹³ And you will be hated by everyone because of My name. But the one who endures to the end will be delivered.ᴱ

¹⁴ "When you see the **abomination that causes desolation**ᶠ standing where it should not" (let the reader understandᴳ), "then those in Judea must flee to the mountains! ¹⁵ A man on the housetop must not come down or go in to get anything out of his house. ¹⁶ And a man in the field must not go back to get his clothes. ¹⁷ Woe to pregnant women and nursing mothers in those days! ¹⁸ Pray itᴴ won't happen in winter. ¹⁹ For those will be days of tribulation, the kind that hasn't been from the beginning of the world,ᴵ which God created, until now and never will be again! ²⁰ Unless the Lord limited those days, no one would survive.ᴶ But He limited those days because of the elect, whom He chose.

²¹ "Then if anyone tells you, 'Look, here is the Messiah! Look—there!' do not believe it! ²² For false messiahsᴷ and false prophets will rise up and will perform signs and wonders to lead astray, if possible, the elect. ²³ And you must watch! I have told you everything in advance.

²⁴ "But in those days, after that tribulation:

The sun will be darkened,
and the moon will not shed its light;
²⁵   the stars will be falling from the sky,
and the celestial powers will be shaken.

²⁶ Then they will see the Son of Man coming in clouds with great power and glory. ²⁷ He will send out the angels and gather His elect from the four winds, from the end of the earth to the end of the sky.

²⁸ "Learn this parable from the fig tree: As soon as its branch becomes tender and sprouts leaves, you know that summer is near. ²⁹ In the same way, when you see these things happening, knowᴸ that Heᴹ is near—at the door! ³⁰ I assure you: This generation will certainly

---

A12:42 Lit dropped in two *lepta*, which is a *quadrans*; the *lepton* was the smallest and least valuable Gk coin in use. The *quadrans*, ¹/₆₄ of a daily wage, was the smallest Roman coin.   **B13:8** Other mss add *and disturbances*   **C13:9** Local Jewish courts or local councils   **D13:10** Or *the gospel*   **E13:13** Or *saved*   **F13:14** Dn 9:27   **G13:14** These are, most likely, Mark's words to his readers.   **H13:18** Other mss read *pray that your escape*   **I13:19** Lit *creation*   **J13:20** Lit *days, all flesh would not survive*   **K13:22** Or *false christs*   **L13:29** Or *you know*   **M13:29** Or *it;* = *summer* not pass away until all these things take place. ³¹Heaven and earth will pass away, but My words will never pass away.

³²"Now concerning that day or hour no one knows—neither the angels in heaven nor the Son—except the Father. ³³Watch! Be alert!ᴬ For you don't know when the time is coming. ³⁴It is like a man on a journey, who left his house, gave authority to his slaves, gave each one his work, and commanded the doorkeeper to be alert. ³⁵Therefore be alert, since you don't know when the master of the house is coming—whether in the evening or at midnight or at the crowing of the rooster or early in the morning. ³⁶Otherwise, he might come suddenly and find you sleeping. ³⁷And what I say to you, I say to everyone: Be alert!"

14 After two days it was the Passover and the Festival of Unleavened Bread. The chief priests and the scribes were looking for a treacherous way to arrest and kill Him. ²"Not during the festival," they said, "or there may be rioting among the people."

³While He was in Bethany at the house of Simon who had a serious skin disease, as He was reclining at the table, a woman came with an alabaster jar of pure and expensive fragrant oil of nard. She broke the jar and poured it on His head. ⁴But some were expressing indignation to one another: "Why has this fragrant oil been wasted? ⁵For this oil might have been sold for more than 300 denarii and given to the poor." And they began to scold her.

⁶Then Jesus said, "Leave her alone. Why are you bothering her? She has done a noble thing for Me. ⁷You always have the poor with you, and you can do what is good for them whenever you want, but you do not always have Me. ⁸She has done what she could; she has anointed My body in advance for burial. ⁹I assure you: Wherever the gospel is proclaimed in the whole world, what this woman has done will also be told in memory of her."

¹⁰Then Judas Iscariot, one of the Twelve, went to the chief priests to hand Him over to them. ¹¹And when they heard this, they were glad and promised to give him silver.ᴮ So he started looking for a good opportunity to betray Him.

¹²On the first day of Unleavened Bread, when they sacrifice the Passover lamb, His disciples asked Him, "Where do You want us to go and prepare the Passover so You may eat it?"

¹³So He sent two of His disciples and told them, "Go into the city, and a man carrying a water jug will meet you. Follow him. ¹⁴Wherever he enters, tell the owner of the house, 'The Teacher says, "Where is the guest room for Me to eat the Passover with My disciples?"' ¹⁵He will show you a large room upstairs, furnished and ready. Make the preparations for us there." ¹⁶So the disciples went out, entered the city, and found it just as He had told them, and they prepared the Passover.

¹⁷When evening came, He arrived with the Twelve. ¹⁸While they were reclining and eating, Jesus said, "I assure you: One of you will betray Me—one who is eating with Me!"

¹⁹They began to be distressed and to say to Him one by one, "Surely not I?"

²⁰He said to them, "It is one of the Twelve—the one who is dipping bread with Me in the bowl. ²¹For the Son of Man will go just as it is written about Him, but woe to that man by whom the Son of Man is betrayed! It would have been better for that man if he had not been born."

²²As they were eating, He took bread, blessed and broke it, gave it to them, and said, "Take it;ᶜ this is My body."

²³Then He took a cup, and after giving thanks, He gave it to them, and so they all drank from it. ²⁴He said to them, "This is My blood that establishes the covenant;ᴰ it is shed for many. ²⁵I assure you: I will no longer drink of the fruit of the vine until that day when I drink it in a new wayᴱ in the kingdom of God." ²⁶After singing psalms,ᶠ they went out to the Mount of Olives.

²⁷Then Jesus said to them, "All of you will run away,ᴳ,ᴴ because it is written:

> I will strike the shepherd,
> and the sheep will be scattered.ᴵ

²⁸But after I have been resurrected, I will go ahead of you to Galilee."

²⁹Peter told Him, "Even if everyone runs away, I will certainly not!"

³⁰"I assure you," Jesus said to him, "today, this very night, before the rooster crows twice, you will deny Me three times!"

ᴬ13:33 Other mss add and pray ᴮ14:11 Or money; in Mt 26:15 it is specified as 30 pieces of silver; see Zch 11:12-13 ᶜ14:22 Other mss add eat; ᴰ14:24 Other mss read the new covenant ᴱ14:25 Or drink new wine; lit drink it new ᶠ14:26 Ps 113–118 were sung during and after the Passover meal. ᴳ14:27 Other mss add because of Me this night ᴴ14:27 Or stumble ᴵ14:27 Zch 13:7

³¹ But he kept insisting, "If I have to die with You, I will never deny You!" And they all said the same thing.

³² Then they came to a place named Gethsemane, and He told His disciples, "Sit here while I pray." ³³ He took Peter, James, and John with Him, and He began to be deeply distressed and horrified. ³⁴ Then He said to them, "My soul is swallowed up in sorrow^A—to the point of death. Remain here and stay awake." ³⁵ Then He went a little farther, fell to the ground, and began to pray that if it were possible, the hour might pass from Him. ³⁶ And He said, "*Abba*, Father! All things are possible for You. Take this cup away from Me. Nevertheless, not what I will, but what You will."

³⁷ Then He came and found them sleeping. "Simon, are you sleeping?" He asked Peter. "Couldn't you stay awake one hour? ³⁸ Stay awake and pray so that you won't enter into temptation. The spirit is willing, but the flesh is weak."

³⁹ Once again He went away and prayed, saying the same thing. ⁴⁰ And He came again and found them sleeping, because they could not keep their eyes open.^B They did not know what to say to Him. ⁴¹ Then He came a third time and said to them, "Are you still sleeping and resting? Enough! The time has come. Look, the Son of Man is being betrayed into the hands of sinners. ⁴² Get up; let's go! See—My betrayer is near."

⁴³ While He was still speaking, Judas, one of the Twelve, suddenly arrived. With him was a mob, with swords and clubs, from the chief priests, the scribes, and the elders. ⁴⁴ His betrayer had given them a signal. "The One I kiss," he said, "He's the One; arrest Him and take Him away under guard." ⁴⁵ So when he came, he went right up to Him and said, "Rabbi!"—and kissed Him. ⁴⁶ Then they took hold of Him and arrested Him. ⁴⁷ And one of those who stood by drew his sword, struck the high priest's slave, and cut off his ear.

⁴⁸ But Jesus said to them, "Have you come out with swords and clubs, as though I were a criminal,^C to capture Me? ⁴⁹ Every day I was among you, teaching in the temple complex, and you didn't arrest Me. But the Scriptures must be fulfilled." ⁵⁰ Then they all deserted Him and ran away.

⁵¹ Now a certain young man,^D having a linen cloth wrapped around his naked body, was following Him. They caught hold of him, ⁵² but he left the linen cloth behind and ran away naked.

⁵³ They led Jesus away to the high priest, and all the chief priests, the elders, and the scribes convened. ⁵⁴ Peter followed Him at a distance, right into the high priest's courtyard. He was sitting with the temple police,^E warming himself by the fire.^F

⁵⁵ The chief priests and the whole Sanhedrin were looking for testimony against Jesus to put Him to death, but they could find none. ⁵⁶ For many were giving false testimony against Him, but the testimonies did not agree. ⁵⁷ Some stood up and were giving false testimony against Him, stating, ⁵⁸ "We heard Him say, 'I will demolish this sanctuary made by human hands, and in three days I will build another not made by hands.'" ⁵⁹ Yet their testimony did not agree even on this.

⁶⁰ Then the high priest stood up before them all and questioned Jesus, "Don't You have an answer to what these men are testifying against You?" ⁶¹ But He kept silent and did not answer anything. Again the high priest questioned Him, "Are You the Messiah, the Son of the Blessed One?"

⁶² "I am," said Jesus, "and all of you^G will see the Son of Man seated at the right hand of the Power and coming with the clouds of heaven."^H

⁶³ Then the high priest tore his robes and said, "Why do we still need witnesses? ⁶⁴ You have heard the blasphemy! What is your decision?"^I

And they all condemned Him to be deserving of death. ⁶⁵ Then some began to spit on Him, to blindfold Him, and to beat Him, saying, "Prophesy!" The temple police also took Him and slapped Him.

⁶⁶ While Peter was in the courtyard below, one of the high priest's servants came. ⁶⁷ When she saw Peter warming himself, she looked at him and said, "You also were with that Nazarene, Jesus."

⁶⁸ But he denied it: "I don't know or understand what you're talking about!" Then he went out to the entryway, and a rooster crowed.^J

---

^A **14:34** Or *I am deeply grieved*   ^B **14:40** Lit *because their eyes were weighed down*   ^C **14:48** Lit *as against a criminal*   ^D **14:51** Perhaps John Mark who later wrote this Gospel   ^E **14:54** Or *the officers;* lit *the servants*   ^F **14:54** Lit *light*   ^G **14:62** Lit *and you*   ^H **14:62** Ps 110:1; Dn 7:13   ^I **14:64** Lit *How does it appear to you?*   ^J **14:68** Other mss omit *and a rooster crowed*

⁶⁹When the servant saw him again she began to tell those standing nearby, "This man is one of them!"

⁷⁰But again he denied it. After a little while those standing there said to Peter again, "You certainly are one of them, since you're also a Galilean!"ᴬ

⁷¹Then he started to curseᴮ and to swear with an oath, "I don't know this man you're talking about!"

⁷²Immediately a rooster crowed a second time, and Peter remembered when Jesus had spoken the word to him, "Before the rooster crows twice, you will deny Me three times." When he thought about it, he began to weep.ᶜ

15 As soon as it was morning, the chief priests had a meeting with the elders, scribes, and the whole Sanhedrin. After tying Jesus up, they led Him away and handed Him over to Pilate.

²So Pilate asked Him, "Are You the King of the Jews?"

He answered him, "You have said it."ᴰ

³And the chief priests began to accuse Him of many things. ⁴Then Pilate questioned Him again, "Are You not answering anything? Look how many things they are accusing You of!" ⁵But Jesus still did not answer anything, so Pilate was amazed.

⁶At the festival it was Pilate's custom to release for the people a prisoner they requested. ⁷There was one named Barabbas, who was in prison with rebels who had committed murder during the rebellion. ⁸The crowd came up and began to ask Pilate to do for them as was his custom. ⁹So Pilate answered them, "Do you want me to release the King of the Jews for you?" ¹⁰For he knew it was because of envy that the chief priests had handed Him over. ¹¹But the chief priests stirred up the crowd so that he would release Barabbas to them instead.

¹²Pilate asked them again, "Then what do you want me to do with the One you call the King of the Jews?"

¹³Again they shouted, "Crucify Him!"

¹⁴Then Pilate said to them, "Why? What has He done wrong?"

But they shouted, "Crucify Him!" all the more.

¹⁵Then, willing to gratify the crowd, Pilate released Barabbas to them. And after having Jesus flogged,ᴱ he handed Him over to be crucified.

¹⁶Then the soldiers led Him away into the courtyard (that is, headquarters) and called the whole company together. ¹⁷They dressed Him in a purple robe, twisted together a crown of thorns, and put it on Him. ¹⁸And they began to salute Him, "Hail, King of the Jews!" ¹⁹They kept hitting Him on the head with a reed and spitting on Him. Getting down on their knees, they were paying Him homage. ²⁰When they had mocked Him, they stripped Him of the purple robe, put His clothes on Him, and led Him out to crucify Him.

²¹They forced a man coming in from the country, who was passing by, to carry Jesus' cross. He was Simon, a Cyrenian, the father of Alexander and Rufus. ²²And they brought Jesus to the place called *Golgotha* (which means Skull Place). ²³They tried to give Him wine mixed with myrrh, but He did not take it. ²⁴Then they crucified Him and divided His clothes, casting lots for them to decide what each would get. ²⁵Now it was nine in the morningᶠ when they crucified Him. ²⁶The inscription of the charge written against Him was:

THE KING OF THE JEWS.

²⁷They crucified two criminalsᴳ with Him, one on His right and one on His left. [²⁸So the Scripture was fulfilled that says: **And He was counted among outlaws.**]ᴴ,ᴵ ²⁹Those who passed by were yelling insults atᴶ Him, shaking their heads, and saying, "Ha! The One who would demolish the sanctuary and build it in three days, ³⁰save Yourself by coming down from the cross!" ³¹In the same way, the chief priests with the scribes were mocking Him to one another and saying, "He saved others; He cannot save Himself! ³²Let the Messiah, the King of Israel, come down now from the cross, so that we may see and believe." Even those who were crucified with Him were taunting Him.

³³When it was noon,ᴷ darkness came over the whole land ᴸ until three in the afternoon.ᴹ ³⁴And at threeᴹ Jesus cried out with a loud

---

ᴬ14:70 Other mss add *and your speech shows it*   ᴮ14:71 To call down curses on himself if what he said weren't true   ᶜ14:72 Or *He burst into tears, or he broke down*   ᴰ15:2 Or *That is true*, an affirmative oath; Mt 26:64; 27:11   ᴱ15:15 Roman flogging was done with a whip made of leather strips embedded with pieces of bone or metal that brutally tore the flesh.   ᶠ15:25 Lit *was the third hour*   ᴳ15:27 Or *revolutionaries*   ᴴ15:28 Other mss omit bracketed text   ᴵ15:28 Is 53:12   ᴶ15:29 Lit *passed by blasphemed*   ᴷ15:33 Lit *the sixth hour*   ᴸ15:33 Or *whole earth*   ᴹ15:33,34 Lit *the ninth hour* voice, ***"Eloi, Eloi, lemá***[A] ***sabachtháni?"*** which is translated, "My God, My God, why have You forsaken Me?"[B]

[35] When some of those standing there heard this, they said, "Look, He's calling for Elijah!" [36] Someone ran and filled a sponge with sour wine, fixed it on a reed, offered Him a drink, and said, "Let's see if Elijah comes to take Him down!"

[37] But Jesus let out a loud cry and breathed His last. [38] Then the curtain of the sanctuary[C] was split in two from top to bottom. [39] When the centurion, who was standing opposite Him, saw the way He[D] breathed His last, he said, "This man really was God's Son!"[E]

[40] There were also women looking on from a distance. Among them were Mary Magdalene, Mary the mother of James the younger and of Joses, and Salome. [41] When He was in Galilee, they would follow Him and help Him. Many other women had come up with Him to Jerusalem.

[42] When it was already evening, because it was preparation day (that is, the day before the Sabbath), [43] Joseph of Arimathea, a prominent member of the Sanhedrin who was himself looking forward to the kingdom of God, came and boldly went in to Pilate and asked for Jesus' body. [44] Pilate was surprised that He was already dead. Summoning the centurion, he asked him whether He had already died. [45] When he found out from the centurion, he gave the corpse to Joseph. [46] After he bought some fine linen, he took Him down and wrapped Him in the linen. Then he placed Him in a tomb cut out of the rock, and rolled a stone against the entrance to the tomb. [47] Now Mary Magdalene and Mary the mother of Joses were watching where He was placed.

16 When the Sabbath was over, Mary Magdalene, Mary the mother of James, and Salome bought spices, so they could go and anoint Him. [2] Very early in the morning, on the first day of the week, they went to the tomb at sunrise. [3] They were saying to one another, "Who will roll away the stone from the entrance to the tomb for us?" [4] Looking up, they observed that the stone—which was very large—had been rolled away. [5] When they entered the tomb, they saw a young man[F] dressed in a long white robe sitting on the right side; they were amazed and alarmed.

[6] "Don't be alarmed," he told them. "You are looking for Jesus the Nazarene, who was crucified. He has been resurrected! He is not here! See the place where they put Him. [7] But go, tell His disciples and Peter, 'He is going ahead of you to Galilee; you will see Him there just as He told you.' "

[8] So they went out and started running from the tomb, because trembling and astonishment overwhelmed them. And they said nothing to anyone, since they were afraid.

[[9] Early on the first day of the week, after He had risen, He appeared first to Mary Magdalene, out of whom He had driven seven demons. [10] She went and reported to those who had been with Him, as they were mourning and weeping. [11] Yet, when they heard that He was alive and had been seen by her, they did not believe it. [12] Then after this, He appeared in a different form to two of them walking on their way into the country. [13] And they went and reported it to the rest, who did not believe them either.

[14] Later, He appeared to the Eleven themselves as they were reclining at the table. He rebuked their unbelief and hardness of heart, because they did not believe those who saw Him after He had been resurrected. [15] Then He said to them, "Go into all the world and preach the gospel to the whole creation. [16] Whoever believes and is baptized will be saved, but whoever does not believe will be condemned. [17] And these signs will accompany those who believe: In My name they will drive out demons; they will speak in new languages; [18] they will pick up snakes;[G] if they should drink anything deadly, it will never harm them; they will lay hands on the sick, and they will get well."

[19] Then after speaking to them, the Lord Jesus was taken up into heaven and sat down at the right hand of God. [20] And they went out and preached everywhere, with the Lord working with them and confirming the word by the accompanying signs.][H]

[A]15:34 Some mss read *lama*; other mss read *lima*   [B]15:34 Ps 22:1   [C]15:38 A heavy curtain separated the inner room of the temple from the outer.   [D]15:39 Other mss read *saw that He cried out like this and*   [E]15:39 Or *the Son of God*; Mk 1:1   [F]16:5 In Mt 28:2, the young man = an angel   [G]16:18 Other mss add *with their hands*   [H]16:9–20 Other mss omit bracketed text

LUKE

1 Many have undertaken to compile a narrative about the events that have been fulfilled[A] among us, [2] just as the original eyewitnesses and servants of the word handed them down to us. [3] It also seemed good to me, since I have carefully investigated everything from the very first, to write to you in an orderly sequence, most honorable Theophilus, [4] so that you may know the certainty of the things about which you have been instructed.[B]

[5] In the days of King Herod of Judea, there was a priest of Abijah's division[C] named Zechariah. His wife was from the daughters of Aaron, and her name was Elizabeth. [6] Both were righteous in God's sight, living without blame according to all the commands and requirements of the Lord. [7] But they had no children[D] because Elizabeth could not conceive,[E] and both of them were well along in years.[F]

[8] When his division was on duty and he was serving as priest before God, [9] it happened that he was chosen by lot, according to the custom of the priesthood, to enter the sanctuary of the Lord and burn incense. [10] At the hour of incense the whole assembly of the people was praying outside. [11] An angel of the Lord appeared to him, standing to the right of the altar of incense. [12] When Zechariah saw him, he was startled and overcome with fear.[G] [13] But the angel said to him:

> Do not be afraid, Zechariah,
> because your prayer has been heard.
> Your wife Elizabeth will bear you a son,
> and you will name him John.
> [14] There will be joy and delight for you,
> and many will rejoice at his birth.
> [15] For he will be great in the sight
> of the Lord
> and will never drink wine or beer.
> He will be filled with the Holy Spirit
> while still in his mother's womb.
> [16] He will turn many of the sons of Israel
> to the Lord their God.
> [17] And he will go before Him
> in the spirit and power of Elijah,
> to turn the hearts of fathers
> to their children,

> and the disobedient
> to the understanding of the righteous,
> to make ready for the Lord
> a prepared people.

[18] "How can I know this?" Zechariah asked the angel. "For I am an old man, and my wife is well along in years."[H]

[19] The angel answered him, "I am Gabriel, who stands in the presence of God, and I was sent to speak to you and tell you this good news. [20] Now listen! You will become silent and unable to speak until the day these things take place, because you did not believe my words, which will be fulfilled in their proper time."

[21] Meanwhile, the people were waiting for Zechariah, amazed that he stayed so long in the sanctuary. [22] When he did come out, he could not speak to them. Then they realized that he had seen a vision in the sanctuary. He kept making signs to them and remained speechless. [23] When the days of his ministry were completed, he went back home.

[24] After these days his wife Elizabeth conceived and kept herself in seclusion for five months. She said, [25] "The Lord has done this for me. He has looked with favor in these days to take away my disgrace among the people."

[26] In the sixth month, the angel Gabriel was sent by God to a town in Galilee called Nazareth, [27] to a virgin engaged to a man named Joseph, of the house of David. The virgin's name was Mary. [28] And the angel came to her and said, "Rejoice, favored woman! The Lord is with you."[I] [29] But she was deeply troubled by this statement, wondering what kind of greeting this could be. [30] Then the angel told her:

> Do not be afraid, Mary,
> for you have found favor with God.
> [31] Now listen:
> You will conceive and give birth to
> a son,
> and you will call His name Jesus.
> [32] He will be great
> and will be called the Son of
> the Most High,
> and the Lord God will give Him
> the throne of His father David.

A 1:1 Or events that have been accomplished, or events most surely believed **B** 1:4 Or informed **C** 1:5 One of the 24 divisions of priests appointed by David for temple service; 1Ch 24:10 **D** 1:7 Lit child **E** 1:7 Lit Elizabeth was sterile or barren **F** 1:7 Lit in her days **G** 1:12 Lit and fear fell on him **H** 1:18 Lit in her days **I** 1:28 Other mss add blessed are you among women

³³ He will reign over the house of Jacob
    forever,
  and His kingdom will have no end.

³⁴ Mary asked the angel, "How can this be, since I have not been intimate with a man?"^A
³⁵ The angel replied to her:

> "The Holy Spirit will come upon you,
>   and the power of the Most High
>   will overshadow you.
> Therefore, the holy One to be born
>   will be called the Son of God.

³⁶ And consider your relative Elizabeth—even she has conceived a son in her old age, and this is the sixth month for her who was called childless. ³⁷ For nothing will be impossible with God."

³⁸ "I am the Lord's slave,"^B said Mary. "May it be done to me according to your word." Then the angel left her.

³⁹ In those days Mary set out and hurried to a town in the hill country of Judah ⁴⁰ where she entered Zechariah's house and greeted Elizabeth. ⁴¹ When Elizabeth heard Mary's greeting, the baby leaped inside her,^C and Elizabeth was filled with the Holy Spirit. ⁴² Then she exclaimed with a loud cry:

> "You are the most blessed of women,
>   and your child will be blessed!^D

⁴³ How could this happen to me, that the mother of my Lord should come to me? ⁴⁴ For you see, when the sound of your greeting reached my ears, the baby leaped for joy inside me!^E ⁴⁵ She who has believed is blessed because what was spoken to her by the Lord will be fulfilled!"

⁴⁶ And Mary said:

> My soul proclaims the greatness
>   of^F the Lord,
> ⁴⁷   and my spirit has rejoiced in God
>   my Savior,
> ⁴⁸ because He has looked with favor
>   on the humble condition of His slave.
> Surely, from now on all generations
>   will call me blessed,
> ⁴⁹ because the Mighty One
>   has done great things for me,
>   and His name is holy.

⁵⁰ His mercy is from generation
>   to generation
>   on those who fear Him.
⁵¹ He has done a mighty deed
>   with His arm;
> He has scattered the proud
>   because of the thoughts of their hearts;
⁵² He has toppled the mighty
>   from their thrones
>   and exalted the lowly.
⁵³ He has satisfied the hungry
>   with good things
>   and sent the rich away empty.
⁵⁴ He has helped His servant Israel,
>   mindful of His mercy,^G
⁵⁵ just as He spoke to our ancestors,
>   to Abraham and his
>   descendants^H forever.

⁵⁶ And Mary stayed with her about three months; then she returned to her home.
⁵⁷ Now the time had come for Elizabeth to give birth, and she had a son. ⁵⁸ Then her neighbors and relatives heard that the Lord had shown her His great mercy,^I and they rejoiced with her.
⁵⁹ When they came to circumcise the child on the eighth day, they were going to name him Zechariah, after his father. ⁶⁰ But his mother responded, "No! He will be called John."
⁶¹ Then they said to her, "None of your relatives has that name." ⁶² So they motioned to his father to find out what he wanted him to be called. ⁶³ He asked for a writing tablet and wrote:

HIS NAME IS JOHN.

And they were all amazed. ⁶⁴ Immediately his mouth was opened and his tongue set free, and he began to speak, praising God. ⁶⁵ Fear came on all those who lived around them, and all these things were being talked about throughout the hill country of Judea. ⁶⁶ All who heard about him took it to heart, saying, "What then will this child become?" For, indeed, the Lord's hand was with him.
⁶⁷ Then his father Zechariah was filled with the Holy Spirit and prophesied:

⁶⁸   Praise the Lord, the God of Israel,
>   because He has visited

---

^A**1:34** Lit *since I do not know a man*   ^B**1:38** Lit *Look, the Lord's slave*   ^C**1:41** Lit *leaped in her abdomen or womb*   ^D**1:42** Lit *and the fruit of your abdomen (or womb) is blessed*   ^E**1:44** Lit *in my abdomen or womb*   ^F**1:46** Or *soul magnifies*   ^G**1:54** Because *He remembered His mercy;* Ps 98:3   ^H**1:55** Or *offspring;* lit *seed*   ^I**1:58** Lit *the Lord magnified His mercy with her*

and provided redemption
for His people.

⁶⁹ He has raised up a horn of salvation^A
for us
in the house of His servant David,

⁷⁰ just as He spoke by the mouth
of His holy prophets in ancient times;

⁷¹ salvation from our enemies
and from the clutches^B of those
who hate us.

⁷² He has dealt mercifully
with our fathers
and remembered His holy covenant—

⁷³ the oath that He swore to our father
Abraham.
He has given us the privilege,

⁷⁴ since we have been rescued
from our enemies' clutches,^C
to serve Him without fear

⁷⁵ in holiness and righteousness
in His presence all our days.

⁷⁶ And child, you will be called
a prophet of the Most High,
for you will go before the Lord
to prepare His ways,

⁷⁷ to give His people knowledge
of salvation
through the forgiveness of their sins.

⁷⁸ Because of our God's merciful
compassion,
the Dawn from on high will visit us

⁷⁹ to shine on those who live in darkness
and the shadow of death,
to guide our feet into the way of peace.

⁸⁰ The child grew up and became spiritually strong, and he was in the wilderness until the day of his public appearance to Israel.

2 In those days a decree went out from Caesar Augustus^D that the whole empire^E should be registered. ²This first registration took place while^F Quirinius was governing Syria. ³So everyone went to be registered, each to his own town.

⁴And Joseph also went up from the town of Nazareth in Galilee, to Judea, to the city of David, which is called Bethlehem, because he was of the house and family line of David, ⁵to be registered along with Mary, who was engaged

to him^G and was pregnant. ⁶While they were there, the time came for her to give birth. ⁷Then she gave birth to her firstborn Son, and she wrapped Him snugly in cloth and laid Him in a feeding trough—because there was no room for them at the lodging place.

⁸In the same region, shepherds were staying out in the fields and keeping watch at night over their flock. ⁹Then an angel of the Lord stood before^H them, and the glory of the Lord shone around them, and they were terrified.^I ¹⁰But the angel said to them, "Don't be afraid, for look, I proclaim to you good news of great joy that will be for all the people:^J ¹¹Today a Savior, who is Messiah the Lord, was born for you in the city of David. ¹²This will be the sign for you: You will find a baby wrapped snugly in cloth and lying in a feeding trough."

¹³Suddenly there was a multitude of the heavenly host with the angel, praising God and saying:

¹⁴ Glory to God in the highest heaven,
and peace on earth to people
He favors!^K,L

¹⁵When the angels had left them and returned to heaven, the shepherds said to one another, "Let's go straight to Bethlehem and see what has happened, which the Lord has made known to us."

¹⁶They hurried off and found both Mary and Joseph, and the baby who was lying in the feeding trough. ¹⁷After seeing them, they reported the message they were told about this child, ¹⁸and all who heard it were amazed at what the shepherds said to them. ¹⁹But Mary was treasuring up all these things^M in her heart and meditating on them. ²⁰The shepherds returned, glorifying and praising God for all they had seen and heard, just as they had been told.

²¹When the eight days were completed for His circumcision, He was named Jesus—the name given by the angel before He was conceived.^N ²²And when the days of their purification according to the law of Moses were finished, they brought Him up to Jerusalem to present Him to the Lord ²³(just as it is written in the law of the Lord: **Every firstborn male**^O **will be dedicated**^P **to the Lord**^Q) ²⁴and to offer

A1:69 = a strong Savior   B1:71 Lit the hand   C1:74 Lit from the hand of enemies   D2:1 Emperor who ruled the Roman Empire 27 B.C.–A.D. 14; also known as Octavian, he established the peaceful era known as the Pax Romana; Caesar was a title of Roman emperors.   E2:1 Or the whole inhabited world   F2:2 Or This registration was the first while, or This registration was before   G2:5 Other mss read was his engaged wife   H2:9 Or Lord appeared to   I2:9 Lit they feared a great fear   J2:10 Or the whole nation   K2:14 Other mss read earth good will to people   L2:14 Or earth to men of good will   M2:19 Lit these words   N2:21 Or conceived in the womb   O2:23 Lit "Every male that opens a womb   P2:23 Lit be called holy   Q2:23 Ex 13:2,12 a sacrifice (according to what is stated in the law of the Lord: **a pair of turtledoves or two young pigeons**[A]).

[25] There was a man in Jerusalem whose name was Simeon. This man was righteous and devout, looking forward to Israel's consolation,[B] and the Holy Spirit was on him. [26] It had been revealed to him by the Holy Spirit that he would not see death before he saw the Lord's Messiah. [27] Guided by the Spirit, he entered[C] the temple complex. When the parents brought in the child Jesus to perform for Him what was customary under the law, [28] Simeon took Him up in his arms, praised God, and said:

[29]   Now, Master,
         You can dismiss Your slave in peace,
            as You promised.
[30]   For my eyes have seen Your salvation.
[31]   You have prepared it
         in the presence of all peoples—
[32]   a light for revelation to the Gentiles[D]
         and glory to Your people Israel.

[33] His father and mother[E] were amazed at what was being said about Him. [34] Then Simeon blessed them and told His mother Mary: "Indeed, this child is destined to cause the fall and rise of many in Israel and to be a sign that will be opposed[F]— [35] and a sword will pierce your own soul—that the thoughts[G] of many hearts may be revealed."

[36] There was also a prophetess, Anna, a daughter of Phanuel, of the tribe of Asher. She was well along in years,[H] having lived with her husband seven years after her marriage,[I] [37] and was a widow for 84 years.[J] She did not leave the temple complex, serving God night and day with fasting and prayers. [38] At that very moment,[K] she came up and began to thank God and to speak about Him to all who were looking forward to the redemption of Jerusalem.[L]

[39] When they had completed everything according to the law of the Lord, they returned to Galilee, to their own town of Nazareth. [40] The boy grew up and became strong, filled with wisdom, and God's grace was on Him.

[41] Every year His parents traveled to Jerusalem for the Passover Festival. [42] When He was

12 years old, they went up according to the custom of the festival. [43] After those days were over, as they were returning, the boy Jesus stayed behind in Jerusalem, but His parents[M] did not know it. [44] Assuming He was in the traveling party, they went a day's journey. Then they began looking for Him among their relatives and friends. [45] When they did not find Him, they returned to Jerusalem to search for Him. [46] After three days, they found Him in the temple complex sitting among the teachers, listening to them and asking them questions. [47] And all those who heard Him were astounded at His understanding and His answers. [48] When His parents saw Him, they were astonished, and His mother said to Him, "Son, why have You treated us like this? Your father and I have been anxiously searching for You."

[49] "Why were you searching for Me?" He asked them. "Didn't you know that I had to be in My Father's house?"[N] [50] But they did not understand what He said to them.

[51] Then He went down with them and came to Nazareth and was obedient to them. His mother kept all these things in her heart. [52] And Jesus increased in wisdom and stature, and in favor with God and with people.

3 In the fifteenth year of the reign of Tiberius Caesar,[O] while Pontius Pilate was governor of Judea, Herod as tetrarch[P] of Galilee, his brother Philip tetrarch of the region of Iturea[Q] and Trachonitis,[Q] and Lysanias tetrarch of Abilene,[R] [2] during the high priesthood of Annas and Caiaphas, God's word came to John the son of Zechariah in the wilderness. [3] He went into all the vicinity of the Jordan, preaching a baptism of repentance[S] for the forgiveness of sins, [4] as it is written in the book of the words of the prophet Isaiah:

      **A voice of one crying out
         in the wilderness:
      Prepare the way for the Lord;
         make His paths straight!**
[5]   **Every valley will be filled,
         and every mountain and hill will be
            made low;[T]**
         **the crooked will become straight,
         the rough ways smooth,**

A2:24 Lv 5:11; 12:8   B2:25 The coming of the Messiah with His salvation for the nation; Is 40:1; 61:2; Lk 2:26,30   C2:27 Lit And in the Spirit, he came into   D2:32 Or the nations   E2:33 Other mss read But Joseph and His mother   F2:34 Or spoken against   G2:35 Or schemes   H2:36 Lit in many days   I2:36 Lit years from her virginity   J2:37 Or she was a widow until the age of 84   K2:38 Lit very hour   L2:38 Other mss read in Jerusalem   M2:43 Other mss read but Joseph and His mother   N2:49 Or be involved in My Father's interests (or things), or be among My Father's people   O3:1 Emperor who ruled the Roman Empire A.D. 14–37   P3:1 Or ruler   Q3:1 A small province northeast of Galilee   R3:1 A small Syrian province   S3:3 Or baptism based on repentance   T3:5 Lit be humbled

⁶ **and everyone**ᴬ **will see the salvation
   of God.**ᴮ

⁷He then said to the crowds who came out to
be baptized by him, "Brood of vipers! Who
warned you to flee from the coming wrath?
⁸Therefore produce fruit consistent with repentance. And don't start saying to yourselves,
'We have Abraham as our father,' for I tell you
that God is able to raise up children for Abraham from these stones! ⁹Even now the ax is
ready to strikeᶜ the root of the trees! Therefore,
every tree that doesn't produce good fruit will
be cut down and thrown into the fire."

¹⁰"What then should we do?" the crowds
were asking him.

¹¹He replied to them, "The one who has
two shirtsᴰ must share with someone who has
none, and the one who has food must do the
same."

¹²Tax collectors also came to be baptized,
and they asked him, "Teacher, what should we
do?"

¹³He told them, "Don't collect any more
than what you have been authorized."

¹⁴Some soldiers also questioned him: "What
should we do?"

He said to them, "Don't take money from
anyone by force or false accusation; be satisfied with your wages."

¹⁵Now the people were waiting expectantly,
and all of them were debating in their mindsᴱ
whether John might be the Messiah. ¹⁶John
answered them all, "I baptize you withᶠ water, but One is coming who is more powerful
than I. I am not worthy to untie the strap of
His sandals. He will baptize you withᶠ the Holy
Spirit and fire. ¹⁷His winnowing shovelᴳ is in
His hand to clear His threshing floor and gather the wheat into His barn, but the chaff He
will burn up with a fire that never goes out."
¹⁸Then, along with many other exhortations,
he proclaimed good news to the people. ¹⁹But
Herod the tetrarch, being rebuked by him
about Herodias, his brother's wife, and about
all the evil things Herod had done, ²⁰added
this to everything else—he locked John up in
prison.

²¹When all the people were baptized, Jesus
also was baptized. As He was praying, heaven
opened, ²²and the Holy Spirit descended on

Him in a physical appearance like a dove. And
a voice came from heaven:

> You are My beloved Son.
> I take delight in You!

²³As He began His ministry, Jesus was about
30 years old and was thought to beᴴ the

24   son of Joseph, sonᴵ of Heli,
         son of Matthat, son of Levi,
         son of Melchi, son of Jannai,
         son of Joseph, ²⁵son of Mattathias,
         son of Amos, son of Nahum,
         son of Esli, son of Naggai,
26   son of Maath, son of Mattathias,
         son of Semein, son of Josech,
         son of Joda, ²⁷son of Joanan,
         son of Rhesa, son of Zerubbabel,
         son of Shealtiel, son of Neri,
28   son of Melchi, son of Addi,
         son of Cosam, son of Elmadam,
         son of Er, ²⁹son of Joshua,
         son of Eliezer, son of Jorim,
         son of Matthat, son of Levi,
30   son of Simeon, son of Judah,
         son of Joseph, son of Jonam,
         son of Eliakim, ³¹son of Melea,
         son of Menna, son of Mattatha,
         son of Nathan, son of David,
32   son of Jesse, son of Obed,
         son of Boaz, son of Salmon,ᴶ
         son of Nahshon, ³³son of Amminadab,
         son of Ram,ᴷ son of Hezron,
         son of Perez, son of Judah,
34   son of Jacob, son of Isaac,
         son of Abraham, son of Terah,
         son of Nahor, ³⁵son of Serug,
         son of Reu, son of Peleg,
         son of Eber, son of Shelah,
36   son of Cainan, son of Arphaxad,
         son of Shem, son of Noah,
         son of Lamech, ³⁷son of Methuselah,
         son of Enoch, son of Jared,
         son of Mahalaleel, son of Cainan,
38   son of Enos, son of Seth,
         son of Adam, son of God.

4 Then Jesus returned from the Jordan, full
of the Holy Spirit, and was led by the Spirit
in the wilderness ²for 40 days to be tempted by
the Devil. He ate nothing during those days,

ᴬ**3:6** Lit *all flesh*   ᴮ**3:4–6** Is 40:3–5   ᶜ**3:9** Lit *the ax lies at*   ᴰ**3:11** Lit *tunics*   ᴱ**3:15** Or *hearts*   ᶠ**3:16** Or *in*   ᴳ**3:17** A wooden farm implement
used to toss threshed grain into the wind so the lighter chaff would blow away and separate from the heavier grain   ᴴ**3:23** People did not
know about His virgin birth; Mt 1:18–25; Lk 1:26–38   ᴵ**3:23** The relationship in some cases may be more distant than a son.   ᴶ**3:32** Other
mss read *Sala*   ᴷ**3:33** Other mss read *Amminadab, son of Aram, son of Joram*; other mss read *Amminadab, son of Admin, son of Arni*

and when they were over,[A] He was hungry. ³The Devil said to Him, "If You are the Son of God, tell this stone to become bread."

⁴But Jesus answered him, "It is written: Man must not live on bread alone."[B,C]

⁵So he took Him up[D] and showed Him all the kingdoms of the world in a moment of time. The Devil said to Him, "I will give You their splendor and all this authority, because it has been given over to me, and I can give it to anyone I want. ⁷If You, then, will worship me,[E] all will be Yours."

⁸And Jesus answered him,[F] "It is written:

Worship the Lord your God,
    and serve Him only."[G]

⁹So he took Him to Jerusalem, had Him stand on the pinnacle of the temple, and said to Him, "If You are the Son of God, throw Yourself down from here. ¹⁰For it is written:

He will give His angels orders
    concerning you,
to protect you,[H] ¹¹and
they will support you with their hands,
    so that you will not strike
    your foot against a stone."[I]

¹²And Jesus answered him, "It is said: Do not test the Lord your God."[J]

¹³After the Devil had finished every temptation, he departed from Him for a time.

¹⁴Then Jesus returned to Galilee in the power of the Spirit, and news about Him spread throughout the entire vicinity. ¹⁵He was teaching in their synagogues, being acclaimed[K] by everyone.

¹⁶He came to Nazareth, where He had been brought up. As usual, He entered the synagogue on the Sabbath day and stood up to read. ¹⁷The scroll of the prophet Isaiah was given to Him, and unrolling the scroll, He found the place where it was written:

¹⁸   The Spirit of the Lord is on Me,
    because He has anointed Me
    to preach good news to the poor.
    He has sent Me[L]
    to proclaim freedom[M] to the captives
    and recovery of sight to the blind,
    to set free the oppressed,

¹⁹   to proclaim the year
        of the Lord's favor.[N,O]

²⁰He then rolled up the scroll, gave it back to the attendant, and sat down. And the eyes of everyone in the synagogue were fixed on Him. ²¹He began by saying to them, "Today as you listen, this Scripture has been fulfilled."

²²They were all speaking well of Him[P] and were amazed by the gracious words that came from His mouth, yet they said, "Isn't this Joseph's son?"

²³Then He said to them, "No doubt you will quote this proverb[Q] to Me: 'Doctor, heal yourself. So all we've heard that took place in Capernaum, do here in Your hometown also.'"

²⁴He also said, "I assure you: No prophet is accepted in his hometown. ²⁵But I say to you, there were certainly many widows in Israel in Elijah's days, when the sky was shut up for three years and six months while a great famine came over all the land. ²⁶Yet Elijah was not sent to any of them—but to a widow at Zarephath in Sidon. ²⁷And in the prophet Elisha's time, there were many in Israel who had serious skin diseases, yet not one of them was healed[R]—only Naaman the Syrian."

²⁸When they heard this, everyone in the synagogue was enraged. ²⁹They got up, drove Him out of town, and brought Him to the edge[S] of the hill that their town was built on, intending to hurl Him over the cliff. ³⁰But He passed right through the crowd and went on His way.

³¹Then He went down to Capernaum, a town in Galilee, and was teaching them on the Sabbath. ³²They were astonished at His teaching because His message had authority. ³³In the synagogue there was a man with an unclean demonic spirit who cried out with a loud voice, ³⁴"Leave us alone![T] What do You have to do with us,[U] Jesus—Nazarene? Have You come to destroy us? I know who You are—the Holy One of God!"

³⁵But Jesus rebuked him and said, "Be quiet and come out of him!"

And throwing him down before them, the demon came out of him without hurting him at all. ³⁶Amazement came over them all, and they kept saying to one another, "What is this message? For He commands the unclean

^A4:2 Lit were completed ^B4:4 Other mss add but on every word of God ^C4:4 Dt 8:3 ^D4:5 Other mss read So the Devil took Him up on a high mountain ^E4:7 Lit will fall down before me ^F4:8 Other mss add "Get behind Me, Satan!" ^G4:8 Dt 6:13 ^H4:10 Ps 91:11 ^I4:11 Ps 91:12 ^J4:12 Dt 6:16 ^K4:15 Or glorified ^L4:18 Other mss add to heal the brokenhearted, ^M4:18 Or release, or forgiveness, ^N4:19 The time of messianic grace ^O4:18-19 Is 61:1-2 ^P4:22 Or They were testifying against Him ^Q4:23 Or parable ^R4:27 Lit cleansed ^S4:29 Lit brow ^T4:34 Or Ha!, or Ah! ^U4:34 Lit What to us and to You spirits with authority and power, and they come out!" ³⁷And news about Him began to go out to every place in the vicinity.

³⁸After He left the synagogue, He entered Simon's house. Simon's mother-in-law was suffering from a high fever, and they asked Him about her. ³⁹So He stood over her and rebuked the fever, and it left her. She got up immediately and began to serve them.

⁴⁰When the sun was setting, all those who had anyone sick with various diseases brought them to Him. As He laid His hands on each one of them, He would heal them. ⁴¹Also, demons were coming out of many, shouting and saying, "You are the Son of God!" But He rebuked them and would not allow them to speak, because they knew He was the Messiah.

⁴²When it was day, He went out and made His way to a deserted place. But the crowds were searching for Him. They came to Him and tried to keep Him from leaving them. ⁴³But He said to them, "I must proclaim the good news about the kingdom of God to the other towns also, because I was sent for this purpose." ⁴⁴And He was preaching in the synagogues of Galilee.ᴬ

5 As the crowd was pressing in on Jesus to hear God's word, He was standing by Lake Gennesaret.ᴮ ²He saw two boats at the edge of the lake;ᶜ the fishermen had left them and were washing their nets. ³He got into one of the boats, which belonged to Simon, and asked him to put out a little from the land. Then He sat down and was teaching the crowds from the boat.

⁴When He had finished speaking, He said to Simon, "Put out into deep water and let downᴰ your nets for a catch."

⁵"Master," Simon replied, "we've worked hard all night long and caught nothing! But at Your word, I'll let down the nets."ᴱ

⁶When they did this, they caught a great number of fish, and their netsᴱ began to tear. ⁷So they signaled to their partners in the other boat to come and help them; they came and filled both boats so full that they began to sink.

⁸When Simon Peter saw this, he fell at Jesus' knees and said, "Go away from me, because I'm a sinful man, Lord!" ⁹For he and all those with him were amazedᶠ at the catch of fish they took, ¹⁰and so were James and John, Zebedee's sons, who were Simon's partners.

"Don't be afraid," Jesus told Simon. "From now on you will be catching people!" ¹¹Then they brought the boats to land, left everything, and followed Him.

¹²While He was in one of the towns, a man was there who had a serious skin disease all over him. He saw Jesus, fell facedown, and begged Him: "Lord, if You are willing, You can make me clean."

¹³Reaching out His hand, He touched him, saying, "I am willing; be made clean," and immediately the disease left him. ¹⁴Then He ordered him to tell no one: "But go and show yourself to the priest, and offer what Moses prescribed for your cleansing as a testimony to them."

¹⁵But the newsᴳ about Him spread even more, and large crowds would come together to hear Him and to be healed of their sicknesses. ¹⁶Yet He often withdrew to deserted places and prayed.

¹⁷On one of those days while He was teaching, Pharisees and teachers of the law were sitting there who had come from every village of Galilee and Judea, and also from Jerusalem. And the Lord's power to heal was in Him. ¹⁸Just then some men came, carrying on a mat a man who was paralyzed. They tried to bring him in and set him down before Him. ¹⁹Since they could not find a way to bring him in because of the crowd, they went up on the roof and lowered him on the mat through the roof tiles into the middle of the crowd before Jesus.

²⁰Seeing their faith He said, "Friend,ᴴ your sins are forgiven you."

²¹Then the scribes and the Pharisees began to think: "Who is this man who speaks blasphemies? Who can forgive sins but God alone?"

²²But perceiving their thoughts, Jesus replied to them, "Why are you thinking this in your hearts?ᴵ ²³Which is easier: to say, 'Your sins are forgiven you,' or to say, 'Get up and walk'? ²⁴But so you may know that the Son of Man has authority on earth to forgive sins"—He told the paralyzed man, "I tell you: Get up, pick up your mat, and go home."

²⁵Immediately he got up before them, picked up what he had been lying on, and went home glorifying God. ²⁶Then everyone was astounded, and they were giving glory to God.

ᴬ4:44 Other mss read Judea   ᴮ5:1 = Sea of Galilee   ᶜ5:2 Lit boats standing by the lake   ᴰ5:4 Lit and you (pl in Gk) let down   ᴱ5:5,6 Other mss read net (Gk sg)   ᶠ5:9 Lit For amazement had seized him and all those with him   ᴳ5:15 Lit the word   ᴴ5:20 Lit Man   ᴵ5:22 Or minds

And they were filled with awe and said, "We have seen incredible things today!"

²⁷After this, Jesus went out and saw a tax collector named Levi sitting at the tax office, and He said to him, "Follow Me!" ²⁸So, leaving everything behind, he got up and began to follow Him.

²⁹Then Levi hosted a grand banquet for Him at his house. Now there was a large crowd of tax collectors and others who were guestsᴬ with them. ³⁰But the Pharisees and their scribes were complaining to His disciples, "Why do you eat and drink with tax collectors and sinners?"

³¹Jesus replied to them, "The healthy don't need a doctor, but the sick do. ³²I have not come to call the righteous, but sinners to repentance."

³³Then they said to Him, "John's disciples fast often and say prayers, and those of the Pharisees do the same, but Yours eat and drink."ᴮ

³⁴Jesus said to them, "You can't make the wedding guestsᶜ fast while the groom is with them, can you? ³⁵But the timeᴰ will come when the groom will be taken away from them—then they will fast in those days."

³⁶He also told them a parable: "No one tears a patch from a new garment and puts it on an old garment. Otherwise, not only will he tear the new, but also the piece from the new garment will not match the old. ³⁷And no one puts new wine into old wineskins. Otherwise, the new wine will burst the skins, it will spill, and the skins will be ruined. ³⁸But new wine should be put into fresh wineskins.ᴱ ³⁹And no one, after drinking old wine, wants new, because he says, 'The old is better.'"ᶠ

6 On a Sabbath,ᴳ He passed through the grainfields. His disciples were picking heads of grain, rubbing them in their hands, and eating them. ²But some of the Pharisees said, "Why are you doing what is not lawful on the Sabbath?"

³Jesus answered them, "Haven't you read what David and those who were with him did when he was hungry— ⁴how he entered the house of God, and took and ate the sacred bread, which is not lawful for any but the priests to eat? He even gave some to those who

were with him." ⁵Then He told them, "The Son of Man is Lord of the Sabbath."

⁶On another Sabbath He entered the synagogue and was teaching. A man was there whose right hand was paralyzed. ⁷The scribes and Pharisees were watching Him closely, to see if He would heal on the Sabbath, so that they could find a charge against Him. ⁸But He knew their thoughts and told the man with the paralyzed hand, "Get up and stand here."ᴴ So he got up and stood there. ⁹Then Jesus said to them, "I ask you: Is it lawful on the Sabbath to do what is good or to do what is evil, to save life or to destroy it?" ¹⁰After looking around at them all, He told him, "Stretch out your hand." He did so, and his hand was restored.ᴵ ¹¹They, however, were filled with rage and started discussing with one another what they might do to Jesus.

¹²During those days He went out to the mountain to pray and spent all night in prayer to God. ¹³When daylight came, He summoned His disciples, and He chose 12 of them—He also named them apostles:

¹⁴   Simon, whom He also named Peter,
        and Andrew his brother;
        James and John;
        Philip and Bartholomew;
¹⁵   Matthew and Thomas;
        James the son of Alphaeus,
        and Simon called the Zealot;
¹⁶   Judas the son of James,
        and Judas Iscariot, who became
            a traitor.

¹⁷After coming down with them, He stood on a level place with a large crowd of His disciples and a great number of people from all Judea and Jerusalem and from the seacoast of Tyre and Sidon. ¹⁸They came to hear Him and to be healed of their diseases; and those tormented by unclean spirits were made well. ¹⁹The whole crowd was trying to touch Him, because power was coming out from Him and healing them all.

²⁰Then looking up atᴶ His disciples, He said:

        You who are poor are blessed,
            because the kingdom of God is yours.
²¹   You who are now hungry are blessed,

ᴬ5:29 Lit *were reclining* (at the table); at important meals the custom was to recline on a mat at a low table and lean on the left elbow. ᴮ5:33 Other mss read *"Why do John's . . . drink?"* (as a question) ᶜ5:34 Or *the friends of the groom*; lit *sons of the bridal chamber* ᴰ5:35 Lit *days* ᴱ5:38 Other mss add *And so both are preserved.* ᶠ5:39 Other mss read *is good* ᴳ6:1 Other mss read *a second-first Sabbath*; perhaps a special Sabbath ᴴ6:8 Lit *stand in the middle* ᴵ6:10 Other mss add *as sound as the other* ᴶ6:20 Lit *Then lifting up His eyes to*

because you will be filled.
You who now weep are blessed,
because you will laugh.
22 You are blessed when people hate you,
when they exclude you, insult you,
and slander your name as evil
because of the Son of Man.

23 "Rejoice in that day and leap for joy! Take note—your reward is great in heaven, for this is the way their ancestors used to treat the prophets.

24 But woe to you who are rich,
for you have received your comfort.
25 Woe to you who are now full,
for you will be hungry.
Woe to you[A] who are now laughing,
for you will mourn and weep.
26 Woe to you[A]
when all people speak well of you,
for this is the way their ancestors
used to treat the false prophets.

27 "But I say to you who listen: Love your enemies, do what is good to those who hate you, 28 bless those who curse you, pray for those who mistreat you. 29 If anyone hits you on the cheek, offer the other also. And if anyone takes away your coat, don't hold back your shirt either. 30 Give to everyone who asks you, and from one who takes your things, don't ask for them back. 31 Just as you want others to do for you, do the same for them. 32 If you love those who love you, what credit is that to you? Even sinners love those who love them. 33 If you do what is good to those who are good to you, what credit is that to you? Even sinners do that. 34 And if you lend to those from whom you expect to receive, what credit is that to you? Even sinners lend to sinners to be repaid in full. 35 But love your enemies, do what is good, and lend, expecting nothing in return. Then your reward will be great, and you will be sons of the Most High. For He is gracious to the ungrateful and evil. 36 Be merciful, just as your Father also is merciful.

37 "Do not judge, and you will not be judged. Do not condemn, and you will not be condemned. Forgive, and you will be forgiven. 38 Give, and it will be given to you; a good measure—pressed down, shaken together, and running over—will be poured into your lap.

For with the measure you use,[B] it will be measured back to you."

39 He also told them a parable: "Can the blind guide the blind? Won't they both fall into a pit? 40 A disciple is not above his teacher, but everyone who is fully trained will be like his teacher.

41 "Why do you look at the speck in your brother's eye, but don't notice the log in your own eye? 42 Or how can you say to your brother, 'Brother, let me take out the speck that is in your eye,' when you yourself don't see the log in your eye? Hypocrite! First take the log out of your eye, and then you will see clearly to take out the speck in your brother's eye.

43 "A good tree doesn't produce bad fruit; on the other hand, a bad tree doesn't produce good fruit. 44 For each tree is known by its own fruit. Figs aren't gathered from thornbushes, or grapes picked from a bramble bush. 45 A good man produces good out of the good storeroom of his heart. An evil man produces evil out of the evil storeroom, for his mouth speaks from the overflow of the heart.

46 "Why do you call Me 'Lord, Lord,' and don't do the things I say? 47 I will show you what someone is like who comes to Me, hears My words, and acts on them: 48 He is like a man building a house, who dug deep[C] and laid the foundation on the rock. When the flood came, the river crashed against that house and couldn't shake it, because it was well built. 49 But the one who hears and does not act is like a man who built a house on the ground without a foundation. The river crashed against it, and immediately it collapsed. And the destruction of that house was great!"

7 When He had concluded all His sayings in the hearing of the people, He entered Capernaum. 2 A centurion's slave, who was highly valued by him, was sick and about to die. 3 When the centurion heard about Jesus, he sent some Jewish elders to Him, requesting Him to come and save the life of his slave. 4 When they reached Jesus, they pleaded with Him earnestly, saying, "He is worthy for You to grant this, 5 because he loves our nation and has built us a synagogue." 6 Jesus went with them, and when He was not far from[D] the house, the centurion sent friends to tell Him, "Lord, don't trouble Yourself, since I am not worthy to have You come under my roof. 7 That is why I didn't even consider myself worthy to

A6:25,26 Other mss omit to you   B6:38 Lit you measure   C6:48 Lit dug and went deep   D7:6 Lit and He already was not far from come to You. But say the word, and my servant will be cured.^A ^8 For I too am a man placed under authority, having soldiers under my command.^B I say to this one, 'Go!' and he goes; and to another, 'Come!' and he comes; and to my slave, 'Do this!' and he does it."

^9 Jesus heard this and was amazed at him, and turning to the crowd following Him, He said, "I tell you, I have not found so great a faith even in Israel!" ^10 When those who had been sent returned to the house, they found the slave in good health.

^11 Soon afterward He was on His way to a town called Nain. His disciples and a large crowd were traveling with Him. ^12 Just as He neared the gate of the town, a dead man was being carried out. He was his mother's only son, and she was a widow. A large crowd from the city was also with her. ^13 When the Lord saw her, He had compassion on her and said, "Don't cry." ^14 Then He came up and touched the open coffin,^C and the pallbearers stopped. And He said, "Young man, I tell you, get up!"

^15 The dead man sat up and began to speak, and Jesus gave him to his mother. ^16 Then fear^D came over everyone, and they glorified God, saying, "A great prophet has risen among us," and "God has visited^E His people." ^17 This report about Him went throughout Judea and all the vicinity.

^18 Then John's disciples told him about all these things. John summoned two of his disciples ^19 and sent them to the Lord, asking, "Are You the One who is to come, or should we look for someone else?"

^20 When the men reached Him, they said, "John the Baptist sent us to ask You, 'Are You the One who is to come, or should we look for someone else?'"

^21 At that time Jesus healed many people of diseases, plagues, and evil spirits, and He granted sight to many blind people. ^22 He replied to them, "Go and report to John the things you have seen and heard: The blind receive their sight, the lame walk, those with skin diseases are healed,^F the deaf hear, the dead are raised, and the poor are told the good news. ^23 And anyone who is not offended because of Me is blessed." ^24 After John's messengers left, He began to speak to the crowds about John: "What did you go out into the wilderness to see? A reed swaying in the wind? ^25 What then did you go out to see? A man dressed in soft robes? Look, those who are splendidly dressed^G and live in luxury are in royal palaces. ^26 What then did you go out to see? A prophet? Yes, I tell you, and far more than a prophet. ^27 This is the one it is written about:

> Look, I am sending My messenger
> ahead of You;^H
> he will prepare Your way before You.^I

^28 I tell you, among those born of women no one is greater than John,^J but the least in the kingdom of God is greater than he."

^29 (And when all the people, including the tax collectors, heard this, they acknowledged God's way of righteousness,^K because they had been baptized with John's baptism. ^30 But since the Pharisees and experts in the law had not been baptized by him, they rejected the plan of God for themselves.)

^31 "To what then should I compare the people of this generation, and what are they like? ^32 They are like children sitting in the marketplace and calling to each other:

> We played the flute for you,
> but you didn't dance;
> we sang a lament,
> but you didn't weep!

^33 For John the Baptist did not come eating bread or drinking wine, and you say, 'He has a demon!' ^34 The Son of Man has come eating and drinking, and you say, 'Look, a glutton and a drunkard, a friend of tax collectors and sinners!' ^35 Yet wisdom is vindicated^L by all her children."

^36 Then one of the Pharisees invited him to eat with him. He entered the Pharisee's house and reclined at the table. ^37 And a woman in the town who was a sinner found out that Jesus was reclining at the table in the Pharisee's house. She brought an alabaster jar of fragrant oil ^38 and stood behind Him at His feet, weeping, and began to wash His feet with her tears. She wiped His feet with the hair of her head, kissing them and anointing them with the fragrant oil.

^39 When the Pharisee who had invited Him saw this, he said to himself, "This man, if He were a prophet, would know who and what kind

---

^A 7:7 Other mss read and let my servant be cured   ^B 7:8 Lit under me   ^C 7:14 Or the bier   ^D 7:16 Or awe   ^E 7:16 Or come to help   ^F 7:22 Lit cleansed   ^G 7:25 Or who have glorious robes   ^H 7:27 Lit messenger before Your face   ^I 7:27 Mal 3:1   ^J 7:28 Other mss read women is not a greater prophet than John the Baptist   ^K 7:29 Lit they justified God   ^L 7:35 Or wisdom is declared right of woman this is who is touching Him—she's a sinner!"

⁴⁰Jesus replied to him, "Simon, I have something to say to you."

"Teacher," he said, "say it."

⁴¹"A creditor had two debtors. One owed 500 denarii, and the other 50. ⁴²Since they could not pay it back, he graciously forgave them both. So, which of them will love him more?"

⁴³Simon answered, "I suppose the one he forgave more."

"You have judged correctly," He told him. ⁴⁴Turning to the woman, He said to Simon, "Do you see this woman? I entered your house; you gave Me no water for My feet, but she, with her tears, has washed My feet and wiped them with her hair. ⁴⁵You gave Me no kiss, but she hasn't stopped kissing My feet since I came in. ⁴⁶You didn't anoint My head with olive oil, but she has anointed My feet with fragrant oil. ⁴⁷Therefore I tell you, her many sins have been forgiven; that's whyᴬ she loved much. But the one who is forgiven little, loves little." ⁴⁸Then He said to her, "Your sins are forgiven."

⁴⁹Those who were at the table with Him began to say among themselves, "Who is this man who even forgives sins?"

⁵⁰And He said to the woman, "Your faith has saved you. Go in peace."

8 Soon afterward He was traveling from one town and village to another, preaching and telling the good news of the kingdom of God. The Twelve were with Him, ²and also some women who had been healed of evil spirits and sicknesses: Mary, called Magdalene (seven demons had come out of her); ³Joanna the wife of Chuza, Herod's steward; Susanna; and many others who were supporting them from their possessions.

⁴As a large crowd was gathering, and people were flocking to Him from every town, He said in a parable: ⁵"A sower went out to sow his seed. As he was sowing, some fell along the path; it was trampled on, and the birds of the sky ate it up. ⁶Other seed fell on the rock; when it sprang up, it withered, since it lacked moisture. ⁷Other seed fell among thorns; the thorns sprang up with it and choked it. ⁸Still other seed fell on good ground; when it sprang up, it produced a crop: 100 times what was sown." As He said this, He called out, "Anyone who has ears to hear should listen!"

⁹Then His disciples asked Him, "What does this parable mean?" ¹⁰So He said, "The secrets of the kingdom of God have been given for you to know, but to the rest it is in parables, so that

> Looking they may not see,
> and hearing they may not understand.ᴮ

¹¹"This is the meaning of the parable:ᶜ The seed is the word of God. ¹²The seed along the path are those who have heard and then the Devil comes and takes away the word from their hearts, so that they may not believe and be saved. ¹³And the seed on the rock are those who, when they hear, welcome the word with joy. Having no root, these believe for a while and depart in a time of testing. ¹⁴As for the seed that fell among thorns, these are the ones who, when they have heard, go on their way and are choked with worries, riches, and pleasures of life, and produce no mature fruit. ¹⁵But the seed in the good ground—these are the ones who,ᴰ having heard the word with an honest and good heart, hold on to it and by enduring, bear fruit.

¹⁶"No one, after lighting a lamp, covers it with a basket or puts it under a bed, but puts it on a lampstand so that those who come in may see its light. ¹⁷For nothing is concealed that won't be revealed, and nothing hidden that won't be made known and come to light. ¹⁸Therefore take care how you listen. For whoever has, more will be given to him; and whoever does not have, even what he thinks he has will be taken away from him."

¹⁹Then His mother and brothers came to Him, but they could not meet with Him because of the crowd. ²⁰He was told, "Your mother and Your brothers are standing outside, wanting to see You."

²¹But He replied to them, "My mother and My brothers are those who hear and do the word of God."

²²One day He and His disciples got into a boat, and He told them, "Let's cross over to the other side of the lake." So they set out, ²³and as they were sailing He fell asleep. Then a fierce windstorm came down on the lake; they were being swamped and were in danger. ²⁴They came and woke Him up, saying, "Master, Master, we're going to die!" Then He got up and rebuked the wind and the raging waves. So

ᴬ7:47 Her love shows that she has been forgiven ᴮ8:10 Is 6:9 ᶜ8:11 Lit But this is the parable: ᴰ8:15 Or these are the kind who they ceased, and there was a calm. 25 He said to them, "Where is your faith?"

They were fearful and amazed, asking one another, "Who can this be?A He commands even the winds and the waves, and they obey Him!"

26 Then they sailed to the region of the Gerasenes,B which is opposite Galilee. 27 When He got out on land, a demon-possessed man from the town met Him. For a long time he had worn no clothes and did not stay in a house but in the tombs. 28 When he saw Jesus, he cried out, fell down before Him, and said in a loud voice, "What do You have to do with me,C Jesus, You Son of the Most High God? I beg You, don't torment me!" 29 For He had commanded the unclean spirit to come out of the man. Many times it had seized him, and though he was guarded, bound by chains and shackles, he would snap the restraints and be driven by the demon into deserted places.

30 "What is your name?" Jesus asked him.

"Legion," he said—because many demons had entered him. 31 And they begged Him not to banish them to the abyss.

32 A large herd of pigs was there, feeding on the hillside. The demons begged Him to permit them to enter the pigs, and He gave them permission. 33 The demons came out of the man and entered the pigs, and the herd rushed down the steep bank into the lake and drowned. 34 When the men who tended them saw what had happened, they ran off and reported it in the town and in the countryside. 35 Then people went out to see what had happened. They came to Jesus and found the man the demons had departed from, sitting at Jesus' feet, dressed and in his right mind. And they were afraid. 36 Meanwhile, the eyewitnesses reported to them how the demon-possessed man was delivered. 37 Then all the people of the Gerasene regionB asked Him to leave them, because they were gripped by great fear. So getting into the boat, He returned.

38 The man from whom the demons had departed kept begging Him to be with Him. But He sent him away and said, 39 "Go back to your home, and tell all that God has done for you." And off he went, proclaiming throughout the town all that Jesus had done for him.

40 When Jesus returned, the crowd welcomed Him, for they were all expecting Him. 41 Just then, a man named Jairus came. He was a leader of the synagogue. He fell down at Jesus' feet and pleaded with Him to come to his house, 42 because he had an only daughter about 12 years old, and she was at death's door.D

While He was going, the crowds were nearly crushing Him. 43 A woman suffering from bleeding for 12 years, who had spent all she had on doctorsE yet could not be healed by any, 44 approached from behind and touched the tassel of His robe. Instantly her bleeding stopped.

45 "Who touched Me?" Jesus asked.

When they all denied it, PeterF said, "Master, the crowds are hemming You in and pressing against You."G

46 "Someone did touch Me," said Jesus. "I know that power has gone out from Me." 47 When the woman saw that she was discovered,H she came trembling and fell down before Him. In the presence of all the people, she declared the reason she had touched Him and how she was instantly cured. 48 "Daughter," He said to her, "your faith has made you well.I Go in peace."

49 While He was still speaking, someone came from the synagogue leader's house, saying, "Your daughter is dead. Don't bother the Teacher anymore."

50 When Jesus heard it, He answered him, "Don't be afraid. Only believe, and she will be made well." 51 After He came to the house, He let no one enter with Him except Peter, John, James, and the child's father and mother. 52 Everyone was crying and mourning for her. But He said, "Stop crying, for she is not dead but asleep."

53 They started laughing at Him, because they knew she was dead. 54 So HeJ took her by the hand and called out, "Child, get up!" 55 Her spirit returned, and she got up at once. Then He gave orders that she be given something to eat. 56 Her parents were astounded, but He instructed them to tell no one what had happened.

9 Summoning the Twelve, He gave them power and authority over all the demons, and power to healK diseases. 2 Then He sent

---

A8:25 Lit Who then is this?   B8:26,37 Other mss read the Gadarenes   C8:28 Lit What to me and to You   D8:42 Lit she was dying   E8:43 Other mss omit who had spent all she had on doctors   F8:45 Other mss add and those with him   G8:45 Other mss add and You say, 'Who touched Me?'   H8:47 Lit she had not escaped notice   I8:48 Or has saved you   J8:54 Other mss add having put them all outside   K9:1 In this passage, different Gk words are translated as heal. In Eng, "to heal" or "to cure" are synonyms with little distinction in meaning. Technically, we do not heal or cure diseases. People are healed or cured from diseases.

them to proclaim the kingdom of God and to heal the sick.

³ "Take nothing for the road," He told them, "no walking stick, no traveling bag, no bread, no money; and don't take an extra shirt. ⁴ Whatever house you enter, stay there and leave from there. ⁵ If they do not welcome you, when you leave that town, shake off the dust from your feet as a testimony against them." ⁶ So they went out and traveled from village to village, proclaiming the good news and healing everywhere.

⁷ Herod the tetrarch heard about everything that was going on. He was perplexed, because some said that John had been raised from the dead, ⁸ some that Elijah had appeared, and others that one of the ancient prophets had risen. ⁹ "I beheaded John," Herod said, "but who is this I hear such things about?" And he wanted to see Him.

¹⁰ When the apostles returned, they reported to Jesus all that they had done. He took them along and withdrew privately to a town called Bethsaida. ¹¹ When the crowds found out, they followed Him. He welcomed them, spoke to them about the kingdom of God, and cured those who needed healing.

¹² Late in the day, the Twelve approached and said to Him, "Send the crowd away, so they can go into the surrounding villages and countryside to find food and lodging, because we are in a deserted place here."

¹³ "You give them something to eat," He told them.

"We have no more than five loaves and two fish," they said, "unless we go and buy food for all these people." ¹⁴ (For about 5,000 men were there.)

Then He told His disciples, "Have them sit down in groups of 50 each." ¹⁵ They did so, and had them all sit down. ¹⁶ Then He took the five loaves and the two fish, and looking up to heaven, He blessed and broke them. He kept giving them to the disciples to set before the crowd. ¹⁷ Everyone ate and was filled. Then they picked up 12 baskets of leftover pieces.

¹⁸ While He was praying in private and His disciples were with Him, He asked them, "Who do the crowds say that I am?"

¹⁹ They answered, "John the Baptist; others, Elijah; still others, that one of the ancient prophets has come back."

²⁰ "But you," He asked them, "who do you say that I am?"

Peter answered, "God's Messiah!"

²¹ But He strictly warned and instructed them to tell this to no one, ²² saying, "The Son of Man must suffer many things and be rejected by the elders, chief priests, and scribes, be killed, and be raised the third day."

²³ Then He said to them all, "If anyone wants to come with Me, he must deny himself, take up his cross daily, and follow Me. ²⁴ For whoever wants to save his life will lose it, but whoever loses his life because of Me will save it. ²⁵ What is a man benefited if he gains the whole world, yet loses or forfeits himself? ²⁶ For whoever is ashamed of Me and My words, the Son of Man will be ashamed of him when He comes in His glory and that of the Father and the holy angels. ²⁷ I tell you the truth: There are some standing here who will not taste death until they see the kingdom of God."

²⁸ About eight days after these words, He took along Peter, John, and James and went up on the mountain to pray. ²⁹ As He was praying, the appearance of His face changed, and His clothes became dazzling white. ³⁰ Suddenly, two men were talking with Him—Moses and Elijah. ³¹ They appeared in glory and were speaking of His death, which He was about to accomplish in Jerusalem. ³² Peter and those with him were in a deep sleep, and when they became fully awake, they saw His glory and the two men who were standing with Him. ³³ As the two men were departing from Him, Peter said to Jesus, "Master, it's good for us to be here! Let us make three tabernacles: one for You, one for Moses, and one for Elijah"—not knowing what he said.

³⁴ While he was saying this, a cloud appeared and overshadowed them. They became afraid as they entered the cloud. ³⁵ Then a voice came from the cloud, saying:

This is My Son, the Chosen One;
listen to Him!

A 9:10 Other mss add deserted place near a   B 9:11 Or healed; in this passage, different Gk words are translated as heal. In Eng, "to heal" or "to cure" are synonyms with little distinction in meaning. Technically, we do not heal or cure diseases. People are healed or cured from diseases.   C 9:12 Lit When the day began to decline   D 9:14 Lit them recline   E 9:17 Lit Then were picked up by them   F 9:19 Lit has risen   G 9:23 Lit come after   H 9:23 Other mss omit daily   I 9:31 Or departure; Gk exodus   J 9:32 Lit were weighed down with sleep   K 9:35 Other mss read the Beloved

³⁶After the voice had spoken, only Jesus was found. They kept silent, and in those days told no one what they had seen.

³⁷The next day, when they came down from the mountain, a large crowd met Him. ³⁸Just then a man from the crowd cried out, "Teacher, I beg You to look at my son, because he's my only child. ³⁹Often a spirit seizes him; suddenly he shrieks, and it throws him into convulsions until he foams at the mouth;ᴬ woundingᴮ him, it hardly ever leaves him. ⁴⁰I begged Your disciples to drive it out, but they couldn't."

⁴¹Jesus replied, "You unbelieving and rebelliousᶜ generation! How long will I be with you and put up with you? Bring your son here."

⁴²As the boy was still approaching, the demon knocked him down and threw him into severe convulsions. But Jesus rebuked the unclean spirit, cured the boy, and gave him back to his father. ⁴³And they were all astonished at the greatness of God.

While everyone was amazed at all the things He was doing, He told His disciples, ⁴⁴"Let these words sink in:ᴰ The Son of Man is about to be betrayed into the hands of men."

⁴⁵But they did not understand this statement; it was concealed from them so that they could not grasp it, and they were afraid to ask Him about it.ᴱ

⁴⁶Then an argument started among them about who would be the greatest of them. ⁴⁷But Jesus, knowing the thoughts of their hearts, took a little child and had him stand next to Him. ⁴⁸He told them, "Whoever welcomesᶠ this little child in My name welcomes Me. And whoever welcomes Me welcomes Him who sent Me. For whoever is least among you—this one is great."

⁴⁹John responded, "Master, we saw someone driving out demons in Your name, and we tried to stop him because he does not follow us."

⁵⁰"Don't stop him," Jesus told him, "because whoever is not against you is for you."ᴳ

⁵¹When the days were coming to a close for Him to be taken up,ᴴ He determinedᴵ to journey to Jerusalem. ⁵²He sent messengers ahead of Him, and on the way they entered a village of the Samaritans to make preparations for Him. ⁵³But they did not welcome Him, because He determined to journey to Jerusalem. ⁵⁴When the disciples James and John saw this, they said, "Lord, do You want us to call down fire from heaven to consume them?"ᴶ

⁵⁵But He turned and rebuked them,ᴷ ⁵⁶and they went to another village.

⁵⁷As they were traveling on the road someone said to Him, "I will follow You wherever You go!"

⁵⁸Jesus told him, "Foxes have dens, and birds of the skyᴸ have nests, but the Son of Man has no place to lay His head." ⁵⁹Then He said to another, "Follow Me."

"Lord," he said, "first let me go bury my father."ᴹ

⁶⁰But He told him, "Let the dead bury their own dead, but you go and spread the news of the kingdom of God."

⁶¹Another also said, "I will follow You, Lord, but first let me go and say good-bye to those at my house."

⁶²But Jesus said to him, "No one who puts his hand to the plow and looks back is fit for the kingdom of God."

10 After this, the Lord appointed 70ᴺ others, and He sent them ahead of Him in pairs to every town and place where He Himself was about to go. ²He told them: "The harvest is abundant, but the workers are few. Therefore, pray to the Lord of the harvest to send out workers into His harvest. ³Now go; I'm sending you out like lambs among wolves. ⁴Don't carry a money-bag, traveling bag, or sandals; don't greet anyone along the road. ⁵Whatever house you enter, first say, 'Peace to this household.' ⁶If a son of peaceᴼ is there, your peace will rest on him; but if not, it will return to you. ⁷Remain in the same house, eating and drinking what they offer, for the worker is worthy of his wages. Don't be moving from house to house. ⁸When you enter any town, and they welcome you, eat the things set before you. ⁹Heal the sick who are there, and tell them, 'The kingdom of God has come near you.' ¹⁰When you enter any town, and they don't welcome you, go out into its streets and say, ¹¹'We are wiping off as a witness against you even the dust of your

ᴬ9:39 Lit convulsions with foam   ᴮ9:39 Or bruising, or mauling   ᶜ9:41 Or corrupt, or perverted, or twisted; Dt 32:5   ᴰ9:44 Lit Put these words in your ears   ᴱ9:45 Lit about this statement   ᶠ9:48 Or receives, throughout the verse   ᴳ9:50 Other mss read against us is for us   ᴴ9:51 His ascension   ᴵ9:51 Lit He stiffened His face to go; Is 50:7   ᴶ9:54 Other mss add as Elijah also did   ᴷ9:55-56 Other mss add and said, "You don't know what kind of spirit you belong to. ³⁶ For the Son of Man did not come to destroy people's lives but to save them."   ᴸ9:58 Wild birds, as opposed to domestic birds   ᴹ9:59 Not necessarily meaning his father was already dead   ᴺ10:1 Other mss read 72   ᴼ10:6 A peaceful person; one open to the message of the kingdom town that clings to our feet. Know this for certain: The kingdom of God has come near.' ¹²I tell you, on that day it will be more tolerable for Sodom than for that town.

¹³"Woe to you, Chorazin! Woe to you, Bethsaida! For if the miracles that were done in you had been done in Tyre and Sidon, they would have repented long ago, sitting in sackcloth and ashes! ¹⁴But it will be more tolerable for Tyre and Sidon at the judgment than for you. ¹⁵And you, Capernaum, will you be exalted to heaven? No, you will go down to Hades! ¹⁶Whoever listens to you listens to Me. Whoever rejects you rejects Me. And whoever rejects Me rejects the One who sent Me."

¹⁷The Seventy[A] returned with joy, saying, "Lord, even the demons submit to us in Your name."

¹⁸He said to them, "I watched Satan fall from heaven like a lightning flash. ¹⁹Look, I have given you the authority to trample on snakes and scorpions and over all the power of the enemy; nothing will ever harm you. ²⁰However, don't rejoice that[B] the spirits submit to you, but rejoice that your names are written in heaven."

²¹In that same hour He[C] rejoiced in the Holy[D] Spirit and said, "I praise[E] You, Father, Lord of heaven and earth, because You have hidden these things from the wise and the learned and have revealed them to infants. Yes, Father, because this was Your good pleasure.[F] ²²All things have[G] been entrusted to Me by My Father. No one knows who the Son is except the Father, and who the Father is except the Son, and anyone to whom the Son desires[H] to reveal Him."

²³Then turning to His disciples He said privately, "The eyes that see the things you see are blessed! ²⁴For I tell you that many prophets and kings wanted to see the things you see yet didn't see them; to hear the things you hear yet didn't hear them."

²⁵Just then an expert in the law stood up to test Him, saying, "Teacher, what must I do to inherit eternal life?"

²⁶"What is written in the law?" He asked him. "How do you read it?"

²⁷He answered:

Love the Lord your God with all your heart, with all your soul, with all your strength, and with all your mind; and your neighbor as yourself.[I]

²⁸"You've answered correctly," He told him. "Do this and you will live."

²⁹But wanting to justify himself, he asked Jesus, "And who is my neighbor?"

³⁰Jesus took up the question and said: "A man was going down from Jerusalem to Jericho and fell into the hands of robbers. They stripped him, beat him up, and fled, leaving him half dead. ³¹A priest happened to be going down that road. When he saw him, he passed by on the other side. ³²In the same way, a Levite, when he arrived at the place and saw him, passed by on the other side. ³³But a Samaritan on his journey came up to him, and when he saw the man, he had compassion. ³⁴He went over to him and bandaged his wounds, pouring on olive oil and wine. Then he put him on his own animal, brought him to an inn, and took care of him. ³⁵The next day[J] he took out two denarii, gave them to the innkeeper, and said, 'Take care of him. When I come back I'll reimburse you for whatever extra you spend.'

³⁶"Which of these three do you think proved to be a neighbor to the man who fell into the hands of the robbers?"

³⁷"The one who showed mercy to him," he said.

Then Jesus told him, "Go and do the same."

³⁸While they were traveling, He entered a village, and a woman named Martha welcomed Him into her home.[K] ³⁹She had a sister named Mary, who also sat at the Lord's[L] feet and was listening to what He said.[M] ⁴⁰But Martha was distracted by her many tasks, and she came up and asked, "Lord, don't You care that my sister has left me to serve alone? So tell her to give me a hand."[N]

⁴¹The Lord[C] answered her, "Martha, Martha, you are worried and upset about many things, ⁴²but one thing is necessary. Mary has made the right choice,[O] and it will not be taken away from her."

11 He was praying in a certain place, and when He finished, one of His disciples said to Him, "Lord, teach us to pray, just as John also taught his disciples."

[2] He said to them, "Whenever you pray, say:

Father,[A]
Your name be honored as holy.
Your kingdom come.[B]
[3] Give us each day our daily bread.[C]
[4] And forgive us our sins,
    for we ourselves also forgive everyone
    in debt to us.[D]
And do not bring us into temptation."[E]

[5] He also said to them: "Suppose one of you[F] has a friend and goes to him at midnight and says to him, 'Friend, lend me three loaves of bread, [6] because a friend of mine on a journey has come to me, and I don't have anything to offer him.'[G] [7] Then he will answer from inside and say, 'Don't bother me! The door is already locked, and my children and I have gone to bed. I can't get up to give you anything.' [8] I tell you, even though he won't get up and give him anything because he is his friend, yet because of his friend's persistence,[H] he will get up and give him as much as he needs.

[9] "So I say to you, keep asking,[I] and it will be given to you. Keep searching,[J] and you will find. Keep knocking,[K] and the door will be opened to you. [10] For everyone who asks receives, and the one who searches finds, and to the one who knocks, the door will be opened. [11] What father among you, his[L] son asks for a fish, will give him a snake instead of a fish? [12] Or if he asks for an egg, will give him a scorpion? [13] If you then, who are evil, know how to give good gifts to your children, how much more will the heavenly Father give[M] the Holy Spirit to those who ask Him?"

[14] Now He was driving out a demon that was mute.[N] When the demon came out, the man who had been mute, spoke, and the crowds were amazed. [15] But some of them said, "He drives out demons by Beelzebul, the ruler of the demons!" [16] And others, as a test, were demanding of Him a sign from heaven.

[17] Knowing their thoughts, He told them: "Every kingdom divided against itself is headed for destruction, and a house divided against itself falls. [18] If Satan also is divided against himself, how will his kingdom stand? For you say I drive out demons by Beelzebul. [19] And if I drive out demons by Beelzebul, who is it your sons[O] drive them out by? For this reason they will be your judges. [20] If I drive out demons by the finger of God, then the kingdom of God has come to you. [21] When a strong man, fully armed, guards his estate, his possessions are secure.[P] [22] But when one stronger than he attacks and overpowers him, he takes from him all his weapons[Q] he trusted in, and divides up his plunder. [23] Anyone who is not with Me is against Me, and anyone who does not gather with Me scatters.

[24] "When an unclean spirit comes out of a man, it roams through waterless places looking for rest, and not finding rest, it then[R] says, 'I'll go back to my house where I came from.' [25] And returning, it finds the house swept and put in order. [26] Then it goes and brings seven other spirits more evil than itself, and they enter and settle down there. As a result, that man's last condition is worse than the first."

[27] As He was saying these things, a woman from the crowd raised her voice and said to Him, "The womb that bore You and the one who nursed You are blessed!"

[28] He said, "Even more, those who hear the word of God and keep it are blessed!"

[29] As the crowds were increasing, He began saying: "This generation is an evil generation. It demands a sign, but no sign will be given to it except the sign of Jonah.[S] [30] For just as Jonah became a sign to the people of Nineveh, so also the Son of Man will be to this generation. [31] The queen of the south will rise up at the judgment with the men of this generation and condemn them, because she came from the ends of the earth to hear the wisdom of Solomon, and look—something greater than Solomon is here! [32] The men of Nineveh will rise up at the judgment with this generation and condemn it, because they repented at Jonah's proclamation, and look—something greater than Jonah is here!

[33] "No one lights a lamp and puts it in the cellar or under a basket,[T] but on a lampstand,

A11:2 Other mss read *Our Father in heaven* B11:2 Other mss add *Your will be done on earth as it is in heaven* C11:3 *Or our bread for tomorrow* D11:4 *Or everyone who wrongs us* E11:4 Other mss add *But deliver us from the evil one* F11:5 Lit *Who of you* G11:6 Lit *I have nothing to set before him* H11:8 *Or annoying persistence, or shamelessness* I11:9 *Or you, ask* J11:9 *Or Search* K11:9 *Or Knock* L11:11 Other mss read *son asks for bread, would give him a stone? Or if he* M11:13 Lit *the Father from heaven will give* N11:14 *A demon that caused the man to be mute* O11:19 *Your exorcists* P11:21 Lit *his possessions are in peace* Q11:22 Gk *panoplia,* the armor and weapons of a foot soldier; Eph 6:11,13 R11:24 Other mss omit *then* S11:29 Other mss add *the prophet* T11:33 Other mss omit *or under a basket* so that those who come in may see its light. [34] Your eye is the lamp of the body. When your eye is good, your whole body is also full of light. But when it is bad, your body is also full of darkness. [35] Take care then, that the light in you is not darkness. [36] If, therefore, your whole body is full of light, with no part of it in darkness, it will be entirely illuminated, as when a lamp shines its light on you."[A]

[37] As He was speaking, a Pharisee asked Him to dine with him. So He went in and reclined at the table. [38] When the Pharisee saw this, he was amazed that He did not first perform the ritual washing[B] before dinner. [39] But the Lord said to him: "Now you Pharisees clean the outside of the cup and dish, but inside you are full of greed and evil. [40] Fools! Didn't He who made the outside make the inside too? [41] But give from what is within to the poor,[C] and then everything is clean for you.

[42] "But woe to you Pharisees! You give a tenth[D] of mint, rue, and every kind of herb, and you bypass[E] justice and love for God.[F] These things you should have done without neglecting the others.

[43] "Woe to you Pharisees! You love the front seat in the synagogues and greetings in the marketplaces.

[44] "Woe to you![G] You are like unmarked graves; the people who walk over them don't know it."

[45] One of the experts in the law answered Him, "Teacher, when you say these things You insult us too."

[46] Then He said: "Woe also to you experts in the law! You load people with burdens that are hard to carry, yet you yourselves don't touch these burdens with one of your fingers.

[47] "Woe to you! You build monuments[H] to the prophets, and your fathers killed them. [48] Therefore, you are witnesses that you approve[I] the deeds of your fathers, for they killed them, and you build their monuments.[J] [49] Because of this, the wisdom of God said, 'I will send them prophets and apostles, and some of them they will kill and persecute,' [50] so that this generation may be held responsible for the blood of all the prophets shed since the foundation of the world[K]— [51] from the blood of Abel to the blood of Zechariah, who perished between the altar and the sanctuary.

"Yes, I tell you, this generation will be held responsible.[L]

[52] "Woe to you experts in the law! You have taken away the key of knowledge! You didn't go in yourselves, and you hindered those who were going in."

[53] When He left there,[M] the scribes and the Pharisees began to oppose Him fiercely and to cross-examine Him about many things; [54] they were lying in wait for Him to trap Him in something He said.[N]

12 In these circumstances,[O] a crowd of many thousands came together, so that they were trampling on one another. He began to say to His disciples first: "Be on your guard against the yeast[P] of the Pharisees, which is hypocrisy. [2] There is nothing covered that won't be uncovered, nothing hidden that won't be made known. [3] Therefore, whatever you have said in the dark will be heard in the light, and what you have whispered in an ear in private rooms will be proclaimed on the housetops.

[4] "And I say to you, My friends, don't fear those who kill the body, and after that can do nothing more. [5] But I will show you the One to fear: Fear Him who has authority to throw people into hell after death. Yes, I say to you, this is the One to fear! [6] Aren't five sparrows sold for two pennies?[Q] Yet not one of them is forgotten in God's sight. [7] Indeed, the hairs of your head are all counted. Don't be afraid; you are worth more than many sparrows!

[8] "And I say to you, anyone who acknowledges Me before men, the Son of Man will also acknowledge him before the angels of God, [9] but whoever denies Me before men will be denied before the angels of God. [10] Anyone who speaks a word against the Son of Man will be forgiven, but the one who blasphemes against the Holy Spirit will not be forgiven. [11] Whenever they bring you before synagogues and rulers and authorities, don't worry about how you should defend yourselves or what you should say. [12] For the Holy Spirit will teach you at that very hour what must be said.

A11:36 Or shines on you with its rays B11:38 Lit He did not first wash C11:41 Or But donate from the heart as charity D11:42 Or a tithe E11:42 Or neglect F11:42 Lit the justice and the love of God G11:44 Other mss read you scribes and Pharisees, hypocrites! H11:47 Or graves I11:48 Lit witnesses and approve J11:48 Other mss omit their monuments K11:50 Lit so that the blood of all . . . world may be required of this generation, L11:51 Lit you, it will be required of this generation M11:53 Other mss read And as He was saying these things to them N11:54 Other mss add so that they might bring charges against Him O12:1 Or Meanwhile, or At this time, or During this period P12:1 Or leaven Q12:6 Lit two assaria; the assarion [sg] was a small copper coin

¹³Someone from the crowd said to Him, "Teacher, tell my brother to divide the inheritance with me."

¹⁴"Friend,"^A He said to him, "who appointed Me a judge or arbitrator over you?" ¹⁵He then told them, "Watch out and be on guard against all greed because one's life is not in the abundance of his possessions."

¹⁶Then He told them a parable: "A rich man's land was very productive. ¹⁷He thought to himself, 'What should I do, since I don't have anywhere to store my crops? ¹⁸I will do this,' he said. 'I'll tear down my barns and build bigger ones and store all my grain and my goods there. ¹⁹Then I'll say to myself, "You^B have many goods stored up for many years. Take it easy; eat, drink, and enjoy yourself."'

²⁰"But God said to him, 'You fool! This very night your life is demanded of you. And the things you have prepared—whose will they be?'

²¹"That's how it is with the one who stores up treasure for himself and is not rich toward God."

²²Then He said to His disciples: "Therefore I tell you, don't worry about your life, what you will eat; or about the body, what you will wear. ²³For life is more than food and the body more than clothing. ²⁴Consider the ravens: They don't sow or reap; they don't have a storeroom or a barn; yet God feeds them. Aren't you worth much more than the birds? ²⁵Can any of you add a cubit to his height^C by worrying? ²⁶If then you're not able to do even a little thing, why worry about the rest?

²⁷"Consider how the wildflowers grow: They don't labor or spin thread. Yet I tell you, not even Solomon in all his splendor was adorned like one of these! ²⁸If that's how God clothes the grass, which is in the field today and is thrown into the furnace tomorrow, how much more will He do for you—you of little faith? ²⁹Don't keep striving for what you should eat and what you should drink, and don't be anxious. ³⁰For the Gentile world eagerly seeks all these things, and your Father knows that you need them.

³¹"But seek His kingdom, and these things will be provided for you. ³²Don't be afraid, little flock, because your Father delights to give you the kingdom. ³³Sell your possessions and give to the poor. Make money-bags for yourselves that won't grow old, an inexhaustible treasure in heaven, where no thief comes near and no moth destroys. ³⁴For where your treasure is, there your heart will be also.

³⁵"Be ready for service^D and have your lamps lit. ³⁶You must be like people waiting for their master to return^E from the wedding banquet so that when he comes and knocks, they can open the door for him at once. ³⁷Those slaves the master will find alert when he comes will be blessed. I assure you: He will get ready,^F have them recline at the table, then come and serve them. ³⁸If he comes in the middle of the night, or even near dawn,^G and finds them alert, those slaves are blessed. ³⁹But know this: If the homeowner had known at what hour the thief was coming, he would not have let his house be broken into. ⁴⁰You also be ready, because the Son of Man is coming at an hour that you do not expect."

⁴¹"Lord," Peter asked, "are You telling this parable to us or to everyone?"

⁴²The Lord said: "Who then is the faithful and sensible manager his master will put in charge of his household servants to give them their allotted food at the proper time? ⁴³That slave whose master finds him working when he comes will be rewarded. ⁴⁴I tell you the truth: He will put him in charge of all his possessions. ⁴⁵But if that slave says in his heart, 'My master is delaying his coming,' and starts to beat the male and female slaves, and to eat and drink and get drunk, ⁴⁶that slave's master will come on a day he does not expect him and at an hour he does not know. He will cut him to pieces^H and assign him a place with the unbelievers.^I ⁴⁷And that slave who knew his master's will and didn't prepare himself or do it^J will be severely beaten. ⁴⁸But the one who did not know and did things deserving of blows will be beaten lightly. Much will be required of everyone who has been given much. And even more will be expected of the one who has been entrusted with more.^K

⁴⁹"I came to bring fire on the earth, and how I wish it were already set ablaze! ⁵⁰But I have a baptism to be baptized with, and how it consumes Me until it is finished! ⁵¹Do you think

^A12:14 Lit Man   ^B12:19 Lit say to your soul, "Soul, you   ^C12:25 Or add one moment to his life-span   ^D12:35 Lit Let your loins be girded; an idiom for tying up loose outer clothing in preparation for action; Ex 12:11   ^E12:36 Lit master, when he should return   ^F12:37 Lit will gird himself   ^G12:38 Lit even in the second or third watch   ^H12:46 Lit him in two   ^I12:46 Or unfaithful, or untrustworthy   ^J12:47 Lit or do toward his will   ^K12:48 Or much that I came here to give peace to the earth? No, I tell you, but rather division! ⁵²From now on, five in one household will be divided: three against two, and two against three.

⁵³ They will be divided, father against son,
son against father,
mother against daughter,
daughter against mother,
mother-in-law against
her daughter-in-law,
and daughter-in-law
against mother-in-law."ᴬ

⁵⁴ He also said to the crowds: "When you see a cloud rising in the west, right away you say, 'A storm is coming,' and so it does. ⁵⁵And when the south wind is blowing, you say, 'It's going to be a scorcher!' and it is. ⁵⁶Hypocrites! You know how to interpret the appearance of the earth and the sky, but why don't you know how to interpret this time?

⁵⁷ "Why don't you judge for yourselves what is right? ⁵⁸As you are going with your adversary to the ruler, make an effort to settle with him on the way. Then he won't drag you before the judge, the judge hand you over to the bailiff, and the bailiff throw you into prison. ⁵⁹I tell you, you will never get out of there until you have paid the last cent."ᴮ

13 At that time, some people came and reported to Him about the Galileans whose blood Pilate had mixed with their sacrifices. ²And Heᶜ responded to them, "Do you think that these Galileans were more sinful than all Galileans because they suffered these things? ³No, I tell you; but unless you repent, you will all perish as well! ⁴Or those 18 that the tower in Siloam fell on and killed—do you think they were more sinful than all the people who live in Jerusalem? ⁵No, I tell you; but unless you repent, you will all perish as well!"

⁶And He told this parable: "A man had a fig tree that was planted in his vineyard. He came looking for fruit on it and found none. ⁷He told the vineyard worker, 'Listen, for three years I have come looking for fruit on this fig tree and haven't found any. Cut it down! Why should it even waste the soil?'

⁸"But he replied to him, 'Sir,ᴰ leave it this year also, until I dig around it and fertilize it.

⁹Perhaps it will bear fruit next year, but if not, you can cut it down.'"

¹⁰As He was teaching in one of the synagogues on the Sabbath, ¹¹a woman was there who had been disabled by a spiritᴱ for over 18 years. She was bent over and could not straighten up at all.ᶠ ¹²When Jesus saw her, He called out to her,ᴳ "Woman, you are free of your disability." ¹³Then He laid His hands on her, and instantly she was restored and began to glorify God.

¹⁴But the leader of the synagogue, indignant because Jesus had healed on the Sabbath, responded by telling the crowd, "There are six days when work should be done; therefore come on those days and be healed and not on the Sabbath day."

¹⁵But the Lord answered him and said, "Hypocrites! Doesn't each one of you untie his ox or donkey from the feeding trough on the Sabbath and lead it to water? ¹⁶Satan has bound this woman, a daughter of Abraham, for 18 years—shouldn't she be untied from this bondage on the Sabbath day?"

¹⁷When He had said these things, all His adversaries were humiliated, but the whole crowd was rejoicing over all the glorious things He was doing.

¹⁸He said, therefore, "What is the kingdom of God like, and what can I compare it to? ¹⁹It's like a mustard seed that a man took and sowed in his garden. It grew and became a tree, and the birds of the sky nested in its branches."

²⁰Again He said, "What can I compare the kingdom of God to? ²¹It's like yeast that a woman took and mixed into 50 poundsᴴ of flour until it spread through the entire mixture."ᴵ

²²He went through one town and village after another, teaching and making His way to Jerusalem. ²³"Lord," someone asked Him, "are there few being saved?"ᴶ

He said to them, ²⁴"Make every effort to enter through the narrow door, because I tell you, many will try to enter and won't be able ²⁵once the homeowner gets up and shuts the door. Then you will standᴷ outside and knock on the door, saying, 'Lord, open up for us!' He will answer you, 'I don't know you or where you're from.' ²⁶Then you will say,ᴸ 'We ate and drank in Your presence, and You taught

---

ᴬ12:53 Mc 7:6   ᴮ12:59 Gk lepton, the smallest and least valuable copper coin in use   ᶜ13:2 Other mss read Jesus   ᴰ13:8 Or Lord   ᴱ13:11 Lit had a spirit of disability   ᶠ13:11 Or straighten up completely   ᴳ13:12 Or He summoned her   ᴴ13:21 Lit 3 sata; about 40 quarts   ᴵ13:21 Or until all of it was leavened   ᴶ13:23 Or are the saved few? (in number); lit are those being saved few?   ᴷ13:25 Lit you will begin to stand   ᴸ13:26 Lit you will begin to say in our streets!' ²⁷But He will say, 'I tell you, I don't know you or where you're from. Get away from Me, all you workers of unrighteousness!' ²⁸There will be weeping and gnashing of teeth in that place, when you see Abraham, Isaac, Jacob, and all the prophets in the kingdom of God, but yourselves thrown out. ²⁹They will come from east and west, from north and south, and recline at the table in the kingdom of God. ³⁰Note this: Some are last who will be first, and some are first who will be last."

³¹At that time some Pharisees came and told Him, "Go, get out of here! Herod wants to kill You!"

³²He said to them, "Go tell that fox, 'Look! I'm driving out demons and performing healings today and tomorrow, and on the third day^A I will complete My work.'^B ³³That I must travel today, tomorrow, and the next day, because it is not possible for a prophet to perish outside of Jerusalem!

³⁴"Jerusalem, Jerusalem! She who kills the prophets and stones those who are sent to her. How often I wanted to gather your children together, as a hen gathers her chicks under her wings, but you were not willing! ³⁵See, your house^C is abandoned to you. And I tell you, you will not see Me until the time comes when you say, '**He who comes in the name of the Lord is the blessed One**'!"^D

14 One Sabbath, when He went to eat^E at the house of one of the leading Pharisees, they were watching Him closely. ²There in front of Him was a man whose body was swollen with fluid.^F ³In response, Jesus asked the law experts and the Pharisees, "Is it lawful to heal on the Sabbath or not?" ⁴But they kept silent. He took the man, healed him, and sent him away. ⁵And to them, He said, "Which of you whose son or ox falls into a well, will not immediately pull him out on the Sabbath day?" ⁶To this they could find no answer.

⁷He told a parable to those who were invited, when He noticed how they would choose the best places for themselves: ⁸"When you are invited to a wedding banquet, don't recline at the best place, because a more distinguished person than you may have been invited by your host.^G ⁹The one who invited both of you may come and say to you, 'Give

your place to this man,' and then in humiliation, you will proceed to take the lowest place.

¹⁰"But when you are invited, go and recline in the lowest place, so that when the one who invited you comes, he will say to you, 'Friend, move up higher.' You will then be honored in the presence of all the other guests. ¹¹For everyone who exalts himself will be humbled, and the one who humbles himself will be exalted."

¹²He also said to the one who had invited Him, "When you give a lunch or a dinner, don't invite your friends, your brothers, your relatives, or your rich neighbors, because they might invite you back, and you would be repaid. ¹³On the contrary, when you host a banquet, invite those who are poor, maimed, lame, or blind. ¹⁴And you will be blessed, because they cannot repay you; for you will be repaid at the resurrection of the righteous."

¹⁵When one of those who reclined at the table with Him heard these things, he said to Him, "The one who will eat bread in the kingdom of God is blessed!"

¹⁶Then He told him: "A man was giving a large banquet and invited many. ¹⁷At the time of the banquet, he sent his slave to tell those who were invited, 'Come, because everything is now ready.'

¹⁸"But without exception^H they all began to make excuses. The first one said to him, 'I have bought a field, and I must go out and see it. I ask you to excuse me.'

¹⁹"Another said, 'I have bought five yoke of oxen, and I'm going to try them out. I ask you to excuse me.'

²⁰"And another said, 'I just got married,^I and therefore I'm unable to come.'

²¹"So the slave came back and reported these things to his master. Then in anger, the master of the house told his slave, 'Go out quickly into the streets and alleys of the city, and bring in here the poor, maimed, blind, and lame!'

²²"'Master,' the slave said, 'what you ordered has been done, and there's still room.'

²³"Then the master told the slave, 'Go out into the highways and lanes and make them come in, so that my house may be filled. ²⁴For I tell you, not one of those men who were invited will enjoy my banquet!'"

^A13:32 Very shortly   ^B13:32 Lit *I will be finished*   ^C13:35 Probably the temple; Jr 12:7; 22:5   ^D13:35 Ps 118:26   ^E14:1 Lit *eat bread; = eat a meal*   ^F14:2 Afflicted with dropsy or edema   ^G14:8 Lit *by him*   ^H14:18 Lit *And from one* (voice)   ^I14:20 Lit *I have married a woman*

²⁵ Now great crowds were traveling with Him. So He turned and said to them: ²⁶ "If anyone comes to Me and does not hate his own father and mother, wife and children, brothers and sisters—yes, and even his own life—he cannot be My disciple. ²⁷ Whoever does not bear his own cross and come after Me cannot be My disciple.

²⁸ "For which of you, wanting to build a tower, doesn't first sit down and calculate the cost to see if he has enough to complete it? ²⁹ Otherwise, after he has laid the foundation and cannot finish it, all the onlookers will begin to make fun of him, ³⁰ saying, 'This man started to build and wasn't able to finish.'

³¹ "Or what king, going to war against another king, will not first sit down and decide if he is able with 10,000 to oppose the one who comes against him with 20,000? ³² If not, while the other is still far off, he sends a delegation and asks for terms of peace. ³³ In the same way, therefore, every one of you who does not say good-bye to^A all his possessions cannot be My disciple.

³⁴ "Now, salt is good, but if salt should lose its taste, how will it be made salty? ³⁵ It isn't fit for the soil or for the manure pile; they throw it out. Anyone who has ears to hear should listen!"

15 All the tax collectors and sinners were approaching to listen to Him. ² And the Pharisees and scribes were complaining, "This man welcomes sinners and eats with them!"

³ So He told them this parable: ⁴ "What man among you, who has 100 sheep and loses one of them, does not leave the 99 in the open field^B and go after the lost one until he finds it? ⁵ When he has found it, he joyfully puts it on his shoulders, ⁶ and coming home, he calls his friends and neighbors together, saying to them, 'Rejoice with me, because I have found my lost sheep!' ⁷ I tell you, in the same way, there will be more joy in heaven over one sinner who repents than over 99 righteous people who don't need repentance.

⁸ "Or what woman who has 10 silver coins,^C if she loses one coin, does not light a lamp, sweep the house, and search carefully until she finds it? ⁹ When she finds it, she calls her women friends and neighbors together, saying, 'Rejoice with me, because I have found

the silver coin I lost!' ¹⁰ I tell you, in the same way, there is joy in the presence of God's angels over one sinner who repents."

¹¹ He also said: "A man had two sons. ¹² The younger of them said to his father, 'Father, give me the share of the estate I have coming to me.' So he distributed the assets^D to them. ¹³ Not many days later, the younger son gathered together all he had and traveled to a distant country, where he squandered his estate in foolish living. ¹⁴ After he had spent everything, a severe famine struck that country, and he had nothing.^E ¹⁵ Then he went to work for^F one of the citizens of that country, who sent him into his fields to feed pigs. ¹⁶ He longed to eat his fill from^G the carob pods^H the pigs were eating, but no one would give him any. ¹⁷ When he came to his senses,^I he said, 'How many of my father's hired hands have more than enough food, and here I am dying of hunger!^J ¹⁸ I'll get up, go to my father, and say to him, Father, I have sinned against heaven and in your sight. ¹⁹ I'm no longer worthy to be called your son. Make me like one of your hired hands.' ²⁰ So he got up and went to his father. But while the son was still a long way off, his father saw him and was filled with compassion. He ran, threw his arms around his neck,^K and kissed him. ²¹ The son said to him, 'Father, I have sinned against heaven and in your sight. I'm no longer worthy to be called your son.'

²² "But the father told his slaves, 'Quick! Bring out the best robe and put it on him; put a ring on his finger^L and sandals on his feet. ²³ Then bring the fattened calf and slaughter it, and let's celebrate with a feast, ²⁴ because this son of mine was dead and is alive again; he was lost and is found!' So they began to celebrate.

²⁵ "Now his older son was in the field; as he came near the house, he heard music and dancing. ²⁶ So he summoned one of the servants and asked what these things meant. ²⁷ 'Your brother is here,' he told him, 'and your father has slaughtered the fattened calf because he has him back safe and sound.'^M

²⁸ "Then he became angry and didn't want to go in. So his father came out and pleaded with him. ²⁹ But he replied to his father, 'Look, I have been slaving many years for you, and

^A14:33 Or does not renounce or leave   ^B15:4 Or the wilderness   ^C15:8 Gk 10 drachmas; a drachma was a silver coin = a denarius   ^D15:12 Or living; lit livelihood   ^E15:14 Lit and he began to be in need   ^F15:15 Lit went and joined with   ^G15:16 Other mss read to fill his stomach with   ^H15:16 Seed casings of a tree used as food for cattle, pigs, and sometimes the poor   ^I15:17 Lit to himself   ^J15:17 Or dying in the famine; v. 14   ^K15:20 Lit He ran, fell on his neck   ^L15:22 Lit hand   ^M15:27 Lit him back healthy

I have never disobeyed your orders, yet you never gave me a young goat so I could celebrate with my friends. ³⁰But when this son of yours came, who has devoured your assets^A with prostitutes, you slaughtered the fattened calf for him.'

³¹"'Son,'^B he said, 'you are always with me, and everything I have is yours. ³²But we had to celebrate and rejoice, because this brother of yours was dead and is alive again; he was lost and is found.'"

16 He also said to the disciples: "There was a rich man who received an accusation that his manager was squandering his possessions. ²So he called the manager in and asked, 'What is this I hear about you? Give an account of your management, because you can no longer be my manager.'

³"Then the manager said to himself, 'What should I do, since my master is taking the management away from me? I'm not strong enough to dig; I'm ashamed to beg. ⁴I know what I'll do so that when I'm removed from management, people will welcome me into their homes.'

⁵"So he summoned each one of his master's debtors. 'How much do you owe my master?' he asked the first one.

⁶"'A hundred measures of olive oil,' he said.

"'Take your invoice,' he told him, 'sit down quickly, and write 50.'

⁷"Next he asked another, 'How much do you owe?'

"'A hundred measures of wheat,' he said.

"'Take your invoice,' he told him, 'and write 80.'

⁸"The master praised the unrighteous manager because he had acted astutely. For the sons of this age are more astute than the sons of light in dealing with their own people.^C ⁹And I tell you, make friends for yourselves by means of the unrighteous money so that when it fails,^D they may welcome you into eternal dwellings. ¹⁰Whoever is faithful in very little is also faithful in much, and whoever is unrighteous in very little is also unrighteous in much. ¹¹So if you have not been faithful with the unrighteous money, who will trust you with what is genuine? ¹²And if you have not been faithful with what belongs to someone else, who will give you what is your own? ¹³No household

slave can be the slave of two masters, since either he will hate one and love the other, or he will be devoted to one and despise the other. You can't be slaves to both God and money."

¹⁴The Pharisees, who were lovers of money, were listening to all these things and scoffing at Him. ¹⁵And He told them: "You are the ones who justify yourselves in the sight of others, but God knows your hearts. For what is highly admired by people is revolting in God's sight.

¹⁶"The Law and the Prophets were^E until John; since then, the good news of the kingdom of God has been proclaimed, and everyone is strongly urged to enter it.^F ¹⁷But it is easier for heaven and earth to pass away than for one stroke of a letter in the law to drop out.

¹⁸"Everyone who divorces his wife and marries another woman commits adultery, and everyone who marries a woman divorced from her husband commits adultery.

¹⁹"There was a rich man who would dress in purple and fine linen, feasting lavishly every day. ²⁰But a poor man named Lazarus, covered with sores, was left at his gate. ²¹He longed to be filled with what fell from the rich man's table, but instead the dogs would come and lick his sores. ²²One day the poor man died and was carried away by the angels to Abraham's side.^G The rich man also died and was buried. ²³And being in torment in Hades, he looked up and saw Abraham a long way off, with Lazarus at his side. ²⁴'Father Abraham!' he called out, 'Have mercy on me and send Lazarus to dip the tip of his finger in water and cool my tongue, because I am in agony in this flame!'

²⁵"'Son,'^H Abraham said, 'remember that during your life you received your good things, just as Lazarus received bad things, but now he is comforted here, while you are in agony. ²⁶Besides all this, a great chasm has been fixed between us and you, so that those who want to pass over from here to you cannot; neither can those from there cross over to us.'

²⁷"'Father,' he said, 'then I beg you to send him to my father's house— ²⁸because I have five brothers—to warn them, so they won't also come to this place of torment.'

²⁹"But Abraham said, 'They have Moses and the prophets; they should listen to them.'

³⁰ "'No, father Abraham,' he said. 'But if someone from the dead goes to them, they will repent.'

³¹ "But he told him, 'If they don't listen to Moses and the prophets, they will not be persuaded if someone rises from the dead.'"

17

He said to His disciples, "Offenses^A will certainly come,^B but woe to the one they come through! ² It would be better for him if a millstone^C were hung around his neck and he were thrown into the sea than for him to cause one of these little ones to stumble. ³ Be on your guard. If your brother sins,^D rebuke him, and if he repents, forgive him. ⁴ And if he sins against you seven times in a day, and comes back to you seven times, saying, 'I repent,' you must forgive him."

⁵ The apostles said to the Lord, "Increase our faith."

⁶ "If you have faith the size of^E a mustard seed," the Lord said, "you can say to this mulberry tree, 'Be uprooted and planted in the sea,' and it will obey you.

⁷ "Which one of you having a slave tending sheep or plowing will say to him when he comes in from the field, 'Come at once and sit down to eat'? ⁸ Instead, will he not tell him, 'Prepare something for me to eat, get ready,^F and serve me while I eat and drink; later you can eat and drink'? ⁹ Does he thank that slave because he did what was commanded?^G ¹⁰ In the same way, when you have done all that you were commanded, you should say, 'We are good-for-nothing slaves; we've only done our duty.'"

¹¹ While traveling to Jerusalem, He passed between^H Samaria and Galilee. ¹² As He entered a village, 10 men with serious skin diseases met Him. They stood at a distance ¹³ and raised their voices, saying, "Jesus, Master, have mercy on us!"

¹⁴ When He saw them, He told them, "Go and show yourselves to the priests." And while they were going, they were healed.^I

¹⁵ But one of them, seeing that he was healed, returned and, with a loud voice, gave glory to God. ¹⁶ He fell facedown at His feet, thanking Him. And he was a Samaritan.

¹⁷ Then Jesus said, "Were not 10 cleansed? Where are the nine? ¹⁸ Didn't any return^J to

give glory to God except this foreigner?" ¹⁹ And He told him, "Get up and go on your way. Your faith has made you well."^K

²⁰ Being asked by the Pharisees when the kingdom of God will come, He answered them, "The kingdom of God is not coming with something observable; ²¹ no one will say,^L 'Look here!' or 'There!' For you see, the kingdom of God is among you."

²² Then He told the disciples: "The days are coming when you will long to see one of the days of the Son of Man, but you won't see it. ²³ They will say to you, 'Look there!' or 'Look here!' Don't follow or run after them. ²⁴ For as the lightning flashes from horizon to horizon and lights up the sky, so the Son of Man will be in His day. ²⁵ But first He must suffer many things and be rejected by this generation.

²⁶ "Just as it was in the days of Noah, so it will be in the days of the Son of Man: ²⁷ People went on eating, drinking, marrying and giving in marriage until the day Noah boarded the ark, and the flood came and destroyed them all. ²⁸ It will be the same as it was in the days of Lot: People went on eating, drinking, buying, selling, planting, building. ²⁹ But on the day Lot left Sodom, fire and sulfur rained from heaven and destroyed them all. ³⁰ It will be like that on the day the Son of Man is revealed. ³¹ On that day, a man on the housetop, whose belongings are in the house, must not come down to get them. Likewise the man who is in the field must not turn back. ³² Remember Lot's wife! ³³ Whoever tries to make his life secure^M,N will lose it, and whoever loses his life will preserve it. ³⁴ I tell you, on that night two will be in one bed: One will be taken and the other will be left. ³⁵ Two women will be grinding grain together: One will be taken and the other left. [³⁶ Two will be in a field: One will be taken, and the other will be left.]^O

³⁷ "Where, Lord?" they asked Him.

He said to them, "Where the corpse is, there also the vultures will be gathered."

18

He then told them a parable on the need for them to pray always and not become discouraged: ² "There was a judge in a certain town who didn't fear God or respect man. ³ And a widow in that town kept coming to him, saying, 'Give me justice against my adversary.'

---

^A17:1 Or Traps, or Bait-sticks, or Causes of stumbling, or Causes of sin   ^B17:1 Lit It is impossible for offenses not to come   ^C17:2 Large stone used for grinding grains into flour   ^D17:3 Other mss add against you   ^E17:6 Lit faith like   ^F17:8 Or eat, gird yourself; lit eat, tuck in your robe   ^G17:9 Other mss add I don't think so   ^H17:11 Or through the middle of   ^I17:14 Lit cleansed   ^J17:18 Lit Were they not found returning   ^K17:19 Or faith has saved you   ^L17:21 Lit they will not say   ^M17:33 Other mss read to save his life   ^N17:33 Or tries to retain his life   ^O17:36 Other mss omit bracketed text

[4] "For a while he was unwilling, but later he said to himself, 'Even though I don't fear God or respect man, [5] yet because this widow keeps pestering me,[A] I will give her justice, so she doesn't wear me out[B] by her persistent coming.'"

[6] Then the Lord said, "Listen to what the unjust judge says. [7] Will not God grant justice to His elect who cry out to Him day and night? Will He delay to help them? [8] I tell you that He will swiftly grant them justice. Nevertheless, when the Son of Man comes, will He find that faith[D] on earth?"

[9] He also told this parable to some who trusted in themselves that they were righteous and looked down on everyone else: [10] "Two men went up to the temple complex to pray, one a Pharisee and the other a tax collector. [11] The Pharisee took his stand[E] and was praying like this: 'God, I thank You that I'm not like other people[F]—greedy, unrighteous, adulterers, or even like this tax collector. [12] I fast twice a week; I give a tenth[G] of everything I get.'

[13] "But the tax collector, standing far off, would not even raise his eyes to heaven but kept striking his chest[H] and saying, 'God, turn Your wrath from me[I]—a sinner!' [14] I tell you, this one went down to his house justified rather than the other; because everyone who exalts himself will be humbled, but the one who humbles himself will be exalted."

[15] Some people were even bringing infants to Him so He might touch them, but when the disciples saw it, they rebuked them. [16] Jesus, however, invited them: "Let the little children come to Me, and don't stop them, because the kingdom of God belongs to such as these. [17] I assure you: Whoever does not welcome the kingdom of God like a little child will never enter it."

[18] A ruler asked Him, "Good Teacher, what must I do to inherit eternal life?"

[19] "Why do you call Me good?" Jesus asked him. "No one is good but One—God. [20] You know the commandments:

Do not commit adultery;
do not murder;
do not steal;
do not bear false witness;
honor your father and mother."[J]

[21] "I have kept all these from my youth," he said.

[22] When Jesus heard this, He told him, "You still lack one thing: Sell all that you have and distribute it to the poor, and you will have treasure in heaven. Then come, follow Me."

[23] After he heard this, he became extremely sad, because he was very rich.

[24] Seeing that he became sad,[K] Jesus said, "How hard it is for those who have wealth to enter the kingdom of God! [25] For it is easier for a camel to go through the eye of a needle than for a rich person to enter the kingdom of God."

[26] Those who heard this asked, "Then who can be saved?"

[27] He replied, "What is impossible with men is possible with God."

[28] Then Peter said, "Look, we have left what we had and followed You."

[29] So He said to them, "I assure you: There is no one who has left a house, wife or brothers, parents or children because of the kingdom of God, [30] who will not receive many times more at this time, and eternal life in the age to come."

[31] Then He took the Twelve aside and told them, "Listen! We are going up to Jerusalem. Everything that is written through the prophets about the Son of Man will be accomplished. [32] For He will be handed over to the Gentiles, and He will be mocked, insulted, spit on; [33] and after they flog Him, they will kill Him, and He will rise on the third day."

[34] They understood none of these things. This saying[L] was hidden from them, and they did not grasp what was said.

[35] As He drew near Jericho, a blind man was sitting by the road begging. [36] Hearing a crowd passing by, he inquired what this meant. [37] "Jesus the Nazarene is passing by," they told him.

[38] So he called out, "Jesus, Son of David, have mercy on me!" [39] Then those in front told him to keep quiet,[M] but he kept crying out all the more, "Son of David, have mercy on me!"

[40] Jesus stopped and commanded that he be brought to Him. When he drew near, He asked him, [41] "What do you want Me to do for you?"

"Lord," he said, "I want to see!"

[42] "Receive your sight!" Jesus told him. "Your faith has healed you."[N] [43] Instantly he could

---

A18:5 Lit widow causes me trouble   B18:5 Or doesn't give me a black eye, or doesn't ruin my reputation   C18:7 Or Will He put up with them?
D18:8 Or faith, or that kind of faith, or any faith, or the faith, or faithfulness; the faith that persists in prayer for God's vindication   E18:11 Or
Pharisee stood by himself   F18:11 Or like the rest of men   G18:12 Or give tithes   H18:13 = mourning   I18:13 Lit God, be propitious to me; = May
Your wrath be turned aside by the sacrifice   J18:20 Ex 20:12-16; Dt 5:16-20   K18:24 Other mss omit he became sad   L18:34 The meaning of
the saying   M18:39 Or those in front rebuked him   N18:42 Or has saved you

see, and he began to follow Him, glorifying God. All the people, when they saw it, gave praise to God.

19 He entered Jericho and was passing through. ²There was a man named Zacchaeus who was a chief tax collector, and he was rich. ³He was trying to see who Jesus was, but he was not able because of the crowd, since he was a short man. ⁴So running ahead, he climbed up a sycamore tree to see Jesus, since He was about to pass that way. ⁵When Jesus came to the place, He looked up and said to him, "Zacchaeus, hurry and come down because today I must stay at your house."

⁶So he quickly came down and welcomed Him joyfully. ⁷All who saw it began to complain, "He's gone to lodge with a sinful man!"

⁸But Zacchaeus stood there and said to the Lord, "Look, I'll giveᴬ half of my possessions to the poor, Lord! And if I have extorted anything from anyone, I'll payᴮ back four times as much!"

⁹"Today salvation has come to this house," Jesus told him, "because he too is a son of Abraham. ¹⁰For the Son of Man has come to seek and to save the lost."ᶜ

¹¹As they were listening to this, He went on to tell a parable because He was near Jerusalem, and they thought the kingdom of God was going to appear right away.

¹²Therefore He said: "A nobleman traveled to a far country to receive for himself authority to be kingᴰ and then return. ¹³He called 10 of his slaves, gave them 10 minas,ᴱ and told them, 'Engage in business until I come back.'

¹⁴"But his subjects hated him and sent a delegation after him, saying, 'We don't want this man to rule over us!'

¹⁵"At his return, having received the authority to be king,ᶠ he summoned those slaves he had given the money to, so he could find out how much they had made in business. ¹⁶The first came forward and said, 'Master, your mina has earned 10 more minas.'

¹⁷"'Well done, goodᴳ slave!' he told him. 'Because you have been faithful in a very small matter, have authority over 10 towns.'

¹⁸"The second came and said, 'Master, your mina has made five minas.'

¹⁹"So he said to him, 'You will be over five towns.'

²⁰"And another came and said, 'Master, here is your mina. I have kept it hidden away in a cloth ²¹because I was afraid of you, for you're a tough man: you collect what you didn't deposit and reap what you didn't sow.'

²²"He told him, 'I will judge you by what you have said,ᴴ you evil slave! If you knew I was a tough man, collecting what I didn't deposit and reaping what I didn't sow, ²³why didn't you put my money in the bank? And when I returned, I would have collected it with interest!' ²⁴So he said to those standing there, 'Take the mina away from him and give it to the one who has 10 minas.'

²⁵"But they said to him, 'Master, he has 10 minas.'

²⁶"'I tell you, that to everyone who has, more will be given; and from the one who does not have, even what he does have will be taken away. ²⁷But bring here these enemies of mine, who did not want me to rule over them, and slaughterⁱ them in my presence.'"

²⁸When He had said these things, He went on ahead, going up to Jerusalem. ²⁹As He approached Bethphage and Bethany, at the place called the Mount of Olives, He sent two of the disciples ³⁰and said, "Go into the village ahead of you. As you enter it, you will find a young donkey tied there, on which no one has ever sat. Untie it and bring it here. ³¹If anyone asks you, 'Why are you untying it?' say this: 'The Lord needs it.'"

³²So those who were sent left and found it just as He had told them. ³³As they were untying the young donkey, its owners said to them, "Why are you untying the donkey?"

³⁴"The Lord needs it," they said. ³⁵Then they brought it to Jesus, and after throwing their robes on the donkey, they helped Jesus get on it. ³⁶As He was going along, they were spreading their robes on the road. ³⁷Now He came near the path down the Mount of Olives, and the whole crowd of the disciples began to praise God joyfully with a loud voice for all the miracles they had seen:

³⁸　**The King who comes
　　in the name of the Lord**ᴶᴷ
　　is the blessed One.
　　Peace in heaven
　　and glory in the highest heaven!

A19:8 Or I give　**B**19:8 Or I pay　**C**19:10 Or save what was lost　**D**19:12 Lit to receive for himself a kingdom or sovereignty　**E**19:13 = Gk coin worth 100 drachmas or about 100 days' wages　**F**19:15 Lit to receive for himself a kingdom or sovereignty　**G**19:17 Or capable　**H**19:22 Lit you out of your mouth　**I**19:27 Or execute　**J**19:38 Luke substitutes "the King" for "He" in Ps 118:26.　**K**19:38 Ps 118:26

³⁹ Some of the Pharisees from the crowd told Him, "Teacher, rebuke Your disciples."

⁴⁰ He answered, "I tell you, if they were to keep silent, the stones would cry out!"

⁴¹ As He approached and saw the city, He wept over it, ⁴² saying, "If you knew this day what would bring peace—but now it is hidden from your eyes. ⁴³ For the days will come on you when your enemies will build an embankment against you, surround you, and hem you in on every side. ⁴⁴ They will crush you and your children within you to the ground, and they will not leave one stone on another in you, because you did not recognize the time of your visitation."

⁴⁵ He went into the temple complex and began to throw out those who were selling,ᴬ ⁴⁶ and He said, "It is written, My house is a house of prayer, but you have made it a den of thieves!"ᴮ

⁴⁷ Every day He was teaching in the temple complex. The chief priests, the scribes, and the leaders of the people were looking for a way to destroy Him, ⁴⁸ but they could not find a way to do it, because all the people were captivated by what they heard.ᶜ

20 One dayᴰ as He was teaching the people in the temple complex and proclaiming the good news, the chief priests and the scribes, with the elders, came up ² and said to Him: "Tell us, by what authority are You doing these things? Who is it who gave You this authority?"

³ He answered them, "I will also ask you a question. Tell Me, ⁴ was the baptism of John from heaven or from men?"

⁵ They discussed it among themselves: "If we say, 'From heaven,' He will say, 'Why didn't you believe him?' ⁶ But if we say, 'From men,' all the people will stone us, because they are convinced that John was a prophet."

⁷ So they answered that they did not know its origin.ᴱ

⁸ And Jesus said to them, "Neither will I tell you by what authority I do these things."

⁹ Then He began to tell the people this parable: "A man planted a vineyard, leased it to tenant farmers, and went away for a long time. ¹⁰ At harvest time he sent a slave to the farmers so that they might give him some fruit

from the vineyard. But the farmers beat him and sent him away empty-handed. ¹¹ He sent yet another slave, but they beat that one too, treated him shamefully, and sent him away empty-handed. ¹² And he sent yet a third, but they wounded this one too and threw him out.

¹³ "Then the owner of the vineyard said, 'What should I do? I will send my beloved son. Perhapsᶠ they will respect him.'

¹⁴ "But when the tenant farmers saw him, they discussed it among themselves and said, 'This is the heir. Let's kill him, so the inheritance will be ours!' ¹⁵ So they threw him out of the vineyard and killed him.

"Therefore, what will the owner of the vineyard do to them? ¹⁶ He will come and destroy those farmers and give the vineyard to others."

But when they heard this they said, "No—never!"

¹⁷ But He looked at them and said, "Then what is the meaning of this Scripture:ᴳ

> The stone that the builders rejected—
> this has become the cornerstone?ᴴᴵ

¹⁸ Everyone who falls on that stone will be broken to pieces, and if it falls on anyone, it will grind him to powder!"

¹⁹ Then the scribes and the chief priests looked for a way to get their hands on Him that very hour, because they knew He had told this parable against them, but they feared the people.

²⁰ Theyᴶ watched closely and sent spies who pretended to be righteous,ᴷ so they could catch Him in what He said,ᴸ to hand Him over to the governor's rule and authority. ²¹ They questioned Him, "Teacher, we know that You speak and teach correctly, and You don't show partiality,ᴹ but teach truthfully the way of God. ²² Is it lawful for us to pay taxes to Caesar or not?"

²³ But detecting their craftiness, He said to them,ᴺ ²⁴ "Show Me a denarius. Whose image and inscription does it have?"

"Caesar's," they said.

²⁵ "Well then," He told them, "give back to Caesar the things that are Caesar's and to God the things that are God's."

ᴬ19:45 Other mss add and buying in it   ᴮ19:46 Is 56:7; Jr 7:11   ᶜ19:48 Lit people hung on what they heard   ᴰ20:1 Lit It happened on one of the days   ᴱ20:7 Or know where it was from   ᶠ20:13 Other mss add when they see him   ᴳ20:17 Lit What then is this that is written   ᴴ20:17 Lit the head of the corner   ᴵ20:17 Ps 118:22   ᴶ20:20 The scribes and chief priests of v. 19   ᴷ20:20 Or upright; that is, loyal to God's law   ᴸ20:20 Lit catch Him in a word   ᴹ20:21 Lit You don't receive a face   ᴺ20:23 Other mss add "Why are you testing Me?

²⁶They were not able to catch Him in what He saidᴬ in public,ᴮ and being amazed at His answer, they became silent.

²⁷Some of the Sadducees, who say there is no resurrection, came up and questioned Him: ²⁸"Teacher, Moses wrote for us that **if a man's brother** has a wife, and **dies childless, his brother should take the wife and produce offspring for his brother.**ᶜ ²⁹Now there were seven brothers. The first took a wife and died without children. ³⁰Also the secondᴰ ³¹and the third took her. In the same way, all seven died and left no children. ³²Finally, the woman died too. ³³In the resurrection, therefore, whose wife will the woman be? For all seven had married her."ᴱ

³⁴Jesus told them, "The sons of this age marry and are given in marriage. ³⁵But those who are counted worthy to take part in that age and in the resurrection from the dead neither marry nor are given in marriage. ³⁶For they cannot die anymore, because they are like angels and are sons of God, since they are sons of the resurrection. ³⁷Moses even indicated in the passage about the burning bush that the dead are raised, where he calls the Lord the **God of Abraham and the God of Isaac and the God of Jacob.**ᶠ ³⁸He is not God of the dead but of the living, because all are living toᴳ Him."

³⁹Some of the scribes answered, "Teacher, You have spoken well." ⁴⁰And they no longer dared to ask Him anything.

⁴¹Then He said to them, "How can they say that the Messiah is the Son of David? ⁴²For David himself says in the Book of Psalms:

> The Lord declared to my Lord,
> 'Sit at My right hand
> 43   until I make Your enemies
>   Your footstool.'ᴴ

⁴⁴David calls Him 'Lord'; how then can the Messiah be his Son?"

⁴⁵While all the people were listening, He said to His disciples, ⁴⁶"Beware of the scribes, who want to go around in long robes and who love greetings in the marketplaces, the front seats in the synagogues, and the places of honor at banquets. ⁴⁷They devour widows'

houses and say long prayers just for show. These will receive greater punishment."ᴵ

21 He looked up and saw the rich dropping their offerings into the temple treasury. ²He also saw a poor widow dropping in two tiny coins.ᴶ ³⁴"I tell you the truth," He said. "This poor widow has put in more than all of them. ⁴For all these people have put in gifts out of their surplus, but she out of her poverty has put in all she had to live on."

⁵As some were talking about the temple complex, how it was adorned with beautiful stones and gifts dedicated to God,ᴷ He said, ⁶"These things that you see—the days will come when not one stone will be left on another that will not be thrown down!"

⁷"Teacher," they asked Him, "so when will these things be? And what will be the sign when these things are about to take place?"

⁸Then He said, "Watch out that you are not deceived. For many will come in My name, saying, 'I am He,' and, 'The time is near.' Don't follow them. ⁹When you hear of wars and rebellions,ᴸ don't be alarmed. Indeed, these things must take place first, but the end won't come right away."

¹⁰Then He told them: "Nation will be raised up against nation, and kingdom against kingdom. ¹¹There will be violent earthquakes, and famines and plagues in various places, and there will be terrifying sights and great signs from heaven. ¹²But before all these things, they will lay their hands on you and persecute you. They will hand you over to the synagogues and prisons, and you will be brought before kings and governors because of My name. ¹³It will lead to an opportunity for you to witness.ᴹ ¹⁴Therefore make up your mindsᴺ not to prepare your defense ahead of time, ¹⁵for I will give you such wordsᴼ and a wisdom that none of your adversaries will be able to resist or contradict. ¹⁶You will even be betrayed by parents, brothers, relatives, and friends. They will kill some of you. ¹⁷You will be hated by everyone because of My name, ¹⁸but not a hair of your head will be lost. ¹⁹By your endurance gainᴾ your lives.

²⁰"When you see Jerusalem surrounded by armies, then recognize that its desolation has come near. ²¹Then those in Judea must flee

---

ᴬ20:26 Lit catch Him in a word ᴮ20:26 Lit in front of the people ᶜ20:28 Dt 25:5 ᴰ20:30 Other mss add took her as wife, and he died without children ᴱ20:33 Lit had her as wife ᶠ20:37 Ex 3:6,15 ᴳ20:38 Or with ᴴ20:42-43 Ps 110:1 ᴵ20:47 Or judgment ᴶ21:2 Lit two lepta; the lepton was the smallest and least valuable Gk coin in use. ᴷ21:5 Gifts given to the temple in fulfillment of vows to God ᴸ21:9 Or insurrections, or revolutions ᴹ21:13 Lit lead to a testimony for you ᴺ21:14 Lit Therefore place (determine) in your hearts ᴼ21:15 Lit you a mouth ᴾ21:19 Other mss read endurance you will gain to the mountains! Those inside the city^A must leave it, and those who are in the country must not enter it, 22because these are days of vengeance to fulfill all the things that are written. 23Woe to pregnant women and nursing mothers in those days, for there will be great distress in the land^B and wrath against this people. 24They will fall by the edge of the sword and be led captive into all the nations, and Jerusalem will be trampled by the Gentiles^C until the times of the Gentiles are fulfilled.

25"Then there will be signs in the sun, moon, and stars; and there will be anguish on the earth among nations bewildered by the roaring sea and waves. 26People will faint from fear and expectation of the things that are coming on the world, because the celestial powers will be shaken. 27Then they will see the Son of Man coming in a cloud with power and great glory. 28But when these things begin to take place, stand up and lift up your heads, because your redemption is near!"

29Then He told them a parable: "Look at the fig tree, and all the trees. 30As soon as they put out leaves you can see for yourselves and recognize that summer is already near. 31In the same way, when you see these things happening, recognize^D that the kingdom of God is near. 32I assure you: This generation will certainly not pass away until all things take place. 33Heaven and earth will pass away, but My words will never pass away.

34"Be on your guard, so that your minds are not dulled^E from carousing,^F drunkenness, and worries of life, or that day will come on you unexpectedly 35like a trap. For it will come on all who live on the face of the whole earth. 36But be alert at all times, praying that you may have strength^G to escape all these things that are going to take place and to stand before the Son of Man."

37During the day, He was teaching in the temple complex, but in the evening He would go out and spend the night on what is called the Mount of Olives. 38Then all the people would come early in the morning to hear Him in the temple complex.

22 The Festival of Unleavened Bread, which is called Passover, was drawing near. 2The chief priests and the scribes were looking for a way to put Him to death, because they were afraid of the people.

3Then Satan entered Judas, called Iscariot, who was numbered among the Twelve. 4He went away and discussed with the chief priests and temple police how he could hand Him over to them. 5They were glad and agreed to give him silver.^H 6So he accepted the offer and started looking for a good opportunity to betray Him to them when the crowd was not present.

7Then the Day of Unleavened Bread came when the Passover lamb had to be sacrificed. 8Jesus sent Peter and John, saying, "Go and prepare the Passover meal for us, so we can eat it."

9"Where do You want us to prepare it?" they asked Him.

10"Listen," He said to them, "when you've entered the city, a man carrying a water jug will meet you. Follow him into the house he enters. 11Tell the owner of the house, 'The Teacher asks you, "Where is the guest room where I can eat the Passover with My disciples?"' 12Then he will show you a large, furnished room upstairs. Make the preparations there."

13So they went and found it just as He had told them, and they prepared the Passover.

14When the hour came, He reclined at the table, and the apostles with Him. 15Then He said to them, "I have fervently desired to eat this Passover with you before I suffer. 16For I tell you, I will not eat it again^I until it is fulfilled in the kingdom of God." 17Then He took a cup, and after giving thanks, He said, "Take this and share it among yourselves. 18For I tell you, from now on I will not drink of the fruit of the vine until the kingdom of God comes."

19And He took bread, gave thanks, broke it, gave it to them, and said, "This is My body, which is given for you. Do this in remembrance of Me."

20In the same way He also took the cup after supper and said, "This cup is the new covenant established by My blood; it is shed for you.^J 21But look, the hand of the one betraying Me is at the table with Me! 22For the Son of Man will go away as it has been determined, but woe to that man by whom He is betrayed!"

---

^A21:21 Lit inside her ^B21:23 Or the earth ^C21:24 Or nations ^D21:31 Or you know ^E21:34 Lit your hearts are not weighed down ^F21:34 Or hangovers ^G21:36 Other mss read you may be counted worthy ^H22:5 Or money; Mt 26:15 specifies 30 pieces of silver; Zch 11:12-13 ^I22:16 Other mss omit again ^J22:19-20 Other mss omit which is given for you (v. 19) through the end of v. 20

²³So they began to argue among themselves which of them it could be who was going to do this thing.

²⁴Then a dispute also arose among them about who should be considered the greatest. ²⁵But He said to them, "The kings of the Gentiles dominate them, and those who have authority over them are called^A 'Benefactors.'^B ²⁶But it must not be like that among you. On the contrary, whoever is greatest among you must become like the youngest, and whoever leads, like the one serving. ²⁷For who is greater, the one at the table or the one serving? Isn't it the one at the table? But I am among you as the One who serves. ²⁸You are the ones who stood by Me in My trials. ²⁹I bestow on you a kingdom, just as My Father bestowed one on Me, ³⁰so that you may eat and drink at My table in My kingdom. And you will sit on thrones judging the 12 tribes of Israel.

³¹"Simon, Simon,^C look out! Satan has asked to sift you^D like wheat. ³²But I have prayed for you^E that your faith may not fail. And you, when you have turned back, strengthen your brothers."

³³"Lord," he told Him, "I'm ready to go with You both to prison and to death!"

³⁴"I tell you, Peter," He said, "the rooster will not crow today until^F you deny three times that you know Me!"

³⁵He also said to them, "When I sent you out without money-bag, traveling bag, or sandals, did you lack anything?"

"Not a thing," they said.

³⁶Then He said to them, "But now, whoever has a money-bag should take it, and also a traveling bag. And whoever doesn't have a sword should sell his robe and buy one. ³⁷For I tell you, what is written must be fulfilled in Me: And He was counted among the outlaws.^G Yes, what is written about Me is coming to its fulfillment!"

³⁸"Lord," they said, "look, here are two swords."

"Enough of that!"^H He told them.

³⁹He went out and made His way as usual to the Mount of Olives, and the disciples followed Him. ⁴⁰When He reached the place, He told them, "Pray that you may not enter into temptation." ⁴¹Then He withdrew from them about a stone's throw, knelt down, and began to pray, ⁴²"Father, if You are willing, take this cup away from Me—nevertheless, not My will, but Yours, be done."

[⁴³Then an angel from heaven appeared to Him, strengthening Him. ⁴⁴Being in anguish, He prayed more fervently, and His sweat became like drops of blood falling to the ground.]^I ⁴⁵When He got up from prayer and came to the disciples, He found them sleeping, exhausted from their grief.^J ⁴⁶"Why are you sleeping?" He asked them. "Get up and pray, so that you won't enter into temptation."

⁴⁷While He was still speaking, suddenly a mob was there, and one of the Twelve named Judas was leading them. He came near Jesus to kiss Him, ⁴⁸but Jesus said to him, "Judas, are you betraying the Son of Man with a kiss?"

⁴⁹When those around Him saw what was going to happen, they asked, "Lord, should we strike with the sword?" ⁵⁰Then one of them struck the high priest's slave and cut off his right ear.

⁵¹But Jesus responded, "No more of this!"^K And touching his ear, He healed him. ⁵²Then Jesus said to the chief priests, temple police, and the elders who had come for Him, "Have you come out with swords and clubs as if I were a criminal?^L ⁵³Every day while I was with you in the temple complex, you never laid a hand on Me. But this is your hour—and the dominion of darkness."

⁵⁴They seized Him, led Him away, and brought Him into the high priest's house. Meanwhile Peter was following at a distance. ⁵⁵They lit a fire in the middle of the courtyard and sat down together, and Peter sat among them. ⁵⁶When a servant saw him sitting in the firelight, and looked closely at him, she said, "This man was with Him too."

⁵⁷But he denied it: "Woman, I don't know Him!"

⁵⁸After a little while, someone else saw him and said, "You're one of them too!"

"Man, I am not!" Peter said.

⁵⁹About an hour later, another kept insisting, "This man was certainly with Him, since he's also a Galilean."

⁶⁰But Peter said, "Man, I don't know what you're talking about!" Immediately, while he

---

^A22:25 Or them call themselves ^B22:25 Title of honor given to those who benefited the public good ^C22:31 Other mss read *Then the Lord said, "Simon, Simon* ^D22:31 In Gk, the word *you* is pl ^E22:32 In Gk, the word *you* is sg ^F22:34 Other mss read *before* ^G22:37 Is 53:12 ^H22:38 Or *It is enough!* ^I22:43-44 Other mss omit bracketed text ^J22:45 Lit *sleeping from grief* ^K22:51 Lit *Permit as far as this* ^L22:52 Lit as against a criminal was still speaking, a rooster crowed. ⁶¹Then the Lord turned and looked at Peter. So Peter remembered the word of the Lord, how He had said to him, "Before the rooster crows today, you will deny Me three times." ⁶²And he went outside and wept bitterly.

⁶³The men who were holding Jesus started mocking and beating Him. ⁶⁴After blindfolding Him, they kept^A asking, "Prophesy! Who hit You?" ⁶⁵And they were saying many other blasphemous things against Him.

⁶⁶When daylight came, the elders^B of the people, both the chief priests and the scribes, convened and brought Him before their Sanhedrin. ⁶⁷They said, "If You are the Messiah, tell us."

But He said to them, "If I do tell you, you will not believe. ⁶⁸And if I ask you, you will not answer. ⁶⁹But from now on, the Son of Man will be seated at the right hand of the Power of God."

⁷⁰They all asked, "Are You, then, the Son of God?"

And He said to them, "You say that I am."

⁷¹"Why do we need any more testimony," they said, "since we've heard it ourselves from His mouth?"

23 Then their whole assembly rose up and brought Him before Pilate. ²They began to accuse Him, saying, "We found this man subverting our nation, opposing payment of taxes to Caesar, and saying that He Himself is the Messiah, a King."

³So Pilate asked Him, "Are You the King of the Jews?"

He answered him, "You have said it."^C

⁴Pilate then told the chief priests and the crowds, "I find no grounds for charging this man."

⁵But they kept insisting, "He stirs up the people, teaching throughout all Judea, from Galilee where He started even to here."

⁶When Pilate heard this,^D he asked if the man was a Galilean. ⁷Finding that He was under Herod's jurisdiction, he sent Him to Herod, who was also in Jerusalem during those days. ⁸Herod was very glad to see Jesus; for a long time he had wanted to see Him because he had heard about Him and was hoping to see some miracle^E performed by Him. ⁹So he kept ask-

ing Him questions, but Jesus did not answer him. ¹⁰The chief priests and the scribes stood by, vehemently accusing Him. ¹¹Then Herod, with his soldiers, treated Him with contempt, mocked Him, dressed Him in a brilliant robe, and sent Him back to Pilate. ¹²That very day Herod and Pilate became friends.^F Previously, they had been hostile toward each other.

¹³Pilate called together the chief priests, the leaders, and the people, ¹⁴and said to them, "You have brought me this man as one who subverts the people. But in fact, after examining Him in your presence, I have found no grounds to charge this man with those things you accuse Him of. ¹⁵Neither has Herod, because he sent Him back to us. Clearly, He has done nothing to deserve death. ¹⁶Therefore, I will have Him whipped^G and then release Him." [¹⁷For according to the festival he had to release someone to them.]^H

¹⁸Then they all cried out together, "Take this man away! Release Barabbas to us!" ¹⁹(He had been thrown into prison for a rebellion that had taken place in the city, and for murder.)

²⁰Pilate, wanting to release Jesus, addressed them again, ²¹but they kept shouting, "Crucify! Crucify Him!"

²²A third time he said to them, "Why? What has this man done wrong? I have found in Him no grounds for the death penalty. Therefore, I will have Him whipped and then release Him."

²³But they kept up the pressure, demanding with loud voices that He be crucified. And their voices^I won out. ²⁴So Pilate decided to grant their demand ²⁵and released the one they were asking for, who had been thrown into prison for rebellion and murder. But he handed Jesus over to their will.

²⁶As they led Him away, they seized Simon, a Cyrenian, who was coming in from the country, and laid the cross on him to carry behind Jesus. ²⁷A large crowd of people followed Him, including women who were mourning and lamenting Him. ²⁸But turning to them, Jesus said, "Daughters of Jerusalem, do not weep for Me, but weep for yourselves and your children. ²⁹Look, the days are coming when they will say, 'The women without children, the wombs that never bore and the breasts that never nursed, are fortunate!' ³⁰Then they will

---

^A22:64 Other mss add *striking Him on the face and*   ^B22:66 Or *council of elders*   ^C23:3 Or *That is true*; an affirmative oath   ^D23:6 Other mss read *heard "Galilee"*   ^E23:8 Or *sign*   ^F23:12 Lit *friends with one another*   ^G23:16 Gk *paideuo*; to discipline or "teach a lesson"; 1Kg 12:11,14 LXX; 2Ch 10:11,14; perhaps a way of referring to the Roman scourging; Lat *flagellatio*   ^H23:17 Other mss omit bracketed text   ^I23:23 Other mss add *and those of the chief priests* begin to say to the mountains, 'Fall on us!' and to the hills, 'Cover us!'ᴬ ³¹For if they do these things when the wood is green, what will happen when it is dry?"

³²Two others—criminals—were also led away to be executed with Him. ³³When they arrived at the place called The Skull, they crucified Him there, along with the criminals, one on the right and one on the left. [³⁴Then Jesus said, "Father, forgive them, because they do not know what they are doing."]ᴮ And they divided His clothes and cast lots.

³⁵The people stood watching, and even the leaders kept scoffing: "He saved others; let Him save Himself if this is God's Messiah, the Chosen One!" ³⁶The soldiers also mocked Him. They came offering Him sour wine ³⁷and said, "If You are the King of the Jews, save Yourself!" ³⁸An inscription was above Him:ᶜ

THIS IS
THE KING OF THE JEWS.

³⁹Then one of the criminals hanging there began to yell insults atᴰ Him: "Aren't You the Messiah? Save Yourself and us!"

⁴⁰But the other answered, rebuking him: "Don't you even fear God, since you are undergoing the same punishment? ⁴¹We are punished justly, because we're getting back what we deserve for the things we did, but this man has done nothing wrong." ⁴²Then he said, "Jesus, remember meᴱ when You come into Your kingdom!"

⁴³And He said to him, "I assure you: Today you will be with Me in paradise."

⁴⁴It was now about noon,ᶠ and darkness came over the whole landᴳ until three,ᴴ ⁴⁵because the sun's light failed.ᴵ The curtain of the sanctuary was split down the middle. ⁴⁶And Jesus called out with a loud voice, "Father, into Your hands I entrust My spirit."ᴶ Saying this, He breathed His last.

⁴⁷When the centurion saw what happened, he began to glorify God, saying, "This man really was righteous!" ⁴⁸All the crowds that had gathered for this spectacle, when they saw what had taken place, went home, striking their chests.ᴷ ⁴⁹But all who knew Him, including the women who had followed Him from Galilee, stood at a distance, watching these things.

⁵⁰There was a good and righteous man named Joseph, a member of the Sanhedrin, ⁵¹who had not agreed with their plan and action. He was from Arimathea, a Judean town, and was looking forward to the kingdom of God. ⁵²He approached Pilate and asked for Jesus' body. ⁵³Taking it down, he wrapped it in fine linen and placed it in a tomb cut into the rock, where no one had ever been placed.ᴸ ⁵⁴It was preparation day, and the Sabbath was about to begin.ᴹ ⁵⁵The women who had come with Him from Galilee followed along and observed the tomb and how His body was placed. ⁵⁶Then they returned and prepared spices and perfumes. And they rested on the Sabbath according to the commandment.

24

On the first day of the week, very early in the morning, theyᴺ came to the tomb, bringing the spices they had prepared. ²They found the stone rolled away from the tomb. ³They went in but did not find the body of the Lord Jesus. ⁴While they were perplexed about this, suddenly two men stood by them in dazzling clothes. ⁵So the women were terrified and bowed down to the ground.ᴼ

"Why are you looking for the living among the dead?" asked the men. ⁶"He is not here, but He has been resurrected! Remember how He spoke to you when He was still in Galilee, ⁷saying, 'The Son of Man must be betrayed into the hands of sinful men, be crucified, and rise on the third day'?" ⁸And they remembered His words.

⁹Returning from the tomb, they reported all these things to the Eleven and to all the rest. ¹⁰Mary Magdalene, Joanna, Mary the mother of James, and the other women with them were telling the apostles these things. ¹¹But these words seemed like nonsense to them, and they did not believe the women. ¹²Peter, however, got up and ran to the tomb. When he stooped to look in, he saw only the linen cloths.ᴾ So he went home, amazed at what had happened.

¹³Now that same day two of them were on their way to a village calledᴼ Emmaus, which was about seven milesᴿ from Jerusalem. ¹⁴Together they were discussing everything that had taken place. ¹⁵And while they were

ᴬ23:30 Hs 10:8 ᴮ23:34 Other mss omit bracketed text ᶜ23:38 Other mss add *written in Greek, Latin, and Hebrew letters* ᴰ23:39 Or *began to blaspheme* ᴱ23:42 Other mss add *Lord* ᶠ23:44 Lit *about the sixth hour* ᴳ23:44 Or *whole earth* ᴴ23:44 Lit *the ninth hour* ᴵ23:45 Other mss read *three, and the sun was darkened* ᴶ23:46 Ps 31:5 ᴷ23:48 = mourning ᴸ23:53 Or *interred, or laid* ᴹ23:54 Lit *was dawning; not in the morning but at sundown Friday* ᴺ24:1 Other mss add *and other women with them* ᴼ24:5 Lit *and inclined their faces to the ground* ᴾ24:12 Other mss add *lying there* ᴼ24:13 Lit *village, which name is* ᴿ24:13 Lit *about 60 stadia; 1 stadion = 600 feet* discussing and arguing, Jesus Himself came near and began to walk along with them. [16]But they[A] were prevented from recognizing Him. [17]Then He asked them, "What is this dispute that you're having[B] with each other as you are walking?" And they stopped walking and looked discouraged.

[18]The one named Cleopas answered Him, "Are You the only visitor in Jerusalem who doesn't know the things that happened there in these days?"

[19]"What things?" He asked them.

So they said to Him, "The things concerning Jesus the Nazarene, who was a Prophet powerful in action and speech before God and all the people, [20]and how our chief priests and leaders handed Him over to be sentenced to death, and they crucified Him. [21]But we were hoping that He was the One who was about to redeem Israel. Besides all this, it's the third day since these things happened. [22]Moreover, some women from our group astounded us. They arrived early at the tomb, [23]and when they didn't find His body, they came and reported that they had seen a vision of angels who said He was alive. [24]Some of those who were with us went to the tomb and found it just as the women had said, but they didn't see Him."

[25]He said to them, "How unwise and slow you are to believe in your hearts all that the prophets have spoken! [26]Didn't the Messiah have to suffer these things and enter into His glory?" [27]Then beginning with Moses and all the Prophets, He interpreted for them the things concerning Himself in all the Scriptures.

[28]They came near the village where they were going, and He gave the impression that He was going farther. [29]But they urged Him: "Stay with us, because it's almost evening, and now the day is almost over." So He went in to stay with them.

[30]It was as He reclined at the table with them that He took the bread, blessed and broke it, and gave it to them. [31]Then their eyes were opened, and they recognized Him, but He disappeared from their sight. [32]So they said to each other, "Weren't our hearts ablaze

within us while He was talking with us on the road and explaining the Scriptures to us?" [33]That very hour they got up and returned to Jerusalem. They found the Eleven and those with them gathered together, [34]who said,[C] "The Lord has certainly been raised, and has appeared to Simon!" [35]Then they began to describe what had happened on the road and how He was made known to them in the breaking of the bread.

[36]And as they were saying these things, He Himself stood among them. He said to them, "Peace to you!" [37]But they were startled and terrified and thought they were seeing a ghost. [38]"Why are you troubled?" He asked them. "And why do doubts arise in your hearts? [39]Look at My hands and My feet, that it is I Myself! Touch Me and see, because a ghost does not have flesh and bones as you can see I have." [40]Having said this, He showed them His hands and feet. [41]But while they still were amazed and unbelieving because of their joy, He asked them, "Do you have anything here to eat?" [42]So they gave Him a piece of a broiled fish,[D] [43]and He took it and ate in their presence.

[44]Then He told them, "These are My words that I spoke to you while I was still with you—that everything written about Me in the Law of Moses, the Prophets, and the Psalms must be fulfilled." [45]Then He opened their minds to understand the Scriptures. [46]He also said to them, "This is what is written:[E] The Messiah would suffer and rise from the dead the third day, [47]and repentance for[F] forgiveness of sins would be proclaimed in His name to all the nations, beginning at Jerusalem. [48]You are witnesses of these things. [49]And look, I am sending you[G] what My Father promised. As for you, stay in the city[H] until you are empowered[I] from on high."

[50]Then He led them out as far as Bethany, and lifting up His hands He blessed them. [51]And while He was blessing them, He left them and was carried up into heaven. [52]After worshiping Him, they returned to Jerusalem with great joy. [53]And they were continually in the temple complex praising God.[J]

[A]24:16 Lit their eyes   [B]24:17 Lit What are these words that you are exchanging   [C]24:34 Gk is specific that this refers to the Eleven and those with them.   [D]24:42 Other mss add and some honeycomb   [E]24:46 Other mss add and thus it was necessary that   [F]24:47 Other mss read repentance and   [G]24:49 Lit upon you   [H]24:49 Other mss add of Jerusalem   [I]24:49 Lit clothed with power   [J]24:53 Other mss read praising and blessing God. Amen.

JOHN

1 In the beginning was the Word,[A]
and the Word was with God,
and the Word was God.
[2] He was with God in the beginning.
[3] All things were created
through Him,
and apart from Him not one thing
was created
that has been created.
[4] Life was in Him,[B]
and that life was the light of men.
[5] That light shines in the darkness,
yet the darkness did not overcome[C] it.

[6] There was a man named John
who was sent from God.
[7] He came as a witness
to testify about the light,
so that all might believe through him.[D]
[8] He was not the light,
but he came to testify about the light.
[9] The true light, who gives light
to everyone,
was coming into the world.[E]

[10] He was in the world,
and the world was created
through Him,
yet the world did not
recognize Him.
[11] He came to His own,[F]
and His own people[F]
did not receive Him.
[12] But to all who did receive Him,
He gave them the right to be[G]
children of God,
to those who believe in His name,
[13] who were born,
not of blood,[H]
or of the will of the flesh,
or of the will of man,[I]
but of God.

[14] The Word became flesh[J]
and took up residence[K] among us.
We observed His glory,
the glory as the One and Only Son[L]
from the Father,
full of grace and truth.
[15] (John testified concerning Him
and exclaimed,
"This was the One of whom I said,
'The One coming after me
has surpassed me,
because He existed before me.'")
[16] Indeed, we have all received grace
after grace
from His fullness,
[17] for the law was given through Moses,
grace and truth came
through Jesus Christ.
[18] No one has ever seen God.[M]
The One and Only Son[N]—
the One who is at the Father's side[O]—
He has revealed Him.

[19] This is John's testimony when the Jews from Jerusalem sent priests and Levites to ask him, "Who are you?"
[20] He did not refuse to answer, but he declared: "I am not the Messiah."
[21] "What then?" they asked him. "Are you Elijah?"
"I am not," he said.
"Are you the Prophet?"[P]
"No," he answered.
[22] "Who are you, then?" they asked. "We need to give an answer to those who sent us. What can you tell us about yourself?"
[23] He said, "I am a **voice of one crying out in the wilderness: Make straight the way of the Lord**[Q]—just as Isaiah the prophet said."
[24] Now they had been sent from the Pharisees. [25] So they asked him, "Why then do you baptize if you aren't the Messiah, or Elijah, or the Prophet?"

A1:1 The *Word* (Gk *Logos*) is a title for Jesus as the communication and the revealer of God the Father; Jn 1:14,18; Rv 19:13.   B1:3-4 Other punctuation is possible: . . . *not one thing was created. What was created in Him was life*   C1:5 Or *grasp, or comprehend, or overtake*; Jn 12:35   D1:7 Or *through it* (the light)   E1:9 Or *The true light who comes into the world gives light to everyone,* or *The true light enlightens everyone coming into the world.*   F1:11 The same Gk adjective is used twice in this verse: the first refers to all that Jesus owned as Creator (*to His own*); the second refers to the Jews (*His own people*).   G1:12 Or *become*   H1:13 Lit *bloods*; the pl form of *blood* occurs only here in the NT. It may refer either to lineal descent (that is, blood from one's father and mother) or to the OT sacrificial system (that is, the various blood sacrifices). Neither is the basis for birth into the family of God.   I1:13 Or *not of human lineage, or of human capacity, or of human volition*   J1:14 The eternally existent Word (vv. 1-2) took on full humanity but without sin; Heb 4:15.   K1:14 Or *and dwelt in a tent*; lit *and tabernacled*; this word occurs only here in John. A related word, referring to the Festival of Tabernacles, occurs only in 7:2; Ex 40:34-38.   L1:14 *Son* is implied from the reference to the Father and from Gk usage.   M1:18 Since God is an infinite being, no one can see Him in His absolute essential nature; Ex 33:18-23.   N1:18 Other mss read *God*   O1:18 Lit *is in the bosom of the Father*   P1:21 Probably the Prophet in Dt 18:15   Q1:23 Is 40:3

²⁶ "I baptize with^A water," John answered them. "Someone stands among you, but you don't know Him. ²⁷ He is the One coming after me,^B whose sandal strap I'm not worthy to untie."

²⁸ All this happened in Bethany^C across the Jordan,^D where John was baptizing.

²⁹ The next day John saw Jesus coming toward him and said, "Here is the Lamb of God, who takes away the sin of the world! ³⁰ This is the One I told you about: 'After me comes a man who has surpassed me, because He existed before me.' ³¹ I didn't know Him, but I came baptizing with^A water so He might be revealed to Israel."

³² And John testified, "I watched the Spirit descending from heaven like a dove, and He rested on Him. ³³ I didn't know Him, but He^E who sent me to baptize with^A water told me, 'The One you see the Spirit descending and resting on—He is the One who baptizes with^A the Holy Spirit.' ³⁴ I have seen and testified that He is the Son of God!"^F

³⁵ Again the next day, John was standing with two of his disciples. ³⁶ When he saw Jesus passing by, he said, "Look! The Lamb of God!"

³⁷ The two disciples heard him say this and followed Jesus. ³⁸ When Jesus turned and noticed them following Him, He asked them, "What are you looking for?"

They said to Him, "Rabbi" (which means "Teacher"), "where are You staying?"

³⁹ "Come and you'll see," He replied. So they went and saw where He was staying, and they stayed with Him that day. It was about 10 in the morning.^G

⁴⁰ Andrew, Simon Peter's brother, was one of the two who heard John and followed Him. ⁴¹ He first found his own brother Simon and told him, "We have found the Messiah!"^H (which means "Anointed One"), ⁴² and he brought Simon to Jesus.

When Jesus saw him, He said, "You are Simon, son of John.^I You will be called Cephas" (which means "Rock").

⁴³ The next day He^J decided to leave for Galilee. Jesus found Philip and told him, "Follow Me!"

⁴⁴ Now Philip was from Bethsaida, the hometown of Andrew and Peter. ⁴⁵ Philip found Nathanael^K and told him, "We have found the One Moses wrote about in the Law (and so did the prophets): Jesus the son of Joseph, from Nazareth!"

⁴⁶ "Can anything good come out of Nazareth?" Nathanael asked him.

"Come and see," Philip answered.

⁴⁷ Then Jesus saw Nathanael coming toward Him and said about him, "Here is a true Israelite; no deceit is in him."

⁴⁸ "How do you know me?" Nathanael asked.

"Before Philip called you, when you were under the fig tree, I saw you," Jesus answered.

⁴⁹ "Rabbi," Nathanael replied, "You are the Son of God! You are the King of Israel!"

⁵⁰ Jesus responded to him, "Do you believe only because I told you I saw you under the fig tree? You^L will see greater things than this."

⁵¹ Then He said, "I assure you: You^M will see heaven opened and the angels of God ascending and descending on the Son of Man."

2 On the third day a wedding took place in Cana of Galilee. Jesus' mother was there, and ² Jesus and His disciples were invited to the wedding as well. ³ When the wine ran out, Jesus' mother told Him, "They don't have any wine."

⁴ "What has this concern of yours to do with Me,^N woman?" Jesus asked. "My hour^O has not yet come."

⁵ "Do whatever He tells you," His mother told the servants.

⁶ Now six stone water jars had been set there for Jewish purification. Each contained 20 or 30 gallons.^P

⁷ "Fill the jars with water," Jesus told them. So they filled them to the brim. ⁸ Then He said to them, "Now draw some out and take it to the chief servant."^Q And they did.

---

^A 1:26,31,33 Or in   ^B 1:27 Other mss add who came before me   ^C 1:28 Other mss read in Bethabara   ^D 1:28 Another Bethany, near Jerusalem, was the home of Lazarus, Martha, and Mary; Jn 11:1.   ^E 1:33 He refers to God the Father, who gave John a sign to help him identify the Messiah. Vv. 32-34 indicate that John did not know that Jesus was the Messiah until the Spirit descended upon Him at His baptism.   ^F 1:34 Other mss read the Chosen One of God   ^G 1:39 Lit about the tenth hour. Various methods of reckoning time were used in the ancient world. John probably used a different method from the other 3 Gospels. If John used the same method of time reckoning as the other 3 Gospels, the translation would be: It was about four in the afternoon.   ^H 1:41 In the NT, the word Messiah translates the Gk word Christos ("Anointed One"), except here and in Jn 4:25 where it translates Messias.   ^I 1:42 Other mss read Simon, son of Jonah   ^J 1:43 Or he, referring either to Simon Peter (vv. 41-42) or Andrew (vv. 40-41)   ^K 1:45 Probably the Bartholomew of the other Gospels and Acts   ^L 1:50 In Gk, the word you is sg and refers to Nathanael.   ^M 1:51 In Gk, the word you is pl and refers to Nathanael and the other disciples.   ^N 2:4 Or You and I see things differently; lit What to Me and to you; Mt 8:29; Mk 1:24; 5:7; Lk 8:28   ^O 2:4 The time of His sacrificial death and exaltation; Jn 7:30; 8:20; 12:23,27; 13:1; 17:1   ^P 2:6 Lit 2 or 3 measures   ^Q 2:8 Lit ruler of the table; perhaps master of the feast, or headwaiter

⁹When the chief servant tasted the water (after it had become wine), he did not know where it came from—though the servants who had drawn the water knew. He called the groom ¹⁰and told him, "Everyone sets out the fine wine first, then, after people have drunk freely, the inferior. But you have kept the fine wine until now."

¹¹Jesus performed this first signᴬ in Cana of Galilee. He displayed His glory, and His disciples believed in Him.

¹²After this, He went down to Capernaum, together with His mother, His brothers, and His disciples, and they stayed there only a few days.

¹³The Jewish Passover was near, so Jesus went up to Jerusalem. ¹⁴In the temple complex He found people selling oxen, sheep, and doves, and He also found the money changers sitting there. ¹⁵After making a whip out of cords, He drove everyone out of the temple complex with their sheep and oxen. He also poured out the money changers' coins and overturned the tables. ¹⁶He told those who were selling doves, "Get these things out of here! Stop turning My Father's house into a marketplace!"ᴮ

¹⁷And His disciples remembered that it is written: **Zeal for Your house will consume Me.**ᶜ

¹⁸So the Jews replied to Him, "What sign of authority will You show us for doing these things?"

¹⁹Jesus answered, "Destroy this sanctuary, and I will raise it up in three days."

²⁰Therefore the Jews said, "This sanctuary took 46 years to build, and will You raise it up in three days?"

²¹But He was speaking about the sanctuary of His body. ²²So when He was raised from the dead, His disciples remembered that He had said this. And they believed the Scripture and the statement Jesus had made.

²³While He was in Jerusalem at the Passover Festival, many trusted in His name when they saw the signs He was doing. ²⁴Jesus, however, would not entrust Himself to them, since He knew them all ²⁵and because He did not need

anyone to testify about man; for He Himself knew what was in man.

3 There was a man from the Pharisees named Nicodemus, a ruler of the Jews. ²This man came to Him at night and said, "Rabbi, we know that You have come from God as a teacher, for no one could perform these signs You do unless God were with him."

³Jesus replied, "I assure you: Unless someone is born again,ᴰ he cannot see the kingdom of God."

⁴"But how can anyone be born when he is old?" Nicodemus asked Him. "Can he enter his mother's womb a second time and be born?"

⁵Jesus answered, "I assure you: Unless someone is born of water and the Spirit,ᴱ he cannot enter the kingdom of God. ⁶Whatever is born of the flesh is flesh, and whatever is born of the Spirit is spirit. ⁷Do not be amazed that I told you that youᶠ must be born again. ⁸The windᴳ blows where it pleases, and you hear its sound, but you don't know where it comes from or where it is going. So it is with everyone born of the Spirit."

⁹"How can these things be?" asked Nicodemus.

¹⁰"Are you a teacherᴴ of Israel and don't know these things?" Jesus replied. ¹¹"I assure you: We speak what We know and We testify to what We have seen, but youᴵ do not accept Our testimony.ᴶ ¹²If I have told you about things that happen on earth and you don't believe, how will you believe if I tell you about things of heaven? ¹³No one has ascended into heaven except the One who descended from heaven—the Son of Man.ᴷ ¹⁴Just as Moses lifted up the snake in the wilderness, so the Son of Man must be lifted up, ¹⁵so that everyone who believes in Him willᴸ have eternal life.

¹⁶"For God loved the world in this way:ᴹ He gave His One and Only Son, so that everyone who believes in Him will not perish but have eternal life. ¹⁷For God did not send His Son into the world that He might condemn the world, but that the world might be saved through Him. ¹⁸Anyone who believes in Him is not condemned, but anyone who does not

---

ᴬ2:11 Lit *this beginning of the signs*; Jn 4:54; 20:30. Seven miraculous signs occur in John's Gospel and are so noted in the headings. ᴮ2:16 Lit *a house of business* ᶜ2:17 Ps 69:9 ᴰ3:3 The same Gk word can mean *again* or *from above* [also in v. 7]. ᴱ3:5 Or *spirit, or wind*; the Gk word *pneuma* can mean *wind, spirit, or Spirit*, each of which occurs in this context. ᶠ3:7 The pronoun is pl in Gk. ᴳ3:8 The Gk word *pneuma* can mean *wind, spirit, or Spirit*, each of which occurs in this context. ᴴ3:10 Or *the teacher* ᴵ3:11 In Gk, the word *you* is pl here and throughout v. 12. ᴶ3:11 The pronouns *we* and *our* refer to Jesus and His authority to speak for the Father. ᴷ3:13 Other mss add *who is in heaven* ᴸ3:15 Other mss add *not perish, but* ᴹ3:16 The Gk word *houtos*, commonly translated in Jn 3:16 as "so" or "so much," occurs over 200 times in the NT. Almost without exception it is an adverb of manner, not degree (for example, see Mt 1:18). It only means "so much" when modifying an adjective (see Gl 3:3; Rv 16:18). Manner seems primarily in view in Jn 3:16, which explains the HCSB's rendering.

believe is already condemned, because he has not believed in the name of the One and Only Son of God.

[19] "This, then, is the judgment: The light has come into the world, and people loved darkness rather than the light because their deeds were evil. [20] For everyone who practices wicked things hates the light and avoids it,[A] so that his deeds may not be exposed. [21] But anyone who lives by[B] the truth comes to the light, so that his works may be shown to be accomplished by God."[C]

[22] After this, Jesus and His disciples went to the Judean countryside, where He spent time with them and baptized. [23] John also was baptizing in Aenon near Salim, because there was plenty of water there. People were coming and being baptized, [24] since John had not yet been thrown into prison.

[25] Then a dispute arose between John's disciples and a Jew[D] about purification. [26] So they came to John and told him, "Rabbi, the One you testified about, and who was with you across the Jordan, is baptizing—and everyone is flocking to Him."

[27] John responded, "No one can receive a single thing unless it's given to him from heaven. [28] You yourselves can testify that I said, 'I am not the Messiah, but I've been sent ahead of Him.' [29] He who has the bride is the groom. But the groom's friend, who stands by and listens for him, rejoices greatly[E] at the groom's voice. So this joy of mine is complete. [30] He must increase, but I must decrease."

[31] The One who comes from above is above all. The one who is from the earth is earthly and speaks in earthly terms.[F] The One who comes from heaven is above all. [32] He testifies to what He has seen and heard, yet no one accepts His testimony. [33] The one who has accepted His testimony has affirmed that God is true. [34] For God sent Him, and He speaks God's words, since He[G] gives the Spirit without measure. [35] The Father loves the Son and has given all things into His hands. [36] The one who believes in the Son has eternal life, but the one who refuses to believe in the Son will not see life; instead, the wrath of God remains on him.

4 When Jesus[H] knew that the Pharisees heard He was making and baptizing more disciples than John [2] (though Jesus Himself was not baptizing, but His disciples were), [3] He left Judea and went again to Galilee. [4] He had to travel through Samaria, [5] so He came to a town of Samaria called Sychar near the property[I] that Jacob had given his son Joseph. [6] Jacob's well was there, and Jesus, worn out from His journey, sat down at the well. It was about six in the evening.[J]

[7] A woman of Samaria came to draw water.

"Give Me a drink," Jesus said to her, [8] for His disciples had gone into town to buy food.

[9] "How is it that You, a Jew, ask for a drink from me, a Samaritan woman?" she asked Him. For Jews do not associate with[K] Samaritans.[L]

[10] Jesus answered, "If you knew the gift of God, and who is saying to you, 'Give Me a drink,' you would ask Him, and He would give you living water."

[11] "Sir," said the woman, "You don't even have a bucket, and the well is deep. So where do You get this 'living water'? [12] You aren't greater than our father Jacob, are You? He gave us the well and drank from it himself, as did his sons and livestock."

[13] Jesus said, "Everyone who drinks from this water will get thirsty again. [14] But whoever drinks from the water that I will give him will never get thirsty again—ever! In fact, the water I will give him will become a well[M] of water springing up within him for eternal life."

[15] "Sir," the woman said to Him, "give me this water so I won't get thirsty and come here to draw water."

[16] "Go call your husband," He told her, "and come back here."

[17] "I don't have a husband," she answered.

"You have correctly said, 'I don't have a husband,'" Jesus said. [18] "For you've had five husbands, and the man you now have is not your husband. What you have said is true."

[19] "Sir," the woman replied, "I see that You are a prophet. [20] Our fathers worshiped on this mountain,[N] yet you Jews say that the place to worship is in Jerusalem."

A3:20 Lit *and does not come to the light*   B3:21 Lit *who does*   C3:25 It is possible that Jesus' words end at v. 15. Ancient Gk did not have quotation marks.   D3:25 Other mss read *and the Jews*   E3:29 Lit *with joy rejoices*   F3:31 Or *of earthly things*   G3:34 Other mss read *since God*   H4:1 Other mss read *the Lord*   I4:5 Lit *piece of land*   J4:6 Lit *the sixth hour*; see note at Jn 1:39; an alt time reckoning would be noon   K4:9 Or *do not share vessels with*   L4:9 Other mss omit *For Jews do not associate with Samaritans.*   M4:14 Or *spring*   N4:20 Mount Gerizim, where there had been a Samaritan temple that rivaled Jerusalem's

²¹Jesus told her, "Believe Me, woman, an hour is coming when you will worship the Father neither on this mountain nor in Jerusalem. ²²You Samaritans^A worship what you do not know. We worship what we do know, because salvation is from the Jews. ²³But an hour is coming, and is now here, when the true worshipers will worship the Father in spirit and truth. Yes, the Father wants such people to worship Him. ²⁴God is spirit, and those who worship Him must worship in spirit and truth."

²⁵The woman said to Him, "I know that Messiah^B is coming" (who is called Christ). "When He comes, He will explain everything to us."

²⁶"I am He," Jesus told her, "the One speaking to you."

²⁷Just then His disciples arrived, and they were amazed that He was talking with a woman. Yet no one said, "What do You want?" or "Why are You talking with her?"

²⁸Then the woman left her water jar, went into town, and told the men, ²⁹"Come, see a man who told me everything I ever did! Could this be the Messiah?" ³⁰They left the town and made their way to Him.

³¹In the meantime the disciples kept urging Him, "Rabbi, eat something."

³²But He said, "I have food to eat that you don't know about."

³³The disciples said to one another, "Could someone have brought Him something to eat?"

³⁴"My food is to do the will of Him who sent Me and to finish His work," Jesus told them. ³⁵"Don't you say, 'There are still four more months, then comes the harvest'? Listen to what I'm telling you: Open^C your eyes and look at the fields, for they are ready^D for harvest. ³⁶The reaper is already receiving pay and gathering fruit for eternal life, so the sower and reaper can rejoice together. ³⁷For in this case the saying is true: 'One sows and another reaps.' ³⁸I sent you to reap what you didn't labor for; others have labored, and you have benefited from^E their labor."

³⁹Now many Samaritans from that town believed in Him because of what the woman said^F when she testified, "He told me everything I ever did." ⁴⁰Therefore, when the Samaritans came to Him, they asked Him to stay with them, and He stayed there two days. ⁴¹Many more believed because of what He said.^G ⁴²And they told the woman, "We no longer believe because of what you said, for we have heard for ourselves and know that this really is the Savior of the world."^H

⁴³After two days He left there for Galilee. ⁴⁴Jesus Himself testified that a prophet has no honor in his own country. ⁴⁵When they entered Galilee, the Galileans welcomed Him because they had seen everything He did in Jerusalem during the festival. For they also had gone to the festival.

⁴⁶Then He went again to Cana of Galilee, where He had turned the water into wine. There was a certain royal official whose son was ill at Capernaum. ⁴⁷When this man heard that Jesus had come from Judea to Galilee, he went to Him and pleaded with Him to come down and heal his son, for he was about to die.

⁴⁸Jesus told him, "Unless you people see signs and wonders, you will not believe."

⁴⁹"Sir," the official said to Him, "come down before my boy dies!"

⁵⁰"Go," Jesus told him, "your son will live." The man believed what^I Jesus said to him and departed.

⁵¹While he was still going down, his slaves met him saying that his boy was alive. ⁵²He asked them at what time he got better. "Yesterday at seven in the morning^J the fever left him," they answered. ⁵³The father realized this was the very hour at which Jesus had told him, "Your son will live." Then he himself believed, along with his whole household.

⁵⁴This, therefore, was the second sign Jesus performed after He came from Judea to Galilee.

5 After this, a Jewish festival took place, and Jesus went up to Jerusalem. ²By the Sheep Gate in Jerusalem there is a pool, called Bethesda^K in Hebrew, which has five colonnades.^L ³Within these lay a large number of the sick—blind, lame, and paralyzed [—waiting for the moving of the water, ⁴because an angel would go down into the pool from time to time and stir up the water. Then the first one who got in after the water was stirred up recovered from whatever ailment he had].^M

⁵One man was there who had been sick for 38 years. ⁶When Jesus saw him lying there and

A4:22 *Samaritans* is implied since the Gk verb and pronoun are pl. **B**4:25 In the NT, the word *Messiah* translates the Gk word *Christos* ("Anointed One"), except here and in Jn 1:41 where it translates *Messias*. **C**4:35 Lit *Raise* **D**4:35 Lit *white* **E**4:38 Lit *you have entered into* **F**4:39 Lit *because of the woman's word* **G**4:41 Lit *because of His word* **H**4:42 Other mss add *the Messiah* **I**4:50 Lit *the word* **J**4:52 Or *seven in the evening; lit at the seventh hour;* see note at Jn 1:39; an alt time reckoning would be *at one in the afternoon* **K**5:2 Other mss read *Bethzatha;* other mss read *Bethsaida* **L**5:2 Rows of columns supporting a roof **M**5:3-4 Other mss omit bracketed text knew he had already been there a long time, He said to him, "Do you want to get well?"

[7] "Sir," the sick man answered, "I don't have a man to put me into the pool when the water is stirred up, but while I'm coming, someone goes down ahead of me."

[8] "Get up," Jesus told him, "pick up your mat and walk!" [9] Instantly the man got well, picked up his mat, and started to walk.

Now that day was the Sabbath, [10] so the Jews said to the man who had been healed, "This is the Sabbath! It's illegal for you to pick up your mat."

[11] He replied, "The man who made me well told me, 'Pick up your mat and walk.'"

[12] "Who is this man who told you, 'Pick up your mat and walk'?" they asked. [13] But the man who was cured did not know who it was, because Jesus had slipped away into the crowd that was there.[A]

[14] After this, Jesus found him in the temple complex and said to him, "See, you are well. Do not sin anymore, so that something worse doesn't happen to you." [15] The man went and reported to the Jews that it was Jesus who had made him well.

[16] Therefore, the Jews began persecuting Jesus[B] because He was doing these things on the Sabbath. [17] But Jesus responded to them, "My Father is still working, and I am working also." [18] This is why the Jews began trying all the more to kill Him: Not only was He breaking the Sabbath, but He was even calling God His own Father, making Himself equal with God.

[19] Then Jesus replied, "I assure you: The Son is not able to do anything on His own, but only what He sees the Father doing. For whatever the Father[C] does, the Son also does these things in the same way. [20] For the Father loves the Son and shows Him everything He is doing, and He will show Him greater works than these so that you will be amazed. [21] And just as the Father raises the dead and gives them life, so the Son also gives life to anyone He wants to. [22] The Father, in fact, judges no one but has given all judgment to the Son, [23] so that all people will honor the Son just as they honor the Father. Anyone who does not honor the Son does not honor the Father who sent Him.

[24] "I assure you: Anyone who hears My word and believes Him who sent Me has eternal life and will not come under judgment but has passed from death to life.

[25] "I assure you: An hour is coming, and is now here, when the dead will hear the voice of the Son of God, and those who hear will live. [26] For just as the Father has life in Himself, so also He has granted to the Son to have life in Himself. [27] And He has granted Him the right to pass judgment, because He is the Son of Man. [28] Do not be amazed at this, because a time is coming when all who are in the graves will hear His voice [29] and come out—those who have done good things, to the resurrection of life, but those who have done wicked things, to the resurrection of judgment.

[30] "I can do nothing on My own. I judge only as I hear, and My judgment is righteous, because I do not seek My own will, but the will of Him who sent Me.

[31] "If I testify about Myself, My testimony is not valid.[D] [32] There is Another who testifies about Me, and I know that the testimony He gives about Me is valid.[E] [33] You have sent messengers to John, and he has testified to the truth. [34] I don't receive man's testimony, but I say these things so that you may be saved. [35] John[F] was a burning and shining lamp, and for a time you were willing to enjoy his light.

[36] "But I have a greater testimony than John's because of the works that the Father has given Me to accomplish. These very works I am doing testify about Me that the Father has sent Me. [37] The Father who sent Me has Himself testified about Me. You have not heard His voice at any time, and you haven't seen His form. [38] You don't have His word living in you, because you don't believe the One He sent. [39] You pore over[G] the Scriptures because you think you have eternal life in them, yet they testify about Me. [40] And you are not willing to come to Me so that you may have life.

[41] "I do not accept glory from men, [42] but I know you—that you have no love for God within you. [43] I have come in My Father's name, yet you don't accept Me. If someone else comes in his own name, you will accept him. [44] How can you believe? While accepting glory from one another, you don't seek the glory that comes from the only God. [45] Do not think that I will accuse you to the Father. Your accuser is Moses, on whom you have set your hope. [46] For if you believed Moses, you would

[A]5:13 Lit slipped away, there being a crowd in that place   [B]5:16 Other mss add and trying to kill Him   [C]5:19 Lit whatever that One   [D]5:31 Or not true   [E]5:32 Or true   [F]5:35 Lit That man   [G]5:39 In Gk this could be a command: Pore over . . .

believe Me, because he wrote about Me. ⁴⁷But if you don't believe his writings, how will you believe My words?"

6 After this, Jesus crossed the Sea of Galilee (or Tiberias). ²And a huge crowd was following Him because they saw the signs that He was performing by healing the sick. ³So Jesus went up a mountain and sat down there with His disciples.

⁴Now the Passover, a Jewish festival, was near. ⁵Therefore, when Jesus looked up and noticed a huge crowd coming toward Him, He asked Philip, "Where will we buy bread so these people can eat?" ⁶He asked this to test him, for He Himself knew what He was going to do.

⁷Philip answered, "Two hundred denarii worth of bread wouldn't be enough for each of them to have a little."

⁸One of His disciples, Andrew, Simon Peter's brother, said to Him, ⁹"There's a boy here who has five barley loaves and two fish—but what are they for so many?"

¹⁰Then Jesus said, "Have the people sit down."

There was plenty of grass in that place, so they sat down. The men numbered about 5,000. ¹¹Then Jesus took the loaves, and after giving thanks He distributed them to those who were seated—so also with the fish, as much as they wanted.

¹²When they were full, He told His disciples, "Collect the leftovers so that nothing is wasted." ¹³So they collected them and filled 12 baskets with the pieces from the five barley loaves that were left over by those who had eaten.

¹⁴When the people saw the sign^A He had done, they said, "This really is the Prophet who was to come into the world." ¹⁵Therefore, when Jesus knew that they were about to come and take Him by force to make Him king, He withdrew again^B to the mountain by Himself.

¹⁶When evening came, His disciples went down to the sea, ¹⁷got into a boat, and started across the sea to Capernaum. Darkness had already set in, but Jesus had not yet come to them. ¹⁸Then a high wind arose, and the sea began to churn. ¹⁹After they had rowed about three or four miles,^C they saw Jesus walking on the sea. He was coming near the boat, and they were afraid.

²⁰But He said to them, "It is I.^D Don't be afraid!" ²¹Then they were willing to take Him on board, and at once the boat was at the shore where they were heading.

²²The next day, the crowd that had stayed on the other side of the sea knew there had been only one boat.^E They also knew that Jesus had not boarded the boat with His disciples, but that His disciples had gone off alone. ²³Some boats from Tiberias came near the place where they ate the bread after the Lord gave thanks. ²⁴When the crowd saw that neither Jesus nor His disciples were there, they got into the boats and went to Capernaum looking for Jesus.

²⁵When they found Him on the other side of the sea, they said to Him, "Rabbi, when did You get here?"

²⁶Jesus answered, "I assure you: You are looking for Me, not because you saw^F the signs, but because you ate the loaves and were filled. ²⁷Don't work for the food that perishes but for the food that lasts for eternal life, which the Son of Man will give you, because God the Father has set His seal of approval on Him."

²⁸"What can we do to perform the works of God?" they asked.

²⁹Jesus replied, "This is the work of God—that you believe in the One He has sent."

³⁰"What sign then are You going to do so we may see and believe You?" they asked. "What are You going to perform? ³¹Our fathers ate the manna in the wilderness, just as it is written: **He gave them bread from heaven to eat.**^G,H

³²Jesus said to them, "I assure you: Moses didn't give you the bread from heaven, but My Father gives you the real bread from heaven. ³³For the bread of God is the One who comes down from heaven and gives life to the world."

³⁴Then they said, "Sir, give us this bread always!"

³⁵"I am the bread of life," Jesus told them. "No one who comes to Me will ever be hungry, and no one who believes in Me will ever be thirsty again. ³⁶But as I told you, you've seen Me,^I and yet you do not believe. ³⁷Everyone the Father gives Me will come to Me, and the one who comes to Me I will never cast out. ³⁸For I have come down from heaven, not to do My will, but the will of Him who sent Me. ³⁹This is the will of Him who sent Me: that I should lose

^A6:14 Other mss read signs   ^B6:15 A previous withdrawal is mentioned in Mk 6:31-32, an event that occurred just before the feeding of the 5,000.   ^C6:19 Lit 25 or 30 stadia; 1 stadion = 600 feet   ^D6:20 Lit I am   ^E6:22 Other mss add into which His disciples had entered   ^F6:26 Or perceived   ^G6:31 Bread miraculously provided by God for the Israelites   ^H6:31 Ex 16:4; Ps 78:24   ^I6:36 Other mss omit Me none of those He has given Me but should raise them up on the last day. ⁴⁰For this is the will of My Father: that everyone who sees the Son and believes in Him may have eternal life, and I will raise him up on the last day."

⁴¹Therefore the Jews started complaining about Him because He said, "I am the bread that came down from heaven." ⁴²They were saying, "Isn't this Jesus the son of Joseph, whose father and mother we know? How can He now say, 'I have come down from heaven'?"

⁴³Jesus answered them, "Stop complaining among yourselves. ⁴⁴No one can come to Me unless the Father who sent Me draws^A him, and I will raise him up on the last day. ⁴⁵It is written in the Prophets: And they will all be taught by God.^B Everyone who has listened to and learned from the Father comes to Me— ⁴⁶not that anyone has seen the Father except the One who is from God. He has seen the Father.

⁴⁷"I assure you: Anyone who believes^C has eternal life. ⁴⁸I am the bread of life. ⁴⁹Your fathers ate the manna in the wilderness, and they died. ⁵⁰This is the bread that comes down from heaven so that anyone may eat of it and not die. ⁵¹I am the living bread that came down from heaven. If anyone eats of this bread he will live forever. The bread that I will give for the life of the world is My flesh."

⁵²At that, the Jews argued among themselves, "How can this man give us His flesh to eat?"

⁵³So Jesus said to them, "I assure you: Unless you eat the flesh of the Son of Man and drink His blood, you do not have life in yourselves. ⁵⁴Anyone who eats My flesh and drinks My blood has eternal life, and I will raise him up on the last day, ⁵⁵because My flesh is real food and My blood is real drink. ⁵⁶The one who eats My flesh and drinks My blood lives in Me, and I in him. ⁵⁷Just as the living Father sent Me and I live because of the Father, so the one who feeds on Me will live because of Me. ⁵⁸This is the bread that came down from heaven; it is not like the manna^D your fathers ate—and they died. The one who eats this bread will live forever."

⁵⁹He said these things while teaching in the synagogue in Capernaum.

⁶⁰Therefore, when many of His disciples heard this, they said, "This teaching is hard! Who can accept^E it?"

⁶¹Jesus, knowing in Himself that His disciples were complaining about this, asked them, "Does this offend you? ⁶²Then what if you were to observe the Son of Man ascending to where He was before? ⁶³The Spirit is the One who gives life. The flesh doesn't help at all. The words that I have spoken to you are spirit and are life. ⁶⁴But there are some among you who don't believe." (For Jesus knew from the beginning those who would not^F believe and the one who would betray Him.) ⁶⁵He said, "This is why I told you that no one can come to Me unless it is granted to him by the Father."

⁶⁶From that moment many of His disciples turned back and no longer accompanied Him. ⁶⁷Therefore Jesus said to the Twelve, "You don't want to go away too, do you?"

⁶⁸Simon Peter answered, "Lord, who will we go to? You have the words of eternal life. ⁶⁹We have come to believe and know that You are the Holy One of God!"^G

⁷⁰Jesus replied to them, "Didn't I choose you, the Twelve? Yet one of you is the Devil!" ⁷¹He was referring to Judas, Simon Iscariot's son,^H,I one of the Twelve, because he was going to betray Him.

7 After this, Jesus traveled in Galilee, since He did not want to travel in Judea because the Jews were trying to kill Him. ²The Jewish Festival of Tabernacles^J,K was near, ³so His brothers said to Him, "Leave here and go to Judea so Your disciples can see Your works that You are doing. ⁴For no one does anything in secret while he's seeking public recognition. If You do these things, show Yourself to the world." ⁵(For not even His brothers believed in Him.)

⁶Jesus told them, "My time has not yet arrived, but your time is always at hand. ⁷The world cannot hate you, but it does hate Me because I testify about it—that its deeds are evil. ⁸Go up to the festival yourselves. I'm not going up to the festival yet,^L because My time has not yet fully come." ⁹After He had said these things, He stayed in Galilee.

¹⁰After His brothers had gone up to the festival, then He also went up, not openly but

---

^A6:44 Or brings, or leads; see the use of this Gk verb in Jn 12:32; 21:6; Ac 16:19; Jms 2:6.   ^B6:45 Is 54:13   ^C6:47 Other mss add in Me   ^D6:58 Other mss omit the manna   ^E6:60 Lit hear   ^F6:64 Other mss omit not   ^G6:69 Other mss read You are the Messiah, the Son of the Living God   ^H6:71 Other mss read Judas Iscariot, Simon's son   ^I6:71 Lit Judas, of Simon Iscariot   ^J7:2 Or Booths   ^K7:2 One of 3 great Jewish religious festivals, along with Passover and Pentecost; Ex 23:14; Dt 16:16   ^L7:8 Other mss omit yet secretly. [11] The Jews were looking for Him at the festival and saying, "Where is He?" [12] And there was a lot of discussion about Him among the crowds. Some were saying, "He's a good man." Others were saying, "No, on the contrary, He's deceiving the people." [13] Still, nobody was talking publicly about Him because they feared the Jews.

[14] When the festival was already half over, Jesus went up into the temple complex and began to teach. [15] Then the Jews were amazed and said, "How does He know the Scriptures, since He hasn't been trained?"

[16] Jesus answered them, "My teaching isn't Mine but is from the One who sent Me. [17] If anyone wants to do His will, he will understand whether the teaching is from God or if I am speaking on My own. [18] The one who speaks for himself seeks his own glory. But He who seeks the glory of the One who sent Him is true, and there is no unrighteousness in Him. [19] Didn't Moses give you the law? Yet none of you keeps the law! Why do you want to kill Me?"

[20] "You have a demon!" the crowd responded. "Who wants to kill You?"

[21] "I did one work, and you are all amazed," Jesus answered. [22] "Consider this: Moses has given you circumcision—not that it comes from Moses but from the fathers—and you circumcise a man on the Sabbath. [23] If a man receives circumcision on the Sabbath so that the law of Moses won't be broken, are you angry at Me because I made a man entirely well on the Sabbath? [24] Stop judging according to outward appearances; rather judge according to righteous judgment."

[25] Some of the people of Jerusalem were saying, "Isn't this the man they want to kill? [26] Yet, look! He's speaking publicly and they're saying nothing to Him. Can it be true that the authorities know He is the Messiah? [27] But we know where this man is from. When the Messiah comes, nobody will know where He is from."

[28] As He was teaching in the temple complex, Jesus cried out, "You know Me and you know where I am from. Yet I have not come on My own, but the One who sent Me is true. You don't know Him; [29] I know Him because I am from Him, and He sent Me."

[30] Then they tried to seize Him. Yet no one laid a hand on Him because His hour[A] had not yet come. [31] However, many from the crowd believed in Him and said, "When the Messiah comes, He won't perform more signs than this man has done, will He?"

[32] The Pharisees heard the crowd muttering these things about Him, so the chief priests and the Pharisees sent temple police to arrest Him.

[33] Then Jesus said, "I am only with you for a short time. Then I'm going to the One who sent Me. [34] You will look for Me, but you will not find Me; and where I am, you cannot come."

[35] Then the Jews said to one another, "Where does He intend to go so we won't find Him? He doesn't intend to go to the Dispersion[B] among the Greeks and teach the Greeks, does He? [36] What is this remark He made: 'You will look for Me, and you will not find Me; and where I am, you cannot come'?"

[37] On the last and most important day of the festival, Jesus stood up and cried out, "If anyone is thirsty, he should come to Me[C] and drink! [38] The one who believes in Me, as the Scripture has said,[D] will have streams of living water flow from deep within him." [39] He said this about the Spirit. Those who believed in Jesus were going to receive the Spirit, for the Spirit[E] had not yet been received[F,G] because Jesus had not yet been glorified.

[40] When some from the crowd heard these words, they said, "This really is the Prophet!"[H] [41] Others said, "This is the Messiah!" But some said, "Surely the Messiah doesn't come from Galilee, does He? [42] Doesn't the Scripture say that the Messiah comes from David's offspring[I] and from the town of Bethlehem, where David once lived?" [43] So a division occurred among the crowd because of Him. [44] Some of them wanted to seize Him, but no one laid hands on Him.

[45] Then the temple police came to the chief priests and Pharisees, who asked them, "Why haven't you brought Him?"

[46] The police answered, "No man ever spoke like this!"[J]

[47] Then the Pharisees responded to them: "Are you fooled too? [48] Have any of the rulers or

A7:30 The time of His sacrificial death and exaltation; Jn 2:4; 8:20; 12:23,27; 13:1; 17:1   B7:35 Jewish people scattered throughout Gentile lands who spoke Gk and were influenced by Gk culture   C7:37 Other mss omit to Me   D7:38 Jesus may have had several OT passages in mind; Is 58:11; Ezk 47:1-12; Zch 14:8   E7:39 Other mss read Holy Spirit   F7:39 Other mss read had not yet been given   G7:39 Lit the Spirit was not yet; the word received is implied from the previous clause.   H7:40 Probably the Prophet in Dt 18:15   I7:42 Lit seed   J7:46 Other mss read like this man

Pharisees believed in Him? [49] But this crowd, which doesn't know the law, is accursed!"

[50] Nicodemus—the one who came to Him previously, being one of them—said to them, [51] "Our law doesn't judge a man before it hears from him and knows what he's doing, does it?"

[52] "You aren't from Galilee too, are you?" they replied. "Investigate and you will see that no prophet arises from Galilee."[A]

8 [[53] So each one went to his house. [1] But Jesus went to the Mount of Olives.

[2] At dawn He went to the temple complex again, and all the people were coming to Him. He sat down and began to teach them.

[3] Then the scribes and the Pharisees brought a woman caught in adultery, making her stand in the center. "Teacher," they said to Him, "this woman was caught in the act of committing adultery. [5] In the law Moses commanded us to stone such women. So what do You say?" [6] They asked this to trap Him, in order that they might have evidence to accuse Him.

Jesus stooped down and started writing on the ground with His finger. [7] When they persisted in questioning Him, He stood up and said to them, "The one without sin among you should be the first to throw a stone at her."

[8] Then He stooped down again and continued writing on the ground. [9] When they heard this, they left one by one, starting with the older men. Only He was left, with the woman in the center. [10] When Jesus stood up, He said to her, "Woman, where are they? Has no one condemned you?"

[11] "No one, Lord,"[B] she answered.

"Neither do I condemn you," said Jesus. "Go, and from now on do not sin anymore."][C]

[12] Then Jesus spoke to them again: "I am the light of the world. Anyone who follows Me will never walk in the darkness but will have the light of life."

[13] So the Pharisees said to Him, "You are testifying about Yourself. Your testimony is not valid."[D]

[14] "Even if I testify about Myself," Jesus replied, "My testimony is valid,[E] because I know where I came from and where I'm going. But you don't know where I come from or where I'm going. [15] You judge by human standards.[F] I judge no one. [16] And if I do judge, My judg-

ment is true, because I am not alone, but I and the Father who sent Me judge together. [17] Even in your law it is written that the witness of two men is valid. [18] I am the One who testifies about Myself, and the Father who sent Me testifies about Me."

[19] Then they asked Him, "Where is Your Father?"

"You know neither Me nor My Father," Jesus answered. "If you knew Me, you would also know My Father." [20] He spoke these words by the treasury,[G] while teaching in the temple complex. But no one seized Him, because His hour[H] had not come.

[21] Then He said to them again, "I'm going away; you will look for Me, and you will die in your sin. Where I'm going, you cannot come."

[22] So the Jews said again, "He won't kill Himself, will He, since He says, 'Where I'm going, you cannot come'?"

[23] "You are from below," He told them, "I am from above. You are of this world; I am not of this world. [24] Therefore I told you that you will die in your sins. For if you do not believe that I am He,[I] you will die in your sins."

[25] "Who are You?" they questioned.

"Precisely what I've been telling you from the very beginning," Jesus told them. [26] "I have many things to say and to judge about you, but the One who sent Me is true, and what I have heard from Him—these things I tell the world."

[27] They did not know He was speaking to them about the Father. [28] So Jesus said to them, "When you lift up the Son of Man, then you will know that I am He, and that I do nothing on My own. But just as the Father taught Me, I say these things. [29] The One who sent Me is with Me. He has not left Me alone, because I always do what pleases Him."

[30] As He was saying these things, many believed in Him. [31] So Jesus said to the Jews who had believed Him, "If you continue in My word,[J] you really are My disciples. [32] You will know the truth, and the truth will set you free."

[33] "We are descendants[K] of Abraham," they answered Him, "and we have never been enslaved to anyone. How can You say, 'You will become free'?"

A7:52 Jonah and probably other prophets did come from Galilee; 2Kg 14:25   B8:11 Or Sir; Jn 4:15,49; 5:7; 6:34; 9:36   C8:11 Other mss omit bracketed text   D8:13 The law of Moses required at least 2 witnesses to make a claim legally valid (v. 17).   E8:14 Or true   F8:15 Lit You judge according to the flesh   G8:20 A place for offerings to be given, perhaps in the court of women   H8:20 The time of His sacrificial death and exaltation; Jn 2:4; 7:30; 12:23,27; 13:1; 17:1   I8:24 Jesus claimed to be deity, but the Pharisees didn't understand His meaning.   J8:31 Or My teaching, or My message   K8:33 Or offspring; lit seed; Jn 7:42

³⁴Jesus responded, "I assure you: Everyone who commits sin is a slave of sin. ³⁵A slave does not remain in the household forever, but a son does remain forever. ³⁶Therefore, if the Son sets you free, you really will be free. ³⁷I know you are descendantsᴬ of Abraham, but you are trying to kill Me because My wordᴮ is not welcome among you. ³⁸I speak what I have seen in the presence of the Father;ᶜ therefore, you do what you have heard from your father."

³⁹"Our father is Abraham!" they replied.

"If you were Abraham's children," Jesus told them, "you would do what Abraham did. ⁴⁰But now you are trying to kill Me, a man who has told you the truth that I heard from God. Abraham did not do this! ⁴¹You're doing what your father does."

"We weren't born of sexual immorality," they said. "We have one Father—God."

⁴²Jesus said to them, "If God were your Father, you would love Me, because I came from God and I am here. For I didn't come on My own, but He sent Me. ⁴³Why don't you understand what I say? Because you cannot listen toᴰ My word. ⁴⁴You are of your father the Devil, and you want to carry out your father's desires. He was a murderer from the beginning and has not stood in the truth, because there is no truth in him. When he tells a lie, he speaks from his own nature,ᴱ because he is a liar and the father of liars.ᶠ ⁴⁵Yet because I tell the truth, you do not believe Me. ⁴⁶Who among you can convict Me of sin? If I tell the truth, why don't you believe Me? ⁴⁷The one who is from God listens to God's words. This is why you don't listen, because you are not from God."

⁴⁸The Jews responded to Him, "Aren't we right in saying that You're a Samaritan and have a demon?"

⁴⁹"I do not have a demon," Jesus answered. "On the contrary, I honor My Father and you dishonor Me. ⁵⁰I do not seek My glory; the One who seeks it also judges. ⁵¹I assure you: If anyone keeps My word, he will never see death—ever!"

⁵²Then the Jews said, "Now we know You have a demon. Abraham died and so did the prophets. You say, 'If anyone keeps My word, he will never taste death—ever!' ⁵³Are You greater than our father Abraham who died? Even the prophets died. Who do You pretend to be?"ᴳ

⁵⁴"If I glorify Myself," Jesus answered, "My glory is nothing. My Father—you say about Him, 'He is our God'—He is the One who glorifies Me. ⁵⁵You've never known Him, but I know Him. If I were to say I don't know Him, I would be a liar like you. But I do know Him, and I keep His word. ⁵⁶Your father Abraham was overjoyed that he would see My day; he saw it and rejoiced."

⁵⁷The Jews replied, "You aren't 50 years old yet, and You've seen Abraham?"ᴴ

⁵⁸Jesus said to them, "I assure you: Before Abraham was, I am."ᴵ

⁵⁹At that, they picked up stones to throw at Him. But Jesus was hiddenᴶ and went out of the temple complex.ᴷ

9 As He was passing by, He saw a man blind from birth. ²His disciples questioned Him: "Rabbi, who sinned, this man or his parents, that he was born blind?"

³"Neither this man nor his parents sinned," Jesus answered. "This came about so that God's works might be displayed in him. ⁴Weᴸ must do the works of Him who sent Meᴹ while it is day. Night is coming when no one can work. ⁵As long as I am in the world, I am the light of the world."

⁶After He said these things He spit on the ground, made some mud from the saliva, and spread the mud on his eyes. ⁷"Go," He told him, "wash in the pool of Siloam" (which means "Sent"). So he left, washed, and came back seeing.

⁸His neighbors and those who formerly had seen him as a beggar said, "Isn't this the man who sat begging?" ⁹Some said, "He's the one." "No," others were saying, "but he looks like him."

He kept saying, "I'm the one!"

¹⁰Therefore they asked him, "Then how were your eyes opened?"

¹¹He answered, "The man called Jesus made mud, spread it on my eyes, and told me, 'Go to Siloam and wash.' So when I went and washed I received my sight."

¹²"Where is He?" they asked.

"I don't know," he said.

ᴬ8:37 Or offspring; lit seed; Jn 7:42 ᴮ8:37 Or My teaching, or My message ᶜ8:38 Other mss read of My Father ᴰ8:43 Or cannot hear ᴱ8:44 Lit from his own things ᶠ8:44 Lit of it ᴳ8:53 Lit Who do You make Yourself? ᴴ8:57 Other mss read and Abraham has seen You? ᴵ8:58 I AM is the name God gave Himself at the burning bush; Ex 3:13-14; see note at Jn 8:24. ᴶ8:59 Or Jesus hid Himself ᴷ8:59 Other mss add and having gone through their midst, He passed by ᴸ9:4 Other mss read I ᴹ9:4 Other mss read sent us

¹³They brought the man who used to be blind to the Pharisees. ¹⁴The day that Jesus made the mud and opened his eyes was a Sabbath. ¹⁵So again the Pharisees asked him how he received his sight.

"He put mud on my eyes," he told them. "I washed and I can see."

¹⁶Therefore some of the Pharisees said, "This man is not from God, for He doesn't keep the Sabbath!" But others were saying, "How can a sinful man perform such signs?" And there was a division among them.

¹⁷Again they asked the blind man,ᴬ "What do you say about Him, since He opened your eyes?"

"He's a prophet," he said.

¹⁸The Jews did not believe this about him —that he was blind and received sight—until they summoned the parents of the one who had received his sight.

¹⁹They asked them, "Is this your son, the one you say was born blind? How then does he now see?"

²⁰"We know this is our son and that he was born blind," his parents answered. ²¹"But we don't know how he now sees, and we don't know who opened his eyes. Ask him; he's of age. He will speak for himself." ²²His parents said these things because they were afraid of the Jews, since the Jews had already agreed that if anyone confessed Him as Messiah, he would be banned from the synagogue. ²³This is why his parents said, "He's of age; ask him."

²⁴So a second time they summoned the man who had been blind and told him, "Give glory to God.ᴮ We know that this man is a sinner!"

²⁵He answered, "Whether or not He's a sinner, I don't know. One thing I do know: I was blind, and now I can see!"

²⁶Then they asked him, "What did He do to you? How did He open your eyes?"

²⁷"I already told you," he said, "and you didn't listen. Why do you want to hear it again? You don't want to become His disciples too, do you?"

²⁸They ridiculed him: "You're that man's disciple, but we're Moses' disciples. ²⁹We know that God has spoken to Moses. But this man—we don't know where He's from!"

³⁰"This is an amazing thing," the man told them. "You don't know where He is from, yet He opened my eyes! ³¹We know that God doesn't listen to sinners, but if anyone is God-fearing and does His will, He listens to him. ³²Throughout historyᶜ no one has ever heard of someone opening the eyes of a person born blind. ³³If this man were not from God, He wouldn't be able to do anything."

³⁴"You were born entirely in sin," they replied, "and are you trying to teach us?" Then they threw him out.ᴰ

³⁵When Jesus heard that they had thrown the man out, He found him and asked, "Do you believe in the Son of Man?"ᴱ

³⁶"Who is He, Sir, that I may believe in Him?" he asked.

³⁷Jesus answered, "You have seen Him; in fact, He is the One speaking with you."

³⁸"I believe, Lord!" he said, and he worshiped Him.

³⁹Jesus said, "I came into this world for judgment, in order that those who do not see will see and those who do see will become blind."

⁴⁰Some of the Pharisees who were with Him heard these things and asked Him, "We aren't blind too, are we?"

⁴¹"If you were blind," Jesus told them, "you wouldn't have sin.ᶠ But now that you say, 'We see'—your sin remains.

10 "I assure you: Anyone who doesn't enter the sheep pen by the door but climbs in some other way, is a thief and a robber. ²The one who enters by the door is the shepherd of the sheep. ³The doorkeeper opens it for him, and the sheep hear his voice. He calls his own sheep by name and leads them out. ⁴When he has brought all his own outside, he goes ahead of them. The sheep follow him because they recognize his voice. ⁵They will never follow a stranger; instead they will run away from him, because they don't recognize the voice of strangers."

⁶Jesus gave them this illustration, but they did not understand what He was telling them.

⁷So Jesus said again, "I assure you, I am the door of the sheep. ⁸All who came before Meᴳ are thieves and robbers, but the sheep didn't listen to them. ⁹I am the door. If anyone enters by Me, he will be saved and will come in and go out and find pasture. ¹⁰A thief comes only to steal and to kill and to destroy. I have come so that they may have life and have it in abundance.

ᴬ9:17 = the man who had been blind   ᴮ9:24 *Give glory to God* was a solemn charge to tell the truth; Jos 7:19.   ᶜ9:32 Lit *From the age*   ᴰ9:34 = they banned him from the synagogue; v. 22   ᴱ9:35 Other mss read *the Son of God*   ᶠ9:41 To have sin is an idiom that refers to guilt caused by sin.   ᴳ10:8 Other mss omit *before Me*

¹¹"I am the good shepherd. The good shepherd lays down his life for the sheep. ¹²The hired man, since he is not the shepherd and doesn't own the sheep, leaves him^A and runs away when he sees a wolf coming. The wolf then snatches and scatters them. ¹³This happens because he is a hired man and doesn't care about the sheep.

¹⁴"I am the good shepherd. I know My own sheep, and they know Me, ¹⁵as the Father knows Me, and I know the Father. I lay down My life for the sheep. ¹⁶But I have other sheep that are not of this fold; I must bring them also, and they will listen to My voice. Then there will be one flock, one shepherd. ¹⁷This is why the Father loves Me, because I am laying down My life so I may take it up again. ¹⁸No one takes it from Me, but I lay it down on My own. I have the right to lay it down, and I have the right to take it up again. I have received this command from My Father."

¹⁹Again a division took place among the Jews because of these words. ²⁰Many of them were saying, "He has a demon and He's crazy! Why do you listen to Him?" ²¹Others were saying, "These aren't the words of someone demon-possessed. Can a demon open the eyes of the blind?"

²²Then the Festival of Dedication^B took place in Jerusalem, and it was winter. ²³Jesus was walking in the temple complex in Solomon's Colonnade.^C ²⁴Then the Jews surrounded Him and asked, "How long are You going to keep us in suspense?^D If You are the Messiah, tell us plainly."^E

²⁵"I did tell you and you don't believe," Jesus answered them. "The works that I do in My Father's name testify about Me. ²⁶But you don't believe because you are not My sheep.^F ²⁷My sheep hear My voice, I know them, and they follow Me. ²⁸I give them eternal life, and they will never perish—ever! No one will snatch them out of My hand. ²⁹My Father, who has given them to Me, is greater than all. No one is able to snatch them out of the Father's hand. ³⁰The Father and I are one."^G

³¹Again the Jews picked up rocks to stone Him.

³²Jesus replied, "I have shown you many good works from the Father. Which of these works are you stoning Me for?"

³³"We aren't stoning You for a good work," the Jews answered, "but for blasphemy, because You—being a man—make Yourself God."

³⁴Jesus answered them, "Isn't it written in your scripture,^H I said, you are gods?¹ ³⁵If He called those whom the word of God came to 'gods'—and the Scripture cannot be broken— ³⁶do you say, 'You are blaspheming' to the One the Father set apart and sent into the world, because I said: I am the Son of God? ³⁷If I am not doing My Father's works, don't believe Me. ³⁸But if I am doing them and you don't believe Me, believe the works. This way you will know and understand^J that the Father is in Me and I in the Father." ³⁹Then they were trying again to seize Him, yet He eluded their grasp.

⁴⁰So He departed again across the Jordan to the place where John had been baptizing earlier, and He remained there. ⁴¹Many came to Him and said, "John never did a sign, but everything John said about this man was true." ⁴²And many believed in Him there.

11 Now a man was sick, Lazarus, from Bethany, the village of Mary and her sister Martha. ²Mary was the one who anointed the Lord with fragrant oil and wiped His feet with her hair, and it was her brother Lazarus who was sick. ³So the sisters sent a message to Him: "Lord, the one You love is sick."

⁴When Jesus heard it, He said, "This sickness will not end in death but is for the glory of God, so that the Son of God may be glorified through it." ⁵Now Jesus loved Martha, her sister, and Lazarus. ⁶So when He heard that he was sick, He stayed two more days in the place where He was. ⁷Then after that, He said to the disciples, "Let's go to Judea again."

⁸"Rabbi," the disciples told Him, "just now the Jews tried to stone You, and You're going there again?"

⁹"Aren't there 12 hours in a day?" Jesus answered. "If anyone walks during the day, he doesn't stumble, because he sees the light of this world. ¹⁰If anyone walks during the night, he does stumble, because the light is not in him." ¹¹He said this, and then He told them, "Our friend Lazarus has fallen asleep, but I'm on My way to wake him up."

---

^A10:12 Lit *leaves the sheep* ^B10:22 Or *Hanukkah*, also called the *Feast of Lights*; this festival commemorated the rededication of the temple in 164 B.C. ^C10:23 Rows of columns supporting a roof ^D10:24 Lit *How long are you taking away our life?* ^E10:24 Or *openly*, or *publicly* ^F10:26 Other mss add *just as I told you* ^G10:30 Lit *I and the Father—We are one.* ^H10:34 Other mss read *in the scripture* ^I10:34 Ps 82:6 ^J10:38 Other mss read *know and believe*

[12] Then the disciples said to Him, "Lord, if he has fallen asleep, he will get well."

[13] Jesus, however, was speaking about his death, but they thought He was speaking about natural sleep. [14] So Jesus then told them plainly, "Lazarus has died. [15] I'm glad for you that I wasn't there so that you may believe. But let's go to him."

[16] Then Thomas (called "Twin") said to his fellow disciples, "Let's go so that we may die with Him."

[17] When Jesus arrived, He found that Lazarus had already been in the tomb four days. [18] Bethany was near Jerusalem (about two miles[A] away). [19] Many of the Jews had come to Martha and Mary to comfort them about their brother. [20] As soon as Martha heard that Jesus was coming, she went to meet Him. But Mary remained seated in the house.

[21] Then Martha said to Jesus, "Lord, if You had been here, my brother wouldn't have died. [22] Yet even now I know that whatever You ask from God, God will give You."

[23] "Your brother will rise again," Jesus told her.

[24] Martha said, "I know that he will rise again in the resurrection at the last day."

[25] Jesus said to her, "I am the resurrection and the life. The one who believes in Me, even if he dies, will live. [26] Everyone who lives and believes in Me will never die—ever. Do you believe this?"

[27] "Yes, Lord," she told Him, "I believe You are the Messiah, the Son of God, who comes into the world."

[28] Having said this, she went back and called her sister Mary, saying in private, "The Teacher is here and is calling for you."

[29] As soon as she heard this, she got up quickly and went to Him. [30] Jesus had not yet come into the village but was still in the place where Martha had met Him. [31] The Jews who were with her in the house consoling her saw that Mary got up quickly and went out. So they followed her, supposing that she was going to the tomb to cry there.

[32] When Mary came to where Jesus was and saw Him, she fell at His feet and told Him, "Lord, if You had been here, my brother would not have died!"

[33] When Jesus saw her crying, and the Jews who had come with her crying, He was angry[B] in His spirit and deeply moved. [34] "Where have you put him?" He asked.

"Lord," they told Him, "come and see."

[35] Jesus wept.

[36] So the Jews said, "See how He loved him!" [37] But some of them said, "Couldn't He who opened the blind man's eyes also have kept this man from dying?"

[38] Then Jesus, angry[C] in Himself again, came to the tomb. It was a cave, and a stone was lying against it. [39] "Remove the stone," Jesus said.

Martha, the dead man's sister, told Him, "Lord, he's already decaying.[D] It's been four days."

[40] Jesus said to her, "Didn't I tell you that if you believed you would see the glory of God?"

[41] So they removed the stone. Then Jesus raised His eyes and said, "Father, I thank You that You heard Me. [42] I know that You always hear Me, but because of the crowd standing here I said this, so they may believe You sent Me." [43] After He said this, He shouted with a loud voice, "Lazarus, come out!" [44] The dead man came out bound hand and foot with linen strips and with his face wrapped in a cloth. Jesus said to them, "Loose him and let him go."

[45] Therefore, many of the Jews who came to Mary and saw Him did believe in Him. [46] But some of them went to the Pharisees and told them what Jesus had done.

[47] So the chief priests and the Pharisees convened the Sanhedrin and said, "What are we going to do since this man does many signs? [48] If we let Him continue in this way, everyone will believe in Him! Then the Romans will come and remove both our place[E] and our nation."

[49] One of them, Caiaphas, who was high priest that year, said to them, "You know nothing at all! [50] You're not considering that it is to your[F] advantage that one man should die for the people rather than that the whole nation perish." [51] He did not say this on his own, but being high priest that year he prophesied that Jesus was going to die for the nation, [52] and not for the nation only, but also to unite the scattered children of God. [53] So from that day on

A11:18 Lit 15 *stadia*; 1 *stadion* = 600 feet   B11:33 The Gk word is very strong and probably indicates Jesus' anger against sin's tyranny and death.   C11:38 See note at 11:33.   D11:39 Lit *he already stinks*   E11:48 The temple or possibly all of Jerusalem   F11:50 Other mss read *to our* they plotted to kill Him. ⁵⁴Therefore Jesus no longer walked openly among the Jews but departed from there to the countryside near the wilderness, to a town called Ephraim. And He stayed there with the disciples.

⁵⁵The Jewish Passover was near, and many went up to Jerusalem from the country to purifyᴬ themselves before the Passover. ⁵⁶They were looking for Jesus and asking one another as they stood in the temple complex: "What do you think? He won't come to the festival, will He?" ⁵⁷The chief priests and the Pharisees had given orders that if anyone knew where He was, he should report it so they could arrest Him.

12 Six days before the Passover, Jesus came to Bethany where Lazarusᴮ was, the one Jesus had raised from the dead. ²So they gave a dinner for Him there; Martha was serving them, and Lazarus was one of those reclining at the table with Him. ³Then Mary took a pound of fragrant oil—pure and expensive nard—anointed Jesus' feet, and wiped His feet with her hair. So the house was filled with the fragrance of the oil.

⁴Then one of His disciples, Judas Iscariot (who was about to betray Him), said, ⁵"Why wasn't this fragrant oil sold for 300 denariiᶜ and given to the poor?" ⁶He didn't say this because he cared about the poor but because he was a thief. He was in charge of the money-bag and would steal part of what was put in it.

⁷Jesus answered, "Leave her alone; she has kept it for the day of My burial. ⁸For you always have the poor with you, but you do not always have Me."

⁹Then a large crowd of the Jews learned He was there. They came not only because of Jesus, but also to see Lazarus the one He had raised from the dead. ¹⁰Therefore the chief priests decided to kill Lazarus also ¹¹because he was the reason many of the Jews were deserting themᴰ and believing in Jesus.

¹²The next day, when the large crowd that had come to the festival heard that Jesus was coming to Jerusalem, ¹³they took palm branches and went out to meet Him. They kept shouting: *"Hosanna!* **He who comes in the name of the Lord is the blessed One**ᴱ—the King of Israel!"

¹⁴Jesus found a young donkey and sat on it, just as it is written: ¹⁵**Fear no more, Daughter Zion. Look, your King is coming, sitting on a donkey's colt.**ᶠ

¹⁶His disciples did not understand these things at first. However, when Jesus was glorified, then they remembered that these things had been written about Him and that they had done these things to Him. ¹⁷Meanwhile, the crowd, which had been with Him when He called Lazarus out of the tomb and raised him from the dead, continued to testify.ᴳ ¹⁸This is also why the crowd met Him, because they heard He had done this sign.

¹⁹Then the Pharisees said to one another, "You see? You've accomplished nothing. Look—the world has gone after Him!"

²⁰Now some Greeks were among those who went up to worship at the festival. ²¹So they came to Philip, who was from Bethsaida in Galilee, and requested of him, "Sir, we want to see Jesus."

²²Philip went and told Andrew; then Andrew and Philip went and told Jesus. ²³Jesus replied to them, "The hour has come for the Son of Man to be glorified.

²⁴"I assure you: Unless a grain of wheat falls to the ground and dies, it remains by itself. But if it dies, it produces a large crop.ᴴ ²⁵The one who loves his life will lose it, and the one who hates his life in this world will keep it for eternal life. ²⁶If anyone serves Me, he must follow Me. Where I am, there My servant also will be. If anyone serves Me, the Father will honor him.

²⁷"Now My soul is troubled. What should I say—Father, save Me from this hour? But that is why I came to this hour. ²⁸Father, glorify Your name!"

Then a voice came from heaven: "I have glorified it, and I will glorify it again!"

²⁹The crowd standing there heard it and said it was thunder. Others said that an angel had spoken to Him.

³⁰Jesus responded, "This voice came, not for Me, but for you. ³¹Now is the judgment of this world. Now the ruler of this world will be cast out. ³²As for Me, if I am lifted upᴶ from the earth I will draw all people to Myself." ³³He

ᴬ11:55 The law of Moses required God's people to purify or cleanse themselves so they could celebrate the Passover. Jews often came to Jerusalem a week early to do this; Nm 9:4-11. ᴮ12:1 Other mss read *Lazarus who died* ᶜ12:5 This amount was about a year's wages for a common worker. ᴰ12:11 Lit *going away* ᴱ12:13 Ps 118:25-26 ᶠ12:15 Zch 9:9 ᴳ12:17 Other mss read *Meanwhile the crowd, which had been with Him, continued to testify that He had called Lazarus out of the tomb and raised him from the dead.* ᴴ12:24 Lit *produces much fruit* ᴶ12:28 Other mss read *Your Son* ᴶ12:32 Or *exalted* said this to signify what kind of death He was about to die.

³⁴Then the crowd replied to Him, "We have heard from the scripture that the Messiah will remain forever. So how can You say, 'The Son of Man must be lifted up'?ᴬ Who is this Son of Man?"

³⁵Jesus answered, "The light will be with you only a little longer. Walk while you have the light so that darkness doesn't overtake you. The one who walks in darkness doesn't know where he's going. ³⁶While you have the light, believe in the light so that you may become sons of light." Jesus said this, then went away and hid from them.

³⁷Even though He had performed so many signs in their presence, they did not believe in Him. ³⁸But this was to fulfill the word of Isaiah the prophet, who said:ᴮ

> Lord, who has believed
>   our message?
> And who has the arm of the Lord
>   been revealed to?ᶜ

³⁹This is why they were unable to believe, because Isaiah also said:

⁴⁰ He has blinded their eyes
>   and hardened their hearts,
> so that they would not see
>   with their eyes
> or understand with their hearts,
>   and be converted,
> and I would heal them.ᴰ

⁴¹Isaiah said these things becauseᴱ he saw His glory and spoke about Him.

⁴²Nevertheless, many did believe in Him even among the rulers, but because of the Pharisees they did not confess Him, so they would not be banned from the synagogue. ⁴³For they loved praise from men more than praise from God.ᶠ

⁴⁴Then Jesus cried out, "The one who believes in Me believes not in Me, but in Him who sent Me. ⁴⁵And the one who sees Me sees Him who sent Me. ⁴⁶I have come as a light into the world, so that everyone who believes in Me would not remain in darkness. ⁴⁷If anyone hears My words and doesn't keep them, I do not judge him; for I did not come to judge the world but to save the world. ⁴⁸The one who

rejects Me and doesn't accept My sayings has this as his judge:ᴳ The word I have spoken will judge him on the last day. ⁴⁹For I have not spoken on My own, but the Father Himself who sent Me has given Me a command as to what I should say and what I should speak. ⁵⁰I know that His command is eternal life. So the things that I speak, I speak just as the Father has told Me."

13 Before the Passover Festival, Jesus knew that His hour had come to depart from this world to the Father. Having loved His own who were in the world, He loved them to the end.ᴴ

²Now by the time of supper, the Devil had already put it into the heart of Judas, Simon Iscariot's son, to betray Him. ³Jesus knew that the Father had given everything into His hands, that He had come from God, and that He was going back to God. ⁴So He got up from supper, laid aside His robe, took a towel, and tied it around Himself. ⁵Next, He poured water into a basin and began to wash His disciples' feet and to dry them with the towel tied around Him.

⁶He came to Simon Peter, who asked Him, "Lord, are You going to wash my feet?"

⁷Jesus answered him, "What I'm doing you don't understand now, but afterward you will know."

⁸"You will never wash my feet—ever!" Peter said.

Jesus replied, "If I don't wash you, you have no part with Me."

⁹Simon Peter said to Him, "Lord, not only my feet, but also my hands and my head."

¹⁰"One who has bathed," Jesus told him, "doesn't need to wash anything except his feet, but he is completely clean. You are clean, but not all of you." ¹¹For He knew who would betray Him. This is why He said, "You are not all clean."

¹²When Jesus had washed their feet and put on His robe, He reclinedⁱ again and said to them, "Do you know what I have done for you? ¹³You call Me Teacher and Lord. This is well said, for I am. ¹⁴So if I, your Lord and Teacher, have washed your feet, you also ought to wash one another's feet. ¹⁵For I have given you an example that you also should do just as I have done for you.

ᴬ12:34 Or exalted   ᴮ12:38 Lit which he said   ᶜ12:38 Is 53:1   ᴰ12:40 Is 6:10   ᴱ12:41 Other mss read when   ᶠ12:43 Lit loved glory of men more than glory of God; v. 41; Jn 5:41   ᴳ12:48 Lit has the one judging him   ᴴ13:1 = completely or always   ⁱ13:12 At important meals the custom was to recline on a mat at a low table and lean on the left elbow.

[16]"I assure you: A slave is not greater than his master,[A] and a messenger is not greater than the one who sent him. [17]If you know these things, you are blessed if you do them. [18]I'm not speaking about all of you; I know those I have chosen. But the Scripture must be fulfilled: The one who eats My bread[B] has raised his heel against Me.[C]

[19]"I am telling you now before it happens, so that when it does happen you will believe that I am He. [20]I assure you: Whoever receives anyone I send receives Me, and the one who receives Me receives Him who sent Me."

[21]When Jesus had said this, He was troubled in His spirit and testified, "I assure you: One of you will betray Me!"

[22]The disciples started looking at one another—uncertain which one He was speaking about. [23]One of His disciples, the one Jesus loved, was reclining close beside Jesus.[D] [24]Simon Peter motioned to him to find out who it was He was talking about. [25]So he leaned back against Jesus and asked Him, "Lord, who is it?"

[26]Jesus replied, "He's the one I give the piece of bread to after I have dipped it." When He had dipped the bread, He gave it to Judas, Simon Iscariot's son.[E] [27]After Judas ate the piece of bread, Satan entered him. Therefore Jesus told him, "What you're doing, do quickly."

[28]None of those reclining at the table knew why He told him this. [29]Since Judas kept the money-bag, some thought that Jesus was telling him, "Buy what we need for the festival," or that he should give something to the poor. [30]After receiving the piece of bread, he went out immediately. And it was night.

[31]When he had gone out, Jesus said, "Now the Son of Man is glorified, and God is glorified in Him. [32]If God is glorified in Him,[F] God will also glorify Him in Himself and will glorify Him at once.

[33]"Children, I am with you a little while longer. You will look for Me, and just as I told the Jews, 'Where I am going you cannot come,' so now I tell you.

[34]"I give you a new command: Love one another. Just as I have loved you, you must also love one another. [35]By this all people will know that you are My disciples, if you have love for one another."

[36]"Lord," Simon Peter said to Him, "where are You going?"

Jesus answered, "Where I am going you cannot follow Me now, but you will follow later."

[37]"Lord," Peter asked, "why can't I follow You now? I will lay down my life for You!"

[38]Jesus replied, "Will you lay down your life for Me? I assure you: A rooster will not crow until you have denied Me three times.

14

"Your heart must not be troubled. Believe[G] in God; believe also in Me. [2]In My Father's house are many dwelling places;[H] if not, I would have told you. I am going away to prepare a place for you. [3]If I go away and prepare a place for you, I will come back and receive you to Myself, so that where I am you may be also. [4]You know the way to where I am going."[I]

[5]"Lord," Thomas said, "we don't know where You're going. How can we know the way?"

[6]Jesus told him, "I am the way, the truth, and the life. No one comes to the Father except through Me.

[7]"If you know Me, you will also know[J] My Father. From now on you do know Him and have seen Him."

[8]"Lord," said Philip, "show us the Father, and that's enough for us."

[9]Jesus said to him, "Have I been among you all this time without your knowing Me, Philip? The one who has seen Me has seen the Father. How can you say, 'Show us the Father'? [10]Don't you believe that I am in the Father and the Father is in Me? The words I speak to you I do not speak on My own. The Father who lives in Me does His works. [11]Believe Me that I am in the Father and the Father is in Me. Otherwise, believe[K] because of the works themselves.

[12]"I assure you: The one who believes in Me will also do the works that I do. And he will do even greater works than these, because I am going to the Father. [13]Whatever you ask in My name, I will do it so that the Father may be glorified in the Son. [14]If you ask Me[L] anything in My name, I will do it.[M]

[15]"If you love Me, you will keep[N] My commands. [16]And I will ask the Father, and He will

^A13:16 Or lord   ^B13:18 Other mss read eats bread with Me   ^C13:18 Ps 41:9   ^D13:23 Lit reclining at Jesus' breast; that is, on His right; Jn 1:18   ^E13:26 Other mss read Judas Iscariot, Simon's son   ^F13:32 Other mss omit If God is glorified in Him   ^G14:1 Or You believe   ^H14:2 The Vg used the Lat term mansio, a traveler's resting place. The Gk word is related to the verb meno, meaning remain or stay, which occurs 40 times in John.   ^I14:4 Other mss read this verse: And you know where I am going, and you know the way   ^J14:7 Other mss read If you had known Me, you would have known   ^K14:11 Other mss read believe Me   ^L14:14 Other mss omit Me   ^M14:14 Other mss omit all of v. 14   ^N14:15 Other mss read If you love Me, keep (as a command) give you another Counselor to be with you forever. [17]He is the Spirit of truth. The world is unable to receive Him because it doesn't see Him or know Him. But you do know Him, because He remains with you and will be[A] in you. [18]I will not leave you as orphans; I am coming to you.

[19]"In a little while the world will see Me no longer, but you will see Me. Because I live, you will live too. [20]In that day you will know that I am in My Father, you are in Me, and I am in you. [21]The one who has My commands and keeps them is the one who loves Me. And the one who loves Me will be loved by My Father. I also will love him and will reveal Myself to him."

[22]Judas (not Iscariot) said to Him, "Lord, how is it You're going to reveal Yourself to us and not to the world?"

[23]Jesus answered, "If anyone loves Me, he will keep My word. My Father will love him, and We will come to him and make Our home with him. [24]The one who doesn't love Me will not keep My words. The word that you hear is not Mine but is from the Father who sent Me.

[25]"I have spoken these things to you while I remain with you. [26]But the Counselor, the Holy Spirit—the Father will send Him in My name—will teach you all things and remind you of everything I have told you.

[27]"Peace I leave with you. My peace I give to you. I do not give to you as the world gives. Your heart must not be troubled or fearful. [28]You have heard Me tell you, 'I am going away and I am coming to you.' If you loved Me, you would have rejoiced that I am going to the Father, because the Father is greater than I. [29]I have told you now before it happens so that when it does happen you may believe. [30]I will not talk with you much longer, because the ruler of the world is coming. He has no power over Me.[B] [31]On the contrary, I am going away[C] so that the world may know that I love the Father. Just as the Father commanded Me, so I do.

"Get up; let's leave this place.

15 "I am the true vine, and My Father is the vineyard keeper. [2]Every branch in Me that does not produce fruit He removes, and He prunes every branch that produces fruit so that it will produce more fruit. [3]You are already clean because of the word I have spoken

to you. [4]Remain in Me, and I in you. Just as a branch is unable to produce fruit by itself unless it remains on the vine, so neither can you unless you remain in Me.

[5]"I am the vine; you are the branches. The one who remains in Me and I in him produces much fruit, because you can do nothing without Me. [6]If anyone does not remain in Me, he is thrown aside like a branch and he withers. They gather them, throw them into the fire, and they are burned. [7]If you remain in Me and My words remain in you, ask whatever you want and it will be done for you. [8]My Father is glorified by this: that you produce much fruit and prove to be[D] My disciples.

[9]"As the Father has loved Me, I have also loved you. Remain in My love. [10]If you keep My commands you will remain in My love, just as I have kept My Father's commands and remain in His love.

[11]"I have spoken these things to you so that My joy may be in you and your joy may be complete. [12]This is My command: Love one another as I have loved you. [13]No one has greater love than this, that someone would lay down his life for his friends. [14]You are My friends if you do what I command you. [15]I do not call you slaves anymore, because a slave doesn't know what his master[E] is doing. I have called you friends, because I have made known to you everything I have heard from My Father. [16]You did not choose Me, but I chose you. I appointed you that you should go out and produce fruit and that your fruit should remain, so that whatever you ask the Father in My name, He will give you. [17]This is what I command you: Love one another.

[18]"If the world hates you, understand that it hated Me before it hated you. [19]If you were of the world, the world would love you as its own. However, because you are not of the world, but I have chosen you out of it, the world hates you. [20]Remember the word I spoke to you: 'A slave is not greater than his master.' If they persecuted Me, they will also persecute you. If they kept My word, they will also keep yours. [21]But they will do all these things to you on account of My name, because they don't know the One who sent Me. [22]If I had not come and spoken to them, they would not have sin.[F] Now they have no excuse for their sin. [23]The one who hates Me also hates My Father. [24]If I had not done the

---

A14:17 Other mss read and is   B14:30 Lit He has nothing in Me   C14:31 Probably refers to the cross   D15:8 Or and become   E15:15 Or lord
F15:22 To have sin is an idiom that refers to guilt caused by sin.

works among them that no one else has done, they would not have sin. Now they have seen and hated both Me and My Father. ²⁵But this happened so that the statement written in their scripture might be fulfilled: **They hated Me for no reason.**ᴬ

²⁶"When the Counselor comes, the One I will send to you from the Father—the Spirit of truth who proceeds from the Father—He will testify about Me. ²⁷You also will testify, because you have been with Me from the beginning.

16 "I have told you these things to keep you from stumbling. ²They will ban you from the synagogues. In fact, a time is coming when anyone who kills you will think he is offering service to God. ³They will do these things because they haven't known the Father or Me. ⁴But I have told you these things so that when their timeᴮ comes you may remember I told them to you. I didn't tell you these things from the beginning, because I was with you.

⁵"But now I am going away to Him who sent Me, and not one of you asks Me, 'Where are You going?' ⁶Yet, because I have spoken these things to you, sorrow has filled your heart. ⁷Nevertheless, I am telling you the truth. It is for your benefit that I go away, because if I don't go away the Counselor will not come to you. If I go, I will send Him to you. ⁸When He comes, He will convict the world about sin, righteousness, and judgment: ⁹About sin, because they do not believe in Me; ¹⁰about righteousness, because I am going to the Father and you will no longer see Me; ¹¹and about judgment, because the ruler of this world has been judged.

¹²"I still have many things to tell you, but you can't bear them now. ¹³When the Spirit of truth comes, He will guide you into all the truth. For He will not speak on His own, but He will speak whatever He hears. He will also declare to you what is to come. ¹⁴He will glorify Me, because He will take from what is Mine and declare it to you. ¹⁵Everything the Father has is Mine. This is why I told you that He takes from what is Mine and will declare it to you.

¹⁶"A little while and you will no longer see Me; again a little while and you will see Me."ᶜ

¹⁷Therefore some of His disciples said to one another, "What is this He tells us: 'A little while and you will not see Me; again a little while and you will see Me'; and, 'because I am going to the Father'?" ¹⁸They said, "What is this He is saying,ᴰ 'A little while'? We don't know what He's talking about!"

¹⁹Jesus knew they wanted to question Him, so He said to them, "Are you asking one another about what I said, 'A little while and you will not see Me; again a little while and you will see Me'? ²⁰"I assure you: You will weep and wail, and the world will rejoice. You will become sorrowful, but your sorrow will turn to joy. ²¹When a woman is in labor she has pain because her time has come. But when she has given birth to a child, she no longer remembers the suffering because of the joy that a person has been born into the world. ²²So also you have sorrowᴱ now. But I will see you again. Your hearts will rejoice, and no one will rob you of your joy. ²³In that day you will not ask Me anything.

"I assure you: Anything you ask the Father in My name, He will give you. ²⁴Until now you have asked for nothing in My name. Ask and you will receive, so that your joy may be complete.

²⁵"I have spoken these things to you in figures of speech. A time is coming when I will no longer speak to you in figures, but I will tell you plainly about the Father. ²⁶In that day you will ask in My name. I am not telling you that I will make requests to the Father on your behalf. ²⁷For the Father Himself loves you, because you have loved Me and have believed that I came from God.ᶠ ²⁸I came from the Father and have come into the world. Again, I am leaving the world and going to the Father."

²⁹"Ah!" His disciples said. "Now You're speaking plainly and not using any figurative language. ³⁰Now we know that You know everything and don't need anyone to question You. By this we believe that You came from God."

³¹Jesus responded to them, "Do you now believe? ³²Look: An hour is coming, and has come, when each of you will be scattered to his own home, and you will leave Me alone. Yet I am not alone, because the Father is with Me. ³³I have told you these things so that in Me you may have peace. You will have suffering in this world. Be courageous! I have conquered the world."

ᴬ15:25 Ps 69:4 ᴮ16:4 Other mss read *when the time* ᶜ16:16 Other mss add *because I am going to the Father* ᴰ16:18 Other mss omit *He is saying* ᴱ16:22 Other mss read *will have sorrow* ᶠ16:27 Other mss read *from the Father*

17 Jesus spoke these things, looked up to heaven, and said:

Father,
the hour has come.
Glorify Your Son
  so that the Son may glorify You,
2 for You gave Him authority
  over all flesh;[A]
  so He may give eternal life
  to all You have given Him.
3 This is eternal life:
  that they may know You,
    the only true God,
  and the One You have sent—
    Jesus Christ.
4 I have glorified You on the earth
  by completing the work You gave Me
    to do.
5 Now, Father, glorify Me
  in Your presence
  with that glory I had with You
  before the world existed.

6 I have revealed Your name
  to the men You gave Me
    from the world.
  They were Yours, You gave them to Me,
  and they have kept Your word.
7 Now they know that all things
  You have given to Me are from You,
8 because the words that You gave Me,
  I have given them.
  They have received them
  and have known for certain
  that I came from You.
  They have believed that You sent Me.
9 I pray[B] for them.
  I am not praying for the world
  but for those You have given Me,
  because they are Yours.
10 Everything I have is Yours,
  and everything You have is Mine,
  and I have been glorified in them.
11 I am no longer in the world,
  but they are in the world,
  and I am coming to You.
  Holy Father,
  protect[C] them by Your name
  that You have given Me,
  so that they may be one as We are one.
12 While I was with them,

I was protecting them by Your name
  that You have given Me.
I guarded them and not one of them
    is lost,
except the son of destruction,[D]
  so that the Scripture may be fulfilled.
13 Now I am coming to You,
  and I speak these things in the world
  so that they may have My joy
    completed in them.
14 I have given them Your word.
  The world hated them
  because they are not of the world,
  as I am not of the world.
15 I am not praying
  that You take them out of the world
  but that You protect them
    from the evil one.
16 They are not of the world,
  as I am not of the world.
17 Sanctify[E] them by the truth;
  Your word is truth.
18 As You sent Me into the world,
  I also have sent them into the world.
19 I sanctify Myself for them,
  so they also may be sanctified
    by the truth.

20 I pray not only for these,
  but also for those who believe in Me
  through their message.
21 May they all be one,
  as You, Father, are in Me and I am
    in You.
  May they also be one[F] in Us,
  so the world may believe You sent Me.
22 I have given them the glory
  You have given Me.
  May they be one as We are one.
23 I am in them and You are in Me.
  May they be made completely one,
  so the world may know You have
    sent Me
  and have loved them as
    You have loved Me.
24 Father,
  I desire those You have given Me
  to be with Me where I am.
  Then they will see My glory,
  which You have given Me
  because You loved Me
    before the world's foundation.

A17:2 Or *people*   B17:9 Lit *ask* (throughout this passage)   C17:11 Lit *keep* (throughout this passage)   D17:12 The one destined for destruction, loss, or perdition   E17:17 Set apart for special use   F17:21 Other mss omit *one*

25 Righteous Father!
The world has not known You.
However, I have known You,
and these have known
that You sent Me.

26 I made Your name known to them
and will make it known,
so the love You have loved Me with
may be in them and I may be in them.

18 After Jesus had said these things, He went out with His disciples across the Kidron Valley, where there was a garden, and He and His disciples went into it. ²Judas, who betrayed Him, also knew the place, because Jesus often met there with His disciples. ³So Judas took a company of soldiers and some temple police from the chief priests and the Pharisees and came there with lanterns, torches, and weapons.

⁴Then Jesus, knowing everything that was about to happen to Him, went out and said to them, "Who is it you're looking for?"

⁵"Jesus the Nazarene," they answered.

"I am He,"^A Jesus told them.

Judas, who betrayed Him, was also standing with them. ⁶When He told them, "I am He," they stepped back and fell to the ground.

⁷Then He asked them again, "Who is it you're looking for?"

"Jesus the Nazarene," they said.

⁸"I told you I am He," Jesus replied. "So if you're looking for Me, let these men go." ⁹This was to fulfill the words He had said: "I have not lost one of those You have given Me."

¹⁰Then Simon Peter, who had a sword, drew it, struck the high priest's slave, and cut off his right ear. (The slave's name was Malchus.)

¹¹At that, Jesus said to Peter, "Sheathe your sword! Am I not to drink the cup the Father has given Me?"

¹²Then the company of soldiers, the commander, and the Jewish temple police arrested Jesus and tied Him up. ¹³First they led Him to Annas, for he was the father-in-law of Caiaphas, who was high priest that year. ¹⁴Caiaphas was the one who had advised the Jews that it was advantageous that one man should die for the people.

¹⁵Meanwhile, Simon Peter was following Jesus, as was another disciple. That disciple was an acquaintance of the high priest; so he went with Jesus into the high priest's courtyard.

¹⁶But Peter remained standing outside by the door. So the other disciple, the one known to the high priest, went out and spoke to the girl who was the doorkeeper and brought Peter in.

¹⁷Then the slave girl who was the doorkeeper said to Peter, "You aren't one of this man's disciples too, are you?"

"I am not!" he said. ¹⁸Now the slaves and the temple police had made a charcoal fire, because it was cold. They were standing there warming themselves, and Peter was standing with them, warming himself.

¹⁹The high priest questioned Jesus about His disciples and about His teaching.

²⁰"I have spoken openly to the world," Jesus answered him. "I have always taught in the synagogue and in the temple complex, where all the Jews congregate, and I haven't spoken anything in secret. ²¹Why do you question Me? Question those who heard what I told them. Look, they know what I said."

²²When He had said these things, one of the temple police standing by slapped Jesus, saying, "Is this the way you answer the high priest?"

²³"If I have spoken wrongly," Jesus answered him, "give evidence^B about the wrong; but if rightly, why do you hit Me?"

²⁴Then Annas sent Him bound to Caiaphas the high priest.

²⁵Now Simon Peter was standing and warming himself. They said to him, "You aren't one of His disciples too, are you?"

He denied it and said, "I am not!"

²⁶One of the high priest's slaves, a relative of the man whose ear Peter had cut off, said, "Didn't I see you with Him in the garden?"

²⁷Peter then denied it again. Immediately a rooster crowed.

²⁸Then they took Jesus from Caiaphas to the governor's headquarters. It was early morning. They did not enter the headquarters themselves; otherwise they would be defiled and unable to eat the Passover.

²⁹Then Pilate came out to them and said, "What charge do you bring against this man?"

³⁰They answered Him, "If this man weren't a criminal,^C we wouldn't have handed Him over to you."

³¹So Pilate told them, "Take Him yourselves and judge Him according to your law."

"It's not legal^D for us to put anyone to death," the Jews declared. ³²They said this so

^A18:5 Lit *I am*; see note at Jn 8:58.　^B18:23 Or *him, testify*　^C18:30 Lit *an evil doer*　^D18:31 According to Roman law that Jesus' words might be fulfilled signifying what kind of death He was going to die.

³³Then Pilate went back into the headquarters, summoned Jesus, and said to Him, "Are You the King of the Jews?"

³⁴Jesus answered, "Are you asking this on your own, or have others told you about Me?"

³⁵"I'm not a Jew, am I?" Pilate replied. "Your own nation and the chief priests handed You over to me. What have You done?"

³⁶"My kingdom is not of this world," said Jesus. "If My kingdom were of this world, My servants^A would fight, so that I wouldn't be handed over to the Jews. As it is, My kingdom does not have its origin here."^B

³⁷"You are a king then?" Pilate asked.

"You say that I'm a king," Jesus replied. "I was born for this, and I have come into the world for this: to testify to the truth. Everyone who is of the truth listens to My voice."

³⁸"What is truth?" said Pilate.

After he had said this, he went out to the Jews again and told them, "I find no grounds for charging Him. ³⁹You have a custom that I release one prisoner to you at the Passover. So, do you want me to release to you the King of the Jews?"

⁴⁰They shouted back, "Not this man, but Barabbas!" Now Barabbas was a revolutionary.^C

19 Then Pilate took Jesus and had Him flogged. ²The soldiers then twisted together a crown of thorns, put it on His head, and threw a purple robe around Him. ³And they repeatedly came up to Him and said, "Hail, King of the Jews!" and were slapping His face.

⁴Pilate went outside again and said to them, "Look, I'm bringing Him outside to you to let you know I find no grounds for charging Him."

⁵Then Jesus came out wearing the crown of thorns and the purple robe. Pilate said to them, "Here is the man!"

⁶When the chief priests and the temple police saw Him, they shouted, "Crucify! Crucify!"

Pilate responded, "Take Him and crucify Him yourselves, for I find no grounds for charging Him."

⁷"We have a law," the Jews replied to him, "and according to that law He must die, because He made Himself^D the Son of God."

⁸When Pilate heard this statement, he was more afraid than ever. ⁹He went back into the headquarters and asked Jesus, "Where are You from?" But Jesus did not give him an answer. ¹⁰So Pilate said to Him, "You're not talking to me? Don't You know that I have the authority to release You and the authority to crucify You?"

¹¹"You would have no authority over Me at all," Jesus answered him, "if it hadn't been given you from above. This is why the one who handed Me over to you has the greater sin."^E

¹²From that moment Pilate made every effort^F to release Him. But the Jews shouted, "If you release this man, you are not Caesar's friend. Anyone who makes himself a king opposes Caesar!"

¹³When Pilate heard these words, he brought Jesus outside. He sat down on the judge's bench in a place called the Stone Pavement (but in Hebrew *Gabbatha*). ¹⁴It was the preparation day for the Passover, and it was about six in the morning.^G Then he told the Jews, "Here is your king!"

¹⁵But they shouted, "Take Him away! Take Him away! Crucify Him!"

Pilate said to them, "Should I crucify your king?"

"We have no king but Caesar!" the chief priests answered.

¹⁶So then, because of them, he handed Him over to be crucified.

Therefore they took Jesus away.^H ¹⁷Carrying His own cross, He went out to what is called Skull Place, which in Hebrew is called *Golgotha*. ¹⁸There they crucified Him and two others with Him, one on either side, with Jesus in the middle. ¹⁹Pilate also had a sign lettered and put on the cross. The inscription was:

JESUS THE NAZARENE THE KING OF THE JEWS.

²⁰Many of the Jews read this sign, because the place where Jesus was crucified was near the city, and it was written in Hebrew,^I Latin, and Greek. ²¹So the chief priests of the Jews said to Pilate, "Don't write, 'The King of the

---

^A18:36 Or *attendants,* or *helpers*   ^B18:36 Lit *My kingdom is not from here*   ^C18:40 Or *robber;* see Jn 10:1,8 for the same Gk word used here   ^D19:7 He claimed to be   ^E19:11 To *have sin* is an idiom that refers to guilt caused by sin.   ^F19:12 Lit *Pilate was trying*   ^G19:14 Lit *the sixth hour;* see note at Jn 1:39; an alt time reckoning would be *about noon*   ^H19:16 Other mss add *and led Him out*   ^I19:20 Or *Aramaic*

Jews,' but that He said, 'I am the King of the Jews.'"

²²Pilate replied, "What I have written, I have written."

²³When the soldiers crucified Jesus, they took His clothes and divided them into two parts, a part for each soldier. They also took the tunic, which was seamless, woven in one piece from the top. ²⁴So they said to one another, "Let's not tear it, but cast lots for it, to see who gets it." They did this to fulfill the Scripture that says: **They divided My clothes among themselves, and they cast lots for My clothing.**ᴬ And this is what the soldiers did.

²⁵Standing by the cross of Jesus were His mother, His mother's sister, Mary the wife of Clopas, and Mary Magdalene. ²⁶When Jesus saw His mother and the disciple He loved standing there, He said to His mother, "Woman, here is your son." ²⁷Then He said to the disciple, "Here is your mother." And from that hour the disciple took her into his home.

²⁸After this, when Jesus knew that everything was now accomplished that the Scripture might be fulfilled, He said, "I'm thirsty!" ²⁹A jar full of sour wine was sitting there; so they fixed a sponge full of sour wine on hyssopᴮ and held it up to His mouth.

³⁰When Jesus had received the sour wine, He said, "It is finished!" Then bowing His head, He gave up His spirit.

³¹Since it was the preparation day, the Jews did not want the bodies to remain on the cross on the Sabbath (for that Sabbath was a specialᶜ day). They requested that Pilate have the men's legs broken and that their bodies be taken away. ³²So the soldiers came and broke the legs of the first man and of the other one who had been crucified with Him. ³³When they came to Jesus, they did not break His legs since they saw that He was already dead. ³⁴But one of the soldiers pierced His side with a spear, and at once blood and water came out. ³⁵He who saw this has testified so that you also may believe. His testimony is true, and he knows he is telling the truth. ³⁶For these things happened so that the Scripture would be fulfilled: **Not one of His bones will be broken.**ᴰ ³⁷Also, another Scripture says: **They will look at the One they pierced.**ᴱ

³⁸After this, Joseph of Arimathea, who was a disciple of Jesus—but secretly because of his fear of the Jews—asked Pilate that he might remove Jesus' body. Pilate gave him permission, so he came and took His body away. ³⁹Nicodemus (who had previously come to Him at night) also came, bringing a mixture of about 75 poundsᶠ of myrrh and aloes. ⁴⁰Then they took Jesus' body and wrapped it in linen cloths with the aromatic spices, according to the burial custom of the Jews. ⁴¹There was a garden in the place where He was crucified. A new tomb was in the garden; no one had yet been placed in it. ⁴²They placed Jesus there because of the Jewish preparation and since the tomb was nearby.

20 On the first day of the week Mary Magdalene came to the tomb early, while it was still dark. She saw that the stone had been removedᴳ from the tomb. ²So she ran to Simon Peter and to the other disciple, the one Jesus loved, and said to them, "They have taken the Lord out of the tomb, and we don't know where they have put Him!"

³At that, Peter and the other disciple went out, heading for the tomb. ⁴The two were running together, but the other disciple outran Peter and got to the tomb first. ⁵Stooping down, he saw the linen cloths lying there, yet he did not go in. ⁶Then, following him, Simon Peter came also. He entered the tomb and saw the linen cloths lying there. ⁷The wrapping that had been on His head was not lying with the linen cloths but was folded up in a separate place by itself. ⁸The other disciple, who had reached the tomb first, then entered the tomb, saw, and believed. ⁹For they still did not understand the Scripture that He must rise from the dead. ¹⁰Then the disciples went home again.

¹¹But Mary stood outside facing the tomb, crying. As she was crying, she stooped to look into the tomb. ¹²She saw two angels in white sitting there, one at the head and one at the feet, where Jesus' body had been lying. ¹³They said to her, "Woman, why are you crying?"

"Because they've taken away my Lord," she told them, "and I don't know where they've put Him." ¹⁴Having said this, she turned around and saw Jesus standing there, though she did not know it was Jesus.

¹⁵"Woman," Jesus said to her, "why are you crying? Who is it you are looking for?"

A19:24 Ps 22:18   **B**19:29 Or with hyssop   **C**19:31 Lit great   **D**19:36 Ex 12:46; Nm 9:12; Ps 34:20   **E**19:37 Zch 12:10   **F**19:39 Lit 100 litrai; a Roman litrai = 12 ounces   **G**20:1 Lit She saw the stone removed

Supposing He was the gardener, she replied, "Sir, if you've removed Him, tell me where you've put Him, and I will take Him away."

¹⁶Jesus said, "Mary."

Turning around, she said to Him in Hebrew, *"Rabbouni!"*ᴬ—which means "Teacher."

¹⁷"Don't cling to Me," Jesus told her, "for I have not yet ascended to the Father. But go to My brothers and tell them that I am ascending to My Father and your Father—to My God and your God."

¹⁸Mary Magdalene went and announced to the disciples, "I have seen the Lord!" And she told them whatᴮ He had said to her.

¹⁹In the evening of that first day of the week, the disciples were gathered together with the doors locked because of their fear of the Jews. Then Jesus came, stood among them, and said to them, "Peace to you!"

²⁰Having said this, He showed them His hands and His side. So the disciples rejoiced when they saw the Lord.

²¹Jesus said to them again, "Peace to you! As the Father has sent Me, I also send you." ²²After saying this, He breathed on them and said,ᶜ "Receive the Holy Spirit. ²³If you forgive the sins of any, they are forgiven them; if you retain the sins of any, they are retained."

²⁴But one of the Twelve, Thomas (called "Twin"), was not with them when Jesus came. ²⁵So the other disciples kept telling him, "We have seen the Lord!"

But he said to them, "If I don't see the mark of the nails in His hands, put my finger into the mark of the nails, and put my hand into His side, I will never believe!"

²⁶After eight days His disciples were indoors again, and Thomas was with them. Even though the doors were locked, Jesus came and stood among them. He said, "Peace to you!"

²⁷Then He said to Thomas, "Put your finger here and observe My hands. Reach out your hand and put it into My side. Don't be an unbeliever, but a believer."

²⁸Thomas responded to Him, "My Lord and my God!"

²⁹Jesus said, "Because you have seen Me, you have believed.ᴰ Those who believe without seeing are blessed."

³⁰Jesus performed many other signs in the presence of His disciples that are not written in this book. ³¹But these are written so that you may believe Jesus is the Messiah, the Son of God,ᴱ and by believing you may have life in His name.

21 After this, Jesus revealed Himself again to His disciples by the Sea of Tiberias.ᶠ He revealed Himself in this way:

²Simon Peter, Thomas (called "Twin"), Nathanael from Cana of Galilee, Zebedee's sons, and two others of His disciples were together.

³"I'm going fishing," Simon Peter said to them.

"We're coming with you," they told him. They went out and got into the boat, but that night they caught nothing.

⁴When daybreak came, Jesus stood on the shore. However, the disciples did not know it was Jesus.

⁵"Men,"ᴳ Jesus called to them, "you don't have any fish, do you?"

"No," they answered.

⁶"Cast the net on the right side of the boat," He told them, "and you'll find some." So they did,ᴴ and they were unable to haul it in because of the large number of fish. ⁷Therefore the disciple, the one Jesus loved, said to Peter, "It is the Lord!"

When Simon Peter heard that it was the Lord, he tied his outer garment around himᴵ (for he was stripped) and plunged into the sea. ⁸But since they were not far from land (about 100 yards ᴶ away), the other disciples came in the boat, dragging the net full of fish. ⁹When they got out on land, they saw a charcoal fire there, with fish lying on it, and bread.

¹⁰"Bring some of the fish you've just caught," Jesus told them. ¹¹So Simon Peter got up and hauled the net ashore, full of large fish—153 of them. Even though there were so many, the net was not torn.

¹²"Come and have breakfast," Jesus told them. None of the disciples dared ask Him, "Who are You?" because they knew it was the Lord. ¹³Jesus came, took the bread, and gave it to them. He did the same with the fish.

¹⁴This was now the third timeᴷ Jesus appearedᴸ to the disciples after He was raised from the dead.

ᴬ20:16 Rabbouni is also used in Mk 10:51 ᴮ20:18 Lit these things [as a question] ᶜ20:31 Or that the Messiah, the Son of God, is Jesus ᶠ21:1 The Sea of Galilee; Sea of Tiberias is used only in John; Jn 6:1,23 ᴳ21:5 Lit Children ᴴ21:6 Lit they cast ᴵ21:7 Lit he girded his garment ᴶ21:8 Lit about 200 cubits ᴷ21:14 The other two are in Jn 20:19-29. ᴸ21:14 Lit was revealed [see v. 1] ᶜ20:22 Lit He breathed and said to them ᴰ20:29 Or have you believed?

¹⁵When they had eaten breakfast, Jesus asked Simon Peter, "Simon, son of John,ᴬ do you loveᴮ Me more than these?"

"Yes, Lord," he said to Him, "You know that I love You."

"Feed My lambs," He told him.

¹⁶A second time He asked him, "Simon, son of John, do you love Me?"

"Yes, Lord," he said to Him, "You know that I love You."

"Shepherd My sheep," He told him.

¹⁷He asked him the third time, "Simon, son of John, do you love Me?"

Peter was grieved that He asked him the third time, "Do you love Me?" He said, "Lord, You know everything! You know that I love You."

"Feed My sheep," Jesus said. ¹⁸"I assure you: When you were young, you would tie your belt and walk wherever you wanted. But when you grow old, you will stretch out your hands and someone else will tie you and carry you where you don't want to go." ¹⁹He said this to signify by what kind of death he would glorify God.ᶜ After saying this, He told him, "Follow Me!"

²⁰So Peter turned around and saw the disciple Jesus loved following them. That disciple was the one who had leaned back against Jesus at the supper and asked, "Lord, who is the one that's going to betray You?" ²¹When Peter saw him, he said to Jesus, "Lord—what about him?"

²²"If I want him to remain until I come," Jesus answered, "what is that to you? As for you, follow Me."

²³So this reportᴰ spread to the brothersᴱ that this disciple would not die. Yet Jesus did not tell him that he would not die, but, "If I want him to remain until I come, what is that to you?"

²⁴This is the disciple who testifies to these things and who wrote them down. We know that his testimony is true.

²⁵And there are also many other things that Jesus did, which, if they were written one by one, I suppose not even the world itself could contain the booksᶠ that would be written.

ACTS

1 I wrote the first narrative, Theophilus, about all that Jesus began to do and teach ²until the day He was taken up, after He had given orders through the Holy Spirit to the apostles He had chosen. ³After He had suffered, He also presented Himself alive to them by many convincing proofs, appearing to them during 40 days and speaking about the kingdom of God.

⁴While He was togetherᴳ with them, He commanded them not to leave Jerusalem, but to wait for the Father's promise. "This," He said, "is what you heard from Me; ⁵for John baptized with water, but you will be baptized with the Holy Spirit not many days from now."

⁶So when they had come together, they asked Him, "Lord, are You restoring the kingdom to Israel at this time?"

⁷He said to them, "It is not for you to know times or periods that the Father has set by His own authority. ⁸But you will receive power when the Holy Spirit has come on you, and you will be My witnesses in Jerusalem, in all Judea and Samaria, and to the endsᴴ of the earth."

⁹After He had said this, He was taken up as they were watching, and a cloud took Him out of their sight. ¹⁰While He was going, they were gazing into heaven, and suddenly two men in white clothes stood by them. ¹¹They said, "Men of Galilee, why do you stand looking up into heaven? This Jesus, who has been taken from you into heaven, will come in the same way that you have seen Him going into heaven."

¹²Then they returned to Jerusalem from the mount called the Mount of Olives, which is near Jerusalem—a Sabbath day's journey

---

ᴬ21:15-17 Other mss read *Simon, son of Jonah*; Mt 16:17; Jn 1:42   ᴮ21:15-17 Two synonyms are translated *love* in this conversation: *agapao*, the first 2 times by Jesus (vv. 15-16); and *phileo*, the last time by Jesus (v. 17) and all 3 times by Peter (vv. 15-17). Peter's threefold confession of love for Jesus corresponds to his earlier threefold denial of Jesus; Jn 18:15-18,25-27.   ᶜ21:19 Jesus predicts that Peter would be martyred. Church tradition says that Peter was crucified upside down.   ᴰ21:23 Lit *this word*   ᴱ21:23 The word *brothers* refers to the late first century Christian community.   ᶠ21:25 Lit *scroll*   ᴳ1:4 Or *He was eating*, or *He was lodging*   ᴴ1:8 Lit *the end* away. ¹³When they arrived, they went to the room upstairs where they were staying:

Peter, John,
James, Andrew,
Philip, Thomas,
Bartholomew, Matthew,
James the son of Alphaeus,
Simon the Zealot,
and Judas the son of James.

¹⁴All these were continually united in prayer,ᴬ along with the women, including Maryᴮ the mother of Jesus, and His brothers.

¹⁵During these days Peter stood up among the brothersᶜ—the number of people who were together was about 120—and said: ¹⁶"Brothers, the Scripture had to be fulfilled that the Holy Spirit through the mouth of David spoke in advance about Judas, who became a guide to those who arrested Jesus. ¹⁷For he was one of our number and was allotted a share in this ministry." ¹⁸Now this man acquired a field with his unrighteous wages. He fell headfirst and burst open in the middle, and all his insides spilled out. ¹⁹This became known to all the residents of Jerusalem, so that in their own language that field is called *Hakeldama* (that is, Field of Blood). ²⁰"For it is written in the Book of Psalms:

**Let his dwelling become desolate;
let no one live in it;**ᴰ and
**Let someone else take
his position.**ᴱ

²¹"Therefore, from among the men who have accompanied us during the whole time the Lord Jesus went in and out among us—²²beginning from the baptism of John until the day He was taken up from us—from among these, it is necessary that one become a witness with us of His resurrection."

²³So they proposed two: Joseph, called Barsabbas, who was also known as Justus, and Matthias. ²⁴Then they prayed, "You, Lord, know the hearts of all; show which of these two You have chosen ²⁵to take the placeᶠ in this apostolic service that Judas left to go to his own place." ²⁶Then they cast lots for them, and the lot fell to Matthias. So he was numbered with the 11 apostles.

2 When the day of Pentecost had arrived, they were all together in one place. ²Suddenly a sound like that of a violent rushing wind came from heaven, and it filled the whole house where they were staying. ³And tongues, like flames of fire that were divided, appeared to them and rested on each one of them. ⁴Then they were all filled with the Holy Spirit and began to speak in different languages, as the Spirit gave them ability for speech.

⁵There were Jews living in Jerusalem, devout men from every nation under heaven. ⁶When this sound occurred, a crowd came together and was confused because each one heard them speaking in his own language. ⁷And they were astounded and amazed, saying,ᴳ "Look, aren't all these who are speaking Galileans? ⁸How is it that each of us can hear in our own native language? ⁹Parthians, Medes, Elamites; those who live in Mesopotamia, in Judea and Cappadocia, Pontus and Asia, ¹⁰Phrygia and Pamphylia, Egypt and the parts of Libya near Cyrene; visitors from Rome, both Jews and proselytes, ¹¹Cretans and Arabs—we hear them speaking the magnificent acts of God in our own languages." ¹²They were all astounded and perplexed, saying to one another, "What could this be?" ¹³But some sneered and said, "They're full of new wine!"

¹⁴But Peter stood up with the Eleven, raised his voice, and proclaimed to them: "Men of Judah and all you residents of Jerusalem, let me explain thisᴴ to you and pay attention to my words. ¹⁵For these people are not drunk, as you suppose, since it's only nine in the morning.ᴵ ¹⁶On the contrary, this is what was spoken through the prophet Joel:

¹⁷   **And it will be** in the last days, says God,
        that **I will pour out My Spirit
        on all humanity;
        then your sons and your daughters
        will prophesy,
        your young men will see visions,
        and your old men will dream dreams.**
¹⁸   **I will even pour out My Spirit
        on My male and female slaves
        in those days,**
        and they will prophesy.
¹⁹   **I will display wonders
        in the heaven** above

and signs on the earth below:
blood and fire and a cloud of smoke.
20 The sun will be turned to darkness
and the moon to blood
before the great and remarkable Day
of the Lord comes.
21 Then everyone who calls
on the name of the Lord
will be saved.^A

22 "Men of Israel, listen to these words: This Jesus the Nazarene was a man pointed out to you by God with miracles, wonders, and signs that God did among you through Him, just as you yourselves know. 23 Though He was delivered up according to God's determined plan and foreknowledge, you used^B lawless people^C to nail Him to a cross and kill Him. 24 God raised Him up, ending the pains of death, because it was not possible for Him to be held by it. 25 For David says of Him:

I saw the Lord ever before me;
because He is at my right hand,
I will not be shaken.
26 Therefore my heart was glad,
and my tongue rejoiced.
Moreover, my flesh will rest in hope,
27 because You will not leave me
in Hades
or allow Your Holy One to see decay.
28 You have revealed the paths of life
to me;
You will fill me with gladness
in Your presence.^D

29 "Brothers, I can confidently speak to you about the patriarch David: He is both dead and buried, and his tomb is with us to this day. 30 Since he was a prophet, he knew that God had sworn an oath to him to seat one of his descendants^E,^F on his throne. 31 Seeing this in advance, he spoke concerning the resurrection of the Messiah:

He^G was not left in Hades,
and His flesh did not
experience decay.^H

32 "God has resurrected this Jesus. We are all witnesses of this. 33 Therefore, since He has been exalted to the right hand of God and has

received from the Father the promised Holy Spirit, He has poured out what you both see and hear. 34 For it was not David who ascended into the heavens, but he himself says:

The Lord declared to my Lord,
'Sit at My right hand,
35 until I make Your enemies
Your footstool.'^I

36 "Therefore let all the house of Israel know with certainty that God has made this Jesus, whom you crucified, both Lord and Messiah!"

37 When they heard this, they came under deep conviction^J and said to Peter and the rest of the apostles: "Brothers, what must we do?"

38 "Repent," Peter said to them, "and be baptized, each of you, in the name of Jesus Christ for the forgiveness of your sins, and you will receive the gift of the Holy Spirit. 39 For the promise is for you and for your children, and for all who are far off,^K as many as the Lord our God will call." 40 And with many other words He testified and strongly urged them, saying, "Be saved from this corrupt^L generation!"

41 So those who accepted His message were baptized, and that day about 3,000 people were added to them. 42 And they devoted themselves to the apostles' teaching, to the fellowship, to the breaking of bread, and to the prayers.

43 Then fear came over everyone, and many wonders and signs were being performed through the apostles. 44 Now all the believers were together and held all things in common. 45 They sold their possessions and property and distributed the proceeds to all, as anyone had a need.^M 46 Every day they devoted themselves to meeting together in the temple complex, and broke bread from house to house. They ate their food with a joyful and humble attitude, 47 praising God and having favor with all the people. And every day the Lord added to them^N those who were being saved.

3 Now Peter and John were going up together to the temple complex at the hour of prayer at three in the afternoon.^O 2 And a man who was lame from birth was carried there and placed every day at the temple gate called Beautiful, so he could beg from those entering the temple complex. 3 When he saw Peter and John about to enter the temple complex, he asked for help.

---

^A2:17-21 Jl 2:28-32 ^B2:23 Other mss read you have taken ^C2:23 Or used the hand of lawless ones ^D2:25-28 Ps 16:8-11 ^E2:30 Other mss add according to the flesh to raise up the Messiah ^F2:30 Lit one from the fruit of his loin ^G2:31 Other mss read His soul ^H2:31 Ps 16:10 ^I2:34-35 Ps 110:1 ^J2:37 Lit they were pierced to the heart ^K2:39 For distant generations or perhaps Gentiles ^L2:40 Or crooked, or twisted ^M2:45 Or to all, according to one's needs ^N2:47 Other mss read to the church ^O3:1 Lit at the ninth hour

⁴Peter, along with John, looked at him intently and said, "Look at us." ⁵So he turned to them,^A expecting to get something from them. ⁶But Peter said, "I don't have silver or gold, but what I have, I give you: In the name of Jesus Christ the Nazarene, get up and walk!" ⁷Then, taking him by the right hand he raised him up, and at once his feet and ankles became strong. ⁸So he jumped up, stood, and started to walk, and he entered the temple complex with them—walking, leaping, and praising God. ⁹All the people saw him walking and praising God, ¹⁰and they recognized that he was the one who used to sit and beg at the Beautiful Gate of the temple complex. So they were filled with awe and astonishment at what had happened to him.

¹¹While he^B was holding on to Peter and John, all the people, greatly amazed, ran toward them in what is called Solomon's Colonnade. ¹²When Peter saw this, he addressed the people: "Men of Israel, why are you amazed at this? Or why do you stare at us, as though we had made him walk by our own power or godliness? ¹³The God of Abraham, Isaac, and Jacob, the God of our fathers, has glorified His Servant Jesus, whom you handed over and denied in the presence of Pilate, when he had decided to release Him. ¹⁴But you denied the Holy and Righteous One and asked to have a murderer given to you. ¹⁵You killed the source^C of life, whom God raised from the dead; we are witnesses of this. ¹⁶By faith in His name, His name has made this man strong, whom you see and know. So the faith that comes through Him has given him this perfect health in front of all of you.

¹⁷"And now, brothers, I know that you did it in ignorance, just as your leaders also did. ¹⁸But what God predicted through the mouth of all the prophets—that His Messiah would suffer—He has fulfilled in this way. ¹⁹Therefore repent and turn back, so that your sins may be wiped out, that seasons of refreshing may come from the presence of the Lord,^D ²⁰and that He may send Jesus, who has been appointed for you as the Messiah. ²¹Heaven must welcome^E Him until the times of the restoration of all things, which God spoke about by the mouth of His holy prophets from the beginning. ²²Moses said:^F

The Lord your God will raise up for you a Prophet like me from among your brothers. You must listen to Him in everything He will say to you. ²³And everyone who will not listen to that Prophet will be completely cut off from the people.^G

²⁴"In addition, all the prophets who have spoken, from Samuel and those after him, have also announced these days. ²⁵You are the sons of the prophets and of the covenant that God made with your ancestors, saying to Abraham, **And all the families of the earth will be blessed through your offspring.^H** ²⁶God raised up His Servant^I and sent Him first to you to bless you by turning each of you from your evil ways."

4 Now as they were speaking to the people, the priests, the commander of the temple police, and the Sadducees confronted them, ²because they were provoked that they were teaching the people and proclaiming the resurrection from the dead, using Jesus as the example.^J ³So they seized them and put them in custody until the next day, since it was already evening. ⁴But many of those who heard the message believed, and the number of the men came to about 5,000.

⁵The next day, their rulers, elders, and scribes assembled in Jerusalem ⁶with Annas the high priest, Caiaphas, John and Alexander, and all the members of the high-priestly family.^K ⁷After they had Peter and John stand before them, they asked the question: "By what power or in what name have you done this?"

⁸Then Peter was filled with the Holy Spirit and said to them, "Rulers of the people and elders: ⁹If we are being examined today about a good deed done to a disabled man—by what means he was healed— ¹⁰let it be known to all of you and to all the people of Israel, that by the name of Jesus Christ the Nazarene—whom you crucified and whom God raised from the dead—by Him this man is standing here before you healthy. ¹¹This Jesus is

the stone rejected by you builders, which has become the cornerstone.^M,N

---

^A3:5 Or he paid attention to them   ^B3:11 Other mss read the lame man who was healed   ^C3:15 Or the Prince, or the Ruler   ^D3:19 Some editors or translators put that seasons . . . the Lord in v. 20   ^E3:21 Or receive, or retain   ^F3:22 Other mss add to the fathers   ^G3:22-23 Dt 18:15-19   ^H3:25 Gn 12:3; 18:18; 22:18; 26:4   ^I3:26 Other mss add Jesus   ^J4:2 Lit proclaiming in Jesus the resurrection from the dead   ^K4:6 Or high-priestly class, or high-priestly clan   ^L4:8 Other mss add of Israel   ^M4:11 Lit the head of the corner   ^N4:11 Ps 118:22

¹²There is salvation in no one else, for there is no other name under heaven given to people, and we must be saved by it."

¹³When they observed the boldness of Peter and John and realized that they were uneducated and untrained men, they were amazed and recognized that they had been with Jesus. ¹⁴And since they saw the man who had been healed standing with them, they had nothing to say in response. ¹⁵After they had ordered them to leave the Sanhedrin, they conferred among themselves, ¹⁶saying, "What should we do with these men? For an obvious sign, evident to all who live in Jerusalem, has been done through them, and we cannot deny it! ¹⁷However, so this does not spread any further among the people, let's threaten them against speaking to anyone in this name again." ¹⁸So they called for them and ordered them not to preach or teach at all in the name of Jesus.

¹⁹But Peter and John answered them, "Whether it's right in the sight of God for us to listen to you rather than to God, you decide; ²⁰for we are unable to stop speaking about what we have seen and heard."

²¹After threatening them further, they released them. They found no way to punish them, because the people were all giving glory to God over what had been done; ²²for this sign of healing had been performed on a man over 40 years old.

²³After they were released, they went to their own people and reported everything the chief priests and the elders had said to them. ²⁴When they heard this, they all raised their voices to God and said, "Master, You are the One who made the heaven, the earth, and the sea, and everything in them. ²⁵You said through the Holy Spirit, by the mouth of our father David Your servant:ᴬ

Why did the Gentiles rage
and the peoples plot futile things?
²⁶ The kings of the earth took their stand
and the rulers assembled together
against the Lord and
against His Messiah.ᴮ

²⁷"For, in fact, in this city both Herod and Pontius Pilate, with the Gentiles and the peopleᶜ of Israel, assembled together against Your holy Servant Jesus, whom You anointed, ²⁸to do whatever Your hand and Your plan had predestined to take place. ²⁹And now, Lord, consider their threats, and grant that Your slaves may speak Your message with complete boldness, ³⁰while You stretch out Your hand for healing, signs, and wonders to be performed through the name of Your holy Servant Jesus." ³¹When they had prayed, the place where they were assembled was shaken, and they were all filled with the Holy Spirit and began to speak God's message with boldness.

³²Now the large group of those who believed were of one heart and mind, and no one said that any of his possessions was his own, but instead they held everything in common. ³³And the apostles were giving testimony with great power to the resurrection of the Lord Jesus, and great grace was on all of them. ³⁴For there was not a needy person among them, because all those who owned lands or houses sold them, brought the proceeds of the things that were sold, ³⁵and laid them at the apostles' feet. This was then distributed for each person's basic needs.ᴰ

³⁶Joseph, a Levite and a Cypriot by birth, the one the apostles called Barnabas, which is translated Son of Encouragement, ³⁷sold a field he owned, brought the money, and laid it at the apostles' feet.

5 But a man named Ananias, with his wife Sapphira, sold a piece of property. ²However, he kept back part of the proceeds with his wife's knowledge, and brought a portion of it and laid it at the apostles' feet. ³Then Peter said, "Ananias, why has Satan filled your heart to lie to the Holy Spirit and keep back part of the proceeds from the field? ⁴Wasn't it yours while you possessed it? And after it was sold, wasn't it at your disposal? Why is it that you planned this thing in your heart? You have not lied to men but to God!" ⁵When he heard these words, Ananias dropped dead, and a great fear came on all who heard. ⁶The young men got up, wrapped his body, carried him out, and buried him.

⁷There was an interval of about three hours; then his wife came in, not knowing what had happened. ⁸"Tell me," Peter asked her, "did you sell the field for this price?"

"Yes," she said, "for that price."

⁹Then Peter said to her, "Why did you agree to test the Spirit of the Lord? Look! The feet of

ᴬ4:25 Other mss read through the mouth of David Your servant ᴮ4:25-26 Ps 2:1-2 ᶜ4:27 Lit peoples ᴰ4:35 Lit person as anyone had need those who have buried your husband are at the door, and they will carry you out!"

¹⁰ Instantly she dropped dead at his feet. When the young men came in, they found her dead, carried her out, and buried her beside her husband. ¹¹ Then great fear came on the whole church and on all who heard these things.

¹² Many signs and wonders were being done among the people through the hands of the apostles. By common consent they would all meet in Solomon's Colonnade. ¹³ None of the rest dared to join them, but the people praised them highly. ¹⁴ Believers were added to the Lord in increasing numbers—crowds of both men and women. ¹⁵ As a result, they would carry the sick out into the streets and lay them on cots and mats so that when Peter came by, at least his shadow might fall on some of them. ¹⁶ In addition, a large group came together from the towns surrounding Jerusalem, bringing sick people and those who were tormented by unclean spirits, and they were all healed.

¹⁷ Then the high priest took action. He and all his colleagues, those who belonged to the party of the Sadducees, were filled with jealousy. ¹⁸ So they arrested^A the apostles and put them in the city jail. ¹⁹ But an angel of the Lord opened the doors of the jail during the night, brought them out, and said, ²⁰ "Go and stand in the temple complex, and tell the people all about this life." ²¹ In obedience to this, they entered the temple complex at daybreak and began to teach.

When the high priest and those who were with him arrived, they convened the Sanhedrin—the full Senate of the sons of Israel—and sent orders to the jail to have them brought. ²² But when the temple police got there, they did not find them in the jail, so they returned and reported, ²³ "We found the jail securely locked, with the guards standing in front of the doors, but when we opened them, we found no one inside!" ²⁴ As^B the commander of the temple police and the chief priests heard these things, they were baffled about them, as to what could come of this.

²⁵ Someone came and reported to them, "Look! The men you put in jail are standing in the temple complex and teaching the people." ²⁶ Then the commander went with the temple police and brought them in without force, be-cause they were afraid the people might stone them. ²⁷ After they brought them in, they had them stand before the Sanhedrin, and the high priest asked, ²⁸ "Didn't we strictly order you not to teach in this name? And look, you have filled Jerusalem with your teaching and are determined to bring this man's blood on us!"

²⁹ But Peter and the apostles replied, "We must obey God rather than men. ³⁰ The God of our fathers raised up Jesus, whom you had murdered by hanging Him on a tree. ³¹ God exalted this man to His right hand as ruler and Savior, to grant repentance to Israel, and forgiveness of sins. ³² We are witnesses of these things, and so is the Holy Spirit whom God has given to those who obey Him."

³³ When they heard this, they were enraged and wanted to kill them. ³⁴ A Pharisee named Gamaliel, a teacher of the law who was respected by all the people, stood up in the Sanhedrin and ordered the men^C to be taken outside for a little while. ³⁵ He said to them, "Men of Israel, be careful about what you're going to do to these men. ³⁶ Not long ago Theudas rose up, claiming to be somebody, and a group of about 400 men rallied to him. He was killed, and all his partisans were dispersed and came to nothing. ³⁷ After this man, Judas the Galilean rose up in the days of the census and attracted a following.^D That man also perished, and all his partisans were scattered. ³⁸ And now, I tell you, stay away from these men and leave them alone. For if this plan or this work is of men, it will be overthrown; ³⁹ but if it is of God, you will not be able to overthrow them. You may even be found fighting against God." So they were persuaded by him. ⁴⁰ After they called in the apostles and had them flogged, they ordered them not to speak in the name of Jesus and released them. ⁴¹ Then they went out from the presence of the Sanhedrin, rejoicing that they were counted worthy to be dishonored on behalf of the Name.^E ⁴² Every day in the temple complex, and in various homes, they continued teaching and proclaiming the good news that Jesus is the Messiah.

6 In those days, as the number of the disciples was multiplying, there arose a complaint by the Hellenistic Jews^F against the Hebraic Jews^G that their widows were being overlooked in the daily distribution. ² Then the Twelve summoned the whole company

---

^A5:18 Lit *laid hands on*   ^B5:24 Other mss add *the high priest and*   ^C5:34 Other mss read *apostles*   ^D5:37 Lit *and drew people after him*   ^E5:41 Other mss add *of Jesus*, or *of Christ*   ^F6:1 Jews of Gk language and culture   ^G6:1 Jews of Aram or Hb language and culture of the disciples and said, "It would not be right for us to give up preaching about God to handle financial matters.[A] ³ Therefore, brothers, select from among you seven men of good reputation, full of the Spirit and wisdom, whom we can appoint to this duty. ⁴ But we will devote ourselves to prayer and to the preaching ministry." ⁵ The proposal pleased the whole company. So they chose Stephen, a man full of faith and the Holy Spirit, and Philip, Prochorus, Nicanor, Timon, Parmenas, and Nicolaus, a proselyte from Antioch. ⁶ They had them stand before the apostles, who prayed and laid their hands on them.[B]

⁷ So the preaching about God flourished, the number of the disciples in Jerusalem multiplied greatly, and a large group of priests became obedient to the faith.

⁸ Stephen, full of grace and power, was performing great wonders and signs among the people. ⁹ Then some from what is called the Freedmen's Synagogue, composed of both Cyrenians and Alexandrians, and some from Cilicia and Asia, came forward and disputed with Stephen. ¹⁰ But they were unable to stand up against his wisdom and the Spirit by whom he was speaking.

¹¹ Then they persuaded some men to say, "We heard him speaking blasphemous words against Moses and God!" ¹² They stirred up the people, the elders, and the scribes; so they came, dragged him off, and took him to the Sanhedrin. ¹³ They also presented false witnesses who said, "This man does not stop speaking blasphemous words against this holy place and the law. ¹⁴ For we heard him say that Jesus, this Nazarene, will destroy this place and change the customs that Moses handed down to us." ¹⁵ And all who were sitting in the Sanhedrin looked intently at him and saw that his face was like the face of an angel.

7 "Is this true?"[C] the high priest asked. ² "Brothers and fathers," he said, "listen: The God of glory appeared to our father Abraham when he was in Mesopotamia, before he settled in Haran, ³ and said to him:

> Get out of your country
> and away from your relatives,
> and come to the land
> that I will show you.[D]

⁴ "Then he came out of the land of the Chaldeans and settled in Haran. From there, after his father died, God had him move to this land you now live in. ⁵ He didn't give him an inheritance in it, not even a foot of ground, but He promised to give it to him as a possession, and to his descendants after him, even though he was childless. ⁶ God spoke in this way:

> His descendants would be strangers
> in a foreign country,
> and they would enslave
> and oppress them 400 years.
> ⁷ I will judge the nation
> that they will serve as slaves, God said.
> After this, they will come out
> and worship Me in this place.[E]

⁸ Then He gave him the covenant of circumcision. After this, he fathered Isaac and circumcised him on the eighth day; Isaac did the same with Jacob, and Jacob with the 12 patriarchs.

⁹ "The patriarchs became jealous of Joseph and sold him into Egypt, but God was with him ¹⁰ and rescued him out of all his troubles. He gave him favor and wisdom in the sight of Pharaoh, king of Egypt, who appointed him ruler over Egypt and over his whole household. ¹¹ Then a famine and great suffering came over all of Egypt and Canaan, and our ancestors could find no food. ¹² When Jacob heard there was grain in Egypt, he sent our ancestors the first time. ¹³ The second time, Joseph was revealed to his brothers, and Joseph's family became known to Pharaoh. ¹⁴ Joseph then invited his father Jacob and all his relatives, 75 people in all, ¹⁵ and Jacob went down to Egypt. He and our ancestors died there, ¹⁶ were carried back to Shechem, and were placed in the tomb that Abraham had bought for a sum of silver from the sons of Hamor in Shechem.

¹⁷ "As the time was drawing near to fulfill the promise that God had made to Abraham, the people flourished and multiplied in Egypt ¹⁸ until a different king who did not know Joseph ruled over Egypt.[F] ¹⁹ He dealt deceitfully with our race and oppressed our ancestors by making them leave their infants outside, so they wouldn't survive.[G] ²⁰ At this time Moses was born, and he was beautiful in God's sight. He was cared for in his father's home three months, ²¹ and when he was left outside, Pha-

raoh's daughter adopted and raised him as her own son. ²²So Moses was educated in all the wisdom of the Egyptians and was powerful in his speech and actions.

²³As he was approaching the age of 40, he decided^A to visit his brothers, the Israelites. ²⁴When he saw one of them being mistreated, he came to his rescue and avenged the oppressed man by striking down the Egyptian. ²⁵He assumed his brothers would understand that God would give them deliverance through him, but they did not understand. ²⁶The next day he showed up while they were fighting and tried to reconcile them peacefully, saying, 'Men, you are brothers. Why are you mistreating each other?'

²⁷But the one who was mistreating his neighbor pushed him^B away, saying:

Who appointed you a ruler and a judge over us? ²⁸Do you want to kill me, the same way you killed the Egyptian yesterday?^C

²⁹At this disclosure, Moses fled and became an exile in the land of Midian, where he fathered two sons. ³⁰After 40 years had passed, an angel^D appeared to him in the wilderness of Mount Sinai, in the flame of a burning bush. ³¹When Moses saw it, he was amazed at the sight. As he was approaching to look at it, the voice of the Lord came: ³²I am the God of your fathers—the God of Abraham, of Isaac, and of Jacob.^E So Moses began to tremble and did not dare to look.

³³Then the Lord said to him:

Remove the sandals from your feet, for the place where you are standing is holy ground. ³⁴I have observed the oppression of My people in Egypt; I have heard their groaning and have come down to rescue them. And now, come, I will send you to Egypt.^F

³⁵This Moses, whom they rejected when they said, Who appointed you a ruler and a judge?^C—this one God sent as a ruler and a redeemer by means of the angel who appeared to him in the bush. ³⁶This man led them out and performed wonders and signs in the land of Egypt, at the Red Sea, and in the wilderness 40 years.

³⁷This is the Moses who said to the Israelites, God^G will raise up for you a Prophet like me from among your brothers.^H ³⁸He is the one who was in the congregation in the wilderness together with the angel who spoke to him on Mount Sinai, and with our ancestors. He received living oracles to give to us. ³⁹Our ancestors were unwilling to obey him, but pushed him away, and in their hearts turned back to Egypt. ⁴⁰They told Aaron:

Make us gods who will go before us. As for this Moses who brought us out of the land of Egypt, we don't know what's happened to him.^I

⁴¹They even made a calf in those days, offered sacrifice to the idol, and were celebrating what their hands had made. ⁴²Then God turned away and gave them up to worship the host of heaven, as it is written in the book of the prophets:

House of Israel, did you bring Me
    offerings and sacrifices
    40 years in the wilderness?
⁴³ No, you took up the tent of Moloch^J
    and the star of your god Rephan,^K
    the images that you made to worship.
    So I will deport you beyond Babylon!^L

⁴⁴Our ancestors had the tabernacle of the testimony in the wilderness, just as He who spoke to Moses commanded him to make it according to the pattern he had seen. ⁴⁵Our ancestors in turn received it and with Joshua brought it in when they dispossessed the nations that God drove out before our fathers, until the days of David. ⁴⁶He found favor in God's sight and asked that he might provide a dwelling place for the God^M of Jacob. ⁴⁷But it was Solomon who built Him a house. ⁴⁸However, the Most High does not dwell in sanctuaries made with hands, as the prophet says:

⁴⁹ Heaven is My throne,
    and earth My footstool.
    What sort of house will you build
        for Me?
    says the Lord,
    or what is My resting place?

^A7:23 Lit 40, it came into his heart   ^B7:27 Moses   ^C7:27-28,35 Ex 2:14   ^D7:30 Other mss add of the Lord   ^E7:32 Ex 3:6,15   ^F7:33-34 Ex 3:5,7-8,10   ^G7:37 Other mss read 'The Lord your God'   ^H7:37 Dt 18:15   ^I7:40 Ex 32:1,23   ^J7:43 Canaanite or Phoenician sky or sun god   ^K7:43 Perhaps an Assyrian star god—the planet Saturn   ^L7:42-43 Am 5:25-27   ^M7:46 Other mss read house

⁵⁰ **Did not My hand make all
these things?**ᴬ

⁵¹"You stiff-necked people with uncircumcised hearts and ears! You are always resisting the Holy Spirit; as your ancestors did, so do you. ⁵²Which of the prophets did your fathers not persecute? They even killed those who announced beforehand the coming of the Righteous One, whose betrayers and murderers you have now become. ⁵³You received the law under the direction of angels and yet have not kept it."

⁵⁴When they heard these things, they were enraged in their heartsᴮ and gnashed their teeth at him. ⁵⁵But Stephen, filled by the Holy Spirit, gazed into heaven. He saw God's glory, withᶜ Jesus standing at the right hand of God, and he said, ⁵⁶"Look! I see the heavens opened and the Son of Man standing at the right hand of God!"

⁵⁷Then they screamed at the top of their voices, covered their ears, and together rushed against him. ⁵⁸They threw him out of the city and began to stone him. And the witnesses laid their robes at the feet of a young man named Saul. ⁵⁹They were stoning Stephen as he called out: "Lord Jesus, receive my spirit!" ⁶⁰Then he knelt down and cried out with a loud voice, "Lord, do not charge them with this sin!" And saying this, he fell asleep.

8 Saul agreed with putting him to death. On that day a severe persecution broke out against the church in Jerusalem, and all except the apostles were scattered throughout the land of Judea and Samaria. ²Devout men buried Stephen and mourned deeply over him. ³Saul, however, was ravaging the church. He would enter house after house, drag off men and women, and put them in prison.

⁴So those who were scattered went on their way preaching the message of good news. ⁵Philip went down to aᴰ city in Samaria and proclaimed the Messiah to them. ⁶The crowds paid attention with one mind to what Philip said, as they heard and saw the signs he was performing. ⁷For unclean spirits, crying out with a loud voice, came out of many who were possessed, and many who were paralyzed and lame were healed. ⁸So there was great joy in that city.

⁹A man named Simon had previously practiced sorcery in that city and astounded the Samaritan people, while claiming to be somebody great. ¹⁰They all paid attention to him, from the least of them to the greatest, and they said, "This man is called the Great Power of God!"ᴱ ¹¹They were attentive to him because he had astounded them with his sorceries for a long time. ¹²But when they believed Philip, as he preached the good news about the kingdom of God and the name of Jesus Christ, both men and women were baptized. ¹³Then even Simon himself believed. And after he was baptized, he went around constantly withᶠ Philip and was astounded as he observed the signs and great miracles that were being performed.

¹⁴When the apostles who were at Jerusalem heard that Samaria had welcomed God's message, they sent Peter and John to them. ¹⁵After they went down there, they prayed for them, so the Samaritans might receive the Holy Spirit. ¹⁶For He had not yet come down onᴳ any of them; they had only been baptized in the name of the Lord Jesus. ¹⁷Then Peter and John laid their hands on them, and they received the Holy Spirit.

¹⁸When Simon saw that the Holyᴴ Spirit was given through the laying on of the apostles' hands, he offered them money, ¹⁹saying, "Give me this power too, so that anyone I lay hands on may receive the Holy Spirit."

²⁰But Peter told him, "May your silver be destroyed with you, because you thought the gift of God could be obtained with money! ²¹You have no part or share in this matter, because your heart is not right before God. ²²Therefore repent of this wickedness of yours, and pray to the Lord that the intent of your heart may be forgiven you. ²³For I see you are poisoned by bitterness and bound by iniquity!"

²⁴"Please prayᴵ to the Lord for me," Simon replied, "so that nothing you have said may happen to me."

²⁵Then, after they had testified and spoken the message of the Lord, they traveled back to Jerusalem, evangelizing many villages of the Samaritans.

²⁶An angel of the Lord spoke to Philip: "Get up and go south to the road that goes down from Jerusalem to Gaza. (This is the desert road.)ᴶ ²⁷So he got up and went. There was an

ᴬ7:49-50 Is 66:1-2   ᴮ7:54 Or were cut to the quick   ᶜ7:55 Lit and   ᴰ8:5 Other mss read the   ᴱ8:10 Or This is the power of God called Great   ᶠ8:13 Or he kept close company with   ᴳ8:16 Or yet fallen on   ᴴ8:18 Other mss omit Holy   ᴵ8:24 Gk words you and pray are pl   ᴶ8:26 Or is a desert place

Ethiopian man, a eunuch and high official of Candace, queen of the Ethiopians,ᴬ who was in charge of her entire treasury. He had come to worship in Jerusalem ²⁸and was sitting in his chariot on his way home, reading the prophet Isaiah aloud.

²⁹The Spirit told Philip, "Go and join that chariot."

³⁰When Philip ran up to it, he heard him reading the prophet Isaiah, and said, "Do you understand what you're reading?"

³¹"How can I," he said, "unless someone guides me?" So he invited Philip to come up and sit with him. ³²Now the Scripture passage he was reading was this:

> He was led like a sheep
>   to the slaughter,
> and as a lamb is silent
>   before its shearer,
> so He does not open His mouth.
> ³³   In His humiliation justice
>   was denied Him.
>   Who will describe His generation?
>   For His life is taken
>   from the earth.ᴮ

³⁴The eunuch replied to Philip, "I ask you, who is the prophet saying this about—himself or another person?" ³⁵So Philip proceededᶜ to tell him the good news about Jesus, beginning from that Scripture.

³⁶As they were traveling down the road, they came to some water. The eunuch said, "Look, there's water! What would keep me from being baptized?" [³⁷And Philip said, "If you believe with all your heart you may." And he replied, "I believe that Jesus Christ is the Son of God."]ᴰ ³⁸Then he ordered the chariot to stop, and both Philip and the eunuch went down into the water, and he baptized him. ³⁹When they came up out of the water, the Spirit of the Lord carried Philip away, and the eunuch did not see him any longer. But he went on his way rejoicing. ⁴⁰Philip appeared inᴱ Azotus,ᶠ and he was traveling and evangelizing all the towns until he came to Caesarea.

9 Meanwhile, Saul was still breathing threats and murder against the disciples of the Lord. He went to the high priest ²and requested letters from him to the synagogues in Damascus, so that if he found any men or women who belonged to the Way, he might bring them as prisoners to Jerusalem. ³As he traveled and was nearing Damascus, a light from heaven suddenly flashed around him. ⁴Falling to the ground, he heard a voice saying to him, "Saul, Saul, why are you persecuting Me?"

⁵"Who are You, Lord?" he said.

"I am Jesus, the One you are persecuting," He replied. ⁶"But get up and go into the city, and you will be told what you must do."

⁷The men who were traveling with him stood speechless, hearing the sound but seeing no one. ⁸Then Saul got up from the ground, and though his eyes were open, he could see nothing. So they took him by the hand and led him into Damascus. ⁹He was unable to see for three days and did not eat or drink.

¹⁰There was a disciple in Damascus named Ananias. And the Lord said to him in a vision, "Ananias!"

"Here I am, Lord!" he said.

¹¹"Get up and go to the street called Straight," the Lord said to him, "to the house of Judas, and ask for a man from Tarsus named Saul, since he is praying there. ¹²In a visionᴳ he has seen a man named Ananias coming in and placing his hands on him so he can regain his sight."

¹³"Lord," Ananias answered, "I have heard from many people about this man, how much harm he has done to Your saints in Jerusalem. ¹⁴And he has authority here from the chief priests to arrest all who call on Your name."

¹⁵But the Lord said to him, "Go! For this man is My chosen instrument to take My name to Gentiles, kings, and the Israelites. ¹⁶I will show him how much he must suffer for My name!"

¹⁷So Ananias left and entered the house. Then he placed his hands on him and said, "Brother Saul, the Lord Jesus, who appeared to you on the road you were traveling, has sent me so that you can regain your sight and be filled with the Holy Spirit."

¹⁸At once something like scales fell from his eyes, and he regained his sight. Then he got up and was baptized. ¹⁹And after taking some food, he regained his strength.

Saul was with the disciples in Damascus for some days. ²⁰Immediately he began proclaiming Jesus in the synagogues: "He is the Son of God."

ᴬ8:27 = Nubia   ᴮ8:32-33 Is 53:7-8   ᶜ8:35 Lit *Philip opened his mouth*   ᴰ8:37 Other mss omit bracketed text   ᴱ8:40 Or *Philip was found at,* or *Philip found himself in*   ᶠ8:40 Or Ashdod   ᴳ9:12 Other mss omit *In a vision*

²¹ But all who heard him were astounded and said, "Isn't this the man who, in Jerusalem, was destroying those who called on this name and then came here for the purpose of taking them as prisoners to the chief priests?"

²² But Saul grew more capable and kept confounding the Jews who lived in Damascus by proving that this One is the Messiah.

²³ After many days had passed, the Jews conspired to kill him, ²⁴ but their plot became known to Saul. So they were watching the gates day and night intending to kill him, ²⁵ but his disciples took him by night and lowered him in a large basket through an opening in the wall.

²⁶ When he arrived in Jerusalem, he tried to associate with the disciples, but they were all afraid of him, since they did not believe he was a disciple. ²⁷ Barnabas, however, took him and brought him to the apostles and explained to them how Saul had seen the Lord on the road and that He had talked to him, and how in Damascus he had spoken boldly in the name of Jesus. ²⁸ Saul was coming and going with them in Jerusalem, speaking boldly in the name of the Lord. ²⁹ He conversed and debated with the Hellenistic Jews,ᴬ but they attempted to kill him. ³⁰ When the brothers found out, they took him down to Caesarea and sent him off to Tarsus.

³¹ So the church throughout all Judea, Galilee, and Samaria had peace, being built up and walking in the fear of the Lord and in the encouragement of the Holy Spirit, and it increased in numbers.

³² As Peter was traveling from place to place,ᴮ he also came down to the saints who lived in Lydda. ³³ There he found a man named Aeneas, who was paralyzed and had been bedridden for eight years. ³⁴ Peter said to him, "Aeneas, Jesus Christ heals you. Get up and make your bed,"ᶜ and immediately he got up. ³⁵ So all who lived in Lydda and Sharon saw him and turned to the Lord.

³⁶ In Joppa there was a disciple named Tabitha, which is translated Dorcas.ᴰ She was always doing good works and acts of charity. ³⁷ In those days she became sick and died. After washing her, they placed her in a room upstairs. ³⁸ Since Lydda was near Joppa, the disciples heard that Peter was there and sent two men to him who begged him, "Don't delay in coming with us." ³⁹ So Peter got up and went with them. When he arrived, they led him to the room upstairs. And all the widows approached him, weeping and showing him the robes and clothes that Dorcas had made while she was with them. ⁴⁰ Then Peter sent them all out of the room. He knelt down, prayed, and turning toward the body said, "Tabitha, get up!" She opened her eyes, saw Peter, and sat up. ⁴¹ He gave her his hand and helped her stand up. Then he called the saints and widows and presented her alive. ⁴² This became known throughout Joppa, and many believed in the Lord. ⁴³ And Peter stayed on many days in Joppa with Simon, a leather tanner.ᴱ

10 There was a man in Caesarea named Cornelius, a centurion of what was called the Italian Regiment. ² He was a devout man and feared God along with his whole household. He did many charitable deeds for the Jewish people and always prayed to God. ³ About three in the afternoonᶠ he distinctly saw in a vision an angel of God who came in and said to him, "Cornelius!"

⁴ Looking intently at him, he became afraid and said, "What is it, lord?"

The angel told him, "Your prayers and your acts of charity have come up as a memorial offering before God. ⁵ Now send men to Joppa and call for Simon, who is also named Peter. ⁶ He is lodging with Simon, a tanner, whose house is by the sea."

⁷ When the angel who spoke to him had gone, he called two of his household slaves and a devout soldier, who was one of those who attended him. ⁸ After explaining everything to them, he sent them to Joppa.

⁹ The next day, as they were traveling and nearing the city, Peter went up to pray on the housetop about noon.ᴳ ¹⁰ Then he became hungry and wanted to eat, but while they were preparing something, he went into a visionary state. ¹¹ He saw heaven opened and an object that resembled a large sheet coming down, being lowered by its four corners to the earth. ¹² In it were all the four-footed animals and reptiles of the earth, and the birds of the sky. ¹³ Then a voice said to him, "Get up, Peter; kill and eat!"

ᴬ9:29 Lit Hellenists; that is, Gk-speaking Jews ᴮ9:32 Lit Peter was passing through all ᶜ9:34 Or and get ready to eat ᴰ9:36 = Gazelle
ᴱ9:43 Tanners were considered ritually unclean because of their occupation. ᶠ10:3 Lit About the ninth hour ᴳ10:9 Lit about the sixth hour

¹⁴"No, Lord!" Peter said. "For I have never eaten anything common^A and ritually unclean!"

¹⁵Again, a second time, a voice said to him, "What God has made clean, you must not call common." ¹⁶This happened three times, and then the object was taken up into heaven.

¹⁷While Peter was deeply perplexed about what the vision he had seen might mean, the men who had been sent by Cornelius, having asked directions to Simon's house, stood at the gate. ¹⁸They called out, asking if Simon, who was also named Peter, was lodging there.

¹⁹While Peter was thinking about the vision, the Spirit told him, "Three men are here looking for you. ²⁰Get up, go downstairs, and accompany them with no doubts at all, because I have sent them."

²¹Then Peter went down to the men and said, "Here I am, the one you're looking for. What is the reason you're here?"

²²They said, "Cornelius, a centurion, an upright and God-fearing man, who has a good reputation with the whole Jewish nation, was divinely directed by a holy angel to call you to his house and to hear a message from you." ²³Peter then invited them in and gave them lodging.

The next day he got up and set out with them, and some of the brothers from Joppa went with him. ²⁴The following day he entered Caesarea. Now Cornelius was expecting them and had called together his relatives and close friends. ²⁵When Peter entered, Cornelius met him, fell at his feet, and worshiped him.

²⁶But Peter helped him up and said, "Stand up! I myself am also a man." ²⁷While talking with him, he went on in and found that many had come together there. ²⁸Peter said to them, "You know it's forbidden for a Jewish man to associate with or visit a foreigner. But God has shown me that I must not call any person common or unclean. ²⁹That's why I came without any objection when I was sent for. So I ask: Why did you send for me?"

³⁰Cornelius replied, "Four days ago at this hour, at three in the afternoon,^B I was^C praying in my house. Just then a man in a dazzling robe stood before me ³¹and said, 'Cornelius, your prayer has been heard, and your acts of charity have been remembered in God's sight. ³²Therefore send someone to Joppa and invite Simon here, who is also named Peter. He is lodging in Simon the tanner's house by the sea.'^D ³³Therefore I immediately sent for you, and you did the right thing in coming. So we are all present before God, to hear everything you have been commanded by the Lord."

³⁴Then Peter began to speak: "Now I really understand that God doesn't show favoritism, ³⁵but in every nation the person who fears Him and does righteousness is acceptable to Him. ³⁶He sent the message to the Israelites, proclaiming the good news of peace through Jesus Christ—He is Lord of all. ³⁷You know the events^E that took place throughout Judea, beginning from Galilee after the baptism that John preached: ³⁸how God anointed Jesus of Nazareth with the Holy Spirit and with power, and how He went about doing good and healing all who were under the tyranny of the Devil, because God was with Him. ³⁹We ourselves are witnesses of everything He did in both the Judean country and in Jerusalem, yet they killed Him by hanging Him on a tree. ⁴⁰God raised up this man on the third day and permitted Him to be seen, ⁴¹not by all the people, but by us, witnesses appointed beforehand by God, who ate and drank with Him after He rose from the dead. ⁴²He commanded us to preach to the people and to solemnly testify that He is the One appointed by God to be the Judge of the living and the dead. ⁴³All the prophets testify about Him that through His name everyone who believes in Him will receive forgiveness of sins."

⁴⁴While Peter was still speaking these words, the Holy Spirit came down on all those who heard the message. ⁴⁵The circumcised believers^F who had come with Peter were astounded because the gift of the Holy Spirit had been poured out on the Gentiles also. ⁴⁶For they heard them speaking in other languages and declaring the greatness of^G "Can anyone withhold water and prevent these people from being baptized, who have received the Holy Spirit just as we have?" ⁴⁸And he commanded them to be baptized in the name of Jesus Christ. Then they asked him to stay for a few days.

---

^A10:14 Perhaps *profane*, or *non-sacred*; Jews ate distinctive food according to OT law and their traditions, similar to modern kosher or non-kosher foods.   ^B10:30 Lit *at the ninth hour*   ^C10:30 Other mss add *fasting and*   ^D10:32 Other mss add *When he arrives, he will speak to you.*   ^E10:37 Or *word*; lit *thing*   ^F10:45 Jewish Christians who stressed circumcision; Ac 11:2; 15:5; Gl 2:12; Col 4:11; Ti 1:10   ^G10:46 Or *and magnifying*

11 The apostles and the brothers who were throughout Judea heard that the Gentiles had welcomed God's message also. [2] When Peter went up to Jerusalem, those who stressed circumcision[A] argued with him, [3] saying, "You visited uncircumcised men and ate with them!"

[4] Peter began to explain to them in an orderly sequence, saying: [5] "I was in the town of Joppa praying, and I saw, in a visionary state, an object that resembled a large sheet coming down, being lowered by its four corners from heaven, and it came to me. [6] When I looked closely and considered it, I saw the four-footed animals of the earth, the wild beasts, the reptiles, and the birds of the sky. [7] Then I also heard a voice telling me, 'Get up, Peter; kill and eat!'

[8] "'No, Lord!' I said. 'For nothing common or ritually unclean has ever entered my mouth!' [9] But a voice answered from heaven a second time, 'What God has made clean, you must not call common.'

[10] "Now this happened three times, and then everything was drawn up again into heaven. [11] At that very moment, three men who had been sent to me from Caesarea arrived at the house where we were. [12] Then the Spirit told me to accompany them with no doubts at all. These six brothers accompanied me, and we went into the man's house. [13] He reported to us how he had seen the angel standing in his house and saying, 'Send[B] to Joppa, and call for Simon, who is also named Peter. [14] He will speak a message[C] to you that you and all your household will be saved by.'

[15] "As I began to speak, the Holy Spirit came down on them, just as on us at the beginning. [16] Then I remembered the word of the Lord, how He said, 'John baptized with water, but you will be baptized with the Holy Spirit.' [17] Therefore, if God gave them the same gift that He also gave to us when we believed on the Lord Jesus Christ, how could I possibly hinder God?"

[18] When they heard this they became silent. Then they glorified God, saying, "So God has granted repentance resulting in life[D] even to the Gentiles!"

[19] Those who had been scattered as a result of the persecution that started because of Stephen made their way as far as Phoenicia, Cyprus, and Antioch, speaking the message to no one except Jews. [20] But there were some of them, Cypriot and Cyrenian men, who came to Antioch and began speaking to the Hellenists,[E,F] proclaiming the good news about the Lord Jesus. [21] The Lord's hand was with them, and a large number who believed turned to the Lord. [22] Then the report about them was heard by the church that was at Jerusalem, and they sent out Barnabas to travel[G] as far as Antioch. [23] When he arrived and saw the grace of God, he was glad and encouraged all of them to remain true to the Lord with a firm resolve of the heart, [24] for he was a good man, full of the Holy Spirit and of faith. And large numbers of people were added to the Lord. [25] Then he[H] went to Tarsus to search for Saul, [26] and when he found him he brought him to Antioch. For a whole year they met with the church and taught large numbers. The disciples were first called Christians at Antioch.

[27] In those days some prophets came down from Jerusalem to Antioch. [28] Then one of them, named Agabus, stood up and predicted by the Spirit that there would be a severe famine throughout the Roman world.[I] This took place during the time of Claudius.[J] [29] So each of the disciples, according to his ability, determined to send relief to the brothers who lived in Judea. [30] They did this, sending it to the elders by means of Barnabas and Saul.

12 About that time King Herod cruelly attacked some who belonged to the church, [2] and he killed James, John's brother, with the sword. [3] When he saw that it pleased the Jews, he proceeded to arrest Peter too, during the days of Unleavened Bread. [4] After the arrest, he put him in prison and assigned four squads of four soldiers each to guard him, intending to bring him out to the people after the Passover. [5] So Peter was kept in prison, but prayer was being made earnestly to God for him by the church.

[6] On the night before Herod was to bring him out for execution, Peter, bound with two chains, was sleeping between two soldiers, while the sentries in front of the door guarded the prison. [7] Suddenly an angel of the Lord appeared, and a light shone in the cell. Striking Peter on the side, he woke him up and said,

A11:2 Lit those of the circumcision B11:13 Other mss add men C11:14 Lit speak words D11:18 Or repentance to life E11:20 Other mss read Greeks F11:20 In this context, a non-Jewish person who spoke Gk. G11:22 Other mss omit to travel H11:25 Other mss read Barnabas I11:28 Or the whole world J11:28 Emperor A.D. 41–54; there was a famine A.D. 47–48.

"Quick, get up!" Then the chains fell off his wrists. [8]"Get dressed," the angel told him, "and put on your sandals." And he did so. "Wrap your cloak around you," he told him, "and follow me." [9]So he went out and followed, and he did not know that what took place through the angel was real, but thought he was seeing a vision. [10]After they passed the first and second guard posts, they came to the iron gate that leads into the city, which opened to them by itself. They went outside and passed one street, and immediately the angel left him.

[11]Then Peter came to himself and said, "Now I know for certain that the Lord has sent His angel and rescued me from Herod's grasp and from all that the Jewish people expected." [12]When he realized this, he went to the house of Mary, the mother of John Mark,[A] where many had assembled and were praying. [13]He knocked at the door in the gateway, and a servant named Rhoda came to answer. [14]She recognized Peter's voice, and because of her joy, she did not open the gate but ran in and announced that Peter was standing at the gateway.

[15]"You're crazy!" they told her. But she kept insisting that it was true. Then they said, "It's his angel!" [16]Peter, however, kept on knocking, and when they opened the door and saw him, they were astounded.

[17]Motioning to them with his hand to be silent, he explained to them how the Lord had brought him out of the prison. "Report these things to James[B] and the brothers," he said. Then he departed and went to a different place.

[18]At daylight, there was a great commotion[C] among the soldiers as to what could have become of Peter. [19]After Herod had searched and did not find him, he interrogated the guards and ordered their execution. Then Herod went down from Judea to Caesarea and stayed there.

[20]He had been very angry with the Tyrians and Sidonians.[D] Together they presented themselves before him. They won over Blastus, who was in charge of the king's bedroom, and through him they asked for peace, because their country was supplied with food from the king's country. [21]So on an appointed day, dressed in royal robes and seated on the throne, Herod delivered a public address to them. [22]The assembled people began to shout, "It's the voice of a god and not of a man!" [23]At once an angel of the Lord struck him because he did not give the glory to God, and he became infected with worms and died. [24]Then God's message flourished and multiplied. [25]After they had completed their relief mission, Barnabas and Saul returned to[E] Jerusalem, taking along John who is called Mark.

13 In the church that was at Antioch there were prophets and teachers: Barnabas, Simeon who was called Niger, Lucius the Cyrenian, Manaen, a close friend of Herod the tetrarch, and Saul.

[2]As they were ministering to[F] the Lord and fasting, the Holy Spirit said, "Set apart for Me Barnabas and Saul for the work I have called them to." [3]Then after they had fasted, prayed, and laid hands on them, they sent them off.

[4]Being sent out by the Holy Spirit, they came down to Seleucia, and from there they sailed to Cyprus. [5]Arriving in Salamis, they proclaimed God's message in the Jewish synagogues. They also had John as their assistant. [6]When they had gone through the whole island as far as Paphos, they came across a sorcerer, a Jewish false prophet named Bar-Jesus. [7]He was with the proconsul, Sergius Paulus, an intelligent man. This man summoned Barnabas and Saul and desired to hear God's message. [8]But Elymas the sorcerer (this is the meaning of his name) opposed them and tried to turn the proconsul away from the faith.

[9]Then Saul—also called Paul—filled with the Holy Spirit, stared straight at the sorcerer [10]and said, "You son of the Devil, full of all deceit and all fraud, enemy of all righteousness! Won't you ever stop perverting the straight paths of the Lord? [11]Now, look! The Lord's hand is against you. You are going to be blind, and will not see the sun for a time." Suddenly a mist and darkness fell on him, and he went around seeking someone to lead him by the hand.

[12]Then the proconsul, seeing what happened, believed and was astonished at the teaching about the Lord.

[13]Paul and his companions set sail from Paphos and came to Perga in Pamphylia. John, however, left them and went back to Jerusalem. [14]They continued their journey from Perga and reached Antioch in Pisidia. On the Sabbath day they went into the synagogue and sat down. [15]After the reading of the Law and

A12:12 Lit John who was called Mark   B12:17 This was James, the Lord's brother; Mk 6:3. This was not James the apostle; Ac 12:2.   C12:18 Or was no small disturbance   D12:20 The people of the area of modern Lebanon   E12:25 Other mss read from   F13:2 Or were worshiping the Prophets, the leaders of the synagogue sent word to them, saying, "Brothers, if you have any message of encouragement for the people, you can speak."

¹⁶Then Paul stood up and motioned with his hand and said: "Men of Israel, and you who fear God, listen! ¹⁷The God of this people Israel chose our ancestors, exalted the people during their stay in the land of Egypt, and led them out of it with a mightyᴬ arm. ¹⁸And for about 40 years He put up with themᴮ in the wilderness; ¹⁹then after destroying seven nations in the land of Canaan, He gave their land to them as an inheritance. ²⁰This all took about 450 years. After this, He gave them judges until Samuel the prophet. ²¹Then they asked for a king, so God gave them Saul the son of Kish, a man of the tribe of Benjamin, for 40 years. ²²After removing him, He raised up David as their king and testified about him: '**I have found David** the son of Jesse, **a man loyal to Me,**ᶜ who will carry out all My will.'

²³"From this man's descendants, according to the promise, God brought the Savior, Jesus,ᴰ to Israel. ²⁴Before He came to public attention,ᴱ John had previously proclaimed a baptism of repentance to all the people of Israel. ²⁵Then as John was completing his life's work, he said, 'Who do you think I am? I am not the One. But look! Someone is coming after me, and I am not worthy to untie the sandals on His feet.'

²⁶"Brothers, sons of Abraham's race, and those among you who fear God, the message of this salvation has been sent to us. ²⁷For the residents of Jerusalem and their rulers, since they did not recognize Him or the voices of the prophets that are read every Sabbath, have fulfilled their wordsᶠ by condemning Him. ²⁸Though they found no grounds for the death penalty, they asked Pilate to have Him killed. ²⁹When they had fulfilled all that had been written about Him, they took Him down from the tree and put Him in a tomb. ³⁰But God raised Him from the dead, ³¹and He appeared for many days to those who came with Him from Galilee to Jerusalem, who are now His witnesses to the people. ³²And we ourselves proclaim to you the good news of the promise that was made to our ancestors. ³³God has

fulfilled this for us, their children, by raising up Jesus, as it is written in the second Psalm:

> **You are My Son;**
> **today I have become Your Father.**ᴳ·ᴴ

³⁴Since He raised Him from the dead, never to return to decay, He has spoken in this way, **I will grant you the faithful covenant blessings**ᶦ **made to David.**ᴶ ³⁵Therefore He also says in another passage, **You will not allow Your Holy One to see decay.**ᴷ ³⁶For David, after serving his own generation in God's plan, fell asleep, was buried with his fathers, and decayed. ³⁷But the One God raised up did not decay. ³⁸Therefore, let it be known to you, brothers, that through this man forgiveness of sins is being proclaimed to you, ³⁹and everyone who believes in Him is justified from everything that you could not be justified from through the law of Moses. ⁴⁰So beware that what is said in the prophets does not happen to you:

> ⁴¹   **Look, you scoffers,**
> **marvel and vanish away,**
> **because I am doing a work**
> **in your days,**
> **a work that you will never believe,**
> **even if someone were to explain it**
> **to you.**"ᴸ

⁴²As theyᴹ were leaving, the peopleᴺ begged that these matters be presented to them the following Sabbath. ⁴³After the synagogue had been dismissed, many of the Jews and devout proselytes followed Paul and Barnabas, who were speaking with them and persuading them to continue in the grace of God.

⁴⁴The following Sabbath almost the whole town assembled to hear the message of the Lord.º ⁴⁵But when the Jews saw the crowds, they were filled with jealousy and began to oppose what Paul was saying by insulting them.

⁴⁶Then Paul and Barnabas boldly said: "It was necessary that God's message be spoken to you first. But since you reject it and consider yourselves unworthy of eternal life, we now turn to the Gentiles! ⁴⁷For this is what the Lord has commanded us:

> **I have made you**
> **a light for the Gentiles**

ᴬ13:17 Lit with an uplifted   ᴮ13:18 Other mss read He cared for them   ᶜ13:22 1Sm 13:14; Ps 89:20   ᴰ13:23 Other mss read brought salvation   ᴱ13:24 Lit Before the face of His entrance   ᶠ13:27 Lit fulfilled them   ᴳ13:33 Or I have begotten You   ᴴ13:33 Ps 2:7   ᴵ13:34 Lit faithful holy things   ᴶ13:34 Is 55:3   ᴷ13:35 Ps 16:10   ᴸ13:41 Hab 1:5   ᴹ13:42 Paul and Barnabas   ᴺ13:42 Other mss read they were leaving the synagogue of the Jews, the Gentiles   º13:44 Other mss read of God

121

to bring salvation
to the ends^A of the earth."^B

^48When the Gentiles heard this, they rejoiced and glorified the message of the Lord, and all who had been appointed to eternal life believed. ^49So the message of the Lord spread through the whole region. ^50But the Jews incited the prominent women, who worshiped God, and the leading men of the city. They stirred up persecution against Paul and Barnabas and expelled them from their district. ^51But they shook the dust off their feet against them and went to Iconium. ^52And the disciples were filled with joy and the Holy Spirit.

14 The same thing happened in Iconium; they entered the Jewish synagogue and spoke in such a way that a great number of both Jews and Greeks believed. ^2But the Jews who refused to believe stirred up and poisoned the minds of the Gentiles against the brothers. ^3So they stayed there for some time and spoke boldly in reliance on the Lord, who testified to the message of His grace by granting that signs and wonders be performed through them. ^4But the people of the city were divided, some siding with the Jews and some with the apostles. ^5When an attempt was made by both the Gentiles and Jews, with their rulers, to assault and stone them, ^6they found out about it and fled to the Lycaonian towns called Lystra and Derbe, and to the surrounding countryside. ^7And there they kept evangelizing.

^8In Lystra a man without strength in his feet, lame from birth,^C and who had never walked, sat ^9and heard Paul speaking. After observing him closely and seeing that he had faith to be healed, ^10Paul said in a loud voice, "Stand upright on your feet!" And he jumped up and started to walk around.

^11When the crowds saw what Paul had done, they raised their voices, saying in the Lycaonian language, "The gods have come down to us in the form of men!" ^12And they started to call Barnabas, Zeus, and Paul, Hermes, because he was the main speaker. ^13Then the priest of Zeus, whose temple was just outside the town, brought oxen and garlands to the gates. He, with the crowds, intended to offer sacrifice.

^14The apostles Barnabas and Paul tore their robes when they heard this and rushed into the crowd, shouting: ^15"Men! Why are you doing these things? We are men also, with the same nature as you, and we are proclaiming good news to you, that you should turn from these worthless things to the living God, **who made the heaven, the earth, the sea, and everything in them.**^D ^16In past generations He allowed all the nations to go their own way, ^17though He did not leave Himself without a witness, since He did what is good by giving you rain from heaven and fruitful seasons and satisfying your^E hearts with food and happiness." ^18Even though they said these things, they barely stopped the crowds from sacrificing to them.

^19Then some Jews came from Antioch and Iconium, and when they had won over the crowds and stoned Paul, they dragged him out of the city, thinking he was dead. ^20After the disciples surrounded him, he got up and went into the town. The next day he left with Barnabas for Derbe.

^21After they had evangelized that town and made many disciples, they returned to Lystra, to Iconium, and to Antioch, ^22strengthening the^F disciples by encouraging them to continue in the faith and by telling them, "It is necessary to pass through many troubles on our way into the kingdom of God." ^23When they had appointed elders in every church and prayed with fasting, they committed them to the Lord in whom they had believed. ^24Then they passed through Pisidia and came to Pamphylia. ^25After they spoke the message in Perga, they went down to Attalia. ^26From there they sailed back to Antioch where they had been entrusted to the grace of God for the work they had now completed. ^27After they arrived and gathered the church together, they reported everything God had done with them and that He had opened the door of faith to the Gentiles. ^28And they spent a considerable time^G with the disciples.

15 Some men came down from Judea and began to teach the brothers: "Unless you are circumcised according to the custom prescribed by Moses, you cannot be saved!" ^2But after Paul and Barnabas had engaged them in serious argument and debate, the church arranged for Paul and Barnabas and some others of them to go up to the apostles and elders in Jerusalem concerning this controversy.

^A13:47 Lit the end ^B13:47 Is 49:6 ^C14:8 Lit *from his mother's womb* ^D14:15 Ex 20:11; Ps 146:6 ^E14:17 Other mss read *our* ^F14:22 Lit *the souls of the* ^G14:28 Or *spent no little time*

³When they had been sent on their way by the church, they passed through both Phoenicia and Samaria, explaining in detail the conversion of the Gentiles, and they created great joy among all the brothers.

⁴When they arrived at Jerusalem, they were welcomed by the church, the apostles, and the elders, and they reported all that God had done with them. ⁵But some of the believers from the party of the Pharisees stood up and said, "It is necessary to circumcise them and to command them to keep the law of Moses!"

⁶Then the apostles and the elders assembled to consider this matter. ⁷After there had been much debate, Peter stood up and said to them: "Brothers, you are aware that in the early days God made a choice among you,ᴬ that by my mouth the Gentiles would hear the gospel message and believe. ⁸And God, who knows the heart, testified to them by givingᴮ the Holy Spirit, just as He also did to us. ⁹He made no distinction between us and them, cleansing their hearts by faith. ¹⁰Now then, why are you testing God by putting a yoke on the disciples' necks that neither our ancestors nor we have been able to bear? ¹¹On the contrary, we believe we are saved through the grace of the Lord Jesus in the same way they are."

¹²Then the whole assembly fell silent and listened to Barnabas and Paul describing all the signs and wonders God had done through them among the Gentiles. ¹³After they stopped speaking, James responded: "Brothers, listen to me! ¹⁴Simeonᶜ has reported how God first intervened to take from the Gentiles a people for His name. ¹⁵And the words of the prophets agree with this, as it is written:

¹⁶   After these things I will return
        and rebuild David's fallen tent.
        I will rebuild its ruins
        and set it up again,
¹⁷   so the rest of humanity
        may seek the Lord—
        even all the Gentiles
        who are called by My name,
        declares the Lord who does
        these things,
¹⁸   known from long ago.ᴰ·ᴱ

¹⁹Therefore, in my judgment, we should not cause difficulties for those among the Gentiles who turn to God, ²⁰but instead we should write to them to abstain from things polluted by idols, from sexual immorality, from eating anything that has been strangled, and from blood. ²¹For since ancient times, Moses has had those who proclaim him in every city, and every Sabbath day he is read aloud in the synagogues."

²²Then the apostles and the elders, with the whole church, decided to select men who were among them and to send them to Antioch with Paul and Barnabas: Judas, called Barsabbas, and Silas, both leading men among the brothers. ²³They wrote this letter to be delivered by them:ᶠ

From the apostles and the elders, your brothers,
To the brothers among the Gentiles in Antioch, Syria, and Cilicia:
Greetings.

²⁴Because we have heard that some without our authorization went out from us and troubled you with their words and unsettled your hearts,ᴳ ²⁵we have unanimously decided to select men and send them to you along with our dearly loved Barnabas and Paul, ²⁶who have risked their lives for the name of our Lord Jesus Christ. ²⁷Therefore we have sent Judas and Silas, who will personally report the same things by word of mouth. ²⁸For it was the Holy Spirit's decision—and ours—to put no greater burden on you than these necessary things: ²⁹that you abstain from food offered to idols, from blood, from eating anything that has been strangled, and from sexual immorality. You will do well if you keep yourselves from these things.
Farewell.

³⁰Then, being sent off, they went down to Antioch, and after gathering the assembly, they delivered the letter. ³¹When they read it, they rejoiced because of its encouragement. ³²Both Judas and Silas, who were also prophets themselves, encouraged the brothers and strengthened them with a long message. ³³After spending some time there, they were sent

ᴬ15:7 Other mss read us   ᴮ15:8 Other mss add them   ᶜ15:14 Simon [Peter]   ᴰ15:17-18 Other mss read says the Lord who does all His works. Known to God from long ago are all His works.   ᴱ15:16-18 Am 9:11-12; Is 45:21   ᶠ15:23 Lit Writing by their hand;   ᴳ15:24 Other mss add by saying, "Be circumcised and keep the law,"   ᴴ15:27 Lit things through word back in peace by the brothers to those who had sent them.[A,B] [35]But Paul and Barnabas, along with many others, remained in Antioch teaching and proclaiming the message of the Lord.

[36]After some time had passed, Paul said to Barnabas, "Let's go back and visit the brothers in every town where we have preached the message of the Lord and see how they're doing." [37]Barnabas wanted to take along John Mark.[C] [38]But Paul did not think it appropriate to take along this man who had deserted them in Pamphylia and had not gone on with them to the work. [39]There was such a sharp disagreement that they parted company, and Barnabas took Mark with him and sailed off to Cyprus. [40]Then Paul chose Silas and departed, after being commended to the grace of the Lord by the brothers. [41]He traveled through Syria and Cilicia, strengthening the churches.

16 Then he went on to Derbe and Lystra, where there was a disciple named Timothy, the son of a believing Jewish woman, but his father was a Greek. [2]The brothers at Lystra and Iconium spoke highly of him. [3]Paul wanted Timothy[D] to go with him, so he took him and circumcised him because of the Jews who were in those places, since they all knew that his father was a Greek. [4]As they traveled through the towns, they delivered the decisions reached by the apostles and elders at Jerusalem for them to observe. [5]So the churches were strengthened in the faith and increased in number daily.

[6]They went through the region of Phrygia and Galatia and were prevented by the Holy Spirit from speaking the message in Asia. [7]When they came to Mysia, they tried to go into Bithynia, but the Spirit of Jesus did not allow him. [8]So, bypassing Mysia, they came down to Troas. [9]During the night a vision appeared to Paul: A Macedonian man was standing and pleading with him, "Cross over to Macedonia and help us!" [10]After he had seen the vision, we[E] immediately made efforts to set out for Macedonia, concluding that God had called us to evangelize them.

[11]Then, setting sail from Troas, we ran a straight course to Samothrace, the next day to Neapolis, [12]and from there to Philippi, a Roman colony, which is a leading city of that district of Macedonia. We stayed in that city for a number of days. [13]On the Sabbath day we went outside the city gate by the river, where we thought there was a place of prayer. We sat down and spoke to the women gathered there. [14]A woman named Lydia, a dealer in purple cloth from the city of Thyatira, who worshiped God, was listening. The Lord opened her heart to pay attention to what was spoken by Paul. [15]After she and her household were baptized, she urged us, "If you consider me a believer in the Lord, come and stay at my house." And she persuaded us.

[16]Once, as we were on our way to prayer, a slave girl met us who had a spirit of prediction.[F] She made a large profit for her owners by fortune-telling. [17]As she followed Paul and us she cried out, "These men, who are proclaiming to you[G] the way of salvation, are the slaves of the Most High God." [18]And she did this for many days.

But Paul was greatly aggravated and turning to the spirit, said, "I command you in the name of Jesus Christ to come out of her!" And it came out right away.[H]

[19]When her owners saw that their hope of profit was gone, they seized Paul and Silas and dragged them into the marketplace to the authorities. [20]Bringing them before the chief magistrates, they said, "These men are seriously disturbing our city. They are Jews [21]and are promoting customs that are not legal for us as Romans to adopt or practice."

[22]Then the mob joined in the attack against them, and the chief magistrates stripped off their clothes and ordered them to be beaten with rods. [23]After they had inflicted many blows on them, they threw them in jail, ordering the jailer to keep them securely guarded. [24]Receiving such an order, he put them into the inner prison and secured their feet in the stocks.

[25]About midnight Paul and Silas were praying and singing hymns to God, and the prisoners were listening to them. [26]Suddenly there was such a violent earthquake that the foundations of the jail were shaken, and immediately all the doors were opened, and everyone's chains came loose. [27]When the jailer woke up and saw the doors of the prison open, he drew his sword and was going to kill himself, since he thought the prisoners had escaped.

[A]15:33 Other mss read the brothers to the apostles   [B]15:33 Other mss add v. 34: But Silas decided to stay there.   [C]15:37 Lit John who was called Mark   [D]16:3 Lit wanted this one   [E]16:10 The use of we in this passage probably indicates that the author Luke is joining Paul's missionary team here.   [F]16:16 Or a spirit by which she predicted the future   [G]16:17 Other mss read us   [H]16:18 Lit out this hour

28 But Paul called out in a loud voice, "Don't harm yourself, because all of us are here!"

29 Then the jailer called for lights, rushed in, and fell down trembling before Paul and Silas. 30 Then he escorted them out and said, "Sirs, what must I do to be saved?"

31 So they said, "Believe on the Lord Jesus, and you will be saved—you and your household." 32 Then they spoke the message of the Lord to him along with everyone in his house. 33 He took them the same hour of the night and washed their wounds. Right away he and all his family were baptized. 34 He brought them into his house, set a meal before them, and rejoiced because he had believed God with his entire household.

35 When daylight came, the chief magistrates sent the police to say, "Release those men!"

36 The jailer reported these words to Paul: "The magistrates have sent orders for you to be released. So come out now and go in peace."

37 But Paul said to them, "They beat us in public without a trial, although we are Roman citizens, and threw us in jail. And now are they going to smuggle us out secretly? Certainly not! On the contrary, let them come themselves and escort us out!"

38 Then the police reported these words to the magistrates. They were afraid when they heard that Paul and Silas were Roman citizens. 39 So they came and apologized to them, and escorting them out, they urged them to leave town. 40 After leaving the jail, they came to Lydia's house where they saw and encouraged the brothers, and departed.

17 Then they traveled through Amphipolis and Apollonia and came to Thessalonica, where there was a Jewish synagogue. 2 As usual, Paul went to the synagogue, and on three Sabbath days reasoned with them from the Scriptures, 3 explaining and showing that the Messiah had to suffer and rise from the dead: "This Jesus I am proclaiming to you is the Messiah." 4 Then some of them were persuaded and joined Paul and Silas, including a great number of God-fearing Greeks, as well as a number[A] of the leading women.

5 But the Jews became jealous, and they brought together some scoundrels from the marketplace, formed a mob, and started a riot in the city. Attacking Jason's house, they searched for them to bring them out to the public assembly. 6 When they did not find them, they dragged Jason and some of the brothers before the city officials, shouting, "These men who have turned the world upside down have come here too, 7 and Jason has received them as guests! They are all acting contrary to Caesar's decrees, saying that there is another king—Jesus!" 8 The Jews stirred up the crowd and the city officials who heard these things. 9 So taking a security bond from Jason and the others, they released them.

10 As soon as it was night, the brothers sent Paul and Silas off to Berea. On arrival, they went into the synagogue of the Jews. 11 The people here were more open-minded than those in Thessalonica, since they welcomed the message with eagerness and examined the Scriptures daily to see if these things were so. 12 Consequently, many of them believed, including a number of the prominent Greek women as well as men. 13 But when the Jews from Thessalonica found out that God's message had been proclaimed by Paul at Berea, they came there too, agitating and disturbing[B] the crowds. 14 Then the brothers immediately sent Paul away to go to the sea, but Silas and Timothy stayed on there. 15 Those who escorted Paul brought him as far as Athens, and after receiving instructions for Silas and Timothy to come to him as quickly as possible, they departed.

16 While Paul was waiting for them in Athens, his spirit was troubled within him when he saw that the city was full of idols. 17 So he reasoned in the synagogue with the Jews and with those who worshiped God and in the marketplace every day with those who happened to be there. 18 Then also, some of the Epicurean and Stoic philosophers argued with him. Some said, "What is this pseudo-intellectual[C] trying to say?"

Others replied, "He seems to be a preacher of foreign deities"—because he was telling the good news about Jesus and the Resurrection.[D]

19 They took him and brought him to the Areopagus,[E] and said, "May we learn about this new teaching you're speaking of? 20 For what you say sounds strange to us, and we want to know what these ideas mean." 21 Now all the Athenians and the foreigners residing there spent their time on nothing else but telling or hearing something new.

A17:4 Lit as well as not a few B17:13 Other mss omit and disturbing C17:18 Lit this seed picker; = one who picks up scraps D17:18 = Gk Anastasis E17:19 Or Mars Hill, the oldest and most famous court in Athens with jurisdiction in moral, religious, and civil matters

²²Then Paul stood in the middle of the Areopagus and said: "Men of Athens! I see that you are extremely religious in every respect. ²³For as I was passing through and observing the objects of your worship, I even found an altar on which was inscribed:

TO AN UNKNOWN GOD.

Therefore, what you worship in ignorance, this I proclaim to you. ²⁴The God who made the world and everything in it—He is Lord of heaven and earth and does not live in shrines made by hands. ²⁵Neither is He served by human hands, as though He needed anything, since He Himself gives everyone life and breath and all things. ²⁶From one manᴬ He has made every nationality to live over the whole earth and has determined their appointed times and the boundaries of where they live. ²⁷He did this so they might seek God, and perhaps they might reach out and find Him, though He is not far from each one of us. ²⁸For in Him we live and move and exist, as even some of your own poets have said, 'For we are also His offspring.'ᴮ ²⁹Being God's offspring then, we shouldn't think that the divine nature is like gold or silver or stone, an image fashioned by human art and imagination.

³⁰"Therefore, having overlooked the times of ignorance, God now commands all people everywhere to repent, ³¹because He has set a day when He is going to judge the world in righteousness by the Man He has appointed. He has provided proof of this to everyone by raising Him from the dead."

³²When they heard about resurrection of the dead, some began to ridicule him. But others said, "We'd like to hear from you again about this." ³³Then Paul left their presence. ³⁴However, some men joined him and believed, including Dionysius the Areopagite, a woman named Damaris, and others with them.

18 After this, heᶜ left Athens and went to Corinth, ²where he found a Jewish man named Aquila, a native of Pontus, who had recently come from Italy with his wife Priscilla because Claudiusᴰ had ordered all the Jews to leave Rome. Paul came to them, ³and being of the same occupation, stayed with them and worked, for they were tentmakersᴱ by trade.

⁴He reasoned in the synagogue every Sabbath and tried to persuade both Jews and Greeks.

⁵When Silas and Timothy came down from Macedonia, Paul was occupied with preaching the messageᶠ and solemnly testified to the Jews that Jesus is the Messiah. ⁶But when they resisted and blasphemed, he shook his robeᴳ and told them, "Your blood is on your own heads! I am innocent.ᴴ From now on I will go to the Gentiles." ⁷So he left there and went to the house of a man named Titius Justus, a worshiper of God, whose house was next door to the synagogue. ⁸Crispus, the leader of the synagogue, believed the Lord, along with his whole household. Many of the Corinthians, when they heard, believed and were baptized.

⁹Then the Lord said to Paul in a night vision, "Don't be afraid, but keep on speaking and don't be silent. ¹⁰For I am with you, and no one will lay a hand on you to hurt you, because I have many people in this city." ¹¹And he stayed there a year and six months, teaching the word of God among them.

¹²While Gallio was proconsul of Achaia, the Jews made a united attack against Paul and brought him to the judge's bench. ¹³"This man," they said, "persuades people to worship God contrary to the law!"

¹⁴As Paul was about to open his mouth, Gallio said to the Jews, "If it were a matter of a crime or of moral evil, it would be reasonable for me to put up with you Jews. ¹⁵But if these are questions about words, names, and your own law, see to it yourselves. I don't want to be a judge of such things." ¹⁶So he drove them from the judge's bench. ¹⁷Then they allᴵ seized Sosthenes, the leader of the synagogue, and beat him in front of the judge's bench. But none of these things concerned Gallio.

¹⁸So Paul, having stayed on for many days, said good-bye to the brothers and sailed away to Syria. Priscilla and Aquila were with him. He shaved his head at Cenchreae because he had taken a vow. ¹⁹When they reached Ephesus he left them there, but he himself entered the synagogue and engaged in discussion withᴶ the Jews. ²⁰And though they asked him to stay for a longer time, he declined, ²¹but he said good-bye

---

ᴬ17:26 Other mss read *one blood*   ᴮ17:28 This citation is from Aratus, a third-century B.C. Gk poet.   ᶜ18:1 Other mss read *Paul*   ᴰ18:2 Roman emperor A.D. 41–54; he expelled all Jews from Rome in A.D. 49.   ᴱ18:3 Or *leatherworkers*, or less likely *manufacturers of theatrical properties*   ᶠ18:5 Other mss read *was urged by the Spirit*   ᴳ18:6 A symbolic display of protest; Mt 10:14; Ac 13:51   ᴴ18:6 Lit *clean*   ᴵ18:17 Other mss read *Then all the Greeks*   ᴶ18:19 Or *and addressed* and stated,^A "I'll come back to you again, if God wills." Then he set sail from Ephesus.

²² On landing at Caesarea, he went up and greeted the church^B and went down to Antioch. ²³ And after spending some time there, he set out, traveling through one place after another in the Galatian territory and Phrygia, strengthening all the disciples.

²⁴ A Jew named Apollos, a native Alexandrian, an eloquent man who was powerful in the use of the Scriptures, arrived in Ephesus. ²⁵ This man had been instructed in the way of the Lord; and being fervent in spirit,^C he spoke and taught the things about Jesus accurately, although he knew only John's baptism. ²⁶ He began to speak boldly in the synagogue. After Priscilla and Aquila heard him, they took him home^D and explained the way of God to him more accurately. ²⁷ When he wanted to cross over to Achaia, the brothers wrote to the disciples urging them to welcome him. After he arrived, he greatly helped those who had believed through grace. ²⁸ For he vigorously refuted the Jews in public, demonstrating through the Scriptures that Jesus is the Messiah.

19 While Apollos was in Corinth, Paul traveled through the interior regions and came to Ephesus. He found some disciples ² and asked them, "Did you receive the Holy Spirit when you believed?"

"No," they told him, "we haven't even heard that there is a Holy Spirit."

³ "Then what baptism were you baptized with?" he asked them.

"With John's baptism," they replied.

⁴ Paul said, "John baptized with a baptism of repentance, telling the people that they should believe in the One who would come after him, that is, in Jesus."

⁵ When they heard this, they were baptized in the name of the Lord Jesus. ⁶ And when Paul had laid his hands on them, the Holy Spirit came on them, and they began to speak in other languages and to prophesy. ⁷ Now there were about 12 men in all.

⁸ Then he entered the synagogue and spoke boldly over a period of three months, engaging in discussion and trying to persuade them about the things of the kingdom of God. ⁹ But when some became hardened and would not believe, slandering the Way in front of the crowd, he withdrew from them and met separately with the disciples, conducting discussions every day in the lecture hall of Tyrannus. ¹⁰ And this went on for two years, so that all the inhabitants of Asia, both Jews and Greeks, heard the message about the Lord.

¹¹ God was performing extraordinary miracles by Paul's hands, ¹² so that even facecloths or work aprons^E that had touched his skin were brought to the sick, and the diseases left them, and the evil spirits came out of them.

¹³ Then some of the itinerant Jewish exorcists attempted to pronounce the name of the Lord Jesus over those who had evil spirits, saying, "I command you by the Jesus that Paul preaches!" ¹⁴ Seven sons of Sceva, a Jewish chief priest, were doing this. ¹⁵ The evil spirit answered them, "I know Jesus, and I recognize Paul—but who are you?" ¹⁶ Then the man who had the evil spirit leaped on them, overpowered them all, and prevailed against them, so that they ran out of that house naked and wounded. ¹⁷ This became known to everyone who lived in Ephesus, both Jews and Greeks. Then fear fell on all of them, and the name of the Lord Jesus was magnified. ¹⁸ And many who had become believers came confessing and disclosing their practices, ¹⁹ while many of those who had practiced magic collected their books and burned them in front of everyone. So they calculated their value and found it to be 50,000 pieces of silver. ²⁰ In this way the Lord's message flourished and prevailed.

²¹ When these events were over, Paul resolved in the Spirit to pass through Macedonia and Achaia and go to Jerusalem. "After I've been there," he said, "I must see Rome as well!" ²² So after sending two of those who assisted him, Timothy and Erastus, to Macedonia, he himself stayed in Asia for a while.

²³ During that time there was a major^F disturbance about the Way. ²⁴ For a person named Demetrius, a silversmith who made silver shrines of Artemis,^G provided a great deal of^H business for the craftsmen. ²⁵ When he had assembled them, as well as the workers engaged in this type of business, he said: "Men, you know that our prosperity is derived

---

A18:21 Other mss add *"By all means it is necessary to keep the coming festival in Jerusalem. But*   **B18:22** The church in Jerusalem   **C18:25** Or *in the Spirit*   **D18:26** Lit *they received him*   **E19:12** Or *that also sweatbands and sweatcloths or handkerchiefs*   **F19:23** Lit *was not a little*   **G19:24** Artemis was the ancient Gk mother goddess believed to control all fertility.   **H19:24** Lit *provided not a little* from this business. ²⁶ You both see and hear that not only in Ephesus, but in almost all of Asia, this man Paul has persuaded and misled a considerable number of people by saying that gods made by hand are not gods! ²⁷ So not only do we run a risk that our business may be discredited, but also that the temple of the great goddess Artemis may be despised and her magnificence come to the verge of ruin—the very one all of Asia and the world adore."

²⁸ When they had heard this, they were filled with rage and began to cry out, "Great is Artemis of the Ephesians!" ²⁹ So the city was filled with confusion, and they rushed all together into the amphitheater, dragging along Gaius and Aristarchus, Macedonians who were Paul's traveling companions. ³⁰ Though Paul wanted to go in before the people, the disciples did not let him. ³¹ Even some of the provincial officials of Asia, who were his friends, sent word to him, pleading with him not to take a chance by going^A into the amphitheater. ³² Meanwhile, some were shouting one thing and some another, because the assembly was in confusion, and most of them did not know why they had come together. ³³ Then some of the crowd gave Alexander advice when the Jews pushed him to the front. So motioning with his hand, Alexander wanted to make his defense to the people. ³⁴ But when they recognized that he was a Jew, a united cry went up from all of them for about two hours: "Great is Artemis of the Ephesians!"

³⁵ However, when the city clerk had calmed the crowd down, he said, "Men of Ephesus! What man is there who doesn't know that the city of the Ephesians is the temple guardian of the great^B Artemis, and of the image that fell from heaven? ³⁶ Therefore, since these things are undeniable, you must keep calm and not do anything rash. ³⁷ For you have brought these men here who are not temple robbers or blasphemers of our^C goddess. ³⁸ So if Demetrius and the craftsmen who are with him have a case against anyone, the courts are in session, and there are proconsuls. Let them bring charges against one another. ³⁹ But if you want something else, it must be decided in a legal assembly. ⁴⁰ In fact, we run a risk of being charged with rioting and have

happened today, since there is no justification that we can give as a reason for this disorderly gathering." ⁴¹ After saying this, he dismissed the assembly.

20 After the uproar was over, Paul sent for the disciples, encouraged them, and after saying good-bye, departed to go to Macedonia. ² And when he had passed through those areas and exhorted them at length, he came to Greece ³ and stayed three months. When he was about to set sail for Syria, a plot was devised against him by the Jews, so a decision was made to go back through Macedonia. ⁴ He was accompanied^D by Sopater son of Pyrrhus^E from Berea, Aristarchus and Secundus from Thessalonica, Gaius from Derbe, Timothy, and Tychicus and Trophimus from Asia. ⁵ These men went on ahead and waited for us in Troas, ⁶ but we sailed away from Philippi after the days of Unleavened Bread. In five days we reached them at Troas, where we spent seven days.

⁷ On the first day of the week, we^F assembled to break bread. Paul spoke to them, and since he was about to depart the next day, he extended his message until midnight. ⁸ There were many lamps in the room upstairs where we were assembled, ⁹ and a young man named Eutychus was sitting on a window sill and sank into a deep sleep as Paul kept on speaking. When he was overcome by sleep, he fell down from the third story and was picked up dead. ¹⁰ But Paul went down, fell on him, embraced him, and said, "Don't be alarmed, for his life is in him!" ¹¹ After going upstairs, breaking the bread, and eating, Paul conversed a considerable time until dawn. Then he left. ¹² They brought the boy home alive and were greatly comforted.

¹³ Then we went on ahead to the ship and sailed for Assos, intending to take Paul on board there. For these were his instructions, since he himself was going by land. ¹⁴ When he met us at Assos, we took him on board and came to Mitylene. ¹⁵ Sailing from there, the next day we arrived off Chios. The following day we crossed over to Samos, and^G the day after, we came to Miletus. ¹⁶ For Paul had decided to sail past Ephesus so he would not have to spend time in Asia, because he was hurrying to be in Jerusalem, if possible, for the day of Pentecost.

---

^A 19:31 Lit not to give himself   ^B 19:35 Other mss add goddess   ^C 19:37 Other mss read your   ^D 20:4 Other mss add to Asia   ^E 20:4 Other mss omit son of Pyrrhus   ^F 20:7 Other mss read the disciples   ^G 20:15 Other mss add after staying at Trogyllium

¹⁷ Now from Miletus, he sent to Ephesus and called for the elders of the church. ¹⁸ And when they came to him, he said to them: "You know, from the first day I set foot in Asia, how I was with you the whole time— ¹⁹ serving the Lord with all humility, with tears, and with the trials that came to me through the plots of the Jews— ²⁰ and that I did not shrink back from proclaiming to you anything that was profitable or from teaching it to you in public and from house to house. ²¹ I testified to both Jews and Greeks about repentance toward God and faith in our Lord Jesus.

²² "And now I am on my way to Jerusalem, bound in my spirit,ᴬ not knowing what I will encounter there, ²³ except that in town after town the Holy Spirit testifies to me that chains and afflictions are waiting for me. ²⁴ But I count my life of no value to myself, so that I may finish my courseᴮ and the ministry I received from the Lord Jesus, to testify to the gospel of God's grace.

²⁵ "And now I know that none of you will ever see my face again—everyone I went about preaching the kingdom to. ²⁶ Therefore I testify to you this day that I am innocentᶜ of everyone's blood, ²⁷ for I did not shrink back from declaring to you the whole plan of God. ²⁸ Be on guard for yourselves and for all the flock that the Holy Spirit has appointed you to as overseers, to shepherd the church of God,ᴰ which He purchased with His own blood. ²⁹ I know that after my departure savage wolves will come in among you, not sparing the flock. ³⁰ And men will rise up from your own number with deviant doctrines to lure the disciples into following them. ³¹ Therefore be on the alert, remembering that night and day for three years I did not stop warning each one of you with tears.

³² "And nowᴱ I commit you to God and to the message of His grace, which is able to build you up and to give you an inheritance among all who are sanctified. ³³ I have not coveted anyone's silver or gold or clothing. ³⁴ You yourselves know that these hands have provided for my needs and for those who were with me. ³⁵ In every way I've shown you that by laboring like this, it is necessary to help the weak and to keep in mind the words of the Lord Jesus, for He said, 'It is more blessed to give than to receive.'"

³⁶ After he said this, he knelt down and prayed with all of them. ³⁷ There was a great deal of weeping by everyone. They embraced Paul and kissed him, ³⁸ grieving most of all over his statement that they would never see his face again. Then they escorted him to the ship.

21 After we tore ourselves away from them and set sail, we came by a direct route to Cos, the next day to Rhodes, and from there to Patara. ² Finding a ship crossing over to Phoenicia, we boarded and set sail. ³ After we sighted Cyprus, leaving it on the left, we sailed on to Syria and arrived at Tyre, because the ship was to unload its cargo there. ⁴ So we found some disciples and stayed there seven days. Through the Spirit they told Paul not to go to Jerusalem. ⁵ When our days there were over, we left to continue our journey, while all of them, with their wives and children, escorted us out of the city. After kneeling down on the beach to pray, ⁶ we said good-bye to one another. Then we boarded the ship, and they returned home.

⁷ When we completed our voyage from Tyre, we reached Ptolemais, where we greeted the brothers and stayed with them one day. ⁸ The next day we left and came to Caesarea, where we entered the house of Philip the evangelist, who was one of the Seven, and stayed with him. ⁹ This man had four virgin daughters who prophesied.

¹⁰ While we were staying there many days, a prophet named Agabus came down from Judea. ¹¹ He came to us, took Paul's belt, tied his own feet and hands, and said, "This is what the Holy Spirit says: 'In this way the Jews in Jerusalem will bind the man who owns this belt and deliver him into Gentile hands.'" ¹² When we heard this, both we and the local people begged him not to go up to Jerusalem. ¹³ Then Paul replied, "What are you doing, weeping and breaking my heart? For I am ready not only to be bound but also to die in Jerusalem for the name of the Lord Jesus." ¹⁴ Since he would not be persuaded, we stopped talking and simply said, "The Lord's will be done!"

¹⁵ After these days we got ready and went up to Jerusalem. ¹⁶ Some of the disciples from Caesarea also went with us and brought us to

ᴬ20:22 Or in the Spirit ᴮ20:24 Other mss add with joy ᶜ20:26 Lit clean ᴰ20:28 Other mss read church of the Lord; other mss read church of the Lord and God ᴱ20:32 Other mss add brothers.

Mnason, a Cypriot and an early disciple, with whom we were to stay.

¹⁷ When we reached Jerusalem, the brothers welcomed us gladly. ¹⁸ The following day Paul went in with us to James, and all the elders were present. ¹⁹ After greeting them, he related in detail what God did among the Gentiles through his ministry.

²⁰ When they heard it, they glorified God and said, "You see, brother, how many thousands of Jews there are who have believed, and they are all zealous for the law. ²¹ But they have been told about you that you teach all the Jews who are among the Gentiles to abandon Moses, by telling them not to circumcise their children or to walk in our customs. ²² So what is to be done?ᴬ They will certainly hear that you've come. ²³ Therefore do what we tell you: We have four men who have obligated themselves with a vow. ²⁴ Take these men, purify yourself along with them, and pay for them to get their heads shaved. Then everyone will know that what they were told about you amounts to nothing, but that you yourself are also careful about observing the law. ²⁵ With regard to the Gentiles who have believed, we have written a letter containing our decision thatᴮ they should keep themselves from food sacrificed to idols, from blood, from what is strangled, and from sexual immorality."

²⁶ Then the next day, Paul took the men, having purified himself along with them, and entered the temple, announcing the completion of the purification days when the offering for each of them would be made. ²⁷ As the seven days were about to end, the Jews from Asia saw him in the temple complex, stirred up the whole crowd, and seized him, ²⁸ shouting, "Men of Israel, help! This is the man who teaches everyone everywhere against our people, our law, and this place. What's more, he also brought Greeks into the temple and has profaned this holy place." ²⁹ For they had previously seen Trophimus the Ephesian in the city with him, and they supposed that Paul had brought him into the temple complex.ᶜ

³⁰ The whole city was stirred up, and the people rushed together. They seized Paul, dragged him out of the temple complex, and at once the gates were shut. ³¹ As they were trying to kill him, word went up to the commander of the regiment that all Jerusalem was in chaos. ³² Taking along soldiers and centurions, he immediately ran down to them. Seeing the commander and the soldiers, they stopped beating Paul. ³³ Then the commander came up, took him into custody, and ordered him to be bound with two chains. He asked who he was and what he had done. ³⁴ Some in the mob were shouting one thing and some another. Since he was not able to get reliable information because of the uproar, he ordered him to be taken into the barracks. ³⁵ When Paul got to the steps, he had to be carried by the soldiers because of the mob's violence, ³⁶ for the mass of people followed, yelling, "Take him away!"

³⁷ As he was about to be brought into the barracks, Paul said to the commander, "Am I allowed to say something to you?"

He replied, "Do you know Greek? ³⁸ Aren't you the Egyptian who raised a rebellion some time ago and led 4,000 Assassinsᴰ,ᴱ into the wilderness?"

³⁹ Paul said, "I am a Jewish man from Tarsus of Cilicia, a citizen of an important city.ᶠ Now I ask you, let me speak to the people."

⁴⁰ After he had given permission, Paul stood on the steps and motioned with his hand to the people. When there was a great hush, he addressed them in the Hebrew language:

22 ¹ "Brothers and fathers, listen now to my defense before you." ² When they heard that he was addressing them in the Hebrew language, they became even quieter.

³ He continued, "I am a Jewish man, born in Tarsus of Cilicia but brought up in this cityᴳ at the feet of Gamaliel and educated according to the strict view of our patriarchal law. Being zealous for God, just as all of you are today, ⁴ I persecuted this Way to the death, binding and putting both men and women in jail, ⁵ as both the high priest and the whole council of elders can testify about me. After I received letters from them to the brothers, I traveled to Damascus to bring those who were prisoners there to be punished in Jerusalem.

⁶ "As I was traveling and near Damascus, about noon an intense light from heaven suddenly flashed around me. ⁷ I fell to the ground

---

ᴬ21:22 Other mss add *A multitude has to come together, since*   ᴮ21:25 Other mss add *they should observe no such thing, except that*
ᶜ21:29 The inner temple court for Jewish men   ᴰ21:38 Lit *4,000 men of the Assassins*   ᴱ21:38 In Lat, the word *Sicarii* is similar to the Eng word "cut-throats."   ᶠ21:39 Lit *of no insignificant city*   ᴳ22:3 Probably Jerusalem, but others think Tarsus

and heard a voice saying to me, 'Saul, Saul, why are you persecuting Me?'

⁸ "I answered, 'Who are You, Lord?'

"He said to me, 'I am Jesus the Nazarene, the One you are persecuting!' ⁹ Now those who were with me saw the light,^ but they did not hear the voice of the One who was speaking to me.

¹⁰ "Then I said, 'What should I do, Lord?'

"And the Lord told me, 'Get up and go into Damascus, and there you will be told about everything that is assigned for you to do.'

¹¹ "Since I couldn't see because of the brightness of that light, I was led by the hand by those who were with me, and came into Damascus. ¹² Someone named Ananias, a devout man according to the law, having a good reputation with all the Jews residing there, ¹³ came and stood by me and said, 'Brother Saul, regain your sight.' And in that very hour I looked up and saw him. ¹⁴ Then he said, 'The God of our fathers has appointed you to know His will, to see the Righteous One, and to hear the sound of His voice.⁸ ¹⁵ For you will be a witness for Him to all people of what you have seen and heard. ¹⁶ And now, why delay? Get up and be baptized, and wash away your sins by calling on His name.'

¹⁷ "After I came back to Jerusalem and was praying in the temple complex, I went into a visionary state ¹⁸ and saw Him telling me, 'Hurry and get out of Jerusalem quickly, because they will not accept your testimony about Me!'

¹⁹ "But I said, 'Lord, they know that in synagogue after synagogue I had those who believed in You imprisoned and beaten. ²⁰ And when the blood of Your witness Stephen was being shed, I was standing by and approving,^C and I guarded the clothes of those who killed him.'

²¹ "Then He said to me, 'Go, because I will send you far away to the Gentiles.'"

²² They listened to him up to this word. Then they raised their voices, shouting, "Wipe this person off the earth—it's a disgrace for him to live!"

²³ As they were yelling and flinging aside their robes and throwing dust into the air, ²⁴ the commander ordered him to be brought into the barracks, directing that he be examined with the scourge, so he could discover

the reason they were shouting against him like this. ²⁵ As they stretched him out for the lash, Paul said to the centurion standing by, "Is it legal for you to scourge a man who is a Roman citizen and is uncondemned?"

²⁶ When the centurion heard this, he went and reported to the commander, saying, "What are you going to do? For this man is a Roman citizen."

²⁷ The commander came and said to him, "Tell me—are you a Roman citizen?"

"Yes," he said.

²⁸ The commander replied, "I bought this citizenship for a large amount of money."

"But I was born a citizen," Paul said.

²⁹ Therefore, those who were about to examine him withdrew from him at once. The commander too was alarmed when he realized Paul was a Roman citizen and he had bound him.

³⁰ The next day, since he wanted to find out exactly why Paul was being accused by the Jews, he released him^D and instructed the chief priests and all the Sanhedrin to convene. Then he brought Paul down and placed him before them. ¹ Paul looked intently at the Sanhedrin and said, "Brothers, I have lived my life before God in all good conscience until this day." ² But the high priest Ananias ordered those who were standing next to him to strike him on the mouth. ³ Then Paul said to him, "God is going to strike you, you whitewashed wall! You are sitting there judging me according to the law, and in violation of the law are you ordering me to be struck?"

⁴ And those standing nearby said, "Do you dare revile God's high priest?"

⁵ "I did not know, brothers, that he was the high priest," replied Paul. "For it is written, **You must not speak evil of a ruler of your people.**"^E ⁶ When Paul realized that one part of them were Sadducees and the other part were Pharisees, he cried out in the Sanhedrin, "Brothers, I am a Pharisee, a son of Pharisees! I am being judged because of the hope of the resurrection of the dead!" ⁷ When he said this, a dispute broke out between the Pharisees and the Sadducees, and the assembly was divided. ⁸ For the Sadducees say there is no resurrection, and no angel or spirit, but the Pharisees affirm them all.

^A22:9 Other mss add and were afraid   ^B22:14 Lit to hear a voice from His mouth   ^C22:20 Other mss add of his murder   ^D22:30 Other mss add from his chains   ^E23:5 Ex 22:28

⁹ The shouting grew loud, and some of the scribes of the Pharisees' party got up and argued vehemently: "We find nothing evil in this man. What if a spirit or an angel has spoken to him?"ᴬ ¹⁰ When the dispute became violent, the commander feared that Paul might be torn apart by them and ordered the troops to go down, rescue him from them, and bring him into the barracks.

¹¹ The following night, the Lord stood by him and said, "Have courage! For as you have testified about Me in Jerusalem, so you must also testify in Rome."

¹² When it was day, the Jews formed a conspiracy and bound themselves under a curse: neither to eat nor to drink until they had killed Paul. ¹³ There were more than 40 who had formed this plot. ¹⁴ These men went to the chief priests and elders and said, "We have bound ourselves under a solemn curse that we won't eat anything until we have killed Paul. ¹⁵ So now you, along with the Sanhedrin, make a request to the commander that he bring him down to youᴮ as if you were going to investigate his case more thoroughly. However, before he gets near, we are ready to kill him."

¹⁶ But the son of Paul's sister, hearing about their ambush, came and entered the barracks and reported it to Paul. ¹⁷ Then Paul called one of the centurions and said, "Take this young man to the commander, because he has something to report to him."

¹⁸ So he took him, brought him to the commander, and said, "The prisoner Paul called me and asked me to bring this young man to you, because he has something to tell you."

¹⁹ Then the commander took him by the hand, led him aside, and inquired privately, "What is it you have to report to me?"

²⁰ "The Jews," he said, "have agreed to ask you to bring Paul down to the Sanhedrin tomorrow, as though they are going to hold a somewhat more careful inquiry about him. ²¹ Don't let them persuade you, because there are more than 40 of them arranging to ambush him, men who have bound themselves under a curse not to eat or drink until they kill him. Now they are ready, waiting for a commitment from you."

²² So the commander dismissed the young man and instructed him, "Don't tell anyone that you have informed me about this."

²³ He summoned two of his centurions and said, "Get 200 soldiers ready with 70 cavalry and 200 spearmen to go to Caesarea at nine tonight.ᶜ ²⁴ Also provide mounts so they can put Paul on them and bring him safely to Felix the governor.

²⁵ He wrote a letter of this kind:

²⁶ Claudius Lysias,
To the most excellent governor Felix: Greetings.

²⁷ When this man had been seized by the Jews and was about to be killed by them, I arrived with my troops and rescued him because I learned that he is a Roman citizen. ²⁸ Wanting to know the charge they were accusing him of, I brought him down before their Sanhedrin. ²⁹ I found out that the accusations were about disputed matters in their law, and that there was no charge that merited death or chains. ³⁰ When I was informed that there was a plot against the man,ᴰ I sent him to you right away. I also ordered his accusers to state their case against him in your presence.ᴱ

³¹ Therefore, the soldiers took Paul during the night and brought him to Antipatris as they were ordered. ³² The next day, they returned to the barracks, allowing the cavalry to go on with him. ³³ When these men entered Caesarea and delivered the letter to the governor, they also presented Paul to him. ³⁴ After heᶠ read it, he asked what province he was from. So when he learned he was from Cilicia, ³⁵ he said, "I will give you a hearing whenever your accusers get here too." And he ordered that he be kept under guard in Herod's palace.

24 After five days Ananias the high priest came down with some elders and a lawyerᴳ named Tertullus. These men presented their case against Paul to the governor. ² When he was called in, Tertullus began to accuse him and said: "Since we enjoy great peace because of you, and reforms are taking place for the benefit of this nation by your foresight, ³ we acknowledge this in every way and everywhere, most excellent Felix, with utmost gratitude. ⁴ However, so that I will not burden you any further, I beg you in your graciousness to give us a brief hearing. ⁵ For we have found this man to be a plague, an agitator among all the Jews throughout the Roman world, and a ringleader of the sect of the Nazarenes! ⁶ He even tried to desecrate the temple, so we apprehended him [and wanted to judge him according to our law. ⁷ But Lysias the commander came and took him from our hands with great force, ⁸ commanding his accusers to come to you.]^A By examining him yourself you will be able to discern all these things we are accusing him of." ⁹ The Jews also joined in the attack, alleging that these things were so.

¹⁰ When the governor motioned to him to speak, Paul replied: "Because I know you have been a judge of this nation for many years, I am glad to offer my defense in what concerns me. ¹¹ You are able to determine that it is no more than 12 days since I went up to worship in Jerusalem. ¹² They didn't find me disputing with anyone or causing a disturbance among the crowd, either in the temple complex or in the synagogues or anywhere in the city. ¹³ Neither can they provide evidence to you of what they now bring against me. ¹⁴ But I confess this to you: I worship my fathers' God according to the Way, which they call a sect, believing all the things that are written in the Law and in the Prophets. ¹⁵ And I have a hope in God, which these men themselves also accept, that there is going to be a resurrection,^B both of the righteous and the unrighteous. ¹⁶ I always do my best to have a clear conscience toward God and men. ¹⁷ After many years, I came to bring charitable gifts and offerings to my nation, ¹⁸ and while I was doing this, some Jews from Asia found me ritually purified in the temple, without a crowd and without any uproar. ¹⁹ It is they who ought to be here before you to bring charges, if they have anything against me. ²⁰ Either let these men here state what wrongdoing they found in me when I stood before the Sanhedrin, ²¹ or about this one statement I cried out while standing among them, 'Today I am being judged before you concerning the resurrection of the dead.'"

²² Since Felix was accurately informed about the Way, he adjourned the hearing, saying, "When Lysias the commander comes down, I will decide your case." ²³ He ordered that the centurion keep Paul^C under guard, though he could have some freedom, and that he should not prevent any of his friends from serving^D him.

²⁴ After some days, when Felix came with his wife Drusilla, who was Jewish, he sent for Paul and listened to him on the subject of faith in Christ Jesus. ²⁵ Now as he spoke about righteousness, self-control, and the judgment to come, Felix became afraid and replied, "Leave for now, but when I find time I'll call for you." ²⁶ At the same time he was also hoping that money would be given to him by Paul.^E For this reason he sent for him quite often and conversed with him.

²⁷ After two years had passed, Felix received a successor, Porcius Festus, and because he wished to do a favor for the Jews, Felix left Paul in prison.

25 Three days after Festus arrived in the province, he went up to Jerusalem from Caesarea. ² Then the chief priests and the leaders of the Jews presented their case against Paul to him; and they appealed, ³ asking him to do them a favor against Paul,^F that he might summon him to Jerusalem. They were preparing an ambush along the road to kill him. ⁴ However, Festus answered that Paul should be kept at Caesarea, and that he himself was about to go there shortly. ⁵ "Therefore," he said, "let the men of authority among you go down with me and accuse him, if there is any wrong in this man."

⁶ When he had spent not more than eight or 10 days among them, he went down to Caesarea. The next day, seated at the judge's bench, he commanded Paul to be brought in. ⁷ When he arrived, the Jews who had come down from Jerusalem stood around him and brought many serious charges that they were not able to prove, ⁸ while Paul made the defense that, "Neither against the Jewish law, nor against the temple, nor against Caesar have I sinned at all."

⁹ Then Festus, wanting to do a favor for the Jews, replied to Paul, "Are you willing to go up to Jerusalem, there to be tried before me on these charges?"

^A24:6-8 Other mss omit bracketed text   ^B24:15 Other mss add of the dead   ^C24:23 Lit him   ^D24:23 Other mss add or visiting   ^E24:26 Other mss add so that he might release him   ^F25:3 Lit asking a favor against him

¹⁰But Paul said: "I am standing at Caesar's tribunal, where I ought to be tried. I have done no wrong to the Jews, as even you can see very well. ¹¹If then I am doing wrong, or have done anything deserving of death, I do not refuse to die, but if there is nothing to what these men accuse me of, no one can give me up to them. I appeal to Caesar!"

¹²After Festus conferred with his council, he replied, "You have appealed to Caesar; to Caesar you will go!"

¹³After some days had passed, King Agrippa[A] and Bernice arrived in Caesarea and paid a courtesy call on Festus. ¹⁴Since they stayed there many days, Festus presented Paul's case to the king, saying, "There's a man who was left as a prisoner by Felix. ¹⁵When I was in Jerusalem, the chief priests and the elders of the Jews presented their case and asked for a judgment against him. ¹⁶I answered them that it's not the Romans' custom to give any man up[B] before the accused confronts the accusers face to face and has an opportunity to give a defense concerning the charges. ¹⁷Therefore, when they had assembled here, I did not delay. The next day I sat at the judge's bench and ordered the man to be brought in. ¹⁸Concerning him, the accusers stood up and brought no charge of the sort I was expecting. ¹⁹Instead they had some disagreements with him about their own religion and about a certain Jesus, a dead man Paul claimed to be alive. ²⁰Since I was at a loss in a dispute over such things, I asked him if he wished to go to Jerusalem and be tried there concerning these matters. ²¹But when Paul appealed to be held for trial by the Emperor, I ordered him to be kept in custody until I could send him to Caesar."

²²Then Agrippa said to Festus, "I would like to hear the man myself."

"Tomorrow you will hear him," he replied.

²³So the next day, Agrippa and Bernice came with great pomp and entered the auditorium with the commanders and prominent men of the city. When Festus gave the command, Paul was brought in. ²⁴Then Festus said: "King Agrippa and all men present with us, you see this man about whom the whole Jewish community has appealed to me, both in Jerusalem and here, shouting that he should not live any longer. ²⁵Now I realized

that he had not done anything deserving of death, but when he himself appealed to the Emperor, I decided to send him. ²⁶I have nothing definite to write to my lord about him. Therefore, I have brought him before all of you, and especially before you, King Agrippa, so that after this examination is over, I may have something to write. ²⁷For it seems unreasonable to me to send a prisoner and not to indicate the charges against him."

26 Agrippa said to Paul, "It is permitted for you to speak for yourself."

Then Paul stretched out his hand and began his defense: ²"I consider myself fortunate, King Agrippa, that today I am going to make a defense before you about everything I am accused of by the Jews, ³especially since you are an expert in all the Jewish customs and controversies. Therefore I beg you to listen to me patiently.

⁴"All the Jews know my way of life from my youth, which was spent from the beginning among my own nation and in Jerusalem. ⁵They had previously known me for quite some time, if they were willing to testify, that according to the strictest party of our religion I lived as a Pharisee. ⁶And now I stand on trial for the hope of the promise made by God to our fathers, ⁷the promise our 12 tribes hope to attain as they earnestly serve Him night and day. King Agrippa, I am being accused by the Jews because of this hope. ⁸Why is it considered incredible by any of you that God raises the dead? ⁹In fact, I myself supposed it was necessary to do many things in opposition to the name of Jesus the Nazarene. ¹⁰I actually did this in Jerusalem, and I locked up many of the saints in prison, since I had received authority for that from the chief priests. When they were put to death, I cast my vote against them. ¹¹In all the synagogues I often tried to make them blaspheme by punishing them. I even pursued them to foreign cities since I was greatly enraged at them.

¹²"I was traveling to Damascus under these circumstances with authority and a commission from the chief priests. ¹³King Agrippa, while on the road at midday, I saw a light from heaven brighter than the sun, shining around me and those traveling with me. ¹⁴We all fell to the ground, and I heard a voice speaking to me in the Hebrew language, 'Saul, Saul, why

---

[A]25:13 Herod Agrippa II ruled Palestine A.D. 52–ca 95.   [B]25:16 Other mss add *to destruction* are you persecuting Me? It is hard for you to kick against the goads.'[A]

¹⁵ "Then I said, 'Who are You, Lord?'

"And the Lord replied: 'I am Jesus, the One you are persecuting. ¹⁶ But get up and stand on your feet. For I have appeared to you for this purpose, to appoint you as a servant and a witness of what you have seen[B] and of what I will reveal to you. ¹⁷ I will rescue you from the people and from the Gentiles. I now send you to them ¹⁸ to open their eyes so they may turn from darkness to light and from the power of Satan to God, that by faith in Me they may receive forgiveness of sins and a share among those who are sanctified.'

¹⁹ "Therefore, King Agrippa, I was not disobedient to the heavenly vision. ²⁰ Instead, I preached to those in Damascus first, and to those in Jerusalem and in all the region of Judea, and to the Gentiles, that they should repent and turn to God, and do works worthy of repentance. ²¹ For this reason the Jews seized me in the temple complex and were trying to kill me. ²² To this very day, I have obtained help that comes from God, and I stand and testify to both small and great, saying nothing else than what the prophets and Moses said would take place— ²³ that the Messiah must suffer, and that as the first to rise from the dead, He would proclaim light to our people and to the Gentiles."

²⁴ As he was making his defense this way, Festus exclaimed in a loud voice, "You're out of your mind, Paul! Too much study is driving you mad!"

²⁵ But Paul replied, "I'm not out of my mind, most excellent Festus. On the contrary, I'm speaking words of truth and good judgment. ²⁶ For the king knows about these matters. It is to him I am actually speaking boldly. For I am convinced that none of these things escapes his notice, since this was not done in a corner. ²⁷ King Agrippa, do you believe the prophets? I know you believe."

²⁸ Then Agrippa said to Paul, "Are you going to persuade me to become a Christian so easily?"

²⁹ "I wish before God," replied Paul, "that whether easily or with difficulty, not only you but all who listen to me today might become as I am—except for these chains."

³⁰ So the king, the governor, Bernice, and those sitting with them got up, ³¹ and when they had left they talked with each other and said, "This man is doing nothing that deserves death or chains."

³² Then Agrippa said to Festus, "This man could have been released if he had not appealed to Caesar."

27 When it was decided that we were to sail to Italy, they handed over Paul and some other prisoners to a centurion named Julius, of the Imperial Regiment. ² So when we had boarded a ship of Adramyttium, we put to sea, intending to sail to ports along the coast of Asia. Aristarchus, a Macedonian of Thessalonica, was with us. ³ The next day we put in at Sidon, and Julius treated Paul kindly and allowed him to go to his friends to receive their care. ⁴ When we had put out to sea from there, we sailed along the northern coast[C] of Cyprus because the winds were against us. ⁵ After sailing through the open sea off Cilicia and Pamphylia, we reached Myra in Lycia. ⁶ There the centurion found an Alexandrian ship sailing for Italy and put us on board. ⁷ Sailing slowly for many days, we came with difficulty as far as Cnidus. Since the wind did not allow us to approach it, we sailed along the south side[C] of Crete off Salmone. ⁸ With yet more difficulty we sailed along the coast and came to a place called Fair Havens near the city of Lasea.

⁹ By now much time had passed, and the voyage was already dangerous. Since the Fast[D] was already over, Paul gave his advice ¹⁰ and told them, "Men, I can see that this voyage is headed toward damage and heavy loss, not only of the cargo and the ship but also of our lives." ¹¹ But the centurion paid attention to the captain and the owner of the ship rather than to what Paul said. ¹² Since the harbor was unsuitable to winter in, the majority decided to set sail from there, hoping somehow to reach Phoenix, a harbor on Crete open to the southwest and northwest, and to winter there.

¹³ When a gentle south wind sprang up, they thought they had achieved their purpose. They weighed anchor and sailed along the shore of Crete. ¹⁴ But not long afterward, a fierce wind called the "northeaster"[E] rushed down from the island. ¹⁵ Since the ship was

---

[A]26:14 Sharp sticks used to prod animals, such as oxen in plowing [B]26:16 Other mss read *things in which you have seen Me* [C]27:4,7 Lit *sailed under the lee* [D]27:9 The Day of Atonement [E]27:14 Lit *Euraquilo*, a violent northeast wind caught and was unable to head into the wind, we gave way to it and were driven along. ¹⁶ After running under the shelter of a little island called Cauda,ᴬ we were barely able to get control of the skiff. ¹⁷ After hoisting it up, they used ropes and tackle and girded the ship. Then, fearing they would run aground on the Syrtis,ᴮ they lowered the drift-anchor, and in this way they were driven along. ¹⁸ Because we were being severely battered by the storm, they began to jettison the cargo the next day. ¹⁹ On the third day, they threw the ship's gear overboard with their own hands.

²⁰ For many days neither sun nor stars appeared, and the severe storm kept raging. Finally all hope that we would be saved was disappearing. ²¹ Since many were going without food, Paul stood up among them and said, "You men should have followed my advice not to sail from Crete and sustain this damage and loss. ²² Now I urge you to take courage, because there will be no loss of any of your lives, but only of the ship. ²³ For this night an angel of the God I belong to and serve stood by me, ²⁴ and said, 'Don't be afraid, Paul. You must stand before Caesar. And, look! God has graciously given you all those who are sailing with you.' ²⁵ Therefore, take courage, men, because I believe God that it will be just the way it was told to me. ²⁶ However, we must run aground on a certain island."

²⁷ When the fourteenth night came, we were drifting in the Adriatic Sea,ᶜ and in the middle of the night the sailors thought they were approaching land.ᴰ ²⁸ They took a sounding and found it to be 120 feetᴱ deep; when they had sailed a little farther and sounded again, they found it to be 90 feetᶠ deep. ²⁹ Then, fearing we might run aground in some rocky place, they dropped four anchors from the stern and prayed for daylight to come.

³⁰ Some sailors tried to escape from the ship; they had let down the skiff into the sea, pretending that they were going to put out anchors from the bow. ³¹ Paul said to the centurion and the soldiers, "Unless these men stay in the ship, you cannot be saved." ³² Then the soldiers cut the ropes holding the skiff and let it drop away.

³³ When it was about daylight, Paul urged them all to take food, saying, "Today is the fourteenth day that you have been waiting and going without food, having eaten nothing. ³⁴ Therefore I urge you to take some food. For this has to do with your survival, since none of you will lose a hair from your head." ³⁵ After he said these things and had taken some bread, he gave thanks to God in the presence of all of them, and when he broke it, he began to eat. ³⁶ They all became encouraged and took food themselves. ³⁷ In all there were 276 of us on the ship. ³⁸ When they had eaten enough, they began to lighten the ship by throwing the grain overboard into the sea.

³⁹ When daylight came, they did not recognize the land but sighted a bay with a beach. They planned to run the ship ashore if they could. ⁴⁰ After casting off the anchors, they left them in the sea, at the same time loosening the ropes that held the rudders. Then they hoisted the foresail to the wind and headed for the beach. ⁴¹ But they struck a sandbar and ran the ship aground. The bow jammed fast and remained immovable, while the stern began to break up by the pounding of the waves.

⁴² The soldiers' plan was to kill the prisoners so that no one could swim away and escape. ⁴³ But the centurion kept them from carrying out their plan because he wanted to save Paul, so he ordered those who could swim to jump overboard first and get to land. ⁴⁴ The rest were to follow, some on planks and some on debris from the ship. In this way, everyone safely reached the shore.

28
Once ashore, we then learned that the island was called Malta. ² The local people showed us extraordinary kindness, for they lit a fire and took us all in, since it was raining and cold. ³ As Paul gathered a bundle of brushwood and put it on the fire, a viper came out because of the heat and fastened itself to his hand. ⁴ When the local people saw the creature hanging from his hand, they said to one another, "This man is probably a murderer, and though he has escaped the sea, Justiceᴳ does not allow him to live!" ⁵ However, he shook the creature off into the fire and suffered no harm. ⁶ They expected that he would swell up or suddenly drop dead. But after they

---

ᴬ27:16 Or *Clauda*   ᴮ27:17 = sandbanks or sandbars near North Africa   ᶜ27:27 Part of the northern Mediterranean Sea; not the modern Adriatic Sea east of Italy   ᴰ27:27 Lit *thought there was land approaching them*   ᴱ27:28 Lit *20 fathoms*   ᶠ27:28 Lit *15 fathoms*   ᴳ28:4 Gk *Dike*, a goddess of justice waited a long time and saw nothing unusual happen to him, they changed their minds and said he was a god.

⁷ Now in the area around that place was an estate belonging to the leading man of the island, named Publius, who welcomed us and entertained us hospitably for three days. ⁸ Publius's father was in bed suffering from fever and dysentery. Paul went to him, and praying and laying his hands on him, he healed him. ⁹ After this, the rest of those on the island who had diseases also came and were cured. ¹⁰ So they heaped many honors on us, and when we sailed, they gave us what we needed.

¹¹ After three months we set sail in an Alexandrian ship that had wintered at the island, with the Twin Brothers^A as its figurehead. ¹² Putting in at Syracuse, we stayed three days. ¹³ From there, after making a circuit along the coast,^B we reached Rhegium. After one day a south wind sprang up, and the second day we came to Puteoli. ¹⁴ There we found believers^C and were invited to stay with them for seven days.

And so we came to Rome. ¹⁵ Now the believers^C from there had heard the news about us and had come to meet us as far as the Forum of Appius and the Three Taverns. When Paul saw them, he thanked God and took courage. ¹⁶ When we entered Rome,^D Paul was permitted to stay by himself with the soldier who guarded him.

¹⁷ After three days he called together the leaders of the Jews. When they had gathered he said to them: "Brothers, although I have done nothing against our people or the customs of our ancestors, I was delivered as a prisoner from Jerusalem into the hands of the Romans. ¹⁸ After they examined me, they wanted to release me, since I had not committed a capital offense. ¹⁹ Because the Jews objected, I was compelled to appeal to Caesar; it was not as though I had any accusation against my nation. ²⁰ For this reason I've asked to see you and speak to you. In fact, it is for the hope of Israel that I'm wearing this chain."

²¹ Then they said to him, "We haven't received any letters about you from Judea. None of the brothers has come and reported or spoken anything evil about you. ²² But we would like to hear from you what you think. For concerning this sect, we are aware that it is spoken against everywhere."

²³ After arranging a day with him, many came to hear him at his lodging. From dawn to dusk he expounded and witnessed about the kingdom of God. He tried to persuade them concerning Jesus from both the Law of Moses and the Prophets. ²⁴ Some were persuaded by what he said, but others did not believe.

²⁵ Disagreeing among themselves, they began to leave after Paul made one statement: "The Holy Spirit correctly spoke through the prophet Isaiah to your^E ancestors ²⁶ when He said,

> Go to these people and say:
> You will listen and listen,
> yet never understand;
> and you will look and look,
> yet never perceive.
> ²⁷ For the hearts of these people
> have grown callous,
> their ears are hard of hearing,
> and they have shut their eyes;
> otherwise they might see
>   with their eyes
> and hear with their ears,
> understand with their heart,
> and be converted,
> and I would heal them.^F

²⁸ Therefore, let it be known to you that this saving work of God has been sent to the Gentiles; they will listen!" [²⁹ After he said these things, the Jews departed, while engaging in a prolonged debate among themselves.]^G

³⁰ Then he stayed two whole years in his own rented house. And he welcomed all who visited him, ³¹ proclaiming the kingdom of God and teaching the things concerning the Lord Jesus Christ with full boldness and without hindrance.

---

^A 28:11 Gk *Dioscuri*, twin sons of Zeus   ^B 28:13 Other mss read *From there, casting off,*   ^C 28:14,15 Lit *brothers*   ^D 28:16 Other mss add *the centurion turned the prisoners over to the military commander; but*   ^E 28:25 Other mss read *our*   ^F 28:26–27 Is 6:9-10   ^G 28:29 Other mss omit bracketed text

ROMANS

1 Paul, a slave of Christ Jesus, called as an apostle[A] and singled out for God's good news— [2] which He promised long ago through His prophets in the Holy Scriptures— [3] concerning His Son, Jesus Christ our Lord, who was a descendant of David[B] according to the flesh [4] and who has been declared to be the powerful Son of God by the resurrection from the dead according to the Spirit of holiness.[C] [5] We have received grace and apostleship through Him to bring about[D] the obedience of faith[E] among all the nations,[F] on behalf of His name, [6] including yourselves who also belong to Jesus Christ by calling:

[7] To all who are in Rome, loved by God, called as saints.

Grace to you and peace from God our Father and the Lord Jesus Christ.

[8] First, I thank my God through Jesus Christ for all of you because the news of your faith[G] is being reported in all the world. [9] For God, whom I serve with my spirit in telling the good news about His Son, is my witness that I constantly mention you, [10] always asking in my prayers that if it is somehow in God's will, I may now at last succeed in coming to you. [11] For I want very much to see you, so I may impart to you some spiritual gift to strengthen you, [12] that is, to be mutually encouraged by each other's faith, both yours and mine.

[13] Now I want you to know,[H] brothers, that I often planned to come to you (but was prevented until now) in order that I might have a fruitful ministry[I] among you, just as among the rest of the Gentiles. [14] I am obligated both to Greeks and barbarians,[J] both to the wise and the foolish. [15] So I am eager to preach the good news to you also who are in Rome.

[16] <u>For I am not ashamed of the gospel,[K] because it is God's power for salvation to everyone who believes, first to the Jew, and also to the Greek.</u> [17] For in it God's righteousness is revealed from faith to faith,[L] just as it is written: **The righteous will live by faith.**[MN]

[18] For God's wrath is revealed from heaven against all godlessness and unrighteousness of people who by their unrighteousness suppress the truth, [19] since what can be known[O] about God is evident among them, because God has shown it to them. [20] For His invisible attributes, that is, His eternal power and divine nature, have been clearly seen since the creation of the world, being understood through what He has made. As a result, people are without excuse. [21] For though they knew God, they did not glorify Him as God or show gratitude. Instead, their thinking became nonsense, and their senseless minds were darkened. [22] Claiming to be wise, they became fools [23] and exchanged the glory of the immortal God for images resembling mortal man, birds, four-footed animals, and reptiles.

[24] Therefore God delivered them over in the cravings of their hearts to sexual impurity, so that their bodies were degraded among themselves. [25] They exchanged the truth of God for a lie, and worshiped and served something created instead of the Creator, who is praised forever. Amen.

[26] This is why God delivered them over to degrading passions. For even their females exchanged natural sexual relations[P] for unnatural ones. [27] The males in the same way also left natural relations[P] with females and were inflamed in their lust for one another. Males committed shameless acts with males and received in their own persons[Q] the appropriate penalty of their error.

[28] And because they did not think it worthwhile to acknowledge God, God delivered them over to a worthless mind to do what is morally wrong. [29] They are filled with all unrighteousness,[R] evil, greed, and wickedness. They are full of envy, murder, quarrels, deceit, and malice. They are gossips, [30] slanderers, God-haters, arrogant, proud, boastful, inventors of evil, disobedient to parents, [31] undiscerning, untrustworthy, unloving,[S] and unmerciful. [32] Although they know full well

---

A[1:1] Or *Jesus, a called apostle* B[1:3] Lit *was of the seed of David* C[1:4] Or *the spirit of holiness, or the Holy Spirit* D[1:5] Or *Him for*; lit *Him into* E[1:5] Or *the obedience that is faith, or the faithful obedience, or the obedience that comes from faith; Rm 16:26* F[1:5] Or *Gentiles* G[1:8] Or *because your faith* H[1:13] Lit *I don't want you to be unaware* I[1:13] Lit *have some fruit* J[1:14] Or *non-Greeks* K[1:16] Other mss add *of Christ* L[1:17] Or *revealed out of faith into faith* M[1:17] Or *The one who is righteous by faith will live* N[1:17] Hab 2:4 O[1:19] Or *what is known* P[1:26,27] Lit *natural use* Q[1:27] Or *in themselves* R[1:29] Other mss add *sexual immorality* S[1:31] Other mss add *unforgiving*

See Romans 2:4, page 138

God's just sentence—that those who practice such things deserve to die^A—they not only do them, but even applaud^B others who practice them.

2 Therefore, any one of you^C who judges is without excuse. For when you judge another, you condemn yourself, since you, the judge, do the same things. ²We know that God's judgment on those who do such things is based on the truth. ³Do you really think—anyone of you who judges those who do such things yet do the same—that you will escape God's judgment? ⁴Or do you despise the riches of His kindness, restraint, and patience, not recognizing^D that God's kindness is intended to lead you to repentance? ⁵But because of your hardness and unrepentant heart you are storing up wrath for yourself in the day of wrath, when God's righteous judgment is revealed. ⁶He will repay each one according to his works:^E ⁷eternal life to those who by persistence in doing good seek glory, honor, and immortality; ⁸but wrath and indignation to those who are selfseeking and disobey the truth but are obeying unrighteousness; ⁹affliction and distress for every human being who does evil, first to the Jew, and also to the Greek; ¹⁰but glory, honor, and peace for everyone who does what is good, first to the Jew, and also to the Greek. ¹¹There is no favoritism with God.

¹²All those who sinned without the law will also perish without the law, and all those who sinned under the law will be judged by the law. ¹³For the hearers of the law are not righteous before God, but the doers of the law will be declared righteous.^F ¹⁴So, when Gentiles, who do not have the law, instinctively do what the law demands, they are a law to themselves even though they do not have the law. ¹⁵They show that the work of the law^G is written on their hearts. Their consciences confirm this. Their competing thoughts will either accuse or excuse them^H ¹⁶on the day when God judges what people have kept secret, according to my gospel through Christ Jesus.

¹⁷Now if^I you call yourself a Jew, and rest in the law, boast in God, ¹⁸know His will, and approve the things that are superior, being instructed from the law, ¹⁹and if you are convinced that you are a guide for the blind, a light to those in darkness, ²⁰an instructor of the ignorant, a teacher of the immature, having the full expression^J of knowledge and truth in the law— ²¹you then, who teach another, don't you teach yourself? You who preach, "You must not steal"—do you steal? ²²You who say, "You must not commit adultery"—do you commit adultery? You who detest idols, do you rob their temples? ²³You who boast in the law, do you dishonor God by breaking the law? ²⁴For, as it is written: **The name of God is blasphemed among the Gentiles because of you.**^K

²⁵For circumcision benefits you if you observe the law, but if you are a lawbreaker, your circumcision has become uncircumcision. ²⁶Therefore if an uncircumcised man keeps the law's requirements, will his uncircumcision not be counted as circumcision? ²⁷A man who is physically uncircumcised, but who fulfills the law, will judge you who are a lawbreaker in spite of having the letter of the law and circumcision. ²⁸For a person is not a Jew who is one outwardly, and true circumcision is not something visible in the flesh. ²⁹On the contrary, a person is a Jew who is one inwardly, and circumcision is of the heart—by the Spirit, not the letter.^L That man's praise^M is not from men but from God.

3 So what advantage does the Jew have? Or what is the benefit of circumcision? ²Considerable in every way. First, they were entrusted with the spoken words of God. ³What then? If some did not believe, will their unbelief cancel God's faithfulness? ⁴Absolutely not! God must be true, even if everyone is a liar, as it is written:

That You may be justified
in Your words
and triumph when You judge.^N

A1:32 Lit *things are worthy of death*   B1:32 Lit *even take pleasure in*   C2:1 Lit *Therefore, O man, every one*   D2:4 Or *patience, because you do not recognize*   E2:6 Ps 62:12; Pr 24:12   F2:13 Or *will be justified or acquitted*   G2:15 The code of conduct required by the law   H2:15 Internal debate, either in a person or among the pagan moralists   I2:17 Other mss read *Look—*   J2:20 Or *the embodiment*   K2:24 Is 52:5   L2:29 Or *heart—spiritually, not literally*   M2:29 In Hb, the words Jew, Judah, and praise are related.   N3:4 Ps 51:4

See Romans 3:23, page 139

⁵But if our unrighteousness highlightsᴬ God's righteousness, what are we to say? I use a human argument:ᴮ Is God unrighteous to inflict wrath? ⁶Absolutely not! Otherwise, how will God judge the world? ⁷But if by my lie God's truth is amplified to His glory, why am I also still judged as a sinner? ⁸And why not say, just as some people slanderously claim we say, "Let us do what is evil so that good may come"? Their condemnation is deserved!

⁹What then? Are we any better?ᶜ Not at all! For we have previously charged that both Jews and Gentilesᴰ are all under sin,ᴱ ¹⁰as it is written:ᶠ

> There is no one righteous,
>   not even one.
> ¹¹ There is no one who understands;
>   there is no one who seeks God.
> ¹² All have turned away;
>   all alike have become useless.
> There is no one who does
>   what is good,
>   not even one.ᴳ
> ¹³ Their throat is an open grave;
>   they deceive with their tongues.ᴴ
> Vipers' venom is under their lips.ᴵ
> ¹⁴ Their mouth is full of cursing
>   and bitterness.ᴶ
> ¹⁵ Their feet are swift to shed blood;
> ¹⁶ ruin and wretchedness are
>   in their paths,
> ¹⁷ and the path of peace
>   they have not known.ᴷ
> ¹⁸ There is no fear of God
>   before their eyes.ᴸ

¹⁹ Now we know that whatever the law says speaks to those who are subject to the law,ᴹ so that every mouth may be shut and the whole world may become subject to God's judgment.ᴺ ²⁰ For no one will be justifiedᴼ in His sight by the works of the law, because the knowledge of sin comes through the law.

²¹ But now, apart from the law, God's righteousness has been revealed—attested by the Law and the Prophetsᴾ ²²—that is, God's righteousness through faith in Jesus Christ,�Q to all who believe, since there is no distinction. ²³ For all have sinned and fall short of theᴿ glory of God. ²⁴ They are justified freely by His grace through the redemption that is in Christ Jesus. ²⁵ God presented Him as a propitiationˢ through faith in His blood, to demonstrate His righteousness, because in His restraint God passed over the sins previously committed. ²⁶ God presented Him to demonstrate His righteousness at the present time, so that He would be righteous and declare righteousᵀ the one who has faith in Jesus.

²⁷ Where then is boasting? It is excluded. By what kind of law?ᵁ By one of works? No, on the contrary, by a lawⱽ of faith. ²⁸ For we conclude that a man is justified by faith apart from the works of the law. ²⁹ Or is God for Jews only? Is He not also for Gentiles? Yes, for Gentiles too, ³⁰ since there is one God who will justify the circumcised by faith and the uncircumcised through faith. ³¹ Do we then cancel the law through faith? Absolutely not! On the contrary, we uphold the law.

4 What then can we say that Abraham, our physical ancestor,ᵂ has found? ²If Abraham was justifiedˣ by works, he has something to brag about—but not before God.ʸ ³For what does the Scripture say?

> Abraham believed God,
>   and it was credited to him
>   for righteousness.ᶻ

⁴Now to the one who works, pay is not considered as a gift, but as something owed. ⁵But to the one who does not work, but believes on Him who declares the ungodly to be righteous,ᴬᴬ his faith is credited for righteousness.

⁶Likewise, David also speaks of the blessing of the man God credits righteousness to apart from works:

> ⁷ How joyful are those whose lawless acts
>   are forgiven

ᴬ3:5 Or shows, or demonstrates　ᴮ3:5 Lit I speak as a man　ᶜ3:9 Are we Jews any better than the Gentiles?　ᴰ3:9 Lit Greeks　ᴱ3:9 Under sin's power or dominion　ᶠ3:10 Paul constructs this charge from a chain of OT quotations, mainly from the Psalms.　ᴳ3:10-12 Ps 14:1-3; 53:1-3; Ec 7:20　ᴴ3:13 Ps 5:9　ᴵ3:13 Ps 140:3　ᴶ3:14 Ps 10:7　ᴷ3:15-17 Is 59:7-8　ᴸ3:18 Ps 36:1　ᴹ3:19 Lit those in the law　ᴺ3:19 Or become guilty before God, or may be accountable to God　ᴼ3:20 Or will be declared righteous, or will be acquitted　ᴾ3:21 When capitalized, the Law and the Prophets = OT　Q3:22 Or through the faithfulness of Jesus Christ　ᴿ3:23 Or and lack the　ˢ3:25 Or as a propitiatory sacrifice, or as an offering of atonement, or as a mercy seat; 2Co 5:21; Heb 9:5　ᵀ3:26 Or and justify, or and acquit　ᵁ3:27 Or what principle?　ⱽ3:27 Or a principle　ᵂ4:1 Lit our ancestor according to the flesh　ˣ4:2 Or was declared righteous, or was acquitted　ʸ4:2 He has no reason for boasting in God's presence.　ᶻ4:3 Gn 15:6　ᴬᴬ4:5 Or who acquits, or who justifies

See Romans 5:8, page 140

and whose sins are covered!
8 **How joyful is the man
the Lord will never charge with sin!**[A]

9 Is this blessing only for the circumcised, then? Or is it also for the uncircumcised? For we say, **Faith was credited to Abraham for righteousness.**[B] 10 In what way then was it credited—while he was circumcised, or uncircumcised? Not while he was circumcised, but uncircumcised. 11 And he received the sign of circumcision as a seal of the righteousness that he had by faith[C] while still uncircumcised. This was to make him the father of all who believe but are not circumcised, so that righteousness may be credited to them also. 12 And he became the father of the circumcised, who are not only circumcised but who also follow in the footsteps of the faith our father Abraham had while he was still uncircumcised.

13 For the promise to Abraham or to his descendants that he would inherit the world was not through the law, but through the righteousness that comes by faith.[C] 14 If those who are of the law are heirs, faith is made empty and the promise is canceled. 15 For the law produces wrath. And where there is no law, there is no transgression.

16 This is why the promise is by faith, so that it may be according to grace, to guarantee it to all the descendants—not only to those who are of the law[D] but also to those who are of Abraham's faith. He is the father of us all 17 in God's sight. As it is written: **I have made you the father of many nations.**[E] He believed in God, who gives life to the dead and calls things into existence that do not exist. 18 He believed, hoping against hope, so that he became **the father of many nations**[E] according to what had been spoken: **So will your descendants be.**[F] 19 He considered[G] his own body to be already dead (since he was about 100 years old) and also considered the deadness of Sarah's womb, without weakening in the faith. 20 He did not waver in unbelief at God's promise but was strengthened in his faith and gave glory to God, 21 because he was

fully convinced that what He had promised He was also able to perform. 22 Therefore, **it was credited to him for righteousness.**[B] 23 Now **it was credited to him** was not written for Abraham alone, 24 but also for us. It will be credited to us who believe in Him who raised Jesus our Lord from the dead. 25 He was delivered up for[H] our trespasses and raised for[H] our justification.[I]

5 Therefore, since we have been declared righteous by faith, we have peace[J] with God through our Lord Jesus Christ. 2 We have also obtained access through Him by faith[K] into this grace in which we stand, and we rejoice in the hope of the glory of God. 3 And not only that, but we also rejoice in our afflictions, because we know that affliction produces endurance, 4 endurance produces proven character, and proven character produces hope. 5 This hope will not disappoint us, because God's love has been poured out in our hearts through the Holy Spirit who was given to us.

6 For while we were still helpless, at the appointed moment, Christ died for the ungodly. 7 For rarely will someone die for a just person—though for a good person perhaps someone might even dare to die. 8 But God proves His own love for us in that while we were still sinners, Christ died for us! 9 Much more then, since we have now been declared righteous by His blood, we will be saved through Him from wrath. 10 For if, while we were enemies, we were reconciled to God through the death of His Son, then how much more, having been reconciled, will we be saved by His life! 11 And not only that, but we also rejoice in God through our Lord Jesus Christ. We have now received this reconciliation through Him.

12 Therefore, just as sin entered the world through one man, and death through sin, in this way death spread to all men, because all sinned.[L] 13 In fact, sin was in the world before the law, but sin is not charged to a person's account when there is no law. 14 Nevertheless, death reigned from Adam to Moses, even over those who did not sin in the likeness of

---

A 4:7-8 Ps 32:1-2   B 4:9,22 Gn 15:6   C 4:11,13 Lit *righteousness of faith*   D 4:16 Or *not to those who are of the law only*   E 4:17,18 Gn 17:5
F 4:18 Gn 15:5   G 4:19 Other mss read *He did not consider*   H 4:25 Or *because of*   I 4:25 Or *acquittal*   J 5:1 Other mss read *faith, let us have peace, which can also be translated faith, let us grasp the fact that we have peace*   K 5:2 Other mss omit *by faith*   L 5:12 Or *have sinned*

See Romans 6:23, page 141

Adam's transgression. He is a prototype[A] of the Coming One.

[15] But the gift is not like the trespass. For if by the one man's trespass the many died, how much more have the grace of God and the gift overflowed to the many by the grace of the one man, Jesus Christ. [16] And the gift is not like the one man's sin, because from one sin came the judgment, resulting in condemnation, but from many trespasses came the gift, resulting in justification.[B] [17] Since by the one man's trespass, death reigned through that one man, how much more will those who receive the overflow of grace and the gift of righteousness reign in life through the one man, Jesus Christ.

[18] So then, as through one trespass there is condemnation for everyone, so also through one righteous act there is life-giving justification[C] for everyone. [19] For just as through one man's disobedience the many were made sinners, so also through the one man's obedience the many will be made righteous. [20] The law came along to multiply the trespass. But where sin multiplied, grace multiplied even more [21] so that, just as sin reigned in death, so also grace will reign through righteousness, resulting in eternal life through Jesus Christ our Lord.

6 What should we say then? Should we continue in sin so that grace may multiply? [2] Absolutely not! How can we who died to sin still live in it? [3] Or are you unaware that all of us who were baptized into Christ Jesus were baptized into His death? [4] Therefore we were buried with Him by baptism into death, in order that, just as Christ was raised from the dead by the glory of the Father, so we too may walk in a new way[D] of life. [5] For if we have been joined with Him in the likeness of His death, we will certainly also be[E] in the likeness of His resurrection. [6] For we know that our old self[F] was crucified with Him in order that sin's dominion over the body[G] may be abolished, so that we may no longer be enslaved to sin, [7] since a person who has died is freed[H] from sin's claims.[I] [8] Now if we died

with Christ, we believe that we will also live with Him, [9] because we know that Christ, having been raised from the dead, will not die again. Death no longer rules over Him. [10] For in light of the fact that He died, He died to sin once for all; but in light of the fact that He lives, He lives to God. [11] So, you too consider yourselves dead to sin but alive to God in Christ Jesus.[J]

[12] Therefore do not let sin reign in your mortal body, so that you obey[K] its desires. [13] And do not offer any parts[L] of it to sin as weapons for unrighteousness. But as those who are alive from the dead, offer yourselves to God, and all the parts[L] of yourselves to God as weapons for righteousness. [14] For sin will not rule over you, because you are not under law but under grace.

[15] What then? Should we sin because we are not under law but under grace? Absolutely not! [16] Don't you know that if you offer yourselves to someone[M] as obedient slaves, you are slaves of that one you obey—either of sin leading to death or of obedience leading to righteousness? [17] But thank God that, although you used to be slaves of sin, you obeyed from the heart that pattern of teaching you were transferred[N] to, [18] and having been liberated from sin, you became enslaved to righteousness. [19] I am using a human analogy[O] because of the weakness of your flesh.[P] For just as you offered the parts[L] of yourselves as slaves to moral impurity, and to greater and greater lawlessness, so now offer them as slaves to righteousness, which results in sanctification. [20] For when you were slaves of sin, you were free from allegiance to righteousness.[Q] [21] So what fruit was produced[R] then from the things you are now ashamed of? For the end of those things is death. [22] But now, since you have been liberated from sin and have become enslaved to God, you have your fruit, which results in sanctification[S]—and the end is eternal life! [23] For the wages of sin is death, but the gift of God is eternal life in Christ Jesus our Lord.

[A] 5:14 Or *figure, or pattern;* = an OT person or thing that prefigures a NT person or thing   [B] 5:16 Or *acquittal*   [C] 5:18 Lit *is justification of life*   [D] 6:4 Or *in newness*   [E] 6:5 Be joined with Him   [F] 6:6 Lit *man;* = the person before conversion   [G] 6:6 Lit *that the body of sin*   [H] 6:7 Or *justified;* lit *acquitted*   [I] 6:7 Lit *from sin*   [J] 6:11 Other mss add *our Lord*   [K] 6:12 Other mss add sin *(lit it)* in   [L] 6:13,19 Or *members*   [M] 6:16 Lit *that to whom you offer yourselves*   [N] 6:17 Or *entrusted*   [O] 6:19 Lit *I speak humanly;* Paul is personifying sin and righteousness as slave masters.   [P] 6:19 Or *your human nature*   [Q] 6:20 Lit *free to righteousness*   [R] 6:21 Lit *what fruit do you have*   [S] 6:22 Or *holiness*

See Romans 10:9-10 and Romans 10:13, page 145

7 Since I am speaking to those who understand law, brothers, are you unaware that the law has authority over someone as long as he lives? ²For example, a married woman is legally bound to her husband while she lives. But if her husband dies, she is released from the law regarding the husband. ³So then, if she gives herself to another man while her husband is living, she will be called an adulteress. But if her husband dies, she is free from that law. Then, if she gives herself to another man, she is not an adulteress.

⁴Therefore, my brothers, you also were put to death in relation to the law through the crucified body of the Messiah, so that you may belong to another—to Him who was raised from the dead—that we may bear fruit for God. ⁵For when we were in the flesh,ᴬ the sinful passions operated through the law in every part of usᴮ and bore fruit for death. ⁶But now we have been released from the law, since we have died to what held us, so that we may serve in the new wayᶜ of the Spirit and not in the old letter of the law.

⁷What should we say then? Is the law sin? Absolutely not! On the contrary, I would not have known sin if it were not for the law. For example, I would not have known what it is to covet if the law had not said, **Do not covet.**ᴰ ⁸And sin, seizing an opportunity through the commandment, produced in me coveting of every kind. For apart from the law sin is dead. ⁹Once I was alive apart from the law, but when the commandment came, sin sprang to life ¹⁰and I died. The commandment that was meant for life resulted in death for me. ¹¹For sin, seizing an opportunity through the commandment, deceived me, and through it killed me. ¹²So then, the law is holy, and the commandment is holy and just and good.

¹³Therefore, did what is good cause my death?ᴱ Absolutely not! On the contrary, sin, in order to be recognized as sin, was producing death in me through what is good, so that through the commandment, sin might become sinful beyond measure. ¹⁴For we know that the law is spiritual, but I am made out

of flesh,ᶠ sold into sin's power. ¹⁵For I do not understand what I am doing, because I do not practice what I want to do, but I do what I hate. ¹⁶And if I do what I do not want to do, I agree with the law that it is good. ¹⁷So now I am no longer the one doing it, but it is sin living in me. ¹⁸For I know that nothing good lives in me, that is, in my flesh. For the desire to do what is good is with me, but there is no ability to do it. ¹⁹For I do not do the good that I want to do, but I practice the evil that I do not want to do. ²⁰Now if I do what I do not want, I am no longer the one doing it, but it is the sin that lives in me. ²¹So I discover this principle:ᴳ When I want to do what is good, evil is with me. ²²For in my inner selfᴴ I joyfully agree with God's law. ²³But I see a different law in the parts of my body,ᴵ waging war against the law of my mind and taking me prisoner to the law of sin in the parts of my body.ᴵ ²⁴What a wretched man I am! Who will rescue me from this dying body? ²⁵I thank God through Jesus Christ our Lord!ᴶ So then, with my mind I myself am a slave to the law of God, but with my flesh, to the law of sin.

8 Therefore, no condemnation now exists for those in Christ Jesus,ᴷ ²because the Spirit's law of life in Christ Jesus has set youᴸ free from the law of sin and of death. ³What the law could not do since it was limitedᴹ by the flesh, God did. He condemned sin in the flesh by sending His own Son in flesh like ours under sin's domain,ᴺ and as a sin offering, ⁴in order that the law's requirement would be accomplished in us who do not walk according to the flesh but according to the Spirit. ⁵For those who liveᴼ according to the flesh think about the things of the flesh, but those who liveᴼ according to the Spirit, about the things of the Spirit. ⁶For the mind-set of the flesh is death, but the mind-set of the Spirit is life and peace. ⁷For the mind-set of the flesh is hostile to God because it does not submit itself to God's law, for it is unable to do so. ⁸Those who are in the flesh cannot please God. ⁹You, however, are not in the flesh, but in the Spirit, sinceᴾ the Spirit

---

ᴬ**7:5** = a person's life before accepting Christ   ᴮ**7:5** Lit of our members   ᶜ**7:6** Lit in newness   ᴰ**7:7** Ex 20:17   ᴱ**7:13** Lit good become death to me?   ᶠ**7:14** Other mss read I am carnal   ᴳ**7:21** Or law   ᴴ**7:22** Lit inner man   ᴵ**7:23** Lit my members   ᴶ**7:25** Or Thanks be to God—(it is done) through Jesus Christ our Lord!   ᴷ**8:1** Other mss add who do not walk according to the flesh but according to the Spirit   ᴸ**8:2** Other mss read me   ᴹ**8:3** Or weak   ᴺ**8:3** Lit in the likeness of sinful flesh   ᴼ**8:5** Or those who are   ᴾ**8:9** Or provided that of God lives in you. But if anyone does not have the Spirit of Christ, he does not belong to Him. ¹⁰Now if Christ is in you, the body is dead^A because of sin, but the Spirit^B is life because of righteousness. ¹¹And if the Spirit of Him who raised Jesus from the dead lives in you, then He who raised Christ from the dead will also bring your mortal bodies to life through^C His Spirit who lives in you.

¹²So then, brothers, we are not obligated to the flesh to live according to the flesh, ¹³for if you live according to the flesh, you are going to die. But if by the Spirit you put to death the deeds of the body, you will live. ¹⁴All those led by God's Spirit are God's sons. ¹⁵For you did not receive a spirit of slavery to fall back into fear, but you received the Spirit of adoption, by whom we cry out, "*Abba*, Father!" ¹⁶The Spirit Himself testifies together with our spirit that we are God's children, ¹⁷and if children, also heirs—heirs of God and coheirs with Christ—seeing that^D we suffer with Him so that we may also be glorified with Him.

¹⁸For I consider that the sufferings of this present time are not worth comparing with the glory that is going to be revealed to us. ¹⁹For the creation eagerly waits with anticipation for God's sons to be revealed. ²⁰For the creation was subjected to futility—not willingly, but because of Him who subjected it—in the hope ²¹that the creation itself will also be set free from the bondage of corruption into the glorious freedom of God's children. ²²For we know that the whole creation has been groaning together with labor pains until now. ²³And not only that, but we ourselves who have the Spirit as the firstfruits—we also groan within ourselves, eagerly waiting for adoption, the redemption of our bodies. ²⁴Now in this hope we were saved, yet hope that is seen is not hope, because who hopes for what he sees? ²⁵But if we hope for what we do not see, we eagerly wait for it with patience.

²⁶In the same way the Spirit also joins to help in our weakness, because we do not know what to pray for as we should, but the Spirit Himself intercedes for us^E with unspoken groanings. ²⁷And He who searches the hearts knows the Spirit's mind-set, because

He intercedes for the saints according to the will of God.

²⁸We know that all things work together^F for the good^G of those who love God: those who are called according to His purpose. ²⁹For those He foreknew He also predestined to be conformed to the image of His Son, so that He would be the firstborn among many brothers. ³⁰And those He predestined, He also called; and those He called, He also justified; and those He justified, He also glorified.

31   What then are we to say
       about these things?
     If God is for us, who is against us?
32   He did not even spare His own Son
       but offered Him up for us all;
     how will He not also with Him grant
       us everything?
33   Who can bring an accusation
       against God's elect?
     God is the One who justifies.
34   Who is the one who condemns?
     Christ Jesus is the One who died,
       but even more, has been raised;
     He also is at the right hand
       of God
     and intercedes for us.
35   Who can separate us from the love
       of Christ?
     Can affliction or anguish
       or persecution
     or famine or nakedness or danger
       or sword?
36   As it is written:
     Because of You
     we are being put to death all day long;
     we are counted as sheep
       to be slaughtered.^H
37   No, in all these things we are
       more than victorious
     through Him who loved us.
38   For I am persuaded that not even death
       or life,
     angels or rulers,
     things present or things to come,
       hostile powers,
39   height or depth, or any other
       created thing

^A8:10 Or *the body will die*   ^B8:10 Or *spirit*   ^C8:11 Other mss read *because of*   ^D8:17 Or *provided that*   ^E8:26 Some mss omit *for us*
^F8:28 Other mss read *that God works together in all things*   ^G8:28 The ultimate good   ^H8:36 Ps 44:22

will have the power
to separate us
from the love of God that is
in Christ Jesus our Lord!

9 I speak the truth in Christ—I am not lying; my conscience is testifying to me
with the Holy Spirit[A]— [2]that I have intense
sorrow and continual anguish in my heart.
[3]For I could almost wish to be cursed and
cut off[B] from the Messiah for the benefit of
my brothers, my own flesh and blood. [4]They
are Israelites, and to them belong the adoption, the glory, the covenants, the giving of
the law, the temple service, and the promises.
[5]The ancestors are theirs, and from them, by
physical descent,[C] came the Messiah, who is
God over all, praised forever.[D] Amen.

[6]But it is not as though the word of God
has failed. For not all who are descended from
Israel are Israel. [7]Neither are they all children
because they are Abraham's descendants.[E] On
the contrary, **your offspring will be traced**
through Isaac.[G] [8]That is, it is not the children
by physical descent[H] who are God's children,
but the children of the promise are considered to be the offspring. [9]For this is the statement of the promise: **At this time I will come,**
and Sarah will have a son.[I] [10]And not only
that, but also Rebekah received a promise
when she became pregnant[J] by one man, our
ancestor Isaac. [11]For though her sons had not
been born yet or done anything good or bad,
so that God's purpose according to election
might stand— [12]not from works but from the
One who calls—she was told: **The older will**
serve the younger.[K] [13]As it is written: **I have**
loved Jacob, but I have hated Esau.[L]

[14]What should we say then? Is there injustice with God? Absolutely not! [15]For He tells
Moses:

I will show mercy
to whom I will show mercy,
and I will have compassion
on whom I will have compassion.[M]

[16]So then it does not depend on human will
or effort[N] but on God who shows mercy. [17]For
the Scripture tells Pharaoh:

I raised you up for this reason
so that I may display My power
in you
and that My name may be proclaimed
in all the earth.[O]

[18]So then, He shows mercy to those He wants
to, and He hardens those He wants to harden.

[19]You will say to me, therefore, "Why then
does He still find fault? For who can resist His
will?" [20]But who are you, a mere man, to talk
back to God? Will what is formed say to the
one who formed it, "Why did you make me
like this?" [21]Or has the potter no right over
the clay, to make from the same lump one
piece of pottery for honor and another for
dishonor? [22]And what if God, desiring to display His wrath and to make His power known,
endured with much patience objects of wrath
ready for destruction? [23]And what if He did
this to make known the riches of His glory on
objects of mercy that He prepared beforehand
for glory— [24]on us, the ones He also called,
not only from the Jews but also from the Gentiles? [25]As He also says in Hosea:

I will call Not My People, My People,
and she who is Unloved, Beloved.[P]
[26] And it will be in the place where
they were told,
you are not My people,
there they will be called sons
of the living God.[Q]

[27]But Isaiah cries out concerning Israel:

Though the number of Israel's sons
is like the sand of the sea,
only the remnant will be saved;
[28] for the Lord will execute His sentence
completely and decisively
on the earth.[R][S]

[29]And just as Isaiah predicted:

A 9:1 Or testifying with me by the Holy Spirit   B 9:3 Lit were anathema   C 9:5 Lit them, according to the flesh   D 9:5 Or the Messiah, the One who is
over all, the God who is blessed forever, or Messiah, God, who is over all, be blessed forever   E 9:7 Lit seed   F 9:7 Lit called   G 9:7 Gn 21:12
H 9:8 Lit children of the flesh   I 9:9 Gn 18:10,14   J 9:10 Or Rebekah conceived by the one act of sexual intercourse   K 9:12 Gn 25:23   L 9:13 Mal
1:2-3   M 9:15 Ex 33:19   N 9:16 Or on the one running; lit on the one willing   O 9:17 Ex 9:16   P 9:25 Hs 2:23   Q 9:26 Hs 1:10   R 9:28 Or land
S 9:27-28 Is 10:22-23; 28:22; Hs 1:10

If the Lord of Hosts[A] **had not left
us offspring,
we would have become like Sodom,
and we would have been made
like Gomorrah.**[B]

[30] What should we say then? Gentiles, who did not pursue righteousness, have obtained righteousness—namely the righteousness that comes from faith. [31] But Israel, pursuing the law for righteousness, has not achieved the righteousness of the law.[C] [32] Why is that? Because they did not pursue it by faith, but as if it were by works.[D] They stumbled over the stumbling stone. [33] As it is written:

**Look! I am putting a stone in Zion
to stumble over
and a rock to trip over,
yet the one who believes on Him
will not be put to shame.**[E]

10 Brothers, my heart's desire and prayer to God concerning them[F] is for their salvation! [2] I can testify about them that they have zeal for God, but not according to knowledge. [3] Because they disregarded the righteousness from God and attempted to establish their own righteousness, they have not submitted themselves to God's righteousness. [4] For Christ is the end[G] of the law for righteousness to everyone who believes. [5] For Moses writes about the righteousness that is from the law: **The one who does these things will live by them.**[H] [6] But the righteousness that comes from faith speaks like this: **Do not say in your heart, "Who will go up to heaven?"**[I] that is, to bring Christ down [7] or, **"Who will go down into the abyss?"**[J] that is, to bring Christ up from the dead. [8] On the contrary, what does it say? **The message is near you, in your mouth and in your heart.**[K] This is the message of faith that we proclaim: [9] If you confess with your mouth, "Jesus is Lord," and believe in your heart that God raised Him from the dead, you will be saved. [10] One believes with the heart, resulting in righteousness, and one confesses with the mouth, resulting in salvation. [11] Now the Scripture says, **Everyone who believes on Him will not be put to shame,**[L] [12] for there is no distinction between Jew and Greek, since the same Lord of all is rich to all who call on Him. [13] For everyone who calls on the name of the Lord will be saved.[M]

[14] But how can they call on Him they have not believed in? And how can they believe without hearing about Him? And how can they hear without a preacher? [15] And how can they preach unless they are sent? As it is written: **How beautiful**[N] **are the feet of those**[O] **who announce the gospel of good things!**[P] [16] But all did not obey the gospel. For Isaiah says, **Lord, who has believed our message?**[Q] [17] So faith comes from what is heard, and what is heard comes through the message about Christ.[R] [18] But I ask, "Did they not hear?" Yes, they did:

**Their voice has gone out to all
the earth,
and their words to the ends
of the inhabited world.**[S]

[19] But I ask, "Did Israel not understand?" First, Moses said:

**I will make you jealous
of those who are not a nation;
I will make you angry by a nation
that lacks understanding.**[T]

[20] And Isaiah says boldly:

**I was found
by those who were not looking
for Me;
I revealed Myself
to those who were not asking
for Me.**[U]

[21] But to Israel he says: **All day long I have spread out My hands to a disobedient and defiant people.**[V]

11 I ask, then, has God rejected His people? Absolutely not! For I too am an Israelite, a descendant of Abraham, from the tribe of Benjamin. [2] God has not rejected His people

A 9:29 Gk *Sabaoth*; this word is a transliteration of the Hb word for *Hosts*, or *Armies*.   **B** 9:29 Is 1:9   **C** 9:31 Other mss read *the law for righteousness*   **D** 9:32 Other mss add *of the law*   **E** 9:33 Is 8:14; 28:16   **F** 10:1 Other mss read *God for Israel*   **G** 10:4 Or *goal*   **H** 10:5 Lv 18:5   **I** 10:6 Dt 9:4; 30:12   **J** 10:7 Dt 30:13   **K** 10:8 Dt 30:14   **L** 10:11 Is 28:16   **M** 10:13 Jl 2:32   **N** 10:15 Or *welcome*, or *timely*   **O** 10:15 Other mss read *feet of those who announce the gospel of peace, of those*   **P** 10:15 Is 52:7; Nah 1:15   **Q** 10:16 Is 53:1   **R** 10:17 Other mss read *God*   **S** 10:18 Ps 19:4   **T** 10:19 Dt 32:21   **U** 10:20 Is 65:1   **V** 10:21 Is 65:2

Turn to page 243

whom He foreknew. Or don't you know what the Scripture says in the passage about Elijah—how he pleads with God against Israel?

³ Lord, they have killed
   Your prophets
and torn down Your altars.
I am the only one left,
and they are trying to take my life!ᴬ

⁴But what was God's reply to him? **I have left 7,000 men for Myself who have not bowed down to Baal.**ᴮ ⁵In the same way, then, there is also at the present time a remnant chosen by grace. ⁶Now if by grace, then it is not by works; otherwise grace ceases to be grace.ᶜ

⁷What then? Israel did not find what it was looking for, but the elect did find it. The rest were hardened, ⁸as it is written:

God gave them a spirit
   of insensitivity,ᴰ
eyes that cannot see
and ears that cannot hear,
   to this day.ᴱ

⁹And David says:

Let their feastingᶠ become a snare
   and a trap,
a pitfall and a retribution to them.
¹⁰ Let their eyes be darkened
   so they cannot see,
and their backs be bent
   continually.ᴳ

¹¹I ask, then, have they stumbled in order to fall? Absolutely not! On the contrary, by their stumbling,ᴴ salvation has come to the Gentiles to make Israel jealous. ¹²Now if their stumblingᴴ brings riches for the world, and their failure riches for the Gentiles, how much more will their full number bring!

¹³Now I am speaking to you Gentiles. In view of the fact that I am an apostle to the Gentiles, I magnify my ministry, ¹⁴if I can somehow make my own peopleᴵ jealous and save some of them. ¹⁵For if their rejection brings reconciliation to the world, what will their acceptance mean but life from the dead? ¹⁶Now if the firstfruits offered up are holy, so

is the whole batch. And if the root is holy, so are the branches.

¹⁷Now if some of the branches were broken off, and you, though a wild olive branch, were grafted in among them and have come to share in the rich rootᴶ of the cultivated olive tree, ¹⁸do not brag that you are better than those branches. But if you do brag—you do not sustain the root, but the root sustains you. ¹⁹Then you will say, "Branches were broken off so that I might be grafted in." ²⁰True enough; they were broken off by unbelief, but you stand by faith. Do not be arrogant, but be afraid. ²¹For if God did not spare the natural branches, He will not spare you either. ²²Therefore, consider God's kindness and severity: severity toward those who have fallen but God's kindness toward you—if you remain in His kindness. Otherwise you too will be cut off. ²³And even they, if they do not remain in unbelief, will be grafted in, because God has the power to graft them in again. ²⁴For if you were cut off from your native wild olive and against nature were grafted into a cultivated olive tree, how much more will these—the natural branches—be grafted into their own olive tree?

²⁵So that you will not be conceited, brothers, I do not want you to be unaware of this mystery: A partial hardening has come to Israel until the full number of the Gentiles has come in. ²⁶And in this way allᴷ Israel will be saved, as it is written:

The Liberator will come
   from Zion;
He will turn away godlessness
   from Jacob.
²⁷ And this will be My covenant
   with themᴸ
when I take away their sins.ᴹ

²⁸Regarding the gospel, they are enemies for your advantage, but regarding election, they are loved because of the patriarchs, ²⁹since God's gracious gifts and calling are irrevocable.ᴺ ³⁰As you once disobeyed God, but now have received mercy through their disobedience, ³¹so they too have now disobeyed,

ᴬ11:3 1Kg 19:10,14 ᴮ11:4 1Kg 19:18 ᶜ11:6 Other mss add *But if of works it is no longer grace; otherwise work is no longer work.* ᴰ11:8 Lit *stupification* ᴱ11:8 Dt 29:4; Is 29:10 ᶠ11:9 Lit *table* ᴳ11:9-10 Ps 69:22-23 ᴴ11:11,12 Or *transgression* ᴵ11:14 Lit *flesh* ᴶ11:17 Other mss read *the root and the richness* ᴷ11:26 Or *And then all* ᴸ11:26-27 Is 59:20-21 ᴹ11:27 Jr 31:31-34 ᴺ11:29 Or *are not taken back* resulting in mercy to you, so that they also now[A] may receive mercy. [32] For God has imprisoned all in disobedience, so that He may have mercy on all.

[33] Oh, the depth of the riches
both of the wisdom and the knowledge
of God!
How unsearchable His judgments
and untraceable His ways!

[34] **For who has known the mind**
of the Lord?
Or who has been His counselor?

[35] **Or who has ever first given to Him,**
and has to be repaid?[B]

[36] For from Him and through Him
and to Him are all things.
To Him be the glory forever. Amen.

12 Therefore, brothers, by the mercies of God, I urge you to present your bodies as a living sacrifice, holy and pleasing to God; this is your spiritual worship.[C] [2] Do not be conformed to this age, but be transformed by the renewing of your mind, so that you may discern what is the good, pleasing, and perfect will of God.

[3] For by the grace given to me, I tell everyone among you not to think of himself more highly than he should think. Instead, think sensibly, as God has distributed a measure of faith to each one. [4] Now as we have many parts in one body, and all the parts do not have the same function, [5] in the same way we who are many are one body in Christ and individually members of one another. [6] According to the grace given to us, we have different gifts:

If prophecy,
use it according to the standard
of one's[D] faith;
[7] if service, in service;
if teaching, in teaching;
[8] if exhorting, in exhortation;
giving, with generosity;
leading, with diligence;
showing mercy, with cheerfulness.

[9] Love must be without hypocrisy. Detest evil; cling to what is good. [10] Show family af-

fection to one another with brotherly love. Outdo one another in showing honor. [11] Do not lack diligence; be fervent in spirit; serve the Lord. [12] Rejoice in hope; be patient in affliction; be persistent in prayer. [13] Share with the saints in their needs; pursue hospitality. [14] Bless those who persecute you; bless and do not curse. [15] Rejoice with those who rejoice; weep with those who weep. [16] Be in agreement with one another. Do not be proud; instead, associate with the humble. Do not be wise in your own estimation. [17] Do not repay anyone evil for evil. Try to do what is honorable in everyone's eyes. [18] If possible, on your part, live at peace with everyone. [19] Friends, do not avenge yourselves; instead, leave room for His[E] wrath. For it is written: **Vengeance belongs to Me; I will repay,**[F] says the Lord. [20] But

If your enemy is hungry, feed him.
If he is thirsty, give him something
to drink.
For in so doing
you will be heaping fiery coals
on his head.[G]

[21] Do not be conquered by evil, but conquer evil with good.

13 Everyone must submit to the governing authorities, for there is no authority except from God, and those that exist are instituted by God. [2] So then, the one who resists the authority is opposing God's command, and those who oppose it will bring judgment on themselves. [3] For rulers are not a terror to good conduct, but to bad. Do you want to be unafraid of the authority? Do what is good, and you will have its approval. [4] For government is God's servant for your good. But if you do wrong, be afraid, because it does not carry the sword for no reason. For government is God's servant, an avenger that brings wrath on the one who does wrong. [5] Therefore, you must submit, not only because of wrath, but also because of your conscience. [6] And for this reason you pay taxes, since the authorities are God's public servants, continually attending to these tasks.[H] [7] Pay your obligations to everyone: taxes to those you owe taxes, tolls to those you owe tolls, respect

A11:31 Other mss omit now   B11:34-35 Jb 41:11; Is 40:13; Jr 23:18   C12:1 Or your reasonable service   D12:6 Or the   E12:19 Lit the
F12:19 Dt 32:35   G12:20 Pr 25:21-22   H13:6 Lit to this very thing

to those you owe respect, and honor to those you owe honor.

⁸Do not owe anyone anything,ᴬ except to love one another, for the one who loves another has fulfilled the law. ⁹The commandments:

> **Do not commit adultery;**
> **do not murder;**
> **do not steal;**ᴮ
> **do not covet;**ᶜ

and whatever other commandment—all are summed up by this: **Love your neighbor as yourself.**ᴰ

¹⁰Love does no wrong to a neighbor. Love, therefore, is the fulfillment of the law.

¹¹Besides this, knowing the time, it is already the hour for youᴱ to wake up from sleep, for now our salvation is nearer than when we first believed. ¹²The night is nearly over, and the daylight is near, so let us discard the deeds of darkness and put on the armor of light. ¹³Let us walk with decency, as in the daylight: not in carousing and drunkenness; not in sexual impurity and promiscuity; not in quarreling and jealousy. ¹⁴But put on the Lord Jesus Christ, and make no plans to satisfy the fleshly desires.

14 Accept anyone who is weak in faith,ᶠ but don't argue about doubtful issues. ²One person believes he may eat anything, but one who is weak eats only vegetables. ³One who eats must not look down on one who does not eat, and one who does not eat must not criticize one who does, because God has accepted him. ⁴Who are you to criticize another's household slave? Before his own Lord he stands or falls. And he will stand. For the Lord is ableᴳ to make him stand.

⁵One person considers one day to be above another day. Someone else considers every day to be the same. Each one must be fully convinced in his own mind. ⁶Whoever observes the day, observes it for the honor of the Lord.ᴴ Whoever eats, eats for the Lord, since he gives thanks to God; and whoever does not eat, it is for the Lord that he does not eat it, yet he thanks God. ⁷For none of us lives to himself, and no one dies to himself. ⁸If we live, we live for the Lord; and if we die, we die for the Lord. Therefore, whether we live or die, we belong to the Lord. ⁹Christ died and came to life for this: that He might rule over both the dead and the living. ¹⁰But you, why do you criticize your brother? Or you, why do you look down on your brother? For we will all stand before the tribunal of God.ᴵ ¹¹For it is written:

> **As I live, says the Lord,**
> **every knee will bow to Me,**
> **and every tongue will give praise**
> **to God.**ᴶ

¹²So then, each of us will give an account of himself to God.

¹³Therefore, let us no longer criticize one another. Instead decide never to put a stumbling block or pitfall in your brother's way. ¹⁴(I know and am persuaded by the Lord Jesus that nothing is unclean in itself. Still, to someone who considers a thing to be unclean, to that one it is unclean.) ¹⁵For if your brother is hurt by what you eat, you are no longer walking according to love. Do not destroy that one Christ died for by what you eat. ¹⁶Therefore, do not let your good be slandered, ¹⁷for the kingdom of God is not eating and drinking, but righteousness, peace, and joy in the Holy Spirit. ¹⁸Whoever serves Christ in this way is acceptable to God and approved by men.

¹⁹So then, we must pursue what promotes peace and what builds up one another. ²⁰Do not tear down God's work because of food. Everything is clean, but it is wrong for a man to cause stumbling by what he eats. ²¹It is a noble thing not to eat meat, or drink wine, or do anything that makes your brother stumble.ᴷ ²²Do you have a conviction?ᴸ Keep it to yourself before God. The man who does not condemn himself by what he approves is blessed. ²³But whoever doubts stands condemned if he eats, because his eating is not from a conviction,ᴹ and everything that is not from a convictionᴹ is sin.

ᴬ13:8 Or Leave no debt outstanding to anyone   ᴮ13:9 Other mss add you shall not bear false witness   ᶜ13:9 Ex 20:13-17; Dt 5:17-21   ᴰ13:9 Lv 19:18   ᴱ13:11 Other mss read for us   ᶠ14:1 Or weak in the Faith   ᴳ14:4 Other mss read For God has the power   ᴴ14:6 Other mss add but whoever does not observe the day, it is to the Lord that he does not observe it   ᴵ14:10 Other mss read of Christ   ᴶ14:11 Is 45:23; 49:18   ᴷ14:21 Other mss add or offended or weakened   ᴸ14:22 Lit have faith   ᴹ14:23 Or faith

15 Now we who are strong have an obligation to bear the weaknesses of those without strength, and not to please ourselves. ² Each one of us must please his neighbor for his good, to build him up. ³ For even the Messiah did not please Himself. On the contrary, as it is written, **The insults of those who insult You have fallen on Me.**[A] ⁴ For whatever was written in the past was written for our instruction, so that we may have hope through endurance and through the encouragement from the Scriptures. ⁵ Now may the God who gives[B] endurance and encouragement allow you to live in harmony with one another, according to the command of Christ Jesus, ⁶ so that you may glorify the God and Father of our Lord Jesus Christ with a united mind and voice.

⁷ Therefore accept one another, just as the Messiah also accepted you, to the glory of God. ⁸ For I say that the Messiah became a servant of the circumcised[C] on behalf of God's truth, to confirm the promises to the fathers, ⁹ and so that Gentiles may glorify God for His mercy. As it is written:

> Therefore I will praise You
>   among the Gentiles,
> and I will sing psalms
>   to Your name.[D]

¹⁰ Again it says: **Rejoice, you Gentiles, with His people![E]** ¹¹ And again:

> Praise the Lord, all you Gentiles;
> all the peoples should praise Him![F]

¹² And again, Isaiah says:

> The root of Jesse will appear,
>   the One who rises to rule
>   the Gentiles;
> the Gentiles will hope in Him.[G]

¹³ Now may the God of hope fill you with all joy and peace as you believe in Him so that you may overflow with hope by the power of the Holy Spirit.

¹⁴ My brothers, I myself am convinced about you that you also are full of goodness, filled with all knowledge, and able to instruct one an-

other. ¹⁵ Nevertheless, I have written to remind you more boldly on some points[H] because of the grace given me by God ¹⁶ to be a minister of Christ Jesus to the Gentiles, serving as a priest of God's good news. My purpose is that the offering of the Gentiles may be acceptable, sanctified by the Holy Spirit. ¹⁷ Therefore I have reason to boast in Christ Jesus regarding what pertains to God. ¹⁸ For I would not dare say anything except what Christ has accomplished through me to make the Gentiles obedient by word and deed, ¹⁹ by the power of miraculous signs and wonders, and by the power of God's Spirit. As a result, I have fully proclaimed the good news about the Messiah from Jerusalem all the way around to Illyricum.[I] ²⁰ My aim is to evangelize where Christ has not been named, so that I will not build on someone else's foundation, ²¹ but, as it is written:

> Those who were not told about Him
>   will see,
> and those who have not heard
>   will understand.[J]

²² That is why I have been prevented many times from coming to you. ²³ But now I no longer have any work to do in these provinces,[K] and I have strongly desired for many years to come to you ²⁴ whenever I travel to Spain.[L] For I hope to see you when I pass through, and to be assisted by you for my journey there, once I have first enjoyed your company for a while. ²⁵ Right now I am traveling to Jerusalem to serve the saints, ²⁶ for Macedonia and Achaia[M] were pleased to make a contribution for the poor among the saints in Jerusalem. ²⁷ Yes, they were pleased, and indeed are indebted to them. For if the Gentiles have shared in their spiritual benefits, then they are obligated to minister to Jews in material needs. ²⁸ So when I have finished this and safely delivered the funds[N] to them, I will visit you on the way to Spain. ²⁹ I know that when I come to you, I will come in the fullness of the blessing[O] of Christ.

³⁰ Now I appeal to you, brothers, through our Lord Jesus Christ and through the love of

A 15:3 Ps 69:9   **B** 15:5 Lit *God of*   **C** 15:8 The Jews   **D** 15:9 2Sm 22:50; Ps 18:49   **E** 15:10 Dt 32:43   **F** 15:11 Ps 117:1   **G** 15:12 Is 11:10
H 15:15 Other mss add *brothers*   **I** 15:19 A Roman province northwest of Greece on the eastern shore of the Adriatic Sea   **J** 15:21 Is 52:15
K 15:23 Lit *now, having no longer a place in these parts*   **L** 15:24 Other mss add *I will come to you.*   **M** 15:26 The churches of these provinces
N 15:28 Lit *delivered this fruit*   **O** 15:29 Other mss add *of the gospel*

the Spirit, to join with me in fervent prayers to God on my behalf. ³¹Pray that I may be rescued from the unbelievers in Judea, that the gift I am bringing to^A Jerusalem may be acceptable to the saints, ³²and that, by God's will, I may come to you with joy and be refreshed together with you.

³³The God of peace be with all of you. Amen.

16 I commend to you our sister Phoebe, who is a servant^B of the church in Cenchreae. ²So you should welcome her in the Lord in a manner worthy of the saints and assist her in whatever matter she may require your help. For indeed she has been a benefactor of many—and of me also.

³Give my greetings to Prisca^C and Aquila, my coworkers in Christ Jesus, ⁴who risked their own necks for my life. Not only do I thank them, but so do all the Gentile churches.
⁵Greet also the church that meets in their home.
Greet my dear friend Epaenetus, who is the first convert^D to Christ from Asia.^E
⁶Greet Mary,^F who has worked very hard for you.^G
⁷Greet Andronicus and Junia,^H my fellow countrymen and fellow prisoners. They are noteworthy in the eyes of the apostles,^I,J and they were also in Christ before me.
⁸Greet Ampliatus, my dear friend in the Lord.
⁹Greet Urbanus, our coworker in Christ, and my dear friend Stachys.
¹⁰Greet Apelles, who is approved in Christ.
Greet those who belong to the household of Aristobulus.
¹¹Greet Herodion, my fellow countryman.
Greet those who belong to the household of Narcissus who are in the Lord.
¹²Greet Tryphaena and Tryphosa, who have worked hard in the Lord.

Greet my dear friend Persis, who has worked very hard in the Lord.
¹³Greet Rufus, chosen in the Lord; also his mother—and mine.
¹⁴Greet Asyncritus, Phlegon, Hermes, Patrobas, Hermas, and the brothers who are with them.
¹⁵Greet Philologus and Julia, Nereus and his sister, and Olympas, and all the saints who are with them.
¹⁶Greet one another with a holy kiss.
All the churches of Christ send you greetings.

¹⁷Now I urge you, brothers, to watch out for those who cause dissensions and obstacles contrary to the doctrine you have learned. Avoid them, ¹⁸for such people do not serve our Lord Christ but their own appetites.^K They deceive the hearts of the unsuspecting with smooth talk and flattering words.

¹⁹The report of your obedience has reached everyone. Therefore I rejoice over you. But I want you to be wise about what is good, yet innocent about what is evil. ²⁰The God of peace will soon crush Satan under your feet. The grace of our Lord Jesus be with you.

²¹Timothy, my coworker, and Lucius, Jason, and Sosipater, my fellow countrymen, greet you.

²²I Tertius, who wrote this letter, greet you in the Lord.^L

²³Gaius, who is host to me and to the whole church, greets you. Erastus, the city treasurer, and our brother Quartus greet you.

[²⁴The grace of our Lord Jesus Christ be with you all.]^M

²⁵Now to Him who has power to strengthen you according to my gospel and the proclamation about Jesus Christ, according to the revelation of the mystery kept silent for long ages ²⁶but now revealed and made known through the prophetic Scriptures, according to the command of the eternal God to advance the obedience of faith^N among all nations— ²⁷to the only wise God, through Jesus Christ—to Him be the glory forever!^O Amen.

^A15:31 Lit that my service for   ^B16:1 Others interpret this term in a technical sense: deacon, or deaconess, or minister, or courier   ^C16:3 Traditionally, Priscilla, as in Ac 18:2,18,26   ^D16:5 Lit the firstfruits   ^E16:5 Other mss read Achaia   ^F16:6 Or Maria   ^G16:6 Other mss read us   ^H16:7 Either a feminine name or "Junias," a masculine name   ^I16:7 Or are outstanding among   ^J16:7 "The apostles" is not always a technical term referring to the 12; cp. 2Co 8:23; Php 2:25 where this word is translated as "messenger."   ^K16:18 Lit belly   ^L16:22 Or letter in the Lord, greet you   ^M16:24 Other mss omit bracketed text; cp. v. 20   ^N16:26 Or the obedience that is faith, or the faithful obedience, or the obedience that comes from faith; Rm 1:5   ^O16:25-27 Other mss have these vv. at the end of chap 14 or 15.

1 CORINTHIANS

1 Paul, called as an apostle of Christ Jesus by God's will, and Sosthenes our brother: ²To God's church at Corinth, to those who are sanctified in Christ Jesus and called as saints, with all those in every place who call on the name of Jesus Christ our Lord—both their Lord and ours.

³Grace to you and peace from God our Father and the Lord Jesus Christ.

⁴I always thank my God for you because of God's grace given to you in Christ Jesus, ⁵that by Him you were enriched in everything—in all speech and all knowledge. ⁶In this way, the testimony about Christ was confirmed among you, ⁷so that you do not lack any spiritual gift as you eagerly wait for the revelation of our Lord Jesus Christ. ⁸He will also strengthen you to the end, so that you will be blameless in the day of our Lord Jesus Christ. ⁹God is faithful; you were called by Him into fellowship with His Son, Jesus Christ our Lord.

¹⁰Now I urge you, brothers, in the name of our Lord Jesus Christ, that all of you agree in what you say, that there be no divisions among you, and that you be united with the same understanding and the same conviction. ¹¹For it has been reported to me about you, my brothers, by members of Chloe's household, that there is rivalry among you. ¹²What I am saying is this: Each of you says, "I'm with Paul," or "I'm with Apollos," or "I'm with Cephas," or "I'm with Christ." ¹³Is Christ divided? Was it Paul who was crucified for you? Or were you baptized in Paul's name? ¹⁴I thank God^{A,B} that I baptized none of you except Crispus and Gaius, ¹⁵so that no one can say you were baptized in my name. ¹⁶I did, in fact, baptize the household of Stephanas; beyond that, I don't know if I baptized anyone else. ¹⁷For Christ did not send me to baptize, but to evangelize—not with clever words, so that the cross of Christ will not be emptied of its effect.

¹⁸For the message of the cross is foolishness to those who are perishing, but it is God's power to us who are being saved. ¹⁹For it is written:

> I will destroy the wisdom
> of the wise,
> and I will set aside the understanding
> of the experts.^C

²⁰Where is the philosopher?^D Where is the scholar? Where is the debater of this age? Hasn't God made the world's wisdom foolish? ²¹For since, in God's wisdom, the world did not know God through wisdom, God was pleased to save those who believe through the foolishness of the message preached. ²²For the Jews ask for signs and the Greeks seek wisdom, ²³but we preach Christ crucified, a stumbling block to the Jews and foolishness to the Gentiles,^E ²⁴Yet to those who are called, both Jews and Greeks, Christ is God's power and God's wisdom, ²⁵because God's foolishness is wiser than human wisdom, and God's weakness is stronger than human strength.

²⁶Brothers, consider your calling: Not many are wise from a human perspective,^F not many powerful, not many of noble birth. ²⁷Instead, God has chosen what is foolish in the world to shame the wise, and God has chosen what is weak in the world to shame the strong. ²⁸God has chosen what is insignificant and despised in the world—what is viewed as nothing—to bring to nothing what is viewed as something, ²⁹so that no one^G can boast in His presence. ³⁰But it is from Him that you are in Christ Jesus, who became God-given wisdom for us—our righteousness, sanctification, and redemption, ³¹in order that, as it is written: **The one who boasts must boast in the Lord.**^H

2 When I came to you, brothers, announcing the testimony^I of God to you, I did not come with brilliance of speech or wisdom. ²For I didn't think it was a good idea to know anything among you except Jesus Christ and Him crucified. ³I came to you in weakness, in fear, and in much trembling. ⁴My speech and

---

^A1:14 Other mss omit *God* ^B1:14 Or *I am thankful* ^C1:19 Is 29:14 ^D1:20 Or *wise* ^E1:23 Other mss read *Greeks* ^F1:26 Lit *wise according to the flesh* ^G1:29 Lit *that not all flesh* ^H1:31 Jr 9:24 ^I2:1 Other mss read *mystery* my proclamation were not with persuasive words of wisdom[A] but with a powerful demonstration by the Spirit, [5]so that your faith might not be based on men's wisdom but on God's power.

[6]However, we do speak a wisdom among the mature, but not a wisdom of this age, or of the rulers of this age, who are coming to nothing. [7]On the contrary, we speak God's hidden wisdom in a mystery, a wisdom God predestined before the ages for our glory. [8]None of the rulers of this age knew this wisdom, for if they had known it, they would not have crucified the Lord of glory. [9]But as it is written:

> What eye did not see and ear
>   did not hear,
> and what never entered
>   the human mind—
> God prepared this for those
>   who love Him.[B]

[10]Now God has revealed these things to us by the Spirit, for the Spirit searches everything, even the depths of God. [11]For who among men knows the thoughts[C] of a man except the spirit of the man that is in him? In the same way, no one knows the thoughts[C] of God except the Spirit of God. [12]Now we have not received the spirit of the world, but the Spirit who comes from God, so that we may understand what has been freely given to us by God. [13]We also speak these things, not in words taught by human wisdom, but in those taught by the Spirit, explaining spiritual things to spiritual people.[D] [14]But the unbeliever[E] does not welcome what comes from God's Spirit, because it is foolishness to him; he is not able to understand it since it is evaluated[F] spiritually. [15]The spiritual person, however, can evaluate[G] everything, yet he himself cannot be evaluated[F] by anyone. [16]For

> who has known the Lord's mind,
>   that he may instruct Him?[H]

But we have the mind of Christ.

3 Brothers, I was not able to speak to you as spiritual people but as people of the flesh, as babies in Christ. [2]I gave you milk to drink, not solid food, because you were not yet ready for it. In fact, you are still not ready, [3]because you are still fleshly. For since there is envy and strife[I] among you, are you not fleshly and living like unbelievers? [4]For whenever someone says, "I'm with Paul," and another, "I'm with Apollos," are you not unspiritual people?[K,L]

[5]What then is Apollos? And what is Paul? They are servants through whom you believed, and each has the role the Lord has given. [6]I planted, Apollos watered, but God gave the growth. [7]So then neither the one who plants nor the one who waters is anything, but only God who gives the growth. [8]Now the one planting and the one watering are one in purpose, and each will receive his own reward according to his own labor. [9]For we are God's coworkers.[M] You are God's field, God's building. [10]According to God's grace that was given to me, I have laid a foundation as a skilled master builder, and another builds on it. But each one must be careful how he builds on it. [11]For no one can lay any other foundation than what has been laid down. That foundation is Jesus Christ. [12]If anyone builds on that foundation with gold, silver, costly stones, wood, hay, or straw, [13]each one's work will become obvious, for the day[N] will disclose it, because it will be revealed by fire; the fire will test the quality of each one's work. [14]If anyone's work that he has built survives, he will receive a reward. [15]If anyone's work is burned up, it will be lost, but he will be saved; yet it will be like an escape through fire.[O]

[16]Don't you yourselves know that you are God's sanctuary and that the Spirit of God lives in you? [17]If anyone destroys God's sanctuary, God will destroy him; for God's sanctuary is holy, and that is what you are.

[18]No one should deceive himself. If anyone among you thinks he is wise in this age, he must become foolish so that he can become wise. [19]For the wisdom of this world is foolishness with God, since it is written: **He**

A2:4 Other mss read *human wisdom*   B2:9 Is 52:15; 64:4   C2:11 Or *things*   D2:13 Or *things with spiritual words*   E2:14 Or *unspiritual; lit natural*   F2:14,15 Or *judged, or discerned*   G2:15 Or *judge, or discern*   H2:16 Is 40:13   I3:3 Other mss add *and divisions*   J3:3 Lit *and walking according to man*   K3:4 Other mss read *are you not carnal*   L3:4 Lit *not just human*   M3:9 Or *are coworkers belonging to God*   N3:13 The day of Christ's judgment of believers   O3:15 Lit *yet so as through fire* catches the wise in their craftiness;[A] [20]and again, **The Lord knows that the reasonings of the wise are meaningless.**[B] [21]So no one should boast in human leaders, for everything is yours— [22]whether Paul or Apollos or Cephas or the world or life or death or things present or things to come—everything is yours, [23]and you belong to Christ, and Christ belongs to God.

4 A person should consider us in this way: as servants of Christ and managers of God's mysteries. [2]In this regard, it is expected of managers that each one of them be found faithful. [3]It is of little importance to me that I should be evaluated by you or by any human court.[C] In fact, I don't even evaluate myself. [4]For I am not conscious of anything against myself, but I am not justified by this. The One who evaluates me is the Lord. [5]Therefore don't judge anything prematurely, before the Lord comes, who will both bring to light what is hidden in darkness and reveal the intentions of the hearts. And then praise will come to each one from God.

[6]Now, brothers, I have applied these things to myself and Apollos for your benefit, so that you may learn from us the saying: "Nothing beyond what is written."[D] The purpose is that none of you will be inflated with pride in favor of one person over another. [7]For who makes you so superior? What do you have that you didn't receive? If, in fact, you did receive it, why do you boast as if you hadn't received it? [8]You are already full! You are already rich! You have begun to reign as kings without us—and I wish you did reign, so that we could also reign with you! [9]For I think God has displayed us, the apostles, in last place, like men condemned to die: We have become a spectacle to the world and to angels and to men. [10]We are fools for Christ, but you are wise in Christ! We are weak, but you are strong! You are distinguished, but we are dishonored! [11]Up to the present hour we are both hungry and thirsty; we are poorly clothed, roughly treated, homeless; [12]we labor, working with our own hands. When we are reviled, we bless; when we are persecuted, we endure it; [13]when we are slandered, we re-

spond graciously. Even now, we are like the world's garbage, like the dirt everyone scrapes off their sandals.

[14]I'm not writing this to shame you, but to warn you as my dear children. [15]For you can have 10,000 instructors in Christ, but you can't have many fathers. For I became your father in Christ Jesus through the gospel. [16]Therefore I urge you to imitate me. [17]This is why I have sent Timothy to you. He is my dearly loved and faithful son in the Lord. He will remind you about my ways in Christ Jesus, just as I teach everywhere in every church. [18]Now some are inflated with pride, as though I were not coming to you. [19]But I will come to you soon, if the Lord wills, and I will know not the talk but the power of those who are inflated with pride. [20]For the kingdom of God is not a matter of talk but of power. [21]What do you want? Should I come to you with a rod, or in love and a spirit of gentleness?

5 It is widely reported that there is sexual immorality among you, and the kind of sexual immorality that is not even tolerated[E] among the Gentiles—a man is living with his father's wife. [2]And you are inflated with pride, instead of filled with grief so that he who has committed this act might be removed from your congregation. [3]For though I am absent in body but present in spirit, I have already decided about the one who has done this thing as though I were present. [4]When you are assembled in the name of our Lord Jesus with my spirit and with the power of our Lord Jesus, [5]turn that one over to Satan for the destruction of the flesh, so that his spirit may be saved in the Day of the Lord.

[6]Your boasting is not good. Don't you know that a little yeast permeates the whole batch of dough? [7]Clean out the old yeast so that you may be a new batch. You are indeed unleavened, for Christ our Passover has been sacrificed.[F] [8]Therefore, let us observe the feast, not with old yeast or with the yeast of malice and evil but with the unleavened bread of sincerity and truth.

[9]I wrote to you in a letter not to associate with sexually immoral people. [10]I did not

[A]3:19 Jb 5:13 [B]3:20 Ps 94:11 [C]4:3 Lit a human day [D]4:6 The words in quotation marks could = the OT, a Jewish maxim, or a popular proverb. [E]5:1 Other mss read named [F]5:7 Other mss add for us mean the immoral people of this world or the greedy and swindlers or idolaters; otherwise you would have to leave the world. ¹¹But now I am writingᴬ not to associate with anyone who claims to be a believerᴮ who is sexually immoral or greedy, an idolater or verbally abusive, a drunkard or a swindler. Do not even eat with such a person. ¹²For what business is it of mine to judge outsiders? Don't you judge those who are inside? ¹³But God judges outsiders. **Put away the evil person from among yourselves.**ᶜ

6 If any of you has a legal dispute against another, do you dare go to court before the unrighteous,ᴰ and not before the saints? ²Or don't you know that the saints will judge the world? And if the world is judged by you, are you unworthy to judge the smallest cases? ³Don't you know that we will judge angels—not to mention ordinary matters? ⁴So if you have cases pertaining to this life, do you select thoseᴱ who have no standing in the church to judge? ⁵I say this to your shame! Can it be that there is not one wise person among you who is able to arbitrate between his brothers? ⁶Instead, believerᶠ goes to court against believer, and that before unbelievers!

⁷Therefore, to have legal disputes against one another is already a moral failure for you. Why not rather put up with injustice? Why not rather be cheated? ⁸Instead, you act unjustly and cheat—and you do this to believers! ⁹Don't you know that the unrighteous will not inherit God's kingdom? Do not be deceived: No sexually immoral people, idolaters, adulterers, or anyone practicing homosexuality,ᴳ ¹⁰no thieves, greedy people, drunkards, verbally abusive people, or swindlers will inherit God's kingdom. ¹¹And some of you used to be like this. But you were washed, you were sanctified, you were justified in the name of the Lord Jesus Christ and by the Spirit of our God.

¹²"Everything is permissible for me,"ᴴ but not everything is helpful. "Everything is permissible for me," but I will not be brought under the control of anything. ¹³"Food for the stomach and the stomach for food," but God will do away with both of them.ᴵ The body is not for sexual immorality but for the Lord, and the Lord for the body. ¹⁴God raised up the Lord and will also raise us up by His power. ¹⁵Don't you know that your bodies are a part of Christ's body? So should I take a part of Christ's body and make it part of a prostitute? Absolutely not! ¹⁶Don't you know that anyone joined to a prostitute is one body with her? For Scripture says, **The two will become one flesh.**ᴶ ¹⁷But anyone joined to the Lord is one spirit with Him.

¹⁸Run from sexual immorality! "Every sin a person can commit is outside the body."ᴷ On the contrary, the person who is sexually immoral sins against his own body. ¹⁹Don't you know that your body is a sanctuary of the Holy Spirit who is in you, whom you have from God? You are not your own, ²⁰for you were bought at a price. Therefore glorify God in your body.ᴸ

7 Now in response to the matters you wroteᴹ about: "It is good for a man not to have relations withᴺ a woman."ᴼ ²But because sexual immorality is so common,ᴾ each man should have his own wife, and each woman should have her own husband. ³A husband should fulfill his marital responsibility to his wife, and likewise a wife to her husband. ⁴A wife does not have the right over her own body, but her husband does. In the same way, a husband does not have the right over his own body, but his wife does. ⁵Do not deprive one another sexually—except when you agree for a time, to devote yourselves toᵠ prayer. Then come together again; otherwise, Satan may tempt you because of your lack of self-control. ⁶I say the followingᴿ as a concession, not as a command. ⁷I wish that all people were just like me. But each has his own gift from God, one person in this way and another in that way.

A5:11 Or now I wrote   B5:11 Lit anyone named a brother   C5:13 Dt 17:7   D6:1 Unbelievers; v. 6   E6:4 Or life, appoint those (as a command)   F6:6–8 Lit brothers   G6:9 Lit adulterers, passive homosexual partners, active homosexual partners   H6:12–13 The words in quotation marks are most likely slogans used by some Corinthian Christians and corrected by Paul.   I6:13 Lit both it and them   J6:16 Gn 2:24   K6:18 See note at 1Co 6:12–13.   L6:20 Other mss add and in your spirit, which belong to God.   M7:1 Other mss add to me   N7:1 Lit not to touch   O7:1 The words in quotation marks are a principle that the Corinthians wrote to Paul about to ask for his view.   P7:2 Lit because of immoralities   Q7:5 Other mss add fasting and to   R7:6 Lit say this; some interpret the word as referring to v. 2, vv. 2-5, v. 5 (wholly or in part), or v. 6

[8] I say to the unmarried and to widows: It is good for them if they remain as I am. [9] But if they do not have self-control, they should marry, for it is better to marry than to burn with desire.

[10] I command the married—not I, but the Lord—a wife is not to leave[A] her husband. [11] But if she does leave, she must remain unmarried or be reconciled to her husband—and a husband is not to leave his wife. [12] But I (not the Lord)[B] say to the rest: If any brother has an unbelieving wife and she is willing to live with him, he must not leave her. [13] Also, if any woman has an unbelieving husband and he is willing to live with her, she must not leave her husband. [14] For the unbelieving husband is set apart for God by the wife, and the unbelieving wife is set apart for God by the husband.[C] Otherwise your children would be corrupt, but now they are set apart for God. [15] But if the unbeliever leaves, let him leave. A brother or a sister is not bound in such cases. God has called you[D] to live in peace. [16] For you, wife, how do you know whether you will save your husband? Or you, husband, how do you know whether you will save your wife?

[17] However, each one must live his life in the situation the Lord assigned when God called him.[E] This is what I command in all the churches. [18] Was anyone already circumcised when he was called? He should not undo his circumcision. Was anyone called while uncircumcised? He should not get circumcised. [19] Circumcision does not matter and uncircumcision does not matter, but keeping God's commands does. [20] Each person should remain in the life situation[F] in which he was called. [21] Were you called while a slave? It should not be a concern to you. But if you can become free, by all means take the opportunity.[G] [22] For he who is called by the Lord as a slave is the Lord's freedman.[H] Likewise he who is called as a free man[I] is Christ's slave. [23] You were bought at a price; do not become slaves of men. [24] Brothers, each person should remain with God in whatever situation he was called.

[25] About virgins: I have no command from the Lord, but I do give an opinion as one who by the Lord's mercy is trustworthy. [26] Therefore I consider this to be good because of the present distress: It is fine for a man to remain as he is. [27] Are you bound to a wife? Do not seek to be loosed. Are you loosed from a wife? Do not seek a wife. [28] However, if you do get married, you have not sinned, and if a virgin marries, she has not sinned. But such people will have trouble in this life,[J] and I am trying to spare you. [29] And I say this, brothers: The time is limited, so from now on those who have wives should be as though they had none, [30] those who weep as though they did not weep, those who rejoice as though they did not rejoice, those who buy as though they did not possess, [31] and those who use the world as though they did not make full use of it. For this world in its current form is passing away.

[32] I want you to be without concerns. An unmarried man is concerned about the things of the Lord—how he may please the Lord. [33] But a married man is concerned about the things of the world—how he may please his wife— [34] and his interests are divided. An unmarried woman or a virgin is concerned about the things of the Lord, so that she may be holy both in body and in spirit. But a married woman is concerned about the things of the world—how she may please her husband. [35] Now I am saying this for your own benefit, not to put a restraint on you, but because of what is proper and so that you may be devoted to the Lord without distraction.

[36] But if any man thinks he is acting improperly toward his virgin,[K] if she is past marriageable age,[L] and so it must be, he can do what he wants. He is not sinning; they can get married. [37] But he who stands firm in his heart (who is under no compulsion, but has control over his own will) and has decided in his heart to keep his own virgin, will do well. [38] So then he who marries[M] his virgin

---

A [7:10](Or separate from, or divorce　B [7:12](Jesus did not address the situation of a marriage in the Gentile world where only one person is a believer.　C [7:14](Lit the brother　D [7:15](Other mss read us　E [7:17](Lit called each　F [7:20](Lit in the calling　G [7:21](Or But even though you can become free, make the most of your position as a slave.　H [7:22](A former slave　I [7:22](A man who was never a slave　J [7:28](Lit in the flesh　K [7:36](a man's fiancée, or his daughter, or his Levirate wife, or a celibate companion　L [7:36](Or virgin, if his passions are strong.　M [7:38](Or marries off does well, but he who does not marry[A] will do better.

[39] A wife is bound[B] as long as her husband is living. But if her husband dies, she is free to be married to anyone she wants—only in the Lord.[C] [40] But she is happier if she remains as she is, in my opinion. And I think that I also have the Spirit of God.

8 About food offered to idols: We know that "we all have knowledge."[D] Knowledge inflates with pride, but love builds up. [2] If anyone thinks he knows anything, he does not yet know it as he ought to know it. [3] But if anyone loves God, he is known by Him.

[4] About eating food offered to idols, then, we know that "an idol is nothing in the world," and that "there is no God but one." [5] For even if there are so-called gods, whether in heaven or on earth—as there are many "gods" and many "lords"—

6   yet for us there is one God, the Father.
       All things are from Him,
           and we exist for Him.
       And there is one Lord, Jesus Christ.
       All things are through Him,
           and we exist through Him.

[7] However, not everyone has this knowledge. In fact, some have been so used to idolatry up until now that when they eat food offered to an idol, their conscience, being weak, is defiled. [8] Food will not make us acceptable to God. We are not inferior if we don't eat, and we are not better if we do eat. [9] But be careful that this right of yours in no way becomes a stumbling block to the weak. [10] For if someone sees you, the one who has this knowledge, dining in an idol's temple, won't his weak conscience be encouraged to eat food offered to idols? [11] Then the weak person, the brother for whom Christ died, is ruined[E] by your knowledge. [12] Now when you sin like this against the brothers and wound their weak conscience, you are sinning against Christ. [13] Therefore, if food causes my brother to fall, I will never again eat meat, so that I won't cause my brother to fall.

9 Am I not free? Am I not an apostle? Have I not seen Jesus our Lord? Are you not my work in the Lord? [2] If I am not an apostle to others, at least I am to you, for you are the seal of my apostleship in the Lord. [3] My defense to those who examine me is this: [4] Don't we have the right to eat and drink? [5] Don't we have the right to be accompanied by a Christian wife[F] like the other apostles, the Lord's brothers, and Cephas? [6] Or do Barnabas and I alone have no right to refrain from working? [7] Who ever goes to war at his own expense? Who plants a vineyard and does not eat its fruit? Or who shepherds a flock and does not drink the milk from the flock? [8] Am I saying this from a human perspective? Doesn't the law also say the same thing? [9] For it is written in the law of Moses, **Do not muzzle an ox while it treads out grain.**[G] Is God really concerned with oxen? [10] Or isn't He really saying it for us? Yes, this is written for us, because he who plows ought to plow in hope, and he who threshes should do so in hope of sharing the crop. [11] If we have sown spiritual things for you, is it too much if we reap material benefits from you? [12] If others have this right to receive benefits from you, don't we even more?

However, we have not made use of this right; instead we endure everything so that we will not hinder the gospel of Christ. [13] Don't you know that those who perform the temple services eat the food from the temple, and those who serve at the altar share in the offerings of the altar? [14] In the same way, the Lord has commanded that those who preach the gospel should earn their living by the gospel. [15] But I have used none of these rights, and I have not written this to make it happen that way for me. For it would be better for me to die than for anyone to deprive me of my boast! [16] For if I preach the gospel, I have no reason to boast, because an obligation is placed on me. And woe to me if I do not preach the gospel! [17] For if I do this willingly, I have a reward, but if unwillingly, I am entrusted with a stewardship. [18] What then is my reward? To preach the gospel and offer it free

A7:38 Or marry her off   B7:39 Other mss add by law   C7:39 Only a believer   D8:1 See note at 1Co 6:12-13.   E8:11 Or destroyed   F9:5 Lit a sister as a wife   G9:9 Dt 25:4

of charge and not make full use of my authority in the gospel.

[19] Although I am a free man and not anyone's slave, I have made myself a slave to everyone, in order to win more people. [20] To the Jews I became like a Jew, to win Jews; to those under the law, like one under the law—though I myself am not under the law[A]—to win those under the law. [21] To those who are without that law, like one without the law—not being without God's law but within Christ's law—to win those without the law. [22] To the weak I became weak, in order to win the weak. I have become all things to all people, so that I may by every possible means save some. [23] Now I do all this because of the gospel, so I may become a partner in its benefits.[B]

[24] Don't you know that the runners in a stadium all race, but only one receives the prize? Run in such a way to win the prize. [25] Now everyone who competes exercises self-control in everything. However, they do it to receive a crown that will fade away, but we a crown that will never fade away. [26] Therefore I do not run like one who runs aimlessly or box like one beating the air. [27] Instead, I discipline my body and bring it under strict control, so that after preaching to others, I myself will not be disqualified.

10 Now I want you to know, brothers, that our fathers were all under the cloud, all passed through the sea, [2] and all were baptized into Moses in the cloud and in the sea. [3] They all ate the same spiritual food, [4] and all drank the same spiritual drink. For they drank from a spiritual rock that followed them, and that rock was Christ. [5] But God was not pleased with most of them, for they were struck down in the wilderness.

[6] Now these things became examples for us, so that we will not desire evil things as they did.[C] [7] Don't become idolaters as some of them were; as it is written, **The people sat down to eat and drink, and got up to play.**[D,E] [8] Let us not commit sexual immorality as some of them did,[F] and in a single day 23,000 people fell dead. [9] Let us not test Christ

as some of them did[G] and were destroyed by snakes. [10] Nor should we complain as some of them did,[H] and were killed by the destroyer.[I] [11] Now these things happened to them as examples, and they were written as a warning to us, on whom the ends of the ages have come. [12] So, whoever thinks he stands must be careful not to fall. [13] No temptation has overtaken you except what is common to humanity. God is faithful, and He will not allow you to be tempted beyond what you are able, but with the temptation He will also provide a way of escape so that you are able to bear it.

[14] Therefore, my dear friends, flee from idolatry. [15] I am speaking as to wise people. Judge for yourselves what I say. [16] The cup of blessing that we give thanks for, is it not a sharing in the blood of Christ? The bread that we break, is it not a sharing in the body of Christ? [17] Because there is one bread, we who are many are one body, for all of us share that one bread. [18] Look at the people of Israel.[J] Do not those who eat the sacrifices participate in what is offered on the altar? [19] What am I saying then? That food offered to idols is anything, or that an idol is anything? [20] No, but I do say that what they[K] sacrifice, they sacrifice to demons and not to God. I do not want you to participate with demons! [21] You cannot drink the cup of the Lord and the cup of demons. You cannot share in the Lord's table and the table of demons. [22] Or are we provoking the Lord to jealousy? Are we stronger than He?

[23] "Everything is permissible,"[L,M] but not everything is helpful. "Everything is permissible,"[L] but not everything builds up. [24] No one should seek his own good, but the good of the other person.

[25] Eat everything that is sold in the meat market, asking no questions for conscience' sake, [26] for **the earth is the Lord's, and all that is in it.**[N] [27] If one of the unbelievers invites you over and you want to go, eat everything that is set before you, without raising questions of conscience. [28] But if someone says to you, "This is food offered to an idol," do not eat it, out of consideration for the one who told you, and for conscience' sake.[O] [29] I do not

---

[A]9:20 Other mss omit *though I myself am not under law*   [B]9:23 Lit *partner of it*   [C]10:6 Lit *they desired*   [D]10:7 Or *to dance*   [E]10:7 Ex 32:6
[F]10:8 Lit *them committed sexual immorality*   [G]10:9 Lit *them tested*   [H]10:10 Lit *them complained*   [I]10:10 Or *the destroying angel*   [J]10:18 Lit
Look at Israel according to the flesh   [K]10:20 Other mss read *Gentiles*   [L]10:23 Other mss add *for me*   [M]10:23 See note at 1Co 6:12-13.
[N]10:26 Ps 24:1   [O]10:28 Other mss add *"For the earth is the Lord's and all that is in it."*

mean your own conscience, but the other person's. For why is my freedom judged by another person's conscience? [30] If I partake with thanks, why am I slandered because of something I give thanks for?

[31] Therefore, whether you eat or drink, or whatever you do, do everything for God's glory. [32] Give no offense to the Jews or the Greeks or the church of God, [33] just as I also try to please all people in all things, not seeking my own profit, but the profit of many, so **11** that they may be saved. [1] Imitate me, as I also imitate Christ.

[2] Now I praise you[A] because you always remember me and keep the traditions just as I delivered them to you. [3] But I want you to know that Christ is the head of every man, and the man is the head of the woman,[B] and God is the head of Christ. [4] Every man who prays or prophesies with something on his head dishonors his head. [5] But every woman who prays or prophesies with her head uncovered dishonors her head, since that is one and the same as having her head shaved. [6] So if a woman's head[C] is not covered, her hair should be cut off. But if it is disgraceful for a woman to have her hair cut off or her head shaved, she should be covered.

[7] A man, in fact, should not cover his head, because he is God's image and glory, but woman is man's glory. [8] For man did not come from woman, but woman came from man. [9] And man was not created for woman, but woman for man. [10] This is why a woman should have a symbol of authority on her head, because of the angels. [11] In the Lord, however, woman is not independent of man, and man is not independent of woman. [12] For just as woman came from man, so man comes through woman, and all things come from God.

[13] Judge for yourselves: Is it proper for a woman to pray to God with her head uncovered? [14] Does not even nature itself teach you that if a man has long hair it is a disgrace to him, [15] but that if a woman has long hair, it is her glory? For her hair is given to her[D] as a covering. [16] But if anyone wants to argue

about this, we have no other[E] custom, nor do the churches of God.

[17] Now in giving the following instruction I do not praise you, since you come together not for the better but for the worse. [18] For to begin with, I hear that when you come together as a church there are divisions among you, and in part I believe it. [19] There must, indeed, be factions among you, so that those who are approved may be recognized among you. [20] Therefore, when you come together, it is not really to eat the Lord's Supper. [21] For at the meal, each one eats his own supper ahead of others. So one person is hungry while another gets drunk! [22] Don't you have houses to eat and drink in? Or do you look down on the church of God and embarrass those who have nothing? What should I say to you? Should I praise you? I do not praise you for this!

[23] For I received from the Lord what I also passed on to you: On the night when He was betrayed, the Lord Jesus took bread, [24] gave thanks, broke it, and said,[F] "This is My body, which is[G] for you. Do this in remembrance of Me."

[25] In the same way, after supper He also took the cup and said, "This cup is the new covenant established by My blood. Do this, as often as you drink it, in remembrance of Me." [26] For as often as you eat this bread and drink the cup, you proclaim the Lord's death until He comes.

[27] Therefore, whoever eats the bread or drinks the cup of the Lord in an unworthy way will be guilty of sin against the body[H] and blood of the Lord. [28] So a man should examine himself; in this way he should eat the bread and drink from the cup. [29] For whoever eats and drinks without recognizing the body,[I] eats and drinks judgment on himself. [30] This is why many are sick and ill among you, and many have fallen asleep. [31] If we were properly evaluating ourselves, we would not be judged, [32] but when we are judged, we are disciplined by the Lord, so that we may not be condemned with the world.

[33] Therefore, my brothers, when you come together to eat, wait for one another. [34] If any-

one is hungry, he should eat at home, so that when you gather together you will not come under judgment. And I will give instructions about the other matters whenever I come.

12 Now concerning what comes from the Spirit:[A] brothers, I do not want you to be unaware. [2]You know that when you were pagans, you used to be led off to the idols that could not speak. [3]Therefore I am informing you that no one speaking by the Spirit of God says, "Jesus is cursed," and no one can say, "Jesus is Lord," except by the Holy Spirit.

[4]Now there are different gifts, but the same Spirit. [5]There are different ministries, but the same Lord. [6]And there are different activities, but the same God activates each gift in each person.[B] [7]A demonstration of the Spirit is given to each person to produce what is beneficial:

[8]   to one is given a message of wisdom
         through the Spirit,
      to another, a message of knowledge
         by the same Spirit,
[9]   to another, faith by the same Spirit,
      to another, gifts of healing
         by the one Spirit,
[10]   to another, the performing of miracles,
      to another, prophecy,
      to another, distinguishing
         between spirits,
      to another, different kinds
         of languages,
      to another, interpretation
         of languages.

[11]But one and the same Spirit is active in all these, distributing to each person as He wills.

[12]For as the body is one and has many parts, and all the parts of that body, though many, are one body—so also is Christ. [13]For we were all baptized by[C] one Spirit into one body—whether Jews or Greeks, whether slaves or free—and we were all made to drink of one Spirit. [14]So the body is not one part but many. [15]If the foot should say, "Because I'm not a hand, I don't belong to the body," in spite of this it still belongs to the body. [16]And if the ear should say, "Because I'm not an eye, I don't belong to the body," in spite of this it still belongs to the body. [17]If the whole body were an eye, where would the hearing be? If the whole body were an ear, where would the sense of smell be? [18]But now God has placed each one of the parts in one body just as He wanted. [19]And if they were all the same part, where would the body be? [20]Now there are many parts, yet one body.

[21]So the eye cannot say to the hand, "I don't need you!" Or again, the head can't say to the feet, "I don't need you!" [22]But even more, those parts of the body that seem to be weaker are necessary. [23]And those parts of the body that we think to be less honorable, we clothe these with greater honor, and our unpresentable parts have a better presentation. [24]But our presentable parts have no need of clothing. Instead, God has put the body together, giving greater honor to the less honorable, [25]so that there would be no division in the body, but that the members would have the same concern for each other. [26]So if one member suffers, all the members suffer with it; if one member is honored, all the members rejoice with it.

[27]Now you are the body of Christ, and individual members of it. [28]And God has placed these in the church:

      first apostles, second prophets,
      third teachers, next miracles,
      then gifts of healing, helping,
      managing, various kinds of languages.
[29]   Are all apostles? Are all prophets?
      Are all teachers? Do all do miracles?
[30]   Do all have gifts of healing?
      Do all speak in other languages?
      Do all interpret?

[31]But desire the greater gifts. And I will show you an even better way.

13 If I speak human or angelic
         languages
      but do not have love,
      I am a sounding gong
         or a clanging cymbal.
[2]   If I have the gift of prophecy
      and understand all mysteries
      and all knowledge,

A12:1 Or concerning spiritual things, or spiritual gifts   B12:6 Lit God acts all things in all   C12:13 Or with, or in

and if I have all faith
so that I can move mountains
but do not have love, I am nothing.
3 And if I donate all my goods to feed
    the poor,
and if I give my body in order
    to boast[A]
but do not have love, I gain nothing.

4 Love is patient, love is kind.
Love does not envy,
is not boastful, is not conceited,
5 does not act improperly,
is not selfish, is not provoked,
and does not keep a record of wrongs.

6 Love finds no joy
    in unrighteousness
but rejoices in the truth.

7 It bears all things, believes all things,
hopes all things, endures all things.

8 Love never ends.
But as for prophecies,
they will come to an end;
as for languages, they will cease;
as for knowledge, it will come
    to an end.

9 For we know in part,
and we prophesy in part.

10 But when the perfect comes,
the partial will come to an end.

11 When I was a child,
I spoke like a child,
I thought like a child,
I reasoned like a child.
When I became a man,
I put aside childish things.

12 For now we see indistinctly,[B] as
    in a mirror,[C]
but then face to face.
Now I know in part,
but then I will know fully,
as I am fully known.

13 Now these three remain:
faith, hope, and love.
But the greatest of these is love.

14 Pursue love and desire spiritual gifts, and above all that you may prophesy. 2For the person who speaks in another language is not speaking to men but to God, since no one understands him; however, he speaks mysteries in the Spirit.[D] 3But the person who prophesies speaks to people for edification, encouragement, and consolation. 4The person who speaks in another language builds himself up, but he who prophesies builds up the church. 5I wish all of you spoke in other languages, but even more that you prophesied. The person who prophesies is greater than the person who speaks in languages, unless he interprets so that the church may be built up.

6But now, brothers, if I come to you speaking in other languages, how will I benefit you unless I speak to you with a revelation or knowledge or prophecy or teaching? 7Even inanimate things that produce sounds—whether flute or harp—if they don't make a distinction in the notes, how will what is played on the flute or harp be recognized? 8In fact, if the trumpet makes an unclear sound, who will prepare for battle? 9In the same way, unless you use your tongue for intelligible speech, how will what is spoken be known? For you will be speaking into the air. 10There are doubtless many different kinds of languages in the world, and all have meaning.[E] 11Therefore, if I do not know the meaning of the language, I will be a foreigner[F] to the speaker, and the speaker will be a foreigner to me. 12So also you—since you are zealous for spiritual gifts,[G] seek to excel in building up the church.

13Therefore the person who speaks in another language should pray that he can interpret. 14For if I pray in another language, my spirit prays, but my understanding is unfruitful. 15What then? I will pray with the spirit, and I will also pray with my understanding. I will sing with the spirit, and I will also sing with my understanding. 16Otherwise, if you praise with the spirit,[H] how will the uninformed person[I] say "Amen" at your giving of thanks, since he does not know what you are saying? [17]For you may very well be giving thanks, but the other person is not being built up. [18]I thank God that I speak in other languages more than all of you; [19]yet in the church I would rather speak five words with my understanding, in order to teach others also, than 10,000 words in another language.

[20]Brothers, don't be childish in your thinking, but be infants in regard to evil and adult in your thinking. [21]It is written in the law:

> I will speak to these people
> by people of other languages
> and by the lips of foreigners,
> and even then, they will not listen
> to Me,[A]

says the Lord. [22]It follows that speaking in other languages is intended as a sign,[B] not for believers but for unbelievers. But prophecy is not for unbelievers but for believers. [23]Therefore, if the whole church assembles together and all are speaking in other languages and people who are uninformed or unbelievers come in, will they not say that you are out of your minds? [24]But if all are prophesying and some unbeliever or uninformed person comes in, he is convicted by all and is judged by all. [25]The secrets of his heart will be revealed, and as a result he will fall facedown and worship God, proclaiming, "God is really among you."

[26]What then is the conclusion, brothers? Whenever you come together, each one[C] has a psalm, a teaching, a revelation, another language, or an interpretation. All things must be done for edification. [27]If any person speaks in another language, there should be only two, or at the most three, each in turn, and someone must interpret. [28]But if there is no interpreter, that person should keep silent in the church and speak to himself and to God. [29]Two or three prophets should speak, and the others should evaluate. [30]But if something has been revealed to another person sitting there, the first prophet should be silent. [31]For you can all prophesy one by one, so that everyone may learn and everyone may be encouraged. [32]And the prophets' spirits

are under the control of the prophets, [33]since God is not a God of disorder but of peace.

As in all the churches of the saints, [34]the women[D] should be silent in the churches, for they are not permitted to speak, but should be submissive, as the law also says. [35]And if they want to learn something, they should ask their own husbands at home, for it is disgraceful for a woman to speak in the church meeting. [36]Did the word of God originate from you, or did it come to you only?

[37]If anyone thinks he is a prophet or spiritual, he should recognize that what I write to you is the Lord's command. [38]But if anyone ignores this, he will be ignored.[E] [39]Therefore, my brothers, be eager to prophesy, and do not forbid speaking in other languages. [40]But everything must be done decently and in order.

15

Now brothers, I want to clarify[F] for you the gospel I proclaimed to you; you received it and have taken your stand on it. [2]You are also saved by it, if you hold to the message I proclaimed to you—unless you believed for no purpose.[G] [3]For I passed on to you as most important what I also received:

> that Christ died for our sins
> according to the Scriptures,
> [4] that He was buried,
> that He was raised on the third day
> according to the Scriptures,
> [5] and that He appeared to Cephas,
> then to the Twelve.
> [6] Then He appeared to over 500 brothers
> at one time;
> most of them are still alive,
> but some have fallen asleep.
> [7] Then He appeared to James,
> then to all the apostles.
> [8] Last of all, as to one abnormally born,[H]
> He also appeared to me.

[9]For I am the least of the apostles, unworthy to be called an apostle, because I persecuted the church of God. [10]But by God's grace I am what I am, and His grace toward me was not ineffective. However, I worked more than any of them, yet not I, but God's grace that

[A]14:21 Is 28:11-12 [B]14:22 Lit that languages are for a sign [C]14:26 Other mss add of you [D]14:34 Other mss read your women [E]14:38 Other mss read he should be ignored [F]15:1 Or I make known [G]15:2 Or believed without careful thought, or believed in vain [H]15:8 Or one whose birth was unusual, He was with me. ¹¹Therefore, whether it is I or they, so we proclaim and so you have believed.

¹²Now if Christ is proclaimed as raised from the dead, how can some of you say, "There is no resurrection of the dead"? ¹³But if there is no resurrection of the dead, then Christ has not been raised; ¹⁴and if Christ has not been raised, then our proclamation is without foundation, and so is your faith.^A ¹⁵In addition, we are found to be false witnesses about God, because we have testified about God that He raised up Christ—whom He did not raise up if in fact the dead are not raised. ¹⁶For if the dead are not raised, Christ has not been raised. ¹⁷And if Christ has not been raised, your faith is worthless; you are still in your sins. ¹⁸Therefore, those who have fallen asleep in Christ have also perished. ¹⁹If we have put our hope in Christ for this life only, we should be pitied more than anyone.

²⁰But now Christ has been raised from the dead, the firstfruits of those who have fallen asleep. ²¹For since death came through a man, the resurrection of the dead also comes through a man. ²²For as in Adam all die, so also in Christ all will be made alive. ²³But each in his own order: Christ, the firstfruits; afterward, at His coming, those who belong to Christ. ²⁴Then comes the end, when He hands over the kingdom to God the Father, when He abolishes all rule and all authority and power. ²⁵For He must reign until He puts all His enemies under His feet. ²⁶The last enemy to be abolished is death. ²⁷For **God has put everything under His feet.**^B But when it says "everything" is put under Him, it is obvious that He who puts everything under Him is the exception. ²⁸And when everything is subject to Christ, then the Son Himself will also be subject to the One who subjected everything to Him, so that God may be all in all.

²⁹Otherwise what will they do who are being baptized for the dead? If the dead are not raised at all, then why are people baptized for them?^C ³⁰Why are we in danger every hour? ³¹I affirm by the pride in you that I have in Christ Jesus our Lord: I die every day! ³²If I

fought wild animals in Ephesus with only human hope,^D what good did that do me?^E If the dead are not raised, **Let us eat and drink, for tomorrow we die.**^F ³³Do not be deceived: "Bad company corrupts good morals."^G ³⁴Come to your senses^H and stop sinning, for some people are ignorant about God. I say this to your shame.

³⁵But someone will say, "How are the dead raised? What kind of body will they have when they come?" ³⁶Foolish one! What you sow does not come to life unless it dies. ³⁷And as for what you sow—you are not sowing the future body, but only a seed,^I perhaps of wheat or another grain. ³⁸But God gives it a body as He wants, and to each of the seeds its own body. ³⁹Not all flesh is the same flesh; there is one flesh for humans, another for animals, another for birds, and another for fish. ⁴⁰There are heavenly bodies and earthly bodies, but the splendor of the heavenly bodies is different from that of the earthly ones. ⁴¹There is a splendor of the sun, another of the moon, and another of the stars; for one star differs from another star in splendor. ⁴²So it is with the resurrection of the dead:

> Sown in corruption, raised
>   in incorruption;
> ⁴³ sown in dishonor, raised in glory;
>   sown in weakness, raised
>   in power;
> ⁴⁴ sown a natural body, raised
>   a spiritual body.

If there is a natural body, there is also a spiritual body. ⁴⁵So it is written: **The first man Adam became a living being;**^J the last Adam became a life-giving Spirit. ⁴⁶However, the spiritual is not first, but the natural, then the spiritual.

> ⁴⁷ The first man was from the earth
>   and made of dust;
>   the second man is^K from heaven.
> ⁴⁸ Like the man made of dust,
>   so are those who are made of dust;
>   like the heavenly man,
>   so are those who are heavenly.

A15:14 Or proclamation is useless, and your faith also is useless, or proclamation is empty, and your faith also is empty   **B15:27** Ps 8:6
C15:29 Other mss read for the dead   **D15:32** Lit Ephesus according to man   **E15:32** Lit what to me the profit?   **F15:32** Is 22:13
G15:33 A quotation from the poet Menander, Thais, 218   **H15:34** Lit Sober up righteously   **I15:37** Lit but a naked seed   **J15:45** Gn 2:7
K15:47 Other mss add the Lord

⁴⁹ And just as we have borne
the image of the man made
of dust,
we will also bear
the image of the heavenly man.

⁵⁰ Brothers, I tell you this: Flesh and blood cannot inherit the kingdom of God, and corruption cannot inherit incorruption. ⁵¹ Listen! I am telling you a mystery:

We will not all fall asleep,
but we will all be changed,
⁵² in a moment, in the blink
of an eye,
at the last trumpet.
For the trumpet will sound,
and the dead will be
raised incorruptible,
and we will be changed.
⁵³ For this corruptible
must be clothed
with incorruptibility,
and this mortal must be clothed
with immortality,
⁵⁴ When this corruptible is clothed
with incorruptibility,
and this mortal is clothed
with immortality,
then the saying that is written
will take place:

**Death has been swallowed up
in victory.**ᴬ

⁵⁵ **Death, where is your victory?
Death, where is your sting?**ᴮ

⁵⁶ Now the sting of death is sin,
and the power of sin is the law.
⁵⁷ But thanks be to God, who gives us
the victory
through our Lord Jesus Christ!

⁵⁸ Therefore, my dear brothers, be steadfast, immovable, always excelling in the Lord's work, knowing that your labor in the Lord is not in vain.

16 Now about the collection for the saints: You should do the same as I instructed the Galatian churches. ² On the first day of the week,ᶜ each of you is to set some-

thing aside and save in keeping with how he prospers, so that no collections will need to be made when I come. ³ When I arrive, I will send with letters those you recommend to carry your gracious gift to Jerusalem. ⁴ If it is suitable for me to go as well, they can travel with me.

⁵ I will come to you after I pass through Macedonia—for I will be traveling through Macedonia— ⁶ and perhaps I will remain with you or even spend the winter, so that you may send me on my way wherever I go. ⁷ I don't want to see you now just in passing, for I hope to spend some time with you, if the Lord allows. ⁸ But I will stay in Ephesus until Pentecost, ⁹ because a wide door for effective ministry has opened for meᴰ—yet many oppose me. ¹⁰ If Timothy comes, see that he has nothing to fear from you, because he is doing the Lord's work, just as I am. ¹¹ Therefore, no one should look down on him. Send him on his way in peace so he can come to me, for I am expecting him with the brothers.ᴱ

¹² About our brother Apollos: I strongly urged him to come to you with the brothers, but he was not at all willing to come now. However, he will come when he has an opportunity.

¹³ Be alert, stand firm in the faith, act like a man, be strong. ¹⁴ Your every action must be done with love.

¹⁵ Brothers, you know the household of Stephanas: They are the firstfruits of Achaia and have devoted themselves to serving the saints. I urge you ¹⁶ also to submit to such people, and to everyone who works and labors with them. ¹⁷ I am pleased to have Stephanas, Fortunatus, and Achaicus present, because these men have made up for your absence. ¹⁸ For they have refreshed my spirit and yours. Therefore recognize such people.

¹⁹ The churches of Asia greet you. Aquila and Priscilla greet you warmly in the Lord, along with the church that meets in their home. ²⁰ All the brothers greet you. Greet one another with a holy kiss.

²¹ This greeting is in my own handᶠ —Paul. ²² If anyone does not love the Lord, a

---

ᴬ15:54 Is 25:8   ᴮ15:55 Hs 13:14   ᶜ16:2 Or Each Sunday   ᴰ16:9 Lit for a door has opened to me, great and effective   ᴱ16:11 With the brothers may connect with Paul or Timothy.   ᶠ16:21 Paul normally dictated his letters to a secretary, but signed the end of each letter himself; Rm 16:22; Gl 6:11; Col 4:18; 2Th 3:17.

curse be on him. *Marana tha* that is, Lord, come!^A ^23 The grace of the Lord Jesus be with you. ^24 My love be with all of you in Christ Jesus.

2 CORINTHIANS

1 Paul, an apostle of Christ Jesus by God's will, and Timothy our^B brother:

To God's church at Corinth, with all the saints who are throughout Achaia.

^2 Grace to you and peace from God our Father and the Lord Jesus Christ.

^3 Praise the God and Father of our Lord Jesus Christ, the Father of mercies and the God of all comfort. ^4 He comforts us in all our affliction,^C so that we may be able to comfort those who are in any kind of affliction, through the comfort we ourselves receive from God. ^5 For as the sufferings of Christ overflow to us, so through Christ our comfort also overflows. ^6 If we are afflicted, it is for your comfort and salvation. If we are comforted, it is for your comfort, which is experienced in your endurance of the same sufferings that we suffer. ^7 And our hope for you is firm, because we know that as you share in the sufferings, so you will share in the comfort.

^8 For we don't want you to be unaware, brothers, of our affliction that took place in Asia: we were completely overwhelmed—beyond our strength—so that we even despaired of life. ^9 Indeed, we personally had a death sentence within ourselves, so that we would not trust in ourselves but in God who raises the dead. ^10 He has delivered us from such a terrible death, and He will deliver us. We have put our hope in Him that He will deliver us again ^11 while you join in helping us by your prayers. Then many will give thanks on our^D behalf for the gift that came to us through the prayers of many.

^12 For this is our confidence: The testimony of our conscience is that we have conducted ourselves in the world, and especially toward you, with God-given sincerity and purity, not by fleshly^E wisdom but by God's grace. ^13 Now we are writing nothing to you other than what you can read and also understand. I hope you will understand completely— ^14 as you have partially understood us—that we are your reason for pride, as you are ours, in the day of our^F Lord Jesus.

^15 I planned with this confidence to come to you first, so you could have a double benefit,^G ^16 and to go on to Macedonia with your help, then come to you again from Macedonia and be given a start by you on my journey to Judea. ^17 So when I planned this, was I irresponsible? Or what I plan, do I plan in a purely human^H way so that I say "Yes, yes" and "No, no" simultaneously? ^18 As God is faithful, our message to you is not "Yes and no." ^19 For the Son of God, Jesus Christ, who was preached among you by us—by me and Silvanus^I and Timothy—did not become "Yes and no"; on the contrary, a final "Yes" has come in Him. ^20 For every one of God's promises is "Yes" in Him. Therefore, the "Amen" is also spoken through Him by us for God's glory. ^21 Now it is God who strengthens us, with you, in Christ and has anointed us. ^22 He has also sealed us and given us the Spirit as a down payment in our hearts.

^23 I call on God as a witness, on my life, that it was to spare you that I did not come to Corinth. ^24 I do not mean that we have control of^J your faith, but we are workers with you for your joy, because you stand by **2** faith. ^1 In fact, I made up my mind about this:^K I would not come to you on another painful visit.^L ^2 For if I cause you pain, then who will cheer me other than the one being hurt by me?^M ^3 I wrote this very thing to you that when I came I wouldn't have pain from those who ought to give me joy, because I am confident about all of you that my joy will also be

A 16:22 Or *Maran atha* (an Aram expression transliterated into Gk) = *Our Lord has come!*   B 1:1 Lit the   C 1:4 Or trouble, or tribulation, or trials, or oppression; the Gk word has a lit meaning of being under pressure.   D 1:11 Other mss read your   E 1:12 The word *fleshly* (characterized by flesh) indicates that the wisdom is natural rather than spiritual.   F 1:14 Other mss omit our   G 1:15 Other mss read a second joy   H 1:17 Or a worldly, or a fleshly, or a selfish   I 1:19 Or Silas; Ac 15:22-32; 16:19-40; 17:1-16   J 1:24 Or we lord it over, or we rule over   K 2:1 Lit I decided this for myself   L 2:1 Lit not again in sorrow to come to you   M 2:2 Lit the one pained yours. ⁴For I wrote to you with many tears out of an extremely troubled and anguished heart—not that you should be hurt, but that you should know the abundant love I have for you.

⁵If anyone has caused pain, he has caused pain not so much to me but to some degree—not to exaggerate—to all of you. ⁶The punishment inflicted by the majority is sufficient for that person. ⁷As a result, you should instead forgive and comfort him. Otherwise, this one may be overwhelmed by excessive grief. ⁸Therefore I urge you to reaffirm your love to him. ⁹I wrote for this purpose: to test your character to see if you are obedient in everything. ¹⁰If you forgive anyone, I do too. For what I have forgiven—if I have forgiven anything—it is for you in the presence of Christ. ¹¹I have done this so that we may not be taken advantage of by Satan. For we are not ignorant of his schemes.

¹²When I came to Troas to preach the gospel of Christ, the Lord opened a door for me. ¹³I had no rest in my spirit because I did not find my brother Titus, but I said good-bye to them and left for Macedonia.

¹⁴But thanks be to God, who always puts us on display^A in Christ^B and through us spreads the aroma of the knowledge of Him in every place. ¹⁵For to God we are the fragrance of Christ among those who are being saved and among those who are perishing. ¹⁶To some we are an aroma of death leading to death, but to others, an aroma of life leading to life. And who is competent for this? ¹⁷For we are not like the many^C who market God's message for profit. On the contrary, we speak with sincerity in Christ, as from God and before God.

3 Are we beginning to commend ourselves again? Or do we need, like some, letters of recommendation to you or from you? ²You yourselves are our letter, written on our hearts, recognized and read by everyone. ³It is clear that you are Christ's letter, produced^D by us, not written with ink but with the Spirit of the living God—not on stone tablets but on tablets that are hearts of flesh.

⁴We have this kind of confidence toward God through Christ. ⁵It is not that we are competent in^E ourselves to consider anything as coming from ourselves, but our competence is from God. ⁶He has made us competent to be ministers of a new covenant, not of the letter, but of the Spirit. For the letter kills, but the Spirit produces life.

⁷Now if the ministry of death, chiseled in letters on stones, came with glory, so that the Israelites were not able to look directly at Moses' face because of the glory from his face—a fading glory— ⁸how will the ministry of the Spirit not be more glorious? ⁹For if the ministry of condemnation had glory, the ministry of righteousness overflows with even more glory. ¹⁰In fact, what had been glorious is not glorious now by comparison because of the glory that surpasses it. ¹¹For if what was fading away was glorious, what endures will be even more glorious.

¹²Therefore, having such a hope, we use great boldness. ¹³We are not like Moses, who used to put a veil over his face so that the Israelites could not stare at the end of what was fading away, ¹⁴but their minds were closed.^F For to this day, at the reading of the old covenant, the same veil remains; it is not lifted, because it is set aside only in Christ. ¹⁵Even to this day, whenever Moses is read, a veil lies over their hearts, ¹⁶but whenever a person turns to the Lord, the veil is removed. ¹⁷Now the Lord is the Spirit, and where the Spirit of the Lord is, there is freedom. ¹⁸We all, with unveiled faces, are looking as in a mirror at^G the glory of the Lord and are being transformed into the same image from glory to glory;^H this is from the Lord who is the Spirit.^I

4 Therefore, since we have this ministry because we were shown mercy, we do not give up. ²Instead, we have renounced shameful secret things, not walking in deceit or distorting God's message, but commending ourselves to every person's conscience in God's sight by an open display of the truth. ³But if our gospel is veiled, it is veiled to those who are perishing. ⁴In their case, the god of

---

^A2:14 Or always leads us in a triumphal procession, or always causes us to triumph　^B2:14 Lit in the Christ, or in the Messiah; 1Co 15:22; Eph 1:10,12,20; 3:11　^C2:17 Other mss read the rest　^D3:3 Lit ministered to　^E3:5 Lit from　^F3:14 Lit their thoughts were hardened　^G3:18 Or are reflecting　^H3:18 Progressive glorification or sanctification　^I3:18 Or from the Spirit of the Lord, or from the Lord, the Spirit this age has blinded the minds of the unbelievers so they cannot see the light of the gospel of the glory of Christ,[A] who is the image of God. [5] For we are not proclaiming ourselves but Jesus Christ as Lord, and ourselves as your slaves because of Jesus. [6] For God who said, "Let light shine out of darkness," has shone in our hearts to give the light of the knowledge of God's glory in the face of Jesus Christ.

[7] Now we have this treasure in clay jars, so that this extraordinary power may be from God and not from us. [8] We are pressured in every way but not crushed; we are perplexed but not in despair; [9] we are persecuted but not abandoned; we are struck down but not destroyed. [10] We always carry the death of Jesus in our body, so that the life of Jesus may also be revealed in our body. [11] For we who live are always given over to death because of Jesus, so that Jesus' life may also be revealed in our mortal flesh. [12] So death works in us, but life in you. [13] And since we have the same spirit of faith in keeping with what is written, **I believed, therefore I spoke,**[B] we also believe, and therefore speak. [14] We know that the One who raised the Lord Jesus will raise us also with Jesus and present us with you. [15] Indeed, everything is for your benefit, so that grace, extended through more and more people, may cause thanksgiving to increase to God's glory.

[16] Therefore we do not give up. Even though our outer person is being destroyed, our inner person is being renewed day by day. [17] For our momentary light affliction[C] is producing for us an absolutely incomparable eternal weight of glory. [18] So we do not focus on what is seen, but on what is unseen. For what is seen is temporary, but what is unseen is eternal.

[5] For we know that if our temporary, earthly dwelling[D] is destroyed, we have a building from God, an eternal dwelling[E] in the heavens, not made with hands. [2] Indeed, we groan in this body, desiring to put on our dwelling from heaven, [3] since, when we are clothed,[F] we will not be found naked. [4] Indeed, we groan while we are in this tent, burdened as we are, because we do not want to be un-

clothed but clothed, so that mortality may be swallowed up by life. [5] And the One who prepared us for this very purpose is God, who gave us the Spirit as a down payment.

[6] So, we are always confident and know that while we are at home in the body we are away from the Lord. [7] For we walk by faith, not by sight, [8] and we are confident and satisfied to be out of the body and at home with the Lord. [9] Therefore, whether we are at home or away, we make it our aim to be pleasing to Him. [10] For we must all appear before the tribunal of Christ, so that each may be repaid for what he has done in the body, whether good or worthless.

[11] Therefore, because we know the fear of the Lord, we seek to persuade people. We are completely open before God, and I hope we are completely open to your consciences as well. [12] We are not commending ourselves to you again, but giving you an opportunity to be proud of us, so that you may have a reply for those who take pride in the outward appearance[G] rather than in the heart. [13] For if we are out of our mind, it is for God; if we have a sound mind, it is for you. [14] For Christ's love compels[H] us, since we have reached this conclusion: If One died for all, then all died. [15] And He died for all so that those who live should no longer live for themselves, but for the One who died for them and was raised.

[16] From now on, then, we do not know[I] anyone in a purely human way.[J] Even if we have known[K] Christ in a purely human way,[L] yet now we no longer know[I] Him in this way. [17] Therefore, if anyone is in Christ, he is a new creation; old things have passed away, and look, new things[M] have come. [18] Everything is from God, who reconciled us to Himself through Christ and gave us the ministry of reconciliation: [19] That is, in Christ, God was reconciling the world to Himself, not counting their trespasses against them, and He has committed the message of reconciliation to us. [20] Therefore, we are ambassadors for Christ, certain that God is appealing through us. We plead on Christ's behalf, "Be reconciled to God." [21] He made the One who did not

A 4:4 Or the gospel of the glorious Christ, or the glorious gospel of Christ   B 4:13 Ps 116:10 LXX   C 4:17 See note at 2Co 1:4.   D 5:1 = our present physical body   E 5:1 = our future body   F 5:3 Other mss read stripped   G 5:12 Lit in face   H 5:14 Or For the love of Christ impels, or For the love of Christ controls   I 5:16 Or regard   J 5:16 Lit anyone according to the flesh   K 5:16 Or have regarded   L 5:16 Lit Christ according to the flesh   M 5:17 Other mss read look, all new things know sin to be sin[A] for us, so that we might become the righteousness of God in Him.

6 Working together[B] with Him, we also appeal to you, "Don't receive God's grace in vain." [2]For He says:

> **I heard you in an acceptable time,**
> **and I helped you in the day**
> **of salvation.**[C]

Look, now is the acceptable time; now is the day of salvation.

[3]We give no opportunity for stumbling to anyone, so that the ministry will not be blamed. [4]But as God's ministers, we commend ourselves in everything:

> by great endurance, by afflictions,
> by hardship, by difficulties,
> [5] by beatings, by imprisonments,
> by riots, by labors,
> by sleepless nights, by times
> of hunger,
> [6] by purity, by knowledge,
> by patience, by kindness,
> by the Holy Spirit, by sincere love,
> [7] by the message of truth,
> by the power of God;
> through weapons of righteousness
> on the right hand and the left,
> [8] through glory and dishonor,
> through slander and good report;
> as deceivers yet true;
> [9] as unknown yet recognized;
> as dying and look—we live;
> as being disciplined yet not killed;
> [10] as grieving yet always rejoicing;
> as poor yet enriching many;
> as having nothing yet
> possessing everything.

[11]We have spoken openly[D] to you, Corinthians; our heart has been opened wide. [12]You are not limited by us, but you are limited by your own affections. [13]I speak as to my children. As a proper response, you should also be open to us.

[14]Do not be mismatched with unbelievers. For what partnership is there between righ-

teousness and lawlessness? Or what fellowship does light have with darkness? [15]What agreement does Christ have with Belial?[E] Or what does a believer have in common with an unbeliever? [16]And what agreement does God's sanctuary have with idols? For we[F] are the sanctuary of the living God, as God said:

> **I will dwell among them**
> **and walk among them,**
> **and I will be their God,**
> **and they will be My people.**[G]
> [17] **Therefore, come out from among them**
> **and be separate, says the Lord;**
> **do not touch any unclean thing,**
> **and I will welcome you.**[H]
> [18] **I will be a Father to you,**
> **and you will be sons and daughters**
> **to Me,**
> **says the Lord Almighty.**[I]

7 Therefore, dear friends, since we have such promises, let us cleanse ourselves from every impurity of the flesh and spirit, completing our sanctification[J] in the fear of God.

[2]Accept us.[K] We have wronged no one, corrupted no one, defrauded no one. [3]I don't say this to condemn you, for I have already said that you are in our hearts, to live together and to die together. [4]I have great confidence in you; I have great pride in you. I am filled with encouragement; I am overcome with joy in all our afflictions.

[5]In fact, when we came into Macedonia, we[L] had no rest. Instead, we were troubled in every way: conflicts on the outside, fears inside. [6]But God, who comforts the humble, comforted us by the arrival of Titus, [7]and not only by his arrival, but also by the comfort he received from you. He told us about your deep longing, your sorrow,[M] and your zeal for me, so that I rejoiced even more. [8]For even if I grieved you with my letter, I do not regret it—even though I did regret it since I saw that the letter grieved you, yet only for a little while. [9]Now I rejoice, not because you were grieved, but because your grief led

to repentance. For you were grieved as God willed, so that you didn't experience any loss from us. ¹⁰For godly grief produces a repentance not to be regretted and leading to salvation, but worldly grief produces death. ¹¹For consider how much diligence this very thing—this grieving as God wills—has produced in you: what a desire to clear yourselves, what indignation, what fear, what deep longing, what zeal, what justice! In every way you showed yourselves to be pure in this matter. ¹²So even though I wrote to you, it was not because of the one who did wrong, or because of the one who was wronged, but in order that your diligence for us might be made plain to you in the sight of God. ¹³For this reason we have been comforted.

In addition to our comfort, we rejoiced even more over the joy Titus had,ᴬ because his spirit was refreshed by all of you. ¹⁴For if I have made any boast to him about you, I have not been embarrassed; but as I have spoken everything to you in truth, so our boasting to Titus has also turned out to be the truth. ¹⁵And his affection toward you is even greater as he remembers the obedience of all of you, and how you received him with fear and trembling. ¹⁶I rejoice that I have complete confidence in you.

8 We want you to know, brothers, about the grace of God granted to the churches of Macedonia: ²During a severe testing by affliction, their abundance of joy and their deep poverty overflowed into the wealth of their generosity. ³I testify that, on their own, according to their ability and beyond their ability, ⁴they begged us insistently for the privilege of sharing in the ministry to the saints, ⁵and not just as we had hoped. Instead, they gave themselves especially to the Lord, then to us by God's will. ⁶So we urged Titus that just as he had begun, so he should also complete this grace to you. ⁷Now as you excel in everything—faith, speech, knowledge, and in all diligence, and in your love for usᴮ—excel also in this grace.

⁸I am not saying this as a command. Rather, by means of the diligence of others, I am testing the genuineness of your love. ⁹For

you know the grace of our Lord Jesus Christ: Though He was rich, for your sake He became poor, so that by His poverty you might become rich. ¹⁰Now I am giving an opinion on this because it is profitable for you, who a year ago began not only to do something but also to desire it.ᶜ ¹¹But now finish the taskᴰ as well, that just as there was eagerness to desire it, so there may also be a completion from what you have. ¹²For if the eagerness is there, it is acceptable according to what one has, not according to what he does not have. ¹³It is not that there may be relief for others and hardship for you, but it is a question of equalityᴱ— ¹⁴at the present time your surplus is available for their need, so their abundance may also become available for our need, so there may be equality. ¹⁵As it has been written:

> **The person who gathered much**
> **did not have too much,**
> **and the person who gathered little**
> **did not have too little.**ᶠ

¹⁶Thanks be to God who put the same concern for you into the heart of Titus. ¹⁷For he accepted our urging and, being very diligent, went out to you by his own choice. ¹⁸We have sent with him the brother who is praised throughout the churches for his gospel ministry.ᴳ ¹⁹And not only that, but he was also appointed by the churches to accompany us with this giftᴴ that is being administered by us for the glory of the Lord Himself and to show our eagerness to help. ²⁰We are taking this precaution so no one can criticize us about this large sum administered by us. ²¹For we are making provision for what is right, not only before the Lord but also before men. ²²We have also sent with them our brother. We have often tested him in many circumstances and found him to be diligent—and now even more diligent because of his great confidence in you. ²³As for Titus, he is my partner and coworker serving you; as for our brothers, they are the messengers of the churches, the glory of Christ. ²⁴Therefore, show them proof before the churches of your love and of our boasting about you.

ᴬ7:13 Lit the joy of Titus ᴮ8:7 Other mss read in our love for you ᶜ8:10 Lit to will ᴰ8:11 Lit finish the doing ᴱ8:13 Lit but from equality
ᶠ8:15 Ex 16:18 ᴳ8:18 Lit churches, in the gospel ᴴ8:19 or grace

9 Now concerning the ministry to the saints, it is unnecessary for me to write to you. ² For I know your eagerness, and I brag about you to the Macedonians:^A "Achaia^B has been prepared since last year," and your zeal has stirred up most of them. ³ But I sent the brothers so our boasting about you in the matter would not prove empty, and so you would be prepared just as I said. ⁴ For if any Macedonians come with me and find you unprepared, we, not to mention you, would be embarrassed in that situation.^C ⁵ Therefore I considered it necessary to urge the brothers to go on ahead to you and arrange in advance the generous gift you promised, so that it will be ready as a gift and not as an extortion.

⁶ Remember this:^D The person who sows sparingly will also reap sparingly, and the person who sows generously will also reap generously. ⁷ Each person should do as he has decided in his heart—not reluctantly or out of necessity, for God loves a cheerful giver. ⁸ And God is able to make every grace overflow to you, so that in every way, always having everything you need, you may excel in every good work. ⁹ As it is written:

> He scattered;
> He gave to the poor;
> **His righteousness endures forever.**^E

¹⁰ Now the One who provides seed for the sower and bread for food will provide and multiply your seed and increase the harvest of your righteousness. ¹¹ You will be enriched in every way for all generosity, which produces thanksgiving to God through us. ¹² For the ministry of this service is not only supplying the needs of the saints, but is also overflowing in many acts of thanksgiving to God. ¹³ They will glorify God for your obedience to the confession of^F the gospel of Christ, and for your generosity in sharing with them and with others through the proof provided by this service. ¹⁴ And they will have deep affection for^G you in their prayers on your behalf because of the surpassing grace of God in you. ¹⁵ Thanks be to God for His indescribable gift.

10 Now I, Paul, make a personal appeal to you by the gentleness and graciousness of Christ—I who am humble among you in person but bold toward you when absent. ² I beg you that when I am present I will not need to be bold with the confidence by which I plan to challenge certain people who think we are behaving in an unspiritual way.^H ³ For though we live in the body,^I we do not wage war in an unspiritual way,^J ⁴ since the weapons of our warfare are not worldly,^K but are powerful through God for the demolition of strongholds. We demolish arguments ⁵ and every high-minded thing that is raised up against the knowledge of God, taking every thought captive to obey Christ. ⁶ And we are ready to punish any disobedience, once your obedience has been confirmed.

⁷ Look at what is obvious.^L If anyone is confident that he belongs to Christ, he should remind himself of this: Just as he belongs to Christ, so do we. ⁸ For if I boast some more about our authority, which the Lord gave for building you up and not for tearing you down, I am not ashamed. ⁹ I don't want to seem as though I am trying to terrify you with my letters. ¹⁰ For it is said, "His letters are weighty and powerful, but his physical presence is weak, and his public speaking is despicable." ¹¹ Such a person should consider this: What we are in the words of our letters when absent, we will be in actions when present.

¹² For we don't dare classify or compare ourselves with some who commend themselves. But in measuring themselves by themselves and comparing themselves to themselves, they lack understanding. ¹³ We, however, will not boast beyond measure but according to the measure of the area of ministry that God has assigned to us, which reaches even to you. ¹⁴ For we are not overextending ourselves, as if we had not reached you, since we have come to you with the gospel of Christ. ¹⁵ We are not bragging beyond measure about other people's labors. But we have the hope that as your faith increases, our area of ministry will be greatly enlarged, ¹⁶ so that we may proclaim the good news to

---

^A 9:2 Macedonia was a Roman province in the northern area of modern Greece.   ^B 9:2 Achaia was the Roman province, south of Macedonia, where Corinth was located.   ^C 9:4 Or in this confidence   ^D 9:6 Lit And this   ^E 9:9 Ps 112:9   ^F 9:13 Or your obedient confession to   ^G 9:14 Or will long for   ^H 10:2 Or are living as a non-Christian; lit are walking according to flesh   ^I 10:3 Lit flesh   ^J 10:3 Lit war according to flesh   ^K 10:4 Lit fleshly   ^L 10:7 Or You are looking at things outwardly the regions beyond you, not boasting about what has already been done in someone else's area of ministry. [17] So **the one who boasts must boast in the Lord.**[A] [18] For it is not the one commending himself who is approved, but the one the Lord commends.

11 I wish you would put up with a little foolishness from me. Yes, do put up with me.[B] [2] For I am jealous over you with a godly jealousy, because I have promised you in marriage to one husband—to present a pure virgin to Christ. [3] But I fear that, as the serpent deceived Eve by his cunning, your minds may be seduced from a complete and pure[C] devotion to Christ. [4] For if a person comes and preaches another Jesus, whom we did not preach, or you receive a different spirit, which you had not received, or a different gospel, which you had not accepted, you put up with it splendidly!

[5] Now I consider myself in no way inferior to the "super-apostles." [6] Though untrained in public speaking, I am certainly not untrained in knowledge. Indeed, we have always made that clear to you in everything. [7] Or did I commit a sin by humbling myself so that you might be exalted, because I preached the gospel of God to you free of charge? [8] I robbed other churches by taking pay from them to minister to you. [9] When I was present with you and in need, I did not burden anyone, for the brothers who came from Macedonia supplied my needs. I have kept myself, and will keep myself, from burdening you in any way. [10] As the truth of Christ is in me, this boasting of mine will not be stopped[D] in the regions of Achaia. [11] Why? Because I don't love you? God knows I do!

[12] But I will continue to do what I am doing, in order to deny[E] the opportunity of those who want an opportunity to be regarded just as our equals in what they boast about. [13] For such people are false apostles, deceitful workers, disguising themselves as apostles of Christ. [14] And no wonder! For Satan disguises himself as an angel of light. [15] So it is no great thing if his servants also disguise themselves

as servants of righteousness. Their destiny[F] will be according to their works.

[16] I repeat: No one should consider me a fool. But if you do, at least accept me as a fool, so I too may boast a little. [17] What I say in this matter[G] of boasting, I don't speak as the Lord would, but foolishly. [18] Since many boast in an unspiritual way,[H] I will also boast. [19] For you, being so wise, gladly put up with fools! [20] In fact, you put up with it if someone enslaves you, if someone devours you, if someone captures you, if someone dominates you, or if someone hits you in the face. [21] I say this to our shame: We have been weak.

But in whatever anyone dares to boast—I am talking foolishly—I also dare:

[22] Are they Hebrews? So am I.
Are they Israelites? So am I.
Are they the seed of Abraham?
So am I.
[23] Are they servants of Christ?
I'm talking like a madman—
I'm a better one:
with far more labors,
many more imprisonments,
far worse beatings, near death[I]
many times.
[24] Five times I received 39 lashes
from Jews.
[25] Three times I was beaten with rods
by the Romans.
Once I was stoned by my enemies.[J]
Three times I was shipwrecked.
I have spent a night and a day
in the open sea.
[26] On frequent journeys, I faced
dangers from rivers,
dangers from robbers,
dangers from my own people,
dangers from the Gentiles,
dangers in the city,
dangers in the open country,
dangers on the sea,
and dangers among false brothers;
[27] labor and hardship,
many sleepless nights,
hunger and thirst,

---

often without food, cold,
and lacking clothing.

[28]Not to mention[A] other things, there is the daily pressure on me: my care for all the churches. [29]Who is weak, and I am not weak? Who is made to stumble, and I do not burn with indignation? [30]If boasting is necessary, I will boast about my weaknesses. [31]The God and Father of the Lord Jesus, who is praised forever, knows I am not lying. [32]In Damascus, the governor under King Aretas[B] guarded the city of the Damascenes in order to arrest me, [33]so I was let down in a basket through a window in the wall and escaped his hands.

12 Boasting is necessary. It is not profitable, but I will move on to visions and revelations of the Lord. [2]I know a man in Christ who was caught up into the third heaven 14 years ago. Whether he was in the body or out of the body, I don't know, God knows. [3]I know that this man—whether in the body or out of the body I don't know, God knows—[4]was caught up into paradise. He heard inexpressible words, which a man is not allowed to speak. [5]I will boast about this person, but not about myself, except of my weaknesses. [6]For if I want to boast, I will not be a fool, because I will be telling the truth. But I will spare you, so that no one can credit me with something beyond what he sees in me or hears from me, [7]especially because of the extraordinary revelations. Therefore, so that I would not exalt myself, a thorn in the flesh was given to me, a messenger[C] of Satan to torment me so I would not exalt myself. [8]Concerning this, I pleaded with the Lord three times to take it away from me. [9]But He said to me, "My grace is sufficient for you, for power[D] is perfected in weakness." Therefore, I will most gladly boast all the more about my weaknesses, so that Christ's power may reside in me. [10]So I take pleasure in weaknesses, insults, catastrophes, persecutions, and in pressures, because of Christ. For when I am weak, then I am strong.

[11]I have become a fool; you forced it on me. I should have been endorsed by you, since I am not in any way inferior to the "super-apostles," even though I am nothing. [12]The signs of an apostle were performed with great endurance among you—not only signs but also wonders and miracles. [13]So in what way were you treated worse than the other churches, except that I personally did not burden you? Forgive me this wrong!

[14]Now I am ready to come to you this third time. I will not burden you, for I am not seeking what is yours, but you. For children are not obligated to save up for their parents, but parents for their children. [15]I will most gladly spend and be spent for you.[E] If I love you more, am I to be loved less? [16]Now granted, I have not burdened you; yet sly as I am, I took you in by deceit! [17]Did I take advantage of you by anyone I sent you? [18]I urged Titus to come, and I sent the brother with him. Did Titus take advantage of you? Didn't we walk in the same spirit and in the same footsteps?

[19]You have thought all along that we were defending ourselves to you.[F] No, in the sight of God we are speaking in Christ, and everything, dear friends, is for building you up. [20]For I fear that perhaps when I come I will not find you to be what I want, and I may not be found by you to be what you want;[G] there may be quarreling, jealousy, outbursts of anger, selfish ambitions, slander, gossip, arrogance, and disorder. [21]I fear that when I come my God will again[H] humiliate me in your presence, and I will grieve for many who sinned before and have not repented of the moral impurity, sexual immorality, and promiscuity they practiced.

13 This is the third time I am coming to you. **Every fact must be established by the testimony[I] of two or three witnesses.**[J] [2]I gave a warning when I was present the second time, and now I give a warning while I am absent to those who sinned before and to all the rest: If I come again, I will not be lenient, [3]since you seek proof of Christ speaking in me. He is not weak toward you, but powerful among you. [4]In fact, He was crucified in weakness, but He lives by God's power. For we

A[11:28] Lit *Apart from*   B[11:32] Aretus IV (9 B.C.–A.D. 40), a Nabatean Arab king   C[12:7] Or *me, an angel*   D[12:9] Other mss read *My power*   E[12:15] Lit *for your souls, or for your lives*   F[12:19] Or *Have you thought . . . to you?*   G[12:20] Lit *be as you want*   H[12:21] Or *come again my God will*   I[13:1] Lit *mouth*   J[13:1] Dt 17:6; 19:15

also are weak in Him, yet toward you we will live with Him by God's power.

⁵ Test yourselves to see if you are in the faith. Examine yourselves. Or do you yourselves not recognize that Jesus Christ is in you?—unless you fail the test.ᴬ ⁶ And I hope you will recognize that we do not fail the test. ⁷ Now we pray to God that you do nothing wrong—not that we may appear to pass the test, but that you may do what is right, even though we may appear to fail. ⁸ For we are not able to do anything against the truth, but only for the truth. ⁹ In fact, we rejoice when we are weak and you are strong. We also pray

that you become fully mature.ᴮ ¹⁰ This is why I am writing these things while absent, that when I am there I will not use severity, in keeping with the authority the Lord gave me for building up and not for tearing down.

¹¹ Finally, brothers, rejoice. Become mature, be encouraged, be of the same mind, be at peace, and the God of love and peace will be with you. ¹² Greet one another with a holy kiss. All the saints greet you.

¹³ The grace of the Lord Jesus Christ, and the love of God, and the fellowship of the Holy Spirit be with all of you.ᶜ

GALATIANS

1 Paul, an apostle—not from men or by man, but by Jesus Christ and God the Father who raised Him from the dead— ² and all the brothers who are with me:

To the churches of Galatia.ᴰ

³ Grace to you and peace from God the Father and our Lordᴱ Jesus Christ, ⁴ who gave Himself for our sins to rescue us from this present evil age, according to the will of our God and Father. ⁵ To whom be the glory forever and ever. Amen.

⁶ I am amazed that you are so quickly turning away from Him who called you by the grace of Christ and are turning to a different gospel— ⁷ not that there is another gospel, but there are some who are troubling you and want to change the good newsᶠ about the Messiah. ⁸ But even if we or an angel from heaven should preach to you a gospel other than what we have preached to you, a curse be on him!ᴳ ⁹ As we have said before, I now say again: If anyone preaches to you a gospel contrary to what you received, a curse be on him!

¹⁰ For am I now trying to win the favor of people, or God? Or am I striving to please people? If I were still trying to please people, I would not be a slave of Christ.

¹¹ Now I want you to know, brothers, that the gospel preached by me is not based on human thought.ᴴ ¹² For I did not receive it from a human source and I was not taught it, but it came by a revelation from Jesus Christ.

¹³ For you have heard about my former way of life in Judaism: I persecuted God's church to an extreme degree and tried to destroy it. ¹⁴ I advanced in Judaism beyond many contemporaries among my people, because I was extremely zealous for the traditions of my ancestors. ¹⁵ But when God, who from my birth set me apart and called me by His grace, was pleased ¹⁶ to reveal His Son in me, so that I could preach Him among the Gentiles, I did not immediately consult with anyone.ᴵ ¹⁷ I did not go up to Jerusalem to those who had become apostles before me; instead I went to Arabia and came back to Damascus.

¹⁸ Then after three years I did go up to Jerusalem to get to know Cephas,ᴶ and I stayed with him 15 days. ¹⁹ But I didn't see any of the other apostles except James, the Lord's brother. ²⁰ Now I am not lying in what I write to you. God is my witness.ᴷ

²¹ Afterward, I went to the regions of Syria and Cilicia. ²² I remained personally unknown to the Judean churches in Christ; ²³ they simply kept hearing: "He who for-

ᴬ13:5 Or you are disqualified, or you are counterfeit ᴮ13:9 Or become complete, or be restored ᶜ13:12-13 Some translations divide these 2 vv. into 3 vv. so that v. 13 begins with All the saints . . . and v. 14 begins with The grace of . . . ᴰ1:2 A Roman province in what is now Turkey ᴱ1:3 Other mss read God our Father and the Lord ᶠ1:7 Or gospel ᴳ1:8 Or you, let him be condemned, or you, let him be condemned to hell; Gk anathema ᴴ1:11 Lit not according to man ᴵ1:16 Lit flesh and blood ᴶ1:18 Other mss read Peter ᴷ1:20 Lit Behold, before God merly persecuted us now preaches the faith he once tried to destroy." ²⁴ And they glorified God because of me.

2 Then after 14 years I went up again to Jerusalem with Barnabas, taking Titus along also. ² I went up according to a revelation and presented to them the gospel I preach among the Gentiles—but privately to those recognized as leaders—so that I might not be running, or have run the race, in vain. ³ But not even Titus who was with me, though he was a Greek, was compelled to be circumcised. ⁴ This issue arose because of false brothers smuggled in, who came in secretly to spy on the freedom that we have in Christ Jesus, in order to enslave us. ⁵ But we did not give up and submit to these people for even an hour, so that the truth of the gospel would be preserved for you.

⁶ Now from those recognized as important (what they really were makes no difference to me; God does not show favoritismᴬ)—they added nothing to me. ⁷ On the contrary, they saw that I had been entrusted with the gospel for the uncircumcised, just as Peter was for the circumcised, ⁸ since the One at work in Peter for an apostleship to the circumcised was also at work in me for the Gentiles. ⁹ When James, Cephas, and John, recognized as pillars, acknowledged the grace that had been given to me, they gave the right hand of fellowship to me and Barnabas, agreeing that we should go to the Gentiles and they to the circumcised. ¹⁰ They asked only that we would remember the poor, which I made every effort to do.

¹¹ But when Cephasᴮ came to Antioch, I opposed him to his face because he stood condemned.ᶜ ¹² For he regularly ate with the Gentiles before certain men came from James. However, when they came, he withdrew and separated himself, because he feared those from the circumcision party. ¹³ Then the rest of the Jews joined his hypocrisy, so that even Barnabas was carried away

by their hypocrisy. ¹⁴ But when I saw that they were deviating from the truth of the gospel, I told Cephasᴮ in front of everyone, "If you, who are a Jew, live like a Gentile and not like a Jew, how can you compel Gentiles to live like Jews?"ᴰ

¹⁵ We who are Jews by birth and not "Gentile sinners" ¹⁶ know that no one is justified by the works of the law but by faith in Jesus Christ.ᴱ And we have believed in Christ Jesus so that we might be justified by faith in Christᶠ and not by the works of the law, because by the works of the law no human being willᴳ be justified. ¹⁷ But if we ourselves are also found to be "sinners" while seeking to be justified by Christ, is Christ then a promoterᴴ of sin? Absolutely not! ¹⁸ If I rebuild the systemᴵ I tore down, I show myself to be a lawbreaker. ¹⁹ For through the law I have died to the law, so that I might live for God. I have been crucified with Christ ᴶ ²⁰ and I no longer live, but Christ lives in me. The life I now live in the body,ᴷ I live by faith in the Son of God, who loved me and gave Himself for me. ²¹ I do not set aside the grace of God, for if righteousness comes through the law, then Christ died for nothing.

3 You foolish Galatians! Who has hypnotized you,ᴸ before whose eyes Jesus Christ was vividly portrayedᴹ as crucified? ² I only want to learn this from you: Did you receive the Spirit by the works of the law or by hearing with faith?ᴺ ³ Are you so foolish? After beginning with the Spirit, are you now going to be made complete by the flesh?ᴼ ⁴ Did you suffer so much for nothing—if in fact it was for nothing? ⁵ So then, does God supply you with the Spirit and work miracles among you by the works of the law or by hearing with faith?ᴺ

⁶ Just as Abraham **believed God, and it was credited to him for righteousness,**ᴾ ⁷ then understand that those who have faith are Abraham's sons. ⁸ Now the Scripture saw in

ᴬ2:6 Or God is not a respecter of persons; lit God does not receive the face of man   ᴮ2:11,14 Other mss read Peter   ᶜ2:11 Or he was in the wrong   ᴰ2:14 Some translations continue the quotation through v. 16 or v. 21.   ᴱ2:16 Or by the faithfulness of Jesus Christ   ᶠ2:16 Or by the faithfulness of Christ   ᴳ2:16 Lit law all flesh will not   ᴴ2:17 Or servant   ᴵ2:18 Lit rebuild those things that   ᴶ2:19 Other textual traditions place I have been crucified with Christ in v. 20.   ᴷ2:20 Or flesh   ᴸ3:1 Other mss add not to obey the truth   ᴹ3:1 Other mss add among you   ᴺ3:2,5 Lit by law works or faith hearing or hearing the message   ᴼ3:3 By human effort   ᴾ3:6 Gn 15:6

advance that God would justify the Gentiles by faith and told the good news ahead of time to Abraham, saying, **All the nations will be blessed through you.**[A] ⁹ So those who have faith are blessed with Abraham, who had faith.[B]

¹⁰ For all who rely on the works of the law are under a curse, because it is written: **Everyone who does not continue doing everything written in the book of the law is cursed.**[C] ¹¹ Now it is clear that no one is justified before God by the law, because the **righteous will live by faith.**[D] ¹² But the law is not based on faith; instead, **the one who does these things will live by them.**[E] ¹³ Christ has redeemed us from the curse of the law by becoming a curse for us, because it is written: **Everyone who is hung on a tree is cursed.**[F] ¹⁴ The purpose was that the blessing of Abraham would come to the Gentiles by Christ Jesus, so that we could receive the promised Spirit through faith.

¹⁵ Brothers, I'm using a human illustration.[G] No one sets aside or makes additions to even a human covenant[H] that has been ratified. ¹⁶ Now the promises were spoken to Abraham and to his seed. He does not say "and to seeds," as though referring to many, but referring to one, **and to your seed,**[I] who is Christ. ¹⁷ And I say this: The law, which came 430 years later, does not revoke a covenant that was previously ratified by God[J] and cancel the promise. ¹⁸ For if the inheritance is from the law, it is no longer from the promise; but God granted it to Abraham through the promise.

¹⁹ Why then was the law given? It was added because of transgressions until the Seed to whom the promise was made would come. The law was put into effect through angels by means of a mediator. ²⁰ Now a mediator is not for just one person, but God is one. ²¹ Is the law therefore contrary to God's promises? Absolutely not! For if a law had been given that was able to give life, then righteousness would certainly be by the law.

²² But the Scripture has imprisoned everything under sin's power,[K] so that the promise by faith in Jesus Christ might be given to those who believe. ²³ Before this faith came, we were confined under the law, imprisoned until the coming faith was revealed. ²⁴ The law, then, was our guardian[L] until Christ, so that we could be justified by faith. ²⁵ But since that faith has come, we are no longer under a guardian, ²⁶ for you are all sons of God through faith in Christ Jesus.

²⁷ For as many of you as have been baptized into Christ have put on Christ like a garment. ²⁸ There is no Jew or Greek, slave or free, male or female; for you are all one in Christ Jesus. ²⁹ And if you belong to Christ, then you are Abraham's seed, heirs according to the promise. ¹ Now I say that as long as the heir is a child, he differs in no way from a slave, though he is the owner of everything. ² Instead, he is under guardians and stewards until the time set by his father. ³ In the same way we also, when we were children, were in slavery under the elemental forces[M] of the world. ⁴ When the time came to completion, God sent His Son, born of a woman, born under the law, ⁵ to redeem those under the law, so that we might receive adoption as sons. ⁶ And because you are sons, God has sent the Spirit of His Son into our[N] hearts, crying, *"Abba,* Father!" ⁷ So you are no longer a slave but a son, and if a son, then an heir through God.

⁸ But in the past, when you didn't know God, you were enslaved to things[O] that by nature are not gods. ⁹ But now, since you know God, or rather have become known by God, how can you turn back again to the weak and bankrupt elemental forces? Do you want to be enslaved to them all over again? ¹⁰ You observe special days, months, seasons, and years. ¹¹ I am fearful for you, that perhaps my labor for you has been wasted.

¹² I beg you, brothers: Become like me, for I also became like you. You have not wronged

---

A3:8 Gn 12:3; 18:18   **B**3:9 Or *with believing Abraham*   **C**3:10 Dt 27:26   **D**3:11 Hab 2:4   **E**3:12 Lv 18:5   **F**3:13 Dt 21:23   **G**3:15 Lit *I speak according to man*   **H**3:15 Or *will, or testament*   **I**3:16 Gn 12:7; 13:15; 17:8; 24:7   **J**3:17 Other mss add *in Christ*   **K**3:22 Lit *under sin*   **L**3:24 The word translated *guardian* in vv. 24-25 is different from the word in Gl 4:2. In our culture, we do not have a slave who takes a child to and from school, protecting the child from harm or corruption. In Gk the word *paidogogos* described such a slave. This slave was not a teacher.   **M**4:3 Or *spirits, or principles*   **N**4:6 Other mss read *your*   **O**4:8 Or *beings* me; [13] you know that previously I preached the gospel to you because of a physical illness. [14] You did not despise or reject me though my physical condition was a trial for you.[A] On the contrary, you received me as an angel of God, as Christ Jesus Himself.

[15] What happened to this sense of being blessed you had? For I testify to you that, if possible, you would have torn out your eyes and given them to me. [16] Have I now become your enemy by telling you the truth? [17] They[B] are enthusiastic about you, but not for any good. Instead, they want to isolate you so you will be enthusiastic about them. [18] Now it is always good to be enthusiastic about good—and not just when I am with you. [19] My children, I am again suffering labor pains for you until Christ is formed in you. [20] I would like to be with you right now and change my tone of voice, because I don't know what to do about you.

[21] Tell me, those of you who want to be under the law, don't you hear the law? [22] For it is written that Abraham had two sons, one by a slave and the other by a free woman. [23] But the one by the slave was born according to the impulse of the flesh, while the one by the free woman was born as the result of a promise. [24] These things are illustrations,[C] for the women represent the two covenants. One is from Mount Sinai and bears children into slavery—this is Hagar. [25] Now Hagar is Mount Sinai in Arabia and corresponds to the present Jerusalem, for she is in slavery with her children. [26] But the Jerusalem above is free, and she is our mother. [27] For it is written:

> Rejoice, childless woman,
> who does not give birth.
> Burst into song and shout,
> you who are not in labor,
> for the children of the desolate
>   are many,
> more numerous than those
>   of the woman who has
>   a husband.[D]

[28] Now you, brothers, like Isaac, are children of promise. [29] But just as then the child born according to the flesh persecuted the one born according to the Spirit, so also now. [30] But what does the Scripture say?

> Drive out the slave and her son, for the
> son of the slave will never be a coheir
> with the son of the free woman.[E]

[31] Therefore, brothers, we are not children of the slave but of the free woman.

5 Christ has liberated us to be free. Stand firm then and don't submit again to a yoke of slavery. [2] Take note! I, Paul, tell you that if you get yourselves circumcised, Christ will not benefit you at all. [3] Again I testify to every man who gets himself circumcised that he is obligated to keep the entire law. [4] You who are trying to be justified by the law are alienated from Christ; you have fallen from grace. [5] For through the Spirit, by faith, we eagerly wait for the hope of righteousness. [6] For in Christ Jesus neither circumcision nor uncircumcision accomplishes anything; what matters is faith working through love.

[7] You were running well. Who prevented you from obeying the truth? [8] This persuasion did not come from the One who called you. [9] A little yeast leavens the whole lump of dough. [10] I have confidence in the Lord you will not accept any other view. But whoever it is that is confusing you will pay the penalty. [11] Now brothers, if I still preach circumcision, why am I still persecuted? In that case the offense of the cross has been abolished. [12] I wish those who are disturbing you might also get themselves castrated!

[13] For you were called to be free, brothers; only don't use this freedom as an opportunity for the flesh, but serve one another through love. [14] For the entire law is fulfilled in one statement: **Love your neighbor as yourself.**[F] [15] But if you bite and devour one another, watch out, or you will be consumed by one another.

[16] I say then, walk by the Spirit and you will not carry out the desire of the flesh. [17] For the flesh desires what is against the Spirit, and

the Spirit desires what is against the flesh; these are opposed to each other, so that you don't do what you want. [18] But if you are led by the Spirit, you are not under the law.

[19] Now the works of the flesh are obvious:[A, B] sexual immorality, moral impurity, promiscuity, [20] idolatry, sorcery, hatreds, strife, jealousy, outbursts of anger, selfish ambitions, dissensions, factions, [21] envy,[C] drunkenness, carousing, and anything similar. I tell you about these things in advance—as I told you before—that those who practice such things will not inherit the kingdom of God.

[22] But the fruit of the Spirit is love, joy, peace, patience, kindness, goodness, faith,[D] [23] gentleness, self-control. Against such things there is no law. [24] Now those who belong to Christ Jesus have crucified the flesh with its passions and desires. [25] Since we live by the Spirit, we must also follow the Spirit. [26] We must not become conceited, provoking one another, envying one another.

6 Brothers, if someone is caught in any wrongdoing, you who are spiritual should restore such a person with a gentle spirit, watching out for yourselves so you also won't be tempted. [2] Carry one another's burdens; in this way you will fulfill the law of Christ. [3] For if anyone considers himself to be something when he is nothing, he deceives himself. [4] But each person should examine his own work, and then he will have a reason for boasting in himself alone, and not in respect to someone else. [5] For each person will have to carry his own load.

[6] The one who is taught the message must share all his good things with the teacher. [7] Don't be deceived: God is not mocked. For whatever a man sows he will also reap, [8] because the one who sows to his flesh will reap corruption from the flesh, but the one who sows to the Spirit will reap eternal life from the Spirit. [9] So we must not get tired of doing good, for we will reap at the proper time if we don't give up. [10] Therefore, as we have opportunity, we must work for the good of all, especially for those who belong to the household of faith.

[11] Look at what large letters I use as I write to you in my own handwriting. [12] Those who want to make a good impression in the flesh are the ones who would compel you to be circumcised—but only to avoid being persecuted for the cross of Christ. [13] For even the circumcised don't keep the law themselves; however, they want you to be circumcised in order to boast about your flesh. [14] But as for me, I will never boast about anything except the cross of our Lord Jesus Christ. The world has been crucified to me through the cross, and I to the world. [15] For[E] both circumcision and uncircumcision mean nothing; what matters instead is a new creation. [16] May peace come to all those who follow this standard, and mercy to the Israel of God!

[17] From now on, let no one cause me trouble, because I bear on my body scars for the cause of Jesus. [18] Brothers, the grace of our Lord Jesus Christ be with your spirit. Amen.

EPHESIANS

1 Paul, an apostle of Christ Jesus by God's will:

To the faithful saints in Christ Jesus at Ephesus.[F]

[2] Grace to you and peace from God our Father and the Lord Jesus Christ.

[3] Praise the God and Father of our Lord Jesus Christ, who has blessed us in Christ with every spiritual blessing in the heavens. [4] For He chose us in Him, before the foundation of the world, to be holy and blameless in His sight.[G] In love[H] [5] He predestined us to be adopted through Jesus Christ for Himself, according to His favor and will, [6] to the praise of His glorious grace that He favored us with in the Beloved.

A5:19 Other mss add *adultery*   B5:19 Lit *obvious, which are*:   C5:21 Other mss add *murders*   D5:22 Or *faithfulness*   E6:15 Other mss add *in Christ Jesus*   F1:1 Other mss omit *at Ephesus*   G1:4 Vv. 3-14 are 1 sentence in Gk.   H1:4 Or *In His sight in love*

⁷We have redemption in Him through His blood, the forgiveness of our trespasses, according to the riches of His grace ⁸that He lavished on us with all wisdom and understanding. ⁹He made known to us the mystery of His will, according to His good pleasure that He planned in Him ¹⁰for the administration^A of the days of fulfillment^B—to bring everything together in the Messiah, both things in heaven and things on earth in Him.

¹¹We have also received an inheritance^C in Him, predestined according to the purpose of the One who works out everything in agreement with the decision of His will, ¹²so that we who had already put our hope in the Messiah might bring praise to His glory.

¹³When you heard the message of truth, the gospel of your salvation, and when you believed in Him, you were also sealed with the promised Holy Spirit. ¹⁴He is the down payment of our inheritance, for the redemption of the possession,^D to the praise of His glory.

¹⁵This is why, since I heard about your faith in the Lord Jesus and your love for all the saints, ¹⁶I never stop giving thanks for you as I remember you in my prayers. ¹⁷I pray that the God of our Lord Jesus Christ, the glorious Father,^E would give you a spirit^F of wisdom and revelation in the knowledge of Him. ¹⁸I pray that the perception of your mind^G may be enlightened so you may know what is the hope of His calling, what are the glorious riches of His inheritance among the saints, ¹⁹and what is the immeasurable greatness of His power to us who believe, according to the working of His vast strength.

²⁰He demonstrated this power in the Messiah by raising Him from the dead and seating Him at His right hand in the heavens— ²¹far above every ruler and authority, power and dominion, and every title given,^H not only in this age but also in the one to come. ²²And **He put everything under His feet**^I and appointed Him as head over everything for the church, ²³which is His body, the fullness of the One who fills all things in every way.

2 And you were dead in your trespasses and sins ²in which you previously walked according to the ways of this world, according to the ruler who exercises authority over the lower heavens,^J the spirit now working in the disobedient.^K ³We too all previously lived among them in our fleshly desires, carrying out the inclinations of our flesh and thoughts, and we were by nature children under wrath as the others were also. ⁴But God, who is rich in mercy, because of His great love that He had for us,^L ⁵made us alive with the Messiah even though we were dead in trespasses. You are saved by grace! ⁶Together with Christ Jesus He also raised us up and seated us in the heavens, ⁷so that in the coming ages He might display the immeasurable riches of His grace through His kindness to us in Christ Jesus. ⁸For you are saved by grace through faith, and this is not from yourselves; it is God's gift— ⁹not from works, so that no one can boast. ¹⁰For we are His creation, created in Christ Jesus for good works, which God prepared ahead of time so that we should walk in them.

¹¹So then, remember that at one time you were Gentiles in the flesh—called "the uncircumcised" by those called "the circumcised," which is done in the flesh by human hands. ¹²At that time you were without the Messiah, excluded from the citizenship of Israel, and foreigners to the covenants of the promise, without hope and without God in the world. ¹³But now in Christ Jesus, you who were far away have been brought near by the blood of the Messiah. ¹⁴For He is our peace, who made both groups one and tore down the dividing wall of hostility. In His flesh, ¹⁵He made of no effect the law consisting of commands and expressed in regulations, so that He might create in Himself one new man from the two, resulting in peace. ¹⁶He did this so that He might reconcile both to God in one body through the cross and put the hostility to death by it.^M ¹⁷When the Messiah came, He proclaimed the good news of peace to you who were far away and peace to those who were near. ¹⁸For through Him we

---

^A1:10 Or dispensation; lit house law (Gk oikonomia)   ^B1:10 Lit the fulfillment of times   ^C1:11 Or we also were chosen as an inheritance, or we were also made an inheritance   ^D1:14 The possession could be either man's or God's   ^E1:17 Or the Father of glory   ^F1:17 Or you the Spirit   ^G1:18 Lit the eyes of your heart   ^H1:21 Lit every name named   ^I1:22 Ps 8:6   ^J2:2 Lit ruler of the domain of the air   ^K2:2 Lit sons of disobedience   ^L2:4 Lit love with which He loved us   ^M2:16 Or death in Himself both have access by one Spirit to the Father. ¹⁹ So then you are no longer foreigners and strangers, but fellow citizens with the saints, and members of God's household, ²⁰ built on the foundation of the apostles and prophets, with Christ Jesus Himself as the cornerstone. ²¹ The whole building, being put together by Him, grows into a holy sanctuary in the Lord. ²² You also are being built together for God's dwelling in the Spirit.

3 For this reason, I, Paul, the prisoner of Christ Jesus on behalf of you Gentiles— ² you have heard, haven't you, about the administration of God's grace that He gave to me for you? ³ The mystery was made known to me by revelation, as I have briefly written above. ⁴ By reading this you are able to understand my insight about the mystery of the Messiah. ⁵ This was not made known to people[A] in other generations as it is now revealed to His holy apostles and prophets by the Spirit: ⁶ The Gentiles are coheirs, members of the same body, and partners of the promise in Christ Jesus through the gospel. ⁷ I was made a servant of this gospel by the gift of God's grace that was given to me by the working of His power.

⁸ This grace was given to me—the least of all the saints—to proclaim to the Gentiles the incalculable riches of the Messiah, ⁹ and to shed light for all about the administration of the mystery hidden for ages in God who created all things. ¹⁰ This is so God's multi-faceted wisdom may now be made known through the church to the rulers and authorities in the heavens. ¹¹ This is according to His eternal purpose accomplished in the Messiah, Jesus our Lord. ¹² In Him we have boldness and confident access through faith in Him.[B] ¹³ So then I ask you not to be discouraged over my afflictions on your behalf, for they are your glory.

¹⁴ For this reason I kneel before the Father[C] ¹⁵ from whom every family in heaven and on earth is named. ¹⁶ I pray that He may grant you, according to the riches of His glory, to be strengthened with power in the inner man through His Spirit, ¹⁷ and that the Messiah may dwell in your hearts through faith. I pray

that you, being rooted and firmly established in love, ¹⁸ may be able to comprehend with all the saints what is the length and width, height and depth of God's love, ¹⁹ and to know the Messiah's love that surpasses knowledge, so you may be filled with all the fullness of God.

²⁰ Now to Him who is able to do above and beyond all that we ask or think according to the power that works in us— ²¹ to Him be glory in the church and in Christ Jesus to all generations, forever and ever. Amen.

4 Therefore I, the prisoner for the Lord, urge you to walk worthy of the calling you have received, ² with all humility and gentleness, with patience, accepting[D] one another in love, ³ diligently keeping the unity of the Spirit with the peace that binds us. ⁴ There is one body and one Spirit—just as you were called to one hope[E] at your calling— ⁵ one Lord, one faith, one baptism, ⁶ one God and Father of all, who is above all and through all and in all.

⁷ Now grace was given to each one of us according to the measure of the Messiah's gift. ⁸ For it says:

> When He ascended on high,
> He took prisoners into captivity;[F]
> He gave gifts to people.[G]

⁹ But what does "He ascended" mean except that He[H] descended to the lower parts of the earth?[I] ¹⁰ The One who descended is also the One who ascended far above all the heavens, that He might fill[J] all things. ¹¹ And He personally gave some to be apostles, some prophets, some evangelists, some pastors and teachers, ¹² for the training of the saints in the work of ministry, to build up the body of Christ, ¹³ until we all reach unity in the faith and in the knowledge of God's Son, growing into a mature man with a stature measured by Christ's fullness. ¹⁴ Then we will no longer be little children, tossed by the waves and blown around by every wind of teaching, by human cunning with cleverness in the techniques of deceit. ¹⁵ But speaking the truth in love, let us grow in every way into Him who is the head—Christ. ¹⁶ From Him the whole

---

[A] 3:5 Lit to the sons of men [B] 3:12 Or through His faithfulness [C] 3:14 Other mss add of our Lord Jesus Christ [D] 4:2 Or tolerating [E] 4:4 Lit called in one hope [F] 4:8 Or He led the captives [G] 4:8 Ps 68:18 [H] 4:9 Other mss add first [I] 4:9 Or the lower parts, namely, the earth [J] 4:10 Or fulfill; Eph 1:23

body, fitted and knit together by every supporting ligament, promotes the growth of the body for building up itself in love by the proper working of each individual part.

¹⁷Therefore, I say this and testify in the Lord: You should no longer walk as the Gentiles walk, in the futility of their thoughts. ¹⁸They are darkened in their understanding, excluded from the life of God, because of the ignorance that is in them and because of the hardness of their hearts. ¹⁹They became callous and gave themselves over to promiscuity for the practice of every kind of impurity with a desire for more and more.ᴬ

²⁰But that is not how you learned about the Messiah, ²¹assuming you heard about Him and were taught by Him, because the truth is in Jesus. ²²You took offᴮ your former way of life, the old selfᶜ that is corrupted by deceitful desires; ²³you are being renewedᴰ in the spirit of your minds; ²⁴you put onᴱ the new self, the one created according to God's likeness in righteousness and purity of the truth.

²⁵Since you put away lying, **Speak the truth, each one to his neighbor,**ᶠ because we are members of one another. ²⁶**Be angry and do not sin.**ᴳ Don't let the sun go down on your anger, ²⁷and don't give the Devil an opportunity. ²⁸The thief must no longer steal. Instead, he must do honest work with his own hands, so that he has something to share with anyone in need. ²⁹No foul language is to come from your mouth, but only what is good for building up someone in need,ᴴ so that it gives grace to those who hear. ³⁰And don't grieve God's Holy Spirit. You were sealed by Himᴵ for the day of redemption. ³¹All bitterness, anger and wrath, shouting and slander must be removed from you, along with all malice. ³²And be kind and compassionate to one another, forgiving one another, just as God also forgave youᴶ in Christ.

5 Therefore, be imitators of God, as dearly loved children. ²And walk in love, as the Messiah also loved us and gave Himself for us, a sacrificial and fragrant offering to God. ³But sexual immorality and any impurity or greed

should not even be heard ofᴷ among you, as is proper for saints. ⁴Coarse and foolish talking or crude joking are not suitable, but rather giving thanks. ⁵For know and recognize this: Every sexually immoral or impure or greedy person, who is an idolater, does not have an inheritance in the kingdom of the Messiah and of God.

⁶Let no one deceive you with empty arguments, for God's wrath is coming on the disobedientᴸ because of these things. ⁷Therefore, do not become their partners. ⁸For you were once darkness, but now you are light in the Lord. Walk as children of light— ⁹for the fruit of the lightᴹ results in all goodness, righteousness, and truth— ¹⁰discerning what is pleasing to the Lord. ¹¹Don't participate in the fruitless works of darkness, but instead expose them. ¹²For it is shameful even to mention what is done by them in secret. ¹³Everything exposed by the light is made clear, ¹⁴for what makes everything clear is light. Therefore it is said:

> Get up, sleeper, and rise up
>   from the dead,
>   and the Messiah will shine on you.ᴺ

¹⁵Pay careful attention, then, to how you walk—not as unwise people but as wise— ¹⁶making the most of the time,ᴼ because the days are evil. ¹⁷So don't be foolish, but understand what the Lord's will is. ¹⁸And don't get drunk with wine, which leads to reckless actions, but be filled by the Spirit:

> ¹⁹ speaking to one another
>   in psalms, hymns, and spiritual songs,
>   singing and making music
>   from your heart to the Lord,
> ²⁰ giving thanks always for everything
>   to God the Father
>   in the name of our Lord Jesus Christ,
> ²¹ submitting to one another
>   in the fear of Christ.

²²Wives, submitᴾ to your own husbands as to the Lord, ²³for the husband is the head of

---

ᴬ4:19 Lit with greediness   ᴮ4:21-22 Or Jesus. This means: take off (as a command)   ᶜ4:22 Lit man; = a person before conversion   ᴰ4:22-23 Or desires; renew (as a command)   ᴱ4:23-24 Or minds; and put on (as a command)   ᶠ4:25 Zch 8:16   ᴳ4:26 Ps 4:4   ᴴ4:29 Lit for the building up of the need   ᴵ4:30 Or Spirit, by whom you were sealed   ᴶ4:32 Other mss read us   ᴷ5:3 Or be named   ᴸ5:6 Lit sons of disobedience   ᴹ5:9 Other mss read fruit of the Spirit   ᴺ5:14 This poem may have been an early Christian hymn based on several passages in Isaiah; Is 9:2; 26:19; 40:1; 51:17; 52:1; 60:1.   ᴼ5:16 Lit buying back the time   ᴾ5:22 Other mss omit submit the wife as Christ is the head of the church. He is the Savior of the body. ²⁴Now as the church submits to Christ, so wives are to submit to their husbands in everything. ²⁵Husbands, love your wives, just as Christ loved the church and gave Himself for her ²⁶to make her holy, cleansing^A her with the washing of water by the word. ²⁷He did this to present the church to Himself in splendor, without spot or wrinkle or anything like that, but holy and blameless. ²⁸In the same way, husbands are to love their wives as their own bodies. He who loves his wife loves himself. ²⁹For no one ever hates his own flesh but provides and cares for it, just as Christ does for the church, ³⁰since we are members of His body.^B

> ³¹ **For this reason a man will leave**
> **his father and mother**
> **and be joined to his wife,**
> **and the two will become one flesh.**^C

³²This mystery is profound, but I am talking about Christ and the church. ³³To sum up, each one of you is to love his wife as himself, and the wife is to respect her husband.

6 Children, obey your parents as you would the Lord,^D because this is right. ²**Honor your father and mother,** which is the first commandment^E with a promise, ³**so that it may go well with you and that you may have a long life in the land.**^F,G ⁴Fathers, don't stir up anger in your children, but bring them up in the training and instruction of the Lord.

⁵Slaves, obey your human^H masters with fear and trembling, in the sincerity of your heart, as to Christ. ⁶Don't work only while being watched, in order to please men, but as slaves of Christ, so God's will from your heart.^I ⁷Serve with a good attitude, as to the Lord and not to men, ⁸knowing that whatever good each one does, slave or free, he will receive this back from the Lord. ⁹And masters, treat your slaves the same way, without threatening them, because you know that both their Master and yours is in heaven, and there is no favoritism with Him.

¹⁰Finally, be strengthened by the Lord and by His vast strength. ¹¹Put on the full armor of God so that you can stand against the tactics^J of the Devil. ¹²For our battle is not against flesh and blood, but against the rulers, against the authorities, against the world powers of this darkness, against the spiritual forces of evil in the heavens. ¹³This is why you must take up the full armor of God, so that you may be able to resist in the evil day, and having prepared everything, to take your stand. ¹⁴Stand, therefore,

> with truth like a belt
>   around your waist,
> righteousness like armor
>   on your chest,
> ¹⁵ and your feet sandaled with readiness
>   for the gospel of peace.^K
> ¹⁶ In every situation take the shield
>   of faith,
> and with it you will be able
>   to extinguish
> all the flaming arrows of the evil one.
> ¹⁷ Take the helmet of salvation,
> and the sword of the Spirit,
>   which is God's word.

¹⁸Pray at all times in the Spirit with every prayer and request, and stay alert in this with all perseverance and intercession for all the saints. ¹⁹Pray also for me, that the message may be given to me when I open my mouth to make known with boldness the mystery of the gospel. ²⁰For this I am an ambassador in chains. Pray that I might be bold enough in Him to speak as I should.

²¹Tychicus, our dearly loved brother and faithful servant^L in the Lord, will tell you all the news about me so that you may be informed. ²²I am sending him to you for this very reason, to let you know how we are and to encourage your hearts.

²³Peace to the brothers, and love with faith, from God the Father and the Lord Jesus Christ. ²⁴Grace be with all who have undying love for our Lord Jesus Christ.^M,N

^A5:26 Or having cleansed ^B5:30 Other mss add and of His flesh and His bones ^C5:31 Gn 2:24 ^D6:1 Lit parents in the Lord ^E6:2 Or is a preeminent commandment ^F6:3 Or life on the earth ^G6:2-3 Ex 20:12 ^H6:5 Lit according to the flesh ^I6:6 Lit from soul ^J6:11 Or schemes, or tricks ^K6:15 Ready to go tell others about the gospel ^L6:21 Or deacon ^M6:24 Other mss add Amen. ^N6:24 Lit all who love our Lord Jesus Christ in incorruption

PHILIPPIANS

1 Paul and Timothy, slaves of Christ Jesus:
To all the saints in Christ Jesus who are in Philippi, including the overseers and deacons.

² Grace to you and peace from God our Father and the Lord Jesus Christ.

³ I give thanks to my God for every remembrance of you,[A] ⁴ always praying with joy for all of you in my every prayer, ⁵ because of your partnership in the gospel from the first day until now. ⁶ I am sure of this, that He who started a good work in you[B] will carry it on to completion until the day of Christ Jesus. ⁷ It is right for me to think this way about all of you, because I have you in my heart,[C] and you are all partners with me in grace, both in my imprisonment and in the defense and establishment of the gospel. ⁸ For God is my witness, how deeply I miss all of you with the affection of Christ Jesus. ⁹ And I pray this: that your love will keep on growing in knowledge and every kind of discernment, ¹⁰ so that you can approve the things that are superior and can be pure and blameless in[D] the day of Christ, ¹¹ filled with the fruit of righteousness that comes through Jesus Christ to the glory and praise of God.

¹² Now I want you to know, brothers, that what has happened to me has actually resulted in the advance of the gospel, ¹³ so that it has become known throughout the whole imperial guard,[E] and to everyone else, that my imprisonment is in the cause of Christ. ¹⁴ Most of the brothers in the Lord have gained confidence from my imprisonment and dare even more to speak the message[F] fearlessly. ¹⁵ To be sure, some preach Christ out of envy and strife, but others out of good will. ¹⁶ These do so out of love, knowing that I am appointed for the defense of the gospel; ¹⁷ the others proclaim Christ out of rivalry, not sincerely, seeking to cause me anxiety in my imprisonment.[H] ¹⁸ What does it matter? Just that in every way, whether out of false motives or true, Christ is proclaimed.

And in this I rejoice. Yes, and I will rejoice ¹⁹ because I know this will lead to my deliverance[I] through your prayers and help from the Spirit of Jesus Christ. ²⁰ My eager expectation and hope is that I will not be ashamed about anything, but that now as always, with all boldness, Christ will be highly honored in my body, whether by life or by death.

²¹ For me, living is Christ and dying is gain. ²² Now if I live on in the flesh, this means fruitful work for me; and I don't know which one I should choose. ²³ I am pressured by both. I have the desire to depart and be with Christ—which is far better— ²⁴ but to remain in the flesh is more necessary for you. ²⁵ Since I am persuaded of this, I know that I will remain and continue with all of you for your progress and joy in the faith, ²⁶ so that, because of me, your confidence may grow in Christ Jesus when I come to you again.

²⁷ Just one thing: Live your life in a manner worthy of the gospel of Christ. Then, whether I come and see you or am absent, I will hear about you that you are standing firm in one spirit, with one mind,[J] working side by side for the faith that comes from the gospel, ²⁸ not being frightened in any way by your opponents. This is a sign of destruction for them, but of your deliverance—and this is from God. ²⁹ For it has been given to you on Christ's behalf not only to believe in Him, but also to suffer for Him, ³⁰ having the same struggle that you saw I had and now hear that I have.

2 If then there is any encouragement in Christ, if any consolation of love, if any fellowship with the Spirit, if any affection and mercy, ² fulfill my joy by thinking the same way, having the same love, sharing the same feelings, focusing on one goal. ³ Do nothing out of rivalry or conceit, but in humility consider others as more important than yourselves. ⁴ Everyone should look out not only for his own interests, but also for the interests of others.

A1:3 Or for your every remembrance of me   B1:6 Or work among you   C1:7 Or because you have me in your heart   D1:10 Or until   E1:13 Lit praetorium, a Lat word that can also refer to a military headquarters, to the governor's palace, or to Herod's palace.   F1:14 Other mss add of God   G1:15 The good will of men, or God's good will or favor   H1:17 Lit sincerely, intending to raise tribulation to my bonds   I1:19 Or vindication   J1:27 Lit soul

⁵Make your own attitude that of Christ Jesus,

⁶ who, existing in the form of God,
did not consider
equality with God
as something to be used
for His own advantage.ᴬ
⁷ Instead He emptied Himself
by assuming the form of a slave,
taking on the likeness of men.
And when He had come
as a man
in His external form,
⁸ He humbled Himself
by becoming obedient
to the point of death—
even to death on a cross.
⁹ For this reason God
highly exalted Him
and gave Him the name
that is above every name,
¹⁰ so that at the name of Jesus
every knee will bow—
of those who are in heaven
and on earth
and under the earth—
¹¹ and every tongue should confess
that Jesus Christ is Lord,ᴮ
to the glory of God the Father.

¹²So then, my dear friends, just as you have always obeyed, not only in my presence, but now even more in my absence, work out your own salvation with fear and trembling. ¹³For it is God who is working in you, enabling you both to desire and to work out His good purpose. ¹⁴Do everything without grumbling and arguing, ¹⁵so that you may be blameless and pure, children of God who are faultless in a crooked and perverted generation, among whom you shine like stars in the world. ¹⁶Hold firmly toᶜ the message of life. Then I can boast in the day of Christ that I didn't run or labor for nothing. ¹⁷But even if I am poured out as a drink offering on the sacrifice and service of your faith, I am glad and rejoice with all of you. ¹⁸In the same way you should also be glad and rejoice with me.

¹⁹Now I hope in the Lord Jesus to send Timothy to you soon so that I also may be encouraged when I hear news about you. ²⁰For I have no one else like-minded who will genuinely care about your interests; ²¹all seek their own interests, not those of Jesus Christ. ²²But you know his proven character, because he has served with me in the gospel ministry like a son with a father. ²³Therefore, I hope to send him as soon as I see how things go with me. ²⁴I am convinced in the Lord that I myself will also come quickly.

²⁵But I considered it necessary to send you Epaphroditus—my brother, coworker, and fellow soldier, as well as your messenger and minister to my need— ²⁶since he has been longing for all of you and was distressed because you heard that he was sick. ²⁷Indeed, he was so sick that he nearly died. However, God had mercy on him, and not only on him but also on me, so that I would not have one grief on top of another. ²⁸For this reason, I am very eager to send him so that you may rejoice when you see him again and I may be less anxious. ²⁹Therefore, welcome him in the Lord with all joy and hold men like him in honor, ³⁰because he came close to death for the work of Christ, risking his life to make up what was lacking in your ministry to me.

3 Finally, my brothers, rejoice in the Lord. To write to you again about this is no trouble for me and is a protection for you.

²Watch out for "dogs,"ᴰ watch out for evil workers, watch out for those who mutilate the flesh. ³For we are the circumcision, the ones who serve by the Spirit of God, boast in Christ Jesus, and do not put confidence in the flesh— ⁴although I once also had confidence in the flesh. If anyone else thinks he has grounds for confidence in the flesh, I have more: ⁵circumcised the eighth day; of the nation of Israel, of the tribe of Benjamin, a Hebrew born of Hebrews; regarding the law, a Pharisee; ⁶regarding zeal, persecuting the church; regarding the righteousness that is in the law, blameless. ⁷But everything that was a gain to me, I have considered to be a loss because of Christ. ⁸More than that, I also consider everything to be a

ᴬ2:6 Or to be grasped, or to be held on to   ᴮ2:11 Gk kurios = Yahweh; Is 42:8 LXX   ᶜ2:16 Or Offer, or Hold out   ᴰ3:2 An expression of contempt for the unclean, those outside the people of God loss in view of the surpassing value of knowing Christ Jesus my Lord. Because of Him I have suffered the loss of all things and consider them filth, so that I may gain Christ [9] and be found in Him, not having a righteousness of my own from the law, but one that is through faith in Christ[A]—the righteousness from God based on faith. [10] My goal is to know Him and the power of His resurrection and the fellowship of His sufferings, being conformed to His death, [11] assuming that I will somehow reach the resurrection from among the dead.

[12] Not that I have already reached the goal or am already fully mature, but I make every effort to take hold of it because I also have been taken hold of by Christ Jesus. [13] Brothers, I do not[B] consider myself to have taken hold of it. But one thing I do: Forgetting what is behind and reaching forward to what is ahead, [14] I pursue as my goal the prize promised by God's heavenly[C] call in Christ Jesus. [15] Therefore, all who are mature should think this way. And if you think differently about anything, God will reveal this also to you. [16] In any case, we should live up to whatever truth we have attained. [17] Join in imitating me, brothers, and observe those who live according to the example you have in us. [18] For I have often told you, and now say again with tears, that many live as enemies of the cross of Christ. [19] Their end is destruction; their god is their stomach; their glory is in their shame. They are focused on earthly things, [20] but our citizenship is in heaven, from which we also eagerly wait for a Savior, the Lord Jesus Christ. [21] He will transform the body of our humble condition into the likeness of His glorious body, by the power that enables Him to subject everything to Himself.

4 So then, my brothers, you are dearly loved and longed for—my joy and crown. In this manner stand firm in the Lord, dear friends. [2] I urge Euodia and I urge Syntyche to agree in the Lord. [3] Yes, I also ask you, true partner,[D] to help these women who have contended for the gospel at my side, along with Clement and the rest of my coworkers whose names are in the book of life. [4] Rejoice in the Lord always. I will say it again: Rejoice! [5] Let

your graciousness be known to everyone. The Lord is near. [6] Don't worry about anything, but in everything, through prayer and petition with thanksgiving, let your requests be made known to God. [7] And the peace of God, which surpasses every thought, will guard your hearts and minds in Christ Jesus.

[8] Finally brothers, whatever is true, whatever is honorable, whatever is just, whatever is pure, whatever is lovely, whatever is commendable—if there is any moral excellence and if there is any praise—dwell on these things. [9] Do what you have learned and received and heard and seen in me, and the God of peace will be with you.

[10] I rejoiced in the Lord greatly that once again you renewed your care for me. You were, in fact, concerned about me but lacked the opportunity to show it. [11] I don't say this out of need, for I have learned to be content in whatever circumstances I am. [12] I know both how to have a little, and I know how to have a lot. In any and all circumstances I have learned the secret of being content—whether well fed or hungry, whether in abundance or in need. [13] I am able to do all things through Him[E] who strengthens me. [14] Still, you did well by sharing with me in my hardship.

[15] And you Philippians know that in the early days of the gospel, when I left Macedonia, no church shared with me in the matter of giving and receiving except you alone. [16] For even in Thessalonica you sent gifts for my need several times. [17] Not that I seek the gift, but I seek the profit[F] that is increasing to your account. [18] But I have received everything in full, and I have an abundance. I am fully supplied, having received from Epaphroditus what you provided—a fragrant offering, an acceptable sacrifice, pleasing to God. [19] And my God will supply all your needs according to His riches in glory in Christ Jesus. [20] Now to our God and Father be glory forever and ever. Amen.

[21] Greet every saint in Christ Jesus. Those brothers who are with me greet you. [22] All the saints greet you, but especially those from Caesar's household. [23] The grace of the Lord Jesus Christ be with your spirit.[G]

COLOSSIANS

1 Paul, an apostle of Christ Jesus by God's will, and Timothy our[A] brother:

²To the saints in Christ at Colossae, who are faithful brothers.

Grace to you and peace from God our Father.[B]

³We always thank God, the Father of our Lord Jesus Christ, when we pray for you, ⁴for we have heard of your faith in Christ Jesus and of the love you have for all the saints ⁵because of the hope reserved for you in heaven. You have already heard about this hope in the message of truth, the gospel ⁶that has come to you. It is bearing fruit and growing all over the world, just as it has among you since the day you heard it and recognized God's grace in the truth.[C] ⁷You learned this from Epaphras, our dearly loved fellow slave. He is a faithful servant of the Messiah on your[D] behalf, ⁸and he has told us about your love in the Spirit.

⁹For this reason also, since the day we heard this, we haven't stopped praying for you. We are asking that you may be filled with the knowledge of His will in all wisdom and spiritual understanding,[E] ¹⁰so that you may walk worthy of the Lord, fully pleasing to Him, bearing fruit in every good work and growing in the knowledge of God. ¹¹May you be strengthened with all power, according to His glorious might, for all endurance and patience, with joy ¹²giving thanks to the Father, who has enabled you[F] to share in the saints'[G] inheritance in the light. ¹³He has rescued us from the domain of darkness and transferred us into the kingdom of the Son He loves. ¹⁴We have redemption,[H] the forgiveness of sins, in Him.

> ¹⁵ He is the image of the invisible God,
> the firstborn over all creation.[I]
> ¹⁶ For everything was created by Him,
> in heaven and on earth,
> the visible and the invisible,
> whether thrones or dominions
> or rulers or authorities—
> all things have been created
> through Him and for Him.
> ¹⁷ He is before all things,
> and by Him all things
> hold together.
> ¹⁸ He is also the head of the body,
> the church;
> He is the beginning,
> the firstborn from the dead,
> so that He might come
> to have
> first place in everything.
> ¹⁹ For God was pleased to have
> all His fullness dwell in Him,
> ²⁰ and through Him to reconcile
> everything to Himself
> by making peace
> through the blood of His cross[J]—
> whether things on earth or things
> in heaven.

²¹Once you were alienated and hostile in your minds because of your evil actions. ²²But now He has reconciled you by His physical body[K] through His death, to present you holy, faultless, and blameless before Him— ²³if indeed you remain grounded and steadfast in the faith and are not shifted away from the hope of the gospel that you heard. This gospel has been proclaimed in all creation under heaven, and I, Paul, have become a servant of it.

²⁴Now I rejoice in my sufferings for you, and I am completing in my flesh what is lacking in Christ's afflictions for His body, that is, the church. ²⁵I have become its servant, according to God's administration that was given to me for you, to make God's message fully known, ²⁶the mystery hidden for ages and generations but now revealed to His saints. ²⁷God wanted to make known among the Gentiles the glorious wealth of this mystery, which is Christ in you, the hope of glory. ²⁸We proclaim Him, warning and teaching

---

A 1:1 Lit *the* B 1:2 Other mss add *and the Lord Jesus Christ* C 1:6 Or *and truly recognized God's grace* D 1:7 Other mss read *our* E 1:9 Or *all spiritual wisdom and understanding* F 1:12 Other mss read *us* G 1:12 Or *holy ones'* H 1:14 Other mss add *through His blood* I 1:15 The One who is preeminent over all creation J 1:20 Other mss add *through Him* K 1:22 His body of flesh on the cross everyone with all wisdom, so that we may present everyone mature in Christ. ²⁹I labor for this, striving with His strength that works powerfully in me.

2 For I want you to know how great a struggle I have for you, for those in Laodicea, and for all who have not seen me in person. ²I want their hearts to be encouraged and joined together in love, so that they may have all the riches of assured understanding and have the knowledge of God's mystery—Christ.^A ³All the treasures of wisdom and knowledge are hidden in Him.

⁴I am saying this so that no one will deceive you with persuasive arguments. ⁵For I may be absent in body, but I am with you in spirit, rejoicing to see how well ordered you are and the strength of your faith in Christ.

⁶Therefore, as you have received Christ Jesus the Lord, walk in Him, ⁷rooted and built up in Him and established in the faith, just as you were taught, overflowing with gratitude.

⁸Be careful that no one takes you captive through philosophy and empty deceit based on human tradition, based on the elemental forces of the world, and not based on Christ. ⁹For the entire fullness of God's nature^B dwells bodily^C in Christ, ¹⁰and you have been filled by Him, who is the head over every ruler and authority. ¹¹You were also circumcised in Him with a circumcision not done with hands, by putting off the body of flesh, in the circumcision of the Messiah.^D ¹²Having been buried with Him in baptism, you were also raised with Him through faith in the working of God, who raised Him from the dead. ¹³And when you were dead in trespasses and in the uncircumcision of your flesh, He made you alive with Him and forgave us all our trespasses. ¹⁴He erased the certificate of debt, with its obligations, that was against us and opposed to us, and has taken it out of the way by nailing it to the cross. ¹⁵He disarmed the rulers and authorities and disgraced them publicly; He triumphed over them by Him.^E

¹⁶Therefore, don't let anyone judge you in regard to food and drink or in the matter of a festival or a new moon or a Sabbath day.^F ¹⁷These are a shadow of what was to come; the substance is^G the Messiah. ¹⁸Let no one disqualify you,^H insisting on ascetic practices and the worship of angels, claiming access to a visionary realm and inflated without cause by his unspiritual^I mind. ¹⁹He doesn't hold on to the head, from whom the whole body, nourished and held together by its ligaments and tendons, develops with growth from God.

²⁰If you died with the Messiah to the elemental forces of this world, why do you live as if you still belonged to the world? Why do you submit to regulations: ²¹"Don't handle, don't taste, don't touch"? ²²All these regulations refer to what is destroyed by being used up; they are commands and doctrines of men. ²³Although these have a reputation of wisdom by promoting ascetic practices, humility, and severe treatment of the body, they are not of any value in curbing self-indulgence.^J

3 So if you have been raised with the Messiah, seek what is above, where the Messiah is, seated at the right hand of God. ²Set your minds on what is above, not on what is on the earth. ³For you have died, and your life is hidden with the Messiah in God. ⁴When the Messiah, who is your^K life, is revealed, then you also will be revealed with Him in glory.

⁵Therefore, put to death what belongs to your worldly nature:^L sexual immorality, impurity, lust, evil desire, and greed, which is idolatry. ⁶Because of these, God's wrath comes on the disobedient,^M ⁷and you once walked in these things when you were living in them. ⁸But now you must also put away all the following: anger, wrath, malice, slander, and filthy language from your mouth. ⁹Do not lie to one another, since you have put off the old self^N with its practices ¹⁰and have put on the new self. You are being renewed in knowledge according to the image of your^O Creator. ¹¹In Christ^P there is not Greek or Jew, circumcision and uncircumcision, barbarian, Scythian,^Q slave and free; but Christ is all and in all.

¹²Therefore, God's chosen ones, holy and

^A2:2 Other mss read mystery of God, both of the Father and of Christ; other ms variations exist on this v.   ^B2:9 Or of the deity   ^C2:9 Or nature lives in a human body   ^D2:11 = His death   ^E2:15 Or them through it; = through the cross   ^F2:16 Or or sabbaths   ^G2:17 Or substance belongs to   ^H2:18 Or no one cheat us out of your prize   ^I2:18 Lit fleshly   ^J2:23 Lit value against indulgence of the flesh   ^K3:4 Other mss read our   ^L3:5 Lit death the members on the earth   ^M3:6 Other mss omit on the disobedient   ^N3:9 Lit man; = a person before conversion   ^O3:10 Lit his   ^P3:11 Lit Where   ^Q3:11 A term for a savage

loved, put on heartfelt compassion, kindness, humility, gentleness, and patience, [13]accepting one another and forgiving one another if anyone has a complaint against another. Just as the Lord has forgiven you, so you must also forgive. [14]Above all, put on love—the perfect bond of unity. [15]And let the peace of the Messiah, to which you were also called in one body, control your hearts. Be thankful. [16]Let the message about the Messiah dwell richly among you, teaching and admonishing one another in all wisdom, and singing psalms, hymns, and spiritual songs, with gratitude in your hearts to God. [17]And whatever you do, in word or in deed, do everything in the name of the Lord Jesus, giving thanks to God the Father through Him.

[18]Wives, be submissive to your husbands, as is fitting in the Lord. [19]Husbands, love your wives and don't be bitter toward them.

[20]Children, obey your parents in everything, for this pleases the Lord. [21]Fathers, do not exasperate your children, so they won't become discouraged.

[22]Slaves, obey your human masters in everything. Don't work only while being watched, in order to please men, but work wholeheartedly, fearing the Lord.

[23]Whatever you do, do it enthusiastically,[A] as something done for the Lord and not for men, [24]knowing that you will receive the reward of an inheritance from the Lord. You serve the Lord Christ. [25]For the wrongdoer will be paid back for whatever wrong he has done, and there is no favoritism.

4 Masters, supply your slaves with what is right and fair, since you know that you too have a Master in heaven.

[2]Devote yourselves to prayer; stay alert in it with thanksgiving. [3]At the same time, pray also for us that God may open a door to us for the message, to speak the mystery of the Messiah, for which I am in prison, [4]so that I may reveal it as I am required to speak. [5]Act wisely toward outsiders, making the most of the time. [6]Your speech should always be gracious, seasoned with salt, so that you may know how you should answer each person.

[7]Tychicus, our dearly loved brother, faithful servant, and fellow slave in the Lord, will tell you all the news about me. [8]I have sent him to you for this very purpose, so that you may know how we are[B] and so that he may encourage your hearts. [9]He is with Onesimus, a faithful and dearly loved brother, who is one of you. They will tell you about everything here.

[10]Aristarchus, my fellow prisoner, greets you, as does Mark, Barnabas's cousin (concerning whom you have received instructions: if he comes to you, welcome him), [11]and so does Jesus who is called Justus. These alone of the circumcision are my coworkers for the kingdom of God, and they have been a comfort to me. [12]Epaphras, who is one of you, a slave of Christ Jesus, greets you. He is always contending for you in his prayers, so that you can stand mature and fully assured[C] in everything God wills. [13]For I testify about him that he works hard[D] for you, for those in Laodicea, and for those in Hierapolis. [14]Luke, the dearly loved physician, and Demas greet you. [15]Give my greetings to the brothers in Laodicea, and to Nympha and the church in her home. [16]When this letter has been read among you, have it read also in the church of the Laodiceans; and see that you also read the letter from Laodicea. [17]And tell Archippus, "Pay attention to the ministry you have received in the Lord, so that you can accomplish it."

[18]This greeting is in my own hand—Paul. Remember my imprisonment. Grace be with you.[E]

[A]3:23 Lit do it from the soul　　[B]4:8 Other mss read that he may know how you are　　[C]4:12 Other mss read and complete　　[D]4:13 Other mss read he has a great zeal　　[E]4:18 Other mss add Amen.

1 Thessalonians

1 Paul, Silvanus,[A] and Timothy:
To the church of the Thessalonians in God the Father and the Lord Jesus Christ.

Grace to you and peace.[B]

[2] We always thank God for all of you, remembering you constantly in our prayers. [3] We recall, in the presence of our God and Father, your work of faith, labor of love, and endurance of hope in our Lord Jesus Christ, [4] knowing your election, brothers loved by God. [5] For our gospel did not come to you in word only, but also in power, in the Holy Spirit, and with much assurance. You know what kind of men we were among you for your benefit, [6] and you became imitators of us and of the Lord when, in spite of severe persecution, you welcomed the message with joy from the Holy Spirit. [7] As a result, you became an example to all the believers in Macedonia and Achaia. [8] For the Lord's message rang out from you, not only in Macedonia and Achaia, but in every place that your faith[C] in God has gone out. Therefore, we don't need to say anything, [9] for they themselves report[D] what kind of reception we had from you: how you turned to God from idols to serve the living and true God [10] and to wait for His Son from heaven, whom He raised from the dead—Jesus, who rescues us from the coming wrath.

2 For you yourselves know, brothers, that our visit with you was not without result. [2] On the contrary, after we had previously suffered, and we were treated outrageously in Philippi, as you know, we were emboldened by our God to speak the gospel of God to you in spite of great opposition. [3] For our exhortation didn't come from error or impurity or an intent to deceive. [4] Instead, just as we have been approved by God to be entrusted with the gospel, so we speak, not to please men, but rather God, who examines our hearts. [5] For we never used flattering speech, as you know, or had greedy motives—God is our witness— [6] and we didn't seek glory from people, either from you or from oth-

ers. [7] Although we could have been a burden as Christ's apostles, instead we were gentle[E] among you, as a nursing mother nurtures her own children. [8] We cared so much for you that we were pleased to share with you not only the gospel of God but also our own lives, because you had become dear to us. [9] For you remember our labor and hardship, brothers. Working night and day so that we would not burden any of you, we preached God's gospel to you. [10] You are witnesses, and so is God, of how devoutly, righteously, and blamelessly we conducted ourselves with you believers. [11] As you know, like a father with his own children, [12] we encouraged, comforted, and implored each one of you to walk worthy of God, who calls you into His own kingdom and glory.

[13] This is why we constantly thank God, because when you received the message about God that you heard from us, you welcomed it not as a human message, but as it truly is, the message of God, which also works effectively in you believers. [14] For you, brothers, became imitators of God's churches in Christ Jesus that are in Judea, since you have also suffered the same things from people of your own country, just as they did from the Jews [15] who killed both the Lord Jesus and the prophets and persecuted us; they displease God and are hostile to everyone, [16] hindering us from speaking to the Gentiles so that they may be saved. As a result, they are always completing the number of their sins, and wrath has overtaken them at last.[F]

[17] But as for us, brothers, after we were forced to leave you for a short time (in person, not in heart), we greatly desired and made every effort to return and see you face to face. [18] So we wanted to come to you—even I, Paul, time and again—but Satan hindered us. [19] For who is our hope or joy or crown of boasting in the presence of our Lord Jesus at His coming? Is it not you? [20] For you are our glory and joy!

3 Therefore, when we could no longer stand it, we thought it was better to be left alone in Athens. [2] And we sent Timothy, our brother and God's coworker[A] in the gospel of Christ, to strengthen and encourage you concerning your faith, [3] so that no one will be shaken by these persecutions. For you yourselves know that we are appointed to[B] this. [4] In fact, when we were with you, we told you previously that we were going to suffer persecution, and as you know, it happened. [5] For this reason, when I could no longer stand it, I also sent him to find out about your faith, fearing that the tempter had tempted you and that our labor might be for nothing.

[6] But now Timothy has come to us from you and brought us good news about your faith and love and reported that you always have good memories of us, wanting to see us, as we also want to see you. [7] Therefore, brothers, in all our distress and persecution, we were encouraged about you through your faith. [8] For now we live, if you stand firm in the Lord. [9] How can we thank God for you in return for all the joy we experience before our God because of you, [10] as we pray very earnestly night and day to see you face to face and to complete what is lacking in your faith?

[11] Now may our God and Father Himself, and our Lord Jesus, direct our way to you. [12] And may the Lord cause you to increase and overflow with love for one another and for everyone, just as we also do for you. [13] May He make your hearts blameless in holiness before our God and Father at the coming of our Lord Jesus with all His saints. Amen.[C]

4 Finally then, brothers, we ask and encourage you in the Lord Jesus, that as you have received from us how you must walk and please God—as you are doing[D]—do so even more. [2] For you know what commands we gave you through the Lord Jesus.

[3] For this is God's will, your sanctification: that you abstain from sexual immorality, [4] so that each of you knows how to control his own body[E] in sanctification and honor, [5] not with lustful desires, like the Gentiles who don't know God. [6] This means one must not trans-

gress against and defraud his brother in this matter, because the Lord is an avenger of all these offenses,[F] as we also previously told and warned you. [7] For God has not called us to impurity but to sanctification. [8] Therefore, the person who rejects this does not reject man, but God, who also gives you His Holy Spirit.

[9] About brotherly love: You don't need me to write you because you yourselves are taught by God to love one another. [10] In fact, you are doing this toward all the brothers in the entire region of Macedonia. But we encourage you, brothers, to do so even more, [11] to seek to lead a quiet life, to mind your own business,[G] and to work with your own hands, as we commanded you, [12] so that you may walk properly[H] in the presence of outsiders[I] and not be dependent on anyone.[J]

[13] We do not want you to be uninformed, brothers, concerning those who are asleep, so that you will not grieve like the rest, who have no hope. [14] Since we believe that Jesus died and rose again, in the same way God will bring with Him those who have fallen asleep through[K] Jesus. [15] For we say this to you by a revelation from the Lord:[L] We who are still alive at the Lord's coming will certainly have no advantage over[M] those who have fallen asleep. [16] For the Lord Himself will descend from heaven with a shout,[N] with the archangel's voice, and with the trumpet of God, and the dead in Christ will rise first. [17] Then we who are still alive will be caught up together with them in the clouds to meet the Lord in the air and so we will always be with the Lord. [18] Therefore encourage[O] one another with these words.

5 About the times and the seasons: Brothers, you do not need anything to be written to you. [2] For you yourselves know very well that the Day of the Lord will come just like a thief in the night. [3] When they say, "Peace and security," then sudden destruction comes on them, like labor pains come on a pregnant woman, and they will not escape. [4] But you, brothers, are not in the dark, for this day to overtake you like a thief. [5] For you are all sons of light and sons of the day. We do not belong to the night or the darkness. [6] So then, we must not sleep,

---

A3:2 Other mss read *servant* B3:3 Or *are destined for* C3:13 Other mss omit *Amen.* D4:1 Lit *walking* E4:4 Or *to acquire his own wife; lit to possess his own vessel* F4:6 Lit *things* G4:11 Or *to practice one's own things* H4:12 Or *may live respectably* I4:12 Non-Christians J4:12 Or *not need anything, or not be in need* K4:14 Or *in* L4:15 Or *a word of the Lord* M4:15 Or *certainly not precede* N4:16 Or *command* O4:18 Or *comfort* like the rest, but we must stay awake and be serious. [7] For those who sleep, sleep at night, and those who get drunk are drunk at night. [8] But since we belong to the day, we must be serious and put the armor of faith and love on our chests, and put on a helmet of the hope of salvation. [9] For God did not appoint us to wrath, but to obtain salvation through our Lord Jesus Christ, [10] who died for us, so that whether we are awake or asleep, we will live together with Him. [11] Therefore encourage one another and build each other up as you are already doing.

[12] Now we ask you, brothers, to give recognition to those who labor among you and lead you in the Lord and admonish you, [13] and to regard them very highly in love because of their work. Be at peace among yourselves. [14] And we exhort you, brothers: warn those who are irresponsible,[A] comfort the discouraged, help the weak, be patient with everyone. [15] See to it that no one repays evil for evil to anyone, but always pursue what is good for one another and for all.

[16] Rejoice always!
[17] Pray constantly.
[18] Give thanks
in everything,
for this is God's will for you
in Christ Jesus.
[19] Don't stifle the Spirit.
[20] Don't despise prophecies,
[21] but test all things.
Hold on to what is good.
[22] Stay away from every kind
of evil.

[23] Now may the God of peace Himself sanctify you completely. And may your spirit, soul, and body be kept sound and blameless for the coming of our Lord Jesus Christ. [24] He who calls you is faithful, who also will do it. [25] Brothers, pray for us also. [26] Greet all the brothers with a holy kiss. [27] I charge you by the Lord that this letter be read to all the brothers. [28] The grace of our Lord Jesus Christ be with you.

2 THESSALONIANS

1 Paul, Silvanus,[B] and Timothy:
To the church of the Thessalonians in God our Father and the Lord Jesus Christ.

[2] Grace to you and peace from God our Father and the Lord Jesus Christ.

[3] We must always thank God for you, brothers. This is right, since your faith is flourishing and the love each one of you has for one another is increasing. [4] Therefore, we ourselves boast about you among God's churches—about your endurance and faith in all the persecutions and afflictions you endure. [5] It is a clear evidence of God's righteous judgment that you will be counted worthy of God's kingdom, for which you also are suffering, [6] since it is righteous for God to repay with affliction those who afflict you [7] and to reward with rest you who are afflicted, along with us. This will take place at the revelation of the Lord Jesus from heaven with His powerful angels, [8] taking vengeance with flaming fire on those who don't know God and on those who don't obey the gospel of our Lord Jesus. [9] These will pay the penalty of eternal destruction from the Lord's presence and from His glorious strength [10] in that day when He comes to be glorified by His saints and to be admired by all those who have believed, because our testimony among you was believed. [11] And in view of this, we always pray for you that our God will consider you worthy of His calling, and will, by His power, fulfill every desire for goodness and the work of faith, [12] so that the name of our Lord Jesus will be glorified by you, and you by Him, according to the grace of our God and the Lord Jesus Christ.

2 Now concerning the coming of our Lord Jesus Christ and our being gathered to Him: We ask you, brothers, [2] not to be easily upset in mind or troubled, either by a spirit or by a message or by a letter as if from us, alleging that the Day of the Lord[C] has come. [3] Don't let anyone deceive you in any way. For

---

[A] 5:14 Or who are disorderly, or who are undisciplined   [B] 1:1 Or Silas; Ac 15:22-32; 16:19-40; 17:1-16   [C] 2:2 Other mss read Christ that day will not come unless the apostasy[A] comes first and the man of lawlessness[B] is revealed, the son of destruction. [4]He opposes and exalts himself above every so-called god or object of worship, so that he sits[C] in God's sanctuary,[D] publicizing that he himself is God.

[5]Don't you remember that when I was still with you I told you about this? [6]And you know what currently restrains him, so that he will be revealed in his time. [7]For the mystery of lawlessness is already at work, but the one now restraining will do so until he is out of the way, [8]and then the lawless one will be revealed. The Lord Jesus will destroy him with the breath of His mouth and will bring him to nothing with the brightness of His coming. [9]The coming of the lawless one is based on Satan's working, with all kinds of false miracles, signs, and wonders, [10]and with every unrighteous deception among those who are perishing. They perish because they did not accept the love of the truth in order to be saved. [11]For this reason God sends them a strong delusion so that they will believe what is false, [12]so that all will be condemned—those who did not believe the truth but enjoyed unrighteousness.

[13]But we must always thank God for you, brothers loved by the Lord, because from the beginning[E] God has chosen you for salvation through sanctification by the Spirit and through belief in the truth. [14]He called you to this through our gospel, so that you might obtain the glory of our Lord Jesus Christ. [15]Therefore, brothers, stand firm and hold to the traditions you were taught, either by our message or by our letter.

[16]May our Lord Jesus Christ Himself and God our Father, who has loved us and given us eternal encouragement and good hope by grace, [17]encourage your hearts and strengthen you in every good work and word.

3 Finally, brothers, pray for us that the Lord's message may spread rapidly and be honored, just as it was with you, [2]and that we may be delivered from wicked and evil men, for not all have faith.[F] [3]But the Lord is faithful; He will strengthen and guard you from the evil one. [4]We have confidence in the Lord about you, that you are doing and will do what we command. [5]May the Lord direct your hearts to God's love and Christ's endurance.

[6]Now we command you, brothers, in the name of our Lord Jesus Christ, to keep away from every brother who walks irresponsibly and not according to the tradition received from us. [7]For you yourselves know how you must imitate us: We were not irresponsible among you; [8]we did not eat anyone's food[G] free of charge; instead, we labored and struggled, working night and day, so that we would not be a burden to any of you. [9]It is not that we don't have the right to support, but we did it to make ourselves an example to you so that you would imitate us. [10]In fact, when we were with you, this is what we commanded you: "If anyone isn't willing to work, he should not eat." [11]For we hear that there are some among you who walk irresponsibly, not working at all, but interfering with the work of others. [12]Now we command and exhort such people by the Lord Jesus Christ that quietly working, they may eat their own food.[G] [13]Brothers, do not grow weary in doing good.

[14]And if anyone does not obey our instruction in this letter, take note of that person; don't associate with him, so that he may be ashamed. [15]Yet don't treat him as an enemy, but warn him as a brother.

[16]May the Lord of peace Himself give you peace always in every way. The Lord be with all of you. [17]This greeting is in my own hand—Paul. This is a sign in every letter; this is how I write. [18]The grace of our Lord Jesus Christ be with all of you.

[A]2:3 Or rebellion   [B]2:3 Other mss read man of sin   [C]2:4 Other mss add as God   [D]2:4 Or temple   [E]2:13 Other mss read because as a firstfruit   [F]3:2 Or for the faith is not in everyone   [G]3:8,12 Or bread

1 TIMOTHY

1 Paul, an apostle of Christ Jesus by the command of God our Savior and of Christ Jesus our hope:

² To Timothy, my true son in the faith.

Grace, mercy, and peace from God the[A] Father and Christ Jesus our Lord.

³ As I urged you when I went to Macedonia, remain in Ephesus so that you may instruct certain people not to teach different doctrine ⁴ or to pay attention to myths and endless genealogies. These promote empty speculations rather than God's plan, which operates by faith. ⁵ Now the goal of our instruction is love that comes from a pure heart, a good conscience, and a sincere faith. ⁶ Some have deviated from these and turned aside to fruitless discussion. ⁷ They want to be teachers of the law, although they don't understand what they are saying or what they are insisting on. ⁸ But we know that the law is good, provided one uses it legitimately. ⁹ We know that the law is not meant for a righteous person, but for the lawless and rebellious, for the ungodly and sinful, for the unholy and irreverent, for those who kill their fathers and mothers, for murderers, ¹⁰ for the sexually immoral and homosexuals, for kidnappers,[B] liars, perjurers, and for whatever else is contrary to the sound teaching ¹¹ based on the glorious gospel of the blessed God, which was entrusted to me.

¹² I give thanks to Christ Jesus our Lord who has strengthened me, because He considered me faithful, appointing me to the ministry— ¹³ one who was formerly a blasphemer, a persecutor, and an arrogant man. But I received mercy because I acted out of ignorance in unbelief. ¹⁴ And the grace of our Lord overflowed, along with the faith and love that are in Christ Jesus. ¹⁵ This saying is trustworthy and deserving of full acceptance: "Christ Jesus came into the world to save sinners"—and I am the worst of them. ¹⁶ But I received mercy for this reason, so that in me, the worst of them, Christ Jesus might demonstrate His extraordinary patience as an example to those who would believe in Him for eternal life. ¹⁷ Now to the King eternal, immortal, invisible, the only[C] God, be honor and glory forever and ever. Amen.

¹⁸ Timothy, my son, I am giving you this instruction in keeping with the prophecies previously made about you, so that by them you may strongly engage in battle, ¹⁹ having faith and a good conscience. Some have rejected these and have suffered the shipwreck of their faith. ²⁰ Hymenaeus and Alexander are among them, and I have delivered them to Satan, so that they may be taught not to blaspheme.

2 First of all, then, I urge that petitions, prayers, intercessions, and thanksgivings be made for everyone, ² for kings and all those who are in authority, so that we may lead a tranquil and quiet life in all godliness and dignity. ³ This is good, and it pleases God our Savior, ⁴ who wants everyone to be saved and to come to the knowledge of the truth.

> ⁵ For there is one God
> and one mediator between God
> and humanity,
> Christ Jesus, Himself human,
> ⁶ who gave Himself—a ransom for all,
> a testimony at the proper time.

⁷ For this I was appointed a herald, an apostle (I am telling the truth;[D] I am not lying), and a teacher of the Gentiles in faith and truth.

⁸ Therefore, I want the men in every place to pray, lifting up holy hands without anger or argument. ⁹ Also, the women are to dress themselves in modest clothing, with decency and good sense, not with elaborate hairstyles, gold, pearls, or expensive apparel, ¹⁰ but with good works, as is proper for women who affirm that they worship God. ¹¹ A woman should learn in silence with full submission. ¹² I do not allow a woman to teach or to have authority over a man; instead, she is to be silent. ¹³ For Adam was created first, then Eve. ¹⁴ And Adam was not deceived, but the woman was deceived and transgressed. ¹⁵ But she will be saved through childbearing, if she

continues^A in faith, love, and holiness, with good judgment.

3 This saying is trustworthy:^B "If anyone aspires to be an overseer, he desires a noble work." ²An overseer, therefore, must be above reproach, the husband of one wife, self-controlled, sensible, respectable, hospitable, an able teacher,^C ³not addicted to wine, not a bully but gentle, not quarrelsome, not greedy— ⁴one who manages his own household competently, having his children under control with all dignity. ⁵(If anyone does not know how to manage his own household, how will he take care of God's church?) ⁶He must not be a new convert, or he might become conceited and fall into the condemnation of the Devil. ⁷Furthermore, he must have a good reputation among outsiders, so that he does not fall into disgrace and the Devil's trap.

⁸Deacons, likewise, should be worthy of respect, not hypocritical, not drinking a lot of wine, not greedy for money, ⁹holding the mystery of the faith with a clear conscience. ¹⁰And they must also be tested first; if they prove blameless, then they can serve as deacons. ¹¹Wives, too, must be worthy of respect, not slanderers, self-controlled, faithful in everything. ¹²Deacons must be husbands of one wife, managing their children and their own households competently. ¹³For those who have served well as deacons acquire a good standing for themselves, and great boldness in the faith that is in Christ Jesus.

¹⁴I write these things to you, hoping to come to you soon. ¹⁵But if I should be delayed, I have written so that you will know how people ought to act in God's household, which is the church of the living God, the pillar and foundation of the truth. ¹⁶And most certainly, the mystery of godliness is great:

> He^D was manifested in the flesh,
> vindicated in the Spirit,
> seen by angels,
> preached among the nations,
> believed on in the world,
> taken up in glory.

4 Now the Spirit explicitly says that in later times some will depart from the faith, paying attention to deceitful spirits and the teachings of demons, ²through the hypocrisy of liars whose consciences are seared. ³They forbid marriage and demand abstinence from foods that God created to be received with gratitude by those who believe and know the truth. ⁴For everything created by God is good, and nothing should be rejected if it is received with thanksgiving, ⁵since it is sanctified by the word of God and by prayer.

⁶If you point these things out to the brothers, you will be a good servant of Christ Jesus, nourished by the words of the faith and the good teaching that you have followed. ⁷But have nothing to do with irreverent and silly myths. Rather, train yourself in godliness, ⁸for

> the training of the body has
> a limited benefit,
> but godliness is beneficial
> in every way,
> since it holds promise
> for the present life
> and also for the life to come.

⁹This saying is trustworthy and deserves full acceptance. ¹⁰In fact, we labor and strive^E for this, because we have put our hope in the living God, who is the Savior of everyone, especially of those who believe.

¹¹Command and teach these things. ¹²Let no one despise your youth; instead, you should be an example to the believers in speech, in conduct, in love,^F in faith, in purity. ¹³Until I come, give your attention to public reading, exhortation, and teaching. ¹⁴Do not neglect the gift that is in you; it was given to you through prophecy, with the laying on of hands by the council of elders. ¹⁵Practice these things; be committed to them, so that your progress may be evident to all. ¹⁶Pay close attention to your life and your teaching; persevere in these things, for by doing this you will save both yourself and your hearers.

5 Do not rebuke an older man, but exhort him as a father, younger men as brothers, ²older women as mothers, and with all propriety, the younger women as sisters.

---

^A2:15 Lit *if they continue* ^B3:1 "This saying is trustworthy" could refer to 1Tm 2:15. ^C3:2 Or *hospitable, skillful in teaching* ^D3:16 Other mss read *God* ^E4:10 Other mss read *and suffer reproach* ^F4:12 Other mss add *in spirit*

³Support^A widows who are genuinely widows. ⁴But if any widow has children or grandchildren, they must learn to practice godliness toward their own family first and to repay their parents, for this pleases God. ⁵The real widow, left all alone, has put her hope in God and continues night and day in her petitions and prayers; ⁶however, she who is self-indulgent is dead even while she lives. ⁷Command this also, so they won't be blamed. ⁸But if anyone does not provide for his own, that is his own household, he has denied the faith and is worse than an unbeliever.

⁹No widow should be placed on the official support list^B unless she is at least 60 years old, has been the wife of one husband, ¹⁰and is well known for good works—that is, if she has brought up children, shown hospitality, washed the saints' feet, helped the afflicted, and devoted herself to every good work. ¹¹But refuse to enroll younger widows, for when they are drawn away from Christ by desire, they want to marry ¹²and will therefore receive condemnation because they have renounced their original pledge. ¹³At the same time, they also learn to be idle, going from house to house; they are not only idle, but are also gossips and busybodies, saying things they shouldn't say. ¹⁴Therefore, I want younger women to marry, have children, manage their households, and give the adversary no opportunity to accuse us. ¹⁵For some have already turned away to follow Satan. ¹⁶If any^C believing woman has widows in her family, she should help them, and the church should not be burdened, so that it can help those who are genuinely widows.

¹⁷The elders who are good leaders should be considered worthy of an ample honorarium,^D especially those who work hard at preaching and teaching. ¹⁸For the Scripture says:

Do not muzzle an ox while it is treading out the grain,^E
and,
the worker is worthy of his wages.

¹⁹Don't accept an accusation against an elder unless it is supported by two or three witnesses. ²⁰Publicly rebuke those who sin, so that the rest will also be afraid. ²¹I solemnly charge you before God and Christ Jesus and the elect angels to observe these things without prejudice, doing nothing out of favoritism. ²²Don't be too quick to appoint^F anyone as an elder, and don't share in the sins of others. Keep yourself pure. ²³Don't continue drinking only water, but use a little wine because of your stomach and your frequent illnesses. ²⁴Some people's sins are obvious, going before them to judgment, but the sins of others surface^G later. ²⁵Likewise, good works are obvious, and those that are not obvious cannot remain hidden.

6 All who are under the yoke as slaves must regard their own masters^H to be worthy of all respect, so that God's name and His teaching will not be blasphemed. ²Those who have believing masters should not be disrespectful to them because they are brothers, but should serve them better, since those who benefit from their service are believers and dearly loved.

Teach and encourage these things. ³If anyone teaches other doctrine and does not agree with the sound teaching of our Lord Jesus Christ and with the teaching that promotes godliness, ⁴he is conceited, understanding nothing, but has a sick interest in disputes and arguments over words. From these come envy, quarreling, slander, evil suspicions, ⁵and constant disagreement among people whose minds are depraved and deprived of the truth, who imagine that godliness^I is a way to material gain.^J ⁶But godliness with contentment is a great gain.

7   For we brought nothing into the world, and^K we can take nothing out.
8   But if we have food and clothing,^L
    we will be content with these.

⁹But those who want to be rich fall into temptation, a trap, and many foolish and harmful desires, which plunge people into

^A5:3 Lit Honor   ^B5:9 Lit be enrolled   ^C5:16 Other mss add believing man or   ^D5:17 Or respect and remuneration; lit of double honor   ^E5:18 Dt 25:4   ^F5:22 Lit to lay hands on = to ordain   ^G5:24 Lit follow   ^H6:1 Or owners   ^I6:5 Referring to religion as a means of financial gain   ^J6:5 Other mss add From such people withdraw yourself.   ^K6:7 Other mss add it is clear that   ^L6:8 Or food and shelter ruin and destruction. ¹⁰For the love of money is a root^A of all kinds of evil, and by craving it, some have wandered away from the faith and pierced themselves with many pains.

¹¹ But you, man of God, run
    from these things,
  and pursue righteousness,
      godliness, faith,
  love, endurance, and gentleness.
¹² Fight the good fight for the faith;
    take hold of eternal life
    that you were called to
    and have made a good
        confession about
      in the presence of
        many witnesses.

¹³In the presence of God, who gives life to all, and of Christ Jesus, who gave a good confession before Pontius Pilate, I charge you ¹⁴to keep the command without fault or failure until the appearing of our Lord Jesus Christ. ¹⁵God will bring this about in His own time. He is

    the blessed and only Sovereign,
    the King of kings,
    and the Lord of lords,
¹⁶   the only One who has immortality,
    dwelling in unapproachable light;
    no one has seen or can see Him,
    to Him be honor and eternal might.
    Amen.

¹⁷Instruct those who are rich in the present age not to be arrogant or to set their hope on the uncertainty of wealth, but on God,^B who richly provides us with all things to enjoy. ¹⁸Instruct them to do what is good, to be rich in good works, to be generous, willing to share, ¹⁹storing up for themselves a good reserve^C for the age to come, so that they may take hold of life that is real.

²⁰Timothy, guard what has been entrusted to you, avoiding irreverent, empty speech and contradictions from the "knowledge" that falsely bears that name. ²¹By professing it, some people have deviated from the faith.

Grace be with all of you.

2 TIMOTHY

1 Paul, an apostle of Christ Jesus by God's will, for the promise of life in Christ Jesus: ²To Timothy, my dearly loved son.

Grace, mercy, and peace from God the Father and Christ Jesus our Lord.

³I thank God, whom I serve with a clear conscience as my ancestors did, when I constantly remember you in my prayers night and day. ⁴Remembering your tears, I long to see you so that I may be filled with joy, ⁵clearly recalling your sincere faith that first lived in your grandmother Lois, then in your mother Eunice, and that I am convinced is in you also.

⁶Therefore, I remind you to keep ablaze^D the gift of God that is in you through the laying on of my hands. ⁷For God has not given us a spirit^E of fearfulness, but one of power, love, and sound judgment.

⁸So don't be ashamed of the testimony about our Lord, or of me His prisoner. Instead, share in suffering for the gospel, relying on the power of God.

⁹ He has saved us and called us
    with a holy calling,
    not according to our works,
    but according to His own purpose
        and grace,
    which was given to us
      in Christ Jesus
    before time began.
¹⁰ This has now been made evident
    through the appearing of our Savior
        Christ Jesus,
    who has abolished death
    and has brought life and immortality
        to light
    through the gospel.

^A6:10 Or is the root   ^B6:17 Other mss read on the living God   ^C6:19 Or foundation   ^D1:6 Or to rekindle   ^E1:7 Or us the Spirit

¹¹ For this gospel I was appointed a herald, apostle, and teacher,^A ¹² and that is why I suffer these things. But I am not ashamed, because I know the One I have believed in and am persuaded that He is able to guard what has been entrusted to me^B until that day.

¹³ Hold on to the pattern of sound teaching that you have heard from me, in the faith and love that are in Christ Jesus. ¹⁴ Guard, through the Holy Spirit who lives in us, that good thing entrusted to you. ¹⁵ This you know: All those in Asia have turned away from me, including Phygelus and Hermogenes. ¹⁶ May the Lord grant mercy to the household of Onesiphorus, because he often refreshed me and was not ashamed of my chains. ¹⁷ On the contrary, when he was in Rome, he diligently searched for me and found me. ¹⁸ May the Lord grant that he obtain mercy from Him on that day. And you know very well how much he ministered at Ephesus.

2 You, therefore, my son, be strong in the grace that is in Christ Jesus. ² And what you have heard from me in the presence of many witnesses, commit to faithful men who will be able to teach others also.

³ Share in suffering as a good soldier of Christ Jesus. ⁴ No one serving as a soldier gets entangled in the concerns of civilian life; he seeks to please the recruiter. ⁵ Also, if anyone competes as an athlete, he is not crowned unless he competes according to the rules. ⁶ The hardworking farmer ought to be the first to get a share of the crops. ⁷ Consider what I say, for the Lord will give you understanding in everything.

⁸ Keep your attention on Jesus Christ as risen from the dead and descended from David. This is according to my gospel. ⁹ I suffer for it to the point of being bound like a criminal, but God's message is not bound. ¹⁰ This is why I endure all things for the elect: so that they also may obtain salvation, which is in Christ Jesus, with eternal glory. ¹¹ This saying is trustworthy:

> For if we have died
> with Him,
> we will also live with Him;

¹²   if we endure,
>   we will also reign with Him;
> if we deny Him, He will also deny us;
¹³   if we are faithless, He remains faithful,
>   for He cannot deny Himself.

¹⁴ Remind them of these things, charging them before God^C not to fight about words; this is in no way profitable and leads to the ruin of the hearers. ¹⁵ Be diligent to present yourself approved to God, a worker who doesn't need to be ashamed, correctly teaching the word of truth. ¹⁶ But avoid irreverent, empty speech, for this will produce an even greater measure of godlessness. ¹⁷ And their word will spread like gangrene; Hymenaeus and Philetus are among them. ¹⁸ They have deviated from the truth, saying that the resurrection has already taken place, and are overturning the faith of some. ¹⁹ Nevertheless, God's solid foundation stands firm, having this inscription:

> **The Lord knows those
> who are His,**^D and
> Everyone who names the name
> of the Lord
> must turn away
> from unrighteousness.

²⁰ Now in a large house there are not only gold and silver bowls, but also those of wood and clay, some for honorable^E use, some for dishonorable.^F ²¹ So if anyone purifies himself from anything dishonorable,^G he will be a special^H instrument, set apart, useful to the Master, prepared for every good work.

²² Flee from youthful passions, and pursue righteousness, faith, love, and peace, along with those who call on the Lord from a pure heart. ²³ But reject foolish and ignorant disputes, knowing that they breed quarrels. ²⁴ The Lord's slave must not quarrel, but must be gentle to everyone, able to teach,^I and patient, ²⁵ instructing his opponents with gentleness. Perhaps God will grant them repentance leading them to the knowledge of the truth. ²⁶ Then they may come to their senses and escape the Devil's trap, having been captured by him to do his will.

^A1:11 Other mss add of the Gentiles   ^B1:12 Or guard what I have entrusted to Him, or guard my deposit   ^C2:14 Other mss read before the Lord   ^D2:19 Nm 16:5   ^E2:20 Or special   ^F2:20 Or ordinary   ^G2:21 Lit from these   ^H2:21 Or an honorable   ^I2:24 Or everyone, skillful in teaching

3 But know this: Difficult times will come in the last days. [2]For people will be lovers of self, lovers of money, boastful, proud, blasphemers, disobedient to parents, ungrateful, unholy, [3]unloving, irreconcilable, slanderers, without self-control, brutal, without love for what is good, [4]traitors, reckless, conceited, lovers of pleasure rather than lovers of God, [5]holding to the form of godliness but denying its power. Avoid these people!

[6]For among them are those who worm their way into households and capture idle women burdened down with sins, led along by a variety of passions, [7]always learning and never able to come to a knowledge of the truth. [8]Just as Jannes and Jambres resisted Moses, so these also resist the truth, men who are corrupt in mind, worthless in regard to the faith. [9]But they will not make further progress, for their lack of understanding will be clear to all, as theirs[A] was also.

[10]But you have followed my teaching, conduct, purpose, faith, patience, love, and endurance, [11]along with the persecutions and sufferings that came to me in Antioch, Iconium, and Lystra. What persecutions I endured! Yet the Lord rescued me from them all. [12]In fact, all those who want to live a godly life in Christ Jesus will be persecuted. [13]Evil people and impostors will become worse, deceiving and being deceived. [14]But as for you, continue in what you have learned and firmly believed. You know those who taught you, [15]and you know that from childhood you have known the sacred Scriptures, which are able to give you wisdom for salvation through faith in Christ Jesus. [16]All Scripture is inspired by God[B] and is profitable for teaching, for rebuking, for correcting, for training in righteousness, [17]so that the man of God may be complete, equipped for every good work.

4 I solemnly charge you before God and Christ Jesus, who is going to judge the living and the dead, and because of His appearing and His kingdom: [2]Proclaim the message; persist in it whether convenient or not; rebuke, correct, and encourage with great patience and teaching. [3]For the time will come when they will not tolerate sound doctrine, but according to their own desires, will multiply teachers for themselves because they have an itch to hear something new.[C] [4]They will turn away from hearing the truth and will turn aside to myths. [5]But as for you, be serious about everything, endure hardship, do the work of an evangelist, fulfill your ministry.

[6]For I am already being poured out as a drink offering, and the time for my departure is close. [7]I have fought the good fight, I have finished the race, I have kept the faith. [8]There is reserved for me in the future the crown of righteousness, which the Lord, the righteous Judge, will give me on that day, and not only to me, but to all those who have loved His appearing.

[9]Make every effort to come to me soon, [10]for Demas has deserted me, because he loved this present world, and has gone to Thessalonica. Crescens has gone to Galatia, Titus to Dalmatia. [11]Only Luke is with me. Bring Mark with you, for he is useful to me in the ministry. [12]I have sent Tychicus to Ephesus. [13]When you come, bring the cloak I left in Troas with Carpus, as well as the scrolls, especially the parchments. [14]Alexander the coppersmith did great harm to me. The Lord will repay him according to his works. [15]Watch out for him yourself because he strongly opposed our words.

[16]At my first defense, no one stood by me, but everyone deserted me. May it not be counted against them. [17]But the Lord stood with me and strengthened me, so that the proclamation might be fully made through me and all the Gentiles might hear. So I was rescued from the lion's mouth. [18]The Lord will rescue me from every evil work and will bring me safely into His heavenly kingdom. To Him be the glory forever and ever! Amen.

[19]Greet Prisca and Aquila, and the household of Onesiphorus. [20]Erastus has remained at Corinth; I left Trophimus sick at Miletus. [21]Make every effort to come before winter. Eubulus greets you, as do Pudens, Linus, Claudia, and all the brothers.

[22]The Lord be with your spirit. Grace be with you.

A3:9 = Jannes and Jambres   B3:16 Lit breathed out by God; the Scripture is the product of God's Spirit working through men; 2Pt 1:20-21.
C4:3 Or to hear what they want to hear; lit themselves, itching in the hearing

TITLES

1 Paul, a slave of God and an apostle of Jesus Christ, to build up[A] the faith of God's elect and their knowledge of the truth that leads[B] to godliness, [2] in the hope of eternal life that God, who cannot lie, promised before time began. [3] In His own time He has revealed His message in the proclamation that I was entrusted with by the command of God our Savior:

[4] To Titus, my true son in our common faith.

Grace and peace from God the Father and Christ Jesus our Savior.

[5] The reason I left you in Crete was to set right what was left undone and, as I directed you, to appoint elders in every town: [6] one who is blameless, the husband of one wife, having faithful[C] children not accused of wildness or rebellion. [7] For an overseer, as God's administrator, must be blameless, not arrogant, not hot-tempered, not addicted to wine, not a bully, not greedy for money, [8] but hospitable, loving what is good, sensible, righteous, holy, self-controlled, [9] holding to the faithful message as taught, so that he will be able both to encourage with sound teaching and to refute those who contradict it.

[10] For there are also many rebellious people, full of empty talk and deception, especially those from Judaism.[D] [11] It is necessary to silence them; they overthrow whole households by teaching what they shouldn't in order to get money dishonestly. [12] One of their very own prophets said,

> Cretans are always liars, evil beasts, lazy gluttons.[E]

[13] This testimony is true. So, rebuke them sharply, that they may be sound in the faith [14] and may not pay attention to Jewish myths and the commands of men who reject the truth.

[15] To the pure, everything is pure, but to those who are defiled and unbelieving nothing is pure; in fact, both their mind and conscience are defiled. [16] They profess to know

God, but they deny Him by their works. They are detestable, disobedient, and disqualified for any good work.

2 But you must say the things that are consistent with sound teaching. [2] Older men are to be level headed, worthy of respect, sensible, and sound in faith, love, and endurance. [3] In the same way, older women are to be reverent in behavior, not slanderers, not addicted to much wine. They are to teach what is good, [4] so they may encourage the young women to love their husbands and to love their children, [5] to be self-controlled, pure, homemakers, kind, and submissive to their husbands, so that God's message will not be slandered.

[6] In the same way, encourage the young men to be self-controlled [7] in everything. Make yourself an example of good works with integrity and dignity[F] in your teaching. [8] Your message is to be sound beyond reproach, so that the opponent will be ashamed, having nothing bad to say about us.

[9] Slaves are to be submissive to their masters in everything, and to be well-pleasing, not talking back [10] or stealing, but demonstrating utter faithfulness, so that they may adorn the teaching of God our Savior in everything.

[11] For the grace of God has appeared with salvation[G] for all people, [12] instructing us to deny godlessness and worldly lusts and to live in a sensible, righteous, and godly way in the present age, [13] while we wait for the blessed hope and appearing of our great God and Savior, Jesus Christ. [14] He gave Himself for us to redeem us from all lawlessness and to cleanse for Himself a people for His own possession, eager to do good works.

[15] Say these things, and encourage and rebuke with all authority. Let no one disregard[H] you.

3 Remind them to be submissive to rulers and authorities, to obey, to be ready for every good work, [2] to slander no one, to avoid fighting, to be kind, always showing

---

[A]1:1 Or *according to*   [B]1:1 Or *corresponds*   [C]1:6 Or *believing*   [D]1:10 Lit *the circumcision*   [E]1:12 This saying is from the Cretan poet Epimenides (6th century B.C.).   [F]2:7 Other mss add *incorruptibility*   [G]2:11 Or *appeared, bringing salvation; or appeared with saving power*   [H]2:15 Or *despise* gentleness to all people. ³For we too were once foolish, disobedient, deceived, enslaved by various passions and pleasures, living in malice and envy, hateful, detesting one another.

⁴ But when the kindness of God
     our Savior and His love
   for mankind appeared,
⁵ He saved us—
     not by works of righteousness
        that we had done,
     but according to His mercy—
        through the washing
        of regeneration
     and renewal by the Holy Spirit.
⁶ He poured out this Spirit
        on us abundantly
     through Jesus Christ our Savior
⁷ so that, having been justified
        by His grace,
     we may become heirs with the hope
        of eternal life.

⁸This saying is trustworthy. I want you to insist on these things, so that those who have believed God might be careful to devote themselves to good works. These are good and profitable for everyone. ⁹But avoid foolish debates, genealogies, quarrels, and disputes about the law, for they are unprofitable and worthless. ¹⁰Reject a divisive person after a first and second warning, ¹¹knowing that such a person is perverted and sins, being self-condemned.

¹²When I send Artemas or Tychicus to you, make every effort to come to me in Nicopolis, for I have decided to spend the winter there. ¹³Diligently help Zenas the lawyer and Apollos on their journey, so that they will lack nothing. ¹⁴And our people must also learn to devote themselves to good works for cases of urgent need, so that they will not be unfruitful. ¹⁵All those who are with me greet you. Greet those who love us in the faith. Grace be with all of you.

PHILEMON

Paul, a prisoner of Christ Jesus, and Timothy our brother:

To Philemon our dear friend and coworker, ²to Apphia our sister,ᴬ to Archippus our fellow soldier, and to the church that meets in your home.

³Grace to you and peace from God our Father and the Lord Jesus Christ.

⁴I always thank my God when I mention you in my prayers, ⁵because I hear of your love and faith towardᴮ the Lord Jesus and for all the saints. ⁶I pray that your participation in the faith may become effective through knowing every good thing that is in usᶜ for the glory of Christ. ⁷For I have great joy and encouragement from your love, because the hearts of the saints have been refreshed through you, brother.

⁸For this reason, although I have great boldness in Christ to command you to do what is right, ⁹I appeal to you, instead, on the basis of love. I, Paul, as an elderly manᴰ and now also as a prisoner of Christ Jesus, ¹⁰appeal to you for my son, Onesimus,ᴱ I fatheredᶠ him while I was in chains. ¹¹Once he was useless to you, but now he is useful both to you and to me. ¹²I am sending him back to you as a part of myself.ᴳ,ᴴ ¹³I wanted to keep him with me, so that in my imprisonment for the gospel he might serve me in your place. ¹⁴But I didn't want to do anything without your consent, so that your good deed might not be out of obligation, but of your own free will. ¹⁵For perhaps this is why he was separated from you for a brief time, so that you might get him back permanently, ¹⁶no longer as a slave, but more than a slave—as a dearly loved brother. He is especially so to me, but even more to you, both in the flesh and in the Lord.ᴵ

¹⁷So if you consider me a partner, accept him as you would me. ¹⁸And if he has wronged you in any way, or owes you any-

thing, charge that to my account. ¹⁹I, Paul, write this with my own hand: I will repay it—not to mention to you that you owe me even your own self. ²⁰Yes, brother, may I have joy from you in the Lord; refresh my heart in Christ. ²¹Since I am confident of your obedience, I am writing to you, knowing that you will do even more than I say. ²²But mean-while, also prepare a guest room for me, for I hope that through your prayers I will be restored to you.

²³Epaphras, my fellow prisoner in Christ Jesus, greets you, and so do ²⁴Mark, Aristarchus, Demas, and Luke, my coworkers.

²⁵The grace of the Lord[A] Jesus Christ be with your spirit.

HEBREWS

1 Long ago God spoke to the fathers by the prophets at different times and in different ways. ²In these last days, He has spoken to us by His Son. God has appointed Him heir of all things and made the universe[B] through Him. ³The Son is the radiance[C] of God's glory and the exact expression[D] of His nature, sustaining all things by His powerful word. After making purification for sins,[E] He sat down at the right hand of the Majesty on high.[F] ⁴So He became higher in rank than the angels, just as the name He inherited is superior to theirs.

⁵For to which of the angels did He ever say,

You are My Son; today I have become Your Father,[G,H] or again, **I will be His Father, and He will be My Son?**[I] ⁶When He again[J] brings His firstborn into the world, He says, **And all God's angels must worship Him.**[K] ⁷And about the angels He says:

He makes His angels winds,[L]
and His servants[M] **a fiery flame,**[N]

⁸but to[O] the Son:

Your throne, God,
is forever and ever,
and the scepter of Your kingdom
is a scepter of justice.
⁹ **You have loved righteousness**
and hated lawlessness;
this is why God, Your God,
has anointed You
with the oil of joy
rather than Your companions.[P,Q]

¹⁰And:

In the beginning, Lord,
You established the earth,
and the heavens are the works
of Your hands;
¹¹ **they will perish, but You remain.**
They will all wear out
like clothing;
¹² **You will roll them up like a cloak,**[R]
and they will be changed
like a robe.
But You are the same,
and Your years will never end.[S]

¹³Now to which of the angels has He ever said:

Sit at My right hand
until I make Your enemies
Your footstool?[T,U]

¹⁴Are they not all ministering spirits sent out to serve those who are going to inherit salvation?

2 We must, therefore, pay even more attention to what we have heard, so that we will not drift away. ²For if the message spoken through angels was legally binding[V] and every transgression and disobedience received a just punishment, ³how will we escape if we neglect such a great salvation? It was first spoken by the Lord and was confirmed to us by those who heard Him. ⁴At the same time, God also testified with signs and wonders, various miracles, and distributions of gifts from the Holy Spirit according to His will.

A25 Other mss read *our Lord* B1:2 Lit *ages* C1:3 Or *reflection* D1:3 Or *representation, or copy, or reproduction* E1:3 Other mss read *for our sins by Himself* F1:3 Or *He sat down on high at the right hand of the Majesty* G1:5 Or *have begotten You* H1:5 Ps 2:7 I1:5 2Sm 7:14; 1Ch 17:13 J1:6 Or *And again, when He* K1:6 Dt 32:43 LXX; Ps 97:7 L1:7 Or *spirits* M1:7 Or *ministers* N1:7 Ps 104:4 O1:8 Or *about* P1:9 Or *associates* Q1:8-9 Ps 45:6-7 R1:12 Other mss omit *like a cloak* S1:10-12 Ps 102:25-27 T1:13 Or *enemies a footstool for Your feet* U1:13 Ps 110:1 V2:2 Or *valid, or reliable*

⁵For He has not subjected to angels the world to come that we are talking about. ⁶But one has somewhere testified:

> What is man that You remember him,
>   or the son of man that You care
>   for him?
> ⁷ You made him lower
>   than the angels
>   for a short time;
> You crowned him with glory
>   and honor^A
> ⁸ and subjected everything
>   under his feet.^B

For in **subjecting everything** to him, He left nothing that is not subject to him. As it is, we do not yet see **everything subjected** to him. ⁹But we do see Jesus—**made lower than the angels for a short time** so that by God's grace He might taste death for everyone—crowned with glory and honor because of His suffering in death.

¹⁰For in bringing many sons to glory, it was entirely appropriate that God—all things exist for Him and through Him—should make the source^C of their salvation perfect through sufferings. ¹¹For the One who sanctifies and those who are sanctified all have one Father.^D That is why Jesus is not ashamed to call them brothers, ¹²saying:

> I will proclaim Your name
>   to My brothers;
> I will sing hymns to You
>   in the congregation.^E

¹³Again, **I will trust in Him.**^F And again, **Here I am with the children God gave Me.**^G

¹⁴Now since the children have flesh and blood in common, Jesus also shared in these, so that through His death He might destroy the one holding the power of death—that is, the Devil— ¹⁵and free those who were held in slavery all their lives by the fear of death. ¹⁶For it is clear that He does not reach out to help angels, but to help Abraham's offspring. ¹⁷Therefore, He had to be like His brothers in every way, so that He could become a merciful and faithful high priest in service^H to

God, to make propitiation for the sins of the people. ¹⁸For since He Himself was tested and has suffered, He is able to help those who are tested.

3 Therefore, holy brothers and companions in a heavenly calling, consider Jesus, the apostle and high priest of our confession; ²He was faithful to the One who appointed Him, just as Moses was in all God's household. ³For Jesus is considered worthy of more glory than Moses, just as the builder has more honor than the house. ⁴Now every house is built by someone, but the One who built everything is God. ⁵Moses was faithful as a servant in all God's household, as a testimony to what would be said in the future. ⁶But Christ was faithful as a Son over His household. And we are that household if we hold on to the courage and the confidence of our hope.^I

⁷Therefore, as the Holy Spirit says:

> Today, if you hear His voice,
> ⁸ do not harden your hearts
>   as in the rebellion,
> on the day of testing
>   in the wilderness,
> ⁹ where your fathers tested Me, tried Me,
>   and saw My works ¹⁰for 40 years.
> Therefore I was provoked
>   with that generation
> and said, "They always go astray
>   in their hearts,
> and they have not known My ways."
> ¹¹ So I swore in My anger,
>   "They will not enter My rest."^J

¹²Watch out, brothers, so that there won't be in any of you an evil, unbelieving heart that departs from the living God. ¹³But encourage each other daily, while it is still called **today,** so that none of you is hardened by sin's deception. ¹⁴For we have become companions of the Messiah if we hold firmly until the end the reality^K that we had at the start. ¹⁵As it is said:

> Today, if you hear His voice,
> do not harden your hearts
>   as in the rebellion.^L

¹⁶ For who heard and rebelled? Wasn't it really all who came out of Egypt under Moses? ¹⁷ And who was He provoked with for 40 years? Was it not with those who sinned, whose bodies fell in the wilderness? ¹⁸ And who did He swear to that they would not enter His rest, if not those who disobeyed? ¹⁹ So we see that they were unable to enter because of unbelief.

4 Therefore, while the promise to enter His rest remains, let us fear that none of you should miss it.ᴬ ² For we also have received the good news just as they did; but the message they heard did not benefit them, since they were not united with those who heard it in faithᴮ ³ (for we who have believed enter the rest), in keeping with whatᶜ He has said:

> So I swore in My anger,
> they will not enter My rest.ᴰ

And yet His works have been finished since the foundation of the world, ⁴ for somewhere He has spoken about the seventh day in this way:

> And on the seventh day
> God rested from all His works.ᴱ

⁵ Again, in that passage He says, **They will never enter My rest.**ᴰ ⁶ Since it remains for some to enter it, and those who formerly received the good news did not enter because of disobedience, ⁷ again, He specifies a certain day—**today**—speaking through David after such a long time, as previously stated:

> Today, if you hear His voice,
> do not harden your hearts.ᶠ

⁸ For if Joshua had given them rest, God would not have spoken later about another day. ⁹ Therefore, a Sabbath rest remains for God's people. ¹⁰ For the person who has entered His rest has rested from his own works, just as God did from His. ¹¹ Let us then make every effort to enter that rest, so that no one will fall into the same pattern of disobedience.

¹² For the word of God is living and effective and sharper than any double-edged sword, penetrating as far as the separation of soul and spirit, joints and marrow. It is able to judge the ideas and thoughts of the heart.

¹³ No creature is hidden from Him, but all things are naked and exposed to the eyes of Him to whom we must give an account.

¹⁴ Therefore, since we have a great high priest who has passed through the heavens—Jesus the Son of God—let us hold fast to the confession. ¹⁵ For we do not have a high priest who is unable to sympathize with our weaknesses, but One who has been tested in every way as we are, yet without sin. ¹⁶ Therefore let us approach the throne of grace with boldness, so that we may receive mercy and find grace to help us at the proper time.

5 For every high priest taken from men is appointed in serviceᴳ to God for the people, to offer both gifts and sacrifices for sins. ² He is able to deal gently with those who are ignorant and are going astray, since he is also subject to weakness. ³ Because of this, he must make a sin offering for himself as well as for the people. ⁴ No one takes this honor on himself; instead, a person is called by God, just as Aaron was. ⁵ In the same way, the Messiah did not exalt Himself to become a high priest, but the One who said to Him, **You are My Son; today I have become Your Father,**ᴴ ⁶ also said in another passage, **You are a priest forever in the order of Melchizedek.**ᴵ

⁷ During His earthly life,ᴶ He offered prayers and appeals with loud cries and tears to the One who was able to save Him from death, and He was heard because of His reverence. ⁸ Though He was God's Son, He learned obedience through what He suffered. ⁹ After He was perfected, He became the source of eternal salvation for all who obey Him, ¹⁰ and He was declared by God a high priest in the order of Melchizedek.

¹¹ We have a great deal to say about this, and it's difficult to explain, since you have become too lazy to understand. ¹² Although by this time you ought to be teachers, you need someone to teach you the basic principles of God's revelation again. You need milk, not solid food. ¹³ Now everyone who lives on milk is inexperienced with the message about righteousness, because he is an infant. ¹⁴ But solid food is for the mature—for those whose

ᴬ4:1 Or that any of you might seem to have missed it   ᴮ4:2 Other mss read since it was not united by faith in those who heard   ᶜ4:3 Or rest], just as   ᴰ4:3,5 Ps 95:11   ᴱ4:4 Gn 2:2   ᶠ4:7 Ps 95:7-8   ᴳ5:1 Lit things   ᴴ5:5 Ps 2:7   ᴵ5:6 Gn 14:18-20; Ps 110:4   ᴶ5:7 Lit In the days of His flesh senses have been trained to distinguish between good and evil.

6 Therefore, leaving the elementary message about the Messiah, let us go on to maturity, not laying again the foundation of repentance from dead works, faith in God, [2] teaching about ritual washings,[A] laying on of hands, the resurrection of the dead, and eternal judgment. [3] And we will do this if God permits.

[4] For it is impossible to renew to repentance those who were once enlightened, who tasted the heavenly gift, became companions with the Holy Spirit, [5] tasted God's good word and the powers of the coming age, [6] and who have fallen away, because,[B] to their own harm, they are recrucifying the Son of God and holding Him up to contempt. [7] For ground that has drunk the rain that has often fallen on it and that produces vegetation useful to those it is cultivated for receives a blessing from God. [8] But if it produces thorns and thistles, it is worthless and about to be cursed, and will be burned at the end.

[9] Even though we are speaking this way, dear friends, in your case we are confident of the better things connected with salvation. [10] For God is not unjust; He will not forget your work and the love[C] you showed for His name when you served the saints—and you continue to serve them. [11] Now we want each of you to demonstrate the same diligence for the final realization of your hope, [12] so that you won't become lazy but will be imitators of those who inherit the promises through faith and perseverance.

[13] For when God made a promise to Abraham, since He had no one greater to swear by, He swore by Himself:

14   **I will indeed bless you,**
      and I will greatly multiply you.[D]

[15] And so, after waiting patiently, Abraham[E] obtained the promise. [16] For men swear by something greater than themselves, and for them a confirming oath ends every dispute. [17] Because God wanted to show His unchangeable purpose even more clearly to the heirs of the promise, He guaranteed it with an oath, [18] so that through two unchangeable

things, in which it is impossible for God to lie, we who have fled for refuge might have strong encouragement to seize the hope set before us. [19] We have this hope as an anchor for our lives, safe and secure. It enters the inner sanctuary behind the curtain. [20] Jesus has entered there on our behalf as a forerunner, because He has become a high priest forever in the order of Melchizedek.

7 For this Melchizedek—

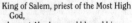

King of Salem, priest of the Most High
    God,
who met Abraham and blessed him
    as he returned from defeating
    the kings,
2   and Abraham gave him a tenth
    of everything;
first, his name means
    king of righteousness,
then also, king of Salem,
    meaning king of peace;
3   without father, mother, or genealogy,
    having neither beginning of days
        nor end of life,
    but resembling the Son of God—

remains a priest forever.

[4] Now consider how great this man was—even Abraham the patriarch gave a tenth of the plunder to him! [5] The sons of Levi who receive the priestly office have a command according to the law to collect a tenth from the people—that is, from their brothers—though they have also descended from Abraham.[F] [6] But one without this[G] lineage collected tenths from Abraham and blessed the one who had the promises. [7] Without a doubt,[H] the inferior is blessed by the superior. [8] In the one case, men who will die receive tenths, but in the other case, Scripture testifies that he lives. [9] And in a sense Levi himself, who receives tenths, has paid tenths through Abraham, [10] for he was still within his ancestor[I] when Melchizedek met him.

[11] If then, perfection came through the Levitical priesthood (for under it the people received the law), what further need was there for another priest to appear, said to be in the order of Melchizedek and not in the order of

A6:2 Or about baptisms   B6:6 Or while   C6:10 Other mss read labor of love   D6:14 Gn 22:17   E6:15 Lit he   F7:5 Lit have come out of Abraham's loins   G7:6 Lit their   H7:7 Or Beyond any dispute   I7:10 Lit still in his father's loins

Aaron? [12]For when there is a change of the priesthood, there must be a change of law as well. [13]For the One these things are spoken about belonged to a different tribe. No one from it has served at the altar. [14]Now it is evident that our Lord came from Judah, and Moses said nothing about that tribe concerning priests.

[15]And this becomes clearer if another priest like Melchizedek appears, [16]who did not become a priest based on a legal command concerning physical[A] descent but based on the power of an indestructible life. [17]For it has been testified:

> You are a priest forever
> in the order of Melchizedek.[B]

[18]So the previous command is annulled because it was weak and unprofitable [19](for the law perfected nothing), but a better hope is introduced, through which we draw near to God.

[20]None of this happened without an oath. For others became priests without an oath, [21]but He became a priest with an oath made by the One who said to Him:

> The Lord has sworn,
> and He will not change His mind,
> You are a priest forever.[B]

[22]So Jesus has also become the guarantee of a better covenant.

[23]Now many have become Levitical priests, since they are prevented by death from remaining in office. [24]But because He remains forever, He holds His priesthood permanently. [25]Therefore, He is always able to save[C] those who come to God through Him, since He always lives to intercede for them.

[26]For this is the kind of high priest we need: holy, innocent, undefiled, separated from sinners, and exalted above the heavens. [27]He doesn't need to offer sacrifices every day, as high priests do—first for their own sins, then for those of the people. He did this once for all when He offered Himself. [28]For the law appoints as high priests men who are weak, but the promise of the oath, which came after the law, appoints a Son, who has been perfected forever.

8 Now the main point of what is being said is this: We have this kind of high priest, who sat down at the right hand of the throne of the Majesty in the heavens, [2]a minister of the sanctuary and the true tabernacle that was set up by the Lord and not man. [3]For every high priest is appointed to offer gifts and sacrifices; therefore it was necessary for this priest also to have something to offer. [4]Now if He were on earth, He wouldn't be a priest, since there are those[D] offering the gifts prescribed by the law. [5]These serve as a copy and shadow of the heavenly things, as Moses was warned when he was about to complete the tabernacle. For God said, **Be careful that you make everything according to the pattern that was shown to you on the mountain.**[E] [6]But Jesus has now obtained a superior ministry, and to that degree He is the mediator of a better covenant, which has been legally enacted on better promises.

[7]For if that first covenant had been faultless, there would have been no occasion for a second one. [8]But finding fault with His people,[F] He says:[G]

> Look, the days are coming,
>   says the Lord,
> when I will make a new covenant
>   with the house of Israel
>   and with the house of Judah—
> [9]   not like the covenant
>   that I made with their ancestors
> on the day I took them by their hands
>   to lead them out of the land of Egypt.
> I disregarded them, says the Lord,
> because they did not continue
>   in My covenant.
> [10]   But this is the covenant
>   that I will make with the house
>   of Israel
> after those days, says the Lord:
> I will put My laws into their minds
>   and write them on their hearts.
> I will be their God,
>   and they will be My people.

A[7:16] Or *fleshy* B[7:17,21] Ps 110:4 C[7:25] Or *He is able to save completely* D[8:4] Other mss read *priests* E[8:5] Ex 25:40 F[8:8] Lit *with them* G[8:8] Other mss read *finding fault, He says to them*

¹¹ And each person will not teach
   his fellow citizen,^A
and each his brother, saying,
   "Know the Lord,"
because they will all know Me,
   from the least to the greatest of them.
¹² For I will be merciful
   to their wrongdoing,
and I will never again remember
   their sins.^B,C

¹³By saying, **a new covenant**, He has declared that the first is old. And what is old and aging is about to disappear.

9 Now the first covenant also had regulations for ministry and an earthly sanctuary. ²For a tabernacle was set up, and in the first room, which is called the holy place, were the lampstand, the table, and the presentation loaves. ³Behind the second curtain, the tabernacle was called the most holy place. ⁴It contained the gold altar of incense and the ark of the covenant, covered with gold on all sides, in which there was a gold jar containing the manna, Aaron's staff that budded, and the tablets of the covenant. ⁵The cherubim of glory were above it overshadowing the mercy seat. It is not possible to speak about these things in detail right now.

⁶With these things set up this way, the priests enter the first room repeatedly, performing their ministry. ⁷But the high priest alone enters the second room, and he does that only once a year, and never without blood, which he offers for himself and for the sins of the people committed in ignorance. ⁸The Holy Spirit was making it clear that the way into the most holy place had not yet been disclosed while the first tabernacle was still standing. ⁹This is a symbol for the present time, during which gifts and sacrifices are offered that cannot perfect the worshiper's conscience. ¹⁰They are physical regulations and only deal with food, drink, and various washings imposed until the time of restoration.

¹¹ But the Messiah has appeared, high priest of the good things that have come.^D In the greater and more perfect tabernacle not made with hands (that is, not of this creation), ¹²He

entered the most holy place once for all, not by the blood of goats and calves, but by His own blood, having obtained eternal redemption. ¹³For if the blood of goats and bulls and the ashes of a young cow, sprinkling those who are defiled, sanctify for the purification of the flesh, ¹⁴how much more will the blood of the Messiah, who through the eternal Spirit offered Himself without blemish to God, cleanse our^E consciences from dead works to serve the living God?

¹⁵Therefore, He is the mediator of a new covenant,^F so that those who are called might receive the promise of the eternal inheritance, because a death has taken place for redemption from the transgressions committed under the first covenant. ¹⁶Where a will exists, the death of the one who made it must be established. ¹⁷For a will is valid only when people die, since it is never in force while the one who made it is living. ¹⁸That is why even the first covenant was inaugurated with blood. ¹⁹For when every command had been proclaimed by Moses to all the people according to the law, he took the blood of calves and goats, along with water, scarlet wool, and hyssop, and sprinkled the scroll itself and all the people, ²⁰saying, **This is the blood of the covenant that God has commanded for you.**^G ²¹In the same way, he sprinkled the tabernacle and all the articles of worship with blood. ²²According to the law almost everything is purified with blood, and without the shedding of blood there is no forgiveness.

²³Therefore it was necessary for the copies of the things in the heavens to be purified with these sacrifices, but the heavenly things themselves to be purified with better sacrifices than these. ²⁴For the Messiah did not enter a sanctuary made with hands (only a model^H of the true one) but into heaven itself, so that He might now appear in the presence of God for us. ²⁵He did not do this to offer Himself many times, as the high priest enters the sanctuary yearly with the blood of another. ²⁶Otherwise, He would have had to suffer many times since the foundation of the world. But now He has appeared one time, at the end of the ages, for

---

^A8:11 Other mss read *neighbor*   ^B8:12 Other mss add *and their lawless deeds*   ^C8:8-12 Jr 31:31-34   ^D9:11 Other mss read *that are to come*   ^E9:14 Other mss read *your*   ^F9:15 The Gk word used here and in vv. 15-18 can be translated *covenant, will,* or *testament.*   ^G9:20 Ex 24:8   ^H9:24 Or *antitype,* or *figure* the removal of sin by the sacrifice of Himself. ²⁷And just as it is appointed for people to die once—and after this, judgment— ²⁸so also the Messiah, having been offered once to bear the sins of many, will appear a second time, not to bear sin, but^A to bring salvation to those who are waiting for Him.

10 Since the law has only a shadow of the good things to come, and not the actual form of those realities, it can never perfect the worshipers by the same sacrifices they continually offer year after year. ²Otherwise, wouldn't they have stopped being offered, since the worshipers, once purified, would no longer have any consciousness of sins? ³But in the sacrifices there is a reminder of sins every year. ⁴For it is impossible for the blood of bulls and goats to take away sins.

⁵Therefore, as He was coming into the world, He said:

> You did not want sacrifice
>   and offering,
> but You prepared a body for Me.
> ⁶ You did not delight
>   in whole burnt offerings
>   and sin offerings.
> ⁷ Then I said, "See—
>   it is written about Me
>   in the volume of the scroll—
>   I have come to do Your will, God!"^B

⁸After He says above, **You did not want or delight in sacrifices and offerings, whole burnt offerings and sin offerings** (which are offered according to the law), ⁹He then says, **See, I have come to do Your will.**^C He takes away the first to establish the second. ¹⁰By this will of God, we have been sanctified through the offering of the body of Jesus Christ once and for all.

¹¹Every priest stands day after day ministering and offering the same sacrifices time after time, which can never take away sins. ¹²But this man, after offering one sacrifice for sins forever, sat down at the right hand of God. ¹³He is now waiting until His enemies are made His footstool. ¹⁴For by one offering He has perfected forever those who are sanctified. ¹⁵The Holy Spirit also testifies to us about this. For after He says:

> ¹⁶ **This is the covenant I will make**
> **with them**
> **after those days, says the Lord:**
> **I will put My laws on their hearts**
> **and write them on their minds,**

¹⁷He adds:

> **I will never again remember**
> **their sins and their lawless acts.**^D

¹⁸Now where there is forgiveness of these, there is no longer an offering for sin.

¹⁹Therefore, brothers, since we have boldness to enter the sanctuary through the blood of Jesus, ²⁰by a new and living way He has opened for us through the curtain (that is, His flesh), ²¹and since we have a great high priest over the house of God, ²²let us draw near with a true heart in full assurance of faith, our hearts sprinkled clean from an evil conscience and our bodies washed in pure water. ²³Let us hold on to the confession of our hope without wavering, for He who promised is faithful. ²⁴And let us be concerned about one another in order to promote love and good works, ²⁵not staying away from our worship meetings, as some habitually do, but encouraging each other, and all the more as you see the day drawing near.

²⁶For if we deliberately sin after receiving the knowledge of the truth, there no longer remains a sacrifice for sins, ²⁷but a terrifying expectation of judgment and the fury of a fire about to consume the adversaries. ²⁸If anyone disregards Moses' law, he dies without mercy, based on the testimony of two or three witnesses. ²⁹How much worse punishment do you think one will deserve who has trampled on the Son of God, regarded as profane^E the blood of the covenant by which he was sanctified, and insulted the Spirit of grace? ³⁰For we know the One who has said, **Vengeance belongs to Me, I will repay,**^F,G and again, **The Lord will judge His people.**^H ³¹It is a terrifying thing to fall into the hands of the living God!

^A9:28 Lit time, apart from sin,   ^B10:5-7 Ps 40:6-8   ^C10:9 Other mss add God   ^D10:16-17 Jr 31:33-34   ^E10:29 Or ordinary   ^F10:30 Other mss add says the Lord   ^G10:30 Dt 32:35   ^H10:30 Dt 32:36

³²Remember the earlier days when, after you had been enlightened, you endured a hard struggle with sufferings. ³³Sometimes you were publicly exposed to taunts and afflictions, and at other times you were companions of those who were treated that way. ³⁴For you sympathized with the prisoners^A and accepted with joy the confiscation of your possessions, knowing that you yourselves have a better and enduring possession.^B ³⁵So don't throw away your confidence, which has a great reward. ³⁶For you need endurance, so that after you have done God's will, you may receive what was promised.

³⁷ For yet in **a very little while,**
   the Coming One will come
      and not delay.
³⁸ **But My righteous one**^C **will live by faith;**
   and if he draws back,
   I have no pleasure in him.^D

³⁹But we are not those who draw back and are destroyed, but those who have faith and obtain life.

11 Now faith is the reality^E of what is hoped for, the proof^F of what is not seen. ²For our ancestors won God's approval by it.

³By faith we understand that the universe was^G created by God's command,^H so that what is seen has been made from things that are not visible.

⁴By faith Abel offered to God a better sacrifice than Cain did. By faith he was approved as a righteous man, because God approved his gifts, and even though he is dead, he still speaks through his faith.

⁵By faith Enoch was taken away so he did not experience death, and **he was not to be found because God took him away.**^I For prior to his removal he was approved, since he had pleased God. ⁶Now without faith it is impossible to please God, for the one who draws near to Him must believe that He exists and rewards those who seek Him.

⁷By faith Noah, after he was warned about what was not yet seen and motivated by godly fear, built an ark to deliver his family. By faith he condemned the world and became an heir of the righteousness that comes by faith.

⁸By faith Abraham, when he was called, obeyed and went out to a place he was going to receive as an inheritance. He went out, not knowing where he was going. ⁹By faith he stayed as a foreigner in the land of promise, living in tents with Isaac and Jacob, coheirs of the same promise. ¹⁰For he was looking forward to the city that has foundations, whose architect and builder is God.

¹¹By faith even Sarah herself, when she was unable to have children, received power to conceive offspring, even though she was past the age, since she^J considered that the One who had promised was faithful. ¹²Therefore from one man—in fact, from one as good as dead—came offspring as numerous as the stars of heaven and as innumerable as the grains of sand by the seashore.

¹³These all died in faith without having received the promises, but they saw them from a distance, greeted them, and confessed that they were foreigners and temporary residents on the earth. ¹⁴Now those who say such things make it clear that they are seeking a homeland. ¹⁵If they were thinking about where they came from, they would have had an opportunity to return. ¹⁶But they now desire a better place—a heavenly one. Therefore God is not ashamed to be called their God, for He has prepared a city for them.

¹⁷By faith Abraham, when he was tested, offered up Isaac. He received the promises and he was offering his unique son, ¹⁸the one it had been said about, **Your seed will be traced**^K **through Isaac.**^L ¹⁹He considered God to be able even to raise someone from the dead, and as an illustration,^M he received him back.

²⁰By faith Isaac blessed Jacob and Esau concerning things to come. ²¹By faith Jacob, when he was dying, blessed each of the sons of Joseph, and **he worshiped, leaning on the top of his staff.**^N ²²By faith Joseph, as he was nearing the end of his life, mentioned the

^A10:34 Other mss read sympathized with my imprisonment   ^B10:34 Other mss add in heaven   ^C10:38 Other mss read the righteous one   ^D10:37-38 Is 26:20 LXX; Hab 2:3-4   ^E11:1 Or assurance   ^F11:1 Or conviction   ^G11:3 Or the worlds were, or the ages were   ^H11:3 Or word   ^I11:5 Gn 5:21-24   ^J11:11 Or By faith Abraham, even though he was past age—and Sarah herself was barren—received the ability to procreate since he   ^K11:18 Lit called   ^L11:18 Gn 21:12   ^M11:19 Or a foreshadowing, or a parable, or a type   ^N11:21 Gn 47:31

exodus of the Israelites and gave instructions concerning his bones.

²³By faith, after Moses was born, he was hidden by his parents for three months, because they saw that the child was beautiful, and they didn't fear the king's edict. ²⁴By faith Moses, when he had grown up, refused to be called the son of Pharaoh's daughter ²⁵and chose to suffer with the people of God rather than to enjoy the short-lived pleasure of sin. ²⁶For he considered the reproach because of the Messiah to be greater wealth than the treasures of Egypt, since his attention was on the reward.

²⁷By faith he left Egypt behind, not being afraid of the king's anger, for Moses persevered as one who sees Him who is invisible. ²⁸By faith he instituted the Passover and the sprinkling of the blood, so that the destroyer of the firstborn might not touch the Israelites. ²⁹By faith they crossed the Red Sea as though they were on dry land. When the Egyptians attempted to do this, they were drowned.

³⁰By faith the walls of Jericho fell down after being encircled by the Israelites for seven days. ³¹By faith Rahab the prostitute received the spies in peace and didn't perish with those who disobeyed.

³²And what more can I say? Time is too short for me to tell about Gideon, Barak, Samson, Jephthah, David, Samuel, and the prophets, ³³who by faith conquered kingdoms, administered justice, obtained promises, shut the mouths of lions, ³⁴quenched the raging of fire, escaped the edge of the sword, gained strength after being weak, became mighty in battle, and put foreign armies to flight. ³⁵Women received their dead—they were raised to life again. Some men were tortured, not accepting release, so that they might gain a better resurrection, ³⁶and others experienced mockings and scourgings, as well as bonds and imprisonment. ³⁷They were stoned,ᴬ they were sawed in two, they died by the sword, they wandered about in sheepskins, in goatskins, destitute, afflicted, and mistreated. ³⁸The world was not worthy of them. They wandered in deserts and on

mountains, hiding in caves and holes in the ground.

³⁹All these were approved through their faith, but they did not receive what was promised, ⁴⁰since God had provided something better for us, so that they would not be made perfect without us.

12 Therefore, since we also have such a large cloud of witnesses surrounding us, let us lay aside every weight and the sin that so easily ensnares us. Let us run with endurance the race that lies before us, ²keeping our eyes on Jesus,ᴮ the source and perfecterᶜ of our faith, who for the joy that lay before Himᴰ endured a cross and despised the shame and has sat down at the right hand of God's throne.

³For consider Him who endured such hostility from sinners against Himself, so that you won't grow weary and lose heart. ⁴In struggling against sin, you have not yet resisted to the point of shedding your blood. ⁵And you have forgotten the exhortation that addresses you as sons:

> My son, do not take the Lord's
>   discipline lightly
> or faint when you are
>   reproved by Him,
> ⁶ for the Lord disciplines the one
>   He loves
>   and punishes every son He receives.ᴱ

⁷Endure suffering as discipline: God is dealing with you as sons. For what son is there that a father does not discipline? ⁸But if you are without discipline—which allᶠ receive�perturbationᴳ—then you are illegitimate children and not sons. ⁹Furthermore, we had natural fathers discipline us, and we respected them. Shouldn't we submit even more to the Father of spirits and live? ¹⁰For they disciplined us for a short time based on what seemed good to them, but He does it for our benefit, so that we can share His holiness. ¹¹No discipline seems enjoyable at the time, but painful. Later on, however, it yields the fruit of peace and righteousness to those who have been trained by it.

ᴬ11:37 Other mss add *they were tempted*   ᴮ12:2 Or *us, looking to Jesus*   ᶜ12:2 Or *the founder and completer*   ᴰ12:2 Or *who instead of the joy lying before Him; that is, the joy of heaven*   ᴱ12:6 Pr 3:11-12   ᶠ12:8 = Christians   ᴳ12:8 Lit *discipline, of which all have become participants*

¹²Therefore strengthen your tired hands and weakened knees, ¹³and make straight paths for your feet, so that what is lame may not be dislocated^A but healed instead.

¹⁴Pursue peace with everyone, and holiness—without it no one will see the Lord. ¹⁵Make sure that no one falls short of the grace of God and that no root of bitterness springs up, causing trouble and by it, defiling many. ¹⁶And make sure that there isn't any immoral or irreverent person like Esau, who sold his birthright in exchange for one meal. ¹⁷For you know that later, when he wanted to inherit the blessing, he was rejected because he didn't find any opportunity for repentance, though he sought it with tears.

¹⁸For you have not come to what could be touched, to a blazing fire, to darkness, gloom, and storm, ¹⁹to the blast of a trumpet, and the sound of words. (Those who heard it begged that not another word be spoken to them, ²⁰for they could not bear what was commanded: **And if even an animal touches the mountain, it must be stoned!**^B ²¹The appearance was so terrifying that Moses said, **I am terrified and trembling.**^C) ²²Instead, you have come to Mount Zion, to the city of the living God (the heavenly Jerusalem), to myriads of angels in festive gathering, ²³to the assembly of the firstborn whose names have been written^D in heaven, to God who is the Judge of all, to the spirits of righteous people made perfect, ²⁴to Jesus (mediator of a new covenant), and to the sprinkled blood, which says better things than the blood of Abel.

²⁵Make sure that you do not reject the One who speaks. For if they did not escape when they rejected Him who warned them on earth, even less will we if we turn away from Him who warns us from heaven. ²⁶His voice shook the earth at that time, but now He has promised, **Yet once more I will shake not only the earth but also heaven.**^E ²⁷This expression, "Yet once more," indicates the removal of what can be shaken—that is, created things—so that what is not shaken might remain. ²⁸Therefore, since we are receiving a kingdom that cannot be shaken, let us hold on to grace.^F By it, we may serve God acceptably, with reverence and awe, ²⁹for our God is a consuming fire.

13 Let brotherly love continue. ²Don't neglect to show hospitality, for by doing this some have welcomed angels as guests without knowing it. ³Remember the prisoners, as though you were in prison with them, and the mistreated, as though you yourselves were suffering bodily.^G ⁴Marriage must be respected by all, and the marriage bed kept undefiled, because God will judge immoral people and adulterers. ⁵Your life should be free from the love of money. Be satisfied with what you have, for He Himself has said, **I will never leave you or forsake you.**^H ⁶Therefore, we may boldly say:

> **The Lord is my helper;
> I will not be afraid.
> What can man do to me?**^I

⁷Remember your leaders who have spoken God's word to you. As you carefully observe the outcome of their lives, imitate their faith. ⁸Jesus Christ is the same yesterday, today, and forever. ⁹Don't be led astray by various kinds of strange teachings; for it is good for the heart to be established by grace and not by foods, since those involved in them have not benefited. ¹⁰We have an altar from which those who serve the tabernacle do not have a right to eat. ¹¹For the bodies of those animals whose blood is brought into the most holy place by the high priest as a sin offering are burned outside the camp. ¹²Therefore Jesus also suffered outside the gate, so that He might sanctify^J the people by His own blood. ¹³Let us then go to Him outside the camp, bearing His disgrace. ¹⁴For we do not have an enduring city here; instead, we seek the one to come. ¹⁵Therefore, through Him let us continually offer up to God a sacrifice of praise, that is, the fruit of our lips that confess His name. ¹⁶Don't neglect to do what is good and to share, for God is pleased with such sacrifices. ¹⁷Obey your leaders^K and submit to them, for they keep watch over your souls as those who will give an account, so

---

^A12:13 Or so that the lame will not be turned aside   ^B12:20 Ex 19:12   ^C12:21 Dt 9:19   ^D12:23 Or registered   ^E12:26 Hg 2:6   ^F12:28 Or let us give thanks, or let us have grace   ^G13:3 Or mistreated, since you are also in a body   ^H13:5 Dt 31:6   ^I13:6 Ps 118:6   ^J13:12 Or set apart, or consecrate   ^K13:17 Or rulers that they can do this with joy and not with grief, for that would be unprofitable for you. ¹⁸Pray for us; for we are convinced that we have a clear conscience, wanting to conduct ourselves honorably in everything. ¹⁹And I especially urge you to pray^A that I may be restored to you very soon.

²⁰Now may the God of peace, who brought up from the dead our Lord Jesus—the great Shepherd of the sheep—with the blood of the everlasting covenant, ²¹equip^B you with all that is good to do His will, working in us what is pleasing in His sight, through Jesus Christ. Glory belongs to Him forever and ever.^C Amen.

²²Brothers, I urge you to receive this message of exhortation, for I have written to you briefly. ²³Be aware that our brother Timothy has been released. If he comes soon enough, he will be with me when I see you. ²⁴Greet all your leaders and all the saints. Those who are from Italy greet you. ²⁵Grace be with all of you.

JAMES

1 James, a slave of God and of the Lord Jesus Christ:

To the 12 tribes in the Dispersion.^D

Greetings.

²Consider it a great joy, my brothers, whenever you experience various trials, ³knowing that the testing of your faith produces endurance. ⁴But endurance must do its complete work, so that you may be mature and complete, lacking nothing.

⁵Now if any of you lacks wisdom, he should ask God, who gives to all generously and without criticizing, and it will be given to him. ⁶But let him ask in faith without doubting. For the doubter is like the surging sea, driven and tossed by the wind. ⁷That person should not expect to receive anything from the Lord. ⁸An indecisive^E man is unstable in all his ways.

⁹The brother of humble circumstances should boast in his exaltation, ¹⁰but the one who is rich should boast in his humiliation because he will pass away like a flower of the field. ¹¹For the sun rises with its scorching heat and dries up the grass; its flower falls off, and its beautiful appearance is destroyed. In the same way, the rich man will wither away while pursuing his activities.

¹²A man who endures trials^F is blessed, because when he passes the test he will receive the crown of life that God^G has promised to those who love Him.

¹³No one undergoing a trial should say, "I am being tempted by God." For God is not tempted by evil,^H and He Himself doesn't tempt anyone. ¹⁴But each person is tempted when he is drawn away and enticed by his own evil desires. ¹⁵Then after desire has conceived, it gives birth to sin, and when sin is fully grown, it gives birth to death.

¹⁶Don't be deceived, my dearly loved brothers. ¹⁷Every generous act and every perfect gift is from above, coming down from the Father of lights; with Him there is no variation or shadow cast by turning. ¹⁸By His own choice, He gave us a new birth by the message of truth^I so that we would be the firstfruits of His creatures.

¹⁹My dearly loved brothers, understand this: Everyone must be quick to hear, slow to speak, and slow to anger, ²⁰for man's anger does not accomplish God's righteousness. ²¹Therefore, ridding yourselves of all moral filth and evil,^J humbly receive the implanted word, which is able to save you.^K

²²But be doers of the word and not hearers only, deceiving yourselves. ²³Because if anyone is a hearer of the word and not a doer, he is like a man looking at his own face^L in a mirror. ²⁴For he looks at himself, goes away, and immediately forgets what kind of man he was. ²⁵But the one who looks intently into the perfect law of freedom and perseveres in

A13:19 Lit to do this   B13:21 Or perfect   C13:21 Other mss omit and ever   D1:1 Jewish people scattered throughout Gentile lands who spoke Gk and were influenced by Gk culture   E1:8 Or A doubting, or A double-minded   F1:12 Lit trial, used as a collective   G1:12 Other mss read that the Lord   H1:13 Or evil persons, or evil things   I1:18 = the gospel   J1:21 Lit evil excess   K1:21 Lit save your souls   L1:23 Lit at the face of his birth it, and is not a forgetful hearer but one who does good works—this person will be blessed in what he does.

²⁶If anyone^A thinks he is religious without controlling his tongue, then his religion is useless and he deceives himself. ²⁷Pure and undefiled religion before our^B God and Father is this: to look after orphans and widows in their distress and to keep oneself unstained by the world.

2 My brothers, do not show favoritism as you hold on to the faith in our glorious Lord Jesus Christ. ²For example, a man comes into your meeting wearing a gold ring and dressed in fine clothes, and a poor man dressed in dirty clothes also comes in. ³If you look with favor on the man wearing the fine clothes and say, "Sit here in a good place," and yet you say to the poor man, "Stand over there," or, "Sit here on the floor by my footstool," ⁴haven't you discriminated among yourselves and become judges with evil thoughts?

⁵Listen, my dear brothers: Didn't God choose the poor in this world to be rich in faith and heirs of the kingdom that He has promised to those who love Him? ⁶Yet you dishonored that poor man. Don't the rich oppress you and drag you into the courts? ⁷Don't they blaspheme the noble name that was pronounced over you at your baptism?

⁸Indeed, if you keep the royal law prescribed in the Scripture, **Love your neighbor as yourself**,^C you are doing well. ⁹But if you show favoritism, you commit sin and are convicted by the law as transgressors. ¹⁰For whoever keeps the entire law, yet fails in one point, is guilty of breaking it all. ¹¹For He who said, **Do not commit adultery**,^D also said, **Do not murder**.^E So if you do not commit adultery, but you do murder, you are a lawbreaker.

¹²Speak and act as those who will be judged by the law of freedom. ¹³For judgment is without mercy to the one who hasn't shown mercy. Mercy triumphs over judgment.

¹⁴What good is it, my brothers, if someone says he has faith but does not have works? Can his faith^F save him?

¹⁵If a brother or sister is without clothes and lacks daily food ¹⁶and one of you says to them, "Go in peace, keep warm, and eat well," but you don't give them what the body needs, what good is it? ¹⁷In the same way faith, if it doesn't have works, is dead by itself.

¹⁸But someone will say, "You have faith, and I have works."^G Show me your faith without works, and I will show you faith from my works.^H ¹⁹You believe that God is one; you do well. The demons also believe—and they shudder.

²⁰Foolish man! Are you willing to learn that faith without works is useless? ²¹Wasn't Abraham our father justified by works when he offered Isaac his son on the altar? ²²You see that faith was active together with his works, and, by works, faith was perfected. ²³So the Scripture was fulfilled that says, **Abraham believed God, and it was credited to him for righteousness**,^I and he was called God's friend. ²⁴You see that a man is justified by works and not by faith alone. ²⁵And in the same way, wasn't Rahab the prostitute also justified by works when she received the messengers and sent them out by a different route? ²⁶For just as the body without the spirit is dead, so also faith without works is dead.

3 Not many should become teachers, my brothers, knowing that we will receive a stricter judgment, ²for we all stumble in many ways. If anyone does not stumble in what he says,^J he is a mature man who is also able to control his whole body.^K

³Now when we put bits into the mouths of horses to make them obey us, we also guide the whole animal.^L ⁴And consider ships: Though very large and driven by fierce winds, they are guided by a very small rudder wherever the will of the pilot directs. ⁵So too, though the tongue is a small part of the body, it boasts great things. Consider how large a forest a small fire ignites. ⁶And the tongue is a fire. The tongue, a world of unrighteousness, is placed among the parts of our bodies. It pollutes the whole body, sets the course of life on fire, and is set on fire by hell.

A1:26 Other mss add among you   B1:27 Or before the   C2:8 Lv 19:18   D2:11 Ex 20:14; Dt 5:18   E2:11 Ex 20:13; Dt 5:17   F2:14 Or Can faith, or Can that faith, or Can such faith   G2:18 The quotation may end here or after v. 18b or v. 19.   H2:18 Other mss read Show me your faith from your works, and from my works I will show you my faith.   I2:23 Gn 15:6   J3:2 Lit in word   K3:2 Lit to bridle the whole body   L3:3 Lit whole body

⁷Every sea creature, reptile, bird, or animal is tamed and has been tamed by man, ⁸but no man can tame the tongue. It is a restless evil, full of deadly poison. ⁹We praise our^A Lord and Father with it, and we curse men who are made in God's likeness with it. ¹⁰Praising and cursing come out of the same mouth. My brothers, these things should not be this way. ¹¹Does a spring pour out sweet and bitter water from the same opening? ¹²Can a fig tree produce olives, my brothers, or a grapevine produce figs? Neither can a saltwater spring yield fresh water.

¹³Who is wise and has understanding among you? He should show his works by good conduct with wisdom's gentleness. ¹⁴But if you have bitter envy and selfish ambition in your heart, don't brag and deny the truth. ¹⁵Such wisdom does not come from above but is earthly, unspiritual, demonic. ¹⁶For where envy and selfish ambition exist, there is disorder and every kind of evil. ¹⁷But the wisdom from above is first pure, then peace-loving, gentle, compliant, full of mercy and good fruits, without favoritism and hypocrisy. ¹⁸And the fruit of righteousness is sown in peace by those who cultivate peace.

4 What is the source of wars and fights among you? Don't they come from the cravings that are at war within you?^B ²You desire and do not have. You murder and covet and cannot obtain. You fight and war. You do not have because you do not ask. ³You ask and don't receive because you ask with wrong motives, so that you may spend it on your evil desires.

⁴Adulteresses!^C,^D Don't you know that friendship with the world is hostility toward God? So whoever wants to be the world's friend becomes God's enemy. ⁵Or do you think it's without reason the Scripture says that the Spirit who lives in us yearns jealously?^E

⁶But He gives greater grace. Therefore He says:

> **God resists the proud,**
> **but gives grace to the humble.**^F

⁷Therefore, submit to God. But resist the Devil, and he will flee from you. ⁸Draw near to God, and He will draw near to you. Cleanse your hands, sinners, and purify your hearts, double-minded people! ⁹Be miserable and mourn and weep. Your laughter must change to mourning and your joy to sorrow. ¹⁰Humble yourselves before the Lord, and He will exalt you.

¹¹Don't criticize one another, brothers. He who criticizes a brother or judges his brother criticizes the law and judges the law. But if you judge the law, you are not a doer of the law but a judge. ¹²There is one lawgiver and judge^G who is able to save and to destroy. But who are you to judge your neighbor?

¹³Come now, you who say, "Today or tomorrow we will travel to such and such a city and spend a year there and do business and make a profit." ¹⁴You don't even know what tomorrow will bring—what your life will be! For you are like smoke that appears for a little while, then vanishes. ¹⁵Instead, you should say, "If the Lord wills, we will live and do this or that." ¹⁶But as it is, you boast in your arrogance. All such boasting is evil. ¹⁷So it is a sin for the person who knows to do what is good and doesn't do it.

5 Come now, you rich people! Weep and wail over the miseries that are coming on you. ²Your wealth is ruined and your clothes are moth-eaten. ³Your silver and gold are corroded, and their corrosion will be a witness against you and will eat your flesh like fire. You stored up treasure in the last days! ⁴Look! The pay that you withheld from the workers who reaped your fields cries out, and the outcry of the harvesters has reached the ears of the Lord of Hosts.^H ⁵You have lived luxuriously on the land and have indulged yourselves. You have fattened your hearts for^I the day of slaughter. ⁶You have condemned—you have murdered—the righteous man; he does not resist you.

⁷Therefore, brothers, be patient until the Lord's coming. See how the farmer waits for the precious fruit of the earth and is patient

---

^A3:9 Or praise the   ^B4:1 Lit war in your members   ^C4:4 Other mss read Adulterers and adulteresses   ^D4:4 Or Unfaithful people!   ^E4:5 Or He who caused the Spirit to live in us yearns jealously, or the spirit He caused to live in us yearns jealously, or He jealously yearns for the Spirit He made to live in us   ^F4:6 Pr 3:34   ^G4:12 Other mss omit and judge   ^H5:4 Gk Sabaoth; this word is a transliteration of the Hb word for Hosts, or Armies.   ^I5:5 Or hearts in with it until it receives the early and the late rains. ⁸You also must be patient. Strengthen your hearts, because the Lord's coming is near.

⁹Brothers, do not complain about one another, so that you will not be judged. Look, the judge stands at the door!

¹⁰Brothers, take the prophets who spoke in the Lord's name as an example of suffering and patience. ¹¹See, we count as blessed those who have endured.[A] You have heard of Job's endurance and have seen the outcome from the Lord. The Lord is very compassionate and merciful.

¹²Now above all, my brothers, do not swear, either by heaven or by earth or with any other oath. Your "yes" must be "yes," and your "no" must be "no," so that you won't fall under judgment.[B]

¹³Is anyone among you suffering? He should pray. Is anyone cheerful? He should sing praises. ¹⁴Is anyone among you sick? He should call for the elders of the church, and they should pray over him after anointing him with olive oil in the name of the Lord. ¹⁵The prayer of faith will save the sick person, and the Lord will restore him to health; if he has committed sins, he will be forgiven. ¹⁶Therefore, confess your sins to one another and pray for one another, so that you may be healed. The urgent request of a righteous person is very powerful in its effect. ¹⁷Elijah was a man with a nature like ours; yet he prayed earnestly that it would not rain, and for three years and six months it did not rain on the land. ¹⁸Then he prayed again, and the sky gave rain and the land produced its fruit.

¹⁹My brothers, if any among you strays from the truth, and someone turns him back, ²⁰let him know that whoever turns a sinner from the error of his way will save his life from death and cover a multitude of sins.

1 PETER

1 Peter, an apostle of Jesus Christ:
To the temporary residents dispersed[C] in Pontus, Galatia, Cappadocia, Asia, and Bithynia, chosen ²according to the foreknowledge of God the Father and set apart by the Spirit for obedience and for sprinkling with the blood of Jesus Christ.

May grace and peace be multiplied to you.

³Praise the God and Father of our Lord Jesus Christ. According to His great mercy, He has given us a new birth into a living hope through the resurrection of Jesus Christ from the dead ⁴and into an inheritance that is imperishable, uncorrupted, and unfading, kept in heaven for you. ⁵You are being protected by God's power through faith for a salvation that is ready to be revealed in the last time. ⁶You rejoice in this,[D] though now for a short time you have had to struggle in various trials ⁷so that the genuineness of your faith—more valuable than gold, which perishes though refined by fire—may result in[E] praise, glory, and honor at the revelation of Jesus Christ. ⁸You love Him, though you have not seen Him. And though not seeing Him now, you believe in Him and rejoice with inexpressible and glorious joy, ⁹because you are receiving the goal of your[F] faith, the salvation of your souls.[G]

¹⁰Concerning this salvation, the prophets who prophesied about the grace that would come to you searched and carefully investigated. ¹¹They inquired into what time or what circumstances[H] the Spirit of Christ within them was indicating when He testified in advance to the messianic sufferings[I] and the glories that would follow.[J] ¹²It was revealed to them that they were not serving themselves but you. These things have now been announced to you through those who preached the gospel to you by the Holy Spirit sent from heaven. Angels desire to look into these things.

A5:11 Or have persevered   B5:12 Other mss read fall into hypocrisy   C1:1 Jewish people scattered throughout Gentile lands who spoke Gk and were influenced by Gk culture   D1:6 Or In this fact rejoice   E1:7 Lit may be found for   F1:9 Other mss read our, or they omit the possessive pronoun   G1:9 Or your lives   H1:11 Or inquired about the person or time   I1:11 Or the sufferings of Christ   J1:11 Lit the glories that after

¹³Therefore, with your minds ready for action,^A be serious and set your hope completely on the grace to be brought to you at the revelation of Jesus Christ. ¹⁴As obedient children, do not be conformed to the desires of your former ignorance. ¹⁵But as the One who called you is holy, you also are to be holy in all your conduct; ¹⁶for it is written, **Be holy, because I am holy.**^B

¹⁷And if you address as Father the One who judges impartially based on each one's work, you are to conduct yourselves in fear during the time of your temporary residence. ¹⁸For you know that you were redeemed from your empty way of life inherited from the fathers, not with perishable things like silver or gold, ¹⁹but with the precious blood of Christ, like that of a lamb without defect or blemish. ²⁰He was chosen^C before the foundation of the world but was revealed at the end of the times for you ²¹who through Him are believers in God, who raised Him from the dead and gave Him glory, so that your faith and hope are in God.

²²By obedience to the truth,^D having purified yourselves^E for sincere love of the brothers, love one another earnestly^F from a pure^G heart, ²³since you have been born again—not of perishable seed but of imperishable—through the living and enduring word of God. ²⁴For

> All flesh is like grass,
> and all its glory like a flower
>   of the grass.
> The grass withers,
>   and the flower falls,
> ²⁵ but the word of the Lord
>   endures forever.^H

And this is the word that was preached as the gospel to you.

2 So rid yourselves of all malice, all deceit, hypocrisy, envy, and all slander. ²Like newborn infants, desire the pure spiritual milk, so that you may grow by it for your salvation,^I ³since **you have tasted that the Lord**

is good.^J ⁴Coming to Him, a living stone—rejected by men but chosen and valuable to God— ⁵you yourselves, as living stones, are being built into a spiritual house for a holy priesthood to offer spiritual sacrifices acceptable to God through Jesus Christ. ⁶For it is contained in Scripture:

> Look! I lay a stone in Zion,
>   a chosen
>   and honored^K cornerstone,^L
> and the one who believes
>   in Him
> will never be put to shame!^M,^N

⁷So honor will come to you who believe, but for the unbelieving,

> The stone that the builders
>   rejected—
> this One has become
>   the cornerstone,^O

⁸and

> A stone to stumble over,^P
> and a rock to trip over.^Q,^R

They stumble because they disobey the message; they were destined for this.

⁹ But you are **a chosen race,**^S,^T
>   **a royal priesthood,**^U
> a holy nation,^V a people
>   for His possession,^W
> so that you may proclaim
>   the praises^X,^Y
> of the One who called you
>   out of darkness
> into His marvelous light.
¹⁰ Once you were not a people,
>   but now you are God's people;
> you had not received mercy,
>   but now you have received mercy.

¹¹Dear friends, I urge you as strangers and temporary residents to abstain from fleshly desires that war against you.^Z ¹²Conduct yourselves honorably among the Gentiles,^AA

---

^A1:13 Lit Therefore, when you have the loins of your mind girded   ^B1:16 Lv 11:44-45; 19:2; 20:7   ^C1:20 Or foreknown   ^D1:22 Other mss add through the Spirit   ^E1:22 Or purified your souls   ^F1:22 Or intensely   ^G1:22 Other mss omit pure   ^H1:24-25 Is 40:6-8   ^I2:2 Other mss omit in your salvation   ^J2:3 Ps 34:8   ^K2:6 Or valuable   ^L2:6 Lit head of the corner   ^M2:6 Or be disappointed   ^N2:6 Is 28:16 LXX   ^O2:7 Ps 118:22   ^P2:8 Or a stone causing stumbling   ^Q2:8 Or a rock to trip over   ^R2:8 Is 8:14   ^S2:9 Or generation, or nation   ^T2:9 Dt 7:6; 10:15; Is 43:20 LXX   ^U2:9 Is 19:6; 23:22 LXX; Is 61:6   ^V2:9 Ex 19:6; 23:22 LXX   ^W2:9 Ex 19:5; 23:22 LXX; Dt 4:20; 7:6; Is 43:21 LXX   ^X2:9 Or the mighty deeds   ^Y2:9 Is 42:12; 43:21   ^Z2:11 Or against the soul   ^AA2:12 Or among the nations, or among the pagans so that in a case where they speak against you as those who do what is evil, they will, by observing your good works, glorify God on the day of visitation.[A]

[13] Submit to every human authority[B] because of the Lord, whether to the Emperor[C] as the supreme authority [14]or to governors as those sent out by him to punish those who do what is evil and to praise those who do what is good. [15]For it is God's will that you silence the ignorance of foolish people by doing good. [16]As God's slaves, live as free people, but don't use your freedom as a way to conceal evil. [17]Honor everyone. Love the brotherhood. Fear God. Honor the Emperor.[C]

[18]Household slaves, submit with all fear to your masters, not only to the good and gentle but also to the cruel.[D] [19]For it brings favor[E] if, mindful of God's will,[F,G] someone endures grief from suffering unjustly. [20]For what credit is there if you sin and are punished, and you endure it? But when you do what is good and suffer, if you endure it, this brings favor with God.

[21]   For you were called to this,
       because Christ also suffered for you,
       leaving you an example,
       so that you should follow
          in His steps.
[22]   He **did not commit sin,
       and no deceit was found
          in His mouth;**[H]
[23]   when He was reviled,
       He did not revile in return;
       when He was suffering,
       He did not threaten
       but entrusted Himself to the One
          who judges justly.
[24]   He Himself bore our sins
       in His body on the tree,
       so that, having died to sins,
       we might live for righteousness;
       you have been healed by His wounds.[I]
[25]   For you **were like sheep
          going astray,**[J]
       but you have now returned

to the Shepherd and Guardian[K]
   of your souls.

3 In the same way, wives, submit yourselves to your own husbands so that, even if some disobey the Christian message, they may be won over[L] without a message by the way their wives live [2]when they observe your pure, reverent lives. [3]Your beauty should not consist of outward things like elaborate hairstyles and the wearing of gold ornaments[M] or fine clothes. [4]Instead, it should consist of what is inside[N] the heart with the imperishable quality of a gentle and quiet spirit, which is very valuable in God's eyes. [5]For in the past, the holy women who put their hope in God also beautified themselves in this way, submitting to their own husbands, [6]just as Sarah obeyed Abraham, calling him lord. You have become her children when you do what is good and are not frightened by anything alarming.

[7]Husbands, in the same way, live with your wives with an understanding of their weaker nature[O] yet showing them honor as coheirs of the grace of life, so that your prayers will not be hindered.

[8]Now finally, all of you should be likeminded and sympathetic, should love believers,[P] and be compassionate and humble,[Q] [9]not paying back evil for evil or insult for insult but, on the contrary, giving a blessing, since you were called for this, so that you can inherit a blessing.

[10] For **the one who wants to love life
          and to see good days
       must keep his tongue from evil
       and his lips from speaking deceit,**
[11] **and he must turn away from evil
       and do what is good.
       He must seek peace and pursue it,**
[12] **because the eyes of the Lord are
          on the righteous
       and His ears are open
          to their request.
       But the face of the Lord is against
          those who do what is evil.**[R]

A2:12 The day when God intervenes in human history, either in grace or in judgment   **B2:13** Or *creature*   **C2:13,17** Lit *king*   **D2:18** Or *unscrupulous; lit crooked*   **E2:19** Other mss add *with God*   **F2:19** Other mss read *if, because of a good conscience*   **G2:19** Lit *if, because of conscience toward God*   **H2:22** Is 53:9   **I2:24** Is 53:5   **J2:25** Is 53:6   **K2:25** Or *Overseer*   **L3:1** Lit *may be gained*   **M3:3** Lit *and of putting around of gold items*   **N3:4** Lit *Instead, the hidden man of*   **O3:7** Lit *understanding as the weaker vessel*   **P3:8** Lit *sympathetic, loving the brothers*   **Q3:8** Other mss read *courteous*   **R3:10-12** Ps 34:12-16

¹³And who will harm^A you if you are deeply committed to what is good?^B ¹⁴But even if you should suffer for righteousness, you are blessed. **Do not fear what they fear or be disturbed,**^C ¹⁵but honor^D the Messiah^E as Lord in your hearts. Always be ready to give a defense to anyone who asks you for a reason^F for the hope that is in you. ¹⁶However, do this with gentleness and respect, keeping your conscience clear,^G,H so that when you are accused,^I those who denounce your Christian life^J will be put to shame. ¹⁷For it is better to suffer for doing good, if that should be God's will,^K than for doing evil.

¹⁸　For Christ also suffered for sins
　　once for all,^L
　　the righteous for the unrighteous,^M
　　that He might bring you^N to God,
　　after being put to death
　　in the fleshly realm^O
　　but made alive in the spiritual realm.^P

¹⁹In that state^Q He also went and made a proclamation to the spirits in prison^R ²⁰who in the past were disobedient, when God patiently waited in the days of Noah while an ark was being prepared. In it a few—that is, eight people^S—were saved through water. ²¹Baptism, which corresponds to this, now saves you (not the removal of the filth of the flesh, but the pledge^T of a good conscience toward God) through the resurrection of Jesus Christ. ²²Now that He has gone into heaven, He is at God's right hand with angels, authorities, and powers subject to Him.

4 Therefore, since Christ suffered^U in flesh,^V equip^W yourselves also with the same resolve^X—because the one who suffered in the flesh has finished with sin^Y— ²in order to live the remaining time in the flesh, no longer for human desires,^Z but for God's will. ³For there has already been enough time spent in doing what the pagans choose to

do:^AA carrying on in unrestrained behavior, evil desires, drunkenness, orgies, carousing, and lawless idolatry. ⁴So they are surprised that you don't plunge with them into the same flood^AB of wild living—and they slander you. ⁵They will give an account to the One who stands ready to judge the living and the dead. ⁶For this reason the gospel was also preached to those who are now dead, so that, although they might be judged by men in the fleshly realm,^O they might live by God in the spiritual realm.^AC

⁷Now the end of all things is near; therefore, be serious and disciplined for prayer. ⁸Above all, maintain an intense love for each other, since **love covers a multitude of sins.**^AD ⁹Be hospitable to one another without complaining. ¹⁰Based on the gift each one has received, use it to serve others, as good managers of the varied grace of God. ¹¹If anyone speaks, it should be as one who speaks God's words; if anyone serves, it should be from the strength God provides, so that God may be glorified through Jesus Christ in everything. To Him belong the glory and the power forever and ever. Amen.

¹²Dear friends, don't be surprised when the fiery ordeal^AE comes among you to test you as if something unusual were happening to you. ¹³Instead, rejoice as you share in the sufferings of the Messiah, so that you may also rejoice with great joy at the revelation of His glory. ¹⁴If you are ridiculed for the name of Christ, you are blessed, because the Spirit of glory and of God rests on you.^AF ¹⁵None of you, however, should suffer as a murderer, a thief, an evildoer, or a meddler.^AG ¹⁶But if anyone suffers as a "Christian," he should not be ashamed but should glorify God in having that name. ¹⁷For the time has come for judgment to begin with God's household, and if it begins with us, what will the outcome be for those who disobey the gospel of God?

^A3:13 Or mistreat, or do evil to   ^B3:13 Or you are partisans for the good; lit you are zealots   ^C3:14 Is 8:12   ^D3:15 Or sanctify; lit set apart   ^E3:15 Other mss read set God   ^F3:15 Or who demands of you an accounting   ^G3:16 Lit good   ^H3:16 Or keeping a clear conscience   ^I3:16 Other mss read when they speak against you as evildoers   ^J3:16 Lit your good behavior in Christ   ^K3:17 Lit if the will of God should will   ^L3:18 Other mss read died for sins on our behalf; other mss read died for our sins; other mss read died for sins on your behalf   ^M3:18 Or the Righteous One in the place of the unrighteous many   ^N3:18 Other mss read us   ^O3:18; 4:6 Or in the flesh   ^P3:18 Or in the spirit, or in the Spirit   ^Q3:19 Or In whom, or At that time, or In which   ^R3:19 Perhaps fallen supernatural beings or angels; 2Pt 2:4; Jd 6   ^S3:20 Lit souls   ^T3:21 Or the appeal   ^U4:1 Other mss read suffered for us   ^V4:1 The phrase "in the flesh" probably means in human experience.   ^W4:1 Or arm   ^X4:1 Or perspective, or attitude   ^Y4:1 Or the one who has suffered in the flesh has ceased from sin   ^Z4:2 Lit for desires of human beings   ^AA4:3 Or Gentiles   ^AB4:4 Lit you don't run with them into the same pouring out   ^AC4:6 Or in the spirit   ^AD4:8 Pr 10:12   ^AE4:12 Lit the burning   ^AF4:12 Other mss add He is blasphemed because of them, but He is glorified because of you.   ^AG4:15 Or as one who defrauds others

¹⁸ And **if a righteous person is saved
    with difficulty,
    what will become of the ungodly
    and the sinner?**ᴬ

¹⁹So those who suffer according to God's will should, while doing what is good, entrust themselves to a faithful Creator.

5 Therefore, as a fellow elder and witness to the sufferings of the Messiah and also a participant in the glory about to be revealed, I exhort the elders among you: ²Shepherd God's flock among you, not overseeingᴮ out of compulsion but freely, according to God's will;ᶜ not for the money but eagerly; ³not lording it over those entrusted to you, but being examples to the flock. ⁴And when the chief Shepherd appears, you will receive the unfading crown of glory.

⁵In the same way, you younger men, be subject to the elders. And all of you clothe yourselves withᴰ humility toward one another, because

**God resists the proud
but gives grace to the humble.**ᴱ

⁶Humble yourselves, therefore, under the mighty hand of God, so that He may exalt you at the proper time,ᶠ ⁷casting all your care on Him, because He cares about you.

⁸Be serious! Be alert! Your adversary the Devil is prowling around like a roaring lion, looking for anyone he can devour. ⁹Resist him and be firm in the faith, knowing that the same sufferings are being experienced by your fellow believers throughout the world.

¹⁰Now the God of all grace, who called you to His eternal glory in Christ Jesus, will personallyᴳ restore, establish, strengthen, and support you after you have suffered a little.ᴴ ¹¹The dominionᴵ belongs to Him forever.ᴶ Amen.

¹²I have written you this brief letter through Silvanusᴷ (I know him to be a faithful brother) to encourage you and to testify that this is the true grace of God. Take your stand in it! ¹³The church in Babylon,ᴸ also chosen, sends you greetings, as does Mark, my son. ¹⁴Greet one another with a kiss of love. Peace to all of you who are in Christ.ᴹ

2 PETER

1 Simeonᴺ Peter, a slave and an apostle of Jesus Christ:

To those who have obtained a faith of equal privilege with oursᴼ through the righteousness of our God and Savior Jesus Christ.

²May grace and peace be multiplied to you through the knowledge of God and of Jesus our Lord.

³Hisᴾ divine power has given us everything required for life and godliness through the knowledge of Him who called us byᑫ His own glory and goodness. ⁴By these He has given us very great and precious promises, so that through them you may share in the divine nature, escaping the corruption that is in the world because of evil desires. ⁵For this very reason, make every effort to supplement your faith with goodness, goodness with

knowledge, ⁶knowledge with self-control, self-control with endurance, endurance with godliness, ⁷godliness with brotherly affection, and brotherly affection with love. ⁸For if these qualities are yours and are increasing, they will keep you from being useless or unfruitful in the knowledge of our Lord Jesus Christ. ⁹The person who lacks these things is blind and shortsighted and has forgotten the cleansing from his past sins. ¹⁰Therefore, brothers, make every effort to confirm your calling and election, because if you do these things you will never stumble. ¹¹For in this way, entry into the eternal kingdom of our Lord and Savior Jesus Christ will be richly supplied to you.

¹²Therefore I will always remind you about these things, even though you know them

ᴬ4:18 Pr 11:31 LXX   ᴮ5:2 Other mss omit *overseeing*   ᶜ5:2 Other mss omit *according to God's will*   ᴰ5:5 Lit *you tie around yourselves*   ᴱ5:5 Pr 3:34 LXX   ᶠ5:6 Lit *in time*   ᴳ5:10 Lit *Himself*   ᴴ5:10 Or *a little while,* or *to a small extent*   ᴵ5:11 Other mss read *dominion and glory;* other mss read *glory and dominion*   ᴶ5:11 Other mss read *forever and ever*   ᴷ5:12 Or *Silas;* Ac 15:22-32; 16:19-40; 17:1-16   ᴸ5:13 Probably refers to Rome   ᴹ5:14 Other mss read *Christ Jesus. Amen.*   ᴺ1:1 Other mss read *Simon*   ᴼ1:1 Or *obtained a faith of the same kind as ours*   ᴾ1:3 Lit *As His*   ᑫ1:3 Or *to* and are established in the truth you have. [13]I consider it right, as long as I am in this bodily tent,[A] to wake you up with a reminder, [14]knowing that I will soon lay aside my tent, as our Lord Jesus Christ has also shown me. [15]And I will also make every effort that you may be able to recall these things at any time after my departure.[B]

[16]For we did not follow cleverly contrived myths when we made known to you the power and coming of our Lord Jesus Christ; instead, we were eyewitnesses of His majesty. [17]For when He received honor and glory from God the Father, a voice came to Him from the Majestic Glory:

This is My beloved Son.[C]
I take delight in Him![D]

[18]And we heard this voice when it came from heaven while we were with Him on the holy mountain. [19]So we have the prophetic word strongly confirmed. You will do well to take attention to it, as to a lamp shining in a dismal place, until the day dawns and the morning star rises in your hearts. [20]First of all, you should know this: No prophecy of Scripture comes from one's own interpretation, [21]because no prophecy ever came by the will of man; instead, men spoke from God as they were moved by the Holy Spirit.

2 But there were also false prophets among the people, just as there will be false teachers among you. They will secretly bring in destructive heresies, even denying the Master who bought them, and will bring swift destruction on themselves. [2]Many will follow their unrestrained ways, and the way of truth will be blasphemed because of them. [3]They will exploit you in their greed with deceptive words. Their condemnation, pronounced long ago, is not idle, and their destruction does not sleep.

[4]For if God didn't spare the angels who sinned but threw them down into Tartarus[E] and delivered them to be kept in chains[F] of darkness until judgment; [5]and if He didn't spare the ancient world, but protected Noah,

a preacher of righteousness, and seven others,[G] when He brought a flood on the world of the ungodly; [6]and if He reduced the cities of Sodom and Gomorrah to ashes and condemned them to ruin,[H] making them an example to those who were going to be ungodly;[I] [7]and if He rescued righteous Lot, distressed by the unrestrained behavior of the immoral [8](for as he lived among them, that righteous man tormented himself day by day with the lawless deeds he saw and heard)— [9]then the Lord knows how to rescue the godly from trials and to keep the unrighteous under punishment until the day of judgment, [10]especially those who follow the polluting desires of the flesh and despise authority.

Bold, arrogant people! They do not tremble when they blaspheme the glorious ones; [11]however, angels, who are greater in might and power, do not bring a slanderous charge against them before the Lord.[J] [12]But these people, like irrational animals—creatures of instinct born to be caught and destroyed— speak blasphemies about things they don't understand, and in their destruction they too will be destroyed, [13]suffering harm as the payment for unrighteousness. They consider it a pleasure to carouse in the daytime. They are spots and blemishes, delighting in their deceptions[K] as they feast with you. [14]They have eyes full of adultery and are always looking for sin. They seduce unstable people and have hearts trained in greed. Children under a curse! [15]They have gone astray by abandoning the straight path and have followed the path of Balaam, the son of Bosor,[L] who loved the wages of unrighteousness [16]but received a rebuke for his transgression: A donkey that could not talk spoke with a human voice and restrained the prophet's irrationality.

[17]These people are springs without water, mists driven by a whirlwind. The gloom of darkness has been reserved for them. [18]For by uttering boastful, empty words, they seduce, with fleshly desires and debauchery, people who have barely escaped[M] from those who

---

A1:13 = Peter's body   **B**1:15 Or *my death*   **C**1:17 Other mss read *My Son, My Beloved*   **D**1:17 = Christ's transfiguration; Mt 17:5   **E**2:4 = Gk name for a place of divine punishment in the underworld.   **F**2:4 Other mss read *in pits*   **G**2:5 Lit *righteousness, as the eighth*   **H**2:6 Other mss omit *to ruin*   **I**2:6 Other mss read *an example of what is going to happen to the ungodly*   **J**2:11 Other mss read *them from the Lord*   **K**2:13 Other mss read *delighting in the love feasts*   **L**2:15 Other mss read *Beor*   **M**2:18 Or *people who are barely escaping* live in error. ¹⁹ They promise them freedom, but they themselves are slaves of corruption, since people are enslaved to whatever defeats them. ²⁰ For if, having escaped the world's impurity through the knowledge of our Lord and Savior Jesus Christ, they are again entangled in these things and defeated, the last state is worse for them than the first. ²¹ For it would have been better for them not to have known the way of righteousness than, after knowing it, to turn back from the holy command delivered to them. ²² It has happened to them according to the true proverb: **A dog returns to its own vomit,**ᴬ and, "a sow, after washing itself, wallows in the mud."

3 Dear friends, this is now the second letter I have written to you; in both letters, I want to develop a genuine understanding with a reminder, ² so that you can remember the words previously spoken by the holy prophets and the command of our Lord and Savior given through your apostles. ³ First, be aware of this: Scoffers will come in the last days to scoff, living according to their own desires, ⁴ saying, "Where is the promise of His coming? Ever since the fathers fell asleep, all things continue as they have been since the beginning of creation." ⁵ They willfully ignore this: Long ago the heavens and the earth were brought about from water and through water by the word of God. ⁶ Through these waters the world of that time perished when it was flooded. ⁷ But by the same word, the present heavens and earth are stored up for fire, being kept until the day of judgment and destruction of ungodly men.

⁸ Dear friends, don't let this one thing escape you: With the Lord one day is like a thousand years, and a thousand years like one day. ⁹ The Lord does not delay His promise, as some understand delay, but is patient with you, not wanting any to perish but all to come to repentance.

¹⁰ But the Day of the Lord will come like a thief;ᴮ on that day the heavens will pass away with a loud noise, the elements will burn and be dissolved, and the earth and the works on it will be disclosed.ᶜ ¹¹ Since all these things are to be destroyed in this way, it is clear what sort of people you should be in holy conduct and godliness ¹² as you wait for and earnestly desire the comingᴰ of the day of God. The heavens will be on fire and be dissolved because of it, and the elements will melt with the heat. ¹³ But based on His promise, we wait for the new heavens and a new earth, where righteousness will dwell.

¹⁴ Therefore, dear friends, while you wait for these things, make every effort to be found at peace with Him without spot or blemish. ¹⁵ Also, regard the patience of our Lord as an opportunity for salvation, just as our dear brother Paul has written to you according to the wisdom given to him. ¹⁶ He speaks about these things in all his letters in which there are some matters that are hard to understand. The untaught and unstable twist them to their own destruction, as they also do with the rest of the Scriptures.

¹⁷ Therefore, dear friends, since you know this in advance, be on your guard, so that you are not led away by the error of lawless people and fall from your own stability. ¹⁸ But grow in the grace and knowledge of our Lord and Savior Jesus Christ. To Him be the glory both now and to the day of eternity.ᴱ Amen.ᶠ

ᴬ2:22 Pr 26:11   ᴮ3:10 Other mss add *in the night*   ᶜ3:10 Other mss read *will be burned up*   ᴰ3:12 Or *and speed the coming*   ᴱ3:18 Or *now and forever*   ᶠ3:18 Other mss omit *Amen.*

1 John

1 What was from the beginning,
   what we have heard,
   what we have seen with our eyes,
   what we have observed
   and have touched with our hands,
   concerning the Word of life—

2 that life was revealed,
   and we have seen it
   and we testify and declare to you
   the eternal life that was
      with the Father
   and was revealed to us—

3 what we have seen and heard
   we also declare to you,
   so that you may have fellowship
      along with us;
   and indeed our fellowship is
      with the Father
   and with His Son Jesus Christ.

4 We are writing these things[A]
   so that our[B] joy may be complete.

5 Now this is the message we have heard from Him and declare to you: God is light, and there is absolutely no darkness in Him. 6 If we say, "We have fellowship with Him," yet we walk in darkness, we are lying and are not practicing[C] the truth. 7 But if we walk in the light as He Himself is in the light, we have fellowship with one another, and the blood of Jesus His Son cleanses us from all sin. 8 If we say, "We have no sin," we are deceiving ourselves, and the truth is not in us. 9 If we confess our sins, He is faithful and righteous to forgive us our sins and to cleanse us from all unrighteousness. 10 If we say, "We don't have any sin," we make Him a liar, and His word is not in us.

2 My little children, I am writing you these things so that you may not sin. But if anyone does sin, we have an advocate with the Father—Jesus Christ the Righteous One. 2 He Himself is the propitiation for our sins, and not only for ours, but also for those of the whole world.

3 This is how we are sure that we have come to know Him: by keeping His commands.

4 The one who says, "I have come to know Him," yet doesn't keep His commands, is a liar, and the truth is not in him. 5 But whoever keeps His word, truly in him the love of God is perfected.[D] This is how we know we are in Him: 6 The one who says he remains in Him should walk just as He walked.

7 Dear friends, I am not writing you a new command but an old command that you have had from the beginning. The old command is the message you have heard. 8 Yet I am writing you a new command, which is true in Him and in you, because the darkness is passing away and the true light is already shining.

9 The one who says he is in the light but hates his brother is in the darkness until now. 10 The one who loves his brother remains in the light, and there is no cause for stumbling in him.[E] 11 But the one who hates his brother is in the darkness, walks in the darkness, and doesn't know where he's going, because the darkness has blinded his eyes.

12 I am writing to you, little children,
   because your sins have
      been forgiven
   because of Jesus' name.

13 I am writing to you, fathers,
   because you have come to know
      the One who is
      from the beginning.
   I am writing to you, young men,
   because you have had victory
      over the evil one.

14 I have written to you, children,
   because you have come to know
      the Father.
   I have written to you, fathers,
   because you have come to know
      the One who is
      from the beginning.
   I have written to you, young men,
   because you are strong,
   God's word remains in you,
   and you have had victory
      over the evil one.

---

¹⁵Do not love the world or the things that belong to^A the world. If anyone loves the world, love for the Father is not in him. ¹⁶For everything that belongs to^B the world—the lust of the flesh, the lust of the eyes, and the pride in one's lifestyle—is not from the Father, but is from the world. ¹⁷And the world with its lust is passing away, but the one who does God's will remains forever.

¹⁸Children, it is the last hour. And as you have heard, "Antichrist is coming," even now many antichrists have come. We know from this that it is the last hour. ¹⁹They went out from us, but they did not belong to us; for if they had belonged to us, they would have remained with us. However, they went out so that it might be made clear that none of them belongs to us.

²⁰But you have an anointing from the Holy One, and all of you have knowledge.^C ²¹I have not written to you because you don't know the truth, but because you do know it, and because no lie comes from the truth. ²²Who is the liar, if not the one who denies that Jesus is the Messiah? This one is the antichrist: the one who denies the Father and the Son. ²³No one who denies the Son can have the Father; he who confesses the Son has the Father as well.

²⁴What you have heard from the beginning must remain in you. If what you have heard from the beginning remains in you, then you will remain in the Son and in the Father. ²⁵And this is the promise that He Himself made to us: eternal life. ²⁶I have written these things to you about those who are trying to deceive you.

²⁷The anointing you received from Him remains in you, and you don't need anyone to teach you. Instead, His anointing teaches you about all things and is true and is not a lie; just as He has taught you, remain in Him. ²⁸So now, little children, remain in Him, so that when He appears we may have boldness and not be ashamed before Him at His coming. ²⁹If you know that He is righteous, you know this as well: Everyone who does

what is right has been born of Him. 3¹Look at how great a love^D the Father has given us that we should be called God's children. And we are! The reason the world does not know us is that it didn't know Him. ²Dear friends, we are God's children now, and what we will be has not yet been revealed. We know that when He appears, we will be like Him because we will see Him as He is. ³And everyone who has this hope in Him purifies himself just as He is pure.

⁴Everyone who commits sin also breaks the law;^E sin is the breaking of law. ⁵You know that He was revealed so that He might take away sins,^F and there is no sin in Him. ⁶Everyone who remains in Him does not sin;^G everyone who^H sins has not seen Him or known Him.

⁷Little children, let no one deceive you! The one who does what is right is righteous, just as He is righteous. ⁸The one who commits^I sin is of the Devil, for the Devil has sinned from the beginning. The Son of God was revealed for this purpose: to destroy the Devil's works. ⁹Everyone who has been born of God does not sin,^J because His^K seed remains in him; he is not able to sin,^L because he has been born of God. ¹⁰This is how God's children—and the Devil's children—are made evident.

Whoever does not do what is right is not of God, especially the one who does not love his brother. ¹¹For this is the message you have heard from the beginning: We should love one another, ¹²unlike Cain, who was of the evil one and murdered^M his brother. And why did he murder him? Because his works were evil, and his brother's were righteous. ¹³Do not be surprised, brothers, if the world hates you. ¹⁴We know that we have passed from death to life because we love our brothers. The one who does not love remains in death. ¹⁵Everyone who hates his brother is a murderer, and you know that no murderer has eternal life residing in him.

¹⁶This is how we have come to know love: He laid down His life for us. We should also lay down our lives for our brothers. ¹⁷If anyone has this world's goods and sees his

^A2:15 Lit things in   ^B2:16 Lit that is in   ^C2:20 Other mss read and you know all things   ^D3:1 Or at what sort of love   ^E3:4 Or also commits iniquity   ^F3:5 Other mss read our sins   ^G3:6 Or not keep on sinning   ^H3:6 Or who keeps on sinning   ^I3:8 Or practices   ^J3:9 Or not practice sin   ^K3:9 God's   ^L3:9 Or to keep on sinning   ^M3:12 Or slaughtered brother in need but closes his eyes to his need—how can God's love reside in him?

[18]Little children, we must not love with word or speech, but with truth and action. [19]This is how we will know we belong to the truth and will convince our conscience in His presence, [20]even if our conscience condemns us, that God is greater than our conscience, and He knows all things.

[21]Dear friends, if our conscience doesn't condemn us, we have confidence before God [22]and can receive whatever we ask from Him because we keep His commands and do what is pleasing in His sight. [23]Now this is His command: that we believe in the name of His Son Jesus Christ, and love one another as He commanded us. [24]The one who keeps His commands remains in Him, and He in him. And the way we know that He remains in us is from the Spirit He has given us.

4 Dear friends, do not believe every spirit, but test the spirits to determine if they are from God, because many false prophets have gone out into the world.

[2]This is how you know the Spirit of God: Every spirit who confesses that Jesus Christ has[A] come in the flesh is from God. [3]But every spirit who does not confess Jesus[B] is not from God. This is the spirit of the antichrist; you have heard that it is coming, and he is already in the world now.

[4]You are from God, little children, and you have conquered them, because the One who is in you is greater than the one who is in the world. [5]They are from the world. Therefore what they say is from the world, and the world listens to them. [6]We are from God. Anyone who knows God listens to us; anyone who is not from God does not listen to us. From this we know the Spirit of truth and the spirit of deception.

[7]Dear friends, let us love one another, because love is from God, and everyone who loves has been born of God and knows God. [8]The one who does not love does not know God, because God is love. [9]God's love was revealed among us in this way:[C] God sent His

One and Only Son into the world so that we might live through Him. [10]Love consists in this: not that we loved God, but that He loved us and sent His Son to be the[D] propitiation for our sins. [11]Dear friends, if God loved us in this way, we also must love one another. [12]No one has ever seen God.[E] If we love one another, God remains in[F] us and His love is perfected in us.

[13]This is how we know that we remain in Him and He in us: He has given assurance to us from His Spirit. [14]And we have seen and we testify that the Father has sent His Son as the world's Savior. [15]Whoever confesses[G] that Jesus is the Son of God—God remains in him and he in God. [16]And we have come to know and to believe the love that God has for us. God is love, and the one who remains in love remains in God, and God remains in him.

[17]In this, love is perfected with us so that we may have confidence in the day of judgment, for we are as He is in this world. [18]There is no fear in love; instead, perfect love drives out fear, because fear involves punishment.[H] So the one who fears has not reached perfection in love. [19]We love[I] because He first loved us. [20]If anyone says, "I love God," yet hates his brother, he is a liar. For the person who does not love his brother he has seen cannot love the God he has not seen.[J] [21]And we have this command from Him: The one who loves God must also love his brother.

5 Everyone who believes that Jesus is the Messiah has been born of God, and everyone who loves the Father also loves the one born of Him. [2]This is how we know that we love God's children when we love God and obey[K] His commands. [3]For this is what love for God is: to keep His commands. Now His commands are not a burden, [4]because whatever has been born of God conquers the world. This is the victory that has conquered the world: our faith. [5]And who is the one who conquers the world but the one who believes that Jesus is the Son of God?

[6]Jesus Christ—He is the One who came by water and blood, not by water only, but by

[A]4:2 Or confesses Jesus to be the Christ   [B]4:3 Other mss read confess that Jesus has come in the flesh   [C]4:9 or revealed in us   [D]4:10 Or a   [E]4:12 Since God is an infinite being, no one can see Him in His absolute essential nature; Ex 33:18-23.   [F]4:12 Or remains among   [G]4:15 Or acknowledges   [H]4:18 Or fear has its own punishment or torment   [I]4:19 Other mss add Him   [J]4:20 Other mss read has seen, how is he able to love . . . seen? (as a question)   [K]5:2 Other mss read keep water and by blood. And the Spirit is the One who testifies, because the Spirit is the truth. [7] For there are three that testify:[A] [8] the Spirit, the water, and the blood—and these three are in agreement. [9] If we accept the testimony of men, God's testimony is greater, because it is God's testimony that He has given about His Son. [10] (The one who believes in the Son of God has this testimony within him. The one who does not believe God has made Him a liar, because he has not believed in the testimony God has given about His Son.) [11] And this is the testimony: God has given us eternal life, and this life is in His Son.

[12] The one who has the Son has life. The one who doesn't have the Son of God does not have life. [13] I have written these things to you who believe in the name of the Son of God, so that you may know that you have eternal life.

[14] Now this is the confidence we have before Him: Whenever we ask anything according to His will, He hears us. [15] And if we know that He hears whatever we ask, we know that we have what we have asked Him for.

[16] If anyone sees his brother committing a sin that does not bring death, he should ask, and God[B] will give life to him—to those who commit sin that doesn't bring death. There is sin[C] that brings death. I am not saying he should pray about that. [17] All unrighteousness is sin, and there is sin that does not bring death.

[18] We know that everyone who has been born of God does not sin, but the One[D] who is born of God keeps him,[E,F] and the evil one does not touch him.

[19] We know that we are of God, and the whole world is under the sway of the evil one.

[20] And we know that the Son of God has come and has given us understanding so that we may know the true One.[G] We are in the true One—that is, in His Son Jesus Christ. He is the true God and eternal life.

[21] Little children, guard yourselves from idols.

2 JOHN

The Elder:[H]
To the elect lady[I] and her children: I love all of you in the truth—and not only I, but also all who have come to know the truth— [2] because of the truth that remains in us and will be with us forever.

[3] Grace, mercy, and peace will be with us from God the Father and from Jesus Christ, the Son of the Father, in truth and love.

[4] I was very glad to find some of your children walking in the truth, in keeping with a command we have received from the Father. [5] So now I urge you, dear lady—not as if I were writing you a new command, but one we have had from the beginning—that we love one another. [6] And this is love: that we walk according to His commands. This is the command as you have heard it from the beginning: you must walk in love.[J]

[7] Many deceivers have gone out into the world; they do not confess the coming of Jesus Christ in the flesh.[K] This is the deceiver and the antichrist. [8] Watch yourselves so you don't lose what we[L] have worked for, but that you may receive a full reward. [9] Anyone who does not remain in Christ's teaching but goes beyond it, does not have God. The one who remains in that teaching, this one has both the Father and the Son. [10] If anyone comes to you and does not bring this teaching, do not receive him into your home, and don't say, "Welcome," to him; [11] for the one who says, "Welcome," to him shares in his evil works.

[12] Though I have many things to write to you, I don't want to do so with paper and ink. Instead, I hope to be with you and talk face to face[M] so that our joy may be complete.

[13] The children of your elect sister send you greetings

A5:7-8 Other mss (Vg and a few late Gk mss) read *testify in heaven: the Father, the Word, and the Holy Spirit, and these three are One.* B *And there are three who bear witness on earth:* B5:16 Lit *He* C5:16 Or *is a sin* D5:18 Jesus Christ E5:18 Other mss read *himself* F5:18 Or *the one who is born of God keeps himself* G5:20 Other mss read *the true God* H1 Or *Presbyter* I1 Or *Kyria,* a proper name; probably a literary figure for a local church known to John; the children would be its members. J6 Lit *in it* K7 Or *confess Jesus Christ as coming in the flesh* L8 Other mss read *you* M12 Lit *mouth to mouth*

3 JOHN

The Elder:
To my dear friend[A] Gaius: I love you in the truth.

[2] Dear friend,[B] I pray that you may prosper in every way and be in good health physically just as you are spiritually.[C] [3] For I was very glad when some brothers came and testified to your faithfulness to the truth—how you are walking in the truth. [4] I have no greater joy than this: to hear that my children are walking in the truth.

[5] Dear friend,[B] you are showing faithfulness[D] by whatever you do for the brothers, especially when they are strangers. [6] They have testified to your love in front of the church. You will do well to send them on their journey in a manner worthy of God, [7] since they set out for the sake of the Name, accepting nothing from pagans. [8] Therefore, we ought to support such men so that we can be coworkers with[E] the truth.

[9] I wrote something to the church, but Diotrephes, who loves to have first place among them, does not receive us. [10] This is why, if I come, I will remind him of the works he is doing, slandering us with malicious words. And he is not satisfied with that! He not only refuses to welcome the brothers himself, but he even stops those who want to do so and expels them from the church.

[11] Dear friend,[B] do not imitate what is evil, but what is good. The one who does good is of God; the one who does evil has not seen God. [12] Demetrius has a good testimony from everyone, and from the truth itself. And we also testify for him, and you know that our testimony is true.

[13] I have many things to write you, but I don't want to write to you with pen and ink. [14] I hope to see you soon, and we will talk face to face.[F]

Peace be with you. The friends send you greetings. Greet the friends by name.

JUDE

Jude, a slave of Jesus Christ and a brother of James:
To those who are the called, loved[G] by God the Father and kept by Jesus Christ.

[2] May mercy, peace, and love be multiplied to you.

[3] Dear friends, although I was eager to write you about the salvation we share, I found it necessary to write and exhort you to contend for the faith that was delivered to the saints once for all. [4] For some men, who were designated for this judgment long ago, have come in by stealth; they are ungodly, turning the grace of our God into promiscuity and denying Jesus Christ, our only Master and Lord.

[5] Now I want to remind you, though you know all these things: The Lord[H] first[I] saved a people out of Egypt and later destroyed those who did not believe; [6] and He has kept, with eternal chains in darkness for the judgment of the great day, the angels who did not keep their own position but deserted their proper dwelling. [7] In the same way, Sodom and Gomorrah and the cities around them committed sexual immorality and practiced perversions,[J] just as angels did, and serve as an example by undergoing the punishment of eternal fire.

[8] Nevertheless, these dreamers likewise defile their flesh, reject authority, and blaspheme glorious ones. [9] Yet Michael the archangel, when he was disputing with the Devil in a debate about Moses' body, did not dare bring an abusive condemnation against him but said, "The Lord rebuke you!" [10] But these people blaspheme anything they don't understand. What they know by instinct like

A1 Or my beloved   B2,5,11 Or Beloved   C2 Lit as your soul prospers   D5 Lit are doing a faithful thing   E8 Or coworkers for   F14 Lit mouth to mouth   G1 Other mss read sanctified   H5 Other mss read Jesus/Joshua, God, or God Christ   I5 Other mss place first after remind you   J7 Lit and went after other flesh unreasoning animals—they destroy themselves with these things. ¹¹Woe to them! For they have traveled in the way of Cain, have abandoned themselves to the error of Balaam for profit, and have perished in Korah's rebellion.

¹²These are the ones who are like dangerous reefs^A at your love feasts. They feast with you, nurturing only themselves without fear. They are waterless clouds carried along by winds; trees in late autumn—fruitless, twice dead, pulled out by the roots; ¹³wild waves of the sea, foaming up their shameful deeds; wandering stars for whom the blackness of darkness is reserved forever!

¹⁴And Enoch, in the seventh generation from Adam, prophesied about them:

> Look! The Lord comes^B
> with thousands of His holy ones
> ¹⁵ to execute judgment on all
> and to convict them^C
> of all their ungodly acts
> that they have done
> in an ungodly way,
> and of all the harsh things
> ungodly sinners
> have said against Him.

¹⁶These people are discontented grumblers, walking according to their desires; their mouths utter arrogant words, flattering people for their own advantage.

¹⁷But you, dear friends, remember what was predicted by the apostles of our Lord Jesus Christ; ¹⁸they told you, "In the end time there will be scoffers walking according to their own ungodly desires." ¹⁹These people create divisions and are unbelievers,^D not having the Spirit.

²⁰But you, dear friends, as you build yourselves up in your most holy faith and pray in the Holy Spirit, ²¹keep yourselves in the love of God, expecting the mercy of our Lord Jesus Christ for eternal life. ²²Have mercy on those who doubt; ²³save others by snatching them from the fire; have mercy on others but with fear, hating even the garment defiled by the flesh.

²⁴Now to Him who is able to protect you from stumbling and to make you stand in the presence of His glory, blameless and with great joy, ²⁵to the only God our Savior, through Jesus Christ our Lord,^E be glory, majesty, power, and authority before all time,^F now and forever. Amen.

REVELATION

1 The revelation of^G Jesus Christ that God gave Him to show His slaves what must quickly^H take place. He sent it and signified it^I through His angel to His slave John, ²who testified to God's word and to the testimony^J about Jesus Christ, in all he saw.^K ³The one who reads this is blessed, and those who hear the words of this prophecy and keep^L what is written in it are blessed, because the time is near!

⁴John:

To the seven churches in Asia.

Grace and peace to you from^M the One who is, who was, and who is coming; from the seven spirits^N before His throne; ⁵and from Jesus Christ, the faithful witness, the firstborn from the dead and the ruler of the kings of the earth.

To Him who loves us and has set us free^O from our sins by His blood, ⁶and made us a kingdom,^P priests^Q to His God and Father—the glory and dominion are His forever and ever. Amen.

> ⁷ Look! He is coming
> with the clouds,
> and every eye will see Him,
> including those who pierced^R Him.
> And all the families of the earth^S,T

^A12 Or like spots ^B14 Or came ^C15 Lit convict all ^D19 Or natural ^E25 Other mss omit through Jesus Christ our Lord ^F25 Other mss omit before all time ^G1:1 Or Revelation of, or A revelation of ^H1:1 Or soon ^I1:1 Made it known through symbols ^J1:2 Or witness ^K1:2 Lit as many as he saw ^L1:3 Or follow, or obey ^M1:4 Other mss add God ^N1:4 Or the sevenfold Spirit ^O1:5 Other mss read has washed us ^P1:6 Other mss read kings and ^Q1:6 Or made us into (or to be) a kingdom of priests; Ex 19:6 ^R1:7 Or impaled ^S1:7 Or all the tribes of the land ^T1:7 Gn 12:3; 28:14; Zch 14:17

will mourn over Him.[A][B]
This is certain. Amen.

[8]"I am the Alpha and the Omega," says the Lord God, "the One who is, who was, and who is coming, the Almighty."

[9]I, John, your brother and partner in the tribulation, kingdom, and endurance that are in Jesus, was on the island called Patmos because of God's word and the testimony about Jesus.[C] [10]I was in the Spirit[D],[E] on the Lord's day,[F] and I heard a loud voice behind me like a trumpet [11]saying, "Write on a scroll[G] what you see and send it to the seven churches: Ephesus, Smyrna, Pergamum, Thyatira, Sardis, Philadelphia, and Laodicea."

[12]I turned to see whose voice it was that spoke to me. When I turned I saw seven gold lampstands, [13]and among the lampstands was One like the Son of Man,[H] dressed in a long robe and with a gold sash wrapped around His chest. [14]His head and hair were white like wool—white as snow—and His eyes like a fiery flame. [15]His feet were like fine bronze as it is fired in a furnace, and His voice like the sound of cascading[I] waters. [16]He had seven stars in His right hand; a sharp double-edged sword came from His mouth, and His face was shining like the sun at midday.[J]

[17]When I saw Him, I fell at His feet like a dead man. He laid His right hand on me and said, "Don't be afraid! I am the First and the Last, [18]and the Living One. I was dead, but look—I am alive forever and ever, and I hold the keys of death and Hades. [19]Therefore write what you have seen, what is, and what will take place after this. [20]The secret of the seven stars you saw in My right hand and of the seven gold lampstands is this: The seven stars are the angels[K] of the seven churches, and the seven lampstands[L] are the seven churches.

2 "Write to the angel[M] of the church in Ephesus.

"The One who holds the seven stars in His right hand and who walks among the seven gold lampstands says: [2]I know your works, your labor, and your endurance, and that you

cannot tolerate evil. You have tested those who call themselves apostles and are not, and you have found them to be liars. [3]You also possess endurance and have tolerated many things because of My name and have not grown weary. [4]But I have this against you: You have abandoned the love you had at first. [5]Remember then how far you have fallen; repent, and do the works you did at first. Otherwise, I will come to you[N] and remove your lampstand from its place—unless you repent. [6]Yet you do have this: You hate the practices of the Nicolaitans, which I also hate.

[7]"Anyone who has an ear should listen to what the Spirit says to the churches. I will give the victor the right to eat from the tree of life, which is in[O] God's paradise.

[8]"Write to the angel of the church in Smyrna:

"The First and the Last, the One who was dead and came to life, says: [9]I know your[P] affliction and poverty, yet you are rich. I know the slander of those who say they are Jews and are not, but are a synagogue of Satan. [10]Don't be afraid of what you are about to suffer. Look, the Devil is about to throw some of you into prison to test you, and you will have affliction for 10 days. Be faithful until death, and I will give you the crown[Q] of life.

[11]"Anyone who has an ear should listen to what the Spirit says to the churches. The victor will never be harmed by the second death.

[12]"Write to the angel of the church in Pergamum:

"The One who has the sharp, double-edged sword says: [13]I know[R] where you live—where Satan's throne is! And you are holding on to My name and did not deny your faith in Me,[S] even in the days of Antipas, My faithful witness who was killed among you, where Satan lives. [14]But I have a few things against you. You have some there who hold to the teaching of Balaam, who taught Balak to place a stumbling block[T] in front of the Israelites: to eat meat sacrificed to idols and to commit

A1:7 Or *will wail because of Him*   **B**1:7 Dn 7:13; Zch 12:10   **C**1:9 Lit *the witness of Jesus*   **D**1:10 Or *in spirit; lit I became in the Spirit*   **E**1:10 John was brought by God's Spirit into a realm of spiritual vision.   **F**1:10 Sunday   **G**1:11 Or *book*   **H**1:13 Or *like a son of man*   **I**1:15 Lit *many*   **J**1:16 Lit *like the sun shines in its power*   **K**1:20 Or *messengers*   **L**1:20 Other mss add *that you saw*   **M**2:1 Or *messenger here and elsewhere*   **N**2:5 Other mss read *will come quickly*   **O**2:7 Other mss read *in the midst of*   **P**2:9 Other mss add *works and*   **Q**2:10 Or *wreath*   **R**2:13 Other mss add *your works and*   **S**2:13 Or *deny My faith*   **T**2:14 Or *to place a trap* sexual immorality.[A] [15]In the same way, you also have those who hold to the teaching of the Nicolaitans.[B] [16]Therefore repent! Otherwise, I will come to you quickly and fight against them with the sword of My mouth.

[17]"Anyone who has an ear should listen to what the Spirit says to the churches. I will give the victor some of the hidden manna.[C] I will also give him a white stone, and on the stone a new name is inscribed that no one knows except the one who receives it.

[18]"Write to the angel of the church in Thyatira:

"The Son of God, the One whose eyes are like a fiery flame and whose feet are like fine bronze,[D] says: [19]I know your works—your love, faithfulness,[E] service, and endurance. Your last works are greater than the first. [20]But I have this against you: You tolerate the woman Jezebel, who calls herself a prophetess and teaches and deceives My slaves to commit sexual immorality[A] and to eat meat sacrificed to idols. [21]I gave her time to repent, but she does not want to repent of her sexual immorality.[F] [22]Look! I will throw her into a sickbed and those who commit adultery with her into great tribulation, unless they repent of her[G] practices. [23]I will kill her children with the plague.[H] Then all the churches will know that I am the One who examines minds[I] and hearts, and I will give to each of you according to your works. [24]I say to the rest of you in Thyatira, who do not hold this teaching, who haven't known the deep things[J] of Satan—as they say—I do not put any other burden on you. [25]But hold on to what you have until I come. [26]The one who is victorious and keeps My works to the end: I will give him authority over the nations—

[27]   and he will shepherd[K] them
            with an iron scepter;
        he will shatter them like pottery[L]—

just as I have received this from My Father. [28]I will also give him the morning star.

[29]"Anyone who has an ear should listen to what the Spirit says to the churches.

3 "Write to the angel of the church in Sardis:

"The One who has the seven spirits of God and the seven stars says: I know your works; you have a reputation[M] for being alive, but you are dead. [2]Be alert and strengthen[N] what remains, which is about to die, for I have not found your works complete before My God. [3]Remember, therefore, what you have received and heard; keep it, and repent. But if you are not alert, I will come[O] like a thief, and you have no idea at what hour I will come against you.[P] [4]But you have a few people[Q] in Sardis who have not defiled[R] their clothes, and they will walk with Me in white, because they are worthy. [5]In the same way, the victor will be dressed in white clothes, and I will never erase his name from the book of life but will acknowledge his name before My Father and before His angels.

[6]"Anyone who has an ear should listen to what the Spirit says to the churches.

[7]"Write to the angel of the church in Philadelphia:

"The Holy One, the True One, the One who has the key of David, who opens and no one will close, and closes and no one opens says: [8]I know your works. Because you have limited strength, have kept My word, and have not denied My name, look, I have placed before you an open door that no one is able to close. [9]Take note! I will make those from the synagogue of Satan, who claim to be Jews and are not, but are lying—note this—I will make them come and bow down at your feet, and they will know that I have loved you. [10]Because you have kept My command to endure,[S] I will also keep you from the hour of testing that is going to come over the whole world to test those who live on the earth. [11]I am coming quickly. Hold on to what you have, so that no one takes your crown. [12]The victor: I will make him a pillar in the sanctuary of My God, and he will never go out again. I will write on him the name of My God and the name of the city of My God—the new Jerusalem, which comes down out of heaven from My God—and My new name.

A2:14,20 Or commit fornication   B2:15 Other mss add which I hate   C2:17 Other mss add to eat   D2:18 Probably gleaming white hot; Rv 1:15
E2:19 Or faith   F2:21 Or her fornication   G2:22 Other mss read their   H2:23 Or I will surely kill her children   I2:23 Lit kidneys   J2:24 Or
the secret things   K2:27 Or rule; see 19:15   L2:27 Ps 2:9   M3:1 Lit have a name   N3:2 Other mss read guard   O3:3 Other mss add upon
you   P3:3 Or upon you   Q3:4 Lit few names   R3:4 Or soiled   S3:10 Lit My word of endurance

[13]"Anyone who has an ear should listen to what the Spirit says to the churches.

[14]"Write to the angel of the church in Laodicea:

"The Amen, the faithful and true Witness, the Originator[A] of God's creation says: [15]I know your works, that you are neither cold nor hot. I wish that you were cold or hot. [16]So, because you are lukewarm, and neither hot nor cold, I am going to vomit[B] you out of My mouth. [17]Because you say, 'I'm rich; I have become wealthy and need nothing,' and you don't know that you are wretched, pitiful, poor, blind, and naked, [18]I advise you to buy from Me gold refined in the fire so that you may be rich, white clothes so that you may be dressed and your shameful nakedness not be exposed, and ointment to spread on your eyes so that you may see. [19]As many as I love, I rebuke and discipline. So be committed[C] and repent. [20]Listen! I stand at the door and knock. If anyone hears My voice and opens the door, I will come in to him and have dinner with him, and he with Me. [21]The victor: I will give him the right to sit with Me on My throne, just as I also won the victory and sat down with My Father on His throne.

[22]"Anyone who has an ear should listen to what the Spirit says to the churches."

4 After this I looked, and there in heaven was an open door. The first voice that I had heard speaking to me like a trumpet said, "Come up here, and I will show you what must take place after this."

[2]Immediately I was in the Spirit,[D] and a throne was set there in heaven. One was seated on the throne, [3]and the One seated[E] looked like jasper[F] and carnelian[G] stone. A rainbow that looked like an emerald surrounded the throne. [4]Around that throne were 24 thrones, and on the thrones sat 24 elders dressed in white clothes, with gold crowns on their heads. [5]Flashes of lightning and rumblings of thunder came from the throne. Seven fiery torches were burning before the throne, which are the seven spirits of God. [6]Something like a sea of glass, similar to crystal, was also before the throne. Four living creatures

covered with eyes in front and in back were in the middle[H] and around the throne. [7]The first living creature was like a lion; the second living creature was like a calf; the third living creature had a face like a man; and the fourth living creature was like a flying eagle. [8]Each of the four living creatures had six wings; they were covered with eyes around and inside. Day and night they never stop,[I] saying:

Holy, holy, holy,[J]
Lord God, the Almighty,
who was, who is, and who is coming.

[9]Whenever the living creatures give glory, honor, and thanks to the One seated on the throne, the One who lives forever and ever, [10]the 24 elders fall down before the One seated on the throne, worship the One who lives forever and ever, cast their crowns before the throne, and say:

[11]   Our Lord and God,[K]
You are worthy to receive
glory and honor and power,
because You have created all things,
and because of Your will
they exist and were created.

5 Then I saw in the right hand of the One seated on the throne a scroll with writing on the inside and on the back, sealed with seven seals. [2]I also saw a mighty angel proclaiming in a loud voice, "Who is worthy to open the scroll and break its seals?" [3]But no one in heaven or on earth or under the earth was able to open the scroll or even to look in it. [4]And I cried and cried because no one was found worthy to open[L] the scroll or even to look in it.

[5]Then one of the elders said to me, "Stop crying. Look! The Lion from the tribe of Judah, the Root of David, has been victorious so that He may open the scroll and[M] its seven seals." [6]Then I saw One like a slaughtered lamb standing between[N] the throne and the four living creatures and among the elders. He had seven horns and seven eyes, which are the seven spirits of God sent into all the earth.

⁷He came and took the scroll^A out of the right hand of the One seated on the throne.

⁸When He took the scroll, the four living creatures and the 24 elders fell down before the Lamb. Each one had a harp and gold bowls filled with incense, which are the prayers of the saints. ⁹And they sang a new song:

> You are worthy to take the scroll
>   and to open its seals,
> because You were slaughtered,
>   and You redeemed^B people^C
>   for God by Your blood
> from every tribe and language
>   and people and nation.
> ¹⁰ You made them a kingdom^D
>   and priests to our God,
>   and they will reign on the earth.

¹¹Then I looked and heard the voice of many angels around the throne, and also of the living creatures and of the elders. Their number was countless thousands, plus thousands of thousands. ¹²They said with a loud voice:

> The Lamb who was slaughtered
>   is worthy
> to receive power and riches
>   and wisdom and strength
> and honor and glory and blessing!

¹³I heard every creature in heaven, on earth, under the earth, on the sea, and everything in them say:

> Blessing and honor and glory
>   and dominion
> to the One seated on the throne,
>   and to the Lamb, forever and ever!

¹⁴The four living creatures said, "Amen," and the elders fell down and worshiped.

6 Then I saw^E the Lamb open one of the seven^F seals, and I heard one of the four living creatures say with a voice like thunder, "Come!"^G,H ²I looked, and there was a white horse. The horseman on it had a bow; a crown was given to him, and he went out as a victor to conquer.^I

³When He opened the second seal, I heard the second living creature say, "Come!"^G,H ⁴Then another horse went out, a fiery red one, and its horseman was empowered^J to take peace from the earth, so that people would slaughter one another. And a large sword was given to him.

⁵When He opened the third seal, I heard the third living creature say, "Come!"^G,H And I looked, and there was a black horse. The horseman on it had a set of scales in his hand. ⁶Then I heard something like a voice among the four living creatures say, "A quart of wheat for a denarius, and three quarts of barley for a denarius—but do not harm the olive oil and the wine."

⁷When He opened the fourth seal, I heard the voice of the fourth living creature say, "Come!"^G,H ⁸And I looked, and there was a pale green^K horse. The horseman on it was named Death, and Hades was following after him. Authority was given to them^L over a fourth of the earth, to kill by the sword, by famine, by plague, and by the wild animals of the earth.

⁹When He opened the fifth seal, I saw under the altar the people^M slaughtered because of God's word and the testimony they had.^N ¹⁰They cried out with a loud voice: "Lord,^O the One who is holy and true, how long until You judge and avenge our blood from those who live on the earth?" ¹¹So a white robe was given to each of them, and they were told to rest a little while longer until the number would be completed of their fellow slaves and their brothers, who were going to be killed just as they had been.

¹²Then I saw Him open^P the sixth seal. A violent earthquake occurred; the sun turned black like sackcloth made of goat hair; the entire moon^Q became like blood; ¹³the stars^R of heaven fell to the earth as a fig tree drops its unripe figs when shaken by a high wind; ¹⁴the sky separated like a scroll being rolled up; and every mountain and island was moved from its place.

A5:7 Other mss exclude *the scroll* B5:9 Or *purchased* C5:9 Other mss read *us* D5:10 Other mss read *them kings* E6:1 Lit *saw when* F6:1 Other mss omit *seven* G6:1,3,5,7 Other mss add *and see* H6:1,3,5,7 Or *Go!* I6:2 Lit *went out conquering and in order to conquer* J6:4 Or *was granted; lit was given* K6:8 Or *a greenish gray* L6:8 Other mss read *him* M6:9 Lit *souls* N6:9 Other mss add *about the Lamb* O6:10 Or *Master* P6:12 Lit *I saw when He opened* Q6:12 Or *the full moon* R6:13 Perhaps *meteors*

¹⁵Then the kings of the earth, the nobles, the military commanders, the rich, the powerful, and every slave and free person hid in the caves and among the rocks of the mountains. ¹⁶And they said to the mountains and to the rocks, "Fall on us and hide us from the face of the One seated on the throne and from the wrath of the Lamb, ¹⁷because the great day of TheirᴬA wrath has come! And who is able to stand?"

7 After this I saw four angels standing at the four corners of the earth, restraining the four winds of the earth so that no wind could blow on the earth or on the sea or on any tree. ²Then I saw another angel, who had the seal of the living God rise up from the east. He cried out in a loud voice to the four angels who were empoweredᴮ to harm the earth and the sea: ³"Don't harm the earth or the sea or the trees until we seal the slaves of our God on their foreheads." ⁴And I heard the number of those who were sealed:

> 144,000 sealed from every tribe
>   of the Israelites:
> ⁵ 12,000 sealed from the tribe of Judah,
>   12,000ᶜ from the tribe of Reuben,
>   12,000 from the tribe of Gad,
> ⁶ 12,000 from the tribe of Asher,
>   12,000 from the tribe of Naphtali,
>   12,000 from the tribe of Manasseh,
> ⁷ 12,000 from the tribe of Simeon,
>   12,000 from the tribe of Levi,
>   12,000 from the tribe of Issachar,
> ⁸ 12,000 from the tribe of Zebulun,
>   12,000 from the tribe of Joseph,
>   12,000 sealed from the tribe
>   of Benjamin.

⁹After this I looked, and there was a vast multitude from every nation, tribe, people, and language, which no one could number, standing before the throne and before the Lamb. They were robed in white with palm branches in their hands. ¹⁰And they cried out in a loud voice:

> Salvation belongs to our God,
>   who is seated on the throne,
>   and to the Lamb!

¹¹All the angels stood around the throne, the elders, and the four living creatures, and they fell facedown before the throne and worshiped God, ¹²saying:

> Amen! Blessing and glory and wisdom
>   and thanksgiving and honor
>   and power and strength
> be to our God forever and ever. Amen.

¹³Then one of the elders asked me, "Who are these people robed in white, and where did they come from?"

¹⁴I said to him, "Sir,ᴰ you know."

Then he told me:

> These are the ones coming out
>   of the great tribulation.
> They washed their robes
>   and made them white
>   in the blood of the Lamb.
> ¹⁵ For this reason they are
>   before the throne of God,
> and they serve Him day and night
>   in His sanctuary.
> The One seated on the throne
>   will shelterᴱ them:
> ¹⁶ They will no longer hunger;
>   they will no longer thirst;
>   the sun will no longer strike them,
>   nor will any heat.
> ¹⁷ For the Lamb who is at the center
>   of the throne
>   will shepherd them;
> He will guide them to springs
>   of living waters,
> and God will wipe away every tear
>   from their eyes.

8 When He opened the seventh seal, there was silence in heaven for about half an hour. ²Then I saw the seven angels who stand in the presence of God; seven trumpets were given to them. ³Another angel, with a gold incense burner, came and stood at the altar. He was given a large amount of incense to offer with the prayers of all the saints on the gold altar in front of the throne. ⁴The smoke of the incense, with the prayers of the saints, went up in the presence of God from the angel's

A6:17 Other mss read *His*   B7:2 Lit *angels to whom it was given*   C7:5-8 Other mss add *sealed* after each number   D7:14 Lit *My lord*
E7:15 Or *will spread His tent over*

hand. ⁵The angel took the incense burner, filled it with fire from the altar, and hurled it to the earth; there were rumblings of thunder, flashes of lightning, and an earthquake. ⁶And the seven angels who had the seven trumpets prepared to blow them.

⁷The first angelᴬ blew his trumpet, and hail and fire, mixed with blood, were hurled to the earth. So a third of the earth was burned up, a third of the trees were burned up, and all the green grass was burned up.

⁸The second angel blew his trumpet, and something like a great mountain ablaze with fire was hurled into the sea. So a third of the sea became blood, ⁹a third of the living creatures in the sea died, and a third of the ships were destroyed.

¹⁰The third angel blew his trumpet, and a great star, blazing like a torch, fell from heaven. It fell on a third of the rivers and springs of water. ¹¹The name of the star is Wormwood, and a third of the waters became wormwood. So, many of the people died from the waters, because they had been made bitter.

¹²The fourth angel blew his trumpet, and a third of the sun was struck, a third of the moon, and a third of the stars, so that a third of them were darkened. A third of the day was without light, and the night as well.

¹³I looked again and heard an eagleᴮ flying high overhead, crying out in a loud voice, "Woe! Woe! Woe to those who live on the earth, because of the remaining trumpet blasts that the three angels are about to sound!"

9 The fifth angel blew his trumpet, and I saw a star that had fallen from heaven to earth. The key to the shaft of the abyss was given to him. ²He opened the shaft of the abyss, and smoke came up out of the shaft like smoke from a greatᶜ furnace so that the sun and the air were darkened by the smoke from the shaft. ³Then locusts came out of the smoke on to the earth, and powerᴰ was given to them like the power that scorpions have on the earth. ⁴They were told not to harm the grass of the earth, or any green plant, or any tree, but only people who do not have God's seal on their foreheads. ⁵They were not per-

mitted to kill them but were to torment them for five months; their torment is like the torment caused by a scorpion when it strikes a man. ⁶In those days people will seek death and will not find it; they will long to die, but death will flee from them.

⁷The appearance of the locusts was like horses equipped for battle. Something like gold crowns was on their heads; their faces were like men's faces; ⁸they had hair like women's hair; their teeth were like lions' teeth; ⁹they had chests like iron breastplates; the sound of their wings was like the sound of chariots with many horses rushing into battle; ¹⁰and they had tails with stingers like scorpions, so that with their tails they had the powerᴰ to harm people for five months. ¹¹They had as their kingᴱ the angel of the abyss; his name in Hebrew is Abaddon,ᶠ and in Greek he has the name Apollyon.ᴳ ¹²The first woe has passed. There are still two more woes to come after this.

¹³The sixth angel blew his trumpet. From the fourᴴ horns of the gold altar that is before God, I heard a voice ¹⁴say to the sixth angel who had the trumpet, "Release the four angels bound at the great river Euphrates." ¹⁵So the four angels who were prepared for the hour, day, month, and year were released to kill a third of the human race. ¹⁶The number of mounted troops was 200 million;ᴵ I heard their number. ¹⁷This is how I saw the horses in my vision: The horsemen had breastplates that were fiery red, hyacinth blue, and sulfur yellow. The heads of the horses were like lions' heads, and from their mouths came fire, smoke, and sulfur. ¹⁸A third of the human race was killed by these three plagues—by the fire, the smoke, and the sulfur that came from their mouths. ¹⁹For the power of the horses is in their mouths and in their tails, for their tails, which resemble snakes, have heads, and they inflict injury with them.

²⁰The rest of the people, who were not killed by these plagues, did not repent of the works of their hands to stop worshiping demons and idols of gold, silver, bronze, stone, and wood, which are not able to see, hear, or walk. ²¹And they did not repent of their mur-

---

ᴬ8:7 Other mss include angel   ᴮ8:13 Other mss read angel   ᶜ9:2 Other mss omit great   ᴰ9:3,10 Or authority   ᴱ9:11 Or as king over them   ᶠ9:11 Or destruction   ᴳ9:11 Or destroyer   ᴴ9:13 Other mss omit four   ᴵ9:16 Other mss read 100 million ders, their sorceries,[A] their sexual immorality, or their thefts.

10 Then I saw another mighty angel coming down from heaven, surrounded by a cloud, with a rainbow over his head.[B] His face was like the sun, his legs[C] were like fiery pillars, [2]and he had a little scroll opened in his hand. He put his right foot on the sea, his left on the land, [3]and he cried out with a loud voice like a roaring lion. When he cried out, the seven thunders spoke with their voices. [4]And when the seven thunders spoke, I was about to write. Then I heard a voice from heaven, saying, "Seal up what the seven thunders said, and do not write it down!"

[5]Then the angel that I had seen standing on the sea and on the land raised his right hand to heaven. [6]He swore an oath by the One who lives forever and ever, who created heaven and what is in it, the earth and what is in it, and the sea and what is in it: "There will no longer be an interval of time,[D] [7]but in the days of the sound of the seventh angel, when he will blow his trumpet, then God's hidden plan will be completed, as He announced to His servants[E] the prophets."

[8]Now the voice that I heard from heaven spoke to me again and said, "Go, take the scroll that lies open in the hand of the angel who is standing on the sea and on the land."

[9]So I went to the angel and asked him to give me the little scroll. He said to me, "Take and eat it; it will be bitter in your stomach, but it will be as sweet as honey in your mouth."

[10]Then I took the little scroll from the angel's hand and ate it. It was as sweet as honey in my mouth, but when I ate it, my stomach became bitter. [11]And I was told,[F] "You must prophesy again about[G] many peoples, nations, languages, and kings."

11 Then I was given a measuring reed like a rod,[H] with these words: "Go[I] and measure God's sanctuary and the altar, and count those who worship there. [2]But exclude the courtyard outside the sanctuary. Don't measure it, because it is given to the nations,[J] and

they will trample the holy city for 42 months. [3]I will empower[K] my two witnesses, and they will prophesy for 1,260 days,[L] dressed in sackcloth."[M] [4]These are the two olive trees and the two lampstands that stand before the Lord[N] of the earth. [5]If anyone wants to harm them, fire comes from their mouths and consumes their enemies; if anyone wants to harm them, he must be killed in this way. [6]These men have the power to close up the sky so that it does not rain during the days of their prophecy. They also have power over the waters to turn them into blood and to strike the earth with every plague whenever they want.

[7]When they finish their testimony, the beast[O] that comes up out of the abyss will make war with them, conquer them, and kill them. [8]Their dead bodies[P] will lie in the public square[Q] of the great city, which prophetically[R] is called Sodom and Egypt, where also their Lord was crucified. [9]And representatives from[S] the peoples, tribes, languages, and nations will view their bodies for three and a half days and not permit their bodies to be put into a tomb. [10]Those who live on the earth will gloat over them and celebrate and send gifts to one another because these two prophets brought judgment to those who live on the earth.

[11]But after 3½ days, the breath[T] of life from God entered them, and they stood on their feet. So great fear fell on those who saw them. [12]Then they heard[U] a loud voice from heaven saying to them, "Come up here." They went up to heaven in a cloud, while their enemies watched them. [13]At that moment a violent earthquake took place, a tenth of the city fell, and 7,000 people were killed in the earthquake. The survivors were terrified and gave glory to the God of heaven. [14]The second woe has passed. Take note: The third woe is coming quickly!

[15]The seventh angel blew his trumpet, and there were loud voices in heaven saying:

> The kingdom of the world has become
> the kingdom

A9:21 Or *magic potions, or drugs;* Gk *pharmakon*   **B**10:1 Or *a halo on his head*   **C**10:1 Or *feet*   **D**10:6 Or *be a delay*   **E**10:7 Or *slaves*   **F**10:11 Lit *And they said to me*   **G**10:11 Or *prophesy again against*   **H**11:1 Other mss add *and the angel stood up*   **I**11:1 Lit *Arise*   **J**11:2 Or *Gentiles*   **K**11:3 Lit *I will give to*   **L**11:3 = 3½ years of 30-day months   **M**11:3 *Mourning garment of coarse, often black, material*   **N**11:4 Other mss read *God*   **O**11:7 Or *wild animal*   **P**11:8 Lit *Their corpse*   **Q**11:8 Or *lie on the broad street*   **R**11:8 Or *spiritually, or symbolically*   **S**11:9 Lit *And from*   **T**11:11 Or *spirit*   **U**11:12 Other mss read *Then I heard*

of our Lord and of His Messiah,
and He will reign forever and ever!

16 The 24 elders, who were seated before God on their thrones, fell facedown and worshiped God, **17** saying:

> We thank You, Lord God,
>   the Almighty,
> who is and who was,^A
> because You have taken
>   Your great power
> and have begun to reign.
> **18**   The nations were angry,
> but Your wrath has come.
> The time has come
>   for the dead to be judged
> and to give the reward
>   to Your servants the prophets,
> to the saints, and to those who fear
>   Your name,
>   both small and great,
> and the time has come to destroy
>   those who destroy the earth.

19 God's sanctuary in heaven was opened, and the ark of His covenant^B appeared in His sanctuary. There were flashes of lightning, rumblings of thunder, an earthquake,^C and severe hail.

12 A great sign^D appeared in heaven: a woman clothed with the sun, with the moon under her feet and a crown of 12 stars on her head. **2** She was pregnant and cried out in labor and agony as she was about to give birth. **3** Then another sign^E appeared in heaven: There was a great fiery red dragon having seven heads and 10 horns, and on his heads were seven diadems.^F **4** His tail swept away a third of the stars in heaven and hurled them to the earth. And the dragon stood in front of the woman who was about to give birth, so that when she did give birth he might devour her child. **5** But she gave birth to a Son—a male who is going to shepherd^G all nations with an iron scepter—and her child was caught up to God and to His throne. **6** The woman fled into the wilderness, where she had a place prepared by God, to be fed there^H for 1,260 days.

7 Then war broke out in heaven: Michael and his angels fought against the dragon. The dragon and his angels also fought, **8** but he could not prevail, and there was no place for them in heaven any longer. **9** So the great dragon was thrown out—the ancient serpent, who is called the Devil^I and Satan,^J the one who deceives the whole world. He was thrown to earth, and his angels with him.

10 Then I heard a loud voice in heaven say:

> The salvation and the power
> and the kingdom of our God
> and the authority of His Messiah
> have now come,
> because the accuser of our brothers
>   has been thrown out:
> the one who accuses them
> before our God day and night.
> **11**   They conquered him
> by the blood of the Lamb
> and by the word of their testimony,
> for they did not love their lives
>   in the face of death.
> **12**   Therefore rejoice, you heavens,
>   and you who dwell in them!
> Woe to the earth and the sea,
> for the Devil has come down to you
>   with great fury,
> because he knows he has a short time.

13 When the dragon saw that he had been thrown to earth, he persecuted the woman who gave birth to the male child. **14** The woman was given two wings of a great eagle, so that she could fly from the serpent's presence to her place in the wilderness, where she was fed for a time, times, and half a time.^K **15** From his mouth the serpent spewed water like a river flowing after the woman, to sweep her away in a torrent. **16** But the earth helped the woman. The earth opened its mouth and swallowed up the river that the dragon had spewed from his mouth. **17** So the dragon was furious with the woman and left to wage war against the rest of her offspring^L—those who

---

^A **11:17** Other mss add *and who is to come*   ^B **11:19** Other mss read *ark of the covenant of the Lord*   ^C **11:19** Other mss omit *an earthquake*   ^D **12:1** Or *great symbolic display;* see Rv 12:3   ^E **12:3** Or *another symbolic display*   ^F **12:3** Or *crowns*   ^G **12:5** Or *rule*   ^H **12:6** Lit *God, that they might feed her there*   ^I **12:9** In Gk, *diabolos* means slanderer.   ^J **12:9** In Hb, *Satan* means adversary.   ^K **12:14** This expression, occurring in Dn 7:25; 12:7, = 3½ years or 42 months (Rv 11:2; 13:5) or 1,260 days (Rv 11:3).   ^L **12:17** Or *seed* keep God's commands and have the testimony about Jesus. [18]He[A] stood on the sand of the sea.[B]

13 And I saw a beast coming up out of the sea. He[C] had 10 horns and seven heads. On his horns were 10 diadems, and on his heads were blasphemous names.[D] [2]The beast I saw was like a leopard, his feet were like a bear's, and his mouth was like a lion's mouth. The dragon gave him his power, his throne, and great authority. [3]One of his heads appeared to be fatally wounded,[E] but his fatal wound was healed. The whole earth was amazed and followed the beast.[F] [4]They worshiped the dragon because he gave authority to the beast. And they worshiped the beast, saying, "Who is like the beast? Who is able to wage war against him?"

[5]A mouth was given to him to speak boasts and blasphemies. He was also given authority to act[G,H] for 42 months. [6]He began to speak[I] blasphemies against God: to blaspheme His name and His dwelling—those who dwell in heaven. [7]And he was permitted to wage war against the saints and to conquer them. He was also given authority over every tribe, people, language, and nation. [8]All those who live on the earth will worship him, everyone whose name was not written from the foundation of the world in the book[J] of life of the Lamb who was slaughtered.[K]

[9]If anyone has an ear, he should listen:

[10] If anyone is destined for captivity,
       into captivity he goes.
       If anyone is to be killed[L] with a sword,
       with a sword he will be killed.

This demands the perseverance[M] and faith of the saints.

[11]Then I saw another beast coming up out of the earth; he had two horns like a lamb,[N] but he sounded like a dragon. [12]He exercises all the authority of the first beast on its behalf and compels the earth and those who live on it to worship the first beast, whose fatal

wound was healed. [13]He also performs great signs, even causing fire to come down from heaven to earth in front of people. [14]He deceives those who live on the earth because of the signs that he is permitted to perform on behalf of the beast, telling those who live on the earth to make an image[O] of the beast who had the sword wound and yet lived. [15]He was permitted to give a spirit[P] to the image of the beast, so that the image of the beast could both speak and cause whoever would not worship the image of the beast to be killed. [16]And he requires everyone—small and great, rich and poor, free and slave—to be given a mark[Q] on his right hand or on his forehead, [17]so that no one can buy or sell unless he has the mark: the beast's name or the number of his name.

[18]Here is wisdom:[R] The one who has understanding must calculate[S] the number of the beast, because it is the number of a man.[T] His number is 666.[U]

14 Then I looked, and there on Mount Zion stood the Lamb, and with Him were 144,000 who had His name and His Father's name written on their foreheads. [2]I heard a sound[V] from heaven like the sound of cascading waters and like the rumbling of loud thunder. The sound I heard was also like harpists playing on their harps. [3]They sang[W] a new song before the throne and before the four living creatures and the elders, but no one could learn the song except the 144,000 who had been redeemed[X] from the earth. [4]These are the ones not defiled with women, for they have kept their virginity. These are the ones who follow the Lamb wherever He goes. They were redeemed[X,Y] from the human race as the firstfruits for God and the Lamb. [5]No lie was found in their mouths; they are blameless.

[6]Then I saw another angel flying high overhead, having the eternal gospel to announce to the inhabitants of the earth—to every nation, tribe, language, and people. [7]He spoke

---

A12:18 Other mss read I. "He" is apparently a reference to the dragon. B12:18 Some translations put Rv 12:18 either in Rv 12:17 or Rv 13:1. C13:1 The beasts in Rv 13:1,11 are customarily referred to as he" or "him" rather than "it." The Gk word for a beast (therion) is grammatically neuter. D13:1 Other mss read heads was a blasphemous name E13:3 Lit be slain to death F13:3 Lit amazed after the beast G13:5 Other mss read wage war H13:5 Or to rule I13:6 Lit He opened his mouth J13:8 Or scroll K13:8 Or written in the book of life of the Lamb who was slaughtered from the foundation of the world L13:10 Other mss read anyone kills M13:10 Lit Here is the perseverance N13:11 Or ram O13:14 Or statue, or likeness P13:15 Or give breath, or give life Q13:16 Or stamp, or brand R13:18 Or This calls for wisdom S13:18 Or count, or figure out T13:18 Or a man's number, or is the number of a person U13:18 Other Gk mss read 616 V14:2 Or voice W14:3 Other mss add as it were X14:3,4 Or purchased T14:4 Other mss add by Jesus with a loud voice: "Fear God and give Him glory, because the hour of His judgment has come. Worship the Maker of heaven and earth, the sea and springs of water."

[8]A second angel[A] followed, saying: "It has fallen, Babylon the Great has fallen,[B] who made all nations drink the wine of her sexual immorality,[C] which brings wrath."

[9]And a third angel[D] followed them and spoke with a loud voice: "If anyone worships the beast and his image and receives a mark on his forehead or on his hand, [10]he will also drink the wine of God's wrath, which is mixed full strength in the cup of His anger. He will be tormented with fire and sulfur in the sight of the holy angels and in the sight of the Lamb, [11]and the smoke of the torment will go up forever and ever. There is no rest[E] day or night for those who worship the beast and his image, or anyone who receives the mark of his name. [12]This demands the perseverance[F] of the saints, who keep God's commands and their faith in Jesus."[G]

[13]Then I heard a voice from heaven saying, "Write: The dead who die in the Lord from now on are blessed."

"Yes," says the Spirit, "let them rest from their labors, for their works follow them!"

[14]Then I looked, and there was a white cloud, and One like the Son of Man[H] was seated on the cloud, with a gold crown on His head and a sharp sickle in His hand. [15]Another angel came out of the sanctuary, crying out in a loud voice to the One who was seated on the cloud, "Use your sickle and reap, for the time to reap has come, since the harvest of the earth is ripe." [16]So the One seated on the cloud swung His sickle over the earth, and the earth was harvested.

[17]Then another angel who also had a sharp sickle came out of the sanctuary in heaven. [18]Yet another angel, who had authority over fire, came from the altar, and he called with a loud voice to the one who had the sharp sickle, "Use your sharp sickle and gather the clusters of grapes from earth's vineyard, because its grapes have ripened." [19]So the angel swung his sickle toward earth and gathered the grapes from earth's vineyard, and he threw them into the great winepress of God's wrath. [20]Then the press was trampled outside the city, and blood flowed out of the press up to the horses' bridles for about 180 miles.[I]

15 Then I saw another great and awe-inspiring sign[J] in heaven: seven angels with the seven last plagues, for with them, God's wrath will be completed. [2]I also saw something like a sea of glass mixed with fire, and those who had won the victory over the beast, his image,[K] and the number of his name, were standing on the sea of glass with harps from God.[L] [3]They sang the song of God's servant Moses and the song of the Lamb:

Great and awe-inspiring are
    Your works,
Lord God, the Almighty;
righteous and true are
    Your ways,
King of the Nations.[M]
[4] Lord, who will not fear
    and glorify Your name?
Because You alone are holy,
for all the nations will come
    and worship before You
because Your righteous acts
    have been revealed.

[5]After this I looked, and the heavenly sanctuary—the tabernacle of testimony—was opened. [6]Out of the sanctuary came the seven angels with the seven plagues, dressed in clean, bright linen, with gold sashes wrapped around their chests. [7]One of the four living creatures gave the seven angels seven gold bowls filled with the wrath of God who lives forever and ever. [8]Then the sanctuary was filled with smoke from God's glory and from His power, and no one could enter the sanctuary until the seven plagues of the seven angels were completed.

16 Then I heard a loud voice from the sanctuary saying to the seven angels, "Go and pour out the seven[N] bowls of God's

[A]14:8 Lit Another angel, a second [B]14:8 Other mss omit the second has fallen [C]14:8 Or wine of her passionate immorality [D]14:9 Lit Another angel, a third [E]14:11 Lit They have no rest [F]14:12 Lit Here is the perseverance [G]14:12 Or and faith in Jesus, or and faithfulness to Jesus [H]14:14 Or like a son of man [I]14:20 Lit 1,600 stadia [J]15:1 Or and awesome symbolic display [K]15:2 Other mss add his mark [L]15:2 Or harps of God; = harps belonging to the service of God [M]15:3 Other mss read ages [N]16:1 Other mss omit seven wrath on the earth." ²The first went and poured out his bowl on the earth, and severely painful sores^A broke out on the people who had the mark of the beast and who worshiped his image.

³The second^B poured out his bowl into the sea. It turned to blood like a dead man's, and all life^C in the sea died.

⁴The third^B poured out his bowl into the rivers and the springs of water, and they became blood. ⁵I heard the angel of the waters say:

You are righteous,
who is and who was,
    the Holy One,
for You have decided
    these things.
⁶ Because they poured out
    the blood of the saints
        and the prophets,
You also gave them blood
    to drink;
they deserve it!

⁷Then I heard someone from the altar say:

Yes, Lord God, the Almighty,
true and righteous
    Your judgments.

⁸The fourth^B poured out his bowl on the sun. He^D was given the power^E to burn people with fire, ⁹and people were burned by the intense heat. So they blasphemed the name of God, who had the power^E over these plagues, and they did not repent and give Him glory.

¹⁰The fifth^B poured out his bowl on the throne of the beast, and his kingdom was plunged into darkness. People^F gnawed their tongues because of their pain ¹¹and blasphemed the God of heaven because of their pains and their sores, yet they did not repent of their actions.

¹²The sixth^B poured out his bowl on the great river Euphrates, and its water was dried up to prepare the way for the kings from the east. ¹³Then I saw three unclean spirits like frogs coming from the dragon's mouth, from the beast's mouth, and from the mouth of the false prophet. ¹⁴For they are spirits of demons performing signs, who travel to the kings of the whole world to assemble them for the battle of the great day of God, the Almighty.

¹⁵"Look, I am coming like a thief. The one who is alert and remains clothed^G so that he may not go around naked and people see his shame is blessed."

¹⁶So they assembled them at the place called in Hebrew, Armagedon.^H,I

¹⁷Then the seventh^B poured out his bowl into the air,^J and a loud voice came out of the sanctuary^K from the throne, saying, "It is done!" ¹⁸There were flashes of lightning and rumblings of thunder. And a severe earthquake occurred like no other since man has been on the earth—so great was the quake. ¹⁹The great city split into three parts, and the cities of the nations^L fell. Babylon the Great was remembered in God's presence; He gave her the cup filled with the wine of His fierce anger. ²⁰Every island fled, and the mountains disappeared.^M ²¹Enormous hailstones, each weighing about 100 pounds,^N fell from the sky on people, and they blasphemed God for the plague of hail because that plague was extremely severe.

17

Then one of the seven angels who had the seven bowls came and spoke with me: "Come, I will show you the judgment of the notorious prostitute^O who sits on many^P waters. ²The kings of the earth committed sexual immorality with her, and those who live on the earth became drunk on the wine of her sexual immorality." ³So he carried me away in the Spirit^Q to a desert. I saw a woman sitting on a scarlet beast that was covered^R with blasphemous names and had seven heads and 10 horns. ⁴The woman was dressed in purple and scarlet, adorned with gold, precious stones, and pearls. She had a gold cup in her hand filled with everything vile and with

---

^A16:2 Lit and a severely painful sore ^B16:3,4,8,10,12,17 Other mss add angel ^C16:3 Lit and every soul of life ^D16:8 Or It ^E16:8,9 Or authority ^F16:10 Lit They ^G16:15 Or and guards his clothes ^H16:16 Other mss read Armageddon; other mss read Harmegedon; other mss read Mageddon; other mss read Magedon ^I16:16 Traditionally the hill of Megiddo, a great city that guarded the pass between the coast and the valley of Jezreel or Esdraelon; Jdg 5:19; 2Kg 9:27 ^J16:17 Or on the air ^K16:17 Other mss add of heaven ^L16:19 Or the Gentile cities ^M16:20 Lit mountains were not found ^N16:21 Lit about a talent; talents varied in weight upwards from 75 pounds ^O17:1 Traditionally translated the great whore ^P17:1 Or by many ^Q17:3 Or in spirit ^R17:3 Lit was filled the impurities of her[A] prostitution. [5]On her forehead a cryptic name was written:

**BABYLON THE GREAT
THE MOTHER OF PROSTITUTES
AND OF THE VILE THINGS
OF THE EARTH.**

[6]Then I saw that the woman was drunk on the blood of the saints and on the blood of the witnesses to Jesus. When I saw her, I was greatly astonished.

[7]Then the angel said to me, "Why are you astonished? I will tell you the secret meaning of the woman and of the beast, with the seven heads and the 10 horns, that carries her. [8]The beast that you saw was, and is not, and is about to come up from the abyss and go to destruction. Those who live on the earth whose names have not been written in the book of life from the foundation of the world will be astonished when they see the beast that was, and is not, and will be present again.

[9]"Here is the mind with wisdom:[B] The seven heads are seven mountains on which the woman is seated. [10]They are also seven kings:[C] Five have fallen, one is, the other has not yet come, and when he comes, he must remain for a little while. [11]The beast that was and is not, is himself an eighth king, yet he belongs to the seven and is going to destruction. [12]The 10 horns you saw are 10 kings who have not yet received a kingdom, but they will receive authority as kings with the beast for one hour. [13]These have one purpose, and they give their power and authority to the beast. [14]These will make war against the Lamb, but the Lamb will conquer them because He is Lord of lords and King of kings. Those with Him are called, chosen, and faithful."

[15]He also said to me, "The waters you saw, where the prostitute was seated, are peoples, multitudes, nations, and languages. [16]The 10 horns you saw, and the beast, will hate the prostitute. They will make her desolate and naked, devour her flesh, and burn her up with fire. [17]For God has put it into their hearts to carry out His plan by having one purpose and to give their kingdom[D] to the beast until God's words are accomplished. [18]And the woman you saw is the great city that has an empire[E] over the kings of the earth."

18 After this I saw another angel with great authority coming down from heaven, and the earth was illuminated by his splendor. [2]He cried in a mighty voice:

> It has fallen,[F]
> Babylon the Great has fallen!
> She has become a dwelling
>   for demons,
> a haunt for every unclean spirit,
> a haunt for every unclean bird,
> and a haunt[G] for every unclean
>   and despicable beast.[H]
> [3] For all the nations have drunk[I]
>   the wine of her sexual immorality,
>   which brings wrath.
> The kings of the earth
> have committed sexual immorality
>   with her,
> and the merchants of the earth
> have grown wealthy
>   from her excessive luxury.

[4]Then I heard another voice from heaven:

> Come out of her, My people,
> so that you will not share in her sins
> or receive any of her plagues.
> [5] For her sins are piled up[J] to heaven,
>   and God has remembered her crimes.
> [6] Pay her back the way she also paid,
>   and double it according to her works.
>   In the cup in which she mixed,
>   mix a double portion for her.
> [7] As much as she glorified herself
>   and lived luxuriously,
>   give her that much torment and grief,
>   for she says in her heart,
>   "I sit as a queen;
>   I am not a widow,
>   and I will never see grief."
> [8] For this reason her plagues will come
>   in one day[K]—
>   death and grief and famine.
>   She will be burned up with fire,

[A]17:4 Other mss read of earth's   [B]17:9 Or This calls for the mind with wisdom   [C]17:10 Some editors or translators put They are also seven kings: in v. 9.   [D]17:17 Or sovereignty   [E]17:18 Or has sovereignty or rulership   [F]18:2 Other mss omit It has fallen   [G]18:2 Or prison   [H]18:2 Other mss omit the words and a haunt for every unclean beast. The words and despicable then refer to the bird of the previous line.   [I]18:3 Some mss read have collapsed; other mss read have fallen   [J]18:5 Or sins have reached up   [K]18:8 Suddenly

because the Lord God who judges her
is mighty.

⁹The kings of the earth who have committed sexual immorality and lived luxuriously
with her will weep and mourn over her when
they see the smoke of her burning. ¹⁰They will
stand far off in fear of her torment, saying:

> Woe, woe, the great city,
> Babylon, the mighty city!
> For in a single hourᴬ
> your judgment has come.

¹¹The merchants of the earth will also weep
and mourn over her, because no one buys their
merchandise any longer— ¹²merchandise of
gold, silver, precious stones, and pearls; fine
fabrics of linen, purple, silk, and scarlet; all
kinds of fragrant wood products; objects of ivo-
ry; objects of expensive wood, brass,ᴮ iron, and
marble; ¹³cinnamon, spice,ᶜ·ᴰ incense, myrrh,ᴱ
and frankincense; wine, olive oil, fine wheat
flour, and grain; cattle and sheep; horses and
carriages; and slavesᶠ and human lives.ᴳ

> ¹⁴ The fruit you craved has left you.
> All your splendid
>   and glamorous things are gone;
> they will never find them again.

¹⁵The merchants of these things, who became
rich from her, will stand far off in fear of her
torment, weeping and mourning, ¹⁶saying:

> Woe, woe, the great city,
> dressed in fine linen, purple,
>   and scarlet,
> adorned with gold, precious stones,
>   and pearls,
> ¹⁷ for in a single hourᴬ
> such fabulous wealth was destroyed!

And every shipmaster, seafarer, the sailors,
and all who do business by sea, stood far off
¹⁸as they watched the smoke from her burning and kept crying out: "Who is like the great
city?" ¹⁹They threw dust on their heads and
kept crying out, weeping, and mourning:

> Woe, woe, the great city,
> where all those who have ships
>   on the sea
> became rich from her wealth,
> for in a single hourᴬ
>   she was destroyed.
> 20 Rejoice over her, heaven,
> and you saints, apostles, and prophets,
> because God has executed
>   your judgment on her!ᴴ

²¹Then a mighty angel picked up a stone
like a large millstone and threw it into the
sea, saying:

> In this way, Babylon the great city
> will be thrown down violently
> and never be found again.
> 22 The sound of harpists, musicians,
> flutists, and trumpeters
> will never be heard in you again;
> no craftsman of any trade
> will ever be found in you again;
> the sound of a mill
> will never be heard in you again;
> 23 the light of a lamp
> will never shine in you again;
> and the voice of a groom and bride
> will never be heard in you again.
> All this will happen
> because your merchants
> were the nobility of the earth,
> because all the nations were deceived
> by your sorcery,ᴵ
> 24 and the blood of prophets and saints,
> and of all those slaughtered on earth,
> was found in you.ᴶ

19 After this I heard something like the
loud voice of a vast multitude in heav-
en, saying:

> Hallelujah!
> Salvation, glory, and power belong
>   to our God,
> 2 because His judgments are trueᴷ
>   and righteous,

ᴬ18:10,17,19 Suddenly   ᴮ18:12 Or bronze, or copper   ᶜ18:13 Other mss omit spice   ᴰ18:13 Or amomum, an aromatic plant   ᴱ18:13 Or
perfume   ᶠ18:13 Or bodies   ᴳ18:13 Slaves; "bodies" was the Gk way of referring to slaves; "souls of men" was the Hb way.   ᴴ18:20 Or God
pronounced on her the judgment she passed on you; see Rv 18:6   ᴵ18:23 Ancient sorcery or witchcraft often used spells and drugs. Here the
term may be non-literal, that is, Babylon drugged the nations with her beauty and power.   ᴶ18:24 Lit in her   ᴷ19:2 Valid; Jn 8:16; 19:35

because He has judged
   the notorious prostitute
who corrupted the earth
   with her sexual immorality;
and He has avenged the blood
   of His slaves
that was on her hands.

³A second time they said:

Hallelujah!
Her smoke ascends forever and ever!

⁴Then the 24 elders and the four living
creatures fell down and worshiped God, who
is seated on the throne, saying:

Amen! Hallelujah!

⁵A voice came from the throne, saying:

Praise our God,
all His slaves, who fear Him,
both small and great!

⁶Then I heard something like the voice of
a vast multitude, like the sound of cascading
waters, and like the rumbling of loud thunder, saying:

Hallelujah, because our Lord God,
   the Almighty,
has begun to reign!
⁷   Let us be glad, rejoice,
      and give Him glory,
   because the marriage of the Lamb
      has come,
   and His wife has prepared herself.
⁸   She was given fine linen to wear, bright
      and pure.

For the fine linen represents the righteous
acts of the saints.

⁹Then heᴬ said to me, "Write: Those invited
to the marriage feast of the Lamb are fortunate!" He also said to me, "These words of
God are true." ¹⁰Then I fell at his feet to worship him, but he said to me, "Don't do that! I
am a fellow slave with you and your brothers
who have the testimony aboutᴮ Jesus. Worship God, because the testimony about Jesus
is the spirit of prophecy."ᶜ

¹¹Then I saw heaven opened, and there was
a white horse. Its rider is called Faithful and
True, and He judges and makes war in righteousness. ¹²His eyes were like a fiery flame,
and many crownsᴰ were on His head. He had a
name written that no one knows except Himself. ¹³He wore a robe stained with blood,ᴱ and
His name is the Word of God. ¹⁴The armies
that were in heaven followed Him on white
horses, wearing pure white linen. ¹⁵A sharpᶠ
sword came from His mouth, so that He
might strike the nations with it. He will shep-
herdᴳ them with an iron scepter. He will also
trample the winepress of the fierce anger of
God, the Almighty. ¹⁶And He has a name written on His robe and on His thigh:

KING OF KINGS
AND LORD OF LORDS.

¹⁷Then I saw an angel standing onᴴ the sun,
and he cried out in a loud voice, saying to all
the birds flying high overhead, "Come, gather
together for the great supper of God, ¹⁸so that
you may eat the flesh of kings, the flesh of
commanders, the flesh of mighty men, the
flesh of horses and of their riders, and the
flesh of everyone, both free and slave, small
and great."

¹⁹Then I saw the beast, the kings of the
earth, and their armies gathered together
to wage war against the rider on the horse
and against His army. ²⁰But the beast was
taken prisoner, and along with him the false
prophet, who had performed the signs in his
presence. He deceived those who accepted
the mark of the beast and those who worshiped his image with these signs. Both of
them were thrown alive into the lake of fire
that burns with sulfur. ²¹The rest were killed
with the sword that came from the mouth of
the rider on the horse, and all the birds were
filled with their flesh.

20 Then I saw an angel coming down
from heaven with the key to the abyss
and a great chain in his hand. ²He seized the
dragon, that ancient serpent who is the Devil
and Satan,ᴵ and bound him for 1,000 years.
³He threw him into the abyss, closed it, and

ᴬ19:9 Probably an angel; Rv 17:1; 22:8-9   ᴮ19:10 Or *to*   ᶜ19:10 Or *the Spirit*   ᴰ19:12 Or *diadems*   ᴱ19:13 Or *a robe dipped in*   ᶠ19:15 Other
mss add *double-edged*   ᴳ19:15 Or *rule*   ᴴ19:17 Or *in*   ᴵ20:2 Other mss add *who deceives the whole world*

put a seal on it so that he would no longer deceive the nations until the 1,000 years were completed. After that, he must be released for a short time.

⁴Then I saw thrones, and people seated on them who were given authority to judge. I also saw the people^A who had been beheaded^B because of their testimony about Jesus and because of God's word, who had not worshiped the beast or his image, and who had not accepted the mark on their foreheads or their hands. They came to life and reigned with the Messiah for 1,000 years. ⁵The rest of the dead did not come to life until the 1,000 years were completed. This is the first resurrection. ⁶Blessed and holy is the one who shares in the first resurrection! The second death has no power^C over them, but they will be priests of God and of the Messiah, and they will reign with Him for 1,000 years.

⁷When the 1,000 years are completed, Satan will be released from his prison ⁸and will go out to deceive the nations at the four corners of the earth, Gog and Magog, to gather them for battle. Their number is like the sand of the sea. ⁹They came up over the surface of the earth and surrounded the encampment of the saints, the beloved city. Then fire came down from heaven^D and consumed them. ¹⁰The Devil who deceived them was thrown into the lake of fire and sulfur where the beast and the false prophet are, and they will be tormented day and night forever and ever.

¹¹Then I saw a great white throne and One seated on it. Earth and heaven fled from His presence, and no place was found for them. ¹²I also saw the dead, the great and the small, standing before the throne, and books were opened. Another book was opened, which is the book of life, and the dead were judged according to their works by what was written in the books.

¹³Then the sea gave up its dead, and Death and Hades gave up their dead; all^E were judged according to their works. ¹⁴Death and Hades were thrown into the lake of fire. This is the second death, the lake of fire.^F ¹⁵And

anyone not found written in the book of life was thrown into the lake of fire.

21 Then I saw a new heaven and a new earth, for the first heaven and the first earth had passed away, and the sea no longer existed. ²I also saw the Holy City, new Jerusalem, coming down out of heaven from God, prepared like a bride adorned for her husband.

³Then I heard a loud voice from the throne:^G

> Look! God's dwelling^H is
>   with humanity,
> and He will live with them.
> They will be His people,
> and God Himself will be with them
>   and be their God.^I
> ⁴ He will wipe away every tear
>   from their eyes.
> Death will no longer exist;
> grief, crying, and pain will exist
>   no longer,
> because the previous things^J
>   have passed away.

⁵Then the One seated on the throne said, "Look! I am making everything new." He also said, "Write, because these words^K are faithful and true." ⁶And He said to me, "It is done! I am the Alpha and the Omega, the Beginning and the End. I will give water as a gift to the thirsty from the spring of life. ⁷The victor will inherit these things, and I will be his God, and he will be My son. ⁸But the cowards, unbelievers,^L vile, murderers, sexually immoral, sorcerers, idolaters, and all liars—their share will be in the lake that burns with fire and sulfur, which is the second death."

⁹Then one of the seven angels, who had held the seven bowls filled with the seven last plagues, came and spoke with me: "Come, I will show you the bride, the wife of the Lamb." ¹⁰He then carried me away in the Spirit^M to a great and high mountain and showed me the holy city, Jerusalem, coming down out of heaven from God, ¹¹arrayed with God's glory. Her radiance was like a very precious stone, like a jasper stone, bright as crystal. ¹²The city

---

^A20:4 Lit souls   ^B20:4 All who had given their lives for their faith in Christ   ^C20:6 Or authority   ^D20:9 Other mss add from God   ^E20:13 Lit each   ^F20:14 Other mss omit the lake of fire   ^G21:3 Other mss read from heaven   ^H21:3 Or tent, or tabernacle   ^I21:3 Other mss omit and be their God   ^J21:4 Or the first things   ^K21:5 Other mss add of God   ^L21:8 Other mss add the sinful   ^M21:10 Or in spirit had a massive high wall, with 12 gates. Twelve angels were at the gates; the names of the 12 tribes of Israel's sons were inscribed on the gates. ¹³There were three gates on the east, three gates on the north, three gates on the south, and three gates on the west. ¹⁴The city wall had 12 foundations, and the 12 names of the Lamb's 12 apostles were on the foundations.

¹⁵The one who spoke with me had a gold measuring rod to measure the city, its gates, and its wall. ¹⁶The city is laid out in a square; its length and width are the same. He measured the city with the rod at 12,000 *stadia*.ᴬ Its length, width, and height are equal. ¹⁷Then he measured its wall, 144 cubits according to human measurement, which the angel used. ¹⁸The building material of its wall was jasper, and the city was pure gold like clear glass.

¹⁹The foundations of the city wall were adorned with every kind of precious stone:

> the first foundation jasper,
> the second sapphire,
> the third chalcedony,
> the fourth emerald,
> ²⁰ the fifth sardonyx,
> the sixth carnelian,
> the seventh chrysolite,
> the eighth beryl,
> the ninth topaz,
> the tenth chrysoprase,
> the eleventh jacinth,
> the twelfth amethyst.

²¹The 12 gates are 12 pearls; each individual gate was made of a single pearl. The broad streetᴮ of the city was pure gold, like transparent glass.

²²I did not see a sanctuary in it, because the Lord God the Almighty and the Lamb are its sanctuary. ²³The city does not need the sun or the moon to shine on it, because God's glory illuminates it, and its lamp is the Lamb. ²⁴The nationsᶜ will walk in its light, and the kings of the earth will bring their glory into it.ᴰ ²⁵Each day its gates will never close because it will never be night there. ²⁶They will bring the glory and honor of the nations into it.ᴱ ²⁷Nothing profane will ever enter it: no one who does what is vile or false, but only those written in the Lamb's book of life.

22 Then he showed me the riverᶠ of living water, sparkling like crystal, flowing from the throne of God and of the Lamb ²down the middle of the broad street of the city. The tree of lifeᴳ was on both sides of the river, bearing 12 kinds of fruit, producing its fruit every month. The leaves of the tree are for healing the nations, ³and there will no longer be any curse. The throne of God and of the Lamb will be in the city,ᴴ and His slaves will serve Him. ⁴They will see His face, and His name will be on their foreheads. ⁵Night will no longer exist, and people will not need lamplight or sunlight, because the Lord God will give them light. And they will reign forever and ever.

⁶Then he said to me, "These words are faithful and true. And the Lord, the God of the spirits of the prophets,ᴵ has sent His angel to show His slaves what must quickly take place."ᴶ

⁷"Look, I am coming quickly! The one who keeps the prophetic words of this book is blessed."

⁸I, John, am the one who heard and saw these things. When I heard and saw them, I fell down to worship at the feet of the angel who had shown them to me. ⁹But he said to me, "Don't do that! I am a fellow slave with you, your brothers the prophets, and those who keep the words of this book. Worship God." ¹⁰He also said to me, "Don't seal the prophetic words of this book, because the time is near. ¹¹Let the unrighteous go on in unrighteousness; let the filthy go on being made filthy; let the righteous go on in righteousness; and let the holy go on being made holy."

¹²"Look! I am coming quickly, and My reward is with Me to repay each person according to what he has done. ¹³I am the Alpha and

ᴬ21:16 A *stadion* (sg) = about 600 feet; 12,000 *stadia* = 1,400 miles.   ᴮ21:21 Or *The public square*   ᶜ21:24 Other mss add *of those who are saved*   ᴰ21:24 Other mss read *will bring to Him the nations' glory and honor*   ᴱ21:26 Other mss add *in order that they might go in*   ᶠ22:1 Other mss read *pure river*   ᴳ22:2 Or *was a tree of life, or, was a tree that gives life*   ᴴ22:3 Lit *in it*   ᴵ22:6 Other mss read *God of the holy prophets*   ᴶ22:6 Or *soon* the Omega, the First and the Last, the Beginning and the End.

14 "Blessed are those who wash their robes,[A] so that they may have the right to the tree of life and may enter the city by the gates. 15 Outside are the dogs, the sorcerers, the sexually immoral, the murderers, the idolaters, and everyone who loves and practices lying.

16 "I, Jesus, have sent My angel to attest these things to you[B] for the churches. I am the Root and the Offspring of David, the Bright Morning Star."

17 Both the Spirit and the bride say, "Come!" Anyone who hears should say, "Come!" And the one who is thirsty should come. Whoever desires should take the living water as a gift.

18 I testify to everyone who hears the prophetic words of this book: If anyone adds to them, God will add to him the plagues that are written in this book. 19 And if anyone takes away from the words of this prophetic book, God will take away his share of the tree of life and the holy city, written in this book.

20 He who testifies about these things says, "Yes, I am coming quickly."

Amen! Come, Lord Jesus!

21 The grace of the Lord Jesus[C] be with all the saints.[D] Amen.[E]

A 22:14 Other mss read who keep His commands   B 22:16 In Gk, you is pl   C 22:21 Other mss add Christ   D 22:21 Other mss omit the saints   E 22:21 Other mss omit Amen.

ARE YOU READY TO RECEIVE
GOD'S INVITATION TO ETERNAL LIFE AND HOPE?

If so, please pray the following prayer. Remember, it is not the words that you use, but the attitude of your heart. If you pray this prayer sincerely, Jesus will come into your life, and in Him you will have eternal life and hope.

"Dear God, I know that Jesus is Your Son and that He died on the cross and was raised from the dead. Because I have sinned and need forgiveness, I ask Jesus to come into my heart. I am willing to change the direction of my life by acknowledging Jesus as my Lord and Savior, and by turning away from my sins. Thank You for giving me forgiveness, eternal life, and hope. In Jesus' name, Amen."

You Are Assured of Eternal Life and Hope Because:

- You can trust God's promise.

- *"For everyone who calls on the name of the Lord will be saved"* (Romans 10:13).

  Did you sincerely ask Jesus into your heart as Lord and Savior? Where is He right now? What does God's Word promise?

- You are a member of God's family.

  "The Spirit Himself testifies together with our spirit that we are God's children" (Romans 8:16).

- Your life is eternally secure in God.

  "For I am persuaded that not even death or life, angels or rulers, things present or things to come, hostile powers, height or depth, or any other created thing will have the power to separate us from the love of God that is in Christ Jesus our Lord!" (Romans 8:38-39)

WHAT HAPPENS AFTER YOU RECEIVE HOPE FROM GOD?

- You will begin to live for God (Romans 12:1-2, 9-18).

- You will publicly profess your faith by being baptized (Matthew 28:19-20; Luke 3:21; Romans 6:4).

- You will share with others what Jesus has done for you (Romans 10:14).

- You will get to know God better through prayer, Bible study and fellowship with other Christians as a member of a local church (Romans 15:4-6).

MY RECORD OF SALVATION

On _____ I, _____ trusted
      (date)   (name)

Jesus as my Savior and gave myself to Him to be Lord of my life.

Witnessed by: _____